Man of War, Man of Peace

DAVID SHARROCK was the *Guardian*'s Ireland correspondent until September 1997 and is now the newspaper's Middle East correspondent.

MARK DEVENPORT is the BBC's Ireland correspondent.

Man of War,

David Sharrock &
Mark Devenport

Man of Peace

The Unauthorized Biography of
GERRY ADAMS

PAN BOOKS

First published 1997 by Macmillan

This edition published 1998 by Pan Books
an imprint of Macmillan Publishers Ltd
25 Eccleston Place, London SW1W 9NF
and Basingstoke

Associated companies throughout the world

ISBN 0 330 35396 9

A CIP catalogue record for this book is available from
the British Library.

Typeset by SetSystems Ltd, Saffron Walden, Essex
Printed and bound in Great Britain by
Mackays of Chatham plc, Chatham, Kent

Acknowledgements

Inevitably in an unauthorized biography, some of the people who have helped us the most would be least impressed to find their names included here – to the many who have assisted us either on or off the record we extend our deep gratitude. A large number of interviews were conducted specifically for this book, and the authors have also drawn on other material gathered in the course of their 'day' jobs – without the understanding of management and colleagues at both the *Guardian* and the BBC this book would not have been possible. Besides material generated first hand, we owe a debt of gratitude to many other journalists and authors, especially John Ware who allowed us to peruse his invaluable archive. Chris Ryder, Stephen Grimason, Mark Simpson, Nick Watt, Shane Harrison, Paul Rocks, Henry McDonald, Rogelio Alonso, Diarmaid MacDermott and Tom McPhail were all generous with their thoughts and time when their guidance and assistance was sought. Yvonne and Ciaran – the Raiders of the Lost Ark of the library world – were forever digging out obscure republican publications for us from the political collection at the Linenhall Library.

Our editor Richard Milner coped stoically with the difficulties of dealing with authors who regularly broke off writing to cover elections, riots, murders, bombings and a new ceasefire.

Mark wishes to thank Patricia for her patience with his frequent absences and her last minute error-spotting, his brothers, sister and his mother Bernadette for their constant love and support, and his father John who was enthusiastic and encouraging when he learnt of this project, but sadly did not live to see the book's publication.

David wishes to thank Marta for coping so well with a frequently preoccupied husband, and Pablo for failing to find – in spite of his many endeavours – the correct key with which to erase this entire book (one chapter wasn't a bad effort) as well as Carlos for his sense of occasion in arriving on cue with the second IRA ceasefire and the conclusion of this book. To his mother and father for their unstinting love and support and to the ever-loyal Lola, for services to stress-busting.

Contents

Introduction

On a grey and chilly November morning in 1995, Northern Ireland's main airport was on its highest ever state of security as the world's most powerful leader touched down aboard Airforce One. Bill Clinton was about to become the first ever serving United States President to visit a corner of the United Kingdom and Ireland whose dual and divided national identity had given birth to one of the world's most terrible terrorist conflicts.

As the presidential entourage swept down the sealed motorway into Belfast, Clinton surveyed a landscape of rich farmland and prosperous villages, defiled by the decades of killing but now transformed in a year of Provisional IRA ceasefire from its customary state of war-weariness to one of daring to hope that the agony might finally be over. A brittle cessation of hostilities by the Provisionals, renowned as one of the world's most efficient and ruthless terrorist organizations, and their loyalist counterparts in the Ulster Volunteer Force and Ulster Defence Association, was holding and the President was here to celebrate the longest period of peace since the Troubles erupted in 1969.

But there was more to the minutely planned tour than that. During the course of the next twenty-four hours, although he would meet all the main political, business and community leaders, out of them all there was only one man who was to be accorded a special pause in the rigorously screened proceedings. A little while after visiting Mackies engineering works, a factory straddling Belfast's infamous 'Peace Line' separating the Catholics and Protestants, where Clinton had delivered a warmly received speech in which he subverted the IRA's slogan 'Our day will come' and warned the terrorists: 'You are the past, your day is over,' the President's convoy drew to a halt at 'Hijack Corner', where the Falls and Springfield Roads meet.

As the President stepped out of his armour-plated Cadillac and the delighted crowds surged towards his alarmed-looking security staff, a tall, dark-haired and full-bearded figure emerged from a bread-shop-cum-café and crossed the pavement to meet him. 'Cead mile failte,' said the smiling man, a hundred thousand Irish welcomes. Gerry Adams extended his hand and the two men shook. It was a crowning moment for the man who had been the Provisionals' prime strategist and most formidable leader for the past quarter-century.

Adams had already met President Clinton in Washington at his annual St Patrick's Day party in the White House earlier in the year, but now the undisputed leader of the Western democracies was bestowing upon him the unique honour of a home-call. They chatted easily to one another, Clinton telling Adams that he had been reading his collection of short stories until dawn and now, standing in the Falls, he understood from where the Sinn Fein President drew his inspiration.

It was true that in the surrounding huddled streets running off the Falls were written the key chapters in the rise of the Provisionals and the history of Irish republican resistance within Northern Ireland to British rule. Only a short distance away was the street in which Adams was born; around the corner was the spot where his father was shot and wounded when police returned fire on the young IRA volunteer in a gun battle; a mere hundred yards away stood Clonard Monastery, crucible of the peace process. These streets had been the scene of countless riots, shootings and bombings, witness to acts of cowardice and heroism and the heartland of a seemingly hopeless and unwinnable struggle where violence had only deepened the differences between the two communities of Northern Ireland.

The two men talked amiably for a while as the crowds pressed forward and the media fought to record the moment when an American president called on a man whose very name was enough to stir strong passions across the religious divide. To the majority of Protestants Adams was the devil incarnate, an overlord of terrorism who had presided over some of the worst atrocities ever perpetrated in their country. But to many Catholics he was a saintly figure, having led the Provisionals away from violence and towards the political path, who was now clinging to authority only by the strength of his reputation within the IRA as the peace process floundered because of the devious machinations of a perfidious British government.

There could be no common ground between the two conflicting images, but somewhere between these extreme caricatures lay a more complex personality, cast in the traditional republican mould of his family, tempered by the radicalism of the 1960s, scorched by the fires of 1969 and now apparently willing to break the mould which for so long had doomed the people of Northern Ireland, the Irish Republic and England to sudden and terrible acts of violence. For much of his adult life Gerry Adams had been a man who played by the rules of war. In spite of the euphoria surrounding President Clinton's visit, he knew as he shook the hand of the President of the United States of America that the IRA ceasefire was already over. Within days a string of Belfast's petty criminals would die at the hands of the Provisionals, working under the alias of 'Direct Action Against Drugs'. Only the timing of the ceasefire's official rupture was in doubt, but the means to bomb London's Canary Wharf were already on the move as Belfast fêted its most famous visitor.

As a former British minister, Richard Needham, who was one of the VIPs at the President's Mackies visit, recalled: 'I went down after Clinton to the city centre and Adams was walking back having shaken Clinton's hand. One of his "heavies" saw me and for the first time in my life I got a cheery wave from someone with "Up the IRA" on his tee-shirt. I did think it was a day of hope, but I was wrong. So was President Clinton and the rest of us, but occasionally you've got to hope these things are going to come right. What was Clinton's wonderful phrase? "You are the past, your day is over." It's still true . . .'

Was Gerry Adams therefore a man destined to continue his role in the unwinnable war for a united Ireland? Or was there a new man of peace working from the inside at the highest levels of the republican movement, frustrated at the obstacles thrown in his path but determined to succeed in finally breaking the near-theological belief in physical force which had reaped such a terrible harvest of human life? From throwing petrol bombs to greeting a world leader in the same narrow patch of ground, Gerry Adams' journey away from war to peace has been a long and often enigma-shrouded affair. With the most important Irish republican leader since Michael Collins and Eamon De Valera still in transit, the future remains uncertain. Only the past offers clues to his ultimate destination.

CHAPTER ONE

Shoot-Out in Sultan Street

It was just before dawn when Gerry Adams stepped furtively out of his overnight billet into a West Belfast street, a revolver nestling in his pocket. Sleep had eluded him in the preceding hours: this was to be a momentous day in the struggle for Irish liberation and he had prepared himself for it according to the instructions of his commanding officer in D Company of the Belfast Brigade of Oglaigh na hEireann, the Irish Republican Army. The young volunteers had all been urged to go to see a priest and make their confessions and then to prepare themselves mentally for the likelihood of death which, if it came, would not be in vain. It was to be another glorious chapter in the story of Ireland's fight for freedom from British domination.

At that early hour of the morning, with the sun barely able to break through the lowering skyline to illuminate the gantries of the dockyards, standing like giant crucifixes across the River Lagan in the east, the streets of terraced houses running off the Falls Road did not really seem to provide the epic scale required for this moment, his first engagement of the enemy. The working-class Catholic district and its Protestant neighbour the Shankill were waking up together in the prosaic routine of another day, with the mills and foundries beckoning. Even so, he could discern the heightened tension and the peelers – the Black Bastards as they were disparagingly called, after the rifle-green colour of their Royal Ulster Constabulary uniform – were everywhere. Overnight they had raided houses in the neighbourhood and arrested a number of terrorist suspects after a police vehicle came under fire from a machine-gun and revolver.

Those arrested were locals and comrades, as were the men killed earlier in the week by the RUC at an IRA arms dump of weapons on the fringes of the city, newly arrived from the South. Then was this morning's offensive revenge pure and simple or was it to be the beginning of an important new push in the 'Brits Out' campaign? Gerry turned the idea over in his mind, already racing at the thought of what lay ahead. In the final analysis it didn't really matter to the volunteers, who had been schooled to look on the hated British uniforms as their enemies and disregard the flesh and blood of their own countrymen inside them. He had been told the operation would commence at eight o'clock, to be ready at that hour and await further instructions.

But time was ticking rapidly by and the senior man who was supposed to give the final orders was nowhere to be seen. Hanging around on street corners with a gun in his pocket was becoming ever more uncomfortable as the pedestrian traffic swelled. The Webley was one of only nine handguns belonging to D Company, the rest of the arsenal including two submachine-guns. His mind raced as he remembered weapons-drill classes. 'The weapon consists of three parts, body, barrel and butt, accurate up to forty yards, shoots up to sixty . . .' He was beginning to attract the unwanted attention of a group of policemen and decided to move on. He buried his head into his chest and gripped the revolver more tightly.

'Hey you, where are you going?' shouted an RUC man and Adams took to his heels. The gun seemed to grow heavier. He pulled it out and it dangled at the end of his wrist as he continued to run. Should he throw it away or fire a warning shot at his pursuers in order to buy more time for his escape? The RUC patrol made his mind up for him. There was the crack of a bullet whistling over his head. Adams swivelled around and immediately returned fire, aiming his first shot at Constable James Lorimer. It missed, but his second bullet hit Constable Robert Elkin. Four more times Gerry Adams pulled the trigger, but on each occasion the revolver misfired. He cursed the bullets, neutered by the damp ground in which they had lain for too long.

The gun now useless, he ran on. He reached the corner of Osman Street by the time Constable Joseph Farr was able to steady his gun and take careful aim at the running youth. Firing three shots in quick succession he watched as Adams fell. The first bullet hit the IRA man's right knee, another buried itself in his groin and the last struck him on his left hand. His captors carried him to a first aid post and there, while consciousness remained, Gerry Adams said a prayer. It was 5 September 1942.

The ground upon which he fell was a short distance from where, more than half a century later, Gerry Adams' first-born son, named after him in keeping with the Irish custom, was to shake hands with the world's most powerful man. The same piece of land too where, twelve months after that historic handshake, another IRA gunman was to shoot and wound another RUC officer. In December 1996 the chosen killing ground was the interior of a children's hospital and the intended target a senior unionist political participant in the peace talks and his wife visiting their critically ill child. One of the would-be assassin's bullets pierced a baby's incubator, mercifully unoccupied at the time. In 1942, when Gerry Adams senior first wielded a gun, these were streets which held little news worthy of the attention of the world beyond Ireland's shores. In the 1960s that would change. They would become all too wearily familiar as the cockpit for a murderous conflict known as the Troubles.

On Monday 7 September 1942 the news of Adams' gunfight lost the battle for space in the Belfast newspapers with headlines detailing events of wider import. The *Newsletter*, the oldest newspaper in the British Isles, reported that a massive German tank assault on Stalingrad had been repelled – a development which dismayed the IRA internees in Crumlin Road prison gleefully plotting the eastward march of Hitler's shock troops. The Red Army was regaining ground in what was referred to as 'the epic defence' of the city. In the North African desert the Germans' Afrika Korps General Erwin Rommel was reported to have suffered a defeat at the hands of General Bernard Montgomery, an Ulsterman of Donegal extraction. Axis forces had been pushed by Monty west of a major minefield, suffering severe losses.

But back in Belfast the IRA volunteers had other things on their minds. Gerry Adams awoke in hospital, under arrest and facing charges of attempted murder. The 'operation' which had proved his undoing was to have been a co-ordinated series of 'aggressive actions' in retaliation for the execution by hanging of Belfast Company Commander Tom Williams, who had been found guilty along with five other IRA men of the murder of a Catholic RUC constable on the Easter weekend of 1942. The war dominating the local newspapers might go on to determine the fates of nations but it was still of secondary interest to the IRA leadership.

It was two decades earlier that Winston Churchill had glumly reflected upon the lack of perspective to be found on the shores of Britain's nearest neighbour and oldest colony. After the Great War, said Churchill, empires had been overturned and the whole map of Europe changed. 'The modes of thought of men, the whole outlook on affairs, the grouping of parties, all have encountered violent and tremendous changes in the deluge of the world, but as the deluge subsides and the waters fall short we see the dreary steeples of Fermanagh and Tyrone emerging once again. The integrity of their quarrel is one of the few institutions that has been unaltered in the cataclysm which has swept the world.'

In Belfast in the third year of the Second World War some people were determined to prove the Prime Minister's words right. As Mr Justice Brown, the judge who was to convict Gerry Adams, observed, far from providing a pause in violence closer to home the war seemed instead to have stimulated IRA activity with Irish republicans calculating that England's difficulty was Ireland's opportunity. 'While the news from abroad is good and cheers the heart,' said the judge, 'the news at home is very disconcerting.' People were well aware that an organization calling itself the Irish Republican Army had been very active, he continued. 'Attacks have been made on lives and property and on the whole there is no subject for congratulation.' The police were doing an excellent job combating the criminals, the judge told the court, but one could well understand 'how difficult police work must be in the blackout and how easy it is for a small boy to throw a bomb along a street and walk off whistling and present himself to the ordinary eye as a quite innocent lad playing in the street'.

At just sixteen years of age, Gerry Adams was one of the boys that Mr Justice Brown seemed to have in mind. To the ordinary eye he appeared every bit the average teenager, five foot four inches tall, of slight build with a shock of black hair and a pair of hazel eyes. The RUC report to the court said that he had been honest, sober, industrious and generally of good character. The character of his relatives, friends and associates was also described as good. This was his first offence and his mother Margaret was willing to receive him and assist him if he was acquitted. With his wounds it would probably be some time before he could resume work as a labourer.

However, the police report did enter strong caveats against the favourable impression of Adams. He had been known to associate with members of the IRA and his family had connections with the

IRA, which, under its Chief of Staff and Northern Commander Hugh McAteer, regarded itself as an underground army fighting an unfinished war. By 1942 the IRA was a shadow of its former self, but to republican purists it was still their only home. In Belfast the membership amounted to around 300 volunteers in four Companies, supplemented by an uncertain number of Auxiliaries – older men whose primary role was defence of their areas against loyalist attacks while the IRA volunteers supposedly went on the offensive – and Cumann na mBan, the women's branch of the movement whose tasks involved carrying weapons and acting as look-outs.

By national standards this was an impressive set-up. When the Southern authorities finally grew intolerant of the IRA activities they were largely successful in stamping them out. The Northern IRA volunteers, on the other hand, had never known a moment's lull in their war and, unlike their Free State comrades, seemed to thrive on hardship. Banks were raided, army camps penetrated and weapons stolen. They even had their own pirate radio transmitter and newspaper. What they lacked in direction they made up for in enthusiasm for physical-force republicanism.

For Hugh McAteer, the slight, sandy-haired and forever grinning former clerk for the Londonderry Corporation, it was enough to keep his men on a war footing. They were after all in occupied territory, where the IRA's role as defenders of the Republic more often than not was rooted firmly in the defence of Catholic areas from sporadic Protestant attacks.

But the IRA's ruling Army Council and General Headquarters Staff were a hundred miles away in Dublin and their first loyalty was to the whole of the Republic, not just the truncated occupied six counties. A generation earlier in December 1921, at the end of Europe's first modern guerrilla war, the IRA leader Michael Collins signed a treaty with the British Prime Minister Lloyd George. Twenty-six of Ireland's thirty-two counties were granted their independence as a self-governing dominion of the British Empire. Members of the Dail, the Irish parliament, were required to swear allegiance to the British King, his heirs and successors, while the 'Irish Free State' also ceded control of a number of strategic Irish ports to the British armed forces.

For Michael Collins and his followers it was a staging post on the road to a fully independent and united Ireland. But for many of his former comrades it was pure and simple treachery to accept colonial status with all the trappings of imperialism as well as partition, with the north-eastern six counties ruled by a regional Protestant unionist parliament. The IRA split and the anti-Treaty forces, led by Eamon De Valera, decided to fight on to achieve those true goals of Irish republicanism which had been declared at the outbreak of the Easter 1916 Rising.

The 1916 proclamation of the provisional government of the Irish Republic, read out on the steps of the General Post Office building in Dublin by the leaders of a self-appointed military vanguard who drew little support from their countrymen and women, declared:

Irishmen and Irishwomen, in the name of God and of the dead generations from which she receives her old tradition of nation-hood, Ireland, through us, summons her children to her flag and strikes for her freedom . . . We declare the rights of the people of Ireland to the ownership of Ireland and to the unfettered control of Irish destinies to be sovereign and indefeasible. The long usurpation of that right by a foreign people and government has not extinguished the right, nor can it ever be extinguished except by the destruction of the Irish people.

In every generation the Irish people have asserted their right to national freedom and sovereignty: six times during the past three hundred years they have asserted it in arms. Standing on that fundamental right and again asserting it in arms in the face of the world, we hereby proclaim the Irish Republic as a sovereign independent state, and we pledge our lives and the lives of our comrades in arms to the cause of its freedom, of its welfare and of its exaltation among the nations.

These words were to ring down the decades, haunting and harrying Irish politicians, reminding the weak where their real duty lay and confirming the strong in their self-righteousness. In the partitioned North their power to rouse the passions of many of the dispossessed nationalists – outnumbered two to one by their Prot-estant overlords – was all the greater. By the example of the men of 1916 would future generations be judged. Blood would flow until their task was completed.

As James Connolly, one of the seven signatories of the proclamation, acknowledged at the commencement of the Easter Rising: 'We are going out to be slaughtered.' And as his co-signatory Padraig Pearse urged: 'We must not faint at the sight of blood. Winning through it we (or those of us who survive) shall come unto great joy.' Both of them were to be executed by the British at Kilmainham jail shortly after the rebellion was swiftly put down, an act which by its pitiless brutality was to reverse the fortunes of the doomed Irish republicans and establish the use of physical force as a guiding principle for a lethal strand of Irish thought which remains virulently potent to this day. The poet W. B. Yeats summed up the consequences of the British exercise in martyr-making in 1916:

> *I write it out in a verse*
> *MacDonagh and MacBride*
> *And Connolly and Pearse*
> *Now and in time to be*
> *Wherever green is worn,*
> *Are changed, changed utterly:*
> *A terrible beauty is born.*

Michael Collins' opponents fought on in the name of the future generations envisaged by the 1916 proclamation, but, although their bullets were to claim his life within a few years of his signing the Treaty with the British, his new state survived the civil war. The quarrel within the family of Irish republicanism had tragic and fatal consequences for its members and the estrangement was to deepen with the passing years. In time Eamon De Valera came to accept Collins' compromise path and resigned from Sinn Fein, the IRA's political wing, in 1926 after the narrow rejection of his proposal that, once the oath of allegiance to the British Crown was removed, 'it becomes a question not of principle but of policy whether or not republican representatives enter the Dail'.

De Valera set up his own party, Fianna Fail, 'the Soldiers of Destiny', who went 'slightly constitutional' and by 1932 were in power. By the start of the Second World War his political and diplomatic successes seemed to be bringing the Republic ever nearer. In 1936 De Valera eliminated the British Crown from the Irish constitution under cover of the abdication of King Edward VIII and a year later consigned the despised Free State – product of the Treaty

– to the history books, replaced under his new constitution with the title Eire/Ireland. Even today the phrase 'Free Stater' is a favourite term of abuse for Northern republicans speaking ill of the South.

De Valera's constitution created another split – the third suffered by the IRA since 1916 – when the chief of staff Sean MacBride and the army's remaining intellectual accepted its *de jure* claim to jurisdiction over all thirty-two counties in the infamous Articles 2 and 3 which define the National Territory as 'the whole island' and speak of 'pending the reintegration' of the six counties. This, MacBride argued, meant that the final realization of the republican goal could now be achieved peacefully and that the IRA therefore no longer had a role.

In 1938 De Valera sprang the news of fresh negotiations with the British Prime Minister Neville Chamberlain which led to a new Anglo-Irish Agreement, the ending of an economic war between the two states and the return of the Treaty ports, a remarkable achievement at a moment when events in continental Europe were leading inexorably towards another war. It was not by accident therefore, nor did it occasion any surprise, that the IRA, still clinging fast to its 1916 principles, was becoming an anachronistic relic, shrinking in support and quality. Its most able members were gradually absorbed into the emerging political life of the new state. But for those trapped on the wrong side of the border there was of course no such opportunity.

The Catholic-dominated South and the mainly Protestant North increasingly turned their backs upon one another. For many of the Catholics left on the wrong side of the haphazardly wriggling Irish border this was the 'nationalist nightmare'. For nearly fifty years they were to be ruled as a minority by a monolithic Ulster Unionist Party, suffering prejudice, discrimination and bigotry at every turn.

For unionists the 'Protestant state for a Protestant people' was a bulwark against the entire island's Catholic majority, a country in which they feared extinction. The Catholics who remained within their partitioned six-county zone were potential Fifth Columnists, who could never be entrusted with their fair share of power lest they use it only to destroy Northern Ireland. This was as far distant a world from the lofty vision of the 1916 proclamation as it was possible to get, yet those who held true to the original ideals, and in so doing longed to smash both the Free State and Northern Ireland, found themselves ever more in the minority in both jurisdictions. The integrity of the quarrel was intact but the real world no longer seemed to care. It was time to move on.

Yet just as James Connolly and Padraig Pearse had believed that the First World War provided a chance to strike at Britain while its resources were committed elsewhere, so Hugh McAteer and his young Northern volunteers viewed the Second World War as another window of opportunity. In retrospect 1942 would be consigned by republicans to the bulging file labelled 'Another Glorious Failure'. But at the time to young idealists like sixteen-year-old Gerry Adams, hungry for his first taste of 'active service', it looked like a fresh beginning. There was an urgent need to keep the flame of physical-force republicanism alive.

In the South, from where leadership traditionally sprang, all was decay, with little clue of which direction would lead the Northern volunteers towards the Republic. A bombing campaign in Britain, which was forced through by the IRA leadership against serious internal dissent from such heavy-hitters as the Cork Flying Column veteran Tom Barry, had finally run its discredited course, bringing the inevitable loss of life to English civilians and IRA volunteers without making an iota of difference to the British government's position on remaining in Northern Ireland.

Accepting that the war was effectively over in the South and that the England bombing campaign had failed, the IRA turned its attention northwards, and planning for a renewed military campaign began. McAteer decided that a symbolic, public display of strength was urgently required. The stage would be the annual commemoration of the Easter Rising in Belfast, which always provided a confrontation between republicans and the RUC. Tom Williams, the teenage commander of C Company, was ordered to create a 'diversion' for the police in his own district of Clonard, off the Falls Road, leaving the remaining republicans free to hold a brief public rally.

On Easter Sunday 1942 six young men lay in wait for the approach of an RUC patrol car driving slowly up Clonard Gardens. Their objective was to fire above the vehicle and create the planned incident. As the vehicle reached a junction with Kashmir Road the IRA men opened fire, loosing off between seven and ten bullets. Only one hit the patrol car, shattering its windscreen but causing no injuries.

Williams and his men ran off, but were pursued by two women

from the Cumann na mBan who were supposed to have lifted their weapons and made off with them to another safe house. The RUC gave hot pursuit, chasing the fugitives into Cawnpore Street. Leading the charge was Constable Patrick Murphy, who attempted to follow his quarry into a house. According to republicans who were in Belfast on the day of the incident, it was Joe Cahill, the quartermaster of C Company, who seized a revolver and opened fire. Constable Murphy fell dead to the floor, still clutching his Webley revolver in his right hand, its chamber emptied a second before into the body of Tom Williams. Police reinforcements poured into the area and surrounded the house. Upstairs in a bedroom Williams lay bleeding from his wounds with two bullets in his left thigh and one in his left arm. Before passing out he gave the only order that was feasible in the circumstances: to surrender.

Patrick Murphy, the symbol of British imperial rule shot down by C Company, was a Catholic who lived with his family locally in Clowney Street. The constable's son Martin played football with some members of the local IRA. Paddy Murphy was generally to be found patrolling his beat on foot and was well liked by the children of the district because he was forever joking and pulling their legs. 'He was the nicest peeler I ever met,' said one former IRA man. Not for the last time, the IRA's struggle to remove Britain from Ireland amounted to neighbour killing neighbour.

The trial of the six IRA men lasted three days. The two young women had their charges dropped but were interned in Armagh women's jail. In a gallant attempt to save the lives of his co-accused Williams 'confessed' that he alone had fired upon Constable Murphy. But the forensic report showed otherwise. The jury returned six guilty verdicts, for which the obligatory sentence for murder was death. A date was set for the hangings, but postponed while an appeal was heard.

Meanwhile an international campaign for leniency was set in train which collected 250,000 signatures, among them those of Pope Pius XII and the United States Secretary of State Cordell Hull, as well as Eamon De Valera. Emotions were running high and nobody could predict what effect the hanging of six IRA men might produce in Ireland, North and South. It was perhaps an easy if painful journey for the British cabinet to make down memory lane to 1916, when the execution of the leaders of the Easter Rising produced the most extraordinary change in fortunes for those who once had seemed nothing more than a band of desperate and doomed adventurers.

In Crumlin Road prison the IRA men awaited their fate. Williams, who wanted to take sole responsibility for the death of Constable Murphy as the officer commanding the botched mission, received a telegram from his father, a member of the British Army Air Corps, who was so disgusted to discover that his son was in the IRA that he could not bring himself to visit him. 'Be brave to the end my son. Goodbye. God bless you,' it read. Williams hardly needed the advice. His commanding officer and chief of staff Hugh McAteer produced a letter purporting to have been sent to him by the condemned man, written in terms which explicitly recalled the romantic, pseudo-religious prison writings of the 1916 leader Padraig Pearse. If the fulfilment of his sentence was not to be avoided, then even in death could Williams and his men make their contribution to the future struggle by providing themselves as a glorious example. 'It is beyond the powers of my humble intellect to describe the pride of my comrades in knowing that they are going to follow in the footsteps of those who have given their lives to Ireland and the Republic,' the letter read.

To describe the courage and coolness shown when sentenced to death. As Joe has previously stated to you. Our sorrow is not being able to attack the court and the 'Northern' Junta. But now you know the reason.

My God can we tell you and our comrades who will carry on the fight, can we tell you of the gladness and joy that is in our hearts. To know that the Irish people are again united, aye, and well may England quake, Irelands awake. After twenty years of slumber our nation will once again strike, Please God, at the despoilers who have infringed the nation's liberty, freedom and murdered her sons, her daughters, who have given us a foreign tongue; shall please God, strike and strike hard and make the tyrants go on their knees for mercy and forgiveness.

But shall we make the mistake of '21, no, no, tis men like you and your staff will see to it. That no farcical so-called Treaty shall in any way be signed by a bunch of weak-kneed and willed Irishmen. Better that the waves of the mighty oceans sweep over Erin than take and divide our nation, murder her true sons again. Better would be that heavens would open and send fire to destroy Erin than to accept another Treaty like it.

In writing this, dear Hugh, do not think that I am saying it to you or the gallant soldiers of Oglaigh na hEireann, it is from my heart that it comes to the weak-willed and ignorant Irish men who may put any trust in England. My only regret is now I will not be with you in the fight and last stand of Ireland's battle for freedom. But with the help of God and his Blessed Mother we may be in heaven looking down upon our dear, beloved, tortured, crucified Erin, and look with pride on the men and women who will carry on the battle until victory.

Well dear Hugh I'll close with the message to Oglaigh na hEireann, 'To carry on, no matter what odds are against you, to carry on, no matter what torments are inflicted on you. The road to freedom is paved with suffering, hardships and torture, carry on my gallant and brave comrades until that certain day.'

Your comrade in Ireland's cause,
Lieut. Tom Williams,
'C' Coy. Belfast Brigade,
Oglaigh na hEireann.

In the event the Stormont government showed leniency to all the IRA men, commuting their sentences to life imprisonment – except for Williams. An example in these dangerous wartime days had to be set, but one example would be enough.

At eight o'clock on the morning of Wednesday 2 September Williams walked in prayer to the scaffold where the English executioner Albert Pierrepoint – who was by now no stranger to meeting IRA men upon the gallows of Southern Ireland either – awaited him. Five minutes after the appointed hour a notice was posted on the gate of Crumlin Road prison, declaring that the judgement of death had been performed.

Crowds had begun gathering outside the prison from the night before. Scores of women knelt, some silent, others reciting prayers. Many wept. But as the moment of the execution arrived the atmosphere of mourning was broken by shouts and jubilant singing from loyalists who burst into renditions of 'God Save the King', 'Land of Hope and Glory' and 'There'll Always Be an England'. The RUC struggled to keep the rival crowds apart. As the news spread that

Pierrepoint's work was complete sections of the nationalist crowd began booing and some gave Nazi salutes in defiance of the British state which they held responsible.

The enmity extended to Britain's allies. Several hundred demonstrators descended upon Belfast City Hall and some girls greeted the hapless American soldiers strolling around the city centre with 'Heil Hitler' salutes. At Durham Street stones were thrown at a passing US Army car. Throughout West Belfast black flags were flown as a mark of respect for the dead man and about a thousand dockers, many of them Protestants, downed tools in sympathy.

If Williams and his men had been unable to strike back at the 'Northern Junta' in revenge, their comrades soon would. The IRA's reaction to the hanging was to try to match death for death and plans had been laid for weeks in advance of the execution. Six hours after Tom Williams was killed twenty armed men crossed the border in a commandeered lorry and wounded a police sergeant and a constable at Cullaville in South Armagh. The police station at Randalstown in County Antrim was the target of a bomb attack and shots were fired at a barracks in Belleek in Fermanagh. In Belfast police patrols were shot at in Leeson Street and Servia Street. And Gerry Adams was shot and wounded as he exchanged fire with the RUC.

When he first appeared in court a month later Adams, still on crutches, faced three charges: attempting to murder Constables James Lorimer and Robert Elkin and two counts of possessing firearms. In reply to the murder charges Adams had told the police that he had been given the gun by a stranger and intended to throw it away but had then opened fire because he feared he was going to be killed. One police witness, however, alleged that Adams had admitted to him that he was going to shoot all three of the constables he had seen but was thwarted by his poor ammunition. In the event only Constable Elkin had been hit with a bullet, which struck him on the foot.

Adams pleaded not guilty to all the charges. It was probably more his tender years than his implausible defence that convinced the authorities to drop the more serious charges against him, leaving him at his trial facing only a lesser count of possession of explosives – the bullets which refused to fire.

When he appeared before Mr Justice Brown he found himself in august Irish republican company. Hugh McAteer, the IRA's chief of staff, was being tried at the same session on a count of treason. Under the Grand Jury system a large number of IRA men could be dealt with in one trial, with the questionable result that the evidence, taken *en masse*, would implicate even those upon whom less guilt might be pinned. With McAteer safely convicted of 'treason felony' and in receipt of a fifteen-year sentence the judge described him to the Crumlin Road Crown Court as 'the ringleader of this movement and the man responsible in Northern Ireland for a great part of the evil work that has been done'. Mr Justice Brown accused McAteer and his close comrades of bringing into the republican movement 'a number of young boys some of whom will be tried by this Commission and who have no sense but to follow where they are led'.

When it was the turn of Gerry Adams for sentence to be passed the judge gave him eight years, adding that he was fortunate in not being in the dock on a far more serious charge. With some bravado for the big occasion Adams replied that 'as a soldier of the Irish Republican Army I do not recognize this court', which lacked a certain consistency with his earlier admissions to the police. As he was led away to begin his prison term he shouted 'Up the Republic' just to emphasize his point.

On 26 November 1942 Gerry Adams became Convict number 365C and was put into the shoemaking department of Crumlin Road prison. The jail was full of IRA men. Sentenced prisoners like himself and Hugh McAteer were placed in A Wing while suspected republicans, including two of his brothers, who had been interned for the duration of the war were put in D Wing. Unlike the son he was to produce, Gerry Adams was a diminutive figure, small in height and build. But he was to prove a handful for the prison authorities.

His jail record, released in 1996, details the many clashes with the warders. For nearly three months in 1943 he refused to wear prison clothing, the official record categorizing him as a 'nudist', the practice which future generations of republican prisoners would know as 'going on the blanket'. The protest cost him two weeks' remission. He was reported for disturbing the peace of the prison by singing, resisting being searched, using threats to an officer, idling at his work after being cautioned, refusing to obey orders and making a false statement by accepting responsibility for a fellow convict's irregular conduct.

His medical notes detail his distinguishing features, a small scar on the right of his nose and a mole to the left of his jaw, as well as his bullet wounds after the shooting in Sultan Street. His left knee had healed but movement was still restricted, and operation scars were still clearly visible on his stomach. The young republican injured himself again while in jail, but only playing football.

Although his good character and respectable family were noted in two police reports there was no doubting his Irish republican pedigree. A local RUC constable had known of Adams four years before his arrest through his involvement in Na Fianna Eireann, the boy scout movement of the IRA. His brothers, Dominic and Patrick, were both regarded as 'notorious republicans' by the city's detectives. A police officer at the time observed that young Gerry's actions might have been 'endeavouring to uphold the republican family traditions'.

Dominic Adams was at one time chief of staff of the IRA in Dublin, spent some time as an internee in the Curragh and is remembered by veteran republicans for his involvement in the 1939 England bombing campaign. During that campaign the IRA set off 127 bombs, including one in Coventry which claimed the lives of five civilians. Two IRA men were sentenced to death for the atrocity, even though the real bomber was safely back in Dublin a day later.

While Gerry Adams mounted protests inside the Crumlin Road jail, his chief of staff, Hugh McAteer, was determined to go much further. On 15 January 1943 the IRA leader and two of his comrades took part in a daring escape from the jail, which involved breaking out on to the prison roof, dropping down into the jail yard and then using a grappling hook to scale the outside walls. McAteer's breakout was a propaganda triumph for the IRA.

But while on the run Hugh McAteer found that the initial enthusiasm for his campaign had ebbed away. There was another prison breakout, this time from Derry prison, which was led by another of Gerry's brothers, Paddy. Then in October 1943 the RUC caught up with McAteer again and he was arrested at his digs in Belfast's Ormeau Road. The man to whom he handed over command of the IRA was captured in Dublin in June 1944, tried before a military tribunal and sentenced to hang for the murder of a sergeant in the Irish police, the Garda Siochana Special Branch two years before. The execution left the IRA, for the first time ever, without a chief of staff, an Army Council or any Headquarters staff.

Despite his youthfulness Gerry Adams did not see fit to petition for release or remission on his sentence. On 9 December 1946 he stepped out of the gates of Crumlin Road prison under a general amnesty for prisoners under twenty-one years of age, leaving Hugh McAteer behind him in the jail. His release on licence by order of the Governor of Northern Ireland came after he had served just over half of his eight-year sentence. All the internees had been released the previous year. The Second World War was over, but the Belfast IRA's wartime campaign had collapsed well before the German surrender. It was time for Gerry Adams to find work again as a labourer and build something approaching an ordinary life. 'From his behaviour he gave no indication that he wished to continue his militant activity,' a detective familiar with the Belfast IRA observed.

Not much more than a year after being released from jail he married Annie Hannaway, a strikingly good-looking woman from an equally staunch republican family and a doffer in one of Belfast's numerous linen mills. Veteran republicans say that she was a member of Cumann na mBan. Annie's three brothers, Tommy, Billy and Alfie, had all been interned too. In the 1990s Alfie Hannaway was still active within the wider Republican family, considered by some a representative of the National Graves Association which looks after IRA graves and a strong advocate of the republican demand that Tom Williams' remains should be exhumed from their resting place in the grounds of the Crumlin Road jail and given a reburial in a specially reserved plot in Belfast's Milltown cemetery.

In September 1995 the Northern Ireland Office announced that 'Her Majesty has signed the warrant for remission.' A few months earlier Belfast High Court had ruled that the Northern Ireland Secretary had the authority to exercise the Royal Prerogative of mercy and order the body exhumed. Campaigners claimed that the NIO had long argued that it would be impossible to locate Tom Williams' unmarked grave among those of fifteen others inside the walls of the Crum, but in the summer of that year the Northern Ireland Secretary Sir Patrick Mayhew was spotted in the grounds of the prison with the governor, perusing a map.

The long IRA ceasefire of August 1994 was entering the finest summer weather that Northern Ireland had experienced in a decade and the news that Tom Williams was finally to get his dying wish chimed with the optimism of the period. It seemed that the past was finally going to be laid to rest. But at the time of writing the reburial ceremony has not yet taken place. The authorities say they can release his bones only to a next of kin and the nearest surviving relative is determined that the republicans will not have them. The IRA has divided many families in Ireland, in certain instances even some of its own. Since the warrant for remission was signed, Tom Williams' unmarked grave has grown even lonelier with the closure of the Crum as a prison.

The newly married Adamses moved in with Gerry's mother in Abercorn Street, back in the Pound Loney where the IRA's D Company still existed, in name at least. It was an inauspicious start to their marriage; the tiny kitchen cottage was already cramped with three of Gerry's brothers, Paddy, Sean and Frank, all living there too. Overcrowding was endemic in working-class Belfast. One of the few compensations of the privations of life in these streets of two-up, two-downs was the strong sense of community and the intimate bonds of family. On 6 October 1948 the crowded household was delighted to welcome a new addition to the family. Annie gave birth, just across the Grosvenor Road, in the Royal Victoria Hospital. Her firstborn was a boy, who took his looks from his mother but was named for his father – Gerry Adams junior.

CHAPTER TWO

Gerry Adams Junior

The birth of Gerry Adams may have delighted his parents and the extended Adams–Hannaway family, but when he was joined by a baby sister, Margaret, a year later, the house in Abercorn Street was ready to burst at its seams. Mother and father and the two toddlers reluctantly departed, taking themselves out of the city along the north shore of Belfast Lough to Greencastle, where they rented a single room in a large house owned by an order of nuns. With its plaster-board walls to give some semblance of privacy to the parents, it was young Gerry's first experience of partition, but to get running water or go to the toilet they had to leave the 'flat' and go upstairs.

It was only a few miles from the Falls Road but it felt much further. They struggled on there for more than four years, during which time Gerry and Margaret were joined by a brother, Paddy, and a sister, Anne. While Annie busied herself with her children – in all she was to bear thirteen, with the deaths in infancy of three boys – her husband was out scouting for work as a labourer. Many potential employers looked askance at his prison record, which was furnished by the employment exchange for every job interview.

Belfast was chronically short of decent housing and a major construction programme was begun in 1947 by the Estates Committee of Belfast Corporation, which acquired fifty-nine acres at the foot of Black Mountain, part of the chain of hills which dominate the city's western skyline. The shortage was in no small part due to the wartime bombing raids, but the damage to people and property had been compounded by the complacency of the Stormont government and the city corporation, which assumed that Belfast was out of range of the German bombers and failed to build enough shelters, arrange proper evacuation or provide fire cover.

In one night in April 1941 the Luftwaffe bombers completely missed their intended targets, the strategically important factories and the docks which the IRA had endeavoured to guide them towards by supplying maps via a German spy in Dublin, and instead hit densely populated areas of North Belfast. More than 700 people were killed, 1,600 houses completely destroyed and a further 28,000 dwellings severely damaged. When the war ended Belfast was a scarred city with a huge homeless population, further swollen by large numbers of returning servicemen, living in hastily erected prefabricated bungalow estates and huts formerly occupied by troops.

Annie Adams dreamed and lobbied in equal measure to get one of the new houses and was ecstatic when she was finally allotted one in Ballymurphy, on the lower slopes of the Black Mountain. She made several pilgrimages to the building site, bringing young Gerry with her to watch the progress of 11 Divismore Park, an end-terrace with its own gable wall and garden. In the early 1950s the Adamses took up residence. By comparison with Greencastle the luxury of having three bedrooms and a bathroom made it seem like a palace.

For young Gerry life in the new estate was a far cry from the gloomy partitioned room the family had inhabited in Greencastle. The corporation moved many more young married couples into the estate, some of them ex-soldiers and their wives who, like the Adams family, went on to have large broods of children. If Gerry tired of playing with his brothers Paddy, Liam, Sean and Dominic or his sisters Margaret, Anne, Frances, Maura and Deirdre there were always plenty of other children around and lots of open space. With its paths and streams the Black Mountain was an adventurous boys' paradise. Adams has recorded his own earliest memories as larking around on the edges of the estate or up on the slopes of the mountain jumping across rivers, swinging on ropes like junior Tarzans and catching frogs. Others who lived in the same street remember a less outgoing child, anxious to heed the orders of his father, known to all and sundry as Pa Adams. 'He was stand-offish, didn't get too involved with the rest of us that much, his Dad gave the impression that they were somehow a cut above the rest of us.'

In spite of its access to the great outdoors the Ballymurphy estate – or 'the Murph' as it was affectionately nicknamed – was not much of a paradise. The hasty construction of so many new homes had been facilitated by the use of cheap materials such as quick-drying concrete instead of the traditional Belfast red brick of the narrow streets further down the Falls into which Gerry had been born. The lack of cavities in the houses created dampness and cold, bequeathing the residents health problems in years to come. There was no church, community hall, shops or school and with so many bored youngsters running wild and nothing to occupy them it wasn't long before vandalism crept in.

Almost half of the estate's households were out of work, subsisting on state handouts. Some of the families rehoused in Ballymurphy when the Ministry of Health and Local Government ordered the closure of the remaining wartime huts brought with them their own problems too. Although there were many Protestant families in the estate, the fact that the Catholic Church had bought a large patch of it and then acquired the two acres of land earmarked for a Protestant primary school tended to underpin the segregation which was already such a feature of the city. All of these factors combined to give Ballymurphy a bad reputation.

'People who lived there couldn't find work because of the name of the estate,' said Joe Camplisson from Turf Lodge, the neighbouring estate. 'We were tuppence hapenny looking down on tuppence, if you like. Ballymurphy was a transit camp. There were vulnerable people there who could be easily manipulated.' It was certainly an estate where many of the inhabitants didn't want to stay too long. Protestants exercised whatever pull they had with the unionist authorities and got themselves allotted homes in better estates. According to one estimate as many as 12,000 familes passed through the estate's 660 houses over a period of fourteen years.

Among the Adamses' neighbours was Andy Tyrie, a quietly spoken youngster who went on to become better known as one of Ulster's most fearsome loyalist leaders. Tyrie's family had moved up from the Shankill like those of a lot of other Protestant ex-servicemen. While he considered the housing to be good, the rents were six times greater than closer to the city centre. 'A lot of Shankill people brought their traditions with them, the flags and so on, but most of the estate's problems came from the outside, the Whiterock Road and the gaelic football and soccer parks. There was an awful lot of decent people but always the extremists seem to overrule. From my own point of view it was a mixed community. I remember people called Killen and the son saying to me whenever we were playing in the street that his father had been an officer in the old Irish Republican Army, but this was an old man.' When he was eight years old Tyrie's family moved across the Springfield Road to New Barnsley, the neighbouring estate, which was almost exclusively Protestant. Ballymurphy was changing, 'everyone who left was being replaced by Roman Catholics, Protestants didn't feel comfortable there any more. The transport system only went down the Falls Road and a big Catholic school was built right in the centre, so the Protestants felt gradually excluded.'

The Adams family didn't move. Annie genuinely loved the house and though her struggle to feed and clothe so many children grew harder with each passing year the sense of community grew. Old friends like the Cahills felt the same way and the families became pillars of a community which was increasingly Catholic and nationalist in character.

When he turned six young Gerry started at St Finian's De La Salle primary school and moved back down the Falls Road to live with his grandmother Margaret Adams in Abercorn Street, a common enough arrangement for large households with meagre resources. St Finian's was run by the Christian Brothers, a religious order renowned in Ireland for their muscular form of Catholicism and stiff classroom discipline.

The Christian Brothers were founded in 1808 as a teaching order of professed celibates without the rank of priesthood by Edmund Rice, who was beatified by Pope John Paul II in 1996. In the spring of the following year its leader Brother Edmund Garvey became the latest Irish Catholic functionary to apologize on behalf of the organization 'for having excessively physically abused and sometimes even sexually abused children in our [the Christian Brothers'] care . . . I am sorry to say that at times, with some of our men, we reflected some of that harshness and cruelty only too adequately. I believe all I can do is ask for forgiveness.' The influence of the Brothers is waning but they have educated many of those who have gone on to make their names in nationalist Ireland. An Irish shamrock nestling alongside more avowedly religious symbols in its emblem makes its belief in Holy Ireland explicit. Gaelic sports and language played a strong role in the life of the schools, trips to the Irish-language-speaking areas of Ireland's west coast were organized in the holidays and history lessons reflected the national sense of grievance at 800 years of English colonialism. Many of the teachers were from the rural South, 'sons of the Sod' with a liberal attitude towards corporal punishment.

'It was almost a form of educational subversion,' recalls one Catholic member of the professional classes whose schooling in Belfast was cared for by the Brothers. 'Everything was driven and directed towards passing examinations and that was out of a sense of siege and grievance. There was no attempt to foster a civic culture. The only culture was Gaelic.' The Brothers' own stated aims and ideals included the striking phrase, 'to fit the pupils under our tuition for the battle of existence', and there seemed evidence aplenty to suggest that this was taken quite literally. Adams remembers being hit by a teacher on his first day at the school, but despite the harsh discipline he seems to have liked the place. The Irish ethos of the school gelled with the family's republican traditions.

These were happy times for him, dividing his time between two homes: the noisy Ballymurphy one where he could sometimes listen to his mother singing republican songs and the quieter home of his grandmother Margaret, the same woman who had promised Mr Justice Brown she would take care of his wounded father if the court acquitted the young IRA man. The IRA had been deep in the family's blood for generations. Margaret's husband, who died when still young in 1938, was once a member of the Irish Republican Brotherhood, the forerunner of the IRA which Michael Collins once commanded. Most of her sons followed their father into the IRA. Her introvert grandson Gerry adored her and relished the undivided attention lavished upon him as the only child in the house. Almost a surrogate mother, it was Margaret who gave Gerry his love for reading, borrowing books for him from the local library.

He enjoyed school and worked hard but never shone at St Finian's. The hopes of every large Irish family rode on the eldest son and the Adamses were ambitious for Gerry. When he failed his Eleven Plus examination they did not give up. His mother trailed him across the Shankill and up the Crumlin Road to St Pat's, which refused him, and then over to St Gabriel's intermediate school above Ardoyne on the Crumlin Road, which gave him another chance. The long walk there every day took him past a Protestant school, but there was never any bother. The pupils walked on different sides of the road. After a year's cramming he tried for the Eleven Plus again and this time passed, qualifying for a place at St Mary's, the Christian Brothers' grammar school. It was Annie, his grandmother, who accompanied him to the school outfitters on Divis Street to buy him his first uniform.

He had lost a year on his contemporaries but there were compensations. He would go to an aunt's house for lunch every day, where he became better acquainted with one of his cousins, Kevin Hannaway, a bond which would prove important within the close knit world of republicanism in later years. Kevin proudly boasted that he could trace his family as far back as Michael Dwyer, one of the very last of the United Irishmen of the 1798 rebellion to surrender and come down from the hills around Dublin.

The United Irishmen, founded by Wolfe Tone and radical Belfast Presbyterians like Henry Joy McCracken, was the only organization in Ireland to succeed, briefly, in uniting Catholic, Protestant and Dissenter against the British. But its military campaign quickly slithered into disarray and bouts of sectarian-motivated slayings of Protestants. In republican circles those with the longest pedigree of activism are held in the highest regard. Judged on that criterion by their contemporaries, the Adamses and the Hannaways had emerald green blood running through their veins.

During these formative years there were three main influences in Gerry's life: the various branches of the Adams and Hannaway families with their intertwined histories of republican activism and his father, the 'dedicated and determined republican with strong views' according to the RUC; the Gaelic-tinged education provided by the Christian Brothers; and the Catholic Church, via weekly confraternity meetings at Clonard Monastery.

Thirty years later, addressing an ecumenical gathering inside the monastery, he told the congregation that he felt very much at home. 'I remember, and some of the priests may have a similar memory, of coming here to Confraternity. We used to call it Confo, and Father McLaughlin was the main man in those days. Thousands of boys would have filed into the pews here and we were in different sections and there used to be great gusty renditions of all the various hymns and we used to particularly enjoy singing Tanto Mergo, make my hair grow.'

St Mary's in Barrack Street was a great red-brick building, a typical old-time grammar school whose students were expected to be sober and industrious. Grammar education was a serious undertaking and the School Boards made certain that the parents of these young scholars appreciated the fact by furnishing them with a letter which posed searching questions. The passing of the 1947 Education Act, which provided free and compulsory secondary education, was in the process of creating the first generation of professional Catholics in Northern Ireland.

But the new system wasn't without its problems. 'Since 1948 so many requests for pupils to be allowed to leave Grammar Schools have been received before the end of the six year course that the Education Committee wish you in your interests, for the happiness of your child and to ensure the profitable expenditure of public funds, to weigh very carefully all the considerations,' one such letter solemnly stated. 'Every parent thinking of a Grammar School education for his child should ask himself the following questions: Is it my firm intention to keep my child at the school for at least six years? Is my child fond of book learning? The child who has no love of reading is not likely to be happy in a Grammar School.'

At the end of it all the possibility of going on to get a well paid job beckoned, perhaps even joining one of the professions. But *en route* the Adams and other families would, as the document explained, have to dig deep:

> Parents of Grammar School pupils will be required to make some financial sacrifice, for example, earning will be deferred until the pupil is seventeen or eighteen years old and money will have to be spent on uniforms, games and other incidentals. At home, if at all possible, the pupil should have a quiet room free from family disturbances to do the school homework that will be required.
>
> How does your child wish to be employed? If a boy wants to become an apprentice to a trade, a course at the Secondary Intermediate or Technical Intermediate would be more suitable as apprenticeships must be entered into at sixteen years of age. A Grammar School pupil should have a capacity for hard work, perseverance and ambition. Experience in the past years shows that some parents have not given sufficient thought at the time of making this important decision.

The Adams family was not put off. Young Gerry, their eldest child, was the first to attend a grammar school and he was getting on in the world, rubbing shoulders with the sons of publicans and doctors and people who could afford foreign holidays. Initially he found the imposing red-brick St Mary's a daunting establishment. 'Quite quickly I had an acute sense that we were being equipped, as young Catholics, to find places within the professions,' he told the *Irish Times*. 'We did a lot of English history to which I didn't object but very little Irish history. Dick Dynan, our elocution teacher who we called Dirty Dick, gave us a local history lesson on one occasion and that kindled in me a lifelong interest in both local and social history.'

Because of the year at St Gabriel's Gerry was now a year older than most of his classmates. Brother Beausang, who taught him Latin and religious education, remembers that Adams 'always sat at the back for the very good reason that he was taller than most of them, he was a big lad you know and very quiet, I would say, even to the point of being a bit taciturn'. In the view of his teacher the young Adams was a boy who would have been good at keeping secrets. 'He was pensive and thoughtful, he was that sort of fellow who kept himself to himself. He wasn't one of the chatterboxes and was quiet and you never knew and I often did wonder myself what was going on in that little head of his and it wasn't such a little head either as he was a fine, big, well-built fellow.'

On one occasion Adams came to his master's aid, when a fellow pupil, the son of a local landlord, fainted. 'Somebody at the bottom of the class shouted out, "man overboard!" So we all ran to where this fellow was down on the floor and the sweat pouring off him. The thing I remember most was young Adams coming up to the middle of the scene and saying, "Open his collar, sir," which was a fantastic piece of advice to have given. I might not in the excitement of the moment have even thought of it. So we did open the collar to give him a bit of fresh air. And I often wondered after that it showed a certain kind of common sense in the midst of calamity. It was very much in his favour.'

Such a vivid recollection is more the exception than the rule. Because of his reluctance to contribute to class Adams made only a fleeting impression on his teachers. Brother Beausang confesses that if a colleague had asked him after one of his lessons whether the young Adams had been in school he would have been hard pressed to remember whether he had been in the classroom or not. In retrospect the teacher now thinks of the silence as impressive and even in some ways reminiscent of the character of one of Adams' legendary republican forebears, Padraig Pearse. 'He was quiet and minded his own business and was never anxious to throw any light on what we were discussing and had his own thoughts about things, and as far as I was concerned that was all right too if that's the way he wanted it. He was in his own quiet way an impressive sort of a fellow. He would impress you by his very quietness, by his silence. Now it strikes me there was a bit of the old Padraig Pearse in him. I would have guessed that he must have been that type of character, the same silent, deep-thinking sort of a guy as Pearse was.'

Academically Beausang didn't consider Adams anything special, although every boy who made it through to grammar school had already achieved something. 'I wouldn't have considered him any great genius because on account of the sort of guy he was. He could have been a genius but you didn't see the flowering then and there, it was all in this hidden kind of a way.' When it came to politics Beausang again noticed little out of the ordinary, but the Christian Brothers at St Mary's assumed that most of their charges from the area around the overwhelmingly Catholic Falls Road were bound to be strongly nationalist in inclination. 'The lads that came to us from the immediate vicinity would all have been to some extent a bit republican, you know, and therefore you didn't notice any great difference between him and the majority of the lads in the class.' As far as Brother Beausang was concerned, 'I never noticed him any more republican than anybody else and nor would I at that stage have seen any signs of leadership, you know, because he didn't show himself to people. He wasn't that sort, he wasn't that outgoing type.'

While the Irish ideals of the Christian Brothers might have reinforced his outlook, Adams' political education was always more likely to have occurred outside the classroom. In recent years Gerry Adams has maintained that he managed to reach the age of thirteen unburdened by political awareness. At this stage his thoughts were of hurling and holidays.

His father had been over to England to find work and had given such serious consideration to taking his large family off to seek a new life in Australia that he had filled in the forms for an assisted passage. In October 1960 he sought to take advantage of the scheme and admitted his past criminal record. A police report was sought on whether he could be safely recommended to the Australian authorities, and Gerry Adams was interviewed twice by the RUC.

While he still declared himself to be a republican he claimed to have abandoned his faith in the use of physical force. A united Ireland could be and would be achieved in time, but through constitutional means, he told his interviewers. Although tabs were kept on him nothing really detrimental was observed, and the police were impressed by his frankness and apparent concern for the welfare of his family. Although it was felt that Gerry Adams could be safely recommended for a new life in Australia, nothing ever came of the scheme and historians can only speculate on the altered course of the looming Troubles if he had taken his family away from Ireland to begin a new life.

Whether or not the patriarchal figure of 11 Divismore Park told his large family that constitutional reform would one day lead them all to the Republic is a moot point. It is hard to imagine that the long evenings before the Adams household acquired a black and white television set in the early 1960s were not taken up in retelling old republican stories. Just as other children brought up during the 1950s learned on their father's knees of what their daddy did during the war, it seems unlikely that the young Gerry did not venture on occasion to discover why his Da was shooting at peelers when he was only sixteen and why he had spent four years of his early life behind bars.

It wasn't as if Gerry Adams senior was averse to talking about the good old days to those close to him. On Saturday nights he used to go out drinking with some of his old IRA pals, raiding the pantry afterwards for a bowl of soup. Often his former jail-mates would come home with him, and out of these impromptu get-togethers was founded the Irish Republican Felons Association, with Gerry Adams senior as its first chairman.

There were more than just his father's exploits for the young Adams to hear about. His paternal grandfather, who had died before the war, had been active in the Irish Republican Brotherhood, the forerunner of the IRA. And there were the occasional trips to Dublin to see his uncle Dominic, a veritable hard man long remembered with something approaching awe back in the narrow streets of the Pound Loney.

His mother's republican pedigree was if anything even more

impressive. Adams' maternal great-grandfather Michael Hannaway, originally from Sligo, had been one of the original Fenians, a radical nationalist movement responsible for bombing England in the nineteenth century. His mother's father Billy Hannaway had worked with the trade unionist Jim Larkin and with James Connolly, who as one of the seven men who had signed the proclamation of Easter 1916 was regarded as a founding father of modern-day republicanism.

Billy Hannaway acted as an election agent for De Valera when he contested the West Belfast constituency on a purist republican platform after the First World War, but parted company with him when he settled for the governance of less than all of Ireland's thirty-two counties. There were family ties with Cumann na mBan, the Women's IRA, not to mention his uncle Liam Hannaway, who served in D Company alongside Gerry senior and was one of the group of older men whose active republican careers were to span both the campaign during the Second World War and the resurgence of Provisional IRA violence in the early 1970s.

When a teenage boy in Belfast wanted to translate into action his commitment to republican values from listening to stories of past glorious deeds there were two options open to him in Belfast in the 1960s. Sinn Fein, the political wing of the republican movement, existed in name if little else, with a small number of members as an adjunct to the IRA. Most had membership of both. Joining the IRA wasn't open to boys until they were at least sixteen or seventeen, and after the collapse of the border campaign in 1962 there followed the suspension of Fianna Eireann, the republicans' answer to the Boy Scouts.

Adams has been open about his decision to join Sinn Fein, a party which during the 1960s was at some stages banned and at other times legal. He says he joined in 1964, almost immediately after the worst rioting for decades broke out around a temporary Sinn Fein office in Divis Street in West Belfast. The disturbances were sparked by that year's general election campaign in the constituency in which Liam McMillen was standing as a republican candidate. McMillen also wore another hat as the leader of the IRA in Belfast.

McMillen's party workers put up an Irish tricolour in the window of their office in defiance of a law passed by the Stormont government banning the flying of the flag. The tricolour was small and its display would probably have gone unnoticed, or at least ignored, by the RUC if it hadn't been for the Reverend Ian Paisley, a firebrand Protestant preacher who at that stage was supporting the agreed unionist candidate for West Belfast, James Kilfedder.

Paisley, the son of a Baptist minister who founded his own Free Presbyterian Church in 1951, was virulently opposed to the Roman Catholic Church. By the early 1960s he was acquiring a following among those Protestants who yearned for the certainties pedalled by nineteenth-century evangelicals such as Roaring Hugh Hanna. Paisley made a characteristically tub-thumping speech during a rally at the Ulster Hall in Belfast demanding that the Irish flag be taken down (the previous year he had demanded that another flag, the Union Jack on City Hall, be raised after it was lowered as a mark of respect to the deceased Pope John XXIII).

Paisley threatened that if the police did not do the job he would lead Protestant marchers into the area to take the flag down himself. The RUC responded by sending in a squad of constables who broke into the Sinn Fein office and removed the tricolour. That evening there was intense rioting in the area. Petrol bombs were hurled, a corporation trolley-bus was set alight and water cannon was deployed for the first time in forty years. The disturbances worsened when Sinn Fein re-erected the flag and the RUC moved in all over again, this time in even greater numbers, to take it down.

Adams portrays this as a seminal moment for him, that at the age of sixteen his naivety was shattered and he realized that the forces of law and order in the Northern Ireland state were inextricably linked with intransigent unionism. In his autobiography he claims to have witnessed what occurred but to have taken no part in the rioting. In an earlier work, *Falls Memories*, he comments more archly that some of the St Mary's schoolboys who watched the disturbances learned swiftly that the RUC didn't discriminate between spectators and full-blooded rioters and it was better to be caught for throwing stones than just staring. Other republicans from that period suggest that young Gerry had been in and out of the Sinn Fein office on several occasions before the riot even took place.

Whether rioter or onlooker, whether political innocent or, more plausibly, someone who had absorbed republicanism from his parents and grandparents, he joined the Sinn Fein effort, folding election leaflets after school. He wasn't discouraged when Liam McMillen lost his deposit.

Despite electoral failure, the rioting gave Belfast's republicans an unexpected but welcome boost, sufficient to permit them to entertain once more the hope that an effective movement could be re-established. The Fianna was taken out of mothballs and Adams joined up, along with his younger brothers, making him almost unique in entering the youth wing of the IRA only after involvement in the grown-up end of the movement.

The Fianna was established by the *grande dame* of Irish republicanism, Countess Markievicz, to counter Baden Powell's Boy Scouts, which was propagating the British way of life among Irish youths. But its first president was Bulmer Hobson, a West Belfast man who rented a field at the bottom of the Whiterock Road, beneath where Ballymurphy was later to sprout, where up to 300 boys regularly played hurling. Camping and woodcraft were all very well, but not if tied to the teachings of one of the most famous defenders of the British Empire.

When the Troubles erupted the Fianna took on a role as active adjunct to the IRA. Its young members would run messages for the older IRA volunteers, warn them if the security forces were in the area or perhaps help in staging an incident which might lure police or soldiers into a trap. In Adams' younger days the function of the organization was more benign, learning the basic lessons of the republican creed and providing colour parties at the commemorations of important anniversaries. As one republican told the authors, the Fianna was part of the rites of passage for any boy in the dozen or so families which made up the movement in Belfast in the 1960s. 'You would have went into the Fianna first, coming into your teens, start going away on camps and so forth. Then when you got to seventeen or eighteen if you were the right material the IRA would take you.'

In 1964 Adams had other things than politics and street riots to worry about. He had to sit his Junior Certificate examination. 'The curriculum was exam driven and in third year I found myself becoming disaffected,' he told the *Irish Times*. 'I wasn't a diligent student but I did well enough in my O levels to put me on track for A levels. I loved English and geography but detested maths, and after five years of Latin and French I can barely remember a word.'

His school report shows that when he first entered St Mary's his best subject was geography, followed by English. In the next three years his results dropped back, so that by Easter of 1964 he was languishing at the bottom of his class. He must have been given a talking to and pulled himself together because he managed to scrape through the Junior Certificate, performing best in Irish and winning credits in English and geography, but failing Latin, arithmetic and algebra.

Despite having made it on to the final two years of Senior Certificate and the possibility of going on to university it is clear that his heart was no longer in it. 'When I was about seventeen I opted out of school and became a barman to the great disappointment of my parents, who had made great sacrifices to send me to grammar school and who tried to persuade me to stay on. They believed that I was passing up an opportunity that they had never had. My decision to leave school was prompted partly by the fact that I had become caught up in the republican movement as a result of the Divis Street riots in 1964 and partly because a lot of my friends outside school were working and I felt the odd man out.' Besides, with his father more out of work than in it, watching his mother's endless struggle to provide for so many mouths got the better of her eldest son, and a sense of duty compelled him to become the breadwinner.

His final examination results at Christmas 1964 record a bare eight marks in history and within a few more months he had left St Mary's to take up a job in a Catholic-owned bar in the Protestant Old Lodge Road in North Belfast. His school principal, under 'remarks', wrote 'Apprentice Barman' at the end of the school record, followed in another hand by a perfunctory 'very satisfactory'. It could hardly have been the true view of his educational mentors, bearing in mind the stern letter furnished to all grammar-school parents at the outset of their children's education, urging them to consider seriously the possibility of failure.

The previous year Adams had witnessed the Divis Street riots and became actively involved in the conspiratorial world of republican politics. In 1965, when the granite façade of the unionist government in Northern Ireland was finally beginning to show its first cracks in more than forty years, Gerry Adams left school and joined the IRA. He was sixteen, the same age as his father had been when he picked up a Webley and shot a policeman.

CHAPTER THREE

The Volunteer

Ask Gerry Adams what his relationship is with the IRA and he will tell you that he does not have one. Ever since he emerged as one of the principal leaders of that organization in the mid-1970s he has stuck doggedly, in spite of the best efforts of hundreds of journalists and even on one occasion of the families of the IRA hunger strikers dying in Long Kesh, to the position that he is not and never has been a member of the IRA. Prior to the reorganization of the IRA in the mid-1970s the leadership in Belfast never made a great secret of who they were. In 1971, for instance, Joe Cahill was introduced to a press conference by the local MP Paddy Kennedy as the Provisional IRA leader in Belfast.

In his preparation of the IRA for a long war Adams changed the rules. In December 1986, at the launch of his book *The Politics of Irish Freedom*, he said, 'I don't have any paramilitary connections . . . I am not a member of the IRA and have not been a member of the IRA.' Such denials provoke plenty of cynical, cross-community laughter in cities such as Belfast, where, to borrow a local phrase, the dogs in the street know his IRA pedigree. The security forces on both sides of the Irish border, his political opponents and even some of his more candid allies regard these denials not in the same category as those of a reformed alcoholic refusing a drink but as a position of convenience.

Adams himself says in the foreword to his autobiography that he is constrained from writing anything which would jeopardize the lives or liberty of others, and it is only natural to assume that he extends the same care to himself. In 1978, after several years in which numerous newspaper reports identified him as a senior IRA leader and in the immediate aftermath of the La Mon bombing, in which twelve people were burned to death and twenty-three others injured, the

RUC arrested Adams and charged him with membership of an illegal organization. But later the same year Northern Ireland's Lord Chief Justice released him, saying that while he might be an IRA commander there was insufficient evidence to bring him to trial.

During the course of research for this book the authors have spoken to former members of the IRA who operated within the organization alongside Gerry Adams. We have also received information from reliable security sources in Northern Ireland and the Irish Republic. On occasion, as such sources readily concede, the picture can be blurred. A tip-off from one agent may reflect the part of the picture to which he or she is privy, but not match exactly the information provided by another. As a secret army, the IRA does not feel obliged to help observers by publishing a prospectus outlining the names and curriculum vitae of its most senior commanders. But we are satisfied that the details of Adams' career in the IRA which are described in this book represent a fair picture of a truth which he himself is bound to deny.

Adams' active involvement in the IRA can be traced to 1965, when he was invited to join by the Belfast O/C (officer commanding) Liam McMillen, then wearing his IRA hat rather than his Sinn Fein one. Adams was sworn in by McMillen's number two in Belfast, Jim Sullivan, and like his father before him joined D Company of the IRA. At that stage D Company was not the force it had been during the Second World War nor what it was to become during the height of the Troubles, when its members were dubbed on the Falls Road 'the Dogs'. It was certainly one of the most dangerous weapons in the IRA's war against the British. McMillen once admitted that in 1962, at the close of the IRA's disastrous border campaign, there had been only twenty-four members in all of Belfast.

Operation Harvest was launched on 12 December 1956 when approximately 150 men attacked targets along the border, including a BBC transmitter, a magistrates' court and a police station. Although the opening shots may have looked impressive, the plan was built upon Alice in Wonderland foundations, relying upon the wholly mistaken belief that the population of the predominantly Catholic border counties would welcome their Southern liberators. In all six RUC members died and nineteen were wounded. The IRA lost two men in action and seven were killed accidentally in premature explosions. There had been 300 major incidents and several hundred minor ones, with damage estimated at one and a half million pounds. At its conclusion Operation Harvest seemed to many like the last throw of the dice, a campaign whose architects had known they could not succeed but who clung to the hope that, as in 1916, the acts of a few brave men would provoke a greater crisis and convert the Catholic people of Northern Ireland into a risen people.

The IRA's ceasefire statement declaring that it was dumping arms in effect admitted the unpalatable truth that Northern Ireland enjoyed at the very least the passive support of its Catholic minority. For the first time in the state's brief history the optimists were able to discern the foundations for Northern Ireland's future. With the IRA beaten, it was time to build trust across the religious divide. But the colossal scale of the restructuring which was required and the reluctance of most unionists to rise to its challenge would have fatal consequences for the Stormont regime by the end of the decade.

There was evidence of new thinking within the IRA too for those with a mind to discover it. Traumatized and exhausted by the failure of the border campaign, the militarists either left the organization or were forced to consider alternative paths to lead them to the Republic. As the physical-force tradition conceded defeat the centre of gravity swung away from the border and back once more to Dublin, where Cathal Goulding replaced Ruairi O Bradaigh as chief of staff. Goulding preferred arguing left-wing politics in bars to plotting further conspiracy. Goulding was contemptuous of the Belfast IRA. 'For them the fight had become an end in itself. They were not planning to *achieve* the freedom of Ireland, they simply wanted to *fight* for it,' he told the authors.

'From 1962 it was dead as a doornail,' says a young recruit to the republican movement in the 1960s from a traditional family background.

What you had from '62 until '66 was ongoing debate with very little membership, on issues like abstentionism, 'Where do we go from here?' The border campaign of blowing up bridges and cows and B Specials [the overwhelmingly Protestant police reserve], the people didn't give a damn. There were members of the republican movement who were taken from their beds and put in prison for four years and their neighbours didn't even know who they were.

The 1964 Divis Street riots reawoke the whole republican organization and gave it a lot more publicity and that would have attracted many more people into it. Then you had the initial discussions of 'Look, we need to be with the people and their problems,' and ongoing at that stage you had the housing situation in Tyrone, Derry and the housing action groups in which members of the republican movement were involved.

It was into this ferment of ideas that Gerry Adams was plunged, but many of the Belfast traditionalists, among whom were planted his family roots, were deeply suspicious of a path which they recognized as leading towards constitutionalism. Orders from Dublin to set up or infiltrate existing tenants associations, trades unions and housing action committees cut against the grain. Soldiers of Ireland fought the Brit enemy, they didn't help prop up the British state by assisting in its reform.

The tumultuous events changing the Western world in the 1960s were penetrating even the inward-looking IRA. Before that decade the very model of a traditional IRA volunteer was Sean South, the pious young Irish-language activist who was killed during the border campaign. Volunteers were expected to be abstemious in their drinking and attend chapel regularly. Inside Crumlin Road prison the Belfast O/C Billy McKee used to order his men to accompany him to Mass. Although the teenage recruits shared the same ambition with their peers of sending the British home they found the old attitudes chafing.

Even so, the new generation was in many respects as conspiratorial and suspicious of the 'unbelievers' as its fathers. Michael Farrell, a student at Queen's University in Belfast who went on to become prominent in the civil rights movement, recalled meeting the teenage Adams and his friend Joe McCann with a view to forging links between the housing action committees set up by the Dublin republican leadership and Belfast's Young Socialists movement. Farrell remembered them as two young working-class activists, with McCann creating a bigger impression than Adams. 'McCann was very charismatic, he was the guy doing all the talking. They were somewhat politically sectarian, the republican movement didn't like working with anybody else. Nothing ever really came of the meeting, I don't think they were very interested in us. We were just students.'

Easter 1966 was a fraught period in Northern Ireland. The Divis Street riots of two years earlier were still a fresh memory and confrontation was expected. Elaborate security measures were taken and the border practically sealed to satisfy paranoid unionists that on the fiftieth anniversary of the Rising the republicans would not stage a *coup d'état*. The approach of the anniversary had raised fears in both London and Dublin that the IRA might be poised to launch a new campaign. One Scotland Yard estimate, forwarded to the Labour Prime Minister Harold Wilson, claimed that '3,000 trained members or supporters could be called out in an emergency' and warned of 'the real threat' from the IRA.

The Orange Order lobbied Stormont Prime Minister Terence O'Neill to ban a commemoration parade in West Belfast but it went ahead and 10,000 people marched to a rally at Casement Park. Gerry Adams, sporting a black beret, was part of the parade's colour party alongside his cousin Kevin Hannaway. It was a position which could only go to a seventeen-year-old with impeccable republican credentials and connections. Given the tense atmosphere in the city and the emergence of a Protestant terrorist organization calling itself the Ulster Volunteer Force it was a miracle that the parade passed off without major incident.

According to an observer from British military intelligence, Brigadier W. M. T. Magan, this was due to three reasons: 'a) the restraint of the Ulster authorities in assisting, rather than obstructing, the organisers of the provocative nationalist parade, b) the closing of the Border which deterred IRA members from risking entry to the North and c) the high order of police work'. In fact the 'intelligence expert' had spectacularly over-estimated the readiness and capacity of the Belfast IRA to create trouble. Many of the older IRA members, the Forties men, had drifted away in disgust at the new leftwards direction favoured by Dublin. The old certainties of a thirty-two-county Irish Republic achieved through violence no longer held sway. The religious piety of some collided with and broke against the modish Marxism of the new direction.

Undoubtedly some of the military traditions persisted. In a briefing to the Irish Prime Minister Jack Lynch, the Justice Department in Dublin had reported in 1966 that IRA strength had grown throughout Ireland from an estimated 650 in March 1962 to approximately 1,000. The Justice Department acknowledged that 'a certain amount of drilling with firearms' had taken place south of the Irish border, although Dublin appeared more relaxed about this than the Stormont government. In a secret letter written in December 1965 O'Neill described the open IRA training as most worrying. 'The sound of gunfire has been audible over a wide area. Instruction at these sessions has included live firing practice, lectures on the use of explosives, the making of booby traps and the mounting of attacks on government buildings. The RUC are aware of 34 such sessions or camps this year but there may, of course, have been many more.'

Some of the locations the RUC had established for these camps were in County Leitrim, near Glenfarne and Ballinamore. Gerry Adams has subsequently written of the days in 1967, a year after the RUC report, when he organized a camp for twenty Belfast republican youths at Drumshanbo, just up the road from Ballinamore. Although he gives little away about what went on, saying the camp was concentrating on scouting and fieldcraft, it is significant that the two people he remembers from this gathering – Kevin Delaney and Jimmy Quigley – are both Provisional IRA men subsequently killed on active service. Gerald McAuley, identified as attending the camp the following year, was a member of the Fianna killed at the outset of the troubles in 1969. Adams recalls that in the year he organized the camp the local priest invited his young republicans to provide a guard of honour at his chapel.

The Belfast Fianna had approximately seventy members at the time that Adams took his *sluagh*, or pack, on holiday to Leitrim. Along with Delaney, who subsequently blew himself up on board the Belfast-to-Dublin train while carrying a bomb, there were his younger brothers Paddy, Liam, Sean and Dominic to look after. While nothing particularly sinister took place (there was no firearms training, although at other Fianna gatherings the older boys would have been taught the basics of firearms) the camp was organized along military lines. Gerry was O/C, and he appointed his own adjutant, quartermaster and training officer as well as section leaders and intelligence officers.

Much of the fortnight was taken up with assembling the old Army bell tents in which the youngsters slept, digging latrines and fieldcraft, which involved learning how to move across open ground without being detected by the enemy. Older republicans visited the camp to give lectures in various subjects, including Irish history. The campers also played both the local Garda contingent and Gaelic Athletics

Association at hurling, a game in which Adams enjoyed some proficiency. At the church parade the Fianna boys formed a colour party and carried the Irish tricolour into church. Amazingly, even though the Fianna was officially illegal in the republic, a photograph of the campers even appeared in the local newspaper featuring Brendan Kielty, a spirit grocer, or publican, from Drumshanbo who fought on the side of the fascist Franco during the Spanish Civil War, just one of the hundreds who flocked to Spain from Ireland to fight in what many saw as a holy war. The authorities along the border turned a blind eye to such technical illegalities, especially when it was a case of supporting their oppressed nationalist kin in the North.

Adams was admired by Fianna members as an able leader. 'He was very astute and shrewd, he always involved everyone in what he was doing, it was "What should we do" rather than "This is what I think."' When not on annual camp many Fianna boys were seconded to run errands for the IRA and about half went on to become full members. Adams fell into that category. 'Anything that was going on he wanted to know, he wanted to be in it,' recalled another scouting chum. But others took a surprisingly different career route. Of the boys on camp with Adams that summer, two went on to join the British Army, one as a Royal Marine Commando and the other in the elite SAS. For some at least it was the thrill of fighting, rather than fighting for Ireland, which was foremost in their youthful minds.

If Adams' camp was a relatively innocent gathering of boys playing at the grown-up world of Irish freedom fighters, there were other meetings taking place along the border with far more serious objectives. As loyalist extremists and the security forces began reacting with ever increasing ferocity to Northern Ireland's fledgling civil rights movement, the tension within the IRA over its political direction was coming to a head. Some of the old Forties men who had dropped out began to get in touch again with their Belfast comrades.

As Cathal Goulding, IRA chief of staff during the 1960s, has admitted to the authors: 'There were training camps during the mid-1960s. That was because there was so much opposition to what I was doing, it was very difficult to please everybody. There was a lot of agitation for some training camps and it was coming from all over.' Goulding's Belfast comrade Liam McMillen readily admitted that in 1965 'the routine work of organizing a physical-force movement continued and although the IRA progressed to a degree, it failed to make an impact on the political scene'.

According to McMillen his dismal vote in the 1964 election had shown that the traditional republican policy of abstentionism, whereby candidates would stand but not take their seats if successful, was dead, but 'the embers of patriotism still smouldered'. Twelve thousand people had marched up the Falls to celebrate the fiftieth anniversary of the Easter Rising and two members of the Belfast Battalion Staff had been jailed for three months for organizing the parade, but it had been a worthwhile exercise. 'The ordinary everyday work of organizing the IRA was going on. Men were still being recruited, organized into sections, companies and units, and were being trained in the use of arms and explosives.' McMillen had succeeded in increasing the movement's numbers, by his own estimate, from its low point of twenty-four in 1962 to well over a hundred by 1968. These figures are disputed by young IRA volunteers, who say that in 1969 there were at best only seventy members, the vast majority of whom had family connections to the republican movement dating back decades.

While the border camps provided evidence that the military traditions were continuing in one shape or another, the radical rethink endorsed by the IRA leadership in Dublin was also moving ahead, albeit against resistance in many quarters. Leaning heavily on theories provided for him by an academic called Roy Johnston, Goulding wanted to reduce the role of physical-force republicanism and promote a left-wing analysis which emphasized class struggle and social and political agitation. His vision was of removing the sectarian barriers between Protestant and Catholic workers in the North, and then enabling them by stages to join with their Southern counterparts in the overthrow of capitalism in Ireland.

At a special meeting in 1964 of the IRA Army Convention, the organization's supreme authority, Goulding and his allies took the heretical step of proposing that republicans should not only stand for elections but also take their seats whether it be in the Dublin, Stormont or Westminster parliaments. The idea angered traditional republicans, who regarded these institutions as illegitimate, the continuing embodiment of the unjustified division of the island. According to the purists, the IRA was the only proper legal authority in the land and would remain so until partition was ended, the British gone and all the Irish people had taken part in a free and fair vote.

The move to end abstentionism was voted down, but Goulding and Johnston carried on with their work, propagating Marxist, secular and non-sectarian values. Some of the traditional Catholic IRA men regarded the left-wing academic with suspicion, especially when Johnston wrote an article for the republican newspaper the *United Irishman* criticizing the reciting of the rosary at IRA commemorations as a 'sectarian practice'. The English-born John Stephenson, who Gaelicized his name to Sean MacStiofain and was to become the first chief of staff of the Provisionals at the impending split, was so incensed that he ordered his men in Cork and Kerry not to sell the newspaper and was suspended for six months by GHQ as a consequence.

For the young Adams, a philosophy which challenged some of the accepted norms of his parents and teachers had its attractions. As a teenager, he once recalled, he had questioned the Catholic creed's tenet that there is 'one holy Catholic and Apostolic church'. He believed it was very sectarian to pray in this exclusive way only for your own denomination and took some persuading from a 'progressive' Catholic that the prayer was intended to refer to all Churches.

If he found the non-sectarian approach of Johnston to his taste, Adams similarly viewed the left-wing philosophy of the Dublin IRA leaders as, at the very least, thought-provoking. In later years he would come to criticize Goulding, drawing a distinction between the Dublin leadership, whose policy of involvement in civil rights agitation was pointing towards mere reform of Northern Ireland rather than its overthrow, the Belfast leadership which mutely went along with Dublin and the rank-and-file activists becoming involved in rising street activity and who took a 'more realistic attitude than that laid down by the Dublin leadership'.

Obviously Adams counted himself among this final category, but while he may have come to these conclusions in later life, and in order to justify the militarist line he pursued inside the Provisionals, it is most unlikely that such thoughts coursed through him at the time. Like any army the IRA of the 1960s had a rigid top–down command structure where bottom-rung volunteers, such as Adams, were expected to follow orders without asking too many questions. None of his contemporaries in the republican and civil rights movement can recall him expressing any strong opinions or doubts at the time. Indeed few can remember him at all. He carried with him the qualities which his teacher Brother Beausang first observed during class at St Mary's.

In any case, there was no alternative to the new direction; the traditional militarists were out in the cold after the fiasco of the border campaign. Agitational politics at least provided an outlet for eager republicans longing for action. Republican Clubs were set up to get round the state ban on Sinn Fein and, under orders from Dublin, the Belfast activists were directed to forge links with other groups, including Catholic and Protestant middle-class reformers, trade unionists and even Communist Party Members. Adams took part enthusiastically in discussion inside the Cyprus Street Gaelic Athletic Association hall on colonialism, partition and the historic role of the Fenians. Within the Wolfe Tone Society, set up at Johnston's behest, Adams debated civil rights and the gerrymandering by which the Unionist Party had deprived nationalists in the North of fair electoral representation. Republicans set up one man–one vote committees to highlight this point.

In 1967 Adams' commitment was rewarded when he was made public relations officer for the Andersonstown Republican Club. It was illegal to sell the *United Irishman*, the movement's newspaper which chronicled the leadership's obsessions of the time: campaigns against angling restrictions and housing action. To attract attention to the ban Adams briefly succeeded in getting himself arrested by hawking it on the street. But the plan for an orderly demonstration went awry when another republican started a fight with the police and was later charged with assault. Adams claims that with the police concentrating on his comrade he was able to walk out of the RUC station where he was being held and join a group of protesters gathered outside.

He was by now a working man, bringing in a weekly pay packet for his needy mother. It was in February 1965 that he left St Mary's, after seeing an advertisement in the *Irish News* for a barman's job. The Ark bar was situated on the corner of Broadbent Street and the Old Lodge Road and drew its custom from the Protestant streets around the Shankill and Crumlin Road. Pat Rooney was typical of the many Catholic landlords who owned and ran pubs in Protestant areas of Belfast, a tradition which sadly was to end with the onset of the Troubles.

Rooney and his wife Kathleen took to Gerry and very soon trusted him with most of the running of the Ark on their behalf. In the mornings he would walk over from Divis Street and open it up and give the small pub a thorough clean, scrubbing its tiled floor and polishing the bar. He became adept at the tricky art of pouring a perfect pint of porter and got on well with the Protestant customers. Kathleen Rooney remembers him as 'a very young lad, only seventeen, and very tidy. He seemed to be well educated, he was a great conversationalist and a brilliant singer. He could sing some of "The Sash" in Irish and sometimes he used to sing republican songs too. On a Saturday night there'd be quite a party going on. We hadn't a mixed house, the clientele were all elderly and Protestants, but they liked the singing well enough. Gerry seemed to me to be very well reared, there was never a wrong word out of him. He seemed to be very good to his family, he just used to go straight home to them after work.'

At closing time the regulars used to sing 'God Save the Queen', while Gerry cleared away the empty glasses. The idyll was not to last. Adams says he was sacked by the owners of the Ark bar as 12 July approached, the high point of the Orange marching-season calendar, for demanding the union rate for working a public holiday. Kathleen Rooney says that she does not recollect why they parted company. 'But I think he was desperate lucky in those days when there were few jobs to be had because he got ten pounds a week, which was a lot of money. I think he got well enough paid.'

Having walked out of the Ark bar in high dudgeon, he was fortunate to have such an active union organization behind him. The Duke of York in the city centre was anxious to recruit an apprentice barman and found Adams through the union. Jimmy Keaveney was one of the most respected landlords in Belfast, with a reputation for keeping a good bottle of Guinness. His pub was in a cobbled alleyway between Donegall Street and Hill Street and it drew in an eclectic mix of drinkers. For many years it was the RUC's favourite bar, not least because Jimmy was happy to send out meals and even drinks to police headquarters in nearby Waring Street. But it was also the focal point of radical Belfast, according to Paddy Devlin, the Health Minister in the ill-fated Sunningdale power-sharing executive. 'The best spielers in the city turned up constantly to display their wares,' he said. Among them were Bud Bossens, the rotund penner of an amusing and thought-provoking daily column called 'As I See It' in the staunchly unionist *Newsletter*, who held daily court in his 'office', a long-legged stool at the end of the bar.

Bossens would be joined by Sam Thompson, author of *Over the Bridge*, a controversial play which laid bare the sectarianism he knew at first hand from working in the Harland and Wolff shipyard. When the unionist authorities tried to suppress the play it became an even greater success, playing to packed audiences for weeks at the Dublin-owned Empire Theatre. There were trade unionists and leading lights in the Northern Ireland Labour Party and republicans like Liam McMillen and Proinsias MacAirt, otherwise known as Frank Card.

Over this great crossroads of intrigue and gossip presided 'wee' Jimmy Keaveney in his apron, keeping an eye on his spick, tightly run, gleaming, low-ceilinged bar. It was here that Adams says he first read the writings of James Connolly, from an edition donated to him by a regular. And he learned a few literary tricks from Bossens. Curiously, however, none of the surviving habitués of the Duke of York can remember Adams contributing to the general ambience. 'He was just a lanky kid cleaning glasses at the end of the bar, always smiling but never saying a word,' is the typical response from regulars prodded to remember the young barman.

Another of the mainstays of the Duke of York was Martin McBirney QC, a non-sectarian socialist who took 43 per cent of the vote in staunchly loyalist East Belfast in the 1966 general election. McBirney, a resident magistrate, was murdered by the Provisional IRA in 1976. Jimmy Keaveney lived above the shop with his mother and sister until the Duke of York was destroyed by a Provisional IRA bomb. The intended target was a regimental tailors a few doors down, but bombs seldom discriminate. In 1976 alone 408 bars were closed down for ever by the Troubles, the majority falling victim to the Provisional IRA's bombing campaign against 'economic targets', a strategy intended to bring Northern Ireland to its knees and make its existence unviable which has been credited to Gerry Adams.

The Belfast historian Jonathan Bardon remembers the night he was in the Duke of York when a bomb exploded. 'It was freezing weather and as we all stumbled out of the wreckage there were two drunks wading through broken glass and one said to the other: "Now mind yourself, Charlie, on that ice, you might slip and hurt yourself."' During the darkest hours of the Troubles the people of Belfast somehow managed to soldier on, sustained by their black humour and refusal to be beaten.

Gerry Adams moved from involvement in republican discussion classes to political action along the lines prescribed by Goulding. Housing was the chosen battleground, and he and others were directed from Dublin to set up the West Belfast Housing Action Committee with the aim of opposing the erection of a new high-rise development: Divis Flats. The group was modelled upon the Dublin Housing Action Committee, formed by Sinn Fein in May 1967. The committee drew the ire of the Roman Catholic Church, which saw the flats as a means to maintaining its hegemony in the area. From another quarter there was similar opposition, but for an entirely different reason. 'We would be out demonstrating and some of the older republicans would cross the street when they saw us. They'd shout "You should be out fighting the Brits not wasting your time with that." There was a real Red scare building up and we were always being accused of being communists. I remember the cry "Ho, Ho, Ho Chi Minh" coming from a lot of them when they saw us.'

Adams and another young republican started a local news-sheet called *Spearhead, Voice of Republican North*, whose motto 'We serve neither Crown nor Kremlin but Ireland' indicates the difficulties Goulding was facing. *Spearhead*'s obsessions were topics such as the invasion of Czechoslovakia, fish-meal factories, 'Free State Hypocrisy', gerrymandering in Derry and the plight of the small farmer. A lyrical description of the final moments of IRA man Tom Williams as he prepared himself for the Crumlin Road gallows – 'to join our martyred host in manhood's dawn' – has a whiff of Adams juvenilia about it and there are advertisements for forthcoming marches. The May 1967 edition announces: '*Spearhead* will still be published in spite of the recent ban imposed by the 6-county government. We request all readers to help us continue our humble work for Ireland by placing a regular order.'

Adams would print the news-sheet on an old hand-cranked Gestetner in a house in Cape Street. 'Everyone was coming of age, you had things to do, places to go,' recalled a contemporary. 'You actually felt you were doing something for a change rather than sitting back and learning Irish history. We realized we had to move away from the flag-waving but the waves that we made didn't please everybody. And Adams was everybody's son, a favourite with everyone.'

The development of Divis Flats rolled on in spite of the IRA opposition, but Adams and his Action Committee had more success when they occupied one of the first flats to be completed in an attempt to get somewhere to live for the Sherlocks, a family made homeless by a domestic fire. About twenty republicans took turns to squat the flat in shifts and such was the novelty of the action at the time that the local television stations turned up with cameras to film the event. Adams was thrust forward by his shy accomplices to act as spokesman. 'We were all just teenagers and Gerry was always good with words, he was smarter than most, always reading and talking. It just seemed the natural thing that he'd speak for us,' said a colleague. The Sherlocks got their flat.

Adams has latterly claimed that he harboured doubts about whether, north of the Irish border, things could ever be as smooth as Goulding and Johnston had envisaged in their gradualist or 'stages' theory. He says he respected Goulding as someone who openly presented himself as an IRA leader but had mixed feelings about the message. A combination of his family's background of violent republicanism and a pinch of scepticism drawn from what he saw on the ground may have made Adams wary of fully embracing the Goulding approach. But no one could have predicted the speed with which the fledgling civil rights campaign would spark a full-scale confrontation with the state and what swiftly degenerated into a sectarian killing campaign.

The civil rights movement had an IRA input from the start – Cathal Goulding was present at the meeting at Maghera in County Derry in 1966 which marked its birth. The Dublin IRA leadership saw the agitation as a good vehicle for its revolutionary creed, although there was never an intention to take it over. Nevertheless, the word went out to Adams and his comrades to redouble their political efforts and to get involved with the Northern Ireland Civil Rights Association.

NICRA was a broad coalition of Catholics and some liberal Protestants demanding one man one vote in local government elections, an end to gerrymandering, fair housing allocation, statutory protection against religious discrimination, repeal of the Special

Powers Act and the disbandment of the police reserve the B Specials. Its Belfast meetings were held in the city centre at St Mary's Hall.

Adams and his IRA comrades were provided by the Dublin leadership with lists of names of the people they were to vote on to the NICRA executive. Only two of the names were republicans, Goulding remaining conscious of the need to keep the civil rights bandwagon rolling as a broad front of reformist voices. 'We called it guided democracy,' he told the authors with a smile. 'You were given a list of names of people who you were to vote for,' said one junior IRA member who took part. 'Nothing was left to chance, we were even instructed on who to cheer, boo and heckle.' Some of the IRA members found their instructions to vote for communists a bridge too far. It had been drummed into their heads from childhood at church and school that Godless communism was as great an evil as British occupation. Adams, who in his contemporary persona has taken to reminding the public that he was a founder member of the civil rights movement, once confessed he found the Belfast meeting at which NICRA's first executive was elected 'a bit boring' and that he had no clear idea of what it would come to mean.

On 5 October 1968 civil rights marchers in Derry taking part in a banned parade were attacked by baton-wielding police – the most notable skull cracked was that of the nationalist MP for West Belfast Gerry Fitt. The sight of blood streaming from Fitt's wound filled television screens on that evening's news, alerting British opinion for the first time to the problem of discrimination in Northern Ireland. Adams, a rare participant in the demonstrations, watched the scenes of violence on the Duke of York's television set.

'In 1968 and 1969 there was a realization that things were going to hot up, that we were going to get something, that we were controlling events,' said one of the IRA's young street activists. 'If you had told me that this was all about reforming the six counties I wouldn't have believed you and I don't think the leadership thought that either. But we weren't doing much thinking at all, it was an opportunity to get into confrontations with the RUC. We were very naive, we didn't realize the hornet's nest we were stirring up. Things were moving too fast, you were such a small movement and you had to be everywhere.'

Adams' boss Jimmy Keaveney knew of his apprentice barman's involvement in republican politics and housing action and was amused by the zeal with which Gerry kept an eye on the building sites and newspaper deaths columns for the demise of single occupants. Keaveney felt rather protective towards Adams, even if he didn't rate him particularly highly as a barman, and thought he had a delicate constitution. He was always reading books, especially James Connolly, James Joyce and George Orwell. With its constant stream of radicals, the Duke of York was a good vantage point from which to monitor the increasingly nervous state of Northern Ireland.

After October 1968 events began to spiral out of control. With the need for reform now apparent, right-wing unionists swore to resist change, and the counter-marches led by Paisley multiplied. The Stormont Prime Minister Terence O'Neill proposed a five-point reform package which included the suspension of the Londonderry Corporation and a review of local government, but not the abolition of the business vote, which favoured Protestants. Facing a split in his cabinet and party he went on television to appeal for calm. 'Ulster stands at the crossroads . . . There are, I know, today some so-called loyalists who talk of independence from Britain, who seem to want a kind of Protestant Sinn Fein . . . Rhodesia, in defying Britain, at least has an air force and an army of her own. Where are the Ulster armoured divisions and the Ulster jet planes? . . . Unionism armed with justice will be a stronger cause than unionism armed merely with strength . . . What kind of Ulster do you want?' he pleaded. 'A happy and respected province in good standing with the rest of the United Kingdom? Or a place continually torn apart by riots and demonstrations?' It was to be the first in a very long line of appeals to the divided people of Northern Ireland to draw breath and pull back from the brink of disaster.

The year ended on a note of nervous optimism. NICRA, impressed by O'Neill's heartfelt speech, announced it was suspending its marches. The Protestant right looked marginalized after the sacking of the hardline Home Affairs Minister William Craig. But a student fringe of the civil rights movement, the People's Democracy, refused to heed the marching moratorium and announced they were going ahead with plans to walk from Belfast to Derry in the New Year.

Adams has claimed in his 1996 autobiography, that when the forty-strong People's Democracy march set off from Belfast City Hall soon after nine o'clock on New Year's Day in uncertain humour he walked with it for a while before having to head off to a busy day's work at the Duke of York. But curiously, for such a small band of people, nobody seems able to remember the young barman's presence. In earlier writings he admits that the IRA leadership was opposed to the People's Democracy's decision to march and he and others were ordered not to take part. Cathal Goulding described the march as a coat-trailing exercise, routed through some strongly Protestant areas. Within a few days Goulding's leadership position was 'submerged', according to Adams, writing twenty years later, 'by the boots, bricks and batons of off-duty B Specials and their associates as the RUC led the marchers into the ambush at Burntollet Bridge'.

A few days into the march, harried all the way by the Loyalist Citizens of Ulster organization, the participants were ambushed at Burntollet Bridge, attacked with heavy stones and nail-studded sticks. Some were forced into a small river and one woman nearly drowned as she lay unconscious in the water. The police stood by, making no attempt to arrest or impede the attackers. The appalling ferocity of the attack and the failure of the RUC altered the face of the crisis. The People's Democracy had staged their own mini-1916 Easter Rising, with a similar objective in mind. As Bernadette Devlin admitted: 'Our function in marching from Belfast to Derry was to break the truce, to relaunch the civil rights movement as a mass movement and to show people that O'Neill was in fact offering them nothing.'

Edwina Stewart, a NICRA official, recalled that the civil rights movement split over tactics at the end of 1968. The 'conservatives' wanted to consolidate their gains and win allies. But the People's Democracy had changed in character from a mass student organization to 'one in the control of Trotskyite forces. They saw the civil rights movement as a way towards an Irish workers' republic, as they called it, and they wanted to push on.' While the carnage at Burntollet Bridge attracted international sympathy to the civil rights movement and united much of the nationalist/Catholic population of Northern Ireland, 'it had a disastrous effect on building up sectarianism in all the places they marched through and among the neutral unionist voters who were prepared to change'. Such marches were guaranteed not to win allies among the majority population but to make enemies. Edwina Stewart remembered Adams as 'very young and quiet and a member of the IRA . . . he was a shy gangly-looking fellow in 1969. I had seen him in the Duke of York, but he never was a public face.'

After the ambush all hope of resisting the quickening descent into conflagration began to vanish. A week later a People's Democracy march in the border town of Newry turned violent when demonstrators attacked police vehicles, setting light to some and pushing Land Rovers into the town's canal. At one stage an attempt was made to occupy the post office. 'It was a big riot and for once we weren't orchestrating it,' recalled an IRA man acting as a steward.

In the first civil rights marches it was accepted by the organizers that IRA men would perform stewarding duties to ensure that trouble did not break out. But as tension grew in Northern Ireland these same men were using their positions to guarantee that conflicts with the RUC erupted. 'After we threw a few police vans in the canal the PD decided to march on the post office,' said the same IRA man. 'I can remember this PD guy with a brick and he couldn't decide whether or not he was going to throw it into the post office. They didn't know what they wanted. So we helped him.'

For the early part of 1969 the focus of activity was Derry. The IRA leader in Belfast Liam McMillen was 'terrified' – according to more than one IRA man of the period – that the inflamed atmosphere, if transferred to Belfast's peculiar geography with its patchwork of segregated Catholic and Protestant 'villages', would rapidly collapse into an orgy of sectarian violence. His fears, and those of Goulding in Dublin, were driven by the knowledge that the IRA was not equipped nor trained for such an outcome. Even so, the activities of Adams and like-minded activists were becoming more diverse.

A further civil rights demonstration in Derry was brutally suppressed and a local man Samuel Devenny was badly beaten up by the RUC. A few months later he died of coronary thrombosis. Although his demise was never linked by medical evidence to the police assault, he had by that time become in many nationalists' minds a symbolic martyr representing all of the Catholic Bogside. Three days later the moderate Derry Citizens Action Committee dominated by the civil rights MP John Hume was brushed aside by a new, more militant group, the Derry Citizens Defence Group.

Belfast republicans reacted with furious violence to the night upon which the Devennys' home was invaded by the RUC, firebombing eleven post offices throughout their city, an operation which was sanctioned by the local leadership. The Stormont government blamed the IRA, but within a week of these first explosions *Sunday Times* reporters had established that the culprits were 'a tiny gang of hot-headed teenagers from the Falls Road Catholic ghetto styling themselves the Belfast Housing Action Group (some were young relatives of members of People's Democracy). One of the youths was injured rescuing an old couple trapped above one of the post offices he had set alight.' Among them, unbeknown to the *Sunday Times*, there were indeed IRA members, including Gerry Adams.

The circumstances of the attack emerged out of a NICRA meeting taking place at the Wellington Park Hotel in South Belfast, which had heard a tape-recording of the Devenny family recounting their ordeal. The IRA element took their cue from it. Twenty minutes after the meeting ended the bombs hit the post offices. 'The Falls Road youths who had been at the meeting had simply stolen a car and milk bottles and made the petrol bombs as they drove along,' reported the *Sunday Times* Insight team. In fact they were using the IRA's 'staff car' and the choice of target was dictated by a desire to hit the Stormont government in the pocket. 'The desire to "take the pressure off Derry" had bred in Belfast a desperate violence. It was the shape of things to come.'

The finely tuned balance of forces within NICRA was coming under greater pressure as the pitch of violence crept higher. The younger IRA element in Belfast was looking for ever more confrontation with the RUC, partly in order to draw RUC strength away from Derry but also because some volunteers were spoiling for a fight with the old enemy. On one occasion Adams and his fellow protesters, supported by a van carrying crates of petrol bombs, confronted a police squad defending Hastings Street station, who then retreated back inside their base. The crowd, with Adams at the helm, followed through by ramming the gate with a telegraph pole. Eventually, in an unpredictable outcome, Adams says the RUC invited him and another man into the station to outline their grievances.

The same night that the post offices were petrol-bombed, loyalist extremists bombed the main water pipeline serving Belfast in the hope of blaming it on the IRA and provoking a political and security crisis. In this they were successful. Terence O'Neill seemed to have staved off his militant wing once again by calling an election in response to demands from twelve of his MPs that he resign. Although he won, it was his announcement that he intended to push through another reform and satisfy the final and most urgent demand of the civil rights demonstrators, the introduction of 'one man one vote', which toppled him. O'Neill was replaced by James Chichester-Clark, soon to be nicknamed 'Chi-chi'.

The loyalist marching season was heading towards its summer high point in the worst of atmospheres. With a dry spring and balmy summer the conditions were perfect for an upsurge in communal rioting. After an anti-police riot in Ardoyne, a Catholic enclave of North Belfast surrounded by Protestant streets, some of the residents began moving to the relative safety and Catholic hegemony of Andersonstown. By July, with clashes an established nightly occurrence as soon as last orders had been called in the city's bars, Adams was involved in 'defence' preparations for both the Ardoyne and Unity Flats, where, at the beginning of August, a loyalist mob tried to storm the Catholic enclave close to Belfast city centre. It was a development which Liam McMillen had at first resisted, conscious that his grand total of resources included no more than twenty-four weapons and less than a hundred volunteers.

This was, according to the young revolutionary, a frustrating time for Adams. The leadership was still engaging in 'semantics'. He claims to have had many arguments with McMillen, yet some of his contemporaries mock the claim, recalling that on one occasion Adams was vexed at being ignored during a meeting in the back room of a Lower Falls bar, only to be finally acknowledged with a dismissive 'You in the glasses at the back'.

By August the stage was set for the final descent into full-scale insurrection. The Stormont government, ignoring advice from the Army, agreed to let the loyalist Apprentice Boys proceed with their traditional parade in Derry. In fact the new Prime Minister Chichester-Clark had personally appealed to Apprentice Boys' leaders to observe a voluntary ban but capitulated when they rebuffed him.

A radicalized Catholic Bogside prepared itself for three weeks in advance to repel the Apprentice Boys. The Scarman tribunal into the 1969 disturbances later heard that while the 'defence' of the Bogside was elaborately prepared, replete with first-aid stations, radio transmitters and even a locally raised fire brigade, arrangements for preserving peace in the first place were pitiful by comparison. The chief steward had no previous experience and was asleep in bed half an hour after the first missiles were thrown from the Bogside at the parade. Even before the 15,000 Apprentice Boys had begun their march, the balance was tilted heavily in favour of trouble.

The parade was halfway through when trouble finally flared. While the Apprentice Boys' stewards kept their hotheads in check, their Bogside equivalents failed to keep their side of the bargain and the skirmishing began. As soon as the RUC made its first assault on the Bogside's defence lines at 7.15 p.m. the defence association's carefully laid plans swung into action. A steady supply of petrol bombs reached the thirty teenagers manning the roof of Rossville Street flats (43,000 milk bottles had gone missing in the four previous days), rendering the Bogside impenetrable, even when the RUC fired CS gas for the first time ever in Northern Ireland. 'Free Derry' had been born.

In response to appeals from the Bogside, civil rights leaders called protest meetings in several towns. In Dungiven the police station was attacked and the Orange Hall and courthouse set alight. In Armagh a group of B Specials opened fire on demonstrators, killing John Gallagher and wounding two others. By Thursday 14 August, after three days of fighting, the British Prime Minister Harold Wilson finally agreed to a request for military assistance from Chichester-Clark. At 5.00 p.m. lorry-loads of the 1st Battalion, the Prince of Wales' Own drove across the Craigavon Bridge and into the heart of Derry.

In Belfast the IRA commander Liam McMillen's nightmare was about to come true. As battle raged in the Bogside a number of prominent figures including Bernadette Devlin and Eamon McCann appealed to NICRA through its chairman Frank Gogarty to take action to draw police away from Derry. Gogarty convened a meeting of the NICRA executive at his home on the morning of 13 August and a decision was taken that demonstrations should be staged that evening in towns across Northern Ireland, including sit-downs and roadblocks. It was also agreed that a delegation would go to Stormont to appeal directly to the Home Affairs Minister Robert Porter to withdraw police from the Bogside. Requests to stage further demonstrations in Belfast were categorically rejected because of the special risk of provoking sectarian violence.

But the IRA's own internal disagreements about its reaction to the deepening crisis dictated that it would respond in its traditional role of 'defender', however ill-prepared they were or ill-conceived the notion. Gerry Adams' own account of the events of 13 August conflict with the public record as set down by the Scarman tribunal and by prominent civil rights activists, none of whom remembers the emergency NICRA meeting held in the Wellington Park Hotel in South Belfast at which he claims to have proposed a protest rally on the Falls Road in the name of the West Belfast Housing Action Committee. 'We left the meeting to make petrol bombs;' he says in his 1986 book *The Politics of Irish Freedom*. By the time of writing his autobiography *Before the Dawn* a decade later, reference to the petrol bombs had been erased, replaced instead with 'a sense of determination that the nationalist people of Derry needed and were going to get our help'. But even his original account is open to doubt, with none of those present at the NICRA meeting contacted by the authors able to remember the young activist's intervention in the debate and his proposal for a Falls Road rally.

The respected Northern Ireland political scientist Kevin Boyle was then NICRA press officer. 'Certainly I have no memory of it and I was very central to those affairs at that time and this man I never heard of or met. When I first read his account, I have a distinct memory of thinking, "Where the hell did this guy come from?" My own view is this was rather a Johnny-come-lately business, trying to put himself centre-stage.' Whether by accident or intent, Adams has taken the April NICRA meeting called to consider the attack on the Devenny family in Derry, after which Belfast post offices were petrol-bombed, and conjoined it with the NICRA executive meeting of 13 August at Gogarty's house, which he was much too junior to attend.

Indeed, according to an IRA contemporary of Adams, all volunteers had already been given their instructions earlier in the day, after the NICRA meeting had rejected demonstrations in Belfast. Whatever McMillen's reservations about inflaming sectarian passions in the streets running between the Catholic Falls and Protestant Shankill, the decision was taken to keep the pressure up on local police stations in an attempt to draw strength away from the Bogside in Derry.

Only some fifteen protesters gathered outside the Boundary bar at Divis Flats shortly before 9.00 p.m. and they decided to march to the Springfield Road RUC station, where a petition would be handed in. Adams has written that he was chairing the protest meeting when the Irish Premier Jack Lynch made a television broadcast in which he claimed that the violence in Derry was a consequence of decades of unionist misrule, demanded the introduction of a United Nations peace-keeping force and called on the British government to enter into negotiations on the constitutional position of Northern Ireland. His government 'can no longer stand by and see innocent people injured and perhaps worse', so the Army was being sent to the border to establish field hospitals.

Roused by this apparent message of imminent salvation from the South, Adams and his comrades set off up the Falls Road singing 'The Soldier's Song', the national anthem of the Irish Republic. Joe McCann carried aloft the Irish tricolour. 'We were very naive, we really thought that the Dublin government was about to come across the border and that would be the end of the six-counties state,' said one of the small band of IRA men present. Adams' co-editor on *Spearhead* was appointed to hand in the petition and by the time they reached the police station their numbers had swelled to about 200. 'When we got to the barracks a couple of guys had been organized with cans of petrol,' said an IRA man who took part in the action. 'Stones and petrol bombs were thrown and it was supposed to take the pressure off Derry. At the same time this was happening at other places in the city, at Glen Road barracks and Oldpark. But this was really the beginnings of the split. You had a handful of older guys outside the movement, older republicans. They were doing a bit of stirring with the younger lads, "This isn't the way to do it," and Adams was the main one they were impressing.' Support for Goulding's leadership was concentrated in the Lower Falls, where McMillen and Jimmy Sullivan held sway, but in other parts of the city the dominant republican families – including Adams' own and the Cahills in Ballymurphy – were increasingly hostile.

Through the night the demonstrators kept up the pressure on the police. After smashing windows at the Springfield Road station but failing to draw any response, the demonstrators moved off in the direction of Hastings Street station, where another attack took place. The local RUC commander ordered the force's armoured Commer personnel carriers, cumbersome vehicles intended for patrolling border areas of the province rather than the tight streets of Belfast, to disperse the crowds. One of the armoured carriers came under gun and grenade attack in Leeson Street. The IRA had few weapons but what they had, including a couple of American Second World War grenades, they were prepared to use. It is important to remember, in view of the onslaught against the Catholic Falls that was to follow, from where the first shots came.

Immediately after the grenade attack the police withdrew, emerging later in Shorland armoured cars. Normally fitted with .30 Browning machine-guns, they were wholly unsuited to the sort of hit and run situation which was steadily developing in the Falls. Luckily, that night, the Brownings had not yet been fitted. A Protestant-owned car showroom and a mill were set on fire by petrol bombs and two uniformed fire officers attacked as they arrived on the scene. More shots were fired from a passing car at Andersonstown police station.

At 1.00 a.m. police in Springfield Road station returned fire for the first time, wounding two of the rioters. An hour later, with the station once again under attack, a police officer shot a burst of automatic gunfire into the sky. Eventually the rioters dispersed, but it was clear to RUC chiefs in Belfast that they should expect very serious trouble the following night. The Shorlands had their machine guns fitted. The IRA too attempted to make its own preparations. 'There was only a handful of rounds for each of the five revolvers we had and we were cycling round between them, like something out of the Keystone Cops. There was a sten gun too but its cocking handle was broken off so you had to pull it back with your finger. There was a mad search on for weapons, people realized that the bubble had burst, it was panic,' said an IRA man involved in the action.

Adams went to work at the Duke of York the next day. But he only stayed long enough to gather as many empty Guinness bottles as he could cram into a couple of brown paper bags for making petrol bombs before disappearing without another word to his boss Jimmy Keaveney, who later went to the trouble of trekking up to the Adams home in Ballymurphy where, amazed by the poverty around him, he handed over Gerry's national insurance card to a sister and left a message. 'Tell him there's a job waiting for him whenever he wants it back.' It was the last time that Gerry Adams would ever be regularly employed.

Adams made his way back to the Lower Falls, where he claims in his autobiography that he argued against the involvement of the IRA in military defence of the Catholic districts. That is disputed by other IRA figures of the same junior rank, who recall that he was ordered back up to Ballymurphy to stand by for any attacks on the area by loyalists. Meanwhile the search for weaponry continued. The Lower Falls volunteers, loyal to McMillen and the Goulding leadership, were denied access to a weapons dump in Andersonstown, its guardian claiming that he required permission from General Headquarters Staff and that it was reserved for a 'doomsday' scenario. 'Later the man turned up with the stuff and his own men and it was pretty clear to me that the ones up the road were all about trying to discredit us, saying we'd been unable to defend the people, because they went with the Provos when the split came.'

Two factors added to the air of expectation that when darkness fell that night there would be violence on a far more serious scale than the previous evening. The Battle of the Bogside was still raging, as were rumours that the Irish Army had crossed the border and entered Newry. It was also the eve of the Feast of the Assumption, a traditional Catholic occasion for lighting bonfires in their streets. Neighbouring Protestants had watched the previous night's rioting on the Falls from their end of the shared streets running between the Falls and the Shankill and concluded that they should make their own defensive preparations.

Crowds of Catholic youths began stoning passing vehicles, breaking up paving stones and preparing petrol bombs. By 10.00 p.m a crowd of around a hundred had assembled and moved off down Divis Street to launch another attack on the Hastings Street RUC station. Protestants in Dover Street and Percy Street, which ran from Divis Street up to meet the Shankill and were home to families of both religions, skirmished with a line of B Specials to get at the Catholic rioters, who in turn invaded Dover Street carrying with them a makeshift shield of corrugated-iron sheeting in a bid to push the Protestants back. A bingo hall and several houses were set alight and RUC armoured vehicles punched a hole in the Catholic line, through which the B Specials and the Protestant crowds swarmed. Similar scenes were taking place all over the district, including the religiously mixed Cupar Street, where around 400 Catholics and Protestants faced one another. A police patrol led a baton charge on the Catholic end of the street, judging their greater numbers to pose the higher threat. An IRA gunman fired in their direction.

The police took cover, returning fire from a submachine-gun. In adjacent Conway Street another IRA unit opened up with gunfire at an attempt by the police to drive the Catholic crowd back into the

Falls Road. Six people – three Protestants, two Catholics and a policeman – were injured in the exchanges. Around midnight the IRA opened fire on Protestant crowds in Dover Street. Herbert Roy, a twenty-six-year-old Protestant, was killed when he was hit in the chest by a .38 round. Three police officers were also injured. Convinced that the insurrection which their intelligence reports forecast had begun, the RUC made the fatal error of ordering three of their heavy Shorland armoured vehicles – now armed with Browning machine-guns – into the mêlée on Divis Street.

Their firepower was grossly at odds with the urban setting and the appearance of these fearsome vehicles made the Catholics scatter, allowing the enraged Protestant crowd to enter Divis Street. The RUC wrongly believed that the shots which killed Herbert Roy and wounded three officers had come from Divis Flats, and the Shorlands opened fire in its direction. One of the bullets passed through the wall of a first-floor flat and hit nine-year-old Patrick Rooney, asleep in his bed, in the head, killing him instantly. Hugh McCabe, a twenty-year-old Catholic trooper in the Queen's Royal Irish Hussars, home on leave, was found dead on the roof of a block of flats opposite Hastings Street RUC station, killed by a single high-velocity bullet which had entered his right cheek.

The Protestants now had the upper hand and were able to exact their revenge, roaming freely and setting light to houses. An IRA unit occupying St Comgall's school, strategically located at the corner of Divis Street and the Falls, was joined by a group of older Forties republicans, men who had resigned from the IRA in disgust at the new political direction pursued by Goulding. They were armed with the Andersonstown weapons which earlier appeals from the Lower Falls IRA leaders had failed to secure. For an hour and a half the IRA team poured fire into the streets beneath them, wounding at least eight Protestant rioters.

Later, when the legends began to be woven in republican circles, this was presented as the only laudable action taken by the IRA on the night of the 'pogrom' by the police and Protestants against the Catholic Falls. The charge that they had failed to 'defend' the local population did not take into account that it was the IRA which had fired the first shots and claimed the first life. As Henry Patterson noted in his critique of modern republicanism *The Politics of Illusion*: 'Given the intensity of communal feelings by August 13th serious disturbance in Belfast was likely. However, the frenzied, systematic burning of Catholic homes in the Lower Falls, Clonard and Ardoyne was not inevitable. The IRA's use of guns contributed powerfully to the remorseless intensity of the Protestant onslaught in these areas.'

The final toll, after three nights of serious unrest, was seven people killed, 750 injured, 1,505 Catholic and 315 Protestant families forced out of their homes and 275 buildings destroyed or seriously damaged. The lesson which the Provisionals, whose birth was now only weeks away, chose to take from those nights of carnage was that they needed more, not less, weaponry. In future they must ensure that nobody would ever again taunt them with the jibe 'IRA, I ran away'.

Gerry Adams claims that he eventually ignored his orders that night and slipped away from peaceful Ballymurphy to join the fray in the Lower Falls. He set down his personal recollections some years later for a republican newspaper. 'He [Adams] thought of August 14th/15th, only a few months past. Cursed nailbombs without detonators. Bulmer complained a lot about that. An RUC Shorland car drove over one. Nothing happened. A waste of time throwing them at anything armed with Browning machine guns. He remembered the scene that night in Divis Street.'

As dawn broke on Friday the religious geography of Belfast began to reshape itself and harden, with hundreds of families on the move, carrying with them what few posessions they could rescue. While the streetscape rearranged itself, Gerry Adams slept in a safe house back up in Andersonstown. By the time he awoke British troops had taken up position on the streets of the Lower Falls, their arrival met by cheers and pots of tea from the grateful Catholics. Adams says he was 'totally and absolutely outraged' to find that they had done nothing to prevent the burning of Bombay Street, close to Clonard Monastery, by Protestants. During the attack Gerald McAuley, a fifteen-year-old Fianna member, was shot dead as he helped to clear a house. Several Protestants were injured by returned gunfire. The Provisionals have since claimed McAuley, one of the boys who attended the Fianna camp which Gerry Adams organized, as the first of their volunteers to die in the present Troubles.

'The British Army was as disorganized as we were, they really didn't have a clue where they were or where they should be,' said an IRA member on active service as they arrived. The Army's first aim was to establish a 'peace line' between the warring Catholic and

Protestant neighbourhoods. But in the case of Clonard, which lies just west of the Falls Road, they only discovered that they were several hundred yards too far away in the maze of narrow streets when it was already too late to prevent the attack on Bombay Street.

The young Gerry Adams and his small band of IRA men were waking up to a changed world and in the weeks ahead they had plenty of time behind the barricades to ruminate on the lessons of the past few days. On the one hand there was a sense of elation over the fact that the security forces of the Stormont government had finally buckled and conceded defeat in the face of the much smaller forces ranged against them. The nationalists of Derry and West Belfast were a risen people.

On the other hand they had swapped one evil for another, and a much better-armed one at that. Even more galling was the reality that the vast majority of Catholics had welcomed the British Army with open arms. 'We definitely thought we were going to get help from the South and that they would've linked up with our units,' said a veteran. 'Instead of that the British Army came in, unbelievable. We were going to have to arm ourselves. I'd say that if the IRA had been armed the people would've definitely seen them as the saviours.'

Yet there was still hope that the tide would turn against their new occupiers. All it would take would be a few mistakes on the part of the British Army, such as the failure to be in the right place when Bombay Street was attacked. Indeed, Bombay Street was to go down in Provisional folklore as another stain on the IRA leadership's record, and as an uneasy calm returned to the barricaded streets and the British soldiers continued to enjoy the support of the Catholic people of the Falls, the simmering row within the IRA began to bubble.

CHAPTER FOUR

A Division in the Ranks

The drive back from Leitrim to Belfast takes about three and a half hours these days, winding past the lakes around Drumshanbo and then on via Fermanagh and Tyrone to Dungannon where you hit Northern Ireland's M1 motorway. Gerry Adams, Liam 'Bulmer' McParland and Mickey O'Neill were nearly home from a trip at the end of October 1969 when they had a serious crash. Liam McParland was taken to hospital, where after ten days he died as a result of his injuries.

The significance of this episode would no doubt be something of a mystery to readers of Gerry Adams' autobiography *Before the Dawn*, where he recalls his shock after the crash and surprise that it was swiftly followed by his suspension from what he calls his local leadership role within Sinn Fein. There is nothing by way of explanation of what that role was or why being caught up in an accident should lead to such a suspension.

In fact the accident coincided with the point in time when growing divisions between IRA volunteers in Belfast were reaching their inevitable conclusion. Adams had been in Leitrim, according to some republicans, organizing training and weapons supplies without authority from the IRA leadership. Jim Sullivan, who was then the IRA's adjutant in Belfast, believed Adams was also trying to bring arms up from the South. 'He wanted to turn round and say to the young lads – look! we've got the stuff.

'If he'd stayed [with the Official IRA],' commented Sullivan, 'he'd have faced a disciplinary charge. No one was allowed to leave the city without permission.' Another member of the Belfast IRA said that Adams was spared from disciplinary action because the episode was an ingredient in the greater drama of the growing split. 'By going with the Provisionals he avoided any action being taken against him,' said the man.

The separation between the two factions was well under way by the time of Adams' temporary suspension from his role within the IRA's Ballymurphy battalion. Acting as quartermaster, he was responsible for the storage and distribution of weapons, although given the scramble for weaponry in the autumn of 1969 his job seemed also to include procurement. A week after the arrival of British troops on the streets of the Falls Adams was asked by Jimmy Steele, one of the Forties men he had got to know through his father, to attend a secret meeting in a school on North King Street. The gathering was packed with men of Steele's generation, who had quit active republicanism: Joe Cahill, John Kelly, Billy Kelly, Leo Martin, Jimmy Drumm, Billy McKee, Seamus Twomey and Dave O'Connell, the sole Southerner and an ally of the IRA's intelligence director Sean MacStiofain in the internal feud with Cathal Goulding. Apart from O'Connell, Adams was the only serving member of the IRA present.

The main item for discussion was the abysmal performance, in their eyes, of the Belfast commander Liam McMillen and his adjutant Jim Sullivan during the crisis. They resolved to remove them from office and then oust Cathal Goulding and his supporters in Dublin, force the British to take their intervention a step further by closing down Stormont and ruling Northern Ireland directly from London, which would inevitably begin a process of disengagement and the reunification of Ireland.

This old guard, fervently Catholic and conservative in their republicanism, had dropped out of the IRA during the decade of Goulding's new direction. In 1969 Gerry Adams occupied an uncomfortable position with a foot in both camps. His head had been occupied with politics, he had taken part enthusiastically in discussion groups and social protests and as a young man of the 1960s he was perhaps temperamentally drawn towards the 'progressive' nature of the left-wing Dublin leadership. But his heart and, more important, his bloodline placed him firmly with the traditionalists. His father had after all fought alongside Joe Cahill in the 1940s, and his uncle Liam Hannaway was on very close terms with Jimmy Steele.

The McParland episode showed Adams tipping over to the rebel camp, who were establishing their own weapons supply-lines independently of the Belfast command and on the brink of going it alone. On

10 November 1969, four days after Liam McParland's death, British troops made no attempt to remove a tricolour from his coffin as it was carried along the Falls Road. Belfast's nationalist newspaper, the *Irish News*, reported that about 300 people attended the funeral. 'The coffin was flanked by six men wearing black berets, slow marching and halting at various intervals on command.' One death notice described the deceased as a 'soldier of Ireland, dedicated and true', and there were others from the Belfast Republican Welfare Association, the staff and volunteers of A Company First Belfast Battalion of the IRA and B Company Belfast Battalion Oglaigh na hEireann. IRA veterans from Canada and America were among those who sent floral tributes.

In a column which he later wrote in the *Republican News* Adams described a military tribute which he paid to the dead man on the night of the funeral. In defiance of an order by the leadership that there should be no volley of shots over the grave Adams and an older comrade made their way to Milltown cemetery.

He thought of the first time he and Bulmer had got together. Bulmer did the driving. They laughed about it afterwards. They had to push the car most of the way. Bulmer didn't drive after that. He volunteered not to. He made up for it in the Murph. Plenty of organising behind the barricades. Standbys, lectures, recruiting, meeting people, getting gear, rushing here, there and everywhere. The standbys were good crack. Up Springhill Avenue or behind Corry's sitting 'til daylight swapping stories.

Bulmer and the man with the cap talked about the 50s while he himself spoofed about riots, about Civil Rights meetings and housing or unemployment agitation . . . Strange thinking of Bulmer going off to arrange the training camp. The car getting two blowouts on the way home. The long hours of waiting at the hospital. The shock of it when he died. The younger man hadn't got used to it yet. They were at the Republican plot. The older man whispered to him. Wreaths lay on the grave where they had been stretched that morning and the newly dug clay glistened where the diggers had shaped it into a ridge.

The two men glanced at each other and then, silently, they stood abreast of the grave. They prayed their silent prayers and the moon, spying them from above, hid behind a cloud. The men stood to attention. A night wind crept down from the mountain and rustled its way through the wreaths. One of the men barked an order. They both raised revolvers towards the sky and three volleys of shots crashed their way over the grave and across the graveyard.

The young man was tense, a little pale. The man with the cap breathed freely. He pocketed his weapon. The younger man shoved his into the waistband of his jeans. They moved off quickly. The moon slid from behind the clouds again, and the wind shook itself and swept across the landscape. All was quiet again . . . They had just engaged in unofficial action. They didn't seem concerned about that.

All may have been quiet that night in Milltown cemetery but within the IRA rancour and internal division were running at fever pitch. Two months earlier, the Belfast IRA commander Liam McMillen convened a meeting of his supporters in a hall in the Lower Falls in order to pick up the threads of his command after getting out of prison (the RUC had rounded up a number of leaders in the aftermath of the Belfast violence). Sixteen armed men, led by the veteran hardliner Billy McKee, invaded the meeting and announced that they were taking over. McMillen refused their demand to hand over power but did agree to a compromise whereby he cut his links with Dublin for a three-month period and accepted six of McKee's men as part of his 'staff'. The unit's funds of £3,500, donations from Catholic businessmen towards relief supplies, would be spent instead on guns. If at the end of the three-month period Goulding had not purged the leadership of socialism he would be removed and replaced by traditionalists. A separate Northern Command for the six counties, as had existed in the 1940s, would be established to run the IRA independently. As a final gesture the dissidents ruled that no Belfast delegates would be sent to an IRA Army Convention called by Goulding for December, at which the divisive question of ending abstentionism and recognizing the Dublin, Stormont and Westminster parliaments was finally settled with a clear majority in favour.

Many of the traditionalists boycotted the Convention – for them it was another act of treachery by those who could not be considered true to the spirit of the Easter Rising. As Ruairi O Bradaigh later put it: 'What had it all been about since 1922 if we were to accept the status quo and walk into Leinster House [the Irish parliament]? We might as well have accepted the bloody Treaty at the start and just be done with it.' Just before Christmas 1969 a new organization, led by Sean MacStiofain, was created by the rebels in Belfast and traditionalist republicans from the South. In a deliberate echo of the words of the Easter 1916 proclamation on behalf of 'The Provisional Government of the Irish Republican' the faction elected a 'Provisional Executive' and a 'Provisional Army Council'. Ever afterwards they would be known as the Provisional IRA.

Adams had taken part in the first meetings of the traditionalists and had incurred the wrath of the Official IRA through his role in the McParland affair. At the same time unlike many of those involved in the new faction he had been involved with the IRA throughout the late 1960s and had participated enthusiastically in the political campaigning encouraged by its Dublin leadership. He claims to have felt a certain loyalty to Liam McMillen, who had been his leader in Belfast.

All over the city, republicans were having to decide which way to go and it was by no means uncommon for families to split down the middle – one brother opting for the Officials, another for the Provisionals, a husband going with the rebels and his wife staying loyal. Many of those supportive of Liam McMillen hoped that Adams' ideological inclinations would make him side with them. Perhaps he encouraged such a view by his habit, noted on many occasions since, of not taking up a position but retreating into silence or answering a question with another question. In any case, when the split was formalized at the Sinn Fein *ard fheis* (annual conference) in January 1970 Gerry Adams was not among those who walked out to form the Provisionals. Contrary to his later claim that he was refused entry to the meeting at Dublin's Intercontinental Hotel and went off to join an anti-apartheid demonstration instead, he stayed in his seat as Sean MacStiofain led the Provisionals out of the hall. It took him another three months to decide which way to jump.

Adams hesitated. He told the newly appointed Provisional leader in Belfast Billy McKee that the Ballymurphy IRA was staying separate until it saw which way things were going to break. For about six weeks Adams and his Ballymurphy supporters maintained a semi-independent existence. An IRA contemporary of Adams at this fraught time well remembers the pressures that young republicans were under from their peers. The man recalls a meeting at a house in West Belfast with two other young people and a leading light of the Officials, who was trying to persuade them not to follow the Provisionals. 'We couldn't disagree with a word that the man said, all his arguments for staying with the Officials were totally right, totally justified. The Provisionals leadership was reactionary and Catholic, they went against what we believed in. But we just said: "Yeah, but what's my da and ma going to say if I go home and tell them that I'm going with the Reds?" There was a real thing about the communist threat about that time. And family tradition counted for a lot.'

In the case of Gerry Adams, Liam McMillen and the Officials were to be disappointed. In later years McMillen was to say that the only 'splitter' who had really surprised him by going with the Provisionals was Adams. He and Jim Sullivan were invited up to Adams' estate, Ballymurphy, to address a gathering of around forty republicans. They put their case but Adams, who had not yet turned twenty-one, spoke in opposition. The majority at the meeting voted to go with the Provisionals. In most published accounts of this encounter Adams is clearly identified as the main speaker on the Provisional side of the argument, but interestingly, in a version given to the author Ciaran De Baroid, Adams himself talks in the third person, describing how the decisive contribution came from the IRA's local officer commanding. That person was none other than Gerry Adams.

In trying to explain the loss of Adams, those who stayed loyal to the Officials have dredged around for reasons. For Jim Sullivan, Adams was guilty of 'cowardice' and an inability to stand up to 'the thugs and bullies' of the Provisionals. But in the ensuing days, when feuding claimed lives on both sides, there was no place in either camp where a coward could feel safe. In fact the practical failings of the Goulding leadership and the inadequacies of the left-wing approach in dealing with the realities of communal conflict in Belfast probably weighed just as much on Adams' mind as did the fact that his family allegiances dictated where he stood.

Others who know him well attribute his choice to more Machiavellian reasons. 'Adams was one of the very few who'd been active in the IRA in the late Sixties to go with the Provies. If he'd stayed with us, there was already a hierarchy and a structure and he wasn't very senior. But by going with them he was able to climb very high very quickly. There were no thinkers in there, just the Glasgow Celtic supporters type. I've always been convinced that Adams knew exactly what he was doing.'

Gerry Adams' father wouldn't have had to ask too many questions to decide where he stood, nor would many of his comrades from D Company. Many of the Forties men who had dropped out of active republican involvement in the years leading up to the Troubles had been openly dismissive of the trendy new political teachings being disseminated from Dublin. As one of Adams' IRA contemporaries in the late 1960s recalls, these old timers were only too keen to blame the obsession with left-wing rhetoric for the IRA's lack of preparedness for the sectarian violence at the outset of the Troubles. 'When the '69 position developed and there wasn't enough equipment to defend the areas the older boys came back and said, "We told youse lads, now we're defenceless, that's this political thing you're going through, this is where it's left us."'

Nor was there a need for Gerry Adams senior to remind his son of where republican purity lay. When the Provisionals broke away they had gone to County Mayo to visit Tom Maguire, the last surviving republican member of the 2nd Dail, the Irish parliament in 1922. These republicans walked out of the parliament in protest over the Treaty with Britain and therefore Maguire, a former IRA commandant, represented the legitimate government of Ireland, a living symbol to the Provisionals of the spirit of unwavering loyalty to the ideals of the Easter Rising of 1916. Maguire came down on the side of the Provisionals, declaring that the Officials had no right to end abstentionism and seek to take parliamentary seats.

In the event almost all the Adams family went with the Provisionals, with the exception of Gerry's sister Margaret, whose fiancé Michael McCorry remained an activist with the Officials. The majority of the family felt sure they had tradition and history on their side. Their fellow Provisional Leo Martin, now officer commanding the six counties, was to sum it up at a commemoration presided over by Gerry Adams senior in December 1971. The ceremony, complete with a colour party made up of members of the Junior IRA, na Fianna Eireann, was in memory of the republican martyrs Liam Mellows, Rory O'Connor, Dick Barrett and Joe McKelvey, who were summarily executed without any proper trial by the Irish Free State in December 1922.

Martin told a large gathering of republicans in Belfast's Milltown cemetery that 'Ireland today is facing a situation similar to that faced by the four martyrs, that is betrayed by former comrades who have deserted republicanism in favour of alien creeds.' He asked where Liam, Rory, Dick and Joe would have stood today on the issue of civil rights. 'I am certain,' he said, 'that their answer would have been – "Damn your concessions, England, we want our country."' Throughout the oration he continually advised the youth of today to study closely the martyrs' lives and to strive their utmost to follow in their footsteps. After that a young Fianna member said a decade of the rosary in Gaelic.

Weighed down by history and family, Adams embarked on his chosen path with the Provisionals, but the legacy of the 'political' IRA as he had known it under Cathal Goulding stayed with him. Adams was not happy with the virulent anti-communism of some of the traditionalists and though he was a Mass-going Catholic he would not have been as ostentatiously pro-clerical as some of his older comrades. Paddy Joe McClean, who was to be interned along with Adams the following year, had a hunch. 'I formed the impression, rightly or wrongly, that Gerry would have thought he was on the wrong side himself. I felt that he knew that the politics he was pushing wasn't going to get him anywhere. I've no proof, but my intuitive feeling was and is that Gerry first and foremost wants to be a politician.'

When Gerry Adams made his decision he went with the side which promised the most active policy of armed defence of Catholic areas and, fairly soon after that, armed attacks in pursuit of the republican goals. Not until the 1980s would Adams be able to devote himself to the kind of open political work for which he had obviously developed a taste. Life in the Provisional IRA would instead be a matter of, in his former comrade Billy McMillen's words, 'the routine work of organizing a physical-force movement'.

CHAPTER FIVE

The Battle of Ballymurphy

As the Provisionals and the Officials vied for supremacy in Belfast's Catholic districts, they were faced with the reality that the presence of a more conventional army on their streets was to become a permanent feature. The first British Army battalion to take up residency in Adams' home estate of Ballymurphy was from the Light Infantry under the command of Major – later Colonel – David Hancock, a soldier but also a diplomat who believed that in the interests of maintaining the peace locally he should endeavour to keep contacts open with both Catholic Ballymurphy and Protestant New Barnsley. Upon his arrival he found a situation where 'the old order of the IRA was disgraced by the freedom of extreme loyalists to burn whole streets; aware of the fact that the civil rights movement achieved more in a year than they had in forty; aware of nationalist distaste for bombs and bullets and confused by the friendly warmth shown by British soldiers on the streets'.

Hancock met the 'old order' of the IRA, people whom he calls 'trenchcoat and revolver men'. Among these he numbered Jimmy Steele and Gerry Adams' father. He had a strangely ambivalent relationship with them. 'Adams senior, for all his lack of education, was a republican first and foremost, a terrorist because of that and Roman Catholic, in that order, with each being important.' Hancock found that the old order harboured 'an irrational hatred of the British' and 'longed for a reason to take up arms'. At the same time the republicans recognized the tactful Army officer as a man with whom they could, potentially, do business. 'The old order had supplied me with intelligence on loyalist gun-running, asked me to sell them guns and accepted my open-handedness.' Hancock used the information he was gathering to keep Army headquarters well informed of the situation on the ground but ran into internal difficulties when he insisted on keeping his sources confidential.

In comparison to some other parts of West and North Belfast, Ballymurphy remained relatively quiet at the outset – a place to which Catholics burned out of their homes in places like Bombay Street came for shelter. At St Bernadette's school a group of local people set up a relief committee, among them Frank Cahill, Joe Cahill's brother. Accommodation had to be found for refugees, food brought in from local bakeries and dairies and medical care provided for some of the shocked and walking wounded. Gerry Adams was one of those who volunteered to help with the relief committee's efforts. The community leaders agreed a local deal with their Protestant neighbours, barricaded into the small New Barnsley estate. The two sides kept in telephone contact and each tried to hold back their people.

Hancock talked to the members of the Ballymurphy Defence Committee, which met at St Bernadette's, a group which included Frank Cahill, Geordie Shannon, Jimmy Steele and Gerry Adams' father. Although Gerry Adams was by now a prominent member of the local IRA, he spent a lot of time away from his home estate touring areas elsewhere in Belfast that were more immediately under threat from sectarian attacks.

In October 1969 Hancock and his soldiers were also diverted away from the relative calm of Ballymurphy – this time to take on Protestants rioting on the Shankill Road. In what became known as the Battle of the Shankill the Army killed two Protestants and wounded many more. An RUC Constable Victor Arbuckle was killed and the soldiers themselves suffered twenty-two injuries. On their return Hancock recalls that 'the local people clapped us but the old order of the IRA noted that the guns were now out!'

The uneasy calm in Ballymurphy couldn't hold – by Easter 1970, when the Junior Orange Order in New Barnsley decided to press ahead with a march from the estate against the wishes of the Ballymurphy leaders, the fragile local peace had reached breaking point. An officer from the Royal Scots Regiment gave the go-ahead for the parade, trying unsuccessfully to wring out an assurance that no 'party tunes' would be played.

In the event the loyalists struck up whatever tune they liked when they came out on to the Springfield Road which marked the sectarian border. Rioting broke out and continued with much more vigour that night. It was the end of Hancock's work building bridges: 'I was there, and so was young Adams, when the West Belfast nationalists turned against the British Army after a Scottish regiment overreacted to strong protests about an Orange parade on the Springfield Road in late March 1970. After one of the Scots Land Rovers disappeared under a haze of hurled milk bottles, one of the old order came up to me. I was standing in the crowd with my radio operator, pleading for restraint. He said, "I think you'd better go, Major, it's going to get rough now." No one had harmed me up till then.'

The going did get rough, not only that night but during the ensuing months. The Ballymurphy area became the scene of increasingly vicious fights between soldiers and local youths, with IRA veterans like Gerry Adams' father playing their part, pulling barbed wire into place behind troops in order to trap them in cul de sacs where they would be attacked by men armed with hurling sticks, stones and bottles. The Adams family found themselves in regular confrontations with the Army – according to Adams, his father was arrested and beaten, a CS gas canister was fired into the house, and a detachment of Scotland Yard detectives wearing tin hats and overcoats visited Divismore Park.

Adams says he was playing a background role at the time but in reality he was a staff officer in the Belfast Provisional IRA as well as its leader in Ballymurphy. 'The Provos had the tacit support of all the waters in which they swam,' remembers one Army officer. The soldier recalls Ballymurphy as:

an extremely lively little patch. We had a riot virtually every single night for four months. These were major riots but ones which I would characterize as of a quite glamorous kind, meaning that we had thousands involved and buses burning but not many people were getting killed, although people were getting hurt. The youths were definitely being spurred on.

Virtually every night as darkness fell the gatherings started around the Adams family home in Divismore Park. I remember it well as it was directly opposite our base . . . Adams senior was a scruffy little man, already getting quite a bit long in the tooth even then. I believe Adams senior to have been a very powerful influence not only on his own son but also on all the youngsters of Ballymurphy. He and others were always at the back of the riots running around and giving orders. Frequently they were masked, willing the rioters on . . . I remember young Adams as seeming to be in his late teens. He was at the centre of it every time.

Some of those in Ballymurphy sympathetic to Adams do not share this view of him and his father as violent ringleaders. Father Des Wilson, a local radical Catholic priest, remembers an episode:

in maybe 1970 or so when the streets were really chaotic and there were riots and there were attacks, CS gas and all kinds of things happening, and I remember going to a public meeting in the local school here and people were very angry and especially the young people were very angry and they wanted to go out on the street and rampage all around them, because what else could they do? And Gerry Adams I remember on the platform, and he was telling the young people especially, 'This is not the way to proceed, this is not the way to get your rights. What we've got to do is we've got to organize ourselves and what we've got to do is to force the British government to act differently. Going out and smashing and breaking is not the answer.'

With the benefit of hindsight Father Wilson reckons that even in these early days Adams was 'trying very hard to create a political rather than a military situation'. But seen through military eyes the Adams family were simply troublemakers and one officer made no bones about the harsh nature of his encounters with Gerry Adams and family: 'I lifted [arrested] him on a number of occasions. I remember one time I told him, "I am fed up with the sight of you. I am fed up with what you're doing, guided or misguided by your father. I am sick and tired of lifting you." At that point young Adams, with immense accuracy and huge volume, spat straight into my face. I have to confess that another soldier promptly head-butted him, something which he should never have done. Young Adams fell to the floor and I can recall the look he gave me, there was pure venom in his eyes – understandable, I suppose, as the other soldier had undoubtedly hurt him. All in all I thought he was a right little toe-rag.'

In July 1970 the local sectarian friction disappeared in a matter of days when more or less the entire Protestant population of New

Barnsley decamped. Adams, who remembers wandering around the deserted estate before assisting in the distribution of flats to needy Catholics, put the exodus down to scaremongering by Paisleyites. What is certain is that in the mid-1960s there was a strong Protestant community in New Barnsley with upwards of 500 children attending Sunday school at the Henry Taggart Memorial Church on the Springfield Road. 'When we used to go away for a day out it used to take eight double-decker buses to carry us all,' recalled a former elder of the church, Wesley McCready.

> There was about a hundred in the girls' brigade and seventy in the boys' brigade. It was the largest Sunday school in Belfast. There once was a big percentage of Protestants in the Ballymurphy estate. We moved out during Internment week. It had been going on over the period of about a year. Easter came and the Junior Orange parade, they were stoning the wee boys as they came home from the Orange Hall. Then it really went to town in June. The people were all scattered to the winds. We just had a morning service but it was a danger going to it and that was the end of the Taggart. We stayed on but had to go about eleven miles on a detour around the mountain to get in. Then we were advised by the security forces to move. We finally got our house sold, the front was just raked with gunfire one night and the police couldn't protect us. The education authority bought it as a headmaster's house for the Christian Brothers school. That whole area, Springfield Road, was predominantly Protestant. The intimidation began about 1964, a crowd got into Ballymurphy and there was anti-Protestant graffiti coming up to the Twelfth [of July] every year. Panic set in and families were encouraged to move out and that was the rock we perished on.

With the Protestants of New Barnsley gone, the issue of Orange marches was no longer of consequence to the Ballymurphy residents. But since the riots of Easter 1970 relations between them and the British Army were on a sharp downward curve and little was required to trigger confrontation. As the weeks passed a new cause for conflict was found, namely the emotive issue of contact between local girls and the British soldiers. Colonel Hancock recalls that in his time the IRA veterans he dealt with 'bitterly resented Catholic girls fraternizing with British soldiers (my soldiers alone married five!)'. When the Army held discos in their local base and invited girls from the area Gerry Adams mobilized the local Sinn Fein *cumann* or branch, named after his old comrade Liam McParland, to mount a picket made up mostly of women outside the entrance to the base.

Predictably, the pickets quickly became slanging matches between the troops and the women and, in that atmosphere, it was difficult to carry on with the discos. If the soldiers' love lives were hampered the same could not be said of Gerry Adams'. During the picketing he met Colette McArdle, who was later to become his wife.

The dispute over the discos did not peak until the end of 1970, when further dances were organized by the Army and fierce riots broke out in Ballymurphy. In a report in January 1971 the Belfast *Sunday News* looked back on several months of trouble, starting with the point when 'two local Sinn Fein clubs' had taken up the complaints from a handful of mothers that their daughters were in 'moral danger'.

> Stories spread – some of them highly coloured – about what happened after the dances. Residents close by were wakened at night by screams and shouts and in several instances local men intervened between over-amorous off-duty soldiers and frightened girls afraid of going too far. Republicans in the district acted immediately. Letters appeared in local papers demanding that the dances be called off and over 100 women in the area signed a petition condemning the dances and calling on teachers at local schools to warn pupils about the 'moral danger' involved in attending them. And then gradually as the story spread there were threats about what would happen to girls who dared to 'fraternise' with the soldiers.

According to the *Sunday News* there were more rowdy pickets of the kind Gerry Adams had previously organized around Christmas 1970, then after a brief lull the issue became the catalyst for serious violence. Stones and petrol bombs flew: 'this time there were more obvious pointers to the fact that Republicans were involved – if not openly, at least behind the scenes. Traditionally there is an understandable enmity between local youths and soldiers in any area where the military are stationed over the affections of young girls who are often more attracted by a uniform and a strange accent than the boy next door.'

For Adams the whole campaign was a successful agitation, directing anger against the British Army. Republicans promised that Ballymurphy was just the start and areas like the Upper Falls would be next. One soldier stationed in the area regarded the issue as just another example of IRA manipulation of the young. He felt a sense of regret about the dances, though, because the dispute resulted in the ritualized punishment of some girls, who were tied to lampposts and then daubed with tar and feathers. 'We had problems with discos during my time. Looking back on it I didn't think it was wrong. It wasn't so much for entertainment as an attempt to get through to the community. But afterwards we ended up with one or two girls tarred and feathered. I firmly believe that the Adamses would have had something to do with that, but that's by deduction, not by fact.'

The trouble in Ballymurphy was just part of what was a deteriorating picture throughout Northern Ireland. The 'honeymoon period' enjoyed by the British soldiers had come to an end. Gunmen from both communities had been in action against each other. Rioting at sectarian frontlines was commonplace. And then there were the first few incidents which suggested that the rift between Official and Provisional republicans had within it the potential for a bloody feud.

During 1970 the Provisionals commenced their bombing campaign of 'economic targets', but they hesitated about escalating the campaign to a direct shooting war versus the troops. The view was that at some point they would go on the offensive but that to do so prematurely would risk the wrath of the wider Catholic community.

The ferocity of the rioting in Ballymurphy in fact posed the Provisional IRA with a problem. While local IRA men like Gerry Adams had been all in favour of the clashes with the military as a way of radicalizing the youth, the Provisionals' leaders were against the riots because they didn't want too much Army attention being brought to an area which was serving a quite separate purpose. As an IRA publication entitled *Freedom Struggle* was to explain in 1973: 'The full truth about this rioting, particularly in the Ballymurphy area, was that it was most dangerous and embarrassing for the IRA . . . the Ballymurphy rioting was bringing large scale British forces into the area where the major part of the training of hundreds of new recruits was going on.'

At one stage IRA men acting under the orders of the Provisional leaders arrived in the area to stop the riots only to find themselves being stoned by the youths they had hoped to bring under control. By January 1971 after seven months of continuous rioting Adams and other local republicans agreed to try to scale the rioting down to facilitate contacts between Provisional IRA leaders and the Army about the future policing of the area. The local IRA even put some of the more pugnacious rioters under arrest.

In a newspaper interview that year the Belfast Provisional leader Joe Cahill claimed that his organization had never fostered the riots, although he did admit that standards had been allowed to slip:

> We insist that our recruits have a stainless character and come from a good family background. A lot of fellows were accepted in 1969 who should never have been. There was a period of slackness and it was not too hard to get into the IRA then. We impose a strict code of behaviour. A criminal record is enough to exclude a man. When someone joins he is interviewed and private inquiries are made about him. If he is accepted he attends recruiting classes for between six and 12 weeks. He gets a grounding in republicanism, security, policy methods and is warned of the risks of imprisonment and death. He then sits an examination. If he passes he makes a declaration of allegiance, not an oath, and then his military training begins.

In an effort to defuse the tension in Ballymurphy and other trouble spots, discreet talks were held between the Army and senior Provisionals. They included the Belfast O/C Billy McKee, Leo Martin, Frank Card and Gerry Adams' uncle and cousin Liam and Kevin Hannaway. Liam Hannaway told the military, 'If you get out of Ballymurphy we can control it without your assistance.' But ultimately there was no deal – Adams blamed the Army for reneging on agreements after Ian Paisley exposed the contacts. Even if some kind of understanding had been reached between the two sides, the likelihood is that it would only have been temporary.

Relations deteriorated rapidly. The Army did not just stop talking to the Hannaways – they also raided the family's house in the Clonard area. Military commanders claimed they had no choice as they had intelligence that the IRA was planning a new shooting campaign and they urgently needed to retrieve documents giving details of a number of Special Branch men which had fallen into the hands of the Provisionals. The Army's second most senior officer in Northern Ireland, General Sir Anthony Farrar-Hockley, went on Ulster TV and named the Hannaways and others as Provisional IRA men 'of some braggadocio'. Asked by the authors about Gerry Adams' profile during this period Farrar-Hockley expressed the view that he was merely 'small fry'. The General believes, however, that Adams' swift ascent up the Provisional IRA's ranks might well have been due to his family connections, with people like Uncle Liam helping him on his way.

The day after Farrar-Hockley's televised comments about Gerry Adams' uncle and cousin, the Provisional IRA claimed the life of the first British soldier to be killed in the Troubles. The Army had been coming under fire during riots all over Belfast since the raid in Clonard. Gunner Robert Curtis was killed in North Belfast during disturbances in Ardoyne. He was only twenty years of age. His killer, IRA man Billy Reid, survived three more months before dying himself in a shoot-out with the Army which happened, by eerie coincidence, in Curtis Street. Reid was just twenty-three years of age.

The day after Gunner Curtis' death the Stormont Prime Minister James Chichester-Clark announced on television that 'Northern Ireland is at war with the Irish Republican Army Provisionals.' The unionists at Stormont were agitating to bring in their favourite tool to put down the IRA: internment, or detention without trial. The Army had misgivings, knowing that its indiscriminate use, if directed entirely against nationalists, had the potential to misfire and arouse sympathy for the IRA among the Catholic community generally. The RUC was in turmoil, facing substantial reorganization as a result of the Hunt inquiry into its performance at the outset of the Troubles. The most public consequence of this was the disbandment of the discredited B Specials, but the implications of the interruption to normal policing were also that the intelligence effort of the force was nothing like what it had been either in the years before the Troubles or in more recent decades.

Mindful that a crackdown might be on the cards, Adams was often staying away from home. It was important to keep on the move not only to avoid the Army and the RUC, but also to stay one jump ahead of his former comrades in the Official IRA. During the course of 1970 the split between republicans had become ever more hostile as each side jockeyed for position. By 1971 the split had real potential for bloody feuding. The most sensitive issue was that of access to guns. Each side was so keen to get its hands on weaponry that they had few qualms about 'liberating' stocks which belonged to the other faction.

On the Lower Falls the Officials lost a substantial quantity of arms as a result of an Army operation which became known as the Falls Curfew or, in more emotive republican mythology, 'The Rape of the Falls'. This operation was sparked by an Army raid on an Official IRA arms cache – the situation escalated when troops came under attack and the soldiers responded by placing a substantial area of the Lower Falls under curfew, while they carried out lengthy arms searches. People elsewhere in West Belfast began to rally in support of those under curfew and the Army cordon was eventually broken by large numbers of women, led by the Sinn Fein vice president Maire Drumm, who took food and drink into the inhabitants in children's prams. When they marched out the women filled the prams up with another cargo – the Official IRA's guns – the bulk of which were then promptly transferred to the Provisionals, who were in control of the areas outside the cordon.

The guns-in-prams tale may have a folksy quality to it, but the rivalry over weaponry was anything but light-hearted. In Ballymurphy shortly after the majority of the local IRA had decided to go with the Provisionals, they commandeered a major arms dump in the area. According to one account, 'It took six or seven big vans to cart it away.'

One of the most sinister tales of rivalry for arms, though, concerns the McGuinness family. On 4 February 1971 a Provisional IRA gunman called at Paddy Joe McGuinness' home in Ballymurphy and demanded that he hand over a cache of guns he was accused of hiding. The guns were thought to have belonged neither to the Provisionals nor to the Officials but to a Citizens Defence Committee which had a semi-independent existence and wanted the arms to defend the Short Strand, a small Catholic enclave in the mainly Protestant east of the city.

McGuinness refused to have anything to do with the Provisional gunman and ordered him away. The next day McGuinness' son, John, a member of the Officials, was near his home when he was approached by a group of Provisionals. Three of the group walked over to the twenty-two-year-old. Two wrestled him to the ground and the third tried to shoot him in the head, but at the fateful moment McGuinness jerked his head back and the bullet entered his neck. He survived the shooting but the bullet frayed his spinal cord, leaving him paralysed. After several years of treatment by specialists at hospitals in Northern Ireland and England he died of his injuries in 1979.

John's father, who is now also dead, talked a great deal about Gerry Adams' alleged involvement in his son's shooting – according to McGuinness, Adams was in the group of Provisionals who watched his son walking home. He also claimed that Adams came to his door the next day and warned the family against seeking revenge. Years after the incident, when Adams was electioneering in Ballymurphy, Paddy Joe McGuinness would continue to confront him angrily about his son's wounding. However, no member of the family would appear on screen when this aspect of the shooting was first highlighted by John Ware on *World in Action* in 1983. Adams condemned the report as 'black propaganda' but didn't sue. 'I could deny all these allegations,' he said, 'but in a way that just lends them credibility. I'm afraid this programme is very biased. I would take legal action but I am told that is very expensive and I don't want to get involved in a long legal wrangle.' Ware stood by his story.

In his recent autobiography Adams claimed that McGuinness had wounded himself with his own weapon 'in a mêleé with two local activists'. John's sister Lily has a vivid memory of the night he was shot. 'I was watching a John Wayne film, *Iwo Jima*, and the bullets were flying everywhere but none of it was for real, nobody was really getting hurt. Somebody rushed in and said, "John's been shot" and I just couldn't believe it.' Nearly three decades on she still cannot forgive the men who seriously injured her brother. On hearing Adams' version of events she remarked contemptuously: 'So he committed suicide, did he?'

Shortly after the shooting a Provisional and close friend of Gerry Adams, Tom Cahill, was shot and seriously wounded by the three Official IRA gunmen while out on his milk round in Ballymurphy early one morning. According to one supporter of the Officials who lived in the estate at the time the shooting was in retaliation for the attack on John McGuinness. 'The Official IRA regarded the McGuinness shooting as an attack on them because it was the Provisionals trying to confiscate weapons . . . So they decided to take action against a leading Provo who they believed to have been involved in the attempt to confiscate the weapons.'

There is a degree of uncertainty about the precise sequence of events because the Officials and Provisionals were engaged in a fratricidal battle not far away in the Lower Falls. The night before Cahill's shooting a group of Officials ambushed Charlie Hughes, the commander of the Provisionals' D Company in the Lower Falls. Hughes was the first man to be killed in a Provisional–Official feud, and at the time the murder of a young man respected within republican ranks marked the high point of the bloodletting. The leaders on either side agreed to call a halt.

Adams took part in a meeting between the Provisional and Official commanders in a bid to sort out the feuding. With his sister Margaret firmly aligned to the Officials, Adams must have been well aware of the potential such a conflict had for tearing his own family apart. The mediation between the two sides, set up after the murder of Charlie Hughes, developed into a more cohesive form later in the 1970s. It was to prove crucial not only in ending disputes before they escalated beyond anyone's control, but also in establishing links between Adams and members of the clergy, which would prove vital in the peace process of the 1990s. But for now Gerry Adams' concern was more personal and immediate, as he remarked to one of his opponents: 'See these boys here – any one of these sixteen-year-olds could come up behind us and blow our brains out.' Maybe Adams had the example of poor John McGuinness in mind.

But shootings which only resulted in a wounding, however serious, were swiftly lost in the rush of events. No-warning bombs, sectarian killings and IRA shoot-outs with the Army vied for space in the headlines. By the summer of 1971 the authorities were ready to strike with the weapon they hoped would curb the flood of violence. At dawn on Monday 9 August Operation Demetrius was launched.

CHAPTER SIX

Demetrius Unbound

Members of the Parachute Regiment were tasked to swoop on Ballymurphy and arrest leading republican suspects in the early hours of 9 August 1971, but when they were given the name of Gerry Adams and his parents' address at an eve-of-Demetrius briefing in Brigade headquarters on the Springfield Road they realized just how hopeless the intelligence gathering was.

The Provisionals were not just expecting Demetrius, they had been actively seeking and looking forward to the introduction of internment. Any repressive measure brought them more sympathy and volunteers. This was graphically explained by the Belfast Provisional leader Joe Cahill to a reporter from *The Times* newspaper just ten days before the Paras moved in to pick up suspects and after an Army 'dry run' exercise had already been carried out. Adams acted as press officer-cum-minder to Cahill, taking him to meet English reporters to explain strategy. In *The Times* acount of the meeting Adams is described in the following terms: 'Present as a silent observer throughout our meeting was a much younger man [than Cahill], bearded, ascetic, very obviously in the prime of life, who watched me carefully.'

Cahill told *The Times* that the Provos' immediate objective was the abolition of Stormont, leading to the imposition of direct rule from Westminster. 'There will then be a direct confrontation between us and the English ... Things are becoming more repressive all the time; arrests, raids, trumped-up charges, brutality by the Army. Of course we are bringing internment closer, we recognize that. It surprises us that it hasn't been reintroduced already.'

As the Paras company commander in Ballymurphy was at pains to point out, the internment list was riddled with 'nonsenses. One of them was Gerry Adams, who was still being logged as living down in Ballymurphy and another chap, Joe McCann, who was supposedly living in Turf Lodge. Neither of them were actually there and we knew it, they hadn't been there for several weeks but nevertheless we were still given them to pick up.'

As a result of the reorganization of the RUC, discredited through its behaviour in the early days of the Troubles, the Army had, according to their local commander, 'no real support from Special Branch'. The military hoped that the dry run might be taken as a threat but, predictably, it served to warn republicans to be even more on their guard and to stay on the move. Adams and his cousin Kevin Hannaway were stopped by soldiers making their way out of a safe house during the dry run at the end of July, but the patrol let them go. Senior officers would no doubt have been heartbroken if they had known.

The Parachute Regiment's commander in Ballymurphy regarded Adams as 'the IRA's brigade commander in Belfast', which was a slightly over-inflated reading of Adams' position. During 1971 the police had received a variety of reports – most identified Adams as O/C of the IRA's 2nd Battalion, which covered the Lower Falls and Clonard areas. Joe Cahill held the most senior Belfast rank, having taken over from Billy McKee following his arrest four months earlier.

When the soldiers hit the streets at five o'clock in the morning Adams was safely in bed at an address unknown to the Army. He was woken by people in the street shouting 'Internment's in!' and watched the operation from the safety of a window.

The noise was deafening – the residents of Ballymurphy activated their primitive but highly effective warning system, banging bin lids on the ground to warn others of the soldiers' approach. At house after house the soldiers were roughly pulling men from their beds. The company commander, surveying his list, had suspected that 'we wouldn't pick up a soul'. But arrests were made. One of them was Liam Mulholland, who at more than seventy years of age was clearly no threat to anyone. As many as fifty pensioners were picked up, a mix-up attributed by the Army to the Irish practice of naming sons after their fathers.

Nevertheless those arrested were hastily processed through the Army's Henry Taggart base – formerly the church of the departed Protestants of New Barnsley – and bused out in armoured cars nicknamed 'Pigs'. Some of the detainees were subjected to insults and beatings, others were selected for an experiment in particularly brutal treatment involving beatings, being made to run a gauntlet of guards and dogs, and finally being pushed backwards out of helicopters – the internees only discovering when they hit the ground that they had been hovering no more than a few feet up in the air. They were hooded for long periods, interrogated, beaten and then had bright lights shone in their eyes. The practices were later condemned by the European Court of Human Rights. Gerry Adams' cousin Kevin Hannaway was one of these 'hooded men'.

Unsurprised to discover that Gerry Adams was not at home, the soldiers who kicked in the door of 11 Divismore Park detained his father and brother Liam instead. Like his predecessor in Ballymurphy the Parachute Regiment commander recalls Gerry Adams senior as 'a bit of a nuisance. He was always at the mini-riots egging people on but never actually taking part. He had a loud voice and obviously carried a bit of clout in the Ballymurphy area. I think probably that may have in part been due to Gerry being the commander for the Belfast Brigade.' Gerry senior was interned, but Liam Adams was too young and after his age was discovered at Girdwood barracks in North Belfast the Army had to release him, dumping him far from his home.

The Adams family home was trashed during the internment swoop. Ornaments and furniture were smashed, the beds soaked in urine and shit. The house was repeatedly rammed by an Army vehicle, Adams later claimed, in order to ensure it was uninhabitable. While an Army officer in the local base disputed that claim, he readily admitted that the Adams home was accorded special treatment during a post-Demetrius operation to clear barricades. As a precaution against ambushes the Paratroopers always made a point of never walking along the street, preferring to head straight through gardens and across fences. The troops dismantling the barricades 'went straight through the Adams home on a number of occasions . . . there would have been damage done to the house, I have no doubt'. Within days Annie Adams had moved out, never to return.

After the first wave of internment arrests, crowds began to gather outside the Henry Taggart. From seven in the morning till seven at night the rioting was incessant leaving the Army holed up and unable to move. Come the evening gunmen began blasting away at the base, a development which the besieged soldiers welcomed. 'The thing exploded and, being August, it was still half light and to be quite honest this was the one thing that the soldiers had in many ways been hoping for. It was the IRA taking us on at our game. We brought in five dead and one wounded.'

Bullets were blazing in every direction, with gunfire from the two military bases, the Henry Taggart and the former Vere Foster school, as well as shooting from the Ballymurphy estate and further gunfire from the adjacent Springmartin area – some of it coming from loyalist weapons and some from the rifles of the Parachute Regiment's support company based there. 'Anyone who had guns was out firing guns,' according to one community worker in the area aligned with the Officials. 'It was a sort of psychological thing, "We're here and we're defending you and don't worry about it," but there wasn't a ghost's chance in hell and the Army, once they took up positions, just shot anything that moved.'

While the Army claimed that some of those killed had been taking part in the attacks on its base, none of the dead were subsequently acknowledged as members by the IRA. One of the victims that night was the local parish priest, Father Hugh Mullan, who had ventured out on to open ground with the intention of administering the last rites to a nineteen-year-old who had been hit. When he got to the body, the priest found that the teenager was still alive and, turning to go for medical help, he too was shot, the bullet almost certainly coming from the gun of one of the soldiers based in Springmartin.

The next morning the Army padre in the Henry Taggart base ventured out to talk to the community worker, 'and he grabbed me and said, "We didn't know he was a priest and I made sure he got the last rites and I made sure I went to as many victims as I could last night." And I just told him to get lost. The whole thing was just savagery of the highest order.'

The savagery carried on for several days. On the evening of 13 August Adams himself almost fell victim to the arbitrary nature of the shooting when he was escorting Joe Cahill through some brickyards in Beechmount and then across the playground of St Peter's school. As they crossed it a gunman opened up on them and they both hit the ground as bullets flew around them. When they made it to Whiterock, where they were due to meet a reporter, they discovered that their attacker was in fact a Provisional IRA man who thought he had been shooting at the UVF. The Provisionals sarcastically nick-named the sniper 'Rifleman' because he was such a bad shot.

The shooting incident came on the same day that the Army and some West Belfast nationalists held news conferences at exactly the same time, giving completely different versions of the events of the past few days. For the Army, Brigadier Marston Tickell insisted that 'we have undoubtedly inflicted a major defeat on the IRA'. At St Peter's school, the nationalists insisted that only two of the very many victims of the last few days had been IRA men. A reporter asked, 'If the IRA are not defeated, where are they?' and at that point the republican Labour Stormont MP Paddy Kennedy said, 'Well, you'd better ask the commander of the Belfast Brigade,' and threw the floor open to Joe Cahill. After this moment of media exposure Cahill moved away from Belfast, heading for Dublin, where he became the IRA's quartermaster general.

Adams says that the period of internment removed older activists from the ground and meant that the responsibilities of leadership fell on to younger people. With Cahill's departure Seamus Twomey took over as the Provisional IRA's O/C in Belfast. Adams was undoubtedly an important influence in the background – more than one republican told the authors that as the 1970s progressed Twomey became 'no more than Gerry Adams' puppet'.

Internment spurred on the IRA's campaign. In the preceding months it had killed eleven soldiers throughout Northern Ireland. Afterwards it claimed the lives of thirty-two in quick succession. The Provisionals' 2nd Belfast Battalion was under Adams' command between May 1971 and March 1972, during which time it killed three policemen, nineteen soldiers and twenty-seven civilians. The security forces took the view that Adams was more a planner than a trigger man. In the words of one retired general, 'I think he kept his hands fairly clean, but was good at ensuring that somebody else was doing it.'

Peter McMullen, an Army deserter who joined Adams' battalion, later explained to journalist John Ware the authority which Adams held: 'As commanding officer he was ultimately responsible for everything which went on within his battalion area . . . discipline, shooting, bombing, robberies, it doesn't matter what it is, he's ultimately responsible.'

In recent years Adams has written a short story, harking back to these days, in which he graphically describes an IRA sniper attack on an Army patrol, resulting in the death of a British officer. Although the context in which Adams places this tale in his book *Before the Dawn* almost appears to be confessional he has insisted that the story is not factual but merely a piece of empathetic fiction. Given his propensity to write and even speak about himself in the third person, such as his account of the firing of shots over Liam McParland's grave, he cannot be surprised if the story raises suspicions.

The Ballymurphy IRA would have been proud of the fight they were putting up, but Adams was concerned that the struggle might be developing into a purely military engagement, focused entirely on an 'elite' IRA and losing touch with the community. Some evidence that he and his supporters were still thinking politically can be adduced from an edition of the Provisionals' paper *Republican News* dated October 1971. Under the headline 'Ballymurphy Resurgence and Co-operation', an unnamed writer documents and praises the work of the community groups in building an area more or less autonomous from many of the institutions of the state. In language which would later become familiar to students of 'Adams-speak' the article continues: 'Our attack on Unionist and British control must be a fusion on a political, social and cultural basis ... Republicans can not do this alone, we must be prepared to co-operate with all groups working for the benefit of the working class people. Where such groups do not exist we must initiate them.'

The intensity of the time created a mood that life was short and had to be lived to the full. It was while flitting from safe house to billet, avoiding another Army raid in the days after internment, that he told his girlfriend Colette McArdle that if they both got out of their latest scrape he would marry her.

The marriage was performed by Father Des Wilson at the back of St John's chapel in Ballymurphy. It was inevitably a bit of a rushed affair – Adams' brother Paddy and a number of other youths kept watch outside in case the Army turned up uninvited. Inside Father Wilson refused to accept his stipend, freeing up a bit more money for the best man to buy a drink for some of the party. The priest has no lasting memories of the service. So much was happening at the time, he told the authors, that it was better not to ask questions and not to remember much.

But given that Gerry and Colette had met while picketing the Army's dances, it is interesting that he should lump the 'quickie wedding' in with another kind of marriage ceremony:

> It was unusual enough in a way . . . but we would have accepted at that time that people would be moving from house to house, or, if you'd like to say, on the run. That did not necessarily imply that they were in the IRA or any other military organization, it implied or it showed that the British authorities thought they were, or found it convenient to pretend that they were . . . to me a man being on the run wouldn't necessarily have the same meaning as it would for propagandists.
>
> The other thing was that we had quite a curious pattern, because in the early seventies girls from Belfast were still marrying British soldiers, so that if people came along to you and said, 'Unfortunately I have to move from house to house,' you didn't think anything much of that, and if somebody came along and said, 'I want to marry a British soldier but I don't want to be very public about it,' you didn't think very much of that either. It was a very curious time and maybe people don't realize just how curious it was.

Such 'fraternization with the enemy', as the Provisionals dubbed it, became less frequent after internment, which drove a wedge between the Catholic community and the Army. Undoubtedly the rift widened into a chasm after the events of 30 January 1972. Adams was travelling back from a trip to Dublin when he heard about the Bloody Sunday killings in Derry – thirteen civilians were shot dead during a civil rights march through the nationalist Bogside estate. Another victim died later. The soldiers responsible were Paratroopers, from the Regiment which had killed the parish priest in Adams' own estate of Ballymurphy. If the killings were the Regiment's way of putting the 'rebels' down, the brutal act had the reverse effect. The British embassy in Dublin was burned, barricades went up in nationalist areas all over Northern Ireland and, in Adams' own estimation, money, guns and recruits flowed into the IRA.

As the death and casualty toll steadily rose, the Provisionals grew more convinced that their objective, the overthrow of the Northern Ireland state, was approaching realization. When in March 1972 the

British Prime Minister Edward Heath accepted the resignation of the unionist Brian Faulkner and announced the suspension of the unionists' Stormont assembly, it was acclaimed by the IRA as a personal victory. Henceforth William Whitelaw was to govern the province as Secretary of State.

But the hostile reaction among both nationalists and unionists to outrages such as the bombing of the Abercorn restaurant in central Belfast, in which two women were killed and other shoppers were horribly maimed, showed that the potential was there too for a popular backlash against the IRA. Nevertheless, with just a few more of their newly developed car bombs, the Provisionals hoped, direct rule from London would soon be rendered impractical and the way would open up for talks leading to a British withdrawal and the Holy Grail of a United Ireland. These were dreams which Adams could only contemplate from behind bars, because by the time Faulkner resigned his luck on the run had expired.

CHAPTER SEVEN

A Most Important Prisoner

At dawn on 14 March 1972 Gerry Adams was lying in the king-sized double bed that he and his wife Colette had been given as a wedding present when the Army burst in to the small house in Harrogate Street which had been loaned to them. He told the soldiers his name was Joseph McGuigan, but in the Springfield Road barracks he was identified by an RUC detective who had stopped him before. Adams continued to maintain the fiction after being moved to Palace Barracks in Holywood just outside Belfast. He hoped that sticking to an alias would frustrate his interrogators.

Adams alleges that inside Palace Barracks he was kicked and beaten around the kidneys and between the legs for hours on end. He has also recalled how an apparently berserk man rushed into the room and tried to shoot him, and another loudly screaming man came at him with a hatchet. There is no doubt that the handling of the interviews did not conform to the standards which would apply in Northern Ireland today. One of the RUC detectives was widely feared and respected in nationalist West Belfast – people knew that he could more than handle himself in a fight. Parents would warn recalcitrant children that if they misbehaved this policeman 'will get you'. Most youngsters, if they knew what was good for them, immediately stopped whatever they were doing.

Father Denis Faul, a Catholic priest and outspoken critic of the Provisionals, was operating as a freelance ombudsman checking out complaints of ill treatment by the police and Army. The Adams family rang him to see if he could intervene on Gerry's behalf. 'It was either his wife or his mother, I never met her, it was all over the telephone. I rang, got a piece of information and passed it on to her. That was all I could do.' Father Faul didn't get any direct evidence of Adams being subjected to ill-treatment, but he says, 'You would take it for granted he got a bit of a thumping, they all did at the time in Palace Barracks, it was very rough.' Adams' interrogator telephoned Faul on one occasion after the priest sounded off about him in public. 'He was a tough boy, he rang me up one time because I was complaining about him and said, "This would be a lovely wee country now if we could only get rid of this violence."' Faul, who had himself seen men whose whole chest and stomachs were left 'just black' after interrogation, was having none of it. 'There's a lot of violence in your place,' he replied and pledged to continue his complaints.

Almost until the end of his lengthy interview Adams continued to deny his real identity. The detectives concluded that 'this man is a very good liar, who will need a long continuous interrogation, an intelligent gentleman well instructed in the methods of interrogation'. Adams finally abandoned the pretence and gave his real name in order to ensure that his wife would be allowed to visit him. He also made a formal complaint about his treatment in custody.

Security sources indicate that that was not all he had to say. In an interview which took place between a quarter-past midnight and half-past one in the morning the detectives got Adams talking on the promise that any information given to them would not be used to press a charge. He then admitted to having joined the IRA seven years previously as one of only fifteen members of Belfast's D Company at that time. Most of the detectives' questions were ignored or answered in such vague terms as to be of no usefulness. Asked about the supply route of explosives going to the Provisional IRA he replied that they came from Eire, the Irish Republic. Questioned about what kind of explosives were brought from Eire he told the RUC, 'whatever they can dig up'. When pressed in more detail about how they were brought to Northern Ireland he maintained that he had no idea.

Having exhausted their line of questioning on the Provisional IRA's acquisition of explosives the interrogators tried firing some questions at Adams about the situation in Belfast. 'Who selects targets for attacks?' they inquired. 'The Brigade staff,' Adams replied. When asked who made the bombs Adams named two men. Tony Lewis and Sean Johnston were in fact two of four men from his own 2nd Belfast Battalion who, less than a week before his arrest, had been killed in a premature explosion while preparing a bomb in a house in Clonard Street.

Because of the circumstances in which these admissions were made, the lateness of the hour and the treatment which Adams had no doubt been subjected to, they were not in future years to form the basis of any case against him. Uncorroborated confession evidence of this kind would be thrown out of any court and the admissions did not feature in the unsuccessful attempt by the RUC later in the 1970s to try to prove that Adams was an IRA member.

By a quarter-past ten the next morning, Adams was denying that he had said anything whatsoever the previous night. The detectives assessed him as an 'important member' of the IRA, with a capacity for leadership. The admissions he had made in the late-night interview were passed on to a tribunal. They were then used by the Commissioner with responsibility for internment to justify Adams' detention without trial. He was taken off to the prison ship the *Maidstone*, where his uncle Liam Hannaway was the O/C of the 150 prisoners on board.

The *Maidstone* was drawn up at a dock in East Belfast. Apart from being cramped and insanitary, it was also not much of a prison. In January of 1972 seven internees succeeded in sawing through a bar across a window and swimming to the shore. They included two close friends of Adams, the Ballymurphy Provisionals Jim Bryson and Tommy 'Toddler' Tolan. After their escape Bryson and Toland spent some time down south before returning to Ballymurphy where Bryson took Adams' old job as local O/C.

When the *Maidstone* was shut down and the prisoners moved to Long Kesh, a large prison camp full of Nissen huts near Lisburn to the south of Belfast, Adams was reunited with his father and his brother Paddy. These were not altogether unhappy times for him. Adams recalls being involved in boisterous pranks inside 'the Kesh', until such a time as his uncle Liam exerted a restraining influence on him and the other younger internees. Tommy Gorman, who was field operations commander for the IRA's 1st Battalion in Andersonstown, remembers that 'streaking', the craze of running naked through a public place, was sweeping the country and that he and Adams were responsible for introducing it to the compounds.

However, Paddy Joe McLean remembers Adams as being fairly quiet and withdrawn, a memory which echoes in some ways the recollections of his school teachers. 'I never could sort of strike up a warm relationship with Gerry, he seemed to me to always be an aloof sort of a person. He was a young fellow compared to us at that time. He had the beard and he had the long hair but I would have seen no change in him between then and now.'

McLean had heard of Adams some time before meeting him via his cousin Kevin Hannaway. Although neither an Official nor a Provisional, McLean had, like Kevin Hannaway, been one of the 'hooded men' subjected to degrading treatment immediately after internment:

> The first time that I heard of Gerry Adams was when I was interned in 1971 to 1972. I was along with a cousin of his, Kevin Hannaway, and he always referred to Gerry and my understanding was that Gerry was O/C of the Provos at that time in Belfast.
>
> That was round about August of '71 to May of '72 and was on the basis of what Kevin told me. By the way other people behaved towards him I was in no doubt that Gerry was 'the Man'. At that time I was secretary of the internees' camp council, which was the body of people that sort of legislated for all internees and regulated classes and visits and parole and all that sort of stuff, a general welfare body, and Gerry would have been sitting on the camp council along with me.

Though not striking up a particularly warm relationship with Adams, McLean recognized him as a man who had more political sophistication than most of his fellow internees: 'The people that I'd associated with who were Provisionals in the camp, people like his cousin Kevin and the other Hannaways, would have had no depth to them in political terms. Now I always felt that Gerry was more than that. Gerry would have educated himself and would have been able to engage in debate as I saw him round the camp council table, and Gerry never was vociferous on behalf of Provisional Sinn Fein. So I wondered to myself, how come Gerry was on that side and did he not want to be on the other side?' McLean put his finger on the crucial differences between Adams and some of his fellow traditionalists within the Provisionals. 'In relation to the role of the Church, Gerry would have had a progressive view at that time, although I don't see that now, I see him very much now in the Catholic mould. Say in debates on integrated schools or things like that, Gerry would have been in my view on the progressive side in all these conversations.

That would be at complete variance at what the Jimmy Drumms or the Sean MacStiofains or the Rory Bradys would have been.'

McLean concluded that whatever Adams' views he was trapped by his roots: 'Gerry comes from that sort of a tradition who like myself would have been interned over the years and who were in a certain kind of a nationalist mould in the ghetto areas, and I saw the same kind of a mould in Derry city, the same in Newry, the same in Strabane, the same in West Belfast. I'm sure it would be much the same if you were in some of the Italian ethnic centres maybe in New York, where people didn't step outside their mould if they wanted to live and be members of that close-knit community. I think family loyalty meant a lot.'

A small group of Official IRA supporters inside the Kesh organized their own lectures. One afternoon Dessie O'Hagan was addressing some prisoners inside the hut known as Cage 2. As a professional teacher this was a task he was well used to, but that day he couldn't wait for the lecture to end as he was suffering greatly from 'the old Duke of Argylls', Belfast rhyming slang for piles. However, as a question and answer session got under way after the talk, Gerry Adams and a companion made his way into the back of the room. O'Hagan bristled and prepared for rhetorical battle, knowing that the young Provisionals were duty bound to try to pick holes in his left-wing Official republican analysis.

Adams duly objected to a number of points O'Hagan was trying to make, but the encounter did not warm up until they and another Official internee moved outside Cage 2. 'When the meeting had finished,' the Official remembers,

> we were outside and we were pushing this line of the unity of Protestant and Catholic workers and I was giving examples of Protestants around my way who lived in just as bad conditions as me.
>
> He says: 'Youse might make some headway but six well-placed car bombs could put years of work down the drain.' Then the question came up, 'What's your objective, how far are you prepared to go, Gerry, to achieve this objective?' and it was then that he made this statement: 'I'm prepared to wade up to my knees in Protestant blood to get to a United Ireland.' I was stunned. From that day to this Gerry is just . . . I would never

consider him a republican. I see him as a nationalist . . . From the point of view of myself adhering to what I would see as the true republicanism of Wolfe Tone, the United Irishmen, and the French revolution onwards, Adams' attitude to the Protestants – 'Protestant blood, wipe them out' and so on – is basically nationalism at its crudest.

This account of the exchange is hotly disputed by Adams, who maintains that it is untrue, a story cynically made up by embittered political opponents. When the story was retold in 1996 on a BBC radio phone-in, Adams challenged the caller by asking him: 'And who is Dessie O'Hagan?' But both O'Hagan and the other former Official stand by their account, conceding that while the exchange may have been a passing indiscretion it nonetheless exposed the true nature of the Provisional IRA's philosophy.

According to the Official the encounter occurred at a time when Adams was on a short hunger strike. The strike was in support of other IRA prisoners in Belfast's Crumlin Road jail led by the former IRA commander in the city, Billy McKee, who were already refusing food. The Crumlin Road prisoners were demanding political status, exactly the same aim which was to lead to another much more devastating hunger strike in 1981.

Adams and the younger prisoners in Long Kesh were keen to launch some kind of protest in support of their comrades in the Crumlin Road. Even though the older prisoners were reluctant to follow McKee's example, the young internees won the day and a hunger strike was begun. Adams' uncle Liam Hannaway, despite his reservations, joined in and it is thought that the damage the protest did to his health led to his early death in 1981.

Adams cracked after fourteen days. By comparison Billy McKee, at the head of the Crumlin's forty IRA hunger strikers, had by this stage been without food for nearly thirty days. The government was worried about the state of his health and wanted the dispute settled. There were bigger moves afoot which might be jeopardized by the making of another republican martyr. And at the centre of these moves was the twenty-three-year-old Adams. He had only quit his hunger strike for a day when he heard his name being bellowed across the compound: 'Adams. Release!'

It had to be him, as his brother and father had been let out about a month before. But so soon after a protest he thought a release was unlikely and reckoned some of the other internees must be winding him up. It wasn't until his uncle Liam told him to head towards the gates of Long Kesh that he began to realize the shouts were for real. At the gate, the republican who'd been keen to break out of detention double-checked with the governor that it really was his name on the list. 'Yes, Adams,' came the reply, 'you're for release.'

CHAPTER EIGHT

Talking to Mr Whitelaw

In June 1972 a bewildered Gerry Adams walked out of Long Kesh and into the arms of Dolours and Marion Price, two young republican sisters who would, just a year later, achieve notoriety for leading the Provos' first bombing campaign in London. They drove him to Andersonstown, where he met Francie McGuigan, another old comrade from the relatively innocent days of housing action around Divis Flats. Adams was informed, to his surprise, that a truce was about to be declared in return for face-to-face talks between the Provisionals and the British government in London.

By any standards this was an astonishing offer from Downing Street. The last time the IRA held official talks with the British was in 1921, when Michael Collins had won Ireland's partial independence. If it seemed to elevate the leadership of the Provisionals, not yet three years old as an organization, to an altogether higher status, Adams was no doubt conscious that the strand of republicanism from which he came regarded Collins as a traitor.

According to Peter McMullen, the Army deserter turned IRA sniper who served alongside Adams and was interviewed at length about him by journalist John Ware in the early 1980s, it was Seamus Twomey who put forward Adams' name as a talks delegate at a Belfast Brigade meeting prior to the truce. This was for two reasons: it would test the sincerity of the British, who would have to release Adams from Long Kesh, and it would exploit his political skills. 'He was a protégé of Seamus Twomey and we thought he could better handle politicians with his experience, even though he was that young, than we could. He was very articulate, smart and very good at tactics. He knew the political picture better than most volunteers or any Brigade officer for that matter,' said McMullen.

Twomey was sceptical from the start about the merits of calling a truce and recognized young Adams' ability to express what the senior Belfast men feared. Adams was therefore chosen as the delegation's other negotiator, a representative of the Belfast belligerents to complement the more politically minded Dave O'Connell. Although the IRA chief of staff Sean MacStiofain didn't know the Adams family well, he liked the fact that Adams came from an impeccably republican background and believed that he had the makings of good political material. MacStiofain was so impressed by him that he once suggested he should stand as vice president of Sinn Fein. Adams declined the offer, replying that he wanted to make his contribution 'in the field'. MacStiofain had the deciding vote on who should accompany him to London and therefore chose Adams because he considered him to be a useful man on the ground and also to test British intentions. If they were serious they would have to let Adams out of prison. The authorities disguised the significance of his release by letting thirteen other internees out along with him.

Adams made his way to the house of Paddy Devlin of the Social Democratic and Labour Party, who along with John Hume was instrumental in arranging the truce between the Provos and Whitelaw. The Devlins gave him and his accomplice Francie McGuigan a key to the house so that they could come and go as they pleased during the next forty-eight hours – Paddy's wife Theresa was annoyed later when the keys were never returned.

On the evening of Adams' release the deal nearly foundered when Billy McKee, the leader of the IRA's convicted prisoners on hunger strike for political status, was taken to hospital. Devlin was informed that the governor of Crumlin Road prison was standing by with hot soup and milk for the striking prisoners, waiting for official word of the agreement reached with Whitelaw.

In the early hours of Tuesday morning, with Whitelaw dragged from his bed by Devlin's persistent telephone calls, the Northern Ireland Secretary finally gave word that political status – or special-category status as the government preferred to call it – had been granted to loyalist and republican prisoners. While the principal factor in allowing prisoners to wear their own clothes and receive more privileges than 'ordinary decent criminals' was the prospect of a ceasefire, the decision to concede the right to special status would have profound consequences for a future British government and the rise of the Provisionals when it was subsequently withdrawn.

But that lay in the future: for the present IRA leadership there was one further meeting before Adams and McGuigan delivered themselves into the hands of Paddy Devlin and set out for Londonderry. Devlin had been provided with letters of safe conduct from the Northern Ireland Office and the Army, stating that he was an MP and was not to be obstructed or interfered with in any way. With these he was able to negotiate the many roadblocks with his precious cargo. The journey across the Sperrin Mountains was uneventful, although the IRA men were distinctly edgy about Devlin's driving skills.

Later the same day Adams and Dave O'Connell met with Whitelaw's official, Frank Steele, in a house outside Derry to finalize the terms of the truce. There was some wrangling over how long an IRA ceasefire would have to last before the London talks were held, with Adams and O'Connell holding out for seven days and the government side insisting on a fortnight. In the end they split the difference, agreeing that the meeting would go ahead ten days after an announcement was made by the Provos.

Adams insisted that any truce would have to be bilateral, with Army arrests, searches and raids suspended. An arrangement was finally agreed and the two sides went their separate ways. Steele later recalled being impressed by Adams:

> I had been briefed that, although Adams was a young man, he was a senior member of the Belfast Battalion and that Battalion had been murdering and shooting and bombing and therefore I expected, putting it frankly, an aggressive street-wise youth.
>
> And I was therefore pleasantly surprised when instead a very personable, likeable, intelligent, articulate and persuasive young man appeared. At one point I said to him, 'You're a young man, you've got your life ahead of you. Do you really want to spend it on the run from us British?' To which he replied no, he didn't. And I said, 'Well, what would you like to do?' He said, 'I'd like to go to university and get a degree.' So I said, 'Well, we're not stopping you. All you've got to do is renounce violence and you can go to university.' To which he said, 'Well I've got to help you British get out of Ireland first.

On 22 June the Irish republican publicity bureau announced that the Provisional IRA would cease all offensive operations from Monday 26 June. In the Commons that afternoon Whitelaw said that the Army 'will obviously reciprocate'.

MacStiofain was determined to show that the Provisionals were not entering a ceasefire from a position of weakness and the next five days witnessed a serious escalation in IRA attacks. Five soldiers and a policeman were murdered. One of the soldiers was shot dead in East Belfast only minutes before the ceasefire was due to begin. There were nearly fifty explosions and a series of armed robberies in Belfast which netted £55,000.

MacStiofain made his final arrangements for the talks, consulting people he trusted on the best ways to approach the meeting. 'Adams wrote that the IRA received a submission which had been requested from Sean MacBride [the former IRA leader and Nobel Peace Prize winner]. No submission was requested. I asked Mr MacBride for advice on tactics and procedures regarding the forthcoming talks in London and I am grateful to him for the advice which he gave us at the time,' MacStiofain said in response to Adams' own account of the meeting.

MacStiofain chose his delegation to reflect the situation on the ground. Three hundred and seventy-nine people had been killed since 1969, there had been 1,682 explosions and 7,258 people injured, including such horrors as the Abercorn bombing, in which two women out shopping for a wedding dress had their legs blown off. 'At this stage it was the military situation that would be the main British preoccupation and they would scarcely be interested in talking to any republicans just yet apart from representatives of the military wing,' MacStiofain later wrote. 'Therefore I rejected a suggestion that our team should include a leading member of Sinn Fein.'

Accordingly he selected Gerry Adams, Dave O'Connell, Seamus Twomey, Ivor Bell and Martin McGuinness. Adams had risen rapidly through the ranks. By the autumn of 1971 he had assumed the position of commanding officer of the 2nd Battalion. On Friday morning the delegation assembled in Derry and prepared to drive to the rendezvous with the British. One of the two cars in which they were travelling broke down, and everyone had to pile unceremoniously into the one vehicle. Adams had consciously dressed down for the occasion, donning a holey jumper which he trusted would make its own political point. MacStiofain dressed for the occasion too, arming himself with a .38 Cobra Special revolver in a shoulder holster.

According to MacStiofain, Adams was still bewildered by his release when the two men met in Derry. 'You owe me one,' MacStiofain joked. In later years he would bitterly reflect that the favour was never repaid by his acolyte. They were flown by helicopter to the military section of Aldergrove airport on the eastern shores of Lough Neagh and then transferred to a plane which took them to RAF Benson in Oxfordshire. On the drive into London, Seamus Twomey requested that the two limousines stop; he wanted to go to the toilet. He strolled around Henley-on-Thames to the consternation of his minders, observing when he finally returned that it seemed a lovely place.

Their destination was the home of Whitelaw's junior minister Paul Channon, an imposing house on Cheyne Walk, near Chelsea Bridge. The meeting was to take place in the library and when Whitelaw breezed into the room he made a beeline for the IRA chief of staff. 'Oh Mr MacStiofain, how do you do?' he said, extending his hand. MacStiofain, who was born John Stephenson in Leytonstone, noted the perfect Irish pronunciation.

After some introductory pleasantries MacStiofain read out a list of IRA demands. He called on the British government to recognize publicly that it was the right of the people of Ireland acting as a unit to decide the future of Ireland and a British declaration of intent to withdraw British forces from Irish soil by 1 January 1975. 'Pending such withdrawal the British forces must be withdrawn immediately from sensitive areas.' A general amnesty for all political prisoners, internees and detainees and for people on the wanted list was also demanded.

In his account of the meeting, Adams says that Seamus Twomey, the IRA man most opposed to negotiations, lost his temper and thumped the table during a particularly tense moment in the meeting. 'There was no shouting or thumping of tables. Whenever a republican spoke during the meeting he did so with dignity and discipline,' according to MacStiofain. They both agree, however, that when Whitelaw ventured to suggest that British troops would never fire on unarmed civilians, Martin McGuinness, then aged only twenty-two, tackled him forcefully about the Bloody Sunday shootings.

According to Adams it was he who proposed an adjournment.

MacStiofain says that Whitelaw and Channon requested the break. In a side room the IRA delegation assessed its presentation. 'Jesus, we have it!' exclaimed MacStiofain, according to Adams, in an account which conveys the impression that his commanding officer seemed to believe Whitelaw was about to accept the IRA terms. Adams, on the other hand, said he believed exactly the opposite. 'I categorically deny saying any such thing!' MacStiofain angrily states. 'I did, however, hear someone saying, "Maybe we'll get the declaration of intent," to which I responded, "I don't think so."'

Whatever the truth of the matter – and to Provisional leaders it would matter a great deal in due course as their internal power struggle intensified – when the meeting resumed it was agreed that the British cabinet would take a week to consider the proposals and that an open-ended truce would be maintained, with each side agreeing to twenty-four hours' notice of their intent to break it. As the meeting adjourned Whitelaw was anxious to press upon the IRA team the need for secrecy. If news of the meeting got out then 'all bets are off', he threatened. Adams, irritated by this, retorted with a blast of machismo: 'That means all bets are off, then.' It was a phrase which he was to hear repeated back to him in less comfortable circumstances.

The flight back to Northern Ireland was more relaxed and Frank Steele chatted with the IRA men. 'I hope you're not going to start your bloody stupid campaign of violence again,' he said to them. If they really wanted a United Ireland they would be far better off trying to persuade their Protestant neighbours of the benefits than reducing Northern Ireland to rubble. The government was not unduly worried by the Army death toll, he said. There were more men lost in traffic accidents in Germany than to the IRA. MacStiofain pointedly asked him if the British Army had suffered twenty fatal road accidents in the past three weeks, to which Steele could only lamely reply, 'You know what I mean.' They did, but they didn't agree. The only way to a United Ireland was through forcing the Brits to leave at the barrel of a gun. As they flew over the Irish Sea, Adams joined Ivor Bell in a lusty rendition of the Republican song 'The Belfast Brigade'.

The twenty-three-year-old's trip to meet the British government was ending on the same note of unreality as it had begun. The IRA had placed a set of wholly unrealistic demands on the table, but the very fact that the meeting had taken place at all confirmed to some members of the delegation that they were indeed on the road to British withdrawal. The meeting had left nothing of consequence to discuss between the two sides. As Whitelaw later recalled: 'The meeting was a non-event. The IRA simply made impossible demands which I told them the British government would never concede.' But to the IRA it displayed weakness on the government's part and a weak resolve for staying in Northern Ireland. The republicans believed it would be only a matter of time before the campaign of violence proved too much for any government to withstand.

In spite of the expressions of intent to continue the truce it was already under serious pressure. Paddy Devlin believed that the intense rivalry within Provisional ranks had sown the seeds of its collapse in advance of the London meeting. There was 'rampant jealousy' of Adams' rising profile. Later that year he was promoted from O/C of the Ballymurphy-based 2nd Battalion to adjutant for the entire Belfast Brigade. According to some republicans, MacStiofain felt besieged by Ruairi O Bradaigh, Dave O'Connell and Joe Cahill after the split with the Officials and saw Adams as a potential ally to strengthen his hand in the North–South axis of the IRA.

Although a truce was in effect, the killings had continued, if at a slightly less manic though no less horrific pace. The days of 'peace' were punctuated by a string of tit-for-tat sectarian murders with, in some cases, the victims being bound and hooded before their despatch and abandonment on waste ground. By the end of Sunday 9 July, the day upon which the Provisionals ended their ceasefire, twenty-four people had been killed since midnight 26 June, ten of whom were IRA victims. Loyalists began throwing up barricades in response to the republican no-go areas and to the growing climate of rumour that the British were about to make concessions to the Provisionals. Some displaced Catholic families from the Rathcoole estate in North Belfast were allocated homes in Lenadoon in the west of the city, from where Protestants, in their turn, had fled.

The loyalist Ulster Defence Association (UDA) threatened to burn down the houses if they were given to the homeless Catholics. The Provisionals' leader Seamus Twomey set the British Army a deadline of four o'clock on Sunday afternoon to move in the families. But when an Army Saracen rammed a lorry carrying the Catholics' belongings into the estate a large crowd began stoning the soldiers, who opened fire with rubber bullets and CS gas. Within minutes the

Provisionals returned fire and a gun battle was under way. As far as both sides were concerned the ceasefire was over, with a vengeance. At seven o'clock that Sunday evening MacStiofain made the formal announcement. 'The campaign will be resumed with the utmost ferocity and ruthlessness,' he told a reporter.

'It was inevitable in view of the behaviour of the British troops in Lenadoon and it broke with tragic results for everybody concerned, for the Irish, for the English people, tragic results for the British troops and the IRA volunteers and for the civilians who have been killed since then,' MacStiofain said in a television interview which has since been recycled into a 1990s IRA propaganda video containing contributions from Gerry Adams and Martin McGuinness. 'I hope the day will come again when British representatives will realize that the only way to a permanent peace in Ireland is to meet representatives of the republican movement and negotiate with them a phased and orderly withdrawal.'

In Ballymurphy that night the Army opened fire from an observation post at two cars, killing three teenagers, one a member of the IRA's youth wing, a priest and a thirty-nine-year-old father of six. When local IRA volunteers returned from the battle at Lenadoon they concentrated heavy fire on the sandbagged Army post, but to little effect. Adams later complained that the IRA was portrayed as the aggressor in this deadly skirmish when it was in fact retaliating. He had spent the truce period at his parents' home with his wife Colette and was at a wedding when news filtered back of Twomey's decision to return fire at Lenadoon. Within the hour he was back on the run, annoyed that he had not been given ample warning of the development.

MacStiofain later expressed some guarded disappointment at this turn of events. A prolongation of the ceasefire might have bought him the time in which to convene a conference of all Ireland's political and religious organizations. He claims to have been in regular contact with Protestant representatives, both lay and clerical, many of whom were astute enough to realize that some form of united Ireland was inevitable. The only realistic prospect of getting Protestants to the negotiating table was to maintain the ceasefire. But when events in Belfast conspired to bring the Army into open confrontation with Catholics, MacStiofain switched back into the IRA's traditional defender role. In an important sense he was determined not to fall back into the trap of 1969, when the IRA was reviled for 'running away'. Besides, the Provisionals had expanded so rapidly since 1970 that it was easier to maintain control over this unruly, youthful army by going with the flow than attempting to innovate. Internment, the Falls Curfew and Bloody Sunday had all proved to be highly successful recruiting sergeants for the IRA, but in the rush to expand the leadership had let its standards slip. The average volunteer had no interest in or aptitude for politics. The driving forces of the hour were the baser sectarian instincts rather than pious abstractions such as the Republic of Protestant, Catholic and Dissenter.

In this environment Adams' obvious leadership qualities did not take long to impress his elders. He was more articulate than his contemporaries, who were impressed by his ability to put into words what they could only feel. As commander of the IRA's 2nd Battalion in Belfast he was in charge of all Ballymurphy and Whiterock, the biggest and busiest wing of the Belfast Brigade, with some 700 men under his command.

According to Peter McMullen the 2nd Battalion was 'probably the family of the IRA', with leading figures such as Seamus Twomey, Joe Cahill, Brendan Hughes and Brian Keenan all from its ranks. As an O/C Adams also served on the Belfast Brigade staff as staff officer. McMullen first came across him when he approached the Brigade staff with a plan to mount a raid on Palace Barracks in Holywood, a few miles east of Belfast. The Provisionals were short of weaponry at the time. Adams was sceptical about the plan and six weeks later it was turned down.

He was more interested in McMullen's intelligence gathering on the movements of senior-ranking British Army officers, including the then O/C of 39 Brigade, Brigadier Sir Frank Kitson. Because of his counter-insurgency measures Kitson was a thorn in the side of the Provisionals. It was a period in which the IRA was examining and refining its military strategy to encompass large-scale commercial bombings and assassinations of high-ranking figures within the Army, police and judiciary. 'Gerry was smart, he had good ideas, good tactics and he gave his officers a lot of leeway. Basically he was very well respected and thought well of,' said McMullen.

Asked if he had ever seen Adams handle a gun McMullen said: 'Oh I'm sure he has. I have never personally seen him handle a gun, but he's been in rooms and areas where there was lots of guns. But you know you can't expect a man of Adams' rank and stature at that time to be carrying a gun ... it would be unwise, you know, to get ten years just for carrying a gun and people of Adams' calibre we needed to keep clean, because we needed the tactics and the advice and the leadership within the movement.'

As commanding officer Adams was ultimately responsible for everything which went on in his battalion area, from discipline to shootings, bombings and robberies. Kneecappings and executions would have to go to Brigade level, according to McMullen. 'I mean not just military but the civilian population as well would fall under his jurisdiction.'

After the Whitelaw talks débâcle and the resumption of the campaign of violence Adams was promoted to adjutant, responsible for discipline and the day-to-day running of the entire Belfast Brigade, including all three battalions. In this role he was routinely consulted about any major operations within the Brigade area. Three weeks later the Provisionals unleashed their most intense burst of violence yet during the space of a few hours in the centre of Belfast. The infamy of the attack immediately earned it the title Bloody Friday. Among its planners was Gerry Adams. Patrick Bishop and Eamon Mallie in their book *The Provisional IRA* claim that Seamus Twomey planned the operation, assisted by Adams' singing partner from the London flight, Ivor Bell, and 'a leading Belfast Provisional who is now a senior member of Sinn Fein'.

Because of the scale of the operation every Belfast Battalion was involved, with the lion's share of planting the car bombs falling to the 3rd Battalion. Over the space of an hour and a quarter, between 2.15 p.m. and 3.30 p.m., twenty-two bombs exploded one after the other, bringing mayhem, terror and death to the busy city centre. Nine people were killed. The carnage was such that the original death toll was put at eleven because so many of the bodies were dismembered. In the worst detonation six people taking shelter in the Oxford Street bus station, including two Welsh Guards and two teenage boys, were killed.

McMullen claimed that Adams was present at several Brigade meetings prior to Bloody Friday 'where all the details were discussed and all the plans were made out ... It had to be a Brigade approved operation because it was so massive.' He went on:

The day before Bloody Friday there was a Brigade meeting which I attended where there was great concern about, I mean we had everything ready, cars, timing devices, detonators, everything like that, but we were waiting for the explosives coming in from the South and like, there was 3,500lb needed. In the whole battalion areas there was probably only 1,000lb. I remember Gerry saying that he was also concerned about the routes to and from the bombing, because those were things that were most important. You know, in a bombing run you've got to watch your routes, make sure nobody is going to cross, have them checked for roadblocks, etcetera.

Gerry Adams has denied Peter McMullen's claims about his involvement in Bloody Friday. The former Sinn Fein Publicity Director Danny Morrison says that, together with Adams, he met McMullen's wife, Eileen, who handed over a letter signed by her husband admitting that he had invented his comments in order to curry favour with the US authorities who were at the time considering an extradition request for him from the UK. Not for the last time, someone who made incriminating remarks about Gerry Adams retracted them swiftly afterwards. McMullen may have been under pressure from the US authorities when he made his original claims, although it is not hard to imagine that McMullen's family back in Northern Ireland might also have been under considerable pressure themselves when they delivered his denial to Sinn Fein.

In his 1996 autobiography Adams dwells on the Bloody Friday massacre at some length and is at pains to point out the media 'distortions'. Accurate warnings had been received about every bomb but in the case of two – including Oxford Street – the RUC and Army 'were either unable or deliberately failed to act on the warnings'. The IRA's intention was to create 'economic damage' and attempted to prevent civilian casualties with warnings of at least thirty minutes. It was 'a moot point' whether the IRA stretched the British too far or whether 'they deliberately failed' to act, but it was clear that the IRA had 'made a mistake' in planting so many bombs. Civilians were killed who should not have been killed. 'This was the IRA's responsibility and a matter of deep regret.'

The purpose of Bloody Friday, as McMullen described it, was to cripple Belfast and Northern Ireland economically:

It's just too easy to go out and shoot British soldiers. We wanted to hit England in its taxpayers' money. I mean, just bring Northern Ireland to a standstill economically, where it wasn't feasible for England to hold on to it. That was the political idea at the time and Gerry Adams was one of the main or the best political tactician that we had. I mean, he was one of the ones who actually thought up the economic bombings.

I think everybody would have known that there would have been the possibility of loss of life but ... it was not discussed. The whole operation was discussed afterwards, but I don't think anybody who was there showed any remorse, no. I mean, understand, you're in a situation where you plant a bomb and you don't expect anybody to be hurt. Although you give warnings and everything else, human error is ... it's just those are the things that happen. You know you're dealing with human beings and bombs and then you turn round and expect nothing to happen. You know, you'd be a fool to think that that could be so.

The government's response was to launch Operation Motorman, the largest British military operation since Suez. An extra 4,000 troops were drafted in, bringing the total to an all-time high of 21,000, to break the IRA's hold of 'Free Derry' and return the no-go zones, in which the terrorist planners were able to go about their work undisturbed, to government control. An IRA unit, allegedly acting without authorization, showed its contempt for the Army operation by exploding three car bombs in the village of Claudy, twelve miles outside Derry. Eight people were killed.

The loyalist response was more chilling. Francis Arthurs, a Catholic, was kidnapped and driven to a Shankill Road social club where he was severely beaten, repeatedly stabbed and then shot. His body was then dumped on waste ground. Arthurs was the first victim of the notorious Shankill Butchers.

A few weeks later Adams was arrested by Paratroopers at an IRA wake, where the tricolour-draped coffin of Robert McCrudden had been given a guard of honour as it was carried into Corpus Christi church, Ballymurphy. He was released a few hours later and told an *Irish News* reporter: 'They asked me my name and when I told them they started to knock me about a bit. I asked why I was being arrested and one of them said: "You know, we know, that's it." They kept pulling and knocking me about. One of them hit me on the head with the barrel of his rifle. An Army doctor had to put two stitches in the cut.' The report continued: 'The soldiers, said Mr Adams, appeared to believe that he had been talking to the Secretary of State Mr Whitelaw. "They might have thought I was somebody else, but I think I was picked up because I was in Long Kesh. They nearly choked me when I was in the Saracen. One of them stuck a rubber bullet gun under my ear and another one kept clicking his rifle. They kept going on with a lot of vile and obscene talk. I got the usual treatment at the barracks. I was forced to stand against a wall and had my legs kicked. Then a Special Branch man asked me all sorts of questions."'

The IRA leadership was coming under greater pressure than ever before, and Whitelaw was convinced that public tolerance of the Provisionals was plummeting. The face of Northern Ireland was in the throes of transformation with a series of massive, heavily fortified security bases under construction. West Belfast looked as if it was under military occupation. In the law courts there was change afoot, with the recommendation of non-jury trials by Lord Diplock in December, which was immediately accepted by the government. Earlier that year the IRA had murdered a Protestant bus driver from East Belfast who was due to give evidence against three Provos accused of hijacking a coach.

In the South too the IRA was increasingly squeezed. The 1969 wave of sympathy for a beleaguered nationalist minority standing up to Protestant oppression briefly rallied again around Bloody Sunday. But tolerance diminished in direct proportion to the increase of IRA violence. Nineteen-seventy-two was the bloodiest year of the Troubles with 467 killings, 10,628 shootings, 1,853 bombs planted and 531 persons charged with terrorist offences. The Irish Prime Minister Jack Lynch reintroduced Section 5 of the Offences Against the State Act, under which suspected terrorists could be convicted on the evidence of a senior Garda officer in Dublin's Special Criminal Court, a juryless chamber presided over by three judges.

After his scrape with the Paras, Adams became a pimpernel figure around West Belfast, moving constantly from safe house to safe house, commanding his men on the run. In recent years, secure in his new image of politician–statesman, Adams has turned folksy about these murderous times. In 1995 he granted a celebrity interview to Hunter Davies for the London *Independent* newspaper. Explaining his beard he said:

> I grew it in 1971 when I was on the run . . . no, let's say badly wanted.
>
> I jumped on a bus one day with my new beard, shoulder-length hair and wearing a Maxi coat. I was sitting quietly on my own reading a book of poems by Seamus Heaney, when the Paratroopers stopped the bus to search everyone. They didn't find anything or recognise me. When they left everyone breathed a sigh of relief. They turned to me, giving the thumbs-up sign, saying 'Phew, that was close, Gerry.' I thought my beard had completely disguised me but everyone on the bus had known all along that it was me.

In contrast, one of the *Irish Times* reporters who covered Belfast during the same period has an altogether less glamorous anecdote to relate about Gerry Adams. Kevin Myers, one of the most courageous correspondents covering Northern Ireland in its darkest hour, remembers the young IRA commander settling an Andersonstown bar-room brawl in which a man had his eye gouged out. 'An account is brought to him of the fracas in the men's room. He listens and he says, as I walk past, "shoot him" . . . meaning kneecap him, not kill him.'

Adams denied the incident ever took place and Myers attracted some critical comment for retelling this story, at the height of the IRA ceasefire in 1995, in the *Spectator* magazine. For many, particularly those Irish nationalists who had worked so hard to bring about the ceasefire, it seemed to offend the spirit of the time. The unofficial line was 'Why drag up the past now when we all should be concentrating on the present peace and turning it into the future?' It certainly cut a deep wound in the contemporary image of Adams. Myers, some said privately, was out of touch, had been away too long and did not understand how things had changed. But the reverse side of the coin was that the *Irish Times* journalist remembered too well: Northern Ireland is a small place with a population of only a million and a half. Nearly everybody has been touched by the Troubles and for a great number of its people it has been a traumatic experience to see Adams fêted as a peace-maker.

After Bloody Friday the IRA was on the defensive, in more ways than one. Apart from the security clampdown that it faced on both sides of the border, the loyalist paramilitaries had entered a new level of activity. The Ulster Defence Association began as its name suggests. When the barricades went up all over Belfast on both sides of the sectarian divide defenders sprang up to man them. But when Stormont was prorogued and the British government held secret talks with the IRA in London the belief grew in loyalist areas that the Provisionals were indeed near the point of bombing and shooting the British out of Northern Ireland.

Army intelligence on the IRA improved after Motorman, with the new General Officer Commanding General Sir Frank King building on the intelligence work initiated by Kitson to turn the detailed reports compiled by stop and search patrols into an intricate web of intelligence. If a price had been paid in that many Catholic areas now looked and felt as if they were in the hands of occupying forces, senior officers believed it was worth paying. Soldiers were now armed under special legislation with the power to arrest and detain terrorist suspects. The pressure was beginning to tell and the IRA strove to adapt to the changing circumstances. While volunteers were exhorted to ever greater efforts in the annually proclaimed 'Year of Victory' it was becoming clearer that British withdrawal might take longer to achieve. The indiscriminate use of car bombs, which had done so much to turn people away from the Provisionals, was reduced and new theatres of war considered.

The last time an England bombing campaign had been mounted was in 1939. It could not have escaped Adams, when his and the thoughts of others turned to a similar enterprise in the 1970s, that his uncle Dominic had played a leading role before the Second World War. The prospects of bombing the British capital were first discussed formally at an Army Council meeting in June 1972 at a hotel in Black Rock, near Dublin, and MacStiofain is credited with having proposed an ambitious plan to send 'sleepers' over the Irish Sea to integrate themselves into civilian life and await orders to strike from time to time before melting back once more into the background. England's main cities all had substantial Irish communities in which it would be easy to merge without arousing suspicions. The idea was taken so seriously that the Belfast IRA were ordered to identify volunteers of sober character in the 18–24 age bracket prepared to undertake the mission, but it foundered on the simple reality of the time that the Provisionals did not have the financial resources to support such a long-term commitment.

They opted instead for a hit-and-run approach in March 1973, exploding car bombs outside the Old Bailey and the Central Army Recruiting Office at Great Scotland Yard. One man died and 180 were injured in the blasts. Two other bombs were defused and all the bombers were picked up while making their exits through Heathrow airport. Six people were jailed, including the Price sisters, who had greeted Gerry Adams on his release from Long Kesh a year earlier, and Gerry Kelly, later to become a very senior figure in the Provisionals.

In November 1972 Sean MacStiofain was arrested by Irish police while being driven around Dublin Bay and, as evidence that the Provisionals could no longer regard the Republic as a safe haven, was charged with IRA membership. In previous months Joe Cahill, Ruairi O Bradaigh and his brother Sean Brady, then serving as Sinn Fein director of publicity, had all faced similar charges and immediately launched hunger strikes. Each was released for lack of evidence, but in Cahill's case not before spending twenty-three days without food. MacStiofain decided to outshine his comrades by immediately commencing a hunger and thirst strike, with the inevitable and desired result that he became the focus of media attention.

After high-level intervention by the Catholic Church MacStiofain agreed on the tenth day of the strike to end his fast and prevent the bloodshed on the streets of Ireland that his death would provoke. This display of weakness sealed his fate, leaving him wide open to the reasonable charge – in republican eyes – that hunger strikes were undermined as a future tactic. His standing was seriously dented, not least because while detained he breached an IRA standing order that prisoners lose all rank and refused to recognize the camp O/C as his senior officer. After his release MacStiofain was never to hold high rank again and, in a final cutting action, republican publications began referring to him as John Stephenson.

It is clear from remarks made in retirement that MacStiofain felt aggrieved that the 'favour' he had granted to Adams by including him in the Cheyne Walk delegation and thereby guaranteeing his release from internment was not returned at this critical moment. MacStiofain was replaced by Joe Cahill as chief of staff, who was in turn replaced, upon his arrest on board the cargo vessel *Claudia* carrying a gift from Colonel Gadaffi of Libya of five tons of arms, by Seamus Twomey. Twomey later escaped from Mountjoy prison by helicopter and resumed command until his recapture in 1977. The series of arrests marked the commencement of the IRA's long period of decline in terms of military successes.

Adams in his turn was finally arrested in July 1973 and was not to emerge from prison until 1977. As events were to show, he was able to turn this setback to his advantage. In the meantime he could look back on the past eighteen months as a period of mixed fortunes. The British Army, the loyalist paramilitaries, the legal establishment and both the British and Irish states had all in their separate ways reduced the effectiveness of the Provisional war machine. Public opinion was running against them too. The SDLP had been founded as a middle-of-the road nationalist party dedicated to Irish unity through constitutional means alone. It offered a political alternative to the wholly militaristic route envisaged by the Provisionals. Bombs had exploded in London for the first time in thirty-three years, forcing the Irish issue into the faces of the British public and politicians. It was a telling response by the Provisionals to the political methods advocated by their nationalist rivals in the SDLP.

CHAPTER NINE

Behind the Wire

In time of war the domestic incidents of a life do not suspend their intrusions. The interior and exterior worlds merge and sometimes clash. When the Provisionals found their military options narrowing in July 1973, Adams was going through the rites of passage of any young married man. He was looking forward to the birth of a child, his wife Colette pregnant for the second time. The first pregnancy had been cut short by miscarriage, just a month after the deaths of two close friends, Dorothy Maguire and Maura Meehan. The two women, sisters and both members of the IRA, were shot dead by soldiers when driving through the Lower Falls with a siren blaring to warn of an Army raid in the area. They were the first members of the Women's IRA, Cumann na mBan, to be killed by the Army.

Gerry Adams later wrote about the close relationship he and his wife had had with the two sisters in one of the columns he published under a pseudonym in *Republican News*. He described how about one o'clock one morning he was coming off an IRA 'stand-by' or sentry duty in the Whiterock area when he found a hedgehog. He took it to the home of Bridget Maguire, the mother of Dorothy and Maura. 'They were not amused,' Adams recalled, 'and Bridget gave off about fleas, as I deposited my prickly friend on her sofa. "What are you going to do with that?" asked a girl who, incidentally, I later married. "I'm going to set it free," I declared. "If the Paras catch you, it'll look good in the papers," Bridget interjected. "IRA man caught with hedgehog". The neighbours laughed, I took a reddener and the hedgehog rolled itself up even tighter.' (The anecdote later appeared under Gerry Adams' own name in his book *Cage Glevon* but with all referenced to his status as an IRA man judiciously edited out.)

The year after the death of the Maguire sisters and the loss of her first baby, Colette had fallen pregnant again. The birth of their child was imminent when in July 1973 Adams' thirteen months of freedom came to an end. Immediately after hearing of his arrest Colette went to the police station on the Springfield Road. According to the *Irish Times* she tried unsuccessfully to see her husband and 'when permission was refused she screamed and wept and had to be helped away'.

Adams had been in a house on the Falls Road, not far from the RUC station, meeting two other IRA men, Brendan 'Darkie' Hughes and Tom Cahill, still suffering from his injuries after being shot by the Officials in Ballymurphy in 1971. The three Provisionals noticed some strange activity outside the house but didn't realize that the Army had them surrounded. When a soldier knocked on the front door Cahill went to answer it and Adams and Hughes tried to make their escape out the back. There, as they tried to hop over a wall, they discovered the area was full of troops. They were placed under arrest, but not before Adams casually lit his pipe with the only piece of paper in the house to contain any incriminating information.

As Colette pleaded with the police at the desk, Adams says that he was again subjected to ill-treatment inside the Springfield Road RUC station. This allegedly consisted of men dressed in plain clothes putting him up against the wall with his legs spread, beating him on the kidneys and around the groin and, on one occasion, a soldier stubbing a cigarette out on his wrist. He again refused to admit his identity and had a health card and documents on him which bore another alias: this time the name was John Davey.

But Adams' interrogators appear to have been in no doubt about his true identity. According to his own account, one of his tormentors threw a bucket of water over him and then made him squat in the corner of the cell, before smiling and asking playfully, 'Well, Gerry, what was it you told Mr Whitelaw? All bets are off?'

Before they let their prize catch be transported off to the Castlereagh interrogation centre in East Belfast the soldiers from the 2nd Battalion Light Infantry wanted to record the moment for posterity and lined up to be photographed individually and in groups with Adams and his IRA comrades. Adams sensed that the soldiers believed they had just won some kind of competition. Certainly there would have been great rivalry among the regiments then based in Belfast to be the one to arrest the IRA's O/C in the city. The arrest gets a special mention in the Light Infantry's Regimental History.

The sense of achievement can be gauged from the tenor of the press coverage, clearly reflecting considerable briefing from the Army and the police. The arrests were linked in some reports to the kneecapping of three Provisionals a short time before, which it was claimed had started a wave of revulsion against the IRA in Catholic areas, leading to the relevant tip-off. Whether this detail was true or a ruse to cover the real source of information is unclear, but the papers were in complete agreement about Adams' status.

The *Guardian*, *Irish Times* and *Irish Independent* all identified him as the IRA Brigade commander in Belfast. In *The Times*, Robert Fisk described Adams as 'an intense, dark haired, bespectacled youth'. Via the media the security forces tried to make Adams' comrades on the outside as anxious as possible about the potential impact of his arrest together with Cahill and Hughes, the *Guardian* speculating that 'the prospect of any one of the three giving information under interrogation must be deeply worrying to the remaining leaders'. But the *Irish Independent* wasn't so sure that Adams would talk: 'There is little doubt that during the next 72 hours, when they can be held under the Emergency Provisions Act, Special Branch officers will attempt to "break" Adams and obtain information about the entire Provisional network throughout the North. It is thought Adams will be, in the words of one member of the security forces, "a hard nut to crack".'

The source of much of this high-grade information was Colin Wallace, a press officer at British Army Headquarters in Lisburn whose remit ran far beyond the daily business of issuing the latest grim statistics. 'We had Information Policy, which was the psychological warfare team hidden inside the press office,' recalled Wallace of the days when his immediate boss was a senior MI6 officer. It was Wallace who first brought Adams to the attention of the British public, via a call to a BBC Television reporter called Keith Graves.

I had a call from Colin Wallace, who said, 'We've pinpointed the new head of the Belfast IRA.' There had been a lot of speculation about his identity, so I went up to see him and another man and they gave me a photograph of Gerry Adams. They said, 'This man is running things in Belfast.' You had to be very careful about Colin's information so I made a few inquiries, including with Maire Drumm [Sinn Fein vice president, later murdered by the UVF] who was a bloody good contact. As a result I came to the conclusion that the story was true and that Gerry Adams was running Belfast, so I did the lead story for the *Nine O'Clock News* using the photograph.

Drumm called me the next day, couldn't get hold of me so she ended up putting someone else into a flat spin. I was told by the BBC to get out of Belfast, which I did. Apparently Adams was livid. A few days later I went back without the BBC knowing and went to see Drumm to sort it all out. She said that Adams was bloody furious. She never said Adams was going to do me but she said some of his people were going to. Then I went to Londonderry, when the Bogside was still a no-go zone, and Martin McGuinness, who I knew very well and was always a source of good stories for me, told me to get the hell out for the same reason.

For Wallace the planting of the story was part of an overall strategy to soften up the Provisionals in advance of negotiating a new ceasefire with them. The arrests of half a dozen key Belfast Brigade members represented 'a major purge of their main command structure and Adams was pulled in with that'. General Sir Frank King, the Army's General Officer Commanding at the time, formulated the strategy of targeting what he called the officer structure of the IRA. 'There were a number of key players and then the rest of the teams weren't quite so good, so if we could take them out the rest of the structure would crumble,' said Wallace.

Effectively that worked because by the end of 1974 my other bosses, who were MI6 at the time, were negotiating the second ceasefire. Our tactic was to take out the Adams strata and that would leave the third- and fourth-division people and it would be much easier to negotiate a ceasefire.

What we were doing in the run-up to the arrests was highlighting some of the players, so that when eventually they were caught from a psychological point of view it was enhancing the security forces' success against the IRA. There was the arrest of the main IRA Ops centre in the Malone Road, there was the Doomsday plan, which we then leaked, about the plan to destroy parts of Belfast and then there was the dealing with the hard core of the IRA, so we could say we had literally destroyed the command structure. So the thing was to identify the key members to the media, so that as we picked them up this would enhance the successes we were having. At that stage Belfast was effectively managed by a small group of people, of which Gerry Adams was one. He was very much the strategist behind much of the '73–'74 activity.

According to Wallace the Belfast IRA took a prominent role in running the England bombing operations. 'It was a fairly hardline team and it was important to remove all Adams' team to get the ceasefire.' After the arrests *Visor*, the Army's magazine, published mugshots of Adams and his comrades. 'At that time he was reckoned to be effectively the Belfast commander or the number two from the operations point of view, and very much a hawk. Neither Gerry Adams nor Martin McGuinness in 1974 would ever have been seen as key figures in a peace initiative. I'm not saying that people don't change over the years. But their presence on the street would have made it much more difficult for us to prepare the way for a ceasefire.' Wallace agreed with Adams' later assessment that by 1975 the Provisionals were close to being defeated. 'In 1974 we were able to write the complete Belfast IRA by name on one chart – they were literally down to their lowest ebb.'

The newspapers were right to speculate about Adams being a hard nut to crack because, in contrast to his first arrest, he gave nothing away to his police interrogators. At Castlereagh, even by his own estimation, the police gave him a relatively easy time. He told them a few things they already knew, that he'd been stopped on several occasions since leaving Long Kesh, and mentioned that he was suffering from an ulcer. Otherwise all was silence until a helicopter arrived to take Adams off to the Kesh, now renamed the Maze prison, where he was to spend a much longer period of detention.

Once installed in Cage 6, Gerry Adams was back among a familiar mixture of friends and relatives. His cousin Kevin was there and his brother Paddy. Another brother Liam was being held in the section of the camp reserved for sentenced prisoners. Shortly after Gerry Adams' transfer to the camp, the prisoners succeeded in smuggling a note out to the press detailing the ill-treatment Adams had suffered during his time at the Springfield Road police station.

The prisoners, who hung on to the jail's old name of the Kesh, spent much of their time plotting how to escape from the camp. Some of the attempts were successful – Brendan Hughes, who was arrested alongside Adams, got out after the prisoners sewed him into an old mattress which they then put out with the rubbish. One of Adams' friends, Ivor Bell, also succeeded in escaping by taking the place of a man due for parole.

But other escape attempts went badly wrong – one plan was to sling a harness under a lorry on its way out of the camp. The prisoners in Adams' hut seriously considered this, and Brendan Hughes tried the harness out, but eventually rejected the plan as too dangerous. Another Cage, however, decided to take up the idea and an internee suffered a broken back when the lorry he had strapped himself under passed over security ramps on its way to the exit.

Adams himself took part in several escape attempts. In his 'Brownie' column in the *Republican News* he described how he had a particular aversion for tunnelling. 'Digging tunnels isn't much crack,' he told his readers.

In fact it's scary, because even in summer, it's impossible to stay above the water level. Dry digging is impossible and the constant seepage, as you may guess, makes sudden shifts in the ground inevitable. Even the shoring is unreliable and prone to collapse at the slightest touch. The water seeps in everywhere because Long Kesh is built on a bog ... I was perfectly willing to bale out water, hide dirt, wash clothes, clean up, cut shoring, make tools or keep watch. I was even prepared to undertake the awesome job of digging through two feet of concrete floor, with only the most basic of home-made chisels. Anything as long as I didn't actually have to go up the tunnel.

But Adams said one day he was instructed to do just that and 'orders is orders'. He didn't like what he found. 'There were two inches of water in the base of the shaft, cold water which lapped, in little waves, around my ankles. The tunnel mouth was only two foot square and as I hunkered down I could see it narrowing as bags of returned dirt bellied their way out from the sides.' Adams was acting as back-up for the main digger a few feet in front of him in the tunnel. 'We were soon hard at work. Slow tortuous work. He scraped at the face with a home-made shovel and I lay on his legs, holding him steady, doing my best to minimise movement, wishing I was somewhere else.' Adams was just growing accustomed to the work when his digging mate's bodily functions intervened: 'We were only down for twenty minutes. I think I could have stuck it longer, lying there petrified, then yer man let off . . . phew! I don't want to make it sound melodramatic, but in the cramped space, far below Long Kesh's tarmac'd and concreted surface, I panicked. Anyhow it was as good, original and as serious an excuse as any other I'd had so we shuffled our way backwards towards the shaft and the abnormality overhead. They never let me go down again. Nobody said anything of course. They just put me to hiding dirt.'

Adams was finally caught trying to break out. On Christmas Eve 1973 he and three others tried to take advantage of a slight fog to make their way to the camp perimeter and then cut through the wire. They were wearing home-made Army uniforms in the hope of being mistaken for soldiers guarding the camp. With bolt cutters and hacksaws at the ready they managed to get out of Cage 6 but were spotted by a patrol near the perimeter fence. In July the following year he tried a different tack, plotting to swap places with a man said to bear an uncanny resemblance to him. Alfred McNiece had been spotted by one of Adams' friends on the outside. McNiece was persuaded to make a visit to Adams' fellow prisoner Ivor Bell, during which he and Adams would swap places.

Preparing for the escape bid Gerry Adams cut his long hair and shaved off his beard to look more like the clean shaven McNiece. But the 'uncanny resemblance' was flawed in one important respect. McNiece was several inches shorter than Adams, and although they did swap places it didn't take long for one of the prison officers to realize something was amiss. 'I knew there was something wrong,' he later told a Belfast court, 'because when this man went in, I was looking down at him. When he came out, I was looking up at him.'

For his pains, Adams was sentenced to eighteen months for one of his escape attempts and three years for the other. To signify his disregard for the court, he sat sewing up an old pair of jeans in the dock. These convictions are the only times Gerry Adams has been found guilty of any offence.

Before then, however, he was to be put to the test within the Maze. In October 1974 a dispute over food, lack of clean sheets and other living conditions inside the jail reached boiling point. The prisoners decided to launch protests. Dumping their food over the wire surrounding their compounds had no effect. So one evening the officer commanding inside the jail, David Morley, gave the order to burn the prison down.

The prisoners began to set the cages on fire and soon most of the camp was in flames. Soldiers arrived and began firing gas canisters into the area; soon baton charges followed and fierce fighting broke out between the troops and the prisoners. Gerry Adams remembers the burning of the camp and its aftermath as a time of great unity among the prisoners, but some of those who shared a cage with him don't agree.

One fellow prisoner, 'John', was younger than Adams. He didn't have much in common with a man whom he saw as a politician not a fighter and as an academic, forever reading books, not someone like himself interested in football and, to use Belfast language, 'a bit of crack'. 'John' says that 'When the order came across from Cage 7, it was well authorized. "Burn the lot," but Adams didn't take the order. The younger generation started ripping the beds up and burning them. Gerry Adams refused to participate in it.' Some of the republican internees made their way out of their burning huts to join the sentenced prisoners at the other end of the camp. After being hit by baton-wielding soldiers the rebellious prisoners were subdued. 'The Brits put us against the wire and kept us standing against it, one or two of us were kicked and beaten.' According to 'John', Adams and his friends didn't help them in the fight, and after their capture 'John' and his group stared resentfully at him. 'We just gave Adams a look, just a look as if to say bugger youse, for not taking part. The Paras came in and we wanted to know "Are we getting into them or what?" But the order was given from somebody to drop it and play it by ear . . . in other words surrender.'

These recollections roughly match the version of events given to other reporters by the camp O/C David Morley, who is now dead. Speaking in the early 1980s Morley told *World in Action* researchers that 'When the Brits came in batoning men to their knees, Adams and his group were five yards away, they did nothing, not even anything to distract the Brits . . . Adams was a compound O/C; he called it [the burning] a "stupid idea" . . . There was a post-mortem – I as O/C did it. It stated in so many words that he had neglected his duty and the men under him, and that he endangered other men, because his was the compound by the main gate. By not burning it he allowed the British to get in quicker.'

Other prisoners disagree. 'Pat' says the reason the internees' hut wasn't burned was because 'there was a tunnel under it, from which an escape bid was mounted shortly afterwards. Adams had, according to this version, made a decision that burning the hut would imperil the chances of the breakout succeeding. The escape attempt went ahead on 6 November 1974, but it was foiled and an IRA prisoner, twenty-four-year-old Hugh Coney, was shot dead by soldiers. David Morley was also critical of Adams in relation to this. He maintained that those involved in the escape were instructed to plead not guilty to any charges. They had no chance of being acquitted and would get longer sentences than if they simply entered guilty pleas, but the tactic was decided upon in order to highlight Coney's death. Morley claimed that Adams told the men involved to ignore the order and plead guilty – the men were subsequently dismissed from the republican movement.

Besides the drama of burning the camp and escape attempts, Adams' time in Long Kesh enabled him to broaden his reading, as well as to arrange lectures on political and military matters and write a series of articles smuggled out for publication in the Sinn Fein newspaper *Republican News*.

'Pat' was in Cage 11, for sentenced prisoners. After his conviction for the attempted breakouts, Adams was moved there and was soon elected Cage O/C. He was a compromise candidate between factions which broadly pitted traditionally republican country areas against young, rowdy Belfast men, many of whom had no background in the movement but who had been caught up in the street fighting. Terence 'Cleeky' Clarke, a tough IRA man from the Beechmount area of West Belfast and a future 'minder' for Adams, was the choice of the city faction. The 'country cousins' despised Clarke and put forward their own candidate, a young man from Newry. Eventually Adams was persuaded to take on the role, insisting that he should be allowed to get on with his work and not be forever encumbered with sorting out squabbles in the hut.

Like 'John', 'Pat' remembers Adams as showing no interest in anything other than the republican movement. He never watched sport on TV but instead spent his days sitting at a table puffing a pipe, meditating and then writing, meditating and then writing again. 'Pat' thought Adams manipulative, distant and cold, and only interested in forming relationships with people whom he thought might be useful to him later on, such as Brendan Hughes and Ivor Bell. But he did recognize that as O/C Adams had a great deal of energy:

> He began an officer-training class. This was to prepare volunteers in their twenties to become IRA section commanders and middle leadership when they went outside. It included military training and the history of Irish republicanism. There was theory relating to the use of weapons and explosives. I would have rated his knowledge of military affairs highly. He presented himself as a hard man. The Green Book of anti-interrogation methods, psychological preparation of volunteers in event of capture and how to handle interrogation, which ran to 100 pages, began life as an idea in his cage. Some of it was written outside prison. It was begun in 1974 and completed in '78. It's now a standard text for volunteers.

On a broader military front, Adams was turning his mind to the problems presented by the revamped intelligence effort by the Army and police in the wake of Operation Motorman. The IRA's traditional structure of battalions and brigades was proving too big and unwieldy and prone to infiltration by the security forces. Any one IRA member, whom the police might persuade into becoming an informer, could provide them with information about other members and operations. Adams, together with Martin McGuinness, is credited with the thinking behind the reorganization into smaller, tighter 'cells' or 'active service units'. These units were four strong and operated on a need-to-know basis.

The idea was that even if the Special Branch did make inroads into the organization the damage would be limited. It was no mean achievement on Adams' part that despite being incarcerated he was still able to play a major part in what amounted to a wholesale reorganization of the IRA. In 1978 the head of Army intelligence inside the Ministry of Defence, Brigadier (later) General Sir James Glover, produced a report on future terrorist trends in which he specifically referred to Adams' role and the partial disruption which his arrest had caused. 'There has been considerable turbulence among the leadership at the lower levels through the campaign,' Glover wrote. 'Relationships between the various groups have altered with the changing personalities. The Northern Command concept has probably been accepted and, although the leadership is still fluid, the chain of command is effective. However, following the arrest of Gerry Adams, the prime architect of the new cellular system based on Active Service Units (ASUs), there was a partial reversion towards the traditional Brigade organisation. Indeed this lack of leadership continuity seems endemic to the Provisionals and is exacerbated by Security Force attrition.'

The cell structure undoubtedly made the IRA less susceptible to the security forces' counter-terrorist effort, although, as Glover noted, its practical impact still depended heavily on events on the ground. 'At that time the Maze was acquiring a reputation as being quite a sophisticated university for terrorism,' the General told the authors. 'There was within the Maze a wide range of literature covering almost all aspects of international terrorism, which were being studied in depth and were being called in particularly by Gerry Adams and his partner at the time, Ivor Bell, although subsequently they did part company. Although there was obviously some thinking outside – probably more in Dublin than in the North – that the time had come to move to a traditional Marxist cellular-based terrorist movement, I think that Adams and Bell between them actually drew up a blueprint for a future structure for the Provisional IRA in the North.'

Glover had no specific interest in Adams when compiling his report but he recognized that the young leader had qualities which put him ahead of most of his fellow Provisionals. 'I at one stage said that at some time in the near future a new charismatic figure might emerge who would succeed in transforming the IRA from the old rather unwieldy organization which it was, based on the traditional army structure, into something much more akin to a modern terrorist movement. And I wrote those words with Gerry Adams very much in mind. But I couldn't claim that I thought that he would become the national political figure and would be as adept and mature a politician as he has subsequently become.'

Many of the books which Adams brought into the jail were theoretical and political in nature. One inmate, Gerry O'Hare, recalls Adams and others splitting 'into small study groups, and we would have sent out for books on people like Marx, Lenin, Stalin, Trotsky,

James Connolly, Che Guevara, Jim Larkin and we would have studied the successes and failures of other revolutions'.

'Pat' shared Adams' interest in left-wing political theory but was not impressed by him. 'He was pretty weak on it, he knew everything that went on in Belfast right back to the 1920s but didn't have a good grasp of broader republicanism. Belfast republicans have a theory that the Republic ends somewhere around Lisburn [seven miles from Belfast].'

During one debate inside the study hut when the argument appeared to be going against him, Adams indulged in a rhetorical flourish, quoting from the writings of one of his favourite historical characters, Liam Mellows, who was executed by Irish Free State forces in 1922. 'Adams must have felt himself in a corner because he quoted from a letter by Liam Mellows, probably the lost leader of the era, a very progressive socialist thinker who was shot with three others without trial. Mellows had written about the tragedy of the civil war. The tragedy was that too many gave their allegiance to the IRA or a particular group or person but not enough people gave their allegiance to the Republic. Adams said, "That's where I stand," and slapped a book down on the table and walked out. And as he walked out a young Belfast lad said, "The gospel according to Gearoid MacAdams."'

One visitor who saw Adams on a regular basis inside prison was Father Denis Faul:

He was very good in jail, he wouldn't discuss much politics with you but he would always attend his Mass on Sunday. With his confession, communion and Mass, he was exemplary. There was a difference between him and the previous head man there, Billy McKee. Billy would bring all the others with him and insist that they should go – he was an old-style Catholic. Gerry wouldn't. Gerry would leave it; he thought religion was a private matter and he was entitled to that opinion. I thought he should perhaps have brought the younger fellas along, encourage them to go to their Mass because they were good for the first few years but about '74 or '75 they began to fall off a bit. But Gerry was most exemplary himself and he did give a good example in that regard and I couldn't fault him for his practice of his religious duties.

Faul had campaigned long and hard against the beating and ill-treatment of prisoners. 'In the seventies when I met him in jail I was totally obsessed with the torture and mistreatment of prisoners and that's what we tended to talk about. Any discussion would have been about that or how best to publicize it. I knew he was a big wheel but I never asked about the IRA campaign much because it was pretty well on free wheel then and you were only wasting your time talking about it.'

Faul spent much of his time telling the prisoners how Manchester United, Celtic or other football clubs were performing – indeed on occasion he would even devote his sermons to soccer. But like 'John' he found that Adams was never interested in trivia. 'No, he had no interest in that. He was a serious man. He was working on these books of his and his lectures. He would never discuss his business with you. He would keep his own counsel. He's a very quiet man and he doesn't give much away.'

During 1975 Adams considered the lengthy ceasefire embarked upon under the leadership of Ruairi O Bradaigh and Dave O'Connell. Some of the sentiments expressed prior to the cessation would be familiar to any observer of the 1994 ceasefire which Adams would eventually deliver. IRA men told Church leaders at Feakle in County Clare that they wanted to see an end to the fighting so their children could grow up in peace. The government said that if there was a ceasefire this would constitute 'a new situation to which the British would naturally respond'. The two sides danced a fandango involving on–off contacts, the decrease of Army patrols and the release of detainees. Then the Labour government's Northern Ireland Secretary Merlyn Rees pledged that if the IRA halted its violence the military would engage in no actions which could be interpreted as harassment, the Army would be brought back to barracks and eventually replaced by the RUC, and internment without trial would be phased out.

Although the two sides remained light years apart in political terms, with the government intent on promoting new arrangements within Northern Ireland and the IRA demanding a constitutional assembly elected by the Irish people North and South, the Provisionals decided to call a halt to their violence in the hope of advancing their aims.

Internees were released, but the old system of detention without trial was replaced with a new emphasis on 'criminalizing' paramilitaries. Incident Centres staffed by Provisionals were set up in Belfast and Derry to deal with provocative situations, but Rees' political initiatives contained nothing to suggest that the government might be considering withdrawal.

According to 'Pat', inside Cage 11 Gerry Adams 'presented himself as a hardliner and was critical of the leadership of the time, particularly during the truce. He said quite often that the leadership could not see the wood for the trees. At the same time he always maintained and said time and time again that the thing that he wanted to avoid at all costs was becoming involved in a split.'

Adams may not have wanted to provoke an open split, but his hardline attitude inside the jail certainly appeared to antagonize the IRA O/C David Morley, and perhaps explains the criticism Morley was later to make of Adams' role during the burning of Long Kesh. Morley was unhappy about the government's determination to abolish political status and make prisoners wear prison clothes. But he was open to some of the authorities' other suggestions, made as part of the 1975 ceasefire arrangements. Some government officials hoped that talks between the paramilitary leaders on prison issues might forge new relations between the factions and plant the seeds of a new politics in Northern Ireland. The prisoners were being offered a 'downtown office' where their various welfare organizations could base themselves. They were also shown their new accommodation in H Blocks, the new prison quarters being constructed for paramilitary prisioners, which some agreed was a great improvement in their living conditions.

'Morley gave tremendous co-operation,' 'Graham', a prison official, recalls.

He was meeting prison officials at least three times a week ... The package on offer included the downtown office – the paramilitary organizations would have had considerable input into it, they would have had offices in it. We took Morley to look at the new H Blocks, he was quite impressed, asked if the prisoners would be locked up, if they would have the same freedom they already enjoyed ... Morley appeared to be 100 per cent for the package on offer, but then the situation started to get critical. He started asking, 'When will we have this building?' He was under considerable pressure. The next time he saw me he was taking a different line. There had been a palace revolution. He let me know that the ones who'd taken over would be totally opposed to what we were proposing and he more or less indicated that prison staff might be at risk. There are articles about this in *Republican News* in March '76 or so on and it was very soon after that that prison staff did get targeted.

'Graham' deduced that Adams was one of the principal thorns in Morley's side. 'While Morley was the IRA O/C, we all knew that Adams was an important individual. When they had parades he would have been there in a leadership role, not just one of the volunteers . . . The indication I got was that people like Adams were behind the palace revolution and he [Morley] talked about changes in Dublin not just in the prison . . . I was very depressed whenever that folded in 1976. Almost twenty prison staff would have been alive that are now dead if we had achieved agreement on that. Adams would have been associated with the other side to Morley . . . I would say he torpedoed it in 1976.'

In the longer term, once Adams consolidated his power, the 1975 ceasefire came to be regarded as a mistake, a time when the organization came close to extinction and made no political gains. Adams sat back in prison, untainted by the leadership's difficulties, as republicans on the outside occupied themselves by engaging in murderous feuds. The internecine killing pitted the Provisionals against the Officials, and the Officials against a new faction which had broken away from them, Seamus Costello's Irish National Liberation Army. One of the most prominent casualties of this period of feuding was Liam McMillen, the man who had introduced Gerry Adams to the IRA ten years previously. Meanwhile loyalist gunmen embarked on an increasingly intense bout of sectarian blood-letting. The Provisional IRA decided to hit back, but as it matched indiscriminate loyalist bombs in Catholic bars with equally indiscriminate IRA bombs in Protestant pubs, it began to lose all pretence of being involved in anything other than a sectarian war.

Gerry Adams says he smuggled a letter out of jail demanding to know what was going on. He thought the fighting between republicans was playing into British hands. He also believed the sectarian tit-for-tat activity would allow the authorities to portray the IRA as nothing but bigots and criminals. He secured the editorship of the

Belfast *Republican News* for two of his closest allies, Tom Hartley and Danny Morrison, who invited him to contribute a column to the publication under the pen-name 'Brownie', the first of which appeared on 16 August 1975.

Adams used his Brownie column to expound his views about possible ways forward for the movement. He stressed the need to avoid sectarian killings, saying that 'only the British reap the benefits'. He was concerned that the IRA should not allow itself to be cut off from its community. Harking back to his radical involvement in housing action in the 1960s and to the degree of autonomy which he believed people in Ballymurphy had developed in the early 1970s, he started to advance the idea of building alternative state structures that would pay no allegiance to the 'illegitimate statelet' of Northern Ireland. Such structures would represent a strike for freedom in themselves and would also create a subculture in which the IRA could immerse itself. Adams feared that as things were developing in 1975 the IRA was losing what it had taken for granted in 1971, namely the control of all the waters in which it swam.

These structures could be anything from street committees to people's taxis in place of the buses, many of which were no longer running through riot-hit areas, and people's militia instead of the RUC. If these ideas at first sight appear to be the product of Sixties student revolutionary thought they also contained more than an element of Irish republican tradition. The first Dail or independent Irish parliament, voted into office before Britain gave up power in Dublin, functioned by ignoring the British state structures and behaving from the outset as if it was the only legitimate government. The difference, of course, was that the first Dail could, unlike the republican movement of 1975, lay claim to the allegiance of a majority of the people.

Adams was developing his political thought, reaching back to his experiences in the 'political' IRA of Cathal Goulding. But he never sought to diminish his commitment to the continued use of violence against the British foe. On 3 April 1976 Brownie argued that 'a determined and concentrated campaign of attacks on selected targets in England and Ireland will provide the key to a British withdrawal'. A month later he emphasized that 'active Republicanism' involved the necessity of using violence, because the enemy would understand nothing else. 'It's hard for me to write that down because God knows, maybe I won't fight again and it will be cast up at me, but still it needs to be said, even by a coward like myself, because at least I will move aside for the fighters.'

In another piece the same month Brownie mulled over the moral problems presented by his use of force. He described his disagreement with a visiting priest who had argued with him that the IRA should not be threatening to kill prison staff because of the proposed changes in the jail regime. Adams contended that such threats were just part and parcel of living in an abnormal society:

> Republicans involved in physical force in Ireland are always portrayed as if they, and they alone, are the men of violence. Sure, we use force, but it's not a role we choose or a conflict we welcome.
>
> The IRA aren't the cause of violence in Ireland. They are a symptom of it. If this was a normal society, we wouldn't have the violence we are now having to endure . . . I tried to explain it all like this. Rightly or wrongly, I'm an IRA volunteer and, rightly or wrongly, I take a course of action as a means to bringing about a situation in which I believe the people of my country will prosper. I believe firmly that the course of action I take, rightly or wrongly, is the only one open to me, because those who have a vested interest in exploiting my people leave me no choice. The course I take involves the use of physical force, but only if I achieve the situation where my people genuinely prosper can my course of action be seen, by me, to have been justified. In taking this action, I also take certain risks. I have to accept these risks. They are a consequence of my actions and I cannot complain if I am hurt, if I am killed, or if I am imprisoned.

Questioned by one of the authors about these written confirmations of involvement in violence, Gerry Adams subsequently maintained that the Brownie articles were not written solely by him but were the work of a number of prisoners. Asked if he therefore wrote the articles which contained no damaging admissions, but not those which did, he replied yes. The exchange provoked a degree of wry amusement among republicans present at the time. The Brownie articles are clearly the work of an individual rather than a committee, and when Brendan McFarlane, the IRA's officer commanding inside the Maze jail, wrote smuggled messages or 'comms' to Gerry Adams during the hunger strike of 1981 he consistently referred to Adams as 'Brownie'.

In February 1977 Brownie announced to his readers that his column was shortly going to come to an end as his release was imminent. Brownie said that he was looking forward to seeing his wife and his son who had been born while he was in jail. 'Hopefully by the time you get to reading this I will be wandering in some secluded spot, hand in hand with mine spouse and our young son who arrived as soon as I left and is thus about to see me in my first patriarchal role as a father figure. It will be most wonderful ... I can't really say I'm going out into freedom. I will be leaving comrades, but their ghosts will call on me for many days to come. Next week will see me as Joe Barnes (the rat) suggests, in Castlereagh [the RUC's interrogation centre] or the Crum [Belfast remand prison]. Or with my good wife, who has waited patiently, in some quiet spot where a Republican can become a daddy and a husband.' One can safely assume that in this instance Brownie and Gerry Adams were one and the same person as Colette had given birth to the couple's only son Gearoid a short time after Gerry Adams' arrest in 1973.

On 19 February 1977 Brownie's last column was published but it was by no means his last appearance in *Republican News*. A few weeks later in April 1977 another article appeared by an IRA prisoner writing under the pseudonym of 'Solon'. The piece was a sardonic tribute to Gerry Adams by an inmate determined to extract maximum humorous vengeance on the recently freed scribbler who had himself picked on the foibles of his fellow prisoners in his own columns.

'For those of you who don't know,' Solon wrote,

Brownie is a lanky, thin bearded, boggin' excuse for a person with gold rimmed glasses and is oft times to be seen, pipe in mouth, fumbling over cheese sandwiches. Cheese sandwiches are about his limit as far as cookery goes too. They are about the only things he ever made in Long Kesh ... His term in charge of our cage will never be forgotten. It's about the only blemish on our record. We were held to ransom for months on end. He revelled in his position and once passed an order that all lights in the huts were to be out for twelve o'clock because he was doing 'bird' [jail] and consequently had insomnia. It also provided him with the opportunity to patronise everyone which he turned to his advantage ... It was sickening too the way he used to suddenly acquire angelic qualities every time a priest came in. 'Would you like tea, Father?' 'A biscuit perhaps?' Little did the Father know what a tyrant he was and that it was the only time during the week that he would make tea.

'Apart from all his sarcasm, deviousness, patronising, backstabbing useless ways he had some endearing qualities,' Solon conceded.

More quaint than endearing I suppose. I mean who couldn't like a guy who talks to stuffed dogs or breeds caterpillars on his window ledge ... or stands on the top of visit room tables with his son singing 'The Trail of the Lonesome Pine' ... This one may embarrass him but he deserves it for his war crimes against his comrades. In the strictest confidence, he one day revealed to a 'friend' a most intimate secret. When he drives a car, particularly tensed up, such as when being chased, due to an odd injury that's an old one in itself and his lanky legs being cramped, how can I put it, he wets himself. The lads in the Cage don't know this yet but I can assure all readers that when they do his name will be a source of disgrace, disgust and a great deal of humour.

If the tone of Solon's article sounds hostile it should be remembered that this was just an extended example of jail humour – the unrelenting slagging which was the norm inside the Maze cages between inmates, and which was obviously particularly enjoyable when directed against a former IRA O/C in the Cage. Solon's description of Gerry Adams' 'arrogant, overbearing posturing' was just part of the usual rough-and-ready banter between prisoners who remained comrades even if they took every opportunity to pick on each other's individual habits.

The underlying affection was revealed in Solon's references to Adams' 'long suffering spouse and innocent child'. Solon concluded: 'to his poor wife we offer our apologies for laying bare her husband's despicable character. We wish her luck for the future and the hope of everyone in the Cage that the youngster will develop her family traits and not be afflicted with his. Because of her long suffering we are certain she will be canonised at some point in time. The Cage have therefore unanimously adopted her as its patron saint "St. Brownie's wife". To Brownie we conclude by saying you have lived up to our expectations and broken every promise you made before your release. It was only to be expected from someone like you.'

CHAPTER TEN

Peace at the Wrong Price

In recent years one of the words most often to be heard on the lips of Gerry Adams is 'peace'. During the elections to a Northern Ireland forum in May 1996 his face stared out of posters around the province emblazoned with the simple message 'Vote Sinn Fein, Vote Peace'. He is constantly looking for ways to further the 'peace process' and one of his autobiographical books and a key Sinn Fein document both contain the phrase 'Towards a Lasting Peace'.

It would be foolish, however, for anyone to assume that the peace Gerry Adams is talking about is a peace at any price. During the period when he was in jail there was in Northern Ireland a great popular upsurge in support of peace, but Adams reacted more with anger than with sympathy.

As the months progressed, the IRA ceasefire of 1975 was to become more and more a ceasefire in name only. On 5 December the Northern Ireland Secretary Merlyn Rees ordered the release of the last internees, or 'detainees' as they were now being called. But far from being a victory for republicans the phasing out of internment without trial was to presage a period in which the British government tried to dispel the sense created in the early 1970s that a war of sorts was being fought on their soil and to install new structures designed to portray the gunmen on both sides as criminals pure and simple.

In 1972 in the face of the hunger strike led by Billy McKee in the Crumlin Road jail, the government under William Whitelaw had conceded 'special-category status' for paramilitary prisoners, in effect a public recognition that their activities were politically motivated. But from March 1976 Rees announced that all paramilitary prisoners would be tried and convicted in the same way as criminals, albeit in courts with no juries, considered the only option because of the high level of juror intimidation in such cases. The ending of special-category status led to some rioting and protests. It also marked for all practical purposes the end of the IRA ceasefire. The restoration of 'political status' became after this a key demand for republicans, but it did not capture the attention of the rest of the world until the start of the 1980s.

With the IRA back in business Danny 'the Dosser' Lennon returned to active service. Lennon had been a friend of Gerry Adams in Cage 11. In August 1976 Lennon and a companion, John Chillingworth, mounted a sniping attack on an Army foot patrol heading out of the Glasmullan camp in West Belfast. After failing to bring down a soldier they dismantled their rifle and threw it into the back of the Ford Cortina they had commandeered before making off.

The foot patrol, however, alerted soldiers by radio further down Finaghy Road North, down which their attackers were escaping. Sure enough, Lennon was spotted at the wheel of the Cortina by a patrol travelling towards the IRA men, who opened fire on the speeding vehicle, hitting the nineteen-year-old driver in the head. The Cortina veered off the road, ploughing into Anne Maguire and her four young children on the footpath. Mrs Maguire was taking her children to the library before visiting their granny and then heading home to make dinner for her husband Jackie, a motor mechanic.

Instead she and three of her children were crushed against some school railings by the out-of-control vehicle. Her fourth child, Mark, was saved only because a passer-by pulled him out of the way. Mrs Maguire suffered multiple injuries, not least to her mind. 'She never saw her children buried and in her own mind refused to accept their deaths,' said her sister Mairead. 'She would often talk about seeing them playing in the garden. She seemed to lock herself into a private world to be with her dead babies.' Four years later she took her own life by cutting her wrists. An unfinished note to her family read, 'Forgive – I love you . . .'

Shortly after the crash Mrs Maguire's sister, Mairead Corrigan, made an emotional appeal on the local Ulster Television station for the violence to end. Her simple passion combined with the facts of the appalling incident struck a hidden public chord which suddenly, spontaneously, started a bandwagon rolling. In Belfast and Derry, Dublin and London, marches for peace attracted thousands of people, the majority of them women. At a rally in Belfast's Ormeau Park the

Women's Peace Movement, later to be known as the Peace People, demanded the right to 'live and love and build a just and peaceful society'.

They rejected 'the use of the bomb and the bullet and all the techniques of violence'. Mairead Corrigan told the crowd that 'everybody has failed so far to get the two sides together and to bring us peace. I believe it is time for the women to have a go and see what the women of both sides, working together, can do.' The rallies and marches had the straightforward aim of bringing Catholics and Protestants together in a common abhorrence of the years of terror to demand that the paramilitaries halt their violence. In due course the collapse of the campaign in acrimony was to prove yet again that nothing is simple for long in Northern Ireland.

Inside Long Kesh Gerry Adams was saddened by the death of his friend Danny Lennon – whom he described as a 'second timer' because, unlike the majority of youngsters jailed in the early 1970s, he had rejoined the campaign of violence upon release from prison – and angry that the press were holding him solely responsible for the Maguire family's tragedy. He claimed it wasn't clear whether the children died as a result of the bullets fired by the soldiers at Lennon or as a result of the IRA man's car ploughing into them.

He accused the authorities of promoting a one-sided version of the event and suppressing the results of autopsies on the children with the intention of laying the blame on the IRA. Danny Lennon, he maintained, was an ordinary nationalist youth from a large Andersonstown family who had joined the IRA to fight on behalf of families like the Maguires. In an article for the republican weekly *An Phoblacht*, called 'In Defence of Danny Lennon', Adams described his former cellmate's death as 'a contradiction of the life he had spent, fighting for children such as they ... Jesus have pity. None of us stands guiltless.'

The difficulty for Adams and fellow republicans in dealing with the Peace People was that their main figureheads, Mairead Corrigan and Betty Williams, were undoubtedly, just like Danny Lennon, ordinary working-class Catholics. Corrigan was a striking and devoutly religious young woman who hailed originally from the Lower Falls. The Divis Street house where she was born and reared later became the local republican campaign office in the 1964 election, the scene of all the fighting over the Irish tricolour which Adams claims started him down the path of politics.

Her family moved to Andersonstown, another strongly nationalist area, and her father, a window cleaner, knew Gerry Adams' family. Their parents would have gone to ceilidhs, Irish dances, together. According to Mairead Corrigan, 'The Emergency laws were not new to them, families like theirs had a history. They were constantly being lifted – if any Royal family came here these families were lifted and held. Most families around them, we somehow knew they were republicans and they'd gone for a while, but it wasn't a great nationalist feeling. It was mostly in the past, almost.'

While the young Adams was being inducted into the republican movement the young Mairead Corrigan devoted herself to a Catholic lay organization, the Legion of Mary, running youth clubs and, after internment in 1972, visiting prisoners inside Long Kesh. There, squelching through the mud towards the Nissen huts on Sunday visits, she sometimes met Gerry Adams' father and the young Martin McGuinness. 'We went in in twos and they knew we were members of the Legion of Mary and I think a lot of them just took us as a bit of a joke, but it was a long Sunday! Some asked us if we would go and visit their wife or mother, just to see they were all right, and some came out for a bit of crack!'

While Corrigan says she wasn't politicized in any way before the tragic deaths of her nephews and nieces, she witnessed the excesses of the Army before and during internment and felt she understood why young men from her community were going out on to the streets and rioting. 'You could understand the reaction of the young people, going and joining the paramilitaries because of their outrage at how the community was being treated. While I never sympathized with republican ideology and most certainly would not be violent, they were our community and you could also feel very angry with them.'

It was her religious convictions which drove her to reflect long and hard on the right to take a gun and use it against state injustice. 'Somebody said there's such a thing as a just war, the Church blesses a just war. There was great ambivalence from all Church quarters, there was no strong non-violent message coming from the pulpits.' Convinced that human life is sacred and it was wrong to kill, she took, what for many people living in her neighbourhood in the early 1970s, was a brave stand. 'Several times the IRA came to the front door [looking for a vehicle] and I refused them the car. People were being intimidated in their homes by the IRA and that continues today. I was always adamant that we would in no way accommodate the Provisional IRA in our area.'

When the Maguire children were buried Corrigan sought out Danny Lennon's mother, who was among the crowd of mourners, and pressed some roses upon her:

> We had the sympathy of the world because of the children and I just felt that Mrs Lennon was a mother who had lost her son and, although I would not agree with the politics or the violent methods used, I felt that I wanted to tell her that we did feel for her.
>
> I went into her home and she was crying that day and her husband showed me several letters that she'd started to write to Jackie Maguire [the father of the dead children] and had torn up because she couldn't get the words, and several letters sent by neighbours which were saying 'Get out . . . we don't need people like you.' That family suffered tremendously as well. So many have.

Corrigan understood that the power of the Peace People lay in the fact that they came from the same community as the Provisionals. 'We were standing up to say that this violence is wrong and it's got to stop and you've got to deal with this problem in another way. We were breaking the silence out of the heart of the Catholic community. I think they understood that the power of the message and the truth of the message would give courage to other people to stand up and say it too. I think that they recognized that there was a strength there that could well turn the tide against them.'

Adams understood that too. So he wrote a lengthy defence of Lennon and what he stood for. It was published in pamphlet form in September 1976 and called *Peace in Ireland – a broad analysis of the present situation.* It was dedicated to 'Danny Lennon, who died for peace, and for the Maguire children who were killed with him'. Adams claimed that 'the leadership of the peace campaign appears to be middle class and there is a definite anti-Republican bias in their attitudes and in their denunciations'.

Realizing that such an accusation would not make much sense when levelled at a secretary employed by a brewery whose father cleaned windows for a living, he also acknowledged that 'there exists within ordinary Irish people, a genuine desire for peace', but went on, 'it is this desire which is, at present, being exploited'. Adams argued that 'no amount of pray-ins and liberalism' would provide a just society and that peace could not be divorced from political change. 'The partitionist regimes at Leinster House and Stormont are not capable of supporting, leading or developing a just or a peaceful society. Peace has not come in their time and because they are founded within artificial statelets and maintained by coercion, state police, concentration camps and terrorism, peace cannot come whilst they remain in control. While this control is upheld by the British government, peace cannot come to Ireland.' Not for the first or last time, he harked back to his early days in Ballymurphy to justify his continued commitment to violence. 'Some people in Ballymurphy, like others throughout Ireland, decided that only a change of system and the establishment of a social system in all Ireland, equal and worthy of the Irish people, could bring about the just and peaceful society they desired. They engaged in revolutionary warfare and the cause of their violence lay in the society they sought to change.'

Republicans like Adams knew that the continued existence of the IRA depended on the tacit support of the people around them. So long as the 'wee woman on the Falls Road' continued to look the other way or, better still, hide a gun under her bed, their position was assured. But this wasn't the first time that the IRA had faced a challenge from ordinary people demanding that the violence stop. In Derry in 1972 a march by 500 women had played an important part in ensuring that the Official IRA called a permanent ceasefire. The women had been protesting about the 'trial' and 'execution' of a nineteen-year-old soldier, Ranger William Best, who had been kidnapped at home in the Creggan estate while visiting his parents.

In the same year the IRA faced similar pressure from women in Andersonstown angry at the death of a local woman caught in the crossfire during a gun battle between the Provisionals and the Army. The Provisional leadership scornfully described them as the 'peace at any cost' brigade, according to Maria McGuire, a confidante of O Bradaigh and O'Connell in 1972. 'Direct action was taken the following day when the formidable republican Maire Drumm led a detachment of Provisional women into their meeting and wrecked it.'

Four years on the war-weariness instilled a far greater mobilization of anti-violence sympathizers. But they soon discovered that their situation could be made just as difficult. In November 1976 the Peace People held a march through West Belfast and refused police protection on the ground that it was their city and they should be able to walk unescorted where they wanted. As Mairead Corrigan remembers, it didn't work out that way:

> The Falls Road rally was particularly terrible. Sinn Fein took over the Peace People platform and we were attacked on the junction of the road right outside Milltown cemetery.
>
> It was raining that day and it was as well that it was raining too because people had their umbrellas. There were stones thrown and people were hurt and ended up having stitches put in at the hospital. Some women tried to come in to get me and pulled my hair out and kicked me, but we just kept marching, and we were very lucky that day because we know for a fact that there were guns on the road. The sad thing for me was that my sister Anne, who had taken a long time to learn to walk again after the crash, had insisted on going to the Falls Park to read the Peace Declaration and when she got into the park Sinn Fein had taken over the platform and she had to literally get out again quickly in case anything happened to her.

On other occasions prominent members of the movement awoke to find their houses daubed with hostile graffiti. 'We were threatened, told to remain silent, not to get involved. We knew the risk we were taking. We could have been shot but we felt it had to be done.'

Adams' line of attack on the Peace People was that they were purely an anti-IRA movement, unprepared to confront excesses by the security forces. 'Any call for peace,' he argued, 'regardless of the sincerity of those involved, which singled out the republican violence and which ignores the nature of the society in which we live, is sadly doomed to failure.' But he also recognized that it was not enough simply to castigate the peace campaigners, there was also a need for the IRA to avoid indulging in activities which would risk the possibility of a popular backlash. 'Republicans must ensure that our cause and our methods remain within the bounds of our consciences ... Revolutionary violence, and this excludes sectarian violence, must be controlled and disciplined – a symbol of our people's resistance and the spearhead of their desire for a peaceful and just society.'

Under pressure from republicans to say where they stood on incidents such as the shooting of a twelve-year-old girl, Majella O'Hare, by soldiers in South Armagh, or the killing by an Army plastic bullet of fourteen-year-old Brian Stewart in West Belfast, the Peace People voiced their concern. But they also made it clear that they did not bracket such killings together with the activities of the IRA and the UVF or UDA. In October 1976 Mairead Corrigan and Betty Williams declared that 'we do not equate the vicious and determined terrorism of the republican and loyalist paramilitary organizations with the occasional instances when members of the security forces may have stepped beyond the rule of law'.

Corrigan and Williams went further, arguing that in the absence of any proper alternative the RUC were the only legally constituted upholders of the rule of law and urging people to provide the police with information. 'We really said to the people in the communities that we came out of, look you have got to stand up against the violence in your community no matter where it comes from and if you see someone going out to plant a bomb, in your conscience you have to ask yourself, "Have I any right not to do anything about this?" It's up to you to use your conscience and do what you can to save and protect life. So we had to put it into people to exercise their conscience to do what was right and not be afraid and we could only do that by giving that example ourselves, standing out ourselves unprotected and saying you're wrong to do this.'

The direct pacifist action did bring astonishing results at first. 'In the nationalist community in the first six months of the Peace People there was a 70 per cent decrease in the rate of violence. We have never, thanks be to God, returned to the rate of violence that was here pre-1976. The Peace People helped create the atmosphere to do that, where people felt more courage to do what they had to do, not give their cars to the Provies, tell if they saw something suspicious in their area. It was working. The paramilitaries were like a fish out of water. Draw off the water and the fish can't swim.'

She could recall a society before the Troubles in which 'policemen where I lived were my neighbours and didn't carry guns and lived in that community very freely'. But while the Peace People coupled their calls for co-operation with the RUC with demands for wide-ranging reforms of the force and the repeal of the panoply of repressive anti-terrorist powers, for many Catholics this was a bridge too far. Deploring violence was one thing, but turning in the boy down the road who used to go to school with your son was quite another. Not only did many people justifiably fear the consequences, since the IRA had made it abundantly clear on several occasions that they would kill informers, but, more than that, providing information still seemed a dishonourable thing to do.

When Mairead Corrigan attended a meeting inside a community centre in the West Belfast estate of Turf Lodge soon after Brian Stewart was killed by a plastic bullet she found herself being shunned, treated like an outsider on her own patch. 'Going into that meeting there were in the front row people sitting whom I had known in Long Kesh and visited their families. But the tension there, the fear, the anger at what happened to young Brian Stewart was so high, and they saw us as betraying this community because we'd somehow stepped out of the community. They saw us almost as enemies.'

The Peace People were squeezed from a number of directions. Like all relatively spontaneous mass movements they suffered from the temporary nature of people's anger, as the images of the Maguire children faded in the mind. In asking the Catholic community to co-operate with the police they were stretching the boundaries of what could be achieved. The vociferous Provisional assault on the movement was also having an impact. But above all she blamed the government. The harsh policies and rhetoric of the Labour Northern Ireland Secretary Roy Mason and reports of brutal treatment of paramilitary suspects, she says, created an adverse impact within the nationalist community and made her message far more difficult to sell. Catholics were prepared to turn IRA men in, she claims, but not if they believed they were then going to be tortured inside the RUC's interrogation centres.

Eventually the Peace People compounded their own difficulties by an act of self-destruction. In October 1977 Mairead and Betty Williams were awarded the Nobel Peace Prize. It brought with it a substantial sum of money, £80,000. Betty Williams decided to keep her portion of the cash and try to make a new life in the United States. Mairead continued to campaign but the stigma of the prize money stuck to the Peace People, who now appeared to the hard-bitten cynics on the Falls and the Shankill as little more than gold-diggers. When Mairead knocked on the doors of West Belfast the more sympathetic told her they felt what had happened to the movement was a pity, while the more sceptical simply sneered.

Adams says the episode left him feeling 'sad' because it represented a 'perversion' of the basic demand of ordinary people for peace. But he must also have been considerably relieved that the apparent potential of the Peace People to end the conflict had come to naught. He was well aware of the need to ensure that a gap should not be allowed to open up between the IRA and the community in which they operated. He knew that as the IRA reorganized itself into secretive cells the potential for such a divorce increased.

The Peace People carried on their work, albeit in a much more low-key way than in the mid-1970s. They ran buses for prisoners' relatives going on visits to Northern Ireland's jails, organized discussions and worked with groups of young people from both sides of the community. Ten years after the dramatic birth of the movement Mairead Corrigan was out and about in West Belfast selling the Peace People's magazine and being filmed for a television documentary which was to tell the story of 'the dream that died'. She bumped into Adams in the street and he told her he had no money to buy a magazine but would take one if she gave him it for free. In a brief televised exchange Corrigan expounded her heartfelt desire for peace, but Adams told her that peace would only come about 'once the Brits go'. It wouldn't happen, he added with unchivalrous relish, 'while movements like the Peace People have such a discredited leadership'.

Although Gerry Adams has told people around the world that he is committed above all to dialogue, one person whose frequent letters asking for meetings he has not responded to is Mairead Corrigan. Once during the IRA ceasefire of 1995 she had a brief exchange with him at a public meeting in the republican Felons Club on the Falls Road, arguing that the crucial problems in Northern Ireland were more to do with the relations between unionists and nationalists in Northern Ireland than with those between the Irish and the British. Adams thanked her, said that he talked regularly to Protestants but dismissed her analysis as too simple.

Corrigan greeted the calling of the IRA's 1994 ceasefire with 'absolute delight'. She was dismayed about the lack of movement during its eighteen months and felt it was a tragedy that it broke down. Today, despite his criticisms of her, she views Gerry Adams with sympathy and understanding:

> He is coming out of a republican family and he is coming out of a situation where during internment they went into his home, they threw his father down the stairs and took him away in a van to Long Kesh.
>
> He is coming out of a tradition that has felt the effect of Army and police laws here. So for those of us who have not travelled that road it's perhaps harder to understand. The thing is that you always hope that people will change and Adams has come a long way and he has changed, I think. I think he has made a contribution to peace and I hope that he will be given the time and the opportunity to make an even better contribution to peace in the future, and I just hope that he can do it.
>
> For me to come out and call for peace, I don't have to look over my shoulder at some who strongly disagree and would shoot me in the back for calling for it. Gerry Adams is in such a position, it took tremendous courage for him and the other leaders of Sinn Fein and for the loyalist leadership to come out and call for a ceasefire. They're in a much more dangerous situation than any of us are in and that courage cannot be denied.

CHAPTER ELEVEN

The Long War

The day after he walked out of jail in the spring of 1977 Gerry Adams left his wife Colette playing with their young son Gearoid and sauntered across Dublin to meet a man on the run. Adams says that he had wanted to take the family he had not seen for four years to a house in County Meath for a short break, but the word had come that the IRA's chief of staff Seamus Twomey wanted to see him, and for Adams IRA business had to come first.

Twomey, formerly the IRA's leader in Belfast, had been moving from house to house in the Irish Republic after a dramatic escape by helicopter from Mountjoy jail in October 1973. No record was kept of what he and Adams discussed, but it is known that around this time the IRA had set up an internal commission, reporting to its General Headquarters Staff, with a brief to look at a wholesale restructuring of the movement. Adams is generally believed to have headed the commission, which began work before he left jail and reached its conclusions after his release.

The IRA had come under increasing pressure since the morale-sapping 1975 ceasefire and under the tougher regime of the Labour government's Northern Ireland Secretary Roy Mason the security forces were making inroads, recruiting informers and arresting key members. The need was for a tighter structure along the lines which Adams had been developing in jail. But at the same time he was reluctant to recommend a plan which would be purely military in content. He strongly believed that success could not be achieved by an IRA 'military elite' cut off from the community in which it operated. If the secret army was to be made more secretive there would also have to be a corresponding commitment to active and dynamic political action to maintain and develop support for the IRA in the wider community.

The conclusions of the internal commission were meant to be for IRA eyes only. But in December 1977 the Irish police had a stroke of luck. They raided a flat in Dun Laoghaire, the ferry terminal town south of Dublin, and arrested Twomey. A meticulous search of the apartment hit the jackpot. Inside a pencil case was hidden a document entitled 'Staff Report'. It was the work of the commission. The document urged that 'the system with which Brits and Branch [the RUC and Garda Siochana Special Branch] are familiar has to be changed. We recommend reorganisation and remotivation, the building of a new Irish Republican Army ... We must gear ourselves towards a long term armed struggle based on putting unknown men and new recruits into a new structure.'

The reference to a 'long term armed struggle' was significant. In the first phase of the Provisionals' campaign, which saw the most violence inflicted upon Northern Ireland in death and bomb damage, confidence was so high it seemed reasonable to believe that the successful achievement of their goals was just around the corner. Nineteen-seventy-two had been designated the Year of Victory, and the year after and the following year. When Victory continued to elude them these slogans became an embarrassing reminder of their naivety. But even in February 1977, in a statement to *Iris*, a republican magazine launched by Adams, the IRA leadership was still insisting optimistically that 'We are now confident of victory as we face the final phase of the war with England.'

The IRA commission was moving towards an entirely different conclusion: that faced with the overwhelming odds of a better trained, better resourced adversary their aims could be achieved only through a campaign of attrition waged upon a broader battlefield. Within the organization the projected struggle became dubbed 'the long war'. The emphasis was upon a reorganized and remotivated IRA and with it a 'return to secrecy and strict discipline'.

The new structure envisaged to fight this long war was based on the four-strong cells which Adams and Martin McGuinness had been advocating from behind bars. The Staff Report recommended these should replace the old system of battalions and companies, especially in urban areas. They should be specialized, carrying out different functions, such as 'sniping cells, executions, bombings, robberies etc'. Crucially the Report went on to spell out the future role envisaged for

Sinn Fein: active and dynamic, yes – but at all times subservient to the IRA:

> Sinn Fein should come under Army organisers at all levels. Sinn Fein should employ full time organisers in big republican areas. Sinn Fein should be radicalised (under Army direction) and should agitate about social and economic issues which attack the welfare of the people. Sinn Fein should be directed to infiltrate other organisations to win support for, and sympathy to, the movement. Sinn Fein should be re-educated and have a big role to play in publicity and propaganda depts, complaints and problems (making no room for RUC opportunism). It gains the respect of the people which in turn leads to increased support for the cell.

Ever since his involvement in agitation in the late 1960s Adams had remained a believer in politics. The difficulty lay in getting the balance right between political action and the central tenet of physical-force republicanism that only through violence could Ireland be liberated. In 1972 the security forces received a report that Adams wanted to take the IRA in a more overtly political direction and wanted it to be recognized as a political party. It was understood that he didn't receive any backing for this from the Belfast Brigade and in order to re-establish his hardline credentials he recommitted himself to the campaign of violence, instructing all IRA volunteers to leave their jobs and take up arms in earnest, urging in particular unemployed volunteers in the South to come north to prosecute the war.

By 1977 Adams believed that a complete fusion of military and political strategy, with Sinn Fein the tool of a more clandestine IRA, was the answer. Although Sinn Fein was to be controlled entirely by the IRA, the role envisaged for the party was far greater than had been the case before, when it had been nothing more than a support network for the armed struggle. Now it was intended to be visible and radical, the organization which put into action the revolutionary ideas cast up in the Brownie column.

The Staff Report was intended to be a secret plan, but there was a need to communicate some of its thinking to Provisional supporters on the ground. Adams decided the best time and place for this would be the Wolfe Tone commemoration at Bodenstown in June 1977. The speech, made every year beside the grave of the founder of the eighteenth-century United Irishmen movement, is traditionally thought of as a keynote address, incorporating not only the usual exhortations for faithful republicans to remain steadfast to the cause, but also providing some sense of where the movement sees itself going in the future. According to one former senior IRA member it is quite simply 'the most important speech of the year'. That year republicans were treated to a Janus-like piece of symbolism, with Adams' new programme delivered by a man of the Old Guard with impeccable traditionalist credentials.

Jimmy Drumm had spent a total of fifteen years in jail for republican activities. His wife Maire, the Sinn Fein vice president, was murdered in 1976 by loyalists posing as doctors at Belfast's Mater Hospital. When he spoke it was with the authority of someone whose whole life had been dedicated to the cause of ridding Ireland of British influence. The words, however, were those of Gerry Adams and Danny Morrison, editor of the Belfast-based *Republican News* and an increasingly important member of a 'Northern clique' which Adams was building around him.

The speech was in many respects a turning point for the Provisionals, and in keeping with such an important moment the script had been worked and reworked both while Adams was in prison and after his release in February. It represented his belief that the Provisionals should stop kidding themselves that victory was just around the corner and that armed action was enough of itself to achieve British withdrawal. Drumm's words were intended to introduce the twin concepts of a long war against the British and the necessity for broad political activity allied to the violence of the IRA. He told the Wolfe Tone commemoration that the 'isolation of socialist republicans around armed struggle is dangerous' and warned the crowd that the struggle against the British was going to be far from easy. 'The British government is not withdrawing from the six counties ... We find that a successful war of liberation cannot be fought exclusively on the backs of the oppressed in the six counties, nor around the physical presence of the British Army. Hatred and resentment of the Army cannot sustain the war.'

Increasingly Adams and his allies introduced militant left-wing rhetoric to the movement, a development which caused anxiety to those traditionalist right-wing Catholics in the older generation who had no difficulty supporting IRA violence but had been taught by their priests that communism was the enemy. A letter writer to the Dublin-based *An Phoblacht* objected to the trend. 'It sickens me to see republicanism being referred to in the context of Karl Marx's writings – a man who believed neither in God nor in nationalism – and I certainly see it as serving no useful purpose to compare republican beliefs with those of Lenin, whose followers torture and crucify, daily, people who dare to express differences of opinion.'

Ruairi O Bradaigh's brother Sean attended Sinn Fein meetings with the 'Northern clique' where they criticized the 'Eire Nua' plan for a Federal Ireland and enforced rigid adherence to their ultra-left-wing ideology. Sean O'Brady wondered whether the socialist rhetoric was for real or just a convenient way for the young Northerners to distinguish themselves from the older Dublin-based leaders:

For a number of years they were rocking the boat, wanting to get rid of federalism because it was a sop to unionism. Also trying to change the social and economic programme – we weren't socialist enough. They produced 'the grey book', a thin, school-book type thing, at an Ard Comhairle [party] meeting in Parnell Square [Sinn Fein's Dublin office], a slim volume which we weren't allowed to take home. Every copy was numbered and they all had to be accounted for at the end of every meeting. All private property was going to be abolished. I remember trying to make reasonable arguments about there being a small measure of private enterprise allowed even in Vietnam but they wouldn't have it. I think in retrospect they didn't really believe in it, they were just using it to destabilize the leadership. The three leading lights were Tom Hartley, Gerry Adams and Danny Morrison. McGuinness didn't get involved in that.

Sean O'Brady always considered Adams to be 'a bit too smart with his answers'. When discussion started on whether republicans should fight elections and take seats in the Irish parliament, 'He would say, "I don't have a view on that, I will leave it up to the Army Council to decide that."' O'Brady thought that was 'not very leader-like ... I was always concerned about their ability to provide a national leadership rather than a local, regional one. They all knew one another fairly well, had been in prison together, they were arrogant, others didn't count.'

The shift in influence to the North wasn't restricted to political meetings or to publicity via the increasingly divergent voice of *Republican News*. It also encompassed the IRA. While the Staff Report had concentrated entirely on the reorganization of the IRA from brigades to cells, Adams and his allies also created a separate Northern Command which would oversee the IRA's campaign within what it regarded as 'the war zone', Northern Ireland and the Irish border counties.

The idea wasn't new. It harked back to the IRA of the 1940s when Hugh McAteer had established a separate Northern Command to run the campaign in which Gerry Adams' father took part. Indeed, it was understood that recreating a Northern Command was a pet subject of Gerry senior, now busy running republican drinking clubs. In August 1977 Gerry junior was believed to be either the adjutant or the chief of staff of the relatively new Northern Command. He was understood to be responsible for organizing all its cells and was especially tasked to co-ordinate and promote closer liaison between the IRA and Sinn Fein.

Some of those associated with the IRA leadership in Dublin were distinctly edgy about the new structure. They noticed that when Northern Command held its meetings some people were unable to attend because the meetings took place inside Northern Ireland and were therefore off-limits for those on the run. They wondered whether this was a convenient ruse to keep potential critics offside.

But 'Mike', a senior IRA member who was in the future to become a critic of Adams, saw no problems with the restructuring. 'It was necessary for military reasons for the leadership to pass to the North, and for the cell structure to be introduced. Seamus Twomey was IRA chief of staff when that happened but he was very much a puppet of Adams. There was a fair amount of input across the board but Adams would have been basically running the show.'

Adams was keen to spend as much of his time as possible pushing his plans for restructuring the IRA but it was inevitable that more short-term concerns would intervene. During 1977 apart from his role on the Northern Command Adams was variously understood to be, from May, a member of the IRA's Belfast Brigade staff and, from June, one of its seven-strong Army Council.

A flavour of what Adams' activities within the IRA were like is provided by the IRA man and former Parachute Regiment soldier Peter McMullen, who met Adams in a Dublin flat in the company of Martin McGuinness and Brian Keenan. 'During the discussion Gerry chipped in and mentioned that he thought it might be a good idea to expand or renew the bombing campaign in England again . . . It was becoming very hard to operate in the North and with the new laws being brought into the South there was going to be no havens any more. So we thought we could expand and bring it back into England, the campaign.' The principal topic of the meeting was to discuss the possibility of assassinating Brigadier Sir Frank Kitson, whose low-intensity operations had done so much to disrupt IRA activity in Belfast.

Kitson was back in England, but in Provisional eyes he was still a highly desirable target. There was new intelligence on his movements; the Provos had discovered where he lived and noted that at weekends his security guard was lowered. The obvious candidate for the task was McMullen, according to the former Para. However, nothing came of the meeting and McMullen left for New York, where he was officially said to be involved in fund-raising. Soon after, he went on the run, claiming to have fallen out with the IRA over a plot to kidnap an American millionaire. For years he evaded both his former IRA comrades and the US authorities before being sent back to England. In 1996 he was convicted for his part in the bombing of an Army barracks in Yorkshire.

During 1977 Adams also spent time in negotiations intended to resolve the latest feud between the Provisionals and the Officials – this time the result of a loyalist bomb attack on the Officials' Easter parade, which they initially blamed on the Provisionals. The meetings took place at Clonard Monastery off the Falls Road and, after uncertain beginnings, became almost weekly occasions designed to solve differences between the two factions before they erupted into violence.

Father Des Wilson, the priest who married Adams, was briefly involved but handed over to the Redemptorist Order at Clonard Monastery. Father Alex Reid won the trust of both sides. Reid was a serious character who never laughed or joked. 'He wouldn't have been pushy or aggressive, would have excused himself when he said something, would say, "Do you mind if I say . . .", certainly saw his place as the facilitator, always wanted to ensure you were happy, if there was anything else you wanted, going out of his way to help,' according to one Official IRA man who took part in the discussions. 'Reid wouldn't have made a contribution unless he saw the situation deteriorating, he would have listened attentively and then if it wasn't going terribly well then he'd speak. He took the thing very serious and put in long hours at it. What we couldn't understand was how he got so much time. There was obviously some agreement from his Order for him to do this. I'd say he was a Christian, my interpretation of why he was so concerned about this all happening was that these are all Catholic boys, although he assured us he was concerned about the loyalists.'

Reid was to become important to Adams in the years to come when he put his mediating skills to use not just in solving feuds but in relation to the wider problems involved in the peace process of the 1990s. For now, though, the agenda was rather more limited and while Adams maintains that he sincerely wanted to bring all the feuding to an end his demeanour at the Clonard meetings didn't impress the Official IRA man with whom he was negotiating:

> I always got the impression that he had an ego problem and his whole attitude was 'Look, I was lucky getting here because the Brits were all over the place and I had to go to this house' and telling me all about it . . . how he had to negotiate with people coming and whispering in his ear 'Gerry this and Gerry that' . . . It's a situation where you're not going in with an open mind, you're going in with a person that you don't like, your gut reaction is you'd love to hit him a dig in the beak, so you're trying to negotiate in those circumstances, you know your bottom line and you don't want to be there with him, you simply want to get what you want and get out. He had this ego problem, as soon as he came in it would be 'Ach what about you?' and that sort of crack. So it was a matter of having to go through with it, which I found distasteful. These meetings could be three or four hours, you had an agenda which consisted of a lot of nasty incidents. It was a case of getting through with it and then getting out.

The Official IRA man preferred to deal with Kevin Hannaway, Adams' cousin. 'Kevin was a much more decent individual, much more genuine and down to earth, whereas Adams always felt he was away up here, important. The priest would ask Adams about his availability and Adams would always say, "I'm not so sure," and the priest would say, "Listen, this is important," and Adams would say "I'll see what I can do, I'll have to cancel this meeting and that meeting" – all Alice in Wonderland stuff!'

The meetings were often heated. 'The priests would have sat in on the initial discussions, because there was a lot of aggression. Their objective was to get it stopped and to work out a mechanism to ensure as far as possible it didn't happen again, which was impossible because these boys, they'd shot each other's mates dead and they were drinking in the same pubs and they were getting pissed up and by about half-eleven the looks, the glances were turning to punches and by one o'clock the guns were out.'

The feud was resolved and the priests, while continuing to keep an eye on conflict between the republican factions, made some tentative steps towards establishing contacts between the Provisionals and the loyalists. Father Wilson helped set up meetings between Adams and Desmond Boal, a barrister, a former Stormont MP and at one time a leading member of Ian Paisley's Democratic Unionist Party. This wasn't Adams' first political contact with Protestants – in 1972 the security forces were aware that he had been trying to assess Protestant reaction to the IRA's bombing campaign.

But the meeting with Boal, while frank and constructive in Adams' estimation, made little progress. A short time later Father Wilson drove Adams to a meeting in South Belfast with John McKeague, a former chairman of the Shankill Defence Association and reputedly a founder of the small loyalist paramilitary group, the Red Hand Commandos. McKeague was one of a number of loyalists whose dissatisfaction with the British government was drawing them towards a flirtation with the notion of an independent Ulster, rather than the maintenance of the union.

Adams and McKeague may have shared a distaste for British politicians but they had little else in common. Although Adams believed a series of encounters he had with McKeague were useful, again they produced no results. McKeague, who besides his paramilitary activities also attracted attention because of his alleged involvement in the sex scandal involving loyalists and the Kincora boys' home in East Belfast, was shot dead by the INLA in 1982.

At the end of 1977 the IRA launched a series of incendiary attacks on economic targets throughout Northern Ireland. Hotels were especially targeted, even though there wasn't really much left of a tourist industry in the province to destroy. The campaign carried on through the New Year, and on the night of 17 February three IRA members from Gerry Adams' home area of Ballymurphy fixed an incendiary to a window of the La Mon House hotel in the strongly unionist countryside of County Down. Inside, the Irish Collie Dog Club was holding its annual dinner dance. The bomb – a cocktail of crystallized ammonium nitrate and aluminium filings attached to gallon tins of petrol – was primed and the Provisionals drove off.

A telephone warning was made shortly before 9.00 p.m. but when police phoned the hotel a male voice said: 'For God's sake get out here, a bomb has already gone off.' A ball of flame rolled through the hotel, enveloping guests and revellers in its path. Within an hour the entire hotel was alight and by eleven o'clock the security services were recovering the first of twelve bodies, most of them barely recognizable as human beings, so badly charred were they. The seven men and five women – all Protestants – had to be identified by jewellery, blood group, hair samples and one person by a process of elimination.

It emerged that the bombers had stopped at the first public telephone box on their route back to West Belfast, only to find that it had been vandalized. By the time they found another phone the bomb, set on a fifty-eight-minute timer, was about to detonate. A UDR soldier who was first on the scene said he thought he had stumbled into hell. 'There was a large tree facing the hotel which had caught the full blast and was all aglow, bright red. It was just one large, pulsating cinder which oddly hadn't collapsed. It was the most evil-looking thing I'd ever seen in my life and then on top of that were these charred bits of flesh that once were people which had to be carried out and identified. I will never forget the scene.'

Northern Ireland reeled in horror at the savagery of the bombing and demanded swift action. Adams was in a house in Beechmount off the Falls Road with Colette and their son Gearoid when he heard of the La Mon massacre. Stunned by what had happened, he broke his rule of changing safe houses every night and stayed with his family. Early next morning police arrested him at the house. Twenty other republicans were also taken in for questioning. The RUC distributed thousands of leaflets showing the remains of one of the victims in a bid to encourage people to ring its confidential telephone line with information about terrorist activity. After being held for the full seven days of detention under Emergency legislation, during which detectives showed him pictures of the charred victims, Adams was charged with IRA membership.

Sinn Fein called the membership charge an act of appeasement to loyalists and British politicians 'who have been screaming for republican blood over the past few weeks'. Adams also put out a warning, for the first but not the last time, that he was contemplating legal action against a number of newspapers which claimed that he was a senior IRA commander in Belfast. The Provisionals put out thousands of their own leaflets, highlighting the injustice of his arrest. The RUC had appeased public opinion, but only now did they start to build the case against Gerry Adams.

CHAPTER TWELVE

Beating the Rap

A few days after Adams was charged with IRA membership a classified advertisement appeared in the Belfast nationalist daily the *Irish News*. 'The officers and members of Clonard Martyrs Sinn Fein Cumann send support and solidarity to our esteemed member Gerry Adams now interned by remand by the British. We also send greetings in this the second anniversary of the removal of political status to the 300 prisoners of war on the blanket protest in H Block Long Kesh, Crumlin Road and Armagh jail.'

Adams was returning to prison in changed circumstances. In 1976 the British government had abolished the 'political' or special-category prisoner status for which Billy McKee had gone on hunger strike. It was part of a concerted drive to 'Ulsterize' the seven-year-old conflict. Primacy was returned to the RUC, with the Army taking a support role, and on the propaganda front the government took every opportunity to portray the IRA as a criminal Mafia-style organization.

Adams served a short spell in Crumlin Road prison, where he was assailed by constant radio pop music courtesy of two young IRA suspects with whom he was sharing a cell, before transfer to Long Kesh, whose new name of the Maze prison was stubbornly ignored by its inmates, where the first sentenced IRA prisoner was into his second year of a protest which was to escalate beyond anybody's imagining. Ciaran Nugent refused to wear prison uniform. 'If they want me to wear a convict's uniform they'll have to nail it to my back,' the defiant prisoner declared.

Adams did not participate in the blanket protest. As a remand prisoner he was allocated his own cell and given his own clothes to wear. At his first court appearance he was faced with the charge that from March 1977 until his arrest he had been an IRA brigade commander. The main evidence against him was a report by the BBC reporter Jeremy Paxman from a December 1977 edition of the *Tonight* current affairs programme. Among the allegedly incriminating admissions by Adams, recorded at that year's Sinn Fein *ard fheis* was: 'In a war zone it is a necessity, if nothing else, to force the republican movement into a complete and utter reliance on the people's support.' Other key pieces of evidence included: 'We cannot survive almost eight years of war, unless the people want to billet us, look after us and drive us about and unless they want to support us,' and 'I think it is a basic principle of republicanism that we fight on for all the people. We are fighting because the people want us to fight and we are struggling for a situation where their welfare will benefit and they will be left in control of their own destiny.'

Adams' solicitor Paddy McGrory told the court: 'Mr Adams was arrested in the aftermath of La Mon. The public and the media, through no fault of theirs, could take it that there is a connection because of the juxtaposition of dates. But after six days of interrogation by the police, this is the only matter to be raised.' As an unemployed barman living off state handouts, Adams was granted legal aid to fight the charge.

Adams hadn't given anything away to the police during his period of questioning. One of the detectives who carried out the interrogation recalls that Adams 'wanted to portray himself very much as the statesman type. He adopted a very cool stance. He was allowed to smoke his pipe. He was certainly very careful about any answers that he gave. He was quite happy to discuss any issues other than those under consideration. In fact I quite enjoyed the interview with him. If I was going out for an evening and I had a choice of him or Ian Paisley I know who I would pick.'

In fact the detectives were somewhat annoyed by having to pursue the case against Adams, which they believed reflected a desire within the government to take a senior Provisional scalp no matter what damage was done to other ongoing investigations. One RUC officer recalls that 'once Adams was charged there was fair bit of scurrying around to get better evidence'. The detective was concerned that he was being asked to draw on evidence which had been painstakingly gathered in the course of a twelve-month investigation into other republicans, and try to work it into a case against Adams.

Two months later the RUC introduced new evidence and back-dated the charge of membership of an illegal organization to cover an Easter parade staged by republican internees and prisoners during his last period of detention. It was taken as a sign that the RUC knew its case was thin. As Paddy McGrory told the court: 'There is no doubt that there were some republicans taking part in the parade who may have been members of the IRA, but there were many who were not,' and he asked if all loyalists who took part in marches inside prison were also going to be charged with UVF membership.

Outside prison a massive publicity campaign was being organized by Danny 'Bangers' Morrison, one of Adams' new inner circle, a bright, articulate figure who revolutionized the republican move-ment's weekly newspaper. As part of his consolidation of his hold on power, Adams had sacked the editor of the Dublin-based *An Phob-lacht*, Gerry O'Hare, and merged it with the Belfast *Republican News*. Morrison eventually became Sinn Fein's director of publicity while also holding high rank within the IRA, courtesy of his loyalty to Adams.

'Stop the show trial,' read the headline of a leaflet publicizing Adams' case. 'Free Gerry Adams!' It claimed a massive increase in government harassment of 'Republican members of the nationalist community in the occupied Six Counties of Ireland. After nine years British troops have failed to defeat Irish resistance to the partition of Ireland. Curfews, internments, torture, summary execution and special courts have failed to defeat the Irish Republican Army which con-tinues its war of national liberation.' The days of imminent victory were clearly a propaganda cry of the past. 'Late last year and continuing into this year the British Government turned their atten-tion against the Sinn Fein political movement [which they had nominally legalized in 1973] and the newspaper *Republican News*. There have been scores of raids on members' homes, offices have been ransacked and files and machinery confiscated,' the leaflet claimed. It was to be the start of a major campaign, 'involving thousands of posters and leaflets to defend Sinn Fein and stop the show trials'. It was also the first green shoots of a strategy to give the IRA's political arm a bigger role in the struggle to end British rule.

Sinn Fein geared up for the trial, inviting the Soviet Union's news agency Tass to cover it in a crude attempt to draw a parallel between the condemnation by 'James Callaghan, David Owen and other leading British hypocrites' of the imprisonment of the dissidents Orlov, Ginzburg and Shcharansky. International jurors would also be present, it warned, while 'we will be mounting a vigorous picket outside the convicting chamber'.

In the event the high-profile campaign proved unnecessary, since the notoriety of Adams ensured blanket coverage. On 6 September the Lord Chief Justice Sir Robert Lowry accepted Paddy McGrory's submission that there was no case to answer. The evidence was insufficient. The judge said that for all he knew Adams was a member of the IRA but speculation could never take the place of evidence. It took him twenty minutes to reach the moment that Adams and his supporters had been waiting eight months to hear. As Sir Robert told him he was free to go, a loud cheer erupted in the public gallery, where Colette was waiting.

Also in court and relieved for somewhat different reasons, was the BBC broadcaster Jeremy Paxman. Having been subpoenaed to give evidence that film footage of Adams was genuine, Paxman had decided he had better attend, even though a colleague had passed on an IRA threat that testifying in the trial could radically shorten his life. Caught between the law and the Provisionals, Paxman was thankful he did not have to stand in the dock.

Rather less relieved was one of the RUC detectives who had worked on the case. He found that the acquittal meant that some of the evidence which he had introduced consisting of documents found in Sinn Fein offices about IRA punishment beatings, could not now be used against those other Provisionals who he believed were more culpable than Adams. 'When the judge threw out the case against Adams it meant a good deal of evidence that we had assembled for use against the others was discredited – it had a bad knock-on effect. Towards the end of the Adams case we were grasping at straws. The evidence required by the courts is of a very high standard. I have no doubt Sinn Fein collectively convicted many of their own people on much more flimsy evidence than on which Mr Adams was cleared by the court that day.'

As they left court arm in arm Gerry and Colette refused to comment. A few days later Adams felt sufficiently prepared to speak. The presence of so many eminent jurists at his trial might have led to the 'political decision' to release him. 'The British government, like Stormont before them, can only rule in the six counties by exercising widespread repression against the nationalist community. The solution to our troubles lies in a British withdrawal and the Irish people being allowed to determine their own future.'

It was a time of high morale on the public front, but anxiety for the state of the military campaign. RUC Special Branch officers noted that while Adams was in prison there had been a lull in commercial bombings. Now he was out, the bombings increased, particularly against the tourist trade. A year earlier the new Labour Northern Ireland Secretary Roy Mason had boasted that he was 'squeezing the IRA like toothpaste'. The number of deaths in 1978 dropped significantly below a hundred for the first time since the beginning of the decade. The reduced capability could be credited to the reorganization of the IRA instituted by Adams and his allies, but it looked from the outside as if Labour's 'get tough' policy was working.

While the founding dream of the Provisionals that they could win a military victory over the British was over, there was consolation to be drawn from an Army document which had fallen into republican hands and which was gleefully published in their newspaper. 'Northern Ireland: Future Terrorist Trends' – the work of General James Glover – commented: 'We see no prospect in the next five years of any political change which would remove PIRA's [Provision IRA] raison d'être.' It went on to observe that 'there is a stratum of intelligent, astute and experienced terrorists who provide the backbone of the organisation . . . our evidence of the calibre of rank-and-file terrorists does not support the view that they are merely mindless hooligans drawn from the unemployed and unemployable.' And 'by reorganising on cellular lines, PIRA has become much less dependent on public support than in the past and is less vulnerable to penetration by informers'.

In November the Provisionals, their restructuring complete, were ready to relaunch their bombing campaign. More than fifty bombs exploded across Northern Ireland and thirty-seven people were injured. With the blanket protest continuing inside the Maze prison, the IRA shot dead its deputy governor Albert Miles at his home in North Belfast. The wives of three prison officers were injured by exploding parcel bombs. And a renewed bombing campaign was launched in England. Police leave was cancelled in London and more than 2,000 uniformed officers were drafted in to the West End to forestall a Christmas bombing campaign.

In the autumn Adams was elected vice president of Sinn Fein, ushering in a period of increasingly strained relations with Ruairi O Bradaigh. 'Immediately what Adams was hitting at was the whole idea of a federal Ireland of four provinces. He used it as big issue, that he had prisoners behind him and all that sort of thing.' O Bradaigh said that Adams was careful not to articulate this criticism himself, but his cohorts would do it with his encouragement. 'Somebody used to make a joke that if there was something critical coming up Danny Morrison would float it. Depending how it got on Martin McGuinness would come out and back it up, and depending on how it gets on at that stage Adams would come out for it. Kite-flying if you like. He would be very sure that the ice was thick enough before he went walking on it.'

In spite of the personal animosity, O Bradaigh could not help admiring Adams. 'I would say that he was always a person with a mind of his own. I don't think he would be going along with the tide. He wasn't part of the '69 tide, he was already involved for years before that. And he did display from the begining an interest in the political aspect of things, which was unusual for a young person in Belfast. I remember in '72 him coming to the *ard fheis* and speaking and proposing motions, which would be unusual for a young person.'

But Adams' release from prison and his success in shaking off charges of IRA membership provided him with the propaganda coup with which to launch his low-profile campaign to replace O Bradaigh and the rest of the Southern leadership.

> He gradually took power. The first thing was he sought the removal of the editor of *An Phoblacht*, Gerry O'Hare. Adams got *Republican News* amalgamated, which meant they came down to Dublin and took over. And then he had his different personnel that he knew and everyone that was in any position of doing a job in the Sinn Fein leadership, he put a shadow on them and was critical of them. Whenever any vacancy occurred he moved his own men over. He built up a shadow leadership. I was aware of it but at the same time you had to think of the good of the movement and you had to see if these were worthy personnel. Often these people had something to contribute. I suppose he could pursue that sort of thing singlemindedly, but people who were there from the leadership since 1956, you had to take the broad view.

By the time he delivered the annual Bodenstown speech in June 1979 Adams had been appointed adjutant general to GHQ Staff in Dublin, following the arrest of the IRA chief of staff Brian Keenan, who was immediately replaced by Martin McGuinness. Adams told supporters at Wolf Tone's graveside that Sinn Fein was 'opposed to all forms and manifestations of imperialism and capitalism. We stand for an Ireland free, united, socialist and Gaelic . . . our most glaring weakness lies in our failure to develop revolutionary politics and to build an alternative to so-called constitutional politics.'

In spite of the rhetoric, security specialists doubted that Adams' reported conversion to Marxism was genuine. An assessment stated: 'No evidence of real understanding of Marxist philosophy. Manipulator. A very capable organiser. No discernible vices.'

On 27 August the IRA proved Roy Mason wrong. A radio-activated bomb attached to the yacht of seventy-nine-year-old Lord Mountbatten killed the Queen's cousin outright, along with three others including his fourteen-year-old grandson. The explosion happened at Mullaghmore, County Sligo, where Mountbatten had holidayed every summer for the previous thirty years, staunchly refusing a bodyguard. Mountbatten had been supreme commander of allied forces in south-east Asia during the Second World War and later the last Viceroy of India. The Indian government announced a week of mourning for him at the news of the atrocity.

Just a few hours later, on the other side of Ireland, eighteen soldiers were killed in an IRA landmine attack at Narrow Water, Warrenpoint, near Newry. It was the Army's greatest loss of life in any one incident since the Second World War. Later *Time* magazine quoted Adams as saying that he believed the assassination of Mountbatten and the soldiers achieved its objective in as much as 'people started paying attention to what was happening in Ireland'. Denying in the same magazine that he was the mastermind he said: 'No one man could have done everything they said I did.'

But the security forces had no doubt that, as a member of the IRA's Army Council, Adams would have had to have given his approval to both atrocities, in particular the murder of Lord Mountbatten, because it took place within the Irish Republic and it was rare for operations to be sanctioned there. The operations were 'spectaculars' in IRA terms, but the long-term effects outweighed the brief boost to morale. First there was an upsurge in the number of Catholics killed in sectarian slayings. The RUC regained outright control of the intelligence and security battle and numbers were increased by a thousand. The following month the Pope visited Ireland but abandoned a visit to Armagh city, seat of the Churches, because of the recent atrocities.

In Drogheda he told a congregation of 250,000: 'On my knees I beg of you to turn away from the paths of violence and to return to the ways of peace . . . do not follow any leaders who train you in the ways of inflicting death. Those who resort to violence always claim that only violence brings about change. You must know that there is a political, peaceful way to justice.' The IRA responded two days later by issuing a statement saying that 'force is by far the only means of removing the evil of the British presence in Ireland . . . we know also that upon victory the Church would have no difficulty in recognising us.'

By the end of the year Adams was confidently writing: 'That the British face military defeat is inevitable and obvious . . . the IRA's struggle would be sufficient to secure victory.' He also openly stated that a united Ireland meant that the Irish Republic's government 'must come down'. The decade of the 1970s was ending on a high note for the Provisionals, but a new kind of front in the war was about to open to Adams.

CHAPTER THIRTEEN

The Hunger Strikes

In the first week of 1980 Adams was arrested. By the time he was released seven days later three Ulster Defence Regiment members had been killed by a 1,000lb booby-trap bomb, bringing the official death toll in the Troubles to 2,000, and a policeman had been shot dead by the IRA inside North Belfast's Seaview soccer ground during an Irish League match. The new decade seemed to be following the same grim pattern as the 1970s.

But if the pattern of IRA attacks on the security forces and the arrests of Provisionals appeared to point to little change, the 1980s was to be the decade when Adams' opportunity to move the republican movement into politics came to fruition and the Armalite, the favourite rifle of the Provisionals, was complemented by the ballot box of Sinn Fein. The circumstances of the shift were unexpected and uninvited. The hunger strikes proved to be a turning point.

The building of a political party was something which even those who never saw eye to eye with Adams could not help but admire. Father Denis Faul often visited Adams in jail. 'If anybody had said to me at the time when he was leaving Long Kesh that the Provos would have had an active political party going after a while I would have laughed at them, I would have said that's insane, they're just physical-force men. It was a major achievement for him, by hook or by crook. I don't know how he did it.'

It was made possible above all by the sacrifices of some of his former prison comrades. But as the decade began his vision of a more overtly political future appeared to be a minority view within the IRA and Sinn Fein. In April 1980 he wrote in *Republican News* that 'a British withdrawal can be secured more quickly and in more favourable conditions if it is achieved not only because of the IRA military threat but also because resistance to British rule has been channelled and built into an alternative political movement'. This questioning of the speed or effectiveness with which the IRA could defeat the British by military means alone provoked some controversy within Provisional leadership circles.

Adams' instinctive interest in political activity wasn't shared by others who were fearful that time and money devoted to politics could be better spent on the war. Although the Sinn Fein *ard fheis* in 1978 had agreed to field candidates in local government elections in the Irish Republic it had turned down the opportunity to fight the 1979 European parliamentary elections.

Thus in June 1979 Adams had been reduced to a place on the sidelines when Bernadette McAliskey, a former Westminster MP, a staunch republican socialist and a heroine of the civil rights campaigns, put her name forward for the election.

The candidate who topped the poll, the Democratic Unionist Party leader Ian Paisley, appealed to his supporters on the basis of strengthening the union and resisting what he portrayed as the overbearing influence of the Catholic Church within the European Community. The SDLP's John Hume promised to fight the scourge of unemployment. But the issue that Bernadette McAliskey chose to fight on was the campaign by republican prisoners protesting against the loss of their political or special-category status.

On the face of it this issue should have been an ideal platform for Sinn Fein. But although McAliskey had the support of some individual IRA prisoners and their relatives, the republican movement as a whole threw their weight against her. McAliskey's decision to press on alone was seen as a challenge to the authority of the IRA Army Council, who had chosen to demonstrate their support for the prisoners not by contesting elections but by murdering prison officers. There were some physical clashes between Provisionals loyal to the leadership and supporters of McAliskey.

In the event McAliskey, buoyed up by her personal reputation and considerable public speaking abilities, drew a respectable level of support. She garnered just under 34,000 votes, which represented 5.9 per cent of the valid poll. The prisoners' grievances on which McAliskey campaigned had their roots in the stategy of 'criminaliza-tion' which the government adopted in the mid-1970s. Ministers believed that just as internment without trial had been an own goal in terms of the international image of the United Kingdom, so the granting of special status to paramilitary prisoners allowed republicans to portray the conflict in Northern Ireland as a war and themselves as soldiers.

After the ceasefires and talks of 1972 and 1975 a new regime was envisaged to coincide with the physical rebuilding of the Maze jail. But the refusal to wear 'a convict's uniform' had been central to previously successful hunger strikes and IRA prisoners felt honour bound to resist any measure which could lead to them being portrayed as common criminals. By the time political or special-category status was removed on 1 March 1976 the IRA had ended its ceasefire and was in no mood to co-operate with the authorities.

The first prisoner to be sentenced under the new regime was Ciaran Nugent, who was found guilty of hijacking a van. As a result of his refusal to wear prison uniform Nugent wore nothing at all and was placed in a cell wrapped in a blanket. Other IRA prisoners, although by no means all of them, followed Nugent's example. The protest by the 'blanket men' continued month after month, but the authorities, for their part, refused to budge.

With neither side prepared to give ground the dispute escalated both inside and outside jail. On the outside, the IRA embarked on a deadly campaign against prison officers. The first victim of this campaign, Peter Dillon, was murdered on 5 April 1976, and by 1980 eighteen prison officers had been killed. Inside the jail in 1978 the prisoners clashed with the authorities over the conditions in which they were allowed to go to the washroom or the toilet. They were allowed a single towel with which to to dry themselves but nothing to cover their bodies. On the ground that this meant they would be naked in the washrooms they refused to leave their cells. This 'no wash' protest quickly developed into a fully fledged 'dirty protest', with the prisoners pouring urine out of the cracks under their cell doors and smearing their excrement on the cell walls.

In 1978 the head of the Catholic Church in Ireland, Tomas O Fiaich, made two visits to the jail. In a public statement after the second visit in July 1978 the Archbishop said that he was 'shocked by the inhumane conditions' inside the H Blocks. 'One would hardly allow an animal to remain in such conditions, let alone a human being. The nearest approach to it that I have seen was the spectacle of hundreds of homeless people living in sewer pipes in the slums of

THE HUNGER STRIKES | 169

Calcutta. The stench and filth in some of the cells, with the remains of rotten food and human excreta scattered around the walls, was almost unbearable. In two of them [the cells] I was unable to speak for fear of vomiting.'

O Fiaich implicitly supported the prisoners' demand for special treatment when he pointed out that:

> the authorities refuse to admit that these prisoners are in a different category from the ordinary, yet everything about their trials and family background indicates that they are different. They were sentenced by special courts without juries. The vast majority were convicted on allegedly voluntary confessions obtained in circumstances which are now placed under grave suspicion by the recent report from Amnesty International. Many are very youthful and come from families which have never been in trouble with the law, though they lived in areas which suffered discrimination in housing and jobs. How can one explain the jump in the prison population of Northern Ireland from 500 to 3,000 unless a new type of prisoner has emerged?

The statement from O Fiaich provoked a storm of controversy, with the Irish primate under attack not only from Protestants in Northern Ireland but also from some of his fellow Catholics in England. The Northern Ireland Office signalled that it had no intention of moving in the face of the dirty protest, saying in a statement: 'These criminals are totally responsible for the situation in which they find themselves. It is they who have been smearing excreta on the walls and pouring urine through cell doors. It is they who by their actions are denying themselves the excellent modern facilities of the prison ... They are not political prisoners; more than 80 have been convicted of murder or attempted murder and more than 80 of explosives offences ... No one who is convicted of a crime carried out after 1 March 1976 – and that includes those involved in the "dirty" protest – will be given any form of special status. As soon as this decision is understood and accepted, conditions in the cell blocks can return to normal.'

As a fellow Provisional and a former jail-mate of many of those involved in the protest inside the Maze, Adams supported the demand for special treatment without question. But there was a reluctance to turn the prisoners issue into the focus of political agitation. The failure to concentrate much attention on the prisoners' grievances was illustrated by a review of the year 1979 in *Republican News*. Amid three pages on the events of the past twelve months Sinn Fein's own journal devoted just one throwaway sentence to the jail dispute: 'And with the H Block struggle three years old that was another thing for Republicans not to be happy about.'

Adams may have still been feeling his way forward politically at the time Bernadette McAliskey fought the 1979 European election, but he learned his lesson well and quickly. On 21 October 1979 he proposed the main motion at a special conference at the Green Briar restaurant in Andersonstown in West Belfast called on behalf of the 'National H Block Armagh Committee', an organization designed to reflect the interests of both the male republican prisoners housed in the H Blocks at the Maze and the females held in Armagh jail.

The Green Briar conference mirrored the meetings of prisoners' relatives which had been a feature of Bernadette McAliskey's European election campaign, but this time McAliskey was away on a trip to America, leaving Gerry Adams and his supporters firmly in charge. Ciaran Nugent, the first blanket man, addressed the conference, describing life in the H Blocks. The protest had by now lasted so long that Nugent had served his sentence and been released. Adams himself tabled Sinn Fein's motion which listed the prisoners' 'five demands'. They were:

1. To be exempt from wearing prison clothes
2. To be exempt from prison work
3. To have freedom of association with fellow political prisoners
4. The right to organize educational and recreational facilities, to have one weekly visit, to receive and send out one letter per week and to receive one parcel per week
5. Entitlement to full remission of sentence

While the specific reference to 'political prisoners' was later dropped the five demands were to remain crucial throughout the developing H Block protest. Adams, by putting forward the demands, had placed himself at the centre of the struggle. He also reversed the previous elitist attitude of the IRA and Sinn Fein to outside assistance. In the run up to McAliskey's campaign Sinn Fein had insisted that anyone who wished to support the prisoners' demands should also be 100 per cent committed to the IRA's violence. In a lurid term it denounced those who opposed the IRA's activities as 'domestic cockroaches'.

Adams realized that this purist position was mistaken. At the Green Briar conference he sought by contrast to promote as broad an alliance as possible, saying 'what we want is these people on the streets, no matter what their reason for supporting us may be'. In a test of just how far this tolerance could extend, the Peace People leader Ciaran McKeown was applauded for supporting the five demands, even though he insisted on telling those present that they should tip off the authorities about any IRA arms caches that they might be aware of.

The H Block campaign at last provided an opportunity for Gerry Adams to add substance to his talk of political activity. But there were risks as well as benefits to be assessed. The failure of the blanket, no-wash or dirty protests to achieve movement, and the steadfast nature of the government's response to the murder of prison officers, meant that the prisoners themselves were considering using a weapon of last resort. Fasting had been a tactic employed by republicans on occasion down through the decades but with mixed results. Those in favour pointed to the hunger strike of Billy McKee in 1972, which had won special status, and to the refusal to take food of Marion and Dolours Price, jailed for their part in bombing the Old Bailey and Scotland Yard in 1973. The Price sisters achieved their demand for a transfer from jail in England back to Northern Ireland after a protest interrupted by forced feeding which lasted more than 200 days.

By contrast there were other protests which had ended in defeat or embarrassment. The former IRA leader Sean MacStiofain embarked on a hunger strike when arrested in the Irish Republic but gave it up without having won his demands. MacStiofain's standing within the IRA was effectively destroyed by the exercise. In 1976 Frank Stagg died after refusing food in Wakefield prison for sixty days. He too had been seeking repatriation to a jail nearer his home. The lasting memory of Stagg's protest had been a macabre struggle between his family and the IRA over who should have the right to bury his emaciated body.

The H Block prisoners had asked for permission to embark on a hunger strike to coincide with the Pope's visit to Ireland in 1979. The

IRA Army Council decided that the time was not ripe. Then in 1980 Martin Meehan, an IRA man from Ardoyne in North Belfast, decided to launch a one-man hunger strike without the IRA leadership's authorization. Meehan's role in the IRA in the early 1970s had been almost legendary, with his public boasts of involvement in a series of IRA attacks, including the longest gun battle with the Army near the border at Dundalk. But Meehan was incensed to find himself in jail on a conviction – conspiracy to kidnap – which he claimed was false. He refused food for sixty-six days but then was persuaded to give up by Cardinal O Fiaich.

Meehan's inconclusive protest damaged his own standing within the IRA and gave the Army Council pause for thought about the H Block prisoners' demand for a larger-scale protest. But eventually the IRA leadership gave the prisoners the go ahead and seven prisoners started to refuse food from 27 October 1980. Adams, reflecting on the mixed results of previous strikes, maintains that he at first resisted the idea of a hunger strike, fearing it would divert attention from his plans to fight elections on broader political themes. But as the 1980 hunger strike got under way he was in day-to-day contact with Bobby Sands, the IRA's officer commanding inside the Maze, whom Adams knew well from their time together in Cage 11. Sands had taken over the job from Brendan 'Darkie' Hughes, who had been arrested alongside Adams back in 1973. Hughes had decided that if there was to be a hunger strike authorized by the Army Council he would have to lead from the front and be one of those refusing food.

The 1980 hunger strike is remembered by Adams as a traumatic time. It would also enter the republican annals as another inconclusive protest. The hunger strikers called their protest off on 18 December at a time when one of them, Sean McKenna, was seriously ill and in danger of losing his sight.

In the face of the strike the government held firm in public, but engaged in a good deal of secret shuttle diplomacy. The 'Mountain Climber', an MI6 agent subsequently identified as Michael Oatley, had been passing messages to Republicans through the 'Angel', a Catholic man acting as a go-between. On 18 December Brendan Hughes found himself in an impossible position. He knew that a message from the Mountain Climber was on its way to the prisoners and he had hopes that it might at last concede the bulk of the five demands. He and the other protesting prisoners were cut off from seeing their O/C, Bobby Sands, to take advice from the outside on what to do. At the same time they were well aware that Sean McKenna had been transferred to hospital in Belfast, where he was said to be dying. Hughes took a chance and called the strike off. It was only later when Hughes learned of the contents of the latest document from the Mountain Climber that he realized that it wasn't the government capitulation he had been hoping for. The hunger strikers, not the government, had given in.

The protest ended in confusion. Some republicans engaged in wild celebration, believing they had won. Adams, who was privy to the fine print of the messages from the government, regarded the compromises on offer as unacceptable. He was despondent, aware that long-term agreement was unlikely and yet hesitant about the prisoners' swiftly expressed desire to embark on a new hunger strike to fight what they saw as an act of betrayal by the authorities.

During the period between the end of the 1980 hunger strike and the start of a new protest in March 1981 Adams kept in touch with the prisoners through the highly organized system of 'comms', messages written in tiny writing on sheets of toilet and cigarette paper which were then passed between prisoners and their visitors. The messages, if intercepted by the authorities, were confiscated, so the 'comms' system depended on secrecy with the little balls of paper, often wrapped in cling film, hidden away in people's mouths, or inside their anal passages.

In January 1981 Adams, referred to under the same pseudonym of 'Brownie' which he had used in *Republican News*, received a message from 'Bik' – Brendan McFarlane, an IRA man imprisoned for bombing the Bayardo bar on the Protestant Shankill Road in 1975, an explosion which killed five people. McFarlane had taken over as the IRA's O/C in the jail. Bobby Sands, like Brendan Hughes before him, had handed over his responsibilities as leader in expectation of a new hunger strike, which Sands intended to lead by example.

McFarlane told Adams how an experimental programme of normalization within the jail was progressing. He was concerned that a week's delay in the simultaneous issue of prison uniforms and civilian clothes might presage an attempt by the prison authorities to induce his men once more into a 'convict's uniform'. McFarlane said the prisoners had told the jail governor that 'as an indication of our good will and willingness and sincerity we had decided that either tomorrow or Saturday ten men from here and ten from H5 would wash, shave etc. This will now be held back till next Tuesday in keeping with AC [Army Council] directive to seek a principled settlement. The Brits may be stalling. We believe they wish to compromise us on the principle of clothes and, by a week's respite, they may gain some ground.' In a somewhat delphic comment which demonstrated Adams' standing, McFarlane added: 'We will comm other blocks on the situation, but if you feel that another AC job is necessary bang one in . . . So take yourself off, you horror picture. See you around. Take care and God Bless – Bik.'

The experiments at normalization broke down, and in February 1981 a new hunger strike was announced to begin the following month. Published 'comms' indicate that the strike was a result of the prisoners' own decision, against the thrust of some of the advice given them by the IRA Army Council. Adams wrote and informed Bobby Sands of his tactical, strategic, physical and moral opposition to another hunger strike. At the same time there was no doubt that this hunger strike, led by Sands as former O/C, had general IRA authorization, and Adams took a central public role as chair of Sinn Fein's hunger strike committee.

The Dungannon priest Father Denis Faul was a frequent visitor to the prisoners – he recognized that they meant business and that in Bobby Sands and Bik McFarlane the prisoners had 'two men with excellent leadership qualities'. Faul felt that prisoners believed that if the 1980 hunger strike had:

> only gone on for a day longer they would have won . . . I don't believe a word of that. But unfortunately I think Sands believed it. He was the newly appointed leader and his strategy, it was a very good strategy, was that he went on himself, so it was Sands face to face [with the British government].
>
> He said to me himself, 'I'll stop the ill-treatment of prisoners in here, I'll stop it.' And I put a lot of points to him about the tragedy for his own family and the grief of his relations and the terrible commotion it would cause in the whole community – people talk about ten dying in Long Kesh, there was sixty died outside – I said to him, 'Bobby this is too big a price to pay,' and he said, 'Well, greater love hath no man than this that a man lays down his life for his friends,' and I said, 'I can't argue with that

Bobby,' so I left it there. I could have argued with it, I could have pointed out that his responsibilities were broader than the prison, but having been in prison nearly all of the seventies he lived in the prison world and he couldn't see a world outside it.

That was his world, he wasn't even interested in seeing his relatives, he loved the prisoners. Bobby Sands always reminded me of the captain of the football team and if a fight started at the other end of the field he wouldn't think about himself, he'd run the length of the field to get into the fight and defend his comrades. But at the same time he was rather an aloof type, you couldn't get in close to him. He could be seen as one of the great prison reformers of the twentieth century.

Sands wasn't ever going to be persuaded by Faul, whom he referred to in 'comms' as 'Denis the Menace' after the popular cartoon character. Sands started to refuse food on 1 March, the fifth anniversary of the end of special-category status. In contrast to the 1980 hunger strike the protesting prisoners staggered the beginning of their hunger strikes so that, if the dispute remained unresolved, their deaths would have a greater, more drawn out impact. On 1 March Sinn Fein held a march in West Belfast, but second time around it was difficult to generate the same level of support: 3,500 people turned out, in contrast to 10,000 four months previously.

The impact of the protest and its significance for Gerry Adams and Sinn Fein were to be changed radically by a death, but not the death of one of the hunger strikers. On 5 March, only five days into Bobby Sands' hunger strike, Frank Maguire, the independent nationalist MP for Fermanagh and South Tyrone, suffered a fatal heart attack. Maguire held the seat at Westminster from 1974 onwards but rarely attended, indeed by the time of his death he had still not made a maiden speech. He did, however, take a strong interest in prisoners' issues and, it was expected that this tradition would be continued by the likely successor, Frank's brother Noel. But Bernadette McAliskey had a different idea. She was recovering from injuries she had sustained in a gun attack by the loyalist Ulster Freedom Fighters at her home in Coalisland. Even though she was still on crutches, McAliskey recognized the potential of a by-election for raising the prisoners' case once again, in the same way she had done in the European election of 1979. While she recognized that the brother of the former MP would benefit from the sense of loyalty felt among Fermanagh nationalists, she was unwilling to stand aside for Noel Maguire, whom she regarded as the candidate of the Catholic establishment.

A McAliskey candidacy would have been a campaign for the hunger strikers by proxy. But some republicans were pondering their mistakes during the 1979 European election and considering whether it wouldn't be more sensible to cut out any middle man or woman. There was sharp division over the wisdom of such a course of action. 'Mike', an IRA member at the time, was an enthusiastic supporter of putting Bobby Sands into the fray. 'I got pulled over the coals. After it came over that Frank Maguire had just died I said that we should put up Sands as a candidate and a member of the Army Council lit on me and said, "It is policy not to contest and I don't want to hear it any more." But it was a golden opportunity, I think we had to grasp it regardless.' He remembers Adams opposing the suggestion. 'I think he was scared of losing. Bobby Sands standing and losing would have been disastrous.'

It was Dave O'Connell who first pushed the idea, but one of Adams' most faithful lieutenants, Jim Gibney, was soon convinced that the by-election had to be fought. Gibney called on McAliskey at her home in Coalisland on 18 March and told her that Bobby Sands was willing to run and Noel Maguire had decided not to stand against the hunger striker. Gibney said the local radio news would soon be carrying a statement from Noel Maguire confirming his decision. The Maguire statement wasn't broadcast but by the evening, when Belfast's Downtown Radio asked McAliskey if she would stand against Sands, she said she would not oppose him but instead would sign his nomination papers and 'work the shirt off my back' to see him elected. Sands' campaign was up and running.

Bringing Noel Maguire on-side was a rather more difficult business. Even Sinn Fein's own organization in Fermanagh was not convinced that a prisoner candidate could win the seat. Adams accompanied Gibney on a visit to the Maguires' home in Lisnaskea, putting forward their argument that republicans only wanted to 'borrow' the Fermanagh and South Tyrone seat in order to save the lives of Sands and his fellow hungers strikers. The SDLP's Austin Currie had made it clear that if Noel Maguire withdrew he would enter the race, while the Catholic hierarchy did not want the field left open to the IRA's candidate.

In the event the scene at the close of nominations outside the local electoral office in Dungannon could hardly have been more dramatic. A crowd of republicans and reporters waited as the 4 p.m. deadline approached to see if Noel Maguire would arrive and withdraw his nomination papers, which had already been lodged. Gerry Adams paced to and fro, a statement tucked in his pocket explaining Sands' withdrawal from the race – a contingency plan in case Maguire decided not to withdraw. Panicking as the minutes ticked by, he even phoned the republican leadership in Dublin to try and persuade them that they should withdraw Sands immediately and save themselves the later humiliation. Then with just thirteen minutes to go Noel Maguire arrived to take himself out of the race.

Some onlookers said Maguire appeared angry – accusations were later made that he had been physically intimidated. But Maguire himself didn't substantiate this, and as the campaign proper got under way he lent his name to Sands' campaign, saying, 'I have been told the only way of saving Bobby Sands' life is by letting him go forward in the elections. I just cannot have the life of another man on my hands. I am calling on my supporters to throw their weight behind Bobby Sands.'

Austin Currie, who was later to move south and become an Irish government minister, was left fulminating on the sidelines. He had positioned one of his supporters inside Noel Maguire's bar in Lisnaskea with orders to alert him if there was any sign that Maguire intended to head to Dungannon to withdraw. But when it came to it the hapless man found that all the available telephone lines were kept busy and Currie was left out of the race.

Adams had been advocating increased political activity – now he found himself at the centre of the most high-profile by-election in many years. He took a role running the Dungannon office. Sands wrote to Adams in a 'comm' from his bed in the prison hospital, 'How are ya! Got your note. Seems we've well and truly entered new realms. Hopefully we'll be successful if only for the Movement's sake ... Seen ya on TV, ya big ugly hunk, you haven't changed a bit. I'm not at all building hopes on anything. I'm afraid I'm just resigned to the worse.'

On the outside Adams had to learn quickly the new arts of electoral politics. It was an education for the Provisionals. Bernadette McAliskey gave a long explanation to some of them about the various procedures involved. When one of them confessed that 'This is more complicated than stripping an Armalite,' McAliskey replied, 'Yes, but more fun.' The by-election campaign mobilized a broad nationalist alliance, including McAliskey, an SDLP councillor Tommy Murray and a radical priest Father Joe McVeigh. It also invoked the deeply held religious beliefs of Fermanagh's predominantly Catholic population, with decades of the rosary recited at the end of election rallies heavy with the pall of Sands' imminent death.

Gerry McGeough remembered Adams' zeal for infiltrating and taking over organizations as beyond the call of duty for many republicans. 'On one occasion Gerry Adams joined a group of us as we prepared to address a large crowd of bingo patrons at the Eglish Gaelic Athletic Association Club near Dungannon. A particularly belligerent little SDLP club-member barred our entry and we were obliged to deliver our message from the sidewalk while the crowd left as opposed to haranguing them from the stage during a gaming interval. Adams' recommendation afterwards, as I recall, was that we should infiltrate such bodies, though quite frankly the prospect of joining the Eglish Bingo Committee was beyond even the intensity of our patriotic zeal.'

The poll took place on 9 April 1981. When he heard the result Adams was listening to his car radio driving back from Clones just south of the border. Sands was victorious, securing 30,492 votes, a majority of 1,446 over his only opponent, unionist Harry West. Adams thumped his steering wheel, shouting, 'Fuck it, we've done it, we've done it!' The contrast struck him between this high-profile victory and his first experience of elections folding leaflets for Liam McMillen, who lost his deposit fighting West Belfast in 1964.

Sands' election made it that much more difficult for the government to portray the hunger strike as a little local difficulty. Now, the man starving to death inside the Maze prison was an elected member of the Westminster parliament. On 28 April President Reagan said the USA would not intervene in the affairs of Northern Ireland but he was 'deeply concerned at the tragic situation'. As Bobby Sands came closer to death the international media focused its attention on the dispute and tension increased on the streets in nationalist areas. A two-man delegation from the European Commission for Human Rights visited the jail and tried to visit Sands in an attempt to mediate but was turned away by the hunger striker because he wanted his 'advisers', Gerry Adams and Danny Morrison, present. A visit from the Pope's envoy Father John Magee also produced nothing in the way of progress. As Sands' condition deteriorated, the convicted bomber Bik McFarlane expressed his frustration in another 'comm' to Adams: 'I think your analysis of the Brit mentality is about as close as anyone can come i.e. their stupidity is unbelievable . . . However, as you said, they will regret their stupidity. How I wish I were out – just to light the blue touch paper and retire if you know what I mean!! Old habits die hard though some of mine had to be re-directed as you well know.'

On Sunday 3 May 1981, Bobby Sands lapsed into a coma, and at 1.17 a.m. on the morning of Tuesday 5 May he died. Adams was in a house in West Belfast when he heard the news. Soon the sound of the bin lids banging on the ground could be heard throughout the area. Adams made his way to the Sinn Fein centre on the Falls Road, where fighting was breaking out between local teenagers and police and Army patrols. Inside he and Danny Morrison started a long round of interviews with the international media about Sands' death. At 2.15 a.m. Brendan McFarlane wrote another emotional 'comm' to Adams:

> Comrade Mor, I just heard the news – I'm shattered – just can't believe it. This is a terrible feeling I have. I don't even know what to say. Comrade, I'm sorry, but I just can't say anything else. May God in his infinite mercy grant eternal rest to his soul. Jesus Christ protect and guide us all.
>   God Bless.
>   xoxo Bik xoxo

Sands' death resounded far beyond the walls of the Maze prison and Northern Ireland's disputed border. Around the world newspapers wrote editorials expressing sympathy with someone who had been willing to sacrifice all for a cause he believed in. Tens of thousands of people lined the route of his funeral procession through West Belfast. The funeral oration was given by Owen Carron, who had been Sands' election agent in Fermanagh and South Tyrone and who would be the man selected by Sinn Fein to fight the by-election made necessary by Sands' death. 'Bobby Sands,' Carron pledged, 'your sacrifice will not be in vain.'

Father Denis Faul summed up the sense of admiration felt by those who entirely disagreed with the IRA's use of violence. 'It amazed me as a Catholic priest. Asceticism and penance is our game, we follow a crucified master, we're supposed to do penance, fasting, abstain and go on retreat and remain in silence locked up for a week every year and here were these boys beating us at our own game. They were making sacrifices, dying for one another, which is our game. We talk about Jesus Christ dying for us, that's the big point of our religion, and in a Christian country this has a colossal effect. In a Christian country like Ireland not only the Catholics couldn't but admire it, but Protestants even couldn't but admire it. They couldn't understand it, it terrified them that these men were prepared to go so far.'

The election and death of Sands represented a high-water mark for republicanism, which had achieved favourable public comment throughout the world and a flood of fresh recruits to the IRA and Sinn Fein closer to home. Denis Faul fulminated against what he saw as the government's stupidity in allowing the strike to go so far. 'You'd have this wake and it was highly organized by Sinn Fein. I remember Jimmy Drumm was the main man and you'd have the wake, this emaciated body in the coffin and these fellas standing guard of honour with balaclavas over their faces, and then if the British could only have stood in the corner and watched this procession of young people, boys and girls, teenagers coming in and stopping and looking into this coffin ... Jesus, they were on a loser. The whole countryside was being swung to Sinn Fein and the IRA, it was unbelievable, especially out in the country.'

But the British government weren't ready to capitulate, and the Provisionals, rather than cash in on their achievements quickly, were determined to push on in the hope of outright victory. Mark Lenaghan, who was one of the IRA's colour party at Bobby Sands' funeral, recalled it as 'a frenzied, very, very tense, highly emotional period for us who were personally and intimately connected with the hunger strikers and their families. We believed passionately in them ... it was a very, very sad, very, very dark period.' Lenaghan had joined the IRA in 1978 and says that 'no one was as committed to the IRA as I was in 1981 ... the IRA just had to say jump and we would have said how high. We wouldn't have asked any questions about the who, the where, or why of it. It was just we had a role, we had a function, and that job was to send as many soldiers as possible home in coffins and boxes back to Britain.'

The rollcall of IRA attacks went on, and inside the jail the conditions of Bobby Sands' fellow hunger strikers continued to deteriorate. Sands had lasted sixty-six days. He was followed by Francis Hughes after fifty-nine days, Raymond McCreesh after 61 days, Patsy O'Hara after sixty-one days and Joe McDonnell after sixty-one days. At McDonnell's funeral Adams became concerned about how large a security operation the police and Army were mounting and how close their vehicles appeared to be to the cortège. When a three-strong IRA colour party emerged to fire a volley of shots over the coffin the Army watched closely from a helicopter hovering above, as the men wearing berets and uniforms melted into the crowd and made their way to a safe house in St Agnes Drive.

An Army unit rushed around to the house in time to challenge a man with a gun who was clambering out of the kitchen window. Lance Corporal Mark Adams shouted, 'Army! Stop or I'll fire.' The man appeared to turn, still holding his gun, so the soldier fired one shot at him. The two other IRA men ran off, escaping from the soldiers with the help of a hail of bricks and bottles thrown by Joe McDonnell's mourners. But the Army broke into the house and found the wounded man. They dragged him into an armoured Saracen vehicle and took him off under arrest. He was Paddy Adams, Gerry Adams' younger brother.

On 27 July 1981 Paddy Adams was charged with the possession of three rifles with intent to endanger life at a special court hearing inside Belfast's Musgrave Park Hospital, where he was recovering from his wounds. On the same day his brother Gerry was giving press interviews denying that he wanted the hunger strike to carry on because of its propaganda value. As the protest continued, its anti-British publicity value was becoming dissipated amid a welter of reports suggesting that it was the IRA not the government which was increasingly the most obdurate party. In a 'comm' from Bik McFarlane, Adams learned that the prisoners were so enthused by Sands' electoral victory that they were seriously contemplating the dropping of abstentionism in the Irish Republic and taking seats in Leinster House where they could be won.

After Sands' death there were a number of attempts to try to find a compromise, involving the Red Cross, the Irish government, constitutional nationalist politicians and most notably the Catholic Church's Irish Commission on Justice and Peace. In June 1981 the ICJP tried to build bridges by proposing that the government give ground on the first three of the hunger strikers' five demands. They pointed out that women prisoners in Armagh already had their own clothes, so there was no good reason why it shouldn't be extended to the men in the Maze; there could be more association between prisoners without it amounting to the military-style organization of the jail, which had been the case during internment; and more emphasis could be placed on work which had educational or cultural value rather than prison work which appeared to be intended to punish or demean.

Rather than embrace this initiative as a creative solution, Adams and Brendan McFarlane looked on it with suspicion – as a compromise of the platform which Bobby Sands and the others had died for and no substitute for their basic requirement, face-to-face talks between republicans and the British. Adams was weighing up a number of factors at this point – the political benefits of continuing the strike were still evident, as two hunger strikers had been elected in the Irish parliamentary elections held in June. McFarlane jocularly congratulated Adams on this: 'We have effected the political change you spoke of. Congratulations, oh wise one!!' Republicans were also involved in further behind-the-scenes negotiations involving the Mountain Climber, Michael Oatley, which they believed would achieve more than the ICJP's public diplomacy.

But dismissing the Church's initiative ran risks of alienating outside support and even opening up doubts among the prisoners' relatives and the hunger strikers themselves. As things began to get more difficult, McFarlane appeared to be looking more and more to Adams for advice. On 16 June he reported that a priest visiting the jail had said that the family of one of the hunger strikers, Kevin Lynch, appeared to becoming more alienated after meeting Adams on the outside. 'The Lynch family intimated to that sagart [priest] that the impression they got from you, Pennies [Danny Morrison] etc. was that you were very unfeeling towards the hunger strikers and that you didn't care whether they died or not . . . I think we need to get those families on the right line of thought.'

In an attempt to explain the Provisionals' unyielding position to the ICJP, Adams breached the confidentiality of his contacts with the Mountain Climber and let the Commission know that back door discussions were under way with the Foreign Office. When the Commission raised this with the government, the Mountain Climber strongly protested about Adams' actions. But the secret contacts continued.

After the death of Joe McDonnell, however, the ICJP's initiative was dismissed by Sinn Fein and the hunger strikers and they were no longer major players. Disquiet continued in the ranks – Joe McDonnell's replacement on the hunger strike, Pat McGeown, expressed the view that they 'should not have cut out the Commission'. McGeown later fell back into line, but throughout this period he showed what was for the Provisionals a worrying tendency towards independent thought.

After the death of Martin Hurson, some of the adverse publicity began to centre not just on Adams but on McFarlane too. It was suggested that he should go on hunger strike himself rather than sit back and select those about to die. The Provisionals decided this was a bad idea, because they wanted an O/C able to run the protest throughout and also because McFarlane's conviction for the bombing of a Protestant pub had strong sectarian overtones and therefore made him a propaganda liability. McFarlane, however, found himself in a meeting with the hunger strikers having to deal with a suggestion from one of them, Thomas McElwee, that maybe he too should join the protest in order to counter reports about the hunger strikers just following orders.

McFarlane put the standard line, but in his heart he wasn't convinced, and it was to Adams, again operating under the pen-name 'Brownie,' that he put his appeal. 'I've always wanted to be in that front line and I haven't changed one iota. I should have been there *sin e* [no more, that's it] and I still want to be there. I've no need to tell you what degree of commitment I have or how much understanding of the situation I have. You know I'd do my best and I know I'd die *sin e*. I'll abide by your decision as I can do little else. If it's negative just say no. Please don't forward any explanations. I just wouldn't accept them and that's the truth, *cara* [friend]. I'd appreciate it also if you'd refrain from giving me a lecture!'

It is striking that given the constant insistence of Adams and other

Provisionals that the hunger strike was run from inside the jail, not outside, when it came to deciding if the O/C should join the protest it fell to Adams to make the decision. McFarlane didn't receive permission and instead continued with his onerous task of selecting others prepared to die.

Father Denis Faul had at first been convinced that the hunger strike was the prisoners' own idea in the face of their leadership's reluctance, but now as he witnessed the dismissal of the ICJP's initiative and the disquiet among hunger strikers' relatives he began to change his view. 'The prisoners might have demanded a hunger strike but once it began and they saw the massive publicity they were getting and the massive money they were getting and the massive build-up of these H Block committees, which were potential Sinn Fein *cumann* [branches], they [the IRA leadership] were all for it. I'm convinced the men were picked outside. A prison officer said to me that there was dead silence when the next name was announced.'

Faul decided he had to do something to break the impasse even if it made him extremely unpopular:

Cardinal O Fiaich had been over in London and he'd met Mrs Thatcher, who he found totally impossible, a woman of no understanding or comprehension at all of Ireland or Irish history. So the final straw was when the thing got rather heated and they decided they should have a drink and Cardinal O Fiaich asked for Irish whiskey and there was no Irish whiskey in Ten Downing Street – that just about finished it . . . We knew that she was a stupid woman and she wasn't going to give in.

I went to see a number of the prisoners' relatives including Mrs Lynch, a very saintly woman, and she says, 'Can nothing be done?' Her son Kevin was the next. And I was presented with this saintly countrywoman who had no interest in politics, despised the INLA and all they stood for but just wanted her son. So I said, 'Yes, we'll have to do something.' I went away and thought about it and prayed about it and then decided to get the relatives together, a couple of weeks after Hurson died. Of course I was well aware of the consequences. I had a lot of influence with the parents and relatives, mainly because of this business of fighting the torture.

Faul decided he had to work with the prisoners' families and, through them, ensure that the hunger strike was called off before more lives were thrown away:

So I got together some people and called the relatives together in the Taggarts Hotel in Toomebridge and we had a meeting there on the night of 28th July. We had a long discussion, Bernadette Devlin [McAliskey] was at it because Matt Devlin, a cousin of hers, was on the strike at that stage so she was able to come and we all agreed in Toomebridge that the thing should be stopped.

I explained the points that they'd got all the publicity that they're going to get and I explained to them, 'You'll probably get the other things when you stop, the Brits being the Brits they won't give you anything until you've stopped . . . Thatcher's not going to stop, the Cardinal's seen her and she's as thick as a wall. She doesn't understand what's going on and she'll just let them die one by one, it won't matter that each death is another nail in her coffin, certainly it's a nail in her policies.' I said six men have died, it's far too many. So we debated away for two or three hours in this hotel and then we came to the unanimous conclusion, everybody there including Bernadette Devlin agreed that we should stop.

Faul and the relatives realized they had two alternatives, either to release a statement to the press or to go to Sinn Fein. Faul told the families that he recalled a comment from Brendan McFarlane to the effect that 'the buck stops with Gerry Adams'.

We rang Sinn Fein HQ and asked Adams would he come up to meet us. Adams said he couldn't come for security reasons. So if the mountain won't go to Mohammed, Mohammed had to move. We said, 'We'll go down and see you.' We piled into our cars and we all went to the Falls Road to the Sinn Fein headquarters and we arrived there about 12.30 at night and stayed until 2.30 and Adams did all the talking.

He's a good talker. For a long time he wouldn't do anything for us. He said he couldn't do it, 'It's nothing to do with me.' One of the relatives from South Armagh, she was determined, her son was on the strike and her husband had died of cancer and she said, 'I'm not going through this a second time.' I went through all the points: 'We've got the clothes, Thatcher's going to let them die, we've got maximum publicity, if they come off they'll get all the other conditions.' By the time they [the families] got down to Adams they were pretty determined and they all spoke, but Adams went through the whole thing, saying he couldn't do anything.

Even though Adams wasn't giving him the answers he wanted to hear Father Faul couldn't help but admire the way in which he worked the families around. 'I remember he said to Mrs McGeown at that meeting, "I'll give you something to do, I'll get you some flags to go up tomorrow and picket [the Irish Prime Minister] Garrett Fitz-gerald's house in Dublin." You see, he has that cleverness that he involves people, he gets them to do little jobs. What the hell good was that to Mrs McGeown going and picketing a house and her husband was dying on hunger strike, but she was flattered. People are flattered to be asked. Irish people yield very easily to flattery. Even Adams yields to flattery. I said to him that night, "Gerry, you've answered all our questions in a wonderful way, even better than any barrister." He was very pleased.'

Faul finally deployed what he thought was his most persuasive line of attack. 'The argument we put in the end was "These are members of the IRA, these hunger strikers, they have to obey orders." Because the leadership had made a false move before that, because in early July they'd ordered everyone to change their solicitors, we knew that, and we used that in the sense that we said, "If the prisoners get orders they'll obey orders." Adams said, "Well, I'm not in the IRA." "No," we said, "but you would have contact with them." "Oh, it would take a long time," he said. We said it wouldn't take a long time. So in the end we said would you see the IRA and tell them it's the unanimous request of the relations that these men are to be ordered off the hunger strike. It's our decision and that's the end of it.'

Even in front of a gathering of the hunger strikers' closest relatives Adams stuck stoically to his line of not being in the IRA, even though he had the authority to decide if the IRA's jail O/C Brendan McFarlane could or could not join the hunger strike. In the words of fellow IRA member 'Mike': 'Adams was very much running the thing.

He would have been basically the main man on the H Block campaign and at that time he would also have been in a very powerful position within the Army Council, he would have held the top position.' 'Mike' says that holding that 'top position' didn't necessarily mean that Adams was the IRA's chief of staff:

The chief of staff doesn't have to be on the Army Council. The Army Council has seven members, all of equal status, and then you have the chairman of the Council. Quite often the chief of staff wouldn't even be on the Army Council. The chief of staff is a military role, he would be reporting to the Army Council; now quite often he is also on the Army Council, but not necessarily. The Army Council is the overall governing body, they would have control and would be directing and the chief of staff would report to them. The thing about Adams was that, if he wasn't chief of staff, whoever was chief of staff was one of his. Like when Twomey was chief of staff, Twomey was basically a puppet for Adams.

Father Faul didn't know precisely what position Adams held in the IRA but 'we knew that he was big in the thing and that his word would go. We knew that he'd be a credible emissary if he went in to Long Kesh and said, "Lads, the IRA say you have to stop." Now the IRA always put out a story that they told them not to start and they were disobeyed from the prison, but I never accepted that. You could have a big debate about whether the hunger strike was run from inside the prison or outside. My personal belief was that it was run from outside. McFarlane was appointed from outside, Sands was appointed from outside. The men to go on hunger strike, it was a combination of inside and outside.'

After two and a half hours' debate Faul said that much to his delight Adams agreed to go into the prison:

We were pleased and happy and we thought he was a decent fellow and that he had humanity. Then the next day I went to Cardinal O Fiaich's house and said we've got to get this man into the jail, he's agreed to go in and ask them to come off. So Cardinal O Fiaich arranged it. Adams went in and he came out, no change. What did dismay me was when I was in Cardinal

O Fiaich's house and I was on the phone to Gerry Adams arranging this, he said, 'I want to bring somebody in with me,' and I said 'Who?' and he says, 'Owen Carron.' My heart sank to my boots because Owen Carron was the candidate for the Fermanagh South Tyrone election for 20th August to take the place of Bobby Sands, an election which they told us they only wanted to 'borrow' to save the life of Bobby Sands.

After having promised that they were only going to borrow the seat they put up a Sinn Fein candidate. His only hope of getting in was the hunger strike. I don't know what transpired inside, whether he saw them individually or whether he saw them in a group, but I know the Lynch brothers came out raging. They wouldn't speak to Adams. I don't know what happened, but I know he didn't do the job he was sent in to do. The feeling I had was that political considerations dominated: from the very start of the hunger strikes Sinn Fein wanted to negotiate face to face with the Brits.

Adams' own account of the crucial meeting inside the jail is, predictably, different in tone to Father Faul's. He describes his encounter inside the jail canteen with Brendan McFarlane and hunger strikers Tom McElwee, Laurence McKeown, Matt Devlin, Pat McGeown, Paddy Quinn and Mickey Devine as a fairly hopeless exercise in trying to point out to men determined to continue their course of action that they had the option to come off the strike at any stage. According to Adams all the hunger strikers remained committed to the five demands as the only price for ending their protest. He warned them that they might well die; they answered 'so be it'. Amid the serious discussion, the strikers took some time to engage in a bit of banter, chiding Adams over the amount of their water which he was drinking. Didn't he realize, they asked, how much the water was costing the British government?

Two hunger strikers were too ill to make it to the canteen – Adams visited Kieran Doherty and found the prisoner and his family very supportive. Kevin Lynch was too ill to talk, but Adams did meet his brother and father and by all accounts this exchange was more difficult. Adams says Kevin Lynch's father told him of his suffering in the face of Britain's failure to concede, saying, 'To rear a son and see him die like this.' Other accounts suggest the old man blamed Adams for his son's impending death and asked him why he didn't take him off the strike, to which Adams replied that the family could take him off but he couldn't. Certainly the exchange must have been more traumatic than Adams' description indicates, because afterwards Brendan McFarlane wrote to Adams that 'Kevin's [family] shattered me. I've never experienced anything like that in my life. How can you get people to understand and view things in a clear light? Looking back I realize you were right in not pursuing the conversation, but I just felt I had to try to get them to see things in a true light. But then what can one say in such a situation?'

The hunger strike continued and 'Denis the Menace' Faul found himself being increasingly vilified in republican newspapers and magazines. 'So after that I said, "Okay, I'll take them off one by one," and I did it from then until October. I went to the relatives and explained the whole thing, most of them were quite agreeable . . . so then the relatives started taking them off.'

The first relative to intervene in this way was Mrs Catherine Quinn, who saw her son Paddy screaming and struggling in an epileptic fit and 'couldn't bear his suffering'. The decision marked a turning point in the protest, but there were to be four more deaths before it was all over. Kevin Lynch's family, despite their anguish, wouldn't go against their son's wishes and take him off the strike. Lynch was followed by Kieran Doherty and Thomas McElwee. The last hunger striker to die, Michael Devine, lasted sixty-six days. The day of his death, 20 August, was also the day of Owen Carron's election in the by-election to replace Bobby Sands. Carron had been chosen because the government had introduced a law preventing any more convicted prisoners like Sands standing for parliament.

Sinn Fein and Gerry Adams had thus squeezed the last drop of electoral advantage out of the hunger strike by the time they realized that they might need Father Faul to help them avoid a situation in which the historic protest ended in ignominy. As Michael Devine died, Pat McGeown's wife was taking her husband off the hunger strike. The families of Matt Devlin and Laurence McKeown followed suit. Father Faul saw that things were moving in his direction:

> They realized they had to stop it, that if they went much further they'd be the laughing stock of the country. So about the last week in September I had a ring from Jim Gibney of Sinn Fein

and he asked me would I like to meet the relatives in the Lake Glen Hotel and I said certainly.

And lo and behold when I lifted the papers on the Sunday next there was a big attack on me, this conniving deceitful priest who'd upset the hunger strike relatives and put unfair pressure on them. When I got to the Lake Glen Hotel there was two or three Sinn Fein people and I said to them, 'Listen, I've read your statement in the Sunday press, now I'd like you to leave the room.' And I spoke to the relatives and a few of them came up to me and they said, 'You talk, we don't know how to talk, we don't want the boy to die, we've no interest in this carry-on, but we can't talk because they'll blackmail us with the boy who's on hunger strike.' There was one family who attacked me all right but I didn't mind because they were highly emotional people at that stage. Then the hunger strikes ended the following Saturday.

Even if at the end there had been some liaison between Faul and Sinn Fein the IRA prisoners were in no mood to forgive him for helping 'break' the hunger strike. 'The next couple of times up at Long Kesh when I went in to say Mass they just got up and walked out and I haven't been allowed into the Provo quarters since. They wouldn't let me in to say Mass. You see, I interfered, they didn't give a damn, I thought, about how many men died, but the important thing was that they should come face to face with the British. And I'm looking at exactly the same scenario now, the whole events of the last two years [1995–6] in connection with the so-called peace process. The whole thing is worked out tactically, there was violence and there was a tactic and then another tactic. As you can see the whole thing has been done to get Sinn Fein face to face with the British.'

The IRA man 'Mike' had, like the prisoners, no time for Father Faul, who he believed was a 'Brit agent using the families against the prisoners'. 'Mike's' criticisms of the IRA leadership during the hunger strike were not to do with their treatment of the prisoners' families but with their failure to engage in as much violence outside the jail as he wanted. But even this hardline republican felt the sense of strain as the deaths in the jail continued. 'I'll certainly never go along with another, never, regardless of the circumstances. It was so painful seeing fellas dying. Probably the whole thing should have been called off as soon as Sands died, because if you didn't get what you were going to get with an MP dying then you were never going to get it. I doubt whether any other politician could have withstood the force of that except Thatcher, she was such a bitch. In hindsight it probably should have been scrubbed earlier.'

The picture that greeted Gerry Adams when he surveyed the landscape after the 1981 hunger strike was one of enormous suffering and tragedy on the part of the hunger strikers themselves but also great gains on a broad front. Inside the jail the prisoners soon got the bulk of their five demands – the term 'political prisoners' was never used but the paramilitaries in the H Blocks wore their own clothes and in large part organized their own lives inside the jail. Politically Sinn Fein had an enormously greater profile. Before the protest Adams' talk of the need for great political activity appeared largely devoid of content; afterwards he could point to successes in two Westminster by-elections and two Irish parliamentary constituencies. Around the country there was a series of H Block committees and associations, some of which were ripe for transformation into Sinn Fein branches or *cumann*.

In September 1981 one IRA prisoner had even written to the Army Council from inside the Maze suggesting that they should think what was in traditional republican terms the unthinkable:

After 12 years of war we [the Movement] have made more gains in the past six months than at any other period of our struggle. We have generated a considerable amount of support, but our most significant gains have been our election victories. We can, technically speaking, claim to have took over from the SDLP as the representative of the population due to the fact that we have a seat in Westminster and the SDLP have none . . . However it is my opinion that a lot of people feel they must have some sort of representation at parliament and therefore the abstentionist policy may not attract them. I don't think Owen Carron going to Westminster would be damaging to our struggle. If he went he could confront Thatcher openly and her death policy in the H Blocks and the plastic bullets issue.

A few days before the IRA prisoner sent his 'comm' about electoral strategy out of the jail, Adams told the *Irish Times* that Sinn

Fein was preparing to fight future elections. He said the hunger strike hadn't been staged in order to achieve electoral success, but 'increasingly over the last 3 or 4 years we have been coming to terms with the need to contest the electoral process. We certainly feel that for too long the Republican movement has neglected this process and we believe that we represent the aspirations of the vast majority of the nationalist people.' Sinn Fein still believed, Adams made clear, that 'legitimate armed action against the British forces' was a necessary ingredient to the Irish nationalist struggle. Adams was speaking immediately after Owen Carron's by-election victory in Fermanagh and South Tyrone. Asked if he would stand for elections himself in the future Gerry Adams replied, 'I have no personal political ambitions.'

CHAPTER FOURTEEN

The Honourable Member

A month after the hunger strike ended, Adams' close associate Danny Morrison made a speech at Sinn Fein's annual conference which summed up the strategy to be pursued by the republican movement during the next decade. Coining a phrase that would become a leitmotif of Sinn Fein/IRA he said: 'Who here really believes that we can win the war through the ballot box?' Then after a dramatic pause he continued: 'But will anyone here object if, with a ballot paper in this hand and an Armalite in this hand, we take power in Ireland?'

Adams was unhappy with the boast, thinking it hyped up what was actually achievable. But Morrison's presentation of the new strategy did keep the most hardline of Provisionals like 'Mike' on board. 'I had no problem at all with the dual strategy, in fact I thought it was very necessary. I was fully supportive of the electoral end, continuing in harmony with the military aspect. Adams was seen as the architect of the dual strategy because he had been preaching the necessity to get involved. Up until then the traditional attitude to Sinn Fein was it held meetings at street corners and so forth and they weren't really a force. It was Adams and Morrison who articulated that this election thing had to go hand in hand.'

As if to emphasize that it was business as usual so far as the Armalite was concerned, the IRA in November 1981 murdered a unionist MP, the Reverend Robert Bradford, at a community centre in Finaghy in South Belfast. The IRA accused Bradford of being 'one of the key people responsible for winding up the loyalist paramilitary sectarian machine'. But the murder of one of the unionist people's elected representatives was widely seen as a deliberate attempt to provoke a loyalist backlash.

The movement's first electoral test after the hunger strikes was not encouraging. In February 1982 Sinn Fein candidates fought the Irish local government elections but compared to the heady days of the hunger strike their vote dropped sharply. Adams noted that a good deal more work would have to be done in the South, but in his own heartland of West Belfast he now had high hopes.

The Northern Ireland Assembly elections – set for 20 October 1982 – provided Adams with his first opportunity after the hunger strike to try his hand at campaigning in West Belfast. He now put into practice what he had learned in the distant days of the mid-1960s, agitating for housing reform and other bread-and-butter reforms in his own back yard. He toured the constituency with a dozen helpers making notes on people's complaints about their day-to-day problems and then assiduously following them up. Republicans and young people who hadn't bothered to vote in the past were encouraged to get their names registered. At one point out canvassing, Adams was involved in a confrontation with some soldiers and, according to Danny Morrison, was thrown to the ground. Morrison said Adams 'wasn't hurt. He is used to this sort of thing.'

In the wider political battle Adams aimed a series of well-placed thrusts at the SDLP, reminding John Hume of his pledge after Bloody Sunday that 'It's a United Ireland or nothing,' a pledge which Adams pointed out was made 'before a United Ireland was ditched in favour of something called power sharing'. Sinn Fein's manifesto strongly suggested that the SDLP wouldn't stick to their declared abstentionist policy. 'The SDLP will sit there [in the Assembly] at the earliest pretext. Sinn Fein candidates will never attend the new Stormont and have never attended the old one . . . the resolution of the national question is delayed because Britain, while it has the help of the SDLP, refuses to face up to the fact that it has no option but to withdraw. The SDLP peddles pacifism, has been regularly elected over the past twelve years, and the violence still continues.'

Mindful that some Provisionals were distinctly uneasy about Sinn Fein's electoral adventure, Adams indicated that the campaign would not be accompanied by any diminution in IRA violence. He said he could not speak for the IRA but he didn't think Sinn Fein's success or failure at the polls would make any difference to the organization as 'the IRA gets its mandate from the fact that the nationalist people are oppressed'. But he conceded that it had become increasingly evident that Sinn Fein could not just be a support group for the IRA but had to begin the process of building a radical alternative to British colonialism in Ireland. And for all Adams said in public, the IRA appeared to be unnaturally quiet in the run-up to the day of the vote.

When the results for West Belfast were posted in Belfast City Hall they showed that Adams had topped the poll. When the successful candidate came out of the room where the votes had been counted unionists shouted 'murderer, murderer' at him. Adams' own supporters countered by raising their fists in the air and singing, 'We are the people'. Adams had received 9,740 votes, compared to 5,207 for the SDLP's Dr Joe Hendron. Like Adams, Sinn Fein's Owen Carron also topped the poll, standing once again in Fermanagh and South Tyrone. Martin McGuinness, Danny Morrison and Jim McAllister were also elected. Sinn Fein took 64,191 first-preference votes, compared to the SDLP's 118,891. That gave the republicans 10.2 per cent of the total vote, behind the SDLP's 18.8 per cent. Gerry Adams could, however, claim to represent 35 per cent of Northern Ireland's nationalist community, a massive step forward for a movement which a few years before the government had been intent on portraying as a collection of common criminals. While some of Sinn Fein's voters were new to the whole business of elections, the SDLP leader John Hume knew that he must have lost some of his natural supporters as a result of the polarization of politics during the hunger strike. 'It is a serious matter,' he said, 'that so many in the community believe the gun is the only solution to political problems.'

Sinn Fein hadn't stinted on the effort or resources they were prepared to throw into the election. Financial returns later showed republicans had spent more than £27,000 on the campaign, more than any other party. Danny Morrison spent £3,925, Martin McGuinness £3,629 and Gerry Adams £1,971. John Hume's campaign had cost, by contrast, £1,390.

During his victory speech in Belfast City Hall, Gerry Adams announced his intention to go on to fight the sitting MP for West Belfast, Gerry Fitt, at the next Westminster election – he challenged Fitt to resign his seat and contest a by-election there and then. Adams was well aware of the scale of the potential achievement if he could replace Fitt as MP. West Belfast, despite its strong Irish republican tradition, had never been represented by a republican. Even when Eamon De Valera had contested the constituency before partition he had been unsuccessful. The sitting MP Gerry Fitt first won the seat under the banner of Republican Labour. But as the Troubles developed so Fitt's opposition to IRA violence had hardened. IRA supporters attacked his home in August 1976, forcing the MP to defend himself and his family with a handgun, his personal protection weapon, issued by the police.

Before embarking on a campaign to unseat Fitt, though, Adams had some internal party business to conclude. At the 1982 Sinn Fein *ard fheis*, held a week after the Assembly elections, the party voted to drop its 'Eire Nua' federalist policy. 'Eirc Nua', meaning New Ireland, had been the creation of the Sinn Fein president Ruairi O Bradaigh and the vote was clearly another step in O Bradaigh's gradual undermining by Adams and his Northern supporters. With Adams riding high on the back of his election victory, O Bradaigh was a beleaguered figure. Father Denis Faul saw the unfolding position as part of the legacy of Adams' handling of the prison protest:

> The hunger strike was his master stroke . . . an awful lot of H Block associations sprang up around Northern Ireland. At one crucial stage just about the time of the first hunger strike in 1980 all these hunger strike associations got instructions that they were to transfer under Belfast . . . and I remember there was a strong one in Newry, I was associated with it, and they refused. They said, 'No, we're running ourselves,' and then they got second instructions they were told, they *had* to transfer. What happened then was when the second hunger strike was nearly over all these hunger strike associations which were then affiliated to Sinn Fein headquarters in Belfast, they were suddenly transformed into Sinn Fein *cumann* [branches]. Then of course Gerry just went down to Dublin with busloads of Sinn Fein *cumann* and outvoted O Bradaigh and company as the Eighties went on.

In an extensive interview for the *Guardian* in November 1982 under the headline 'A coming of age for the political wing', Adams spelt out the relationship between his party and the gunmen. 'Sinn Fein and the IRA have the same objectives. The IRA is engaged in armed struggle. Sinn Fein would not only defend the IRA's right to wage armed struggle but have the job, increasingly, of popularising support. I honestly see no other way by which the British can be forced to withdraw from this country, except by a mixture of struggle which involves properly controlled inter-active armed struggle.' Adams said sectarian shootings should not play a part in that struggle. But he was unmistakably unapologetic when asked about the IRA's killing of the eighty-six-year-old former speaker of the Stormont parliament, Sir Norman Stronge, and his son James at their home at Tynan Abbey in January 1981. Adams expressed regret that Sir Norman was so old when he was killed but justified the murder by describing the victim as 'part of the Orange and unionist ascendancy' and 'one of the key people involved in building up that system of patronage and discrimination . . . The only complaint I have heard from nationalists or anti-unionists is that he was not shot 40 years ago.'

Adams had again recently denied ever being a member of the IRA, so he was questioned about why he hadn't joined. 'Because I have had no great reason to join the IRA . . . I have seen my role primarily as a political role. The IRA appears to have no lack of soldiers.' He also appeared on the BBC's *Panorama* and denied being a 'Shogun-like' figure in the IRA, an epithet coined by the journalist and author Tim Pat Coogan. But senior IRA figures from this period have since cast greater light on his standing in the republican movement and their views are supported by senior members of the security forces on both sides of the border.

Sean O'Callaghan, the Garda agent who held high office in Sinn Fein and the IRA during the 1970s and 1980s, said: 'I talked to Adams in both his capacities. From October 1982 he stopped playing an operational IRA role and never actually resumed a day-to-day IRA involvement, while he remained probably the most senior person at the leadership of the IRA. But he certainly distanced himself from day-to-day IRA activity.' O'Callaghan claims that the shift occurred as Adams entered the political field as a candidate:

> I would have met him quite a lot at Sinn Fein national executive meetings, but I certainly have been involved in other business with him, after October 1982 as well. He was really only attending Army Council meetings after then. Prior to that he was adjutant general of the IRA, he was never chief of staff. He stayed on the IRA Army Council and remained in that position. Although he never resumed the day-to-day role he was by far their senior strategist.

In the mid-1980s Adams and Ivor Bell, who has since been expelled, came up with the idea of a revolutionary council. It was a think-tank basically, which incorporated some senior Sinn Fein people and some senior IRA people. I was at a couple of its meetings, and the idea was that this would eventually be the ruling body of the republican movement.

O'Callaghan said he believes its purpose was to provide a cover for Adams and other senior figures to wield control over the IRA at the highest level while diverting accusations that they were politicians by day and terrorists by night. Security sources in the Irish Republic and Northern Ireland maintain that throughout the 1980s and up to the present day Gerry Adams has retained a seat on the Army Council.

Adams' increased profile as a result of the hunger strikes and the Assembly elections won him some political allies further afield than his West Belfast fiefdom. In the British capital the radical Labour leader of the Greater London Council Ken Livingstone supported the hunger strikes, which he said were 'about the struggle to bring about a free, United Ireland'. Now he invited Adams, Morrison and McGuinness to visit the GLC in December 1982.

But just a few days before the three were due to make the trip, bombers set off a device at the Droppin' Well Pub at Ballykelly in County Derry. Seventeen people died, eleven of them soldiers stationed at the Army base near by. The perpetrators were not from the IRA but the smaller Irish National Liberation Army. Even so, the authorities decided to prevent a high-profile Provisional trip so soon after the bombing and the Home Secretary William Whitelaw, who as Northern Ireland Secretary had invited Adams and McGuinness to London for talks in 1972, stepped in to impose exclusion orders banning them from the British mainland.

The Home Office said it had applied for the orders 'based on intelligence of the men involved in terrorist activities in the past'. Adams criticized the government's decision as 'stupid', reflecting on the irony that 'William Whitelaw invited me to go to England, and brought me there at the taxpayers' expense, to discuss ways of getting peace in Ireland. This time, ten years later, Mr Whitelaw stops another British politician from doing exactly the same thing.' Less predictably, the exclusion orders also drew criticism from unionists. Harold

McCusker, the MP for Armagh, described the decision as 'breathtaking hypocrisy'. 'The corollary of this,' McCusker argued, 'is that they should ban Sinn Fein and declare them the agents of terrorism . . . They are not allowed to walk the streets of London but they can walk the streets of Belfast with impunity.'

On the streets of Belfast the fresh taste of notoriety in England did Adams no harm at all as a general election drew closer. The challenge was on to supplant the SDLP as the main voice of the nationalist community and Adams began 1983 with a blistering attack on a party which he argued was 'becoming increasingly irrelevant'. Speaking in Derry at the eleventh-anniversary commemorations of Bloody Sunday, Adams argued that the people knew that the real terrorists were the British. He said the SDLP leadership also knew this but had chosen the British side and because of that were now a party in decline. 'This process, whether it be lengthy or otherwise, has commenced already and Sinn Fein, with youth and principle on its side, is going to ensure that never again will the nationalist people be sold out by careerist politicians . . . Those who kow-tow with the terrorists in Downing Street have everything to lose. That is why they squeal so loudly. We have everything to gain and that is the reason we struggle so determinedly.'

South of the border the Irish government gave its backing to the New Ireland Forum, a body intended to represent constitutional nationalism north and south of the border, attended by the SDLP and the major Southern parties. The Forum was the brainchild of John Hume, who wanted to create an agreed nationalist strategy, but from the outset Sinn Fein were excluded because of their support for violence. Adams, sensing that his party had John Hume on the run, lampooned the Forum as the Irish Prime Minister Garrett Fitzgerald's 'lifeline to the SDLP'.

'Since the historic hunger strikes,' Adams argued,

it has been obvious to most observers that the SDLP leadership were badly out of step with their nationalist supporters. The SDLP's failure to engage in principled support for the political prisoners and against the British government at that time was being compared to Mr Hume's eagerness to kow-tow to loyalism . . . A rethink led Mr Hume into the realms of fantasy and his Forum for a New Ireland. Sinn Fein's recent electoral successes gave some urgency to this task and persuaded the Leinster House party leaders to throw in with him in this short-term publicity exercise. Far from being the most powerful political initiative since 1920 – and it should not be forgotten that even the limited freedom conceded by the British government at that time to the Irish Free State was won by the IRA – the so-called Forum for a New Ireland is doomed, like Sunningdale and Darlington, to dismal failure.

So the 'Uncle Toms' of the SDLP were firmly in Adams' sights. The rivalry was obviously bitter but on the surface, at any rate, purely political. Subsequently, however, Sean O'Callaghan claimed that in 1982 Adams asked him whether the IRA should kill Hume.

It was 1982 and what actually happened was that I went to Dublin to see Joe Cahill about this possibility of an arms deal which never came off. And we were standing talking just inside the door at the bottom of the stairs in 44 [Parnell Square, Sinn Fein's Dublin office] when Adams came down and Cahill explained to him and Adams said to me: 'Unfortunately Big — is out of the country.' That was a guy who was sort of heavily involved in that sort of business. And when the conversation moved on, what Adams actually said to me was really in effect 'Do the guys think we should kill Hume?', in other words, what is IRA feeling on the ground about it?

I didn't really answer him in those terms. I said to myself, you might be off your bloody head, you are bloody daft. If two IRA men are caught down the road after killing Hume no matter how you portray it Sinn Fein would be wiped out, the whole credibility would be destroyed. I actually believe that Adams agreed with that, that he himself thought, 'It is too much of a gamble to do this.' But you have to look at that in context. From about 1975 the great regret among the IRA leadership and Sinn Fein was that they hadn't killed Gerry Fitt, John Hume, Austin Currie and the rest of them in the very early Seventies, wiped them out. That was a huge regret, because in those days Sinn Fein was not contesting elections [so] it couldn't have had an electoral impact. By the time Sinn Fein began contesting elections it was even more clear to them that they should have got rid of John Hume ten years before, because he was the big electoral rival.

But because they were contesting elections the gamble was far too big. People like —, who was chief of staff of the IRA at the time, would have said, 'Fucking kill him.' And Adams would have had no objections to it except it was a major political gamble to take, no matter how you portrayed it. My reply was that it was complete madness. Basically that the gamble of doing it was such that if it was ever tied to the IRA the political credibility would be destroyed. He didn't say much, but he never does, except he kind of nods. It was a real option within the republican movement to kill John Hume until 1983. So he had to be dealt with and they had to come up with an alternative strategy of dealing with it.

Some of O'Callaghan's claims, such as his story of saving Prince Charles and Princess Diana from an IRA attack on a London theatre, were later substantiated by the authorities – in this case corroboration was provided by the former Irish Prime Minister Garrett Fitzgerald. But the decisive nature of O'Callaghan's conversion from his past republican beliefs, allied to the fact that he was never charged with his involvement in the murder of another informer, has led some to question his credibility. The story about assassinating Hume came to prominence as part of a constant trickle of revelations from O'Callaghan following his release from prison late in 1996. Adams' own response to the allegation was to dismiss O'Callaghan as unworthy of belief.

'It's total rubbish, it's a lie,' he protested. 'The man's obviously a fruit and nut case ... the guy's obviously flipped his lid once again ... some so-called mainstream media outlets actually carry allegations like this, that shows the MI5 agenda is finding some echo among some sections of the media ... this is one in a long series of very bizarre and increasingly ridiculous allegations. I never had any of these discussions about killing anyone at any time and I certainly didn't have any discussion about the SDLP with Sean O Callaghan.' But while Hume himself maintained an enigmatic silence, the *Irish Times* ran a story quoting IRA sources in Belfast which effectively corroborated O'Callaghan's story.

While Adams was keen to define the SDLP as his principal political target, when it came to West Belfast and the general election of June 1983, he was undoubtedly helped by the fact that the sitting MP Gerry Fitt was an independent. Fitt had been a founder member of the SDLP but had split from the party on the grounds that it was too traditionally nationalist and not socialist enough. In the 1979 general election when he was still part of the SDLP Fitt had eased comfortably past all the opposition, retaining his seat with a majority of 8,235 votes. But in 1983 he faced opposition on two fronts – the ballot-box and Armalite candidature of Adams and an officially recognized SDLP candidate in the shape of local GP Dr Joe Hendron. Thus while Adams could consolidate his gains from the time of the hunger strikes and the Assembly elections, constitutional nationalist voters faced a dilemma between backing John Hume's party or staying loyal to the sitting MP.

The IRA and Sinn Fein girded their loins once again for an electoral battle. Financial resources were channelled away from the IRA's military campaign and towards the electoral battle. The party by now had four advice centres up and running, at a cost of approximately £30,000 each, to deal with people's complaints and working out how to get the best out of the welfare system for constituents. At the helm, 'Mike' recalls, the candidate appeared assured. 'Adams was good on the doorsteps, though he was preaching to a converted audience. There were good vibes out campaigning.'

Some IRA members were unhappy about the transfer of cash and the way that military operations appeared to be taking a back seat to the election. But Adams was careful not to say anything which appeared to disown the IRA – in April 1983 he told a commemoration in Donegal that, so long as the British government retained a hold on any part of Ireland, Sinn Fein would unapologetically defend the right of the IRA to engage in armed struggle. At the end of May, with polling only days away, he endorsed the IRA's campaign of assassinating British and foreign businessmen to discourage investment in Northern Ireland. 'I accept that what we have to achieve in this country is a situation where the British government cannot govern, the British government cannot propagate to the world that we have a normal system here.'

While the rhetoric remained hardline there was some evidence of the IRA being persuaded to desist from actions which might cost valuable votes. Armed robberies as a means of fundraising were curtailed and some attempts were made to cut down on the number of kneecappings of youths deemed guilty of 'anti-social behaviour'. During the traditional Easter oration at Milltown cemetery in Belfast in 1983 Martin McGuinness had announced that the IRA was ending its policy of shooting youths in the legs in so-called punishment attacks and would pursue 'more socially involved' and 'preventative' methods of dealing with delinquents. Nevertheless kneecappings still remained a problem issue for Adams as the election campaign reached its latter stages, provoking criticism from Joe Hendron that the IRA was exploiting the unemployed youth of West Belfast. Adams replied that it was 'obvious that the people of West Belfast, while rejecting the RUC, demanded a degree of policing from the IRA'. Joe Hendron, he claimed, 'was fully aware of the fact that the IRA were for the last three years reviewing their policy on punishment shootings'. Strangely it appears that an 'end' to the practice of kneecappings in April had by May become merely a 'review'.

During the course of the campaign Adams became well aware that he was up against a tougher opponent than any one particular party – namely the hierarchy of the Catholic Church in the diocese of Down and Conor, headed by Bishop Cahal Daly, who consistently questioned the morality of voting for republicans while the IRA's campaign continued. Adams claimed that the Bishop was bringing his high office into disrepute when early in May Daly told his faithful that they should be conscious that their vote for Sinn Fein would be interpreted as a vote for violence.

But neither Cahal Daly, Joe Hendron nor Gerry Fitt could stop the Adams bandwagon rolling when the people of West Belfast went to the polls. The count took place the next day inside Belfast City Hall. Adams topped the poll with 16,379 votes, a majority of 5,500 over the SDLP's Joe Hendron, who received 10,934 votes. Gerry Fitt, after seventeen years as local MP, came third with 10,326 votes.

As Gerry Adams watched the ballot papers being sorted into piles inside Belfast City Hall news was just coming through of the murder of a soldier in his home area of Ballymurphy. Mark Curtis died at 8.40 a.m., twenty minutes before Adams' votes started to be counted. Curtis, a private in the Light Infantry Regiment who came from Grimsby, was part of a mixed patrol of soldiers and police officers which had set out shortly before from their New Barnsley base. The twenty-year-old soldier crouched down on his hunkers beside a lamppost in Glenalina Park unaware that the IRA had hidden a 15lb bomb behind the garden wall he was leaning against. A police officer across the road shouted to the young private to watch himself, a warning triggered not by any knowledge of how real the threat was but just the general wariness of the security forces in operating in an area like Ballymurphy. At that instant the bomber pressed the button on his command wire and Curtis' body was flung into the street.

From the IRA's point of view it was a classic operation – mounted after polls closed, it couldn't deter any floating voters from opting for Sinn Fein. It also meant that whatever the result of the election the Provisionals would figure in the headlines. The IRA admission distributed via Sinn Fein's Falls Road press office proclaimed that 'as long as armed British soldiers patrol the streets of Ireland, enforcing British rule, they must expect Irishmen to resist their presence'. The IRA had added another statistic to the Troubles and provided Ballymurphy's own successful candidate with a few extra sentences for his victory speech.

Adams began that speech with a few words in Irish, then told his supporters that they had won 'an historic election victory . . . It will be welcomed by Irish people at home and abroad. I don't consider it to be a personal victory, although I take personal satisfaction from it. It is a victory for all those people who worked over the past two or three weeks and all those who have suffered over the decades . . . This morning a British soldier was killed in Ballymurphy. The responsibility for his death lies with the British government. The tragedy of Ireland rests with the British government. That British soldier should not have been in Ballymurphy.'

After what reporters regarded as a somewhat subdued oration, Adams had to rely on RUC protection to get out of the City Hall running a cordon of loyalists shouting 'murderer' and 'thug'. The celebrations at the Sinn Fein offices on the Falls Road were more euphoric. For 'Mike', 'it was a massive victory and a tremendous achievement. The feeling was just so high, cavalcades all round the areas. There was a lot of work put into it.'

The defeated SDLP candidate Joe Hendron urged Adams to take his seat at Westminster and 'call the paramilitaries off'. If not, Hendron argued, the new MP would be condemning the youth of West Belfast to 'the dole queues and the graveyards'.

Looking back on the result some years later, the outgoing MP Gerry Fitt blamed the SDLP for splitting the anti-violence vote:

> Since the creation of West Belfast the republican vote was always minuscule, two or three thousand votes – there was never a serious republican vote in West Belfast except in 1983. Now that vote was brought out at a terrible cost. Sinn Fein purchased that vote by allowing ten men to die in prison in 1981 and if you remember the terrible emotions there were then, emotions were pulled apart, pulled asunder, terrible hostility was engendered in both communities and that was why Sinn Fein won the seat in 1983 ... The SDLP knew very well that by putting up a candidate they'd split the vote, that they would allow Gerry Adams to take the seat, because everyone could detect the emotion that was there, and they deliberately did it. Maybe at that time in 1983 they were prepared to accept Gerry Adams in place of me.

The unsuccessful candidates could fight over who was to blame, but in 1983 Adams was the victor and to him went the spoils. The day after the result was announced the Home Office withdrew its exclusion order, well aware that it could not sustain an order which would prevent an elected member of parliament taking up his seat. The government, however, firmed up their line on no contact with Sinn Fein, a change from the position just a few months previously when Adams had been able to stride up the steps at Stormont on his way to meet the housing minister. Now the Northern Ireland Secretary Jim Prior rejected the new MP's claim that Britain was responsible for its soldiers dying on the streets of Belfast and declared that he wouldn't meet Gerry Adams unless he renounced violence.

Shortly after his election the Irish Foreign Minister Peter Barry referred disparagingly to Adams and those like him as 'gunmen'. On Southern Irish soil at the traditional Bodenstown commemoration Adams tossed this remark mockingly back in Barry's face, addressing the crowd as 'Friends, fellow Irishmen and Irishwomen, fellow gunmen and gunwomen'. Adams paid tribute to the 'freedom fighters of the IRA', continuing: 'the IRA is the assertion and the guarantee that our will to be free is stronger than the will of the British government, including Margaret Thatcher, to enslave us'. Despite his recent success at the ballot box he again enunciated the traditional republican argument that the IRA did not need an electoral mandate because it derived its mandate from the presence of a foreign government on Irish soil. He finished his speech by declaring, 'Victory to the IRA.'

Back on the Falls Road a mob attacked the SDLP office – Adams spoke out against the attack, which he claimed did a disservice to Sinn Fein. But at the same time he continued his political barrage on the constitutional nationalists, lambasting John Hume for taking the oath and going to Westminster. 'Only hard struggle will bring Ireland to Britain's attention,' he argued, 'the type of struggle which John Hume is incapable of mounting.'

The month after his election Adams decided to go to Westminster, not to take his seat, but to mount a propaganda assault on the British in the heart of the enemy capital. He first held talks with Ken Livingstone and Tony Benn in the GLC building immediately across the Thames from the Palace of Westminster. Then he made his way into the Houses of Parliament to Room 19 in the Upper Committee corridor for a meeting with a number of left-wing Labour MPs, including Jeremy Corbyn, Bob Clay, Ernie Roberts, Clare Short, Harry Cohen and Tony Banks.

The publicity attendant on this trip far outweighed the attention given any other new MP who was willing to take his or her seat in the House of Commons. At Heathrow Adams was met by a large number of policemen who escorted him to a waiting car. No fewer than seventy-three media people crammed into his news conference at the GLC. Ken Livingstone justified the invitation by saying it was in the interests of people in the British capital. 'The overwhelming majority of Londoners want to see an end to the fighting. The only way we are going to stop the killing is by talking.'

Gerry Adams echoed that sentiment, arguing that he was visiting London in order to bring about conditions where 'the war which affects British and Irish people' could be brought to an end. Adams claimed to be nonplussed by the angry opposition to his visit. 'I don't see why there should be any objection to my coming to London when the Irish people have to suffer 30,000 fully armed British troops in their midst.' This was something of an exaggeration, as the Army had 10,000 regular troops in the province, together with 7,200 members of the locally recruited Ulster Defence Regiment.

As Gerry Adams made his way from the GLC building across Westminster Bridge towards Parliament a number of passers-by recognized him and some shouted, 'IRA murderer!' When the West Belfast MP walked into the House of Commons one woman near the entrance shouted, 'Take the vote from the Irish and hang that man, he's a murderer.'

Lest anyone misunderstood his intention in going to parliament, Adams stressed that his abstentionism remained intact. 'In relation to Ireland, Westminster is a foreign parliament. Would you expect a Tory MP to take his seat in Dublin or in Paris?' The new MP pointedly did not enter the Commons chamber. He likened the IRA struggle to 'the patriotic duty that any Englishman would have felt if invaded by the Nazis,' and added: 'If I was not in Sinn Fein I would find myself in the IRA.'

As a PR exercise the trip clearly served its purpose. Adams effortlessly upstaged the Irish Foreign Minister Peter Barry, who was also visiting London at the time. Barry complained that 'Mr Adams is here as part of his mission of destruction. The vast majority of people in Ireland and the Irish in Britain reject his approach.' Certainly the British tabloids shared that assessment. The *Daily Express* claimed that Adams had 'stormed' into the Commons, almost knocking down an old lady in his wake. Other newspapers complained about his 'bullying bodyguards'. The *Sun* summed up the trip by declaring the West Belfast MP to be 'surely the most unwanted visitor to Britain since Hitler's raiders'.

Although during the day Adams and sympathizers within the Labour Party had spoken as one, in the evening, during a meeting at Finsbury Town Hall, there was evidence of the divergence between them. Labour's Chris Smith was heckled when he made clear his opposition to violence. Adams got a standing ovation from the 250-strong audience when he finished his speech with the IRA slogan, 'Our day will come!'

In August 1983 amid a series of street riots and disturbances associated with the anniversary of internment, Belfast man Thomas Reilly was caught up in a fracas with soldiers – one of them, Private Ian Thain, pointed his gun at Reilly and shot him dead. Thain was found guilty of murder, and the family of Reilly, a roadie with several well-known pop groups, received compensation. Later the killing was to cause more controversy when Thain was let out of jail and back into the Army. In 1983 it provoked hijackings and burnings of vehicles and clashes between the Army and the people of West Belfast.

In this tense atmosphere, Gerry Adams addressed a 1,500-strong rally at Dunville Park in West Belfast, treating them to probably his most strident endorsement yet of the IRA. Adams argued that it was the patriotic duty of Irishmen and women to engage in 'legitimate armed struggle'. He added that, while legally he could not appeal to people to join the IRA, those who wished had to make up their own minds on the issue. In an attempt to wind the clock back to the 'revolutionary' days of the early 1970s Adams called for people to resume the practice of raising the alarm by bashing bin lids and blowing whistles when Army patrols came along.

In the weeks after Thomas Reilly's death many of the women of Ballymurphy took up Gerry Adams' suggestion of banging their bin lids whenever soldiers were in the area. In what appeared yet another throwback to the early 1970s the Army once again decided that Gerry Adams senior's house should be targeted for a series of searches. Adams' mother Annie reacted with glum stoicism to what she claimed was half a dozen raids in the course of a week. 'They nearly broke down the front door tonight,' she told the nationalist *Irish News*. 'I saw the policemen around the back first and asked what they were doing and they pushed me a bit and told me to mind my own business. I told him I would not and he got more heated so I moved inside the house. They woke up the father when they came in and they stormed up the stairs and he ran up after them.'

The Army and the RUC may have been paying some attention to his relatives, but it was the West Belfast MP who remained a prime target, as the security forces sought evidence which would enable them to pull his political veil away. In September 1983 the police thought they might have had the breakthrough they were hoping for in the shape of Robert 'Beano' Lean, a thirty-seven-year-old father of five from Ballymurphy who was a known associate of Adams and had decided to turn informer.

The early 1980s was the era of the 'supergrass', the mocking name given to those former paramilitaries who took up the RUC's offer to testify against their comrades in return for indemnity against prosecution and offers of a new life and identity far away from Northern Ireland. The use of supergrass evidence sent a chill through the ranks of both republican and loyalist paramilitaries, but its apparent successes came to naught when judges decided that the character of several key informers was unworthy of belief and dozens were freed on appeal.

Robert Lean didn't get even that far, but when he signalled his initial intention to co-operate the authorities were overjoyed. Press reports appeared, clearly reflecting police thinking at the time, stating that Lean was the second in command of the IRA in Belfast and suggesting that Provisionals in West Belfast were fearful that his evidence could put them behind bars. Lean was said to have information on attacks going back more than a decade, including the assassination of the unionist MP Robert Bradford. A senior RUC officer told the *Daily Mail* that the police were 'now in a position to clean up some of the most unpleasant people. Those who may not necessarily have pulled the trigger but most certainly planned and ordered countless killings.'

Adams, who was pictured in some papers together with Lean during the West Belfast election campaign, said that he himself expected to be arrested. He described Lean as a man of 'dubious credibility'. Asked if Lean was second in command of the Belfast IRA, Adams responded that 'he was a fairly hard-working member of Sinn Fein. I can't speak for the IRA, but I would be surprised if someone like Bobby Lean, who was just a grassroots member of Sinn Fein, would reach such a high status.' Adams was clearly unsettled by what had occurred. 'The way they have projected Robert Lean and the people they have arrested all stinks. To us it is just another "We have the IRA on the run" campaign . . . These boasts if true show the total and discredited reliance of the RUC on the use of hired perjurers and show trials. The silent collusions of the Catholic hierarchy and the SDLP is explained by the fact that they view the RUC's strategy as aimed at smashing republicanism and the morale of militant nationalist people.'

Before joining Sinn Fein, Lean had had a chequered career. The son of a mixed marriage he was brought up on the Protestant Shankill Road. He became involved with the Official IRA, but was kneecapped by them in 1975. This was during a time of feuding between the Officials and the breakaway faction from their ranks which became the Irish National Liberation Army, republicans who regarded themselves as left-wing socialists. When he was jailed in 1976 for arms possession he was identified as a member of the INLA's political wing, the Irish Republican Socialist Party. He served his time in the INLA's compound inside the Maze prison. After his release in 1977 Lean drifted towards the Provisionals, getting involved in Sinn Fein during the era of the hunger strikes. Newspaper photographers captured him tagging along not only beside Adams but also with Danny Morrison and Richard McAuley, who was in the future to take over as Adams' press aide.

In September 1983 another informer, William John Skelly, gave evidence implicating Lean in an IRA rocket attack and a kneecapping. The RUC picked Lean up and offered him a deal – information for immunity against any criminal charges. Lean talked and a series of arrests followed, among them Ivor Bell, who had accompanied Gerry Adams to the IRA's talks with William Whitelaw in 1972, a leading Belfast republican Eddie Carmichael, and Evelyn Glenholmes, who was to become well known later when she eluded extradition from the Irish Republic.

Lean's allegations included conspiracy to murder soldiers, attempts to kidnap the wife of another supergrass and conspiracy to murder an informer. But Lean was later to claim that the detectives only had one person on their mind, 'the one in particular was Gerry Adams who they wanted most of all'. Lean claimed he had been at an IRA meeting together with Eddie Carmichael and Gerry Adams at which the subject of punishment shootings in Ballymurphy was discussed. Lean stated that 'Adams was there and said that they should be stopped, that the IRA should cease them.'

Adams, unlike the others whom Lean had named, was never arrested. Lean refused to confront him with the allegations – something which the police asked supergrasses to do with those they implicated. Asked why he wouldn't confront Adams, Lean said it was 'because I have a lot of respect for the man and I didn't want to bring unnecessary pressure on to my family outside'.

Family connections were indeed to prove the undoing of many supergrasses, including Lean. Initially Lean's wife Geraldine, mother of his five children, moved out of their house in Ballymurphy and joined her husband under police protection at Palace barracks in Holywood, far away from home turf. After a month Geraldine decided she couldn't carry on. Back in Ballymurphy she publicly appealed to her husband to withdraw his evidence. 'I just hope to God that he retracts but I don't know if he will. I thought by staying he would change his mind. I always said I would come back. I told him all these people he has informed on were our friends who stood by me when he was in prison.'

Without his wife and family's support Lean lasted another three weeks. Then one night he took the keys to a car and headed out of the safety of police protection and back to the certainties of home. The following day he talked to reporters at the republican Felons Club in Andersonstown and insisted that his statements about Gerry Adams and all those accused on the basis of his evidence had been works of invention, concocted by the detectives who interviewed him. 'The RUC did all the writing, read it over to me and I signed it . . . I signed all the statements. I was intimidated all along. I didn't feel safe in their custody.'

Shortly after Lean's retraction those jailed on his word were released. Ivor Bell and Eddie Carmichael were met by Gerry Adams and a group of republicans and whisked away in a fleet of waiting cars to a news conference organized by the 'Show Trials Committee'. Ivor Bell claimed that a high ranking police officer called Mr Hunt had asked him to implicate Gerry Adams and said that he could name his own price if he signed a statement naming Adams, Martin McGuinness and Danny Morrison. Eddie Carmichael alleged he was offered £300,000 to 'shop' Gerry Adams.

After being rearrested by the police Lean was freed. He and his wife left Ballymurphy to start a new life south of the Irish border. William Skelly, the informer who had originally implicated Lean, also withdrew his evidence. Given his retraction, Lean's allegations carry little weight. Nevertheless, if, as the supergrass claimed, the whole story was the invention of RUC detectives, it is curious to say the least that they chose to fabricate a scenario which appears to redound so much to Gerry Adams' credit. Rather than inventing a story about Adams ordering death and destruction, the allegation portrays him arguing for a diminution of punishment shootings.

The damaging aspect for Adams was that he allegedly put this laudable argument within an internal IRA meeting. This was at a time in the run-up to his election as an MP when Adams was telling Joe Hendron in public that the IRA was reviewing its policy on kneecapping and Adams' ally Martin McGuinness was promising publicly that the practice would stop. Certainly whatever the provenance of the statement which Lean signed, a debate about paramilitary punishments was under way at this stage within the IRA's ranks.

The debate continued, but without the resolution that Martin McGuinness had promised. In May 1984 *Republican News* carried an article which argued that something more constructive than punishment shootings and beatings was required in dealing with 'hoods', the slang term for petty criminals or those deemed guilty of anti-social behaviour. But just a week later the IRA demonstrated once again the gap between theory and practice when it shot one man in both legs and killed another, Jimmy Campbell. Campbell was a former IRA man who the organization alleged indulged in freelance bank robbery, a practice he persisted with despite warnings and punishment shootings.

Once free of Robert Lean's clutches, Gerry Adams was able to continue his ascent to political power. He squeezed more publicity from visiting England by turning up at the Labour Party's conference in Brighton in October 1983. Addressing a fringe meeting, he told delegates that 'republicanism will never be beaten. There is no way that the British government is winning in Ireland. It would be much better for all of us if we had your support in not being beaten.' He drew on his personal experiences, which he told the Labour Party members were not untypical, describing how soldiers had wrecked his family home in the early 1970s and claiming that he once had to carry his baby brother unconscious from the house. He talked of being arrested and taken to the Castlereagh interrogation centre, where 'I was beaten senseless then had a bucket of cold water thrown over me so that I could be beaten senseless again'. Adams touched on the death of his cousin Ciaran Murphy from Ardoyne: 'My cousin was butchered by loyalists who saw themselves as British and had to kill Catholics to prove it.' But then he went on to justify violence from another quarter: 'I will not be prepared to condemn the legitimate use of armed struggle by the republicans against the British.'

On paper Adams had been number two in Sinn Fein since his appointment as vice president of the party in 1979. In practice since his release from jail in the mid-1970s his combination of military leadership and political profile was increasingly putting him into an unassailable position. In November 1983 all that remained was to replace the nominal head of Sinn Fein, Ruairi O Bradaigh and assume the leadership in name as well as in fact.

The transition was carefully stage managed, with journalists being fed the line that O Bradaigh was ill and for that reason had no option but to go. Not surprisingly O Bradaigh didn't like this tactic and made it clear that although he had a kidney complaint it wasn't serious and not a factor in his decision. He was left with no choice, however, when it became clear that the IRA Army Council backed Adams. O Bradaigh disagreed with Adams over whether Sinn Fein candidates in the following year's European elections should, if successful, take their seats. Adams, although ruling himself out as a candidate, wanted any elected Sinn Feiner to go to the Strasbourg parliament, whereas O Bradaigh felt the electoral platform should remain abstentionist. O Bradaigh's ally Dave O'Connell criticized the increasingly Northern leadership as unrepresentative of Sinn Fein as a whole.

After at least five years planning the eclipse of O Bradaigh and the Dublin old guard, Adams presented himself as a reluctant leader. He said he would have preferred it if the party had been headed by a Southerner as so much emphasis needed to be placed on the Irish Republic. He denied that his election as Sinn Fein president represented a 'Northern takeover'. He also said it didn't mean that he was going to lead Sinn Fein into taking seats in the Dublin parliament, Leinster House. 'My election means neither of those things.'

Adams said that the IRA wasn't engaged in a campaign intended to overthrow the Irish Republic: 'it needs to be made clear that republicans are not interested in armed struggle in the twenty-six counties, aimed at the takeover of the state', but north of the border the commitment remained undiluted. 'Armed struggle is a necessary and morally correct form of resistance in the six counties against a government whose presence is rejected by the vast majority of the Irish people.'

O Bradaigh did not go quietly, warning that Sinn Fein was on a slippery slope to lifting the ban on abstentionism. It would eventually cause a split and that had been the sad history of republicanism, 'splits, splits, splits'.

Adams also called on Protestants to play their part in a democratic United Ireland. A week later gunmen walked into the Pentecostal Church Hall in Darkley close to the County Armagh border and indiscriminately attacked worshippers. Three Protestant elders were killed. The massacre was admitted by the Catholic Reaction Force, a name of convenience used most frequently by elements associated with the INLA when claiming particularly horrific killings. Adams, speaking at an IRA commemoration at Kilmichael in County Cork, described sectarian murders such as those at Darkley as 'unjustifiable morally or tactically . . . It is of paramount importance that I use this platform today, not only to reiterate the republican abhorrence of sectarianism, not only to repudiate the Darkley killings, but also to deny those involved any justification, moral, tactical or strategic, for a repeat of such actions.'

Considerable attention was paid to Adams' appearance at Kilmichael because it was a ceremony organized by veterans of the 'old IRA' of the Irish War of Independence and thus was considered more respectable than Sinn Fein occasions. The veterans had always in the past been able to borrow Irish Army guns and blank ammunition to fire a volley at their ceremony, but in protest at Adams' invitation the Irish government withdrew this courtesy.

When Adams arrived at Kilmichael he used the occasion to associate the 'good old IRA' of the County Cork veterans with their Northern successors. Asked whether he would like to see young people joining the IRA he replied, 'Of course I would. The people engaged in the IRA, whether men or women, are freedom fighters and the people who were commemorated today at Kilmichael were also freedom fighters.' Questioned about whether he would personally be prepared to kill a soldier or an RUC man, he was equally blunt. 'I have answered this question many times before. If my role lay within the IRA and within an armed struggle, I would have no compunction at all. I have no reluctance in my support for armed struggle and if that was where my role lay, then that is where I would be.'

As a creature from far-off Belfast, Gerry Adams was as much a rarity in the southernmost county of Cork as he would have been on his visits to England. The *Irish Independent* reported, approving his style if not his content, that he 'could have been taken for the local school teacher instead of the leader of the political wing of an underground military organisation. His grooming was perfect. A greenish coloured tie complemented his jacket. By his side were his wife Colette and 10 yr old son Gearoid.' The County Cork IRA veterans felt vindicated when they had a chance to look over their immaculately turned out guest of honour. He was not, they told reporters, the monster he had been made out to be.

Elsewhere in the South, though, Adams was experiencing more consumer resistance. In the fruit and vegetable market in Dublin's Moore Street one of the notoriously plain-speaking traders had told him, 'I'll vote for no gunman – we're not any of your gunwomen either.' Adams' jibe at Peter Barry had been turned back on him. In Galway's Eyre Square as he laid a wreath in honour of the executed republican Liam Mellows an elderly man shouted at him, 'There's no room for Armalite politics in Galway. You're a disgrace to the memory of Liam Mellows.'

On 7 December 1983, the day before that confrontation in Galway, the IRA had murdered an Ulster Unionist member of the Northern Ireland Assembly, Edgar Graham, shot dead at Belfast's Queen's University where he lectured in law. Within ten days of this killing IRA men shot dead an Irish soldier and an Irish police officer involved in the rescue of a Dublin supermarket executive Don Tidey, who had been held hostage by gunmen for the previous three weeks. The next day an IRA car bomb exploded outside the famous London store Harrods, killing five people and injuring eighty.

Adams appeared on the ropes, fielding questions from reporters about the sectarian slaughter of a Protestant politician, the murder of a police officer and soldier serving a state which he had said the IRA wasn't interested in overthrowing and the senseless killing of English civilians out doing their Christmas shopping. The Sinn Fein president developed the defensive formulation which he was to deploy on many future occasions, replying that he regretted but wouldn't condemn the deaths. As for the murders of the Irish policeman and soldier: 'It is no reflection on the IRA volunteers that were involved because they were in a position where they were doing their duty.'

Asked if there was tension over the increasing role for Sinn Fein above the IRA, Adams said he did not believe there was any conscious attempt by any republican element to undermine or thwart his attempt to develop a thirty-two-county political struggle: 'I think that what we have to understand is that there are contradictions between our struggle and political structure in the same way as there are contradictions in Irish society.'

As for the impact a ban might have on Sinn Fein, he tried to play down the party's image as being purely a group of cheerleaders for

IRA violence. 'Sinn Fein's policy isn't limited to the armed struggle,' he told his critics. 'It's a policy of a lot of things and we will attempt to develop a strategy which encompasses the widest possible support for the right of the Irish people to self-determination.'

Any fledgling attempt to break loose from the IRA label was met with a deadly journalistic rejoinder when John Ware, then reporting for Granada's *World in Action*, broadcast his unrelenting and extensively researched exposé of Adams' paramilitary roots, *The Honourable Member for West Belfast*. News of Ware's programme had been greeted with protests by unionist politicians and British ministers, who believed it would just be another PR puff for Adams – but when they saw the documentary they quickly changed their tune. Ware covered for the first time incidents like the shooting of John McGuinness in Ballymurphy in February 1971 and, most damaging of all, carried a lengthy contribution from the former IRA man Peter McMullen detailing Adams' career inside the organization. Ware included Dessie O'Hagan's anecdote about Adams being prepared to wade up to his knees in Protestant blood. Cheekily the reporter had also managed to hide a radio microphone inside the Sinn Fein *ard fheis* recording the words of a masked IRA man whose speech was supposedly for republican ears only.

The Northern Ireland Secretary Jim Prior praised *World in Action* for producing 'a very good programme in that it showed what this man really is'. The former MP Bernadette McAliskey apologized to Adams for her participation in the programme and protested about the editing of her interview. Adams himself denounced the documentary as 'black propaganda'. Interviewed by David Frost on TV AM Adams took particular exception to Dessie O'Hagan's claims, saying he found the assertion that he would make such sectarian comments to be 'very offensive'. He stuck by his claim that he had never been in the IRA but told Frost, 'I would have considered it an honour to have been in the IRA.'

Discussion of sectarianism led Frost to probe Adams on how he reconciled the Catholic Church's teachings with the activities of the IRA. 'I don't have to listen to what the Church says,' Adams responded. 'But any human being including myself must have a moral dilemma about the taking of human life. I can live with my conscience.' Father Dominic Johnson, a Benedictine priest based at Glenstal Abbey, in County Limerick begged to differ. He told newspapers that he would refuse to give Adams holy communion because he wasn't following the commandment 'Thou Shalt Not Kill'. 'If this person were to come to the altar for communion,' Father Johnson explained, 'I would in conscience have to by pass him. I could not serve him.'

In February 1984 Adams addressed a meeting of around 300 Sinn Fein members in Dublin setting out his analysis of where the republican movement had been and where it was going to. He recalled the halcyon days of 1969 when events happened quickly and people were 'simply absorbed' into the movement, then the mid-1970s when the authorities launched their effective counter-attack. He now said openly what before he had only implied, that the 1975 ceasefire had been an unmitigated disaster. 'The period confused 99 per cent of the republican base, and is, in my view, the one period in the last fifteen years when republicans were almost beaten, almost shattered . . . In the six counties, the disillusionment and confusion was at a maximum.'

Adams then touched on the radical reviews of both Sinn Fein and the IRA which he had played a key role in during the mid-1970s, aimed at broadening Sinn Fein's political base and making the IRA more efficient and impervious to security-force penetration. 'Around the time of Jimmy Drumm's speech at Bodenstown [in 1977] when we told republicans that the British were not getting out, there was a return of confidence among republicans that the struggle wasn't over.' He went on, somewhat archly, 'At the same time, as we have been told by IRA spokespersons in numerous interviews since, the IRA had also carried out a review and reorganization, and were able to rebuild strength and confidence'.

Adams updated the story by reference to Sinn Fein's 'electoral interventions', which he maintained had been planned, but then 'by sheer coincidence' were accelerated by the hunger strikes. The hiccup, however, that the party had suffered in the Irish elections of February 1982 showed the need not just for one-off electoral interventions but a sustained electoral policy. That policy, Adams fondly hoped, would have to be developed not just north of the border but also in the South.

Amid the usual heavy political debate, the early months of 1984 provided two examples of the absurd. In January a Scottish Conservative MP Albert McQuarrie angrily demanded that legislation should be passed enabling Adams to be ousted from parliament. What had provoked McQuarrie's ire was not another of the Sinn Fein leader's pronouncements on IRA violence but the fact that he had spotted a coathanger in the House of Commons cloakroom reserved for 'Gerry Adams MP for West Belfast'. This was simply too much for the Tory, who decided the whole thing was 'a mockery of parliament'.

The following month Adams and his wife Colette were sleeping in a house in Clones in County Monaghan just south of the border with Northern Ireland when they awoke to find 'three machine-gun-toting men' in the bedroom. The men were Irish police officers. Adams complained bitterly about this latest example of harassment, but the local Garda Chief Superintendent J. J. McNally was having none of it, implying strongly that Adams should not have been sleeping in so late. 'It was a routine search,' the Chief Superintendent said. 'When they went into a bedroom they found Mr Adams and his wife in bed. They searched a suitcase and looked around the house before leaving and did not harass anyone, unless Mr Adams doesn't like being disturbed at eleven o'clock in the morning.'

Gerry Adams couldn't see the funny side of the incident – but his lack of humour when it came to strangers with guns could be forgiven, bearing in mind what the next few days were to bring.

CHAPTER FIFTEEN

Living Dangerously

It was inevitable given the kind of existence Gerry Adams led that from time to time his life would come under threat. The most constant danger for a prominent Irish republican undoubtedly came from the loyalist terrorists of the UVF and the UDA. Adams himself often also claimed that the Army and the police would like to see him dead, and on a number of occasions individual members of the security forces have taken it upon themselves to shoot members and supporters of his party. In the 1990s as he steered the IRA in what was to some Provisional hardliners an unacceptable direction, the greatest threat at times appeared to be from among his own. It is a tribute to the control he has exerted over his supporters that at the time of writing that danger remains hypothetical.

Adams says that as a result of his contacts with the loyalist leader John McKeague he had learned that he had been a top priority target for the UVF in the 1970s. This was hardly surprising given that he was at this stage being named publicly as an IRA leader. Because of Adams' dexterity in moving from house to house, he not only kept one step ahead of the security forces, he also managed to evade on most occasions the would-be killers.

The UVF informer Joe Bennett described one of the many unsuccessful loyalist plots to kill Adams, which he claimed he had heard about over a drink in the Kings Inn Bar in Dundonald in East Belfast in February 1981. Bennett was chatting to John Wilson, whom he identified as the UVF's battalion commander in East Belfast, about the UVF murder the previous night of thirty-three-year-old James 'Skipper' Burns. Burns had been interned in the early 1970s and is identified in the republican roll of honour as a member of the IRA's 2nd Belfast Battalion. He was shot four times as he lay asleep in his bed. Bennett claimed Wilson had described the killing as 'a good job well done', adding that 'Gerry Adams will be next.' He said the UVF regarded Burns as Adams' 'SIC' or second in command. Wilson and another loyalist Robert Seymour were convicted of Burns' murder but won their case when the appeal court found Bennett's testimony unworthy of belief. That didn't stop the IRA murdering Seymour in 1988, at which time the UVF admitted he was one of their members.

In December 1982 an RUC detective inspector visited Adams and told him that he, Danny Morrison, Tom Hartley and another prominent Sinn Fein member Joe Austin were in danger from loyalists. The UDA magazine carried a 'Wanted' poster of Adams. Even so, because of his IRA connections he was refused a licence to carry a personal protection weapon.

As the campaign for the West Belfast seat raised his profile during 1983 Adams became the target for more threats, some of them quite outlandish in their style and content. At one stage the Post Office intercepted letters containing bullets mailed to Adams and two other republicans. At the end of 1983 Adams showed off a letter which he said he'd received in June, purporting to come from the father of a policeman. The letter writer said that, if anything happened to his son in the RUC, Adams would be killed, although first he would know the 'anguish' of attending his wife Colette's funeral. 'Do not depend on Monaghan's hoods to save you,' the writer continued, employing his most colourful prose, 'they will be useless against the violence I will bring upon you – no matter where you are.' Adams claimed this threat arrived on RUC notepaper. The police said he had supplied them with only a poor photostat and they therefore weren't able to carry out forensic tests on the original.

Clearly death was always a possibility, and Adams knew it. He took precautions like avoiding obvious routes and always carried a toothbrush, as he never knew where he would be staying overnight. In November 1982 he answered a question about his political aspirations by referring to the possibility of assassination. 'If I live the life that God would give me to live – and not some loyalist or British soldier – then I think I will certainly see a Britless Ireland.' In January 1984 he was more specific, telling reporters that he believed there was a 90 per cent chance that he would be killed. 'I have been involved in republican politics for a long time and if it happens, it happens. I am fearful I may be assassinated at any time.'

Two months after making that prediction Gerry Adams had to go to the magistrates' court in the centre of Belfast to appear on a relatively minor public order charge. The day before the 1983 Westminster election, Adams and his team had been campaigning in and around the strongly nationalist New Lodge area of North Belfast, where the sectarian borderlines are especially fuzzy. The police were turning a blind eye to their flying of the Irish tricolour within their own area, even though it contravened Northern Ireland's Flags and Emblems law which is designed to crack down on the parading of symbols in public guaranteed to enrage the other community's sensibilities. However, when the campaigners strayed out on to a main road while crossing from one street to another the RUC pounced and a mêlée ensued. Adams and his helpers were arrested, something which probably did them no harm in terms of election propaganda, and were charged with obstructing the police and disorderly behaviour, a rather less politically contentious charge than one under the Flags and Emblems Act. When the arresting officers asked Gerry Adams his occupation he replied, 'Representative of the republican people of Ireland.'

At lunchtime on 14 April 1984 Adams and his co-accused were leaving the magistrates' court for lunch after spending the morning contesting the charges. It was the second day of their case – they knew that arriving and leaving the court presented them with particular dangers, so they'd asked if they could stay inside over the lunch break, but this request had been refused. They delayed their departure for some time to put any potential assassins off, then made their move. When the driver of their gold-coloured Cortina pulled up they crossed the road and jumped in quickly and drove towards West Belfast, where they intended to get some fish and chips. The danger seemed to be behind them, said Adams, so 'we started to relax as we got to the City Hall. Then there was a terrific sound of gunfire very close up and the window came in around me.'

The Ulster Freedom Fighters had sprung their trap. The UFF is a *nom de guerre* for the Ulster Defence Association, Northern Ireland's largest loyalist paramilitary organization. Three UFF terrorists had been watching, waiting to ambush Adams whenever he left the court building. They pulled up alongside his car and opened fire twenty times.

Bob Murray, who was travelling with Adams, hit the floor of the vehicle so quickly that afterwards some West Belfast wags were to dub him 'Hit the Deck' Murray. He remembers, 'We were talking about where we would get lunch and so forth and then the shooting started and I knew immediately when it started what it was and ducked down to the floor of the car and at the same time turned to my right. It's amazing, it feels like it's happening in slow motion – the window had shattered but it was still in one piece and all I could see was holes appearing in it. It happened very very quickly. At the time it seems as if it's never going to end and I came up and I asked Adams if he had been hit and he said he had been and Kevin said I've also been hit.'

Murray was the only one in the car unhurt. Kevin Rooney, the driver, had been hit in the body. Sean Keenan was wounded in the face and arm, Joe Keenan had been hit a number of times in the upper body and arms, while Adams had been struck by four bullets. Murray urged Kevin Rooney to get them to the Royal Victoria Hospital. 'The hospital was just less than a mile from the shooting incident in a perfectly straight line so I just encouraged him to keep driving not to worry about red lights, just to run red lights and keep going, keep going. When we got into the hospital I got into the emergency room and shouted to the staff that there was four men in the car who had been shot and the medical teams came rushing out.'

Inside the Royal Victoria the surgeon on duty in the resuscitation room was William Rutherford. 'I think I was standing at the door when Adams was wheeled in on the trolley. It was quickly obvious that he had been shot in the chest. I knew he could bleed outside his lung and quickly get into a dangerous situation and so I moved straight into the necessary things that needed to be done.'

Rutherford put in a chest drain, ordered X rays and then passed Adams on. 'I don't think he was particularly close to death from the actual injury he sustained. A few inches one way or another, it wouldn't have taken the bullet wounds to have been very different, slightly shifted down the chest, and they would have been right through the heart. So in one way it was near enough, but from the actual injury which he sustained I think had he had to travel for half an hour before he got to a hospital, provided the right things were done at that point I don't see why he shouldn't have survived.'

Back at the scene of the shooting Adams and his companions weren't the only ones injured. An off-duty Ulster Defence Regiment soldier who had witnessed the shooting chased the gunmen's car, before forcing it to halt in Howard Street. There, joined by two plain-clothes members of the Royal Military Police, he arrested the three attackers. Two were taken from the car – one remained inside, bleeding heavily. The soldiers had not opened fire, but the UFF man had been hit by one of his comrades' bullets. One of the loyalists wept openly as he stood against some railings under arrest, waiting to be taken away.

The fact that three members of the Army were in the immediate vicinity stoked suspicions among both republicans and loyalists that the security forces had prior knowledge. Sinn Fein's Danny Morrison claimed that the British were involved in setting up the attack and then in turn setting up the UFF in order to get the credit for the arrests. The UDA, the UFF's *alter ego*, claimed the soldiers involved were not from the UDR or the Royal Military Police but were in fact members of the SAS who had been shadowing and protecting Adams.

These claims were compounded by contradictions in the RUC's official versions of the event. Initially it had been reported that the off-duty UDR soldier had driven the wrong way down a one-way street to intercept the attackers, a manoeuvre which would not only have shown great presence of mind but would also have implied that he must have had a very good idea of which way the UFF men would be making their escape in order to block their path. Later the RUC said this version had been the result of confusion immediately after the shooting and the UDR soldier had never driven against the flow of traffic. However, discrepancies remained – for instance, the RUC described the Royal Military policemen involved as off-duty, while the Army said they were on duty, but on an unrelated mission.

Back in hospital Adams was described as satisfactory – he had one bullet removed when he was in casualty and a further two in the operating theatre. The remaining bullet wasn't removed until three months later. Adams himself believed that the Army had known what had been afoot. 'I think the British might have had information that it was going to happen. I don't think it was an attack planned by the British, or carried out by them, but I think they were aware it was going to happen. The people who have most to gain from my execution – the execution of any Irish republican – is the British government.' According to Adams, the British wanted to have the best of both worlds, watching the shooting and then arresting those responsible 'to get the kudos'.

Outside the hospital the attempted murder provoked an outcry. The UFF statement acknowledging responsibility described Adams as the 'Chief of Staff of the Provisional IRA'. The UFF claimed he was 'responsible for the continuing murder campaign being waged against Ulster Protestants and is therefore regarded as a legitimate target of war'. The loyalist terrorists continued that 'in the absence of any effective security measures taken to protect the lives of Ulster Protestants we are determined to seek out and destroy any or all key personnel within the republican terror organizations as they become amenable'. The other loyalist paramilitary organization, the UVF, stayed silent, but they may have well been cursing the UFF/UDA – in later years they claimed that they had also had a unit waiting to ambush Adams on his way from court but had been foiled by the UFF beating them to the punch.

The wider unionist and loyalist community wept few tears over Adams' wounds. George Seawright, a firebrand Scottish Protestant who became notorious for expressing the belief that all Catholics should be burned, was at this stage a representative of Ian Paisley's DUP in the Assembly at Stormont. Inside the Assembly he expressed his 'deep regret' that the murder attempt had not succeeded. Other DUP members weighed in, the Mid-Ulster MP and fundamentalist preacher the Reverend William McCrea saying that 'as one who believes in the death penalty, I believe the removal of Gerry Adams from this country would have been a bonus for the law-abiding people of this land'.

McCrea's party leader Ian Paisley didn't go so far, but in condemning the shooting he added, 'I'm saying that it's the natural law that you reap what you sow. That is God's law and that cannot be escaped. Evidently Mr Adams has been caught up in a harvest of his own making.' The SDLP leader John Hume, who was then on one of his frequent visits to the USA, said he was appalled to hear of the murder bid. Gerry Fitt, whom Adams had supplanted as West Belfast MP, also condemned the assassination attempt but, like Paisley, added some very heavy qualifications. 'Mr Adams has become a victim of a war in which he believes. Five Protestants were murdered in very cruel, brutal circumstances in Northern Ireland this week and I am quite certain that Mr Adams, even from his hospital bed, would refuse to condemn those murders.' Fitt added that he could understand the lack of sympathy towards Adams felt by unionists: 'the overwhelming majority of the Protestant population will, I am quite certain, say "Well hell slap it into him because he supports the IRA and their murder campaign."'

One Protestant who was pondering more than most the rights and wrongs of what had occurred was William Rutherford, the surgeon who had first come to Adams' aid. A Presbyterian, Rutherford was, unlike most of his co-religionists, not a unionist. He had been brought up in Dublin and had worked in India, where he had witnessed British withdrawal and he was of the view that an independent self-governing Ireland was the only way forward. That said, he was passionately opposed to violence from any quarter. In the hospital Rutherford had witnessed the aftermath of innumerable terrible incidents – the thirteen-year-old boy whom he couldn't save who had been shot because he had a toy gun tucked in the belt of his trousers, the policeman whom Rutherford met one moment when he brought a seriously ill family member to the hospital and whom he then had to treat a few minutes later when he ventured outside to move his car and was shot and fatally wounded by the IRA. Seeing such atrocities at first hand had stirred Rutherford to get involved in peace and cross-community work.

The doctor had first become aware of Adams in the early 1970s when a couple of Protestant professional friends who'd come across the young Provisional had mentioned him as someone worth watching. They suspected he might end up being a positive influence inside militant republicanism. But as Adams had risen to prominence the hardline rhetoric of some of his pronouncements hadn't impressed Rutherford. The surgeon stared down at the man with the chest wound he was treating and reflected on the strange power that he now had over Adams' fate.

What interested me was that often statements that he had made had irritated me quite a bit and I suppose I looked on him as being a kind of enemy figure and I had often wondered what it would be like if I found myself in the position [of treating him]. But actually at the point where I had to take action it was like any other patient. You always have to exclude your normal emotions, if you don't you'd never survive. So I just did exactly the same thing, for he got no more and no less than anyone would have got ... and yet a wee voice inside me was saying isn't it interesting, you're just feeling as if he was a totally ordinary man and it is not in any way worrying you that you're doing this.

On the night of the shooting a bus was hijacked in Andersonstown and an attempt was made, by no means for the first time, to set fire to Gerry Fitt's house. Adams got out of hospital five days after the attack, saying that what had occurred wouldn't change his support for the IRA. He told reporters that he still believed in armed struggle and 'the republican movement is bigger than me or any individual'.

Interviewed by Peter Taylor on the BBC's *Inside Story* some years later, one of the UFF gunmen, John Gregg, expressed no remorse about what had occurred. Gregg told Taylor that he'd pulled the trigger but hadn't killed his target, whom he identified only as 'a prominent member of Sinn Fein'. The UFF man said he was aware of the potential consequences but that hadn't deterred him as 'I believed I was right.' Gregg rejected the notion of Sinn Fein as a 'normal' political party. 'Well, it may be a legal political party,' he countered, but 'to me they're the same as the IRA. It's just the IRA under a different name.'

Gregg's description of how he became caught up in the world of the paramilitaries could be swapped more or less word for word for that of many IRA members. 'I was very young when I got involved, but that was just the nature of the Troubles in the early 1970s. The majority of young men from working-class districts all became involved in one loyalist organization or another. I don't think I realized why I was getting involved, but I certainly know now. There's nothing sectarian in what I'm in here for. Basically I thought I should be doing something for my own people. Twenty years now loyalist people have been getting slaughtered and now somebody has to do something.' Asked if he had any regrets about shooting Adams, Gregg replied, 'Only that I didn't succeed.' There was only one way to beat the IRA, the loyalist argued, and that was 'at their own game'.

Adams continued to harbour the belief that Gregg and his fellow gunmen hadn't acted alone. Writing in the *Irish News* in 1992 Adams again claimed that the British had had advance notice of the assassination attempt. He relied on an anecdote recounted by the journalist Mark Urban in his book *Big Boy's Rules*, in which Urban said an unnamed senior member of the security forces had confirmed that an agent within the UDA had tipped them off about the shooting before it happened. Urban said the security forces' information 'did not tell us the exact time and street where the attack would take place, but did give us the basic information that there would be an attempt on his life when he went to the court house'.

Adams was reflecting on this in 1992 because of revelations about another UDA/UFF plot to kill him. This further murder plot had come to light as a result of the arrest of Brian Nelson, a former soldier who led a double life as a UDA intelligence officer and an agent for Army intelligence. Nelson had been involved in a reconnaissance mission for the UDA at a housing office near Belfast city centre which Adams visited regularly. The UDA planned to kill Adams by attaching a limpet mine to the roof of his car. Nelson told his Army handlers what was planned and the security forces stopped the planned assassination.

In a journal which he kept in jail Nelson wrote:

It was told to me by my handlers that the assassination of Adams, had it gone ahead, would have been totally counterproductive, particularly considering the delicate balance of power within Sinn Fein. The party was split into two camps, on the one side there was Adams and his supporters who were committed to following the political path towards a solution. On the other side was Martin McGuinness and the PIRA army council who were seeking to intensify their military campaign. From their sources the intelligence services knew that Adams was just about holding sway, but it would not take much to tip this delicate state of balance in favour of McGuinness and his hawks.

Adams himself was dismissive about Nelson's story of the British moving in to save his life. Preferring to believe that the security forces were quite happy to see him dead, Adams described it as 'unsubstantiated' and 'an obvious ploy by a senior intelligence officer to paint his agent and the intelligence services as impartial institutions when, in fact, they are part of a conspiracy which we may never hear the truth about'. This was, however, written in 1992 when the IRA ceasefire was still two years away. Adams can always be relied upon to dismiss any story which appears to paint the British Army and their agents in a good light, but at this stage he would have been doubly reticent about giving any credence to the apparent insight which Nelson had gained concerning the behind-the-scenes diplomacy related to the peace process.

In 1994, when more of that diplomacy was out in the open, William Rutherford, the surgeon who had treated Adams a decade earlier, once again saw him in the flesh. This time it was inside the Conway Mill just off the Falls Road, a building regularly used by Sinn Fein for news conferences and meetings and which had recently been highlighted by the investigative television reporter Roger Cook as the nerve centre of the IRA's financial operations. The occasion was a meeting of one of the party's sessions of its 'Peace Commission', an exercise in consultation with the public which was part of the Provisional choreography running up to the announcement of the 1994 ceasefire. On the way in one of the authors met the former MP Bernadette McAliskey, who had by now identified herself as one of the prime sceptics concerning the 'peace process' of the 1990s. Asked if she had been attending the Peace Commission McAliskey scoffed and said, 'No, I've been here on honourable business.'

Inside, however, one man who decided that it was honourable to talk about peace was William Rutherford, who had decided to respond to an invitation sent him by Adams' close colleague Tom Hartley. Adams was in the same room as the man who had helped save his life, but the two didn't exchange words. At this stage the IRA still hadn't given any definite indication that it would cease its violence, so Rutherford decided in a submission which he read to the Sinn Fein activists to be as direct as possible:

> After returning to Ireland in 1967 I got a job in the Casualty in the Royal Victoria Hospital. There in 1969 I stared in disbelief at the first bullet wound I had seen in twenty-five years of surgery. Not long afterwards I saw my first death from the Troubles, and found myself faced with having to convey this news to the family. This harrowing experience was repeated many many times, with Catholics and with Protestants. In the resuscitation room again and again I was faced with gravely injured people. Some of these were left paralysed, blind or without a limb. One thing became clear to me: in the extremes of life and death, a man is just a man, a woman a woman, a family a family. I mourn for them all, I grieve for them all. I used to listen to speeches by your president.

To me they seemed to carry tones of bitterness and hate. Yet when he was wheeled in with bullet wounds in his chest, he too was just a wounded man in need of treatment, and I was glad to fight for his life.

Rutherford went on to welcome comments from Martin McGuinness recognizing the need to find a new way to relate to Protestants and unionists. But in declaring himself a believer in a United Ireland he emphasized that such an arrangement could be achieved only by persuasion, not by violence.

I know that persuading and convincing the unionist community that a United Ireland is truly their best option is an enormously difficult task. Success would not be possible in weeks or months. We must be prepared to think in decades. But the real alternative to such peaceful persuasion is not just continued warfare, it is escalating warfare. I am asking you to bring to an end your support for the armed struggle. If you find that you cannot take that step, I hope that you will have the courage and honesty to admit that you cannot yet support the call for peace. The worst of all outcomes for this Peace or War Commission would be to opt for the words of peace and the acts of war. That a period of confusion is inevitable in the final days of war I understand and accept. But in the end politics are incompatible with Armalites, and peace negotiations are incompatible with mortar attacks and incendiary bombs. Is it not the wish of the overwhelming majority of the people of Ireland that we begin now to make some sense of all the deaths and suffering of the past twenty-six years? In the name of God and for the sake of all our people, I beg you to choose clearly the path of peace.

It was undoubtedly a powerful oration which captured considerable press attention. In the succeeding months Rutherford was to find himself prey to contrasting emotions, as he, like others in Northern Ireland, tried to make sense of the flow of events. Was this a period of confusion at the end of a war or a sign that his call had been rejected? After the IRA launched a mortar attack on Heathrow airport Rutherford heard Adams justify it as something which had focused international attention on Ireland, as a reminder that the conflict was unresolved and which 'should have a major accelerating effect on the British government'. The surgeon was depressed, regarding this as 'the clearest reply I got from him to the submission that I had made. It seemed to me that he was very pleased that the armed struggle had put this on in order to up the political pressure.'

But then when the ceasefire was called on 31 August 1994 Rutherford was extremely heartened by it. Despite the return to violence in February 1996 he inclined towards a sympathetic view of his former patient:

> My guess, and it can be no more than that, is that he would like to be allowed the freedom to fight this in a totally political way . . . that he would like a ceasefire and even a ceasefire where people were promising that it would be permanent. But he has tremendous pressures on him too. I saw the slogan up on the wall where some group didn't like how peaceful he was being and they were comparing him to Collins and asking him to remember what happened to Collins. That was a very severe threat from people within his own community, so it can't be easy. My reading is that he is trying, but that it is a very delicate road that he walks along and that he maybe is now in as much danger from people on his own side as from anywhere else.

CHAPTER SIXTEEN

'We Only Have to Be Lucky Once'

On 15 September 1984 an old friend and former jail-mate of Gerry Adams booked into Room 629 of the Grand Hotel in Brighton. Patrick Magee already had a police record of burglary and petty crime by the time his parents brought the family back home to Belfast in 1970 after seventeen years spent living in England. He quickly turned his talents over to the use of the IRA in the north of the city, and by 1973 found himself in the Long Kesh internment camp, sharing the same cage as Gerry Adams. By the time he was released two years later the prison experience had turned him into one of the IRA's most ruthless and dedicated operators.

A small and intense man, in 1979 he was listed by Scotland Yard's anti-terrorist squad as wanted after an arms and explosives cache was discovered in a London flat. He fled to Holland, from where the Dutch authorities refused to extradite him back to Britain. Released from custody, he slipped quietly back to Belfast and remained active. In 1981 he lost part of a finger when a loyalist gunman opened fire in the Dublin offices of the republican movement's newspaper. Two years later he was being tailed by Special Branch officers in the north of England. But by the time he checked into the Grand Hotel he had shaken them off.

As one of their most experienced operators, Magee was chosen by the IRA's General Headquarters Staff to plant the 30lb Semtex bomb which would come within an ace of wiping out Margaret Thatcher and her cabinet. He checked in under the name of Roy Walsh, a member of the IRA team which bombed the Old Bailey in 1973, asking for a room on an upper floor with a sea view. Within hours he found the perfect hiding place: a partition wall separating the bathroom of Room 629 from Room 628. An IRA explosives expert arrived with the bomb, set it on a long-delay timer to detonate in the early hours of 12 October and the two men ordered a bottle of vodka to celebrate a job well done. Magee would be arrested in June 1985 and sentenced on fingerprint evidence to thirty-five years' imprisonment.

When the bomb exploded, the ensuing fire and the collapsing building killed five people and injured thirty-four as rescuers tore in the darkness at the rubble in a desperate rush to find the victims. Mrs Thatcher and her cabinet survived, but the world was left to ponder the audacity of the Provisionals and what might have been if they had succeeded. The IRA sent a chilling message to Mrs Thatcher claiming responsibility: 'Today we were unlucky but remember, we only have to be lucky once. You will have to be lucky always.'

Gerry Adams gave his reaction the same day. 'The IRA action in Brighton was the inevitable result of the British occupation of the six counties. The way to end such incidents and stop the suffering of people in Ireland is of course in a British withdrawal. Someday, someone in power in Britain will realize that.' And in his presidential address at the Sinn Fein *ard fheis* in Dublin in November he called the attack 'a blow for democracy'. The near success of the bombing, and the huge propaganda dividend it reaped for the Provisionals, illustrated perfectly Adams' concept of 'armed propaganda' and the reforms wrought by him inside the republican movement, the move into political activity and the fine-tuning of the military machine into a leaner, more effective fighting force.

Although overall violence in Northern Ireland was continuing to decrease, the IRA's share in it was going up substantially under the new venture into politics, leading many to the reasonable supposition that in order to reassure the militarists that this new political odyssey would not end the same way as all previous ventures had, in the absorption of the revolutionary movement by the constitutional parties, the Adams leadership was giving a long rein to the volunteers. As well as the murder of the daughter of a Catholic magistrate, two off-duty soldiers had been killed and ten others injured in a car bomb explosion as they competed in a fishing competition in Fermanagh. The Provisionals had intensified their campaign in the countryside, murdering twenty-two local Protestant members of the security forces in the first nine months of the year. Many Protestants living in vulnerable areas along the border and west of the River Bann came to the conclusion, as they saw how many of their religion fled to safer areas after a killing, that the IRA was carrying out a sustained campaign of ethnic cleansing. But another reason for this changing pattern of murder was the increasing effectiveness of the Army and RUC in Belfast.

In 1985 the IRA claimed that it had used more explosives than in any previous year of its campaign, as a major bombing campaign was launched with the intention of wrecking the political process leading towards the Anglo-Irish Agreement. A number of deadly innovations made their debut, including a single-tube mortar for firing 50lb bombs and ever larger mobile bombs. In May a 1,000lb trailer bomb killed four policemen at Killeen on the border and the following month another 1,000lb bomb killed a policeman. The recorder's court in Belfast and a commercial centre at Ballynahinch in County Down were destroyed. The IRA widened its range of 'legitimate targets' when it began murdering building contractors for 'collaborating' with the security forces. Seamus McEvoy, a Catholic businessman from Dublin, was the first victim. But even this renewed offensive was a fraction of the violence committed in 1971 and 1972 when the British government had been forced to meet the IRA.

The rural assassinations, where counter-terrorist surveillance was lighter and local intelligence was reliable, gave the Troubles an even darker countenance, as the career of the former IRA intelligence officer Eamon Collins has testified. Collins was a disaffected Marxist law student who joined the Customs service and was soon giving the details of Protestant colleagues to the Provisionals for 'stiffing'. His chilling account in his autobiography *Killing Rage* of how the 'hidden enemy' preyed upon their Protestant neighbours, often stalking them for years before delivering the *coup de grâce*, stripped away the IRA's military veneer. Collins revealed how in the early 1980s the IRA in South Armagh, renowned as the hardest and most efficient unit in the organization, directed him to join and take control of Sinn Fein in the border town of Newry because they were so concerned that the movement was becoming too political and losing sight of the age-old republican maxim that the British could only be removed from Ireland by force. The diversion into politics, via the huge mobilization of public support for the hunger strikers, had brought unwelcome developments for the pure militarists.

On the other hand, the European poll result in June 1984 seemed to identify Sinn Fein's ceiling of acceptability among the nationalist electorate of Northern Ireland (in the Irish Republic they had attracted less than 2 per cent support). But while Adams might be left feeling frustrated he was not about to call it a day. 'The SDLP can draw only temporary comfort from this election. For our part we will continue to progress electorally,' he said, adjusting his sights to another long war. Nevertheless, the Sinn Fein vote dropped another percentage point the following May in the local government elections, although the party now had fifty-nine councillors spread across Northern Ireland who, for the first time, took their seats. When Seamus Kerr appeared in Omagh District Council two weeks later he made his opening comments in Irish and the chamber erupted. Similar scenes across the province would, for years to come, show local politics at their bleakest and most bitter as unionists reluctantly came to terms with the presence of a new order in their midst.

Although the seemingly unstoppable Sinn Fein bandwagon had been exposed as a sham, much to the relief of London, Dublin and the SDLP, Adams was increasingly confident that his nonetheless solid electoral following had given him a political veto just as effective as any other in Northern Ireland on the shape of the final outcome of the conflict. The events of the next few years would demonstrate that, however industriously the SDLP, the unionist parties or the British and Irish governments contrived to work at a solution, without Adams it could not stand the test of time.

But while he tinkered with the balance between Armalite and ballot box and mused publicly about the inevitability of reaching the same destination by either the military or the political route, his close ally Martin McGuinness was happy to send an unambiguous reminder to the republican faithful where the real power lay. 'The Irish Republican Army offers the only resolution to the present situation,' he told mourners at a republican funeral. 'We recognize the value and the limitations of electoral success. We recognize that only disciplined revolutionary armed struggle by the IRA will ever end British rule. Without the IRA we are on our knees. Without the IRA we are slaves. For fifteen years this generation of republicans have been off their knees. We will never be slaves again.'

Margaret Thatcher's 'Out! Out! Out!' speech, when she rejected options to end the Troubles drawn up by Ireland's constitutional nationalist parties, was welcome propaganda to Gerry Adams, who used it to good effect in showing up the failure of the SDLP to influence the British government. 'I repeat my call to John Hume that if he really wants to demonstrate nationalist alienation then he should withdraw from the foreign parliament at Westminster where as a faithful Uncle Tom he has also been a dartboard for Mrs Thatcher's insults.' But in spite of the British Premier's negative outburst senior civil servants continued to work behind the scenes to put flesh on the bones of ending the 'nationalist nightmare' in Northern Ireland and creating greater security co-operation between the two states.

Before those negotiations came to fruition, there was a serious matter of internal dissent for Adams to deal with. At Easter 1985 he discovered he was facing the strongest challenge to his leadership since wresting control of the Provisionals from the Southerners in the late 1970s. But the challenge was coming from his native Belfast, led by his old prison comrade and companion to the 1972 London talks, Ivor Bell. A veteran O/C of Belfast, Bell went with Adams when the old IRA split and was closely involved with him in the reconstruction of the Provos nearly a decade earlier. He also played a key role in setting up the arms supply line from Libya in 1981. Now he was touring republican areas, canvassing support for an extraordinary general army convention at which Adams' leadership would be challenged.

His supporters complained that Paddy Adams, recently released from prison, had been imposed as the IRA's commander in Belfast as part of the leadership's policy of scaling down military activity in the city. Paddy's big brother acted swiftly to stifle the dissent. All of the figures approached by Bell were interviewed and made to swear statements. A court martial was called in June 1985 but when Bell failed to appear he was found guilty in his absence and expelled from the IRA, with a parting warning that his role in ridding Ireland of British rule was finished, for ever.

'I don't know that Ivor had any great problems with abstentionism or anything else,' said 'Tony', a close ally of both Bell and Adams in the 1980s. 'I think that he saw a problem with the leadership rather than with anything else. Ivor probably did it the wrong way, he started organizing clandestine meetings, which is always a dangerous thing to do rather than doing it up front. He was probably not happy with the dual strategy in that he would have seen too much of the resources going towards the political thing, but in a revolutionary army you have to fairly ruthless about the way you deal with dissent.'

Along with Bell went Eddie Carmichael, Anto Murray, Anne Boyle and Danny McCann, all military hardliners. But McCann, an important intelligence operative, was later allowed to rejoin and was subsequently killed by the SAS in Gibraltar during an attempt to explode a bomb on the British colony at the southern tip of Spain. Adams' success in stamping out this challenge to his authority from figures of high republican calibre is a good indication of the ruthlessness and cold efficiency which even his admirers highlight when asked to sum up his qualities.

Adams managed his electoral setbacks by charting a new course in his relations with the SDLP. He began making overtures to John Hume at the moment when he realized that the leading voice of nationalism was not going to give up his position as easily or swiftly as was imagined during the first heady days of Sinn Fein electoral success. On a radio panel with Hume he said he would like talks with the SDLP to discuss what he described as 'pan-nationalist interests'. In a lively exchange Hume accused Adams of fudging the issue of who really controlled the republican movement. 'As I understand the Provisional republican movement, Sinn Fein are subject in all matters to the Army Council . . . I want to talk to the people who are making the decisions . . . in order to ask them to cease their campaign of violence,' he said. The differences between the SDLP and Sinn Fein 'are so fundamental that it would be impossible to enter into electoral arrangements' with them. 'The division in Ireland is a division in the minds of people. You cannot heal that division by force of arms.'

Within twenty-four hours the IRA, in a statement penned by the ubiquitous 'P. O'Neill', accepted Hume's request for talks. 'We have plenty to discuss. We are also confident that Mr Hume can take adequate security precautions for the meeting. We await his response and will be in contact.' Hume responded by declaring that the IRA statement was 'an implicit admission that the leadership of the Provisional IRA were the real leaders of the republican movement,' but added: 'I would welcome an opportunity to meet them face to face.' Sinn Fein immediately put in another request for a meeting with Hume, who dismissed them as 'mere surrogates'.

The political establishment in Dublin was at one in its reaction to Hume's initiative. The Irish Labour Party leader Dick Spring said: 'No talks should be held with the IRA in advance of their declaring a truce,' while the Taoiseach Garrett Fitzgerald warned that any meeting would be 'broken up' and 'members of the Army Council, if identified, would be arrested'. In the event the arrangements for the meeting did not run as smoothly as the IRA had promised. They sent Seamus Twomey and the Maze prison escaper Brendan 'Bik' McFarlane to meet Hume in a private house in County Sligo, but were delayed by a shortage of vehicles in leaving Dublin. In the end it was Sean O'Callaghan, then O/C Southern Command, who had to arrange their transport, by which time Hume had spent more than thirty hours in the IRA's 'virtual custody'. McFarlane arrived armed with a video camera, saying that the meeting was to be recorded. When Hume refused to be filmed, arguing that he would have no control over its future use, he was told the meeting was off.

Hume went home empty-handed to pen a statement. 'Since the IRA has now confirmed beyond a shadow of doubt that they believe that only an "armed struggle" can solve the problems of this community there is no point whatsoever in discussing politics with their political wing.' The angry words were in stark contrast with his tenacious refusal to abandon Adams during the peace process of the 1990s. Hume had already made several efforts in the 1970s to woo the Provisionals away from violence. In the run-up to the 1972 ceasefire he told Dave O'Connell that the best of the republican movement and the SDLP combined would create an unstoppable nationalist force, but after giving it some consideration O'Connell chose to stick with the physical-force tradition.

In September 1985, after describing a call from Cahal Daly for an IRA ceasefire as 'a call to surrender' and following his refusal to condemn the IRA for murdering a Ballymurphy couple, Catherine and Gerard Mahon, as alleged informers, Adams told a BBC religious affairs programme that 'I do my best to be as good a Catholic as I can.' He criticized the Church for condemning IRA but not RUC violence. 'Thinking people are put into a difficult situation. Involvement in defending physical force or involvement in physical force presents a dilemma. The job of Christians – and I do not profess to be a great Christian – is not to stand up and be one-sided in one's condemnation but to actually give a lead in changing the situation and conditions in which violence flourishes as it does at the moment.'

The first real test of Adams' political acumen would come when he responded to the publication of the Anglo-Irish Agreement in November 1985. According to Sean O'Callaghan, Adams told him that there were ongoing secret contacts with British and Irish govern-ment representatives, the latter party keeping Sinn Fein informed of the likely contents of the Agreement. For their part the unionists were kept in the dark by Downing Street and exploded with rage when, without a word of consultation, Mrs Thatcher and Dr Fitzgerald unveiled at Hillsborough on 15 November the most significant treaty between the two states since the 1920 Treaty negotiations.

The centrepiece of the Agreement was a new Intergovernmental Conference with a permanent secretariat outside Belfast at Maryfield. Within this anonymous but heavily guarded office block Irish civil servants would, in the legalistic phrasing of the Agreement, 'put forward views and proposals on matters relating to Northern Ireland within the field of activity of the conference'. In other words, Dublin was finally being granted an input into the day-to-day running of the political, security and legal life of Northern Ireland. Unionists were appalled, finding Mrs Thatcher's concession to Dublin incomprehen-sible in light of her 'Out! Out! Out!' speech. A massive campaign of opposition was launched, with the largest ever demonstration in Northern Ireland held outside Belfast's City Hall, the resignations of MPs to create a mini-election and many marches and rallies often ending in violence. The RUC Chief Constable Sir John Hermon faced down the unrest, at considerable cost to his predominantly Protestant police force. Three hundred police houses were damaged in the first six months of the Agreement, forcing many officers to move to safer areas.

In his public comments Adams was no fan of the Agreement either, saying it was all about 'stabilizing British interests' and co-opting Dublin to act as 'the new guarantor of partition'. The Agreement would prolong the struggle, he said. He drew particular attention to Article Seven, which promised a new cross-border security deal to make life for the Provisionals hard in the South. He could find himself, for once, in agreement with Mrs Thatcher, who later admitted to regretting she had signed the Agreement once the new get-tough policy failed to materialize in the Republic. Adams declared that it was aimed at defeating the IRA, which in his view was doing 'very well' after sixteen years' fighting. 'I would be only too happy to call on the IRA to declare a ceasefire in the event of a British withdrawal but not only would such an appeal fall on deaf ears, quite rightly it would be a wasted exercise and be in fact a surrender to Margaret

Thatcher and an acceptance by myself as a republican of Britain's right to rule in this part of Ireland.'

With the benefit of hindsight and the peace process some journalists have come to believe that in private Adams and his inner circle gave the Hillsborough accord a warmer reception. That is a view denied by such senior figures as the Sinn Fein vice president Pat Doherty. The evidence from the time points in the other direction, with numerous attacks by Adams on the Agreement. But in 1993 its chief Irish architect Michael Lillis, a senior Dublin civil servant, met Adams twice to discuss its significance. The two men had a long and detailed discussion of political developments since 1985 and Lillis said that his principal concern was to convince Adams that the Agreement was not being worked fully and that it recognized the legitimacy of those who wished to work for Irish unity by peaceful means. 'It was quite clear that privately he and his colleagues saw it as a very significant event and one which was much more positive and significant than the way they reacted to it in public. One of the reasons they reacted to it negatively in public was that it was presented wrongly, including by my own side, as being an attempt to take the ground away from the IRA and its supporters.' A senior Northern Ireland Office official said that the purpose of the Agreement was 'a come-on and a threat', in other words that if Adams wanted to be part of reshaping Northern Ireland he could do so by going constitutional, but if he persisted with terrorism he would be left increasingly isolated. If a long game of coaxing the Provisional leadership down the road to peace was being played here, Adams was giving very little away

Lillis admired Adams, thinking him serious, sincere and intellectually gifted. He argued the Irish government case forcefully to the Sinn Fein leader that the Anglo-Irish Agreement demonstrated that the British preference was for withdrawal, 'but that they cannot exercise that preference because it would be wrong to do so'. Lillis said he formed the impression that Adams was not interested in a 'black and white unitary Irish state' but that in the long term he believed that the Irish border would be removed. Asked by BBC *Panorama*'s John Ware if he thought he had succeeded in convincing Adams of the true nature, as he understood it, of British intentions Lillis said: 'Well, I certainly argued that strongly to him and he listened and from the questions he asked me . . . I want to be fair to him now, I think it would be inaccurate of me to say that that is his conviction, but from the questions that he put repeatedly on several occasions I believe that he is convinced that that's the case, that the British would like to go.'

If Lillis was right it could be reasonably argued that Adams' own belief in the twin-track strategy of the Armalite and the ballot box was, if anything, strengthened by the Anglo-Irish Agreement. A more flexible attitude in turning off the violence to seize political ground and then switching it back on again whenever the British needed a bit more assistance, to help them do what they really wanted anyway, could be the way forward. Crucially, Lillis admitted to Ware that when it came to the moral question of the use of violence to serve political ends Adams had not wavered. 'I think it would be inaccurate certainly to suggest that he was in any way ashamed of the campaign of violence, of the Provisional IRA. I would say actually on the contrary, that he believed that it had produced useful political effects.'

Sean O'Callaghan remembers a Sinn Fein executive meeting shortly before the Anglo-Irish Agreement was published when its contents were being discussed, where he decided to carry out an experiment and he suggested that perhaps there were positive elements in it. 'After the meeting Adams came over to me and said, "Too early, Sean, too early."'

O'Callaghan was one of the coterie of senior Sinn Fein/IRA members watching Adams like a hawk during 1984 and 1985, wondering just where he intended leading the republican movement in the coming years, whether towards or away from the constitutionalism which had failed them so many times before and which was still strongly resisted by the grassroots. Looking back on the period O'Callaghan believed that Adams learned two important lessons: first that John Hume was a much bigger and stronger nationalist leader than he and therefore somebody who had to be dealt with in a sophisticated manner. And secondly that the British government were in fact prepared to ride roughshod over the feelings and wishes of Northern Ireland's unionist majority when and if it suited their political objectives.

> I will say one thing that I would bet with anybody on. Adams will not be involved in giving up the option of armed struggle unless it is taken from him, he is not going to just throw that

option away. Adams' intention has always been that you should negotiate and make war at the same time, that to do anything else, to throw away your option of armed struggle just for simple negotiation is madness. He wants an IRA answerable to the political leadership.

The difficulty is that when Adams says there can be no military victory on either side, democratic politicians make a leap immediately thinking, 'Oh, well if there is not going to be military victory that means he wants compromise.' I just believe that Adams has never bothered to tell them that when he believes there is no military victory certainly there is a political victory for nationalism and that's the one he is interested in.

The same month that the Anglo-Irish Agreement was signed Sinn Fein held its annual party conference. Another step down the constitutional path was taken when the conference debated the question of abstaining from taking seats in the Irish parliament, the Dail. Two years earlier, when Adams took over from Ruairi O Bradaigh as Sinn Fein president, delegates threw out an historic rule that even discussion of abstentionism was forbidden, so sacred a tenet of republicanism had it been until then. The refusal to recognize Dail Eireann, which went hand in hand with the IRA's claim to be the only legitimate government in Ireland, was the very essence of the republican birthright.

Even so, IRA volunteers were encouraged to discuss the issue freely among themselves in their units up and down the country. The conference motion was that it should be treated as a matter of tactics rather than principle. It was an echo of the attempt made by Eamon De Valera to get the republican movement to step down off its lofty plinth of idealism and work with what was available in the real world. De Valera failed, and split with Sinn Fein to go and form his 'Soldiers of Destiny', Fianna Fail. Within a few years he was in power.

Adams publicly took no position on the issue and, in his by now familiar tactic of sending a deputy out into no-man's land, he chose Danny Morrison to speak for him. Confronting the issue head on by asking delegates to end abstentionism was considered exceedingly risky by Adams, so he reasoned with his famous caution that if the movement could be persuaded that it was only a tactic rather than a principle in time the leadership would be able to convince the rank and file that taking seats in Leinster House was an acceptable strategy so long as it advanced the republican cause. When he got up to speak Morrison began by reminding the conference that the IRA gave its support to developing electoral intervention and he promised that there would be no winding down of the campaign of violence. He carried the hall, but not by the two-thirds majority required to change policy. Nevertheless the result was helpful in identifying where resistance lay, and Adams began to plan for the following year's conference.

He had dared to repeat De Valera's gamble and win. Just as he had been able to cap De Valera's successes in the North by winning the West Belfast seat which had eluded the Irish President, now his control of the republican movement was so strong that he was on the verge of accomplishing what many believed impossible. Republicans are supposed to have long memories, but on that day the majority of delegates seemed unable to recall the same conference two years earlier when Adams had told them he was not going to lead Sinn Fein into the Dail.

Where Adams' real leadership quality showed itself was in the way he always secured the ground before moving into it himself. He was taking the movement in the same direction as his old IRA chief of staff Cathal Goulding had tried in the 1960s, but was determined not to end up like the 'Stickies', as Goulding's Official IRA were called in Belfast slang, and be devoured by the sharks. Whenever he encountered resistance he swam back into the shoal. Nevertheless, by the mid-1980s he was confident enough in the changes to tell the RTE investigative reporter Brendan O'Brien that the 1977 IRA Staff Report document which had brought in the cell-structure system and had instructed that Sinn Fein came under army direction at all times no longer applied quite so rigidly.

Sinn Fein and the IRA were now 'on a par', even while recognizing that the army was the supreme authority. In practice, Adams told O'Brien, this meant that 'Sinn Fein people could work away without going to the IRA for say-so.' The 'Falls Road Think Tank' was part of these developments. But Adams' critics lampooned the notion and just how seriously Adams took the charge of being a 'closet Stickie' can be gauged by the treatment of Eamon Collins, who publicly challenged him at the funeral of IRA man Brendan Watters in August

1984. Watters had blown himself up when a bomb he intended throwing at an RUC patrol exploded prematurely.

Collins was annoyed that Adams was managing to calm the angry crowd of mourners when he thought that a violent confrontation with the police was grist to the Provisionals' mill. Afterwards Collins said he felt his blood boil to hear Adams' men discussing the Watters funeral as if it was a football match. Adams chided Collins for encouraging the mourners to stamp their feet, telling him that it smacked of militarism and fascism. Before Adams could say another word, Collins spat at him: '"That sounds like something the Sticks would come out with!" Adams' hand slipped from my shoulder. He looked shocked. I had hit him with the accusation that his competitors within the Provisional republican movement had been levelling at him since he first became the movement's most charismatic figure since Padraig Pearse and Michael Collins.'

Although no more was said that day, the jibe would come back to haunt Collins, with verbal threats levelled at him and friends from Adams supporters. Later, after Collins had buckled under police interrogation, agreed to turn 'supergrass' but then retracted, only to be almost miraculously cleared of serious terrorism offences by a judge who decided that his admissions may have been prised out of him by RUC detectives using excessive force or menace, he was given some bad news by his solicitor, the late Paddy McGrory, a man of great compassion and intellect who was also a close friend of Adams. Collins told McGrory that he intended to go back home to Newry. '"Newry," echoed Paddy, almost sighing. He hesitated again before speaking. In a roundabout, hesitant way he said that he had been speaking to Gerry Adams quite recently and that this present case and its progress happened to come up in the general conversation. He had mentioned the possibility – however slight – of my release. He "got the impression from him" that "interested parties" with an axe to grind wouldn't want me back in Newry. Gerry had said: "South Armagh is a notorious area where they would kill their own granny if they had to."'

Even though Collins protested that he had been promised an amnesty by the IRA if he retracted, McGrory told him that he had never before come across such bitterness and jealousy from republicans as that directed towards him and that it was probably because the high-grade information that he had passed on to the RUC had been especially damaging in Belfast, where he had outlined the divisions, frictions and power struggles in the movement. 'I think you should go to somewhere like Waterford in the Republic and lead a very quiet life,' McGrory advised him.

The by-elections caused by the unionist reaction to the Anglo-Irish Agreement carried more bad news for Adams. The Sinn Fein vote in Newry and Armagh, a strongly republican area, dropped from 21 per cent to 13 per cent, delivering an impressive victory to the SDLP's Seamus Mallon. But Adams' electoral strategy was going to be kept on the rails by the peculiarly Provisional logic of underwriting it with a massive injection of arms. It was in keeping with Adams' pragmatic approach and he correctly calculated that most volunteers involved in the war were more interested in fighting the Brits than questions of republican theology. The waverers could be bought off with the promise of a huge escalation of the campaign, armed by Colonel Gadaffi of Libya.

In all there were four arms shipments from Libya to Ireland, the first in August 1985, the last in October 1987. The first three, successful shipments imported 105 tons of weapons and explosives, including the powerful Czech-made Semtex and SAM-7 missiles. Only when the fourth shipment, on board the *Eksund*, was captured off France did the scale of the operation become clear to the intelligence services in London, Dublin and Belfast. By the time Adams made his move in the second half of 1986 the vast new armoury was already buried in custom-built underground bunkers across Southern Ireland. He went to that year's Sinn Fein conference with a large cheque to cash.

Before that there was an IRA Army Convention, the first to be held since the IRA split of 1969. Adams remembered only too well the bad blood spilt back then and the savage feud which ensued. He resolved never to let it happen again, and to do so meant bringing the IRA with him *en masse*. Ivor Bell had already been expelled and other precautions were taken, such as the escalation of the war effort. Changes in the Belfast command structure were authorized and promises made to drop the women's right to choose their position on the abortion issue to placate the conservatives. But the ace card was the Libyan leader's gift. In playing it Adams knew that he would have to beat Ruairi O Bradaigh once and for all.

O Bradaigh had a strong hunch where Adams was leading the movement from early 1982, although, as he puts it, it was 'impossible to pin down'. 'Adams wasn't seen to be actively pursuing it but he had other people pursuing it and his role was to give those other people protection, give them scope, hold the ring for them which was much the same as what Goulding did in the sixties. When the thing got big enough he jumps in on their side. I have seen it happen before and it was extraordinary to see people who had left with the Officials and then become disenchanted with them and then go into the H Block Committees and eventually back into Sinn Fein and sixteen years later were saying the very same things that had been said in 1969. That was very hard to take.'

O Bradaigh claimed that the Army Convention was 'sprung' on the movement so that Adams' opponents had little time to organize:

> The Army Convention took place and, from what I was made aware of, it was unrepresentative. People had been purged, new structures were created. Units were put together where there would be one Against, and two other ones who were For would be joined with it, no matter how grotesque the gerrymandering. The result was that the one who was Against wouldn't be heard at all. Of course it was prepared over a long time but as far as the rank and file were concerned it was done over a week or two.
>
> On the army side the voting was something like, I believe, seventy-five to twenty-five [in favour of ending abstentionism]. But then there was no word of it in public until about two and a half weeks before the *ard fheis*.

The Convention was held in County Meath under cover of an Irish language conference and in a statement published almost a month later the IRA said it had opened 'with a unanimous pledge of rededication to the armed struggle and confidence in the armed struggle as being the means of breaking the British connection and bringing about Irish independence. Several sections of the Constitution of Oglaigh na hEireann were amended and, by more than the required two-thirds majority, the delegates passed two particular resolutions. The first removed the ban on volunteers discussing or advocating the taking of parliamentary seats. The second removed the ban on supporting successful republican candidates who take their seats in Leinster House.'

What the statement did not reveal was that the leadership of Adams had encountered strong resistance from South Armagh and Dundalk as well as Kerry and Mid-Ulster. The Convention had to be reconvened, where the required majority was obtained only after important concessions were granted to the traditionalists. These in effect amounted to guarantees that the 'war' would be escalated. Martin McGuinness was confirmed as the man in charge of Northern Command as well as the Army Council and a number of hardliners expelled for favouring Ivor Bell were readmitted and returned to active service in Belfast. Kevin Hannaway, Adams' cousin, became adjutant general, number two to McGuinness. Local IRA units were given 'local commander prerogative', in other words greater independence. In time this loosening of the knots was to contribute to a number of setbacks for the movement.

'There was a mad scramble,' said O Bradaigh, recalling the few weeks between the IRA convention and Sinn Fein *ard fheis*. 'We found some of our people excluded, others their cards were gone. Afterwards we found the counterfoils of the admission cards were shredded the next morning in Parnell Square, so that you couldn't get inquiries going.'

According to O Bradaigh, Adams looked for guarantees from him that he would not walk out of the conference if the vote went against him. 'We refused to give them guarantees. We couldn't because he was asking us, from our way of looking at it, to destroy the movement, after all that time, sixty-five years, to remove its revolutionary content.'

A few days before Sinn Fein gathered for its annual conference in Dublin a letter published in the Belfast nationalist *Irish News* sought to damage Adams. It was written by his old comrade and friend Bob Murray, the man who was in the car during the loyalist assassination attempt. Murray said the abstention debate was like watching history repeat itself. 'Are we once again to witness the classic counter-revolutionary tactic in action?' he asked. 'Leaders can be wrong and very often are. Four years ago I remember Gerry Adams saying, "When you talk about constitutional politics in an Irish context it is British constitutionalism to which you refer." What happened, Gerry? Where did it go wrong? What changed? Where and when did it change, or had the decisions already been taken, even then as your oration at Bodenstown would suggest?'

According to some sources in Belfast, Murray received a visit shortly afterwards and was threatened. The reports remain unproven, however, because Murray has remained silent ever since. With less than a week to go to the *ard fheis*, O Bradaigh and his followers who would shortly form the nucleus of the breakaway Republican Sinn Fein were asked to Sunday lunch by Adams. In spite of advice from some supporters to ignore the invitation, O Bradaigh decided to go. Sitting alongside Adams were Martin McGuinness and Danny Morrison. 'They invited a number of us to it and asked us for guarantees that we wouldn't do anything at the conference. I just sat there and said nothing. Des Long said that he was going to walk out anyhow. Pat Ward, who was an invalid as a result of repeated hunger strikes, became quite agitated and he brought down the blackthorn stick which he had to use on the table when he told them what he thought of them.'

Clearly Adams was working overtime to bring the old-timers into line behind him. Adams appeared at a number of old IRA gatherings to reinforce his image as the republican Everyman. But in one important mission he failed. Just as the Provisionals, when they split from the old IRA in 1969, went in search of endorsement as the legitimate republican movement from Tom Maguire, the sole surviving member of the Second Dail – the last all-Ireland parliament before the Treaty – so now did Adams send emissaries seeking the old man's approval for the ending of abstentionism and the recognition of Leinster House, the creation of the hated Free State.

'They made the case that they couldn't win a military war,' one hardliner remembering, 'and Maguire stood up and brought them over to show them a picture of the faithful members of the Second Dail who handed over their authority to the Army Council and he said, "If this is true you've found yourselves in the same position that these people did, but they did not betray the Republic. Now leave," and he dismissed them.' Like his predecessor Cathal Goulding, Adams had been divested of the moral authority which still resided in Maguire. Symbolically it may have been important to the purist, but Adams was in a far better position than Goulding. He had the military men behind him as well as the politicians.

'They were sending army people to Sinn Fein meetings and saying, "The fighting men in the North want this, who the fuck are you to sit down here and tell them they can't have it?"' said 'Tony'. 'That's how they were getting the support, the army people were going in and laying the heavy on them. I argued that you can't ride two horses in opposite directions. If you're going to go fully political you can't be going into Leinster House and shooting people in the back at the same time.'

On the afternoon of Saturday 1 November Gerry Adams rose to deliver his presidential address inside Dublin's Mansion House. He told delegates that he could understand 'that some comrades view a change in the abstention policy as a betrayal of republican principles'. But then he played his IRA ace card. 'The decisions of a general army convention are not binding on Sinn Fein *ard fheiseanna*, but the logic of those who would consider withdrawing support from Sinn Fein if we change the abstentionist policy must be applied also to your attitude to the army. And the logic which would dictate withdrawal of support from Sinn Fein if decisions go against you means that you have already decided to withdraw solidarity and support from the IRA and the armed struggle.'

He admitted that he had once opposed lending republican support to nationalist and republican labour figures such as Gerry Fitt, Paddy Devlin and Paddy Kennedy – all of whom had been Stormont or Westminster MPs. But removing abstentionism would 'initiate an increase in our party membership and could change the political complexion of the party'. Abstentionism was 'merely a deeply rooted and emotive symptom of the lack of republican politics and the failure of successive generations of republicans to grasp the centrality, the primacy and the fundamental need for republican politics. This truth must be grasped. It is a difficult one for many to accept given the conspiratorial and repressive nature of our past, our distrust for "politics and politicians" and a belief that "politics" is inherently corrupt. But once it is grasped then everything else follows logically, especially the need to develop our struggle at the level of people's understanding.' At the end of his speech the floor erupted into several minutes of clapping and cheering. When the actual debate took place the next day it was a foregone conclusion that he had won.

'Adams had done his homework well and made sure that the army wouldn't split,' said 'Mike', a former Adams ally who went with O Bradaigh. 'Even people who agreed with us, their cop-out was "We don't care what happens at the political end of things, we are staying with the army." Because you have to remember at this time they had got all sorts of gear from Libya, so people were being assured, "Listen, this is only a tactic, the war's going on, we're going to pursue it," when there was no intention of doing so.'

The debate gave O Bradaigh one final chance to put his case. Just as he was about to begin speaking he felt a tap on his shoulder and, turning around, discovered a beaming Gerry Adams with his hand outstretched. O Bradaigh observed tartly as he reluctantly returned the gesture: 'I'll shake hands with any man, any time, not just for the cameras.' His speech was received in an eerie silence with only the occasional burst of applause from the sidelines. Martin McGuinness then rose to reply, to the many gathered in the Mansion House the very embodiment of the IRA military tradition. McGuinness launched a vitriolic attack on the old guard, calling 'shame, shame, shame' at their efforts to portray the leaderships of the IRA and Sinn Fein as the same old 'Stickies' of the 1960s movement led by Cathal Goulding.

'Our position is clear and it will never, never, never change. The war against British rule must continue until freedom is achieved,' he said. The reality, after sixty-five years, was that they had failed to convince the majority in the Republic 'that the republican movement has any relevance to them. By ignoring reality we remain alone and isolated on the high altar of abstentionism, divorced from the people of the twenty-six counties and easily dealt with by those who wish to defeat us.' McGuinness said the debate was not only about abstention-ism but about the quality of the movement's leadership. 'The reality is that the former leadership of this movement has never been able to come to terms with this leadership's criticism of the disgraceful attitude adopted by them during the disastrous eighteen-months ceasefire in the mid-1970s. Instead of accepting the validity of our case, as others who have remained have done, they chose to withhold their wholehearted support from the leadership which replaced them . . . If you allow yourselves to be led out of this hall today the only place you're going – is home. You will be walking away from the struggle. Don't go, my friends. We will lead you to the Republic.'

As the Dublin current affairs magazine *Magill* observed, it 'was only thinly disguised as the authentic statement of the IRA army council'. It was beginning to get dark when the results of the vote were read out: 429 delegates had voted to end abstentionism, 161 had voted to retain it. O Bradaigh and Dave O'Connell walked out of the hall, followed by far fewer than those who had voted with them, and reconvened at a hotel under the banner of Republican Sinn Fein.

'When the constitutional bug bites it's an incurable disease,' O Bradaigh observed. 'Armed struggle without ideology is very dangerous.' Adams ended the Mansion House gathering on a high note, his leadership endorsed and with a decision to register Sinn Fein at Leinster House as a political party. A woman's 'right to choose' whether or not to have an abortion was dropped.

At the end of the month Adams was interviewed by *An Phoblacht*. He explained that the difference between the Dail and Westminster was that the people in the twenty-six counties accepted the former's authority whereas the nationalist people in the six counties did not accept the British parliament. For the first time in sixty years republicans in the twenty-six counties had a clear role and their hard graft would be the seed from which – nurtured by some unknown future event – the revolution would break out. The *Andersonstown News* reported him as saying that if Sinn Fein ever renounced the Provisional IRA's campaign he would leave the party. 'The IRA have remained united. There was no walk-out from the IRA and they are the people with the guns.'

At the end of the year he published his second book, *The Politics of Irish Freedom*. Adams gave his view in the book that it was only when the British left Ireland that peace would come and that loyalists would be 'pragmatic' after the withdrawal. Answering the charge that the IRA is sectarian he claimed that given its resources and ability to mount operations its members could slaughter ordinary Protestants if they so wished yet had refrained.

At a press conference to launch the book he was asked about the apparent gap in his writings between the civil rights days and more recent times. 'I don't have any paramilitary connections. I could have written a detailed, sensational version of events over the last sixteen to seventeen years but I felt that would exploit the struggle. I am not a member of the IRA and have not been a member of the IRA.' Any money made from his writings was said to be donated to republican charities, leaving Adams in the clear when it came to collecting his weekly social security benefit from the British government. On occasion there would be stories in London newspapers that Adams was about to have this 'revolutionary tax' cut off and that the unemployed barman would have to make himself available for work, but nothing ever came of it.

Only when he published his autobiography in 1996 did Adams

finally decide to turn himself into a professional writer, assisted in this by the reported £100,000 he received for a manuscript which bore striking resemblance to sections of his earlier books. The financial arrangements of the Adams family have never ceased to intrigue Belfast. A few months after publication of *The Politics of Irish Freedom* he was fined £15 for taking part in an illegal parade on the Falls Road. Although the magistrate said that this was at the lowest range of the scale for such an offence it was Adams' address, given as Norfolk Drive in West Belfast, which surprised many. While close to the ugly security base at the corner of the Andersonstown Road, Norfolk Drive is situated in one of the more sought-after districts of West Belfast.

His writings and the victory at the *ard fheis* were an implicit admission that there was no all-Ireland revolution to complete. The people of the South already had their nation and the struggle was inevitably restricted to the mainly ghetto areas of the North. Anti-imperialism was a dead, or dying, issue; the border had only a limited resonance for Irish people. So now began the search for new allies within constitutional nationalism itself. The problem was that, while he continued to lend his voice in support of the IRA and its campaign, the constitutionalists of North and South would shun him. At least that was the case in public, because it is from this post-abstentionist period that the first green shoots of the peace process began to emerge.

CHAPTER SEVENTEEN

Talking Peace, Waging War

The political battle won against the old guard, it was now time to make good on the promises to the IRA. The military campaign was to be continued and intensified, and the elite of the British establishment would be placed firmly in the firing line. On the morning of Saturday 25 April 1987 the IRA murdered Northern Ireland's second highest judge and his wife. Seventy-three-year-old Lord Justice Maurice Gibson and Cecily were crossing the border at Killeen, County Armagh after returning to Ireland by ferry from Liverpool. At Dublin harbour they were given a Garda escort to the border, where they shook hands with the Irish police before driving alone along the mile-long stretch of road to reach the RUC at the far end. A bomb hidden at the roadside blew them apart before they could reach their Northern escort.

Lord Justice Gibson was a particular hate figure for the IRA, having presided over the trial of a number of RUC members linked to the killing of three IRA men in 1982 whose deaths prompted shoot-to-kill allegations and the subsequent investigation by the Greater Manchester Deputy Chief Constable John Stalker. Lord Justice Gibson had dismissed the case and commended the RUC officers for sending the Provisionals 'to the final court of justice'. Admitting the murders, the IRA said they had sent the judge to 'the final court of justice'. The same day a Provisional unit murdered William Graham, an off-duty Ulster Defence Regiment soldier at his farm in Pomeroy, County Tyrone.

It was a good day for the IRA, two successful operations in its terms. But the jubilation was not to last for very long. Less than a fortnight later the British elite Army unit, the SAS, in conjunction with the RUC and other security-force units, ambushed and killed eight IRA men as they launched an attack on the RUC station at Loughgall, County Armagh. The IRA men were using a digger to ram their way into the police station and drop off a bomb, when they came under withering fire from all directions. The security-force action wiped out most of the East Tyrone Brigade, the IRA's single biggest loss since 1920. A civilian was also killed, and another seriously injured.

Gerry Adams gave the oration at the funeral of one of the IRA dead, former Sinn Fein Monaghan councillor Jim Lynagh. Adams did his best to portray the defeat as a success, warning that in time 'Loughgall will become a tombstone for British policy in Ireland and a bloody milestone in the struggle for freedom, justice and peace.' At the funeral of Tony Gormley, Adams said that republicans would 'avenge the deaths' of the IRA squad. 'Margaret Thatcher and Tom King and all the other rich and powerful people will be sorry in time that Loughgall ever happened.'

One family, the McKearneys from Moy, did not allow Adams or any of the other leaders of the movement to make an oration at their son Padraig's funeral. In the aftermath of the killings, the McKearneys were bitter about whoever passed the information about the attack to the authorities. Padraig's sister Margaret, herself once named by Scotland Yard as 'the most dangerous and active woman terrorist operating' in England, said she was unsure why her brother had been betrayed. 'I can't make up my mind whether someone just went and took British gold to put my brother in the grave or whether it was part of a preconceived plan for internal reasons – with their little plots and schemes to become part of the constitutional process – when there were men like Padraig who would stand there and say "No" . . . Padraig would have stood firm against any sell-out after twenty years. He was taken out for pure greed or because he stood in the way.' Years later Padraig's brother Tommy McKearney was to declare that he was siding with Ruairi O Bradaigh in the division within the republican movement.

The month after Loughgall, Gerry Adams had to do battle once again for his parliamentary seat in West Belfast. Any observer of the election would easily have been forgiven for forming the impression that Adams and John Hume were implacable political enemies, destined to struggle for ever in competition for the allegiance of nationalists in Northern Ireland. In the run-up to the election Adams was scathing about Hume and his party, describing them as 'Mrs Thatcher's preferred candidates'. He contrasted John Hume's comment after Bloody Sunday that 'It's a United Ireland or nothing' with the SDLP's more recent policies which Adams characterized as 'It's the Hillsborough Treaty or nothing.' Adams also personally attacked Hume over his failure to attend Westminster. Since Seamus Mallon had been elected as MP for Newry and Armagh in January 1986, Adams claimed, John Hume hadn't been present at a single recorded vote concerning Northern Ireland at Westminster. This might seem like a curious criticism for an avowedly abstentionist candidate to make, but Adams' point was that voters may as well return a politician who wouldn't go to Westminster on principle as one who didn't turn up there in practice.

The invective between the nationalists was not all one way. Adams' rival in West Belfast, the SDLP's Joe Hendron, described the Sinn Fein policy paper Scenario for Peace as a 'contemptible little document . . . an attempt to dupe a war-weary public as an election approaches'. Adams showed little sign of being concerned about such attacks. On being informed that bookmakers had placed Joe Hendron as a slight favourite to win the West Belfast seat, Adams predicted that 'There are an awful lot of punters in this constituency who will be saying "Thank you, Mr Eastwood."' This jocular reference to the catch-phrase of champion boxer Barry McGuigan, who ritually thanked his manager, bookmaker Barney Eastwood, after every fight, was to come in handy for Adams again on polling day. 'Thank you very, very much, Mr Eastwood,' he quipped after being returned once again as MP.

Adams claimed a victory, but when the dust of the election battle had settled he and his fellow stategists in Sinn Fein knew that the party's direction had to be realigned if it was not to start sliding backwards in its bid for political influence. The Anglo-Irish Agreement had bolstered constitutional nationalism at the expense of physical-force republicanism. Adams had held his own in West Belfast but throughout Northern Ireland the SDLP had captured the initiative and blunted the rise in the Sinn Fein vote. It fell to 11.4 per cent of the overall poll, 2 per cent down on the 1983 general election. The slippage meant that Adams could no longer claim to have the backing of over 100,000 voters: the total number of ballot papers cast for his party in 1987 was 83,389. Reviewing these developments, Adams talked more and more about the need to build broad fronts and seek allies beyond the immediate movement, but as things stood he appeared to be in a cul-de-sac and it was John Hume who effortlessly won friends and influence in Ireland, America and Europe.

But if the SDLP and Sinn Fein were battling it out in public during the 1987 election campaign, behind the scenes moves were afoot to set up talks between them once the polls had closed. The instigator of these contacts was Father Alex Reid, the Redemptorist priest who had been involved in mediating feuds between the Provisionals and the Officials in the 1970s. Reid had continued to play an important but low profile role during other disputes between paramilitaries and had been active at the time of the hunger strikes until the stress of his work caused him to suffer a nervous breakdown. After a period of rehabilitation he was now back, but working on a wider prospectus, intent not just on solving feuds but on building a broader unity among nationalists and from there seeking answers to the intractable problems which underpinned the Troubles.

Reid became Adams' most important single conduit to the world outside the closed ranks of republicanism. He arranged secret contacts between the Irish Catholic Primate Cardinal O Fiaich and Adams. He unsuccessfully tried to persuade the Irish Prime Minister Charles Haughey to meet Adams, but did succeed in setting up a couple of private meetings between the Sinn Fein president and Haughey's adviser on Northern affairs, Martin Mansergh, and the Fianna Fail County Louth deputy Dermot Ahern. The link with the academic, Oxford-educated Mansergh was to prove particularly important as Adams and others involved in the complex diplomacy of succeeding years tried to circumvent the wearying integrity of the Irish dispute by resorting to ever more circuitous and convoluted terminology.

Now Father Reid approached Mark Durkan, principal aide to Hume. He put it to Durkan that Sinn Fein and the IRA should not be treated like lepers, but instead should be talked to with the aim of persuading them of the error of their ways. Reid had an especially high opinion of Adams, with whom he had dealt on a regular basis during the feud negotiations at Clonard. The priest believed that Adams' influence could provide the key to bringing the Provisionals in from the cold.

For the SDLP any kind of meeting during the rough and tumble of an election campaign would have been unthinkable. Hume didn't see Reid until after the election was over. After a series of conversations, he assented to the priest's request that he should explore the possibility of opening up negotiations with Adams. During a number of secret meetings in the latter months of 1987, the two political leaders agreed that their parties would hold more formal discussions in the following year, 1988. Adams' intention was to use the meetings to challenge Hume's assertion that the signing of the Anglo-Irish Agreement had rendered the British a neutral party in the Irish conflict. For his part, Hume wished to press Adams on IRA violence, which he regarded as unjustifiable under any circumstances.

Hume's point was made for him by the IRA itself on the morning of Sunday 8 November in Fermanagh's county town, Enniskillen. People were gathering for a Remembrance Sunday service at the town's war memorial when a 40lb gelignite bomb exploded, bringing down the wall of a community hall. Men, women and children were buried in the rubble. Eleven were crushed to death under the weight of masonry. Amateur video captured the scenes of panic as survivors tried to dig the injured out of the debris. One man, Gordon Wilson, spoke movingly of how he held the hand of his twenty-year-old daughter Marie and tried to keep her talking as they waited for someone to help. Her last words were 'Daddy, I love you very much.' Almost unbelievably, Wilson found the generosity in his soul to tell the bombers that he forgave them and bore them no ill will.

With the revulsion felt in Britain and Northern Ireland matched by the sense of horror which swept across the Irish Republic, Gerry Adams knew that beyond the unshakeable hard core of Sinn Fein and the IRA's support the bombing was bound to have a devastating impact. Adams extended his 'sympathy and condolences to the families and friends of those killed and injured'. He added that 'I do not try to justify yesterday's bombing. I regret very much that it occurred.' The Ulster Unionist leader Jim Molyneaux responded by describing the sentiment as 'nauseating double-talk and humbug'. Adams later acknowledged that 'our efforts to broaden our base have most certainly been upset in all the areas we have selected for expansion. This is particularly true for the South and internationally. Our plans for expansion will have been dealt a body blow.'

To try to deflect the blame the IRA lied, claiming that British Army radio signals had triggered the bomb. In fact it had been a device fitted with a timer which hadn't detonated as intended, before the service when police and soldiers were carrying out a security

Gerry Adams Snr. and Jnr. Taken from *Greater Ballymurphy – 25 Years of Struggle*. Reproduced by permission of Kelvin Boyes Photography.

Gerry Adams at an Easter Parade in Belfast, 1971. Reproduced by
permission of Kelvin Boyes Photography.

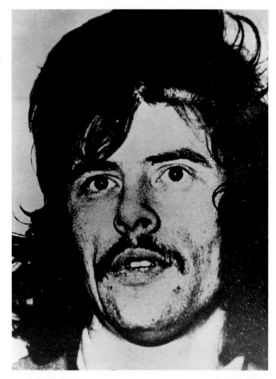

Right: Army/police shot used in *Visor* magazine, 1974. Reproduced by permission of Kelvin Boyes Photography.

Below: Gerry Adams outside Sinn Fein HQ, 20/1/84. © Pacemaker Press Intl. Ltd.

Gerry Adams carrying the coffin of IRA Shankill bomber Thomas Begley,
27/10/93. © Pacemaker Press Intl. Ltd.

Historic meeting in Dublin between Gerry Adams, John Hume and
Irish Prime Minister Albert Reynolds, 6/9/94. © Pacemaker Press Intl. Ltd.

sweep. Several years later the IRA announced that the unit responsible had been disbanded.

A fortnight after the bombing Gerry Adams told the *Irish Times* that the attack had been 'a terrible mistake'. He said that 'the onus is on the IRA to make sure this never happens again and I feel very strongly about that. The IRA must have the safety of civilians as a paramount factor.' Nevertheless he maintained that the relationship between Sinn Fein and the IRA was 'much as it has always been . . . We defend the right of the IRA to engage in its armed struggle. It is true to say that we have been critical of the IRA because of Enniskillen but we still accept the IRA as freedom fighters.'

Within this context it would have been easy for John Hume to have backed away from Father Alec Reid's initiative. Hume had already been given a taste of the likely vilification he would be subjected to when he had carried out his abortive talks with the IRA two years previously. The Enniskillen bombing had come shortly after the discovery of the *Eksund*, the freighter loaded with Libyan arms for the IRA, nationwide searches in the Irish Republic for IRA arms and the discovery of some IRA prisoners still on the run from the mass breakout from the Maze. But Hume had never been convinced that a security response would be enough to marginalize the IRA. He believed that the problem was one of politics and identity and it would only be through political progress and painstaking diplomacy that a solution could be found.

Impressed by Father Reid's arguments in favour of meeting Adams, Hume decided it was worth the risk of embarking on a series of discussions with Sinn Fein. The year was beginning in confusing circumstances, with the Provisionals seemingly pulling in opposite directions. An IRA spokesman told the Belfast political magazine *Fortnight* that 1988 was to be the year of the big push: 'This is the final phase. The next eighteen months to two years will be critical because the IRA has the resources and will know then if it has the capacity to end it.' For the first time since the very early 1970s the IRA was talking about taking territory and holding it in huge setpiece battles with the security forces, rather than staying with the hit-and-run approach.

The venue for Adams' first encounter with Hume was St Gerard's, a Redemptorist retreat house set amid trees on the lower slopes of Belfast's Cavehill. Adams was accompanied by Mitchel McLaughlin, an up and coming Sinn Fein strategist from Derry, and two of his old Belfast allies Danny Morrison and Tom Hartley. Hume's team included his deputy Seamus Mallon, Sean Farren, a senior party member from County Antrim, and Austin Currie, a long-term member of the party who was later to travel south of the Irish border and start a new political career within the Fine Gael party, rising to be an Irish government minister.

The two sides circled around each other, exercising their long-established differences over Britain's role and IRA violence. Adams demanded of Hume, 'Give us an alternative to armed struggle,' but never once gave any indication that he thought the IRA had hit a brick wall with its campaign of violence. Hume replied by telling Adams that, while the Provisionals might think it was noble to die for Ireland, there was a thin line between it and killing for Ireland.

The only chink of light appeared to be some meeting of minds on the notion that the Irish people as a whole had a right to national self-determination. Hume agreed to this concept but registered his disapproval of the Provisionals' use of it as a justification for an armed campaign. After the meeting Hume said that violence was 'utterly counter-productive . . . The talks were about how we achieve peace, which means how to achieve an end to violence.' In response to speculation that an IRA ceasefire might be in the offing Adams insisted that 'no military agenda' was involved.

Predictably the meeting sparked controversy. The DUP leader Ian Paisley joined in claiming that 'the SDLP has more in common with Sinn Fein than with constitutional unionists'. Adams told 'our unionist detractors' to 'catch themselves on', a Northern Ireland phrase admonishing those who should know better. Adams told *Fortnight* that critics of his meeting with Hume were 'tribal leaders who feed off the sick little mess which they and their political masters created in this squalid political slum'. The IRA and the security forces were, he contended, 'locked in a stalemate which has paralysed all other political potential among their supporters and opponents'. It was the responsibility of leaders to try to find a way forward.

After their first publicized encounter Adams and Hume agreed to develop 'further dialogue if it were thought to be productive'. A second meeting was held in February and there were more discussions as the year wore on. Hume's purpose was to convince Adams that the British were neutral on Northern Ireland's present and future status and that he should build bridges to the unionists. Adams predicted that in time he would be sitting down around a table with the unionists. 'I have talked to minor unionist politicians in the past and to loyalist paramilitaries in the past. I have no doubt that, as part of the process of rebuilding, Sinn Fein members will have talks with representatives of the unionist electorate.'

Adams continued to deny that an IRA ceasefire was under discussion with the SDLP but gave this long-term hint: 'Perhaps we can start a process which would unravel the way towards a situation whereby the conditions for a permanent peace can be created.'

But the continued violence on the streets gave little sense of hope that any breakthrough was possible and put very real pressure on the SDLP to call the discussions off. The spring of 1988 was a particularly dark time in West Belfast, when an IRA plan to mount a spectacular attack on a military band in the British colony of Gibraltar set off a grotesque chain of events. Three of the four IRA members involved, Danny McCann, Mairead Farrell and Sean Savage, were shot dead in controversial circumstances by the SAS. McCann had been one of the IRA members who had crossed swords with Adams during the falling out with Ivor Bell in the mid-1980s, but he had since been readmitted to the ranks.

A fourth IRA member escaped – the person has been named by several newspapers as Siobhan O'Hanlon, a cousin of Joe Cahill's who worked later as Gerry Adams' personal assistant and a member of Sinn Fein's negotiating team. When the bodies of the three victims were brought back to Belfast it was always clear that their funerals would be high-profile IRA events. What no one could have predicted was that a maverick loyalist would mount a near suicidal one-man bid to kill Gerry Adams and other Provisional leaders in front of the mourners at Milltown cemetery.

Michael Stone regarded himself as a freelance – a loyalist who would carry out killings on behalf of paramilitary organizations, while staying semi-independent from their structures. From 1980 onwards the loyalist leader whom Stone was closest to was John McMichael, who headed the Ulster Defence Association, the man who in 1984 had given the order that Adams should be killed and who paid for his decision when he was himself killed by an IRA booby-trap bomb in December 1987.

Stone, angry about the death of his leader, and intent on

vengeance both for John McMichael and for the Enniskillen bombing, had for some time looked upon the prospect of a large Provisional funeral with relish – believing it presented an opportunity to target people such as Gerry Adams and Martin McGuinness. As the coffins of the Gibraltar victims were being transported home to Belfast, Stone was trying to persuade associates of the assassinated McMichael that an attack at Milltown cemetery was feasible. They were sceptical, thinking such an assault in a crowd would prove suicidal. But eventually Stone obtained grenades and a Browning pistol from members of another loyalist paramilitary organization, the UVF, and pressed ahead with his plan. He mingled with the crowds heading up the Falls Road to attend the Gibraltar victims' funerals. According to his own account, at one stage he found himself on the steps of St Agnes' church in Andersonstown just behind Gerry Adams and a Sinn Fein councillor, Joe Austin. He considered killing Adams but instead decided to delay his attack until the mourners were gathered at the gravesides in Milltown cemetery, where he hoped to kill both Adams and McGuinness together.

At Milltown cemetery Stone was assisted in his endeavours by the absence of the customary police or Army presence. After lobbying from the Catholic hierarchy and nationalist politicians the security forces were hanging back and keeping a low profile so as to avoid any recurrence of the kind of clashes between the RUC and mourners which had been a feature of several previous IRA funerals. The third of the three coffins was just being lowered into the ground when Michael Stone began his attack, lobbing hand grenades into the crowd and warding off anyone who tried to stop him with aimed shots from the Browning.

Stone claims he called to Gerry Adams and Martin McGuinness, who were standing shoulder to shoulder beside one of the graves, to come towards him, but they refused. Instead Adams and his minders crouched down behind the gravestones. Adams emerged a few seconds later, grabbing a microphone and telling the crowd around him to stay where they were. Already, though, some of the younger mourners had set off with what looked like almost insane courage in pursuit of the slightly portly figure of Stone who began to amble back towards the M1 motorway at the lower end of the cemetery where he hoped, in vain, that his accomplices were waiting to help him escape. Stone knew that he had blown his opportunity to kill Adams and should have tried to shoot him either at the church or as he made his way into the cemetery. Now in the mêlée and confusion any mourner would do.

Eventually Stone ran out of bullets and some of the crowd caught him on the motorway, beat him and bundled him into a hijacked car. The loyalist killer was saved by the RUC, who stopped the vehicle and pulled him from the hands of his captors. Back at the cemetery ambulances had been called to take the injured to hospital. Three of the mourners were beyond help. Stone had shot dead twenty-year-old Thomas McErlean, twenty-six-year-old John Murray and thirty-year-old Kevin Brady, who alone among the dead was a member of the IRA.

Thus it was that three IRA funerals were followed within days by three more funerals. The tension caused by the killings in Gibraltar was compounded by Stone's one-man assault. After the Milltown cemetery attack there was a series of arson attacks on Protestant homes in North Belfast. Adams condemned the attacks and for those who were not used to him using the language of condemnation he added this explanation. 'The term "condemnation" is abused by many politicians. Only on one other occasion have I used the word in any statement. That was after the Darkley shooting. I use it again to express Sinn Fein's absolute opposition to the arson attacks on Protestant homes last night. I am relieved that no one was injured or killed.'

In the immediate aftermath of the Milltown attack Adams alleged that it must have involved some kind of collusion between loyalists and the security forces; claiming that two gunmen had got out of a Transit van in full view of the security forces, he went on to assert that the killer had prior notice that the security presence in the cemetery would be minimal. The van, which had been parked on the M1 motorway close to the cemetery, was the subject of much speculation. The RUC later insisted to sceptical journalists that it was a traffic-patrol vehicle which had rushed away from the scene when the officers inside realized something was happening which they were not equipped to deal with.

Despite one throwaway comment that his mate 'had fucked off and left him' Stone, for his part, stuck stubbornly to his version that he had acted alone. No 'second gunman' was ever traced by the police. Stone expressed regret that he hadn't achieved his aim, 'the termination of the president and vice president of Provisional Sinn Fein (PIRA)', but affirmed that 'I alone carried out the military operation as a retaliatory strike against Provisional Sinn Fein/IRA in response to the slaughter of innocents at La Mon, Darkley, Brighton and Enniskillen. I would state that I am a dedicated freelance loyalist paramilitary. No surrender.'

The international media which flooded into Belfast for the setpiece Gibraltar funerals could have been forgiven for thinking that, after the Milltown cemetery killings, things might calm down. But at the funeral of the IRA member Kevin Brady events took yet another macabre turn. The mourners, including Gerry Adams again, were obviously on edge in case any other loyalist sought to emulate what Michael Stone had done – Stone was already being celebrated as a hero in hardline loyalist areas. As they made their way again from St Agnes' church in Andersonstown towards Milltown cemetery the mourners were suddenly confronted by the sight of a car driving at speed towards them.

The vehicle behaved erratically, mounting the pavement, ploughing on through the lead cars and the first group of mourners, trying unsuccessfully to veer up a side alley, then attempting to reverse away from the crowd. The mourners pounced on the car, momentarily convinced that an attack of some kind was under way. What happened next was captured by the cameras present and seen with horror by TV viewers around the world. One of the men inside the car fired a shot from a handgun to try to ward off the crowd around him. But the mourners smashed their way into the vehicle, dragged out the two occupants and began to give them a severe beating.

One of the most obvious assailants clearly visible on the TV footage was Terence 'Cleeky' Clarke, long-term prison friend and later bodyguard to Gerry Adams. Clarke smashed his way through the front windscreen using a wheel brace and was later convicted for his part in the assault. The two occupants of the car were then carried off to a nearby Gaelic sports ground, Casement Park, where they were horribly tortured. Here it was established that they were not loyalists but British soldiers, Corporal Robert Howes and Corporal Derek Wood, who carried identity cards from the Royal Signals Corps. In the view of the crowd at an IRA funeral, however, this served as no recommendation of character. The two corporals were bundled into a taxi and taken to a patch of rough ground where, still fighting for their lives, they were shot in the head by an IRA gunman. Police and Army units alerted by the helicopter filming the whole affair from above arrived too late to save the two soldiers. No conclusive explanation has ever been provided for the corporals' presence in West Belfast so close to an IRA funeral. Republicans harboured suspicions they were involved in undercover surveillance work, but some military sources suggested that either ignorance of the local geography or an act of misplaced bravado had led to the atrocity.

Due to the tenacity and persistence of the camera crews and reporters on the ground who resisted attempts by republicans to take their films and subsequent death threats, TV viewers were able to witness for themselves the first stages of the lynching. A sense of revulsion gripped Britain at the fate which had befallen the corporals. Adams, whose close associates had been amongst those involved in the mob action, did his best to counter it, telling a republican commemoration shortly afterwards that the people of West Belfast were good and honest and that 'those who seek to criminalise them, whether Catholic bishops, English newspaper editors or politicians, are feeding on their own ignorance and prejudice'.

One of the most moving pictures which appeared in the press showed a priest kneeling down trying to administer last rites to the dying corporals. Father Alec Reid, who had seen more than his fair share of bloodshed through the feuds and Troubles he had encountered in Belfast, was now once again face to face with the consequences of violence. Although one of the soldiers was alive when he knelt beside him there was nothing Father Reid could do to stop his life ebbing away. The experience, however, galvanized him in his conviction that there had to be a better way forward.

Gerry Adams could claim that the death of the corporals was part of a spiral of events in which all sides, the IRA, the SAS, the loyalists, had played their part. But further bloodshed later in 1988 could be laid at the IRA's door alone and the Sinn Fein president continued where he had left off after the Enniskillen bombing, issuing what sounded like ever more half-hearted apologies or statements of regret. In June the IRA killed six soldiers taking part in a fun run in Lisburn when it detonated a booby-trap bomb attached to their minibus. Adams said this was 'vastly preferable' to killing UDR or RUC members, first because it had a greater propaganda impact in Britain and secondly because it removed the 'worst of the agony from Ireland'.

In July two of Gerry Adams' own constituents, sixty-year-old Elizabeth Hamill and twenty-four-year-old Eamonn Gilroy, were killed when the IRA took the flagrantly dangerous step of planting a bomb at the Falls Road swimming baths in an attempt to ambush an Army patrol. A bomb-disposal officer, John Howard, died when he triggered a booby-trap bomb placed at the scene of the earlier explosion.

Adams expressed his 'deep regret' at the deaths of the two civilians, although not the bomb-disposal officer, and he once again wrestled with the word 'condemnation': 'I have never tried to justify any actions in which there were civilian fatalities or casualties. At the same time I am not in the business of condemning the IRA. To condemn them would suggest that I do not understand and that would be dishonest.'

Adams referred to a 'series of unfortunate mistakes' by the IRA and added that 'the onus is on the IRA to sort all of that out . . . to get its house in order. I remain confident that they will do that.' Within days IRA bombers triggered a 1,000lb bomb planted near where the main Dublin-to-Belfast road crosses the Irish border. They thought the jeep-like vehicle they were blowing up was being driven by a member of the Northern Ireland judiciary, Mr Justice Higgins. Instead they killed Robin and Maureen Hanna and their six-year-old son David. Adams, in what seemed an insulting understatement at the time, said he was 'shocked and annoyed by what happened'.

In August two elderly men, William Hassard and Fred Love, were murdered in a hail of bullets as they left Belleek RUC station, where they had been carrying out routine maintenance. Adams said: 'They did not have to take the contracts. There's a war going on and they took sides.'

Within this context, no matter what discussions the two party leaders were having, John Hume was never likely to resist the temptation to press home his arguments about the futility of IRA violence. In August 1988 Hume made a speech in which he pointed out that 'Since Enniskillen 42 per cent of the killings carried out by the IRA have been described as "mistakes" which they regretted.

How long would any politician last if 42 per cent of his actions on behalf of his people were admitted to be mistakes?'

Adams' response showed that the contacts between the two sides were beginning to dry up. 'Mr Hume has consistently explained his involvement in this process by asserting that he is seeking an end to all military and violent activity and not merely an IRA ceasefire. His statement today is at variance with this sentiment. Given the sensitive and important nature of our discussions and the stage they are at, I am surprised and disappointed at the timing and content of today's statement.'

At the end of August 1988 the IRA scored what was in their terms a major success, targeting a bus full of soldiers *en route* from Belfast International Airport to a base in the west of Northern Ireland. Bombers triggered a device hidden in a trailer beside the road which leads from Ballygawley in County Tyrone to Omagh. Eight soldiers died in the attack, the largest number of casualties suffered by the Army in any single incident since the Warrenpoint killings in 1979.

The attack was the work of the IRA's East Tyrone Brigade, which had lost many senior members at Loughgall a year earlier. Adams, who many remembered had warned that the Loughgall deaths would be avenged, was relieved that this was not another IRA mistake and beat the Provisional drum. 'Attempting to defeat the IRA is not a viable and sensible option and it will only prolong the suffering and agony,' he argued, adding for good measure that 'for as long as there is British interference there will be an Irish rejection of that interference and for as long as there is rejection there will be an IRA'.

Comments like that provoked the DUP MP William McCrea to say, 'It is time this spokesman for terror is removed from circulation.' Quite how this should happen the Reverend McCrea did not specify. But inside Downing Street Mrs Thatcher demanded action. Her ministers dissuaded her from her immediate urge to reintroduce internment without trial, so instead the government lit on a measure which they felt would hamper Sinn Fein's propaganda effort. The Independent Television programme *After Dark* had withdrawn an invitation to Adams to appear shortly after the Ballygawley explosion, but other current affairs broadcasters in both the BBC and ITV had been proving troublesome, in particular the Thames Television and BBC Northern Ireland current affairs teams, which had insisted on investigating the precise circumstances of the SAS shootings in Gibraltar.

So the notion of a broadcasting ban on republicans appeared to kill two birds with one stone. Moves began to stop Sinn Fein spokespersons' words being carried on radio or television. The era of Gerry Adams as the man whose voice could not be heard on British television had begun. When the authorities eventually announced the measure in October 1988 they were able to defend their decision by pointing to the fact that the Irish Republic already had similar restrictions in force.

The month after the Ballygawley attack the talks with the SDLP so painstakingly arranged by Father Reid broke up amid mutual recrimination. Adams accused Hume's negotiators of not responding seriously to his party's copious documents. Nevertheless he maintained that the talks had been worth while. 'Given past opposition to face-to-face talks, the laying aside of that prejudice, I am sure you will agree, was a breakthrough in itself.' In the magazine *Living Marxism* Adams described the talks as a genuine attempt to examine the possibility of the development of an unarmed strategy by which justice and peace could be pushed forward: 'Our view is that armed struggle in these current conditions is legitimate. It's up to those who don't believe it's legitimate to come up with alternatives, not to restrict themselves to meaningless denunciations. We went there to look, to listen and to be persuaded that there was some other alternative and the conclusion showed we weren't persuaded.' Asked if an IRA ceasefire was therefore not an option Adams replied negatively. 'I think the IRA has made quite clear its terms for a cessation and what we want is a permanent cessation, a permanent demilitarisation, not just of the IRA but of all the forces, a secure society in which there could be the basis for durable peace, for justice.'

In his speech to the SDLP annual conference Hume gave what sounded like an epilogue to the talks with Adams. Since the beginning of the year the IRA had murdered eighteen civilians – 'non-combatants' as defined by the Provisionals. Hume told the conference that their attitude towards self-determination had all the hallmarks of 'undiluted fascism'. They also had the other hallmark of the fascist – the scapegoat. The Brits were to blame for everything, even the Provos' own atrocities. He detailed the death toll of the last twenty years: 2,705 people had died, 44 per cent of them at the hands of the

Provisionals and a further 18 per cent by their 'fellow travelling republican paramilitaries'. In the past two decades republicans had killed more than twice as many Catholics as the security forces and in the last ten years they had killed more than the loyalists. 'The Irish people as a whole have a right to national self-determination,' Hume argued, 'but since there is a very deep division among the people of this island as to how that right is to be exercised, it is the search for agreement on the exercise of that right that is the real search for peace.'

The formal contacts were over in a flurry of recriminations, but behind the scenes Hume and Adams kept talking, turning over the same narrow ground which was now reduced to the arid phrases of 'self-determination' and 'agreement' on how it should be exercised. It was pitiless work, but both men surely realized they were laying the foundations of the 1994 IRA ceasefire.

CHAPTER EIGHTEEN

The Mountain Climber Returns

The break-up of the talks with the SDLP ushered in another period of relative isolation for Gerry Adams, unable to get his voice heard on the airwaves and not in formal contact with other nationalists of note. Provisionals gathered in sombre mood at Sinn Fein's *ard fheis* in January 1989. Since April 1987 the IRA had lost twenty-five volunteers, fourteen of them in SAS ambushes. Adams was calling for a broad anti-imperialist front. But yet again he had to deal with the subject of IRA mistakes – the violence which was costing him the allies he wanted. He admitted that there had been an 'exceptional and regrettable level of civilian casualties' and lectured the IRA that they had 'to be careful and careful again'. But he insisted that in his view armed struggle remained 'a necessary and morally correct form of resistance in the six counties'.

Martin McGuinness lent his voice to the appeal. 'We must not, in challenging British rule, be the initiators of further injustices,' he said. A number of speakers said that Sinn Fein could not win the struggle on their own and some ventured so far as to say that they wanted the IRA campaign to end soon.

Even so, the IRA in East Tyrone went on in March 1989 to murder three Protestants, garage owner Leslie Dallas, sixty-two-year-old Austin Nelson and seventy-two-year-old Ernest Rankin at Dallas' garage in the village of Coagh not far from the shores of Lough Neagh. The IRA claimed that Leslie Dallas was a member of the UVF, which was denied. The killings provoked the SDLP's Denis Haughey to liken Adams to a man of straw reduced to pleading from the sidelines for the IRA to stop slaughtering non-combatants. Haughey described the IRA as an organization akin to the Mafia which had grown out of a movement for independence but which had reached the stage where the end justified any means.

In April 1989 Adams frankly admitted that the link between the IRA and Sinn Fein might cost his party votes in the forthcoming local government elections. He said that Sinn Fein and the IRA were going through a difficult period which could depend on the IRA heeding Sinn Fein warnings about mistakes like a bomb attack on the RUC station at Warrenpoint which had cost the life of a twenty-year-old Catholic girl, Joanne Reilly. Adams said some people were questioning 'the value of operations which do not advance the broad republican struggle'.

But later in the year he argued that Sinn Fein shouldn't get the blame for the IRA's mistakes. 'Sinn Fein should not be seen as the conscience of the IRA. And neither is Sinn Fein going to be a scapegoat for the IRA. Whatever mistakes the IRA made were genuine though deplorable mistakes. If people are affronted by these mistakes to the point that they are going to desert Sinn Fein then I think they should think twice because that is not going to help anyone except the anti-republican elements, except the British government.' Even as he made this argument, though, he must have known that it would cut little ice with the voters. Sinn Fein candidates went through the indignity – in their terms – of signing a new anti-violence declaration in order to avoid being ruled out of standing for election. But in the local elections in May they saw their share of the vote drop by 1 per cent.

In the European parliamentary elections shortly afterwards Sinn Fein's vote again fell – Danny Morrison received 48,914 votes, 40,000 fewer than he had polled five years before. John Hume's vote also fell, but as a percentage share the SDLP held up much better than Sinn Fein. The SDLP now took 25.5 per cent of the vote, up from 22.1 per cent in 1984, while Sinn Fein's support fell to 9.2 per cent, down from 13.3 per cent in 1984. Sinn Fein's vote also fell in the general election south of the Irish border – they now represented less than 2 per cent of the Southern electorate, confounding their hopes of expanding on a thirty-two-county basis.

Gerry Adams blamed the government's broadcast ban on Sinn Fein for the poor showing. But he was well aware that the IRA's mistakes had played their part. So too did the perception in the wake of the Anglo-Irish Agreement that constitutional nationalism was finding a way forward, with John Hume lobbying in the corridors of power and Irish civil servants based at the Maryfield secretariat taking up Northern nationalists' concerns about policing, justice and other matters with their British counterparts.

At this low point in Sinn Fein's political fortunes, the British Prime Minister Margaret Thatcher conducted a reshuffle in her cabinet and gave a new man the top job at the Northern Ireland Office. Peter Brooke gave the superficial impression of being a slightly bumbling patrician, but in fact he followed the nuances of any debate within republicanism closely and with an acute understanding which he put down in part to his Irish roots.

Brooke understood that any progress in his new job was likely to be measured in inches rather than miles. So while he set about trying to encourage the unionists and the SDLP to get together to talk about developments in the short to medium term, he also scanned Sinn Fein's documents and news-sheets in an attempt to discern any trends which might bear fruit over the long term. Brooke remembers how in 1966 he travelled to Ireland with his first wife to look for the village and the house in County Cavan where his family had lived between 1650 and 1800:

> As we approached the village my wife said we must look for the oldest inhabitant and I said, 'We haven't lived here for 170 years, I don't think the oldest inhabitant is going to do us much good.'
>
> There was an old man in the street when we got there. My wife must have been driving because she wound down her window and said, 'Can you tell me if there's a house called 'Rantaven' in this neighbourhood because it's of great interest to my husband's family.' It was no more than a farmhouse. And the old man didn't ask her any questions, she didn't give him any more information and he simply said to me, 'You must be one of the Brookes.' Now if you have an oral tradition in a small village going back 170 years about a family which moved out 170 years ago then you're not in a society where things are going to happen very fast. You've just got to take a long view.

In as grudging a compliment as he was likely to get Gerry Adams once said that Brooke 'was one of the more interested and thoughtful ministers, compared to some of the dimwits they have sent'. Brooke acquired his knowledge through three main sources – the government's intelligence infrastructure, his extensive contacts with the SDLP leader John Hume and his own detailed reading of the columns of *Republican News*. The first public sign that Brooke was prepared to think laterally came in one of a series of interviews given to mark his first hundred days at Stormont.

Asked if he could ever imagine the government talking to Sinn Fein, given that the two sides were 'basically in a Mexican stand-off', Brooke replied that 'it is difficult to envisage a military defeat' of the IRA, even though 'the security forces can exercise a policy of containment to enable, boadly speaking, normal life to go on within the Province'. He went on to imagine what the situation would be 'if in fact the terrorists were to decide that the moment had come when they wished to withdraw from their activities'. In such circumstances, he said, 'I think the government would need to be imaginative ... because of the welcome which would be given to a return to peaceful conditions in the Province by everybody living here, I hope that the government at that stage would be imaginative in how it responded.'

When the journalist who posed the question commented that it was remarkable that he should indicate he might consider speaking to Gerry Adams or Martin McGuinness, Brooke replied: 'Let me remind you of the move towards independence in Cyprus and a British minister stood up in the House of Commons and used the word "never" in a way which within two years there had been a retreat from that word. All I'm saying is that I would hope that the British government on a long term basis would be sufficiently flexible, that if flexibility were required it could be used, but I am in no way predicating or predicting what those circumstances might be.'

The comments provoked criticism from Labour, some Conservative backbenchers and unionists. Brooke denies that he used the interview deliberately to send out a message to the Provisionals – insisting rather that he simply gave a straight answer to a straight question. But although he later expressed regret about mentioning Cyprus, a colonial analogy which was rather too much to Sinn Fein's liking, he was happy that his words did resonate in the opposing camp. 'I did know from intelligence that there was a debate going on and indeed the material which has come out since the 1994 ceasefire has suggested that certainly as far back as 1986 and possibly earlier there were minds turning to how the matter was going to be brought to a conclusion. Therefore if that was so it was sensible to communicate, because we had no direct communication at all, to indicate that, if they reached the point of having a ceasefire which was a precondition to negotiation, negotiation was possible.'

Publically Adams responded in uncompromising terms to Brooke's statement, insisting that talks with the government were 'inevitable' and accusing Brooke of prolonging the conflict and delaying the process by indicating that there might be talks in the future if the IRA renounced violence. 'Republicans have had talks with the British government in the past. We will have talks again in the future. Sinn Fein is ready at any time to discuss the conditions in which justice and peace can be established. It is Peter Brooke who is delaying this process. It is his government which is prolonging this conflict.'

In later comments Adams argued that 'if the British accept this reality [that the IRA cannot be defeated] they have a responsibility to talk now rather than later and to end a war which they publicly accept they cannot win but which brings tragedy and suffering to both the Irish and British people'. On yet another occasion he claimed that Peter Brooke had the power to end the war in Ireland: 'With a new and imaginative approach he can begin the peace process. Without such flexibility he is simply perpetuating a war which he has admitted the British will never win.'

But behind this tough talk the very volume of Gerry Adams' responses to Brooke's comments demonstrated the intense interest they had provoked within Sinn Fein and the IRA. In an interview in April 1990 for Channel Four's *Dispatches* programme, voiced-over in the dulcet tones of Ulster actor Stephen Rea, Adams' favourite for the job, the Sinn Fein president spoke in rather less truculent terms about Brooke. 'This was a man,' he acknowledged, 'who has a far less hysterical approach to the problems of Ireland than any previous British Secretary of State.' Adams went on to make what sounded like an offer, saying that, if Britain initiated talks aimed at bringing about a permanent solution, the IRA would consider a cessation of violence. Adams said he was not talking about calling off the violence but of 'trying to develop a situation wherein there's a complete cessation of all hostilities'. Faced with the possibility of 'meaningful talks', he added, republicans 'would not be found wanting'.

Neither Brooke nor Adams was speaking in a vacuum. The years

1989 and 1990 were ones of great change in the wider world. Ireland remained divided but Germany's years of division were coming to an end. On 10 November 1989 the Berlin Wall came down, and that same month Czechoslovakia experienced its Velvet Revolution. Within three months Nelson Mandela was walking free from his years of imprisonment in South Africa. None of these events had any immediate impact on the 'dreary steeples' of Fermanagh and Tyrone, but they set the more politically acute minds in Ireland thinking what had seemed the impossible – that there might in the not too distant future be a break in the logjam which had dominated the situation in Ulster.

Adams took on board the developments in the wider world and tried to turn them to his own nationalist advantage. In a series of speeches he claimed that change in Eastern Europe had come about because the Soviet government had recognized the right of nations to decide their own future and that Britain should do likewise regarding Ireland. He urged Mrs Thatcher to emulate Mikhail Gorbachev by directing her government to stop interfering in Irish affairs.

Peter Brooke drew rather different conclusions, believing that the sense of change might promote radical thinking among republicans. 'The Berlin Wall was coming down, things were changing in Russia, South Africa was changing and the Middle East was changing. It was certainly said to me by people who I think were reasonably close to Sinn Fein that there was an anxiety, and certainly a wider anxiety in Ireland as a whole, that Ireland was going to be left as the last unsolved problem and that was going to put pressure on them and that was going to be bad for Ireland's reputation. Then they were let off the hook by Yugoslavia, which let them off the hook totally because that just produced a huge new ethnic dispute which dwarfed everything else afterwards.'

Brooke had lengthy conversations with John Hume, who told the Secretary of State all about his talks with Sinn Fein in 1988 and his failure to budge the Provisionals from their conviction that Britain remained a colonial power and could not be regarded as playing a 'neutral' role in Ireland. Pondering on this, Brooke decided to go further. Interviewed for this book he recalled:

I had appreciated, and no doubt that came through in conversation with John, the thesis because I was reading *Republican*

News every week; the thesis was that we were a colonial power. And since the arguments and motivations for colonialism are one, defence, and two, economics, down the centuries, I simply wanted to put on record that that analysis was wholly wrong since we had no defence interest, no selfish strategic interest.

Because in the nuclear age your back door ceases to be of the importance that it was under conventional warfare. And secondly since the British government was pouring in huge sums of money from the British taxpayer and Northern Ireland was a substantial net receiver of government money, there was no economic advantage either. I simply wanted to put that on the record and did and I gather it did have a certain resonance and reverberation. John Hume in no way sought to discourage me from doing it because he actually thought it was an important message to send.

This second, more deliberate message was delivered in a speech in Peter Brooke's Westminster constituency in November 1990. Until then John Hume had had to rely for his arguments over Britain's neutrality on the text of the Anglo-Irish Agreement, which had made it clear that if the majority of the population of Northern Ireland favoured a constitutional change Britain would not stand in their way. Now Hume was given another weapon – Brooke's statement that 'The British government has no selfish strategic or economic interest in Northern Ireland: our role is to help, enable and encourage. Britain's purpose, as I have sought to describe it, is not to occupy, oppress or exploit, but to ensure democratic debate and free democratic choice.'

Hume eagerly used the ammunition Brooke had given him:

For the first time a Secretary of State has taken them on on the political reasons that they give for what they are doing. They do it, they say, because Britain is here defending her interests by force, therefore we have a right to use force. What are those interests, I asked them, and they said those interests are economic and strategic. Peter Brooke has made it very clear that Britain is not here defending interests by force either strategic or economic, and he has also made it clear that if the people who live in this island reach agreement among themselves then that agreement will be honoured by the British government. That means that the problem today, whatever it was in the past, is our relationships with one another and they cannot be resolved by force. And any organization that is using force is in fact part of the problem, not part of the solution, because force is only making the problem worse.

If the One Hundred Days comments had been relatively off the cuff, here the shape of a more organized, yet arm's-length diplomacy was emerging in public. Adams issued a lengthy statement in response to Brooke's speech, calling on both London and Dublin to make a United Ireland a policy objective. 'The IRA has stated clearly on a number of occasions that for republicans armed struggle is not a dogma. The IRA says that armed struggle is a method of political struggle adopted reluctantly and as a last resort in the absence of any viable alternative . . . The onus is on those who claim that there is an alternative to the IRA's armed struggle to prove that is the case.'

While this arm's-length diplomacy was continuing, so was IRA violence. In the period between Peter Brooke's One Hundred Days comments and his Westminster 'no selfish strategic interest' speech the IRA killed three Paratroopers with a landmine at Mayobridge in County Down, two soldiers in an attack on a border checkpoint at Rosslea in Fermanagh, four UDR soldiers when a bomb exploded under their Land Rover in Downpatrick, and two RUC officers in a close-quarters shooting in the centre of Belfast.

Outside Northern Ireland there were frequent IRA attacks in England and Europe. The Stock Exchange in the City of London was bombed, the exclusive Carlton Club attacked and Tory MP Ian Gow, a harsh critic of the IRA and a close friend of Mrs Thatcher, was killed by a booby-trap bomb placed under his car. In Europe, British soldiers in West Germany were targeted – and alongside the military casualties the IRA murdered the German wife of a soldier, the six-month-old daughter of an RAF corporal and then two Australian tourists, Nick Spanos and Stephen Melrose, whom they had mistaken for off-duty soldiers.

Although Adams described the double murder as 'inexcusable and unjustifiable', he refused to criticize the IRA's campaign in Europe in general. 'What is happening in Germany,' he reasoned, 'is the consequence of what is happening in Ireland. The IRA has a legitimate right to engage in resistance and the operational matters are for them to work out.' Asked if he would call on the IRA to end its campaign in Europe, he replied, 'That is a question for the IRA. I don't want to give the impression that I am critical of the IRA. I believe they have a genuine right to engage in armed actions. I believe they are freedom fighters.'

Back in Northern Ireland two IRA operations – one a partial 'mistake', the other a 'success' – illustrated the consequences of the fight for freedom. In July 1990 a thirty-seven-year-old nun, Catherine Dunne, was killed when the IRA detonated a landmine as a police patrol passed by – three RUC officers also died in the blast. In October IRA men forced a civilian cook who worked for the security forces, Patrick Gillespie, to drive a van packed with explosives into a border checkpoint near Londonderry. They tied him into place in the vehicle which they then detonated by remote control without giving Gillespie time to escape – he died together with five soldiers on duty at the checkpoint. Another soldier was killed at the Newry border checkpoint in one of two similar attacks mounted by the IRA at exactly the same time.

The violence wasn't all one way. A fortnight before the human-bomb attacks, undercover soldiers ambushed and killed two IRA men seen carrying AK47 rifles in a field near Loughgall in County Armagh. One of the IRA men, Dessie Grew, was believed to have been involved in many of the recent attacks in Europe, including the murder of the RAF corporal and his young daughter. The other man, Martin McCaughey, led a double existence, an IRA gunman by night and a Sinn Fein councillor by day. McCaughey's death on active service served once again to emphasize the inextricable links between Gerry Adams' party and the IRA.

Against this backdrop it was impossible for Peter Brooke or any other government representative to contemplate taking up Gerry Adams' challenge to meet for talks. But Brooke was prepared to take risks in secret in the hope of finding some way to end the violence. In the autumn of 1990 he gave authority for John Deverell, a senior MI5 officer based in the Northern Ireland Office, to open up a line of communication with the IRA, using a go-between who had been in place since the days of the hunger strikes.

According to Brooke,

The intelligence people came to me and said, 'We are considering doing this but it obviously needs to have political endorsement. Are you prepared to give the political endorsement?' And I said I was ... There's no question at all that my permanent preoccupation right back to the Hundred Days' comments was that I couldn't know precisely what was happening in smoke-filled rooms on the other side of the hill. But if what was happening on the other side of the hill was important then I had to communicate that I had some sense of what was going on and I had to seek to lay out clearly what the parameters were of government policy. Now there's no question that there was an interest on the part of Sinn Fein in testing just what I was meaning. Did these things mean what their own interpretation might be? So there was inevitably an element that the private contacts were unquestionably used simply to test and to verify that what they thought was being said was in fact being said.

Gerry Adams didn't take it on himself to conduct the secret contacts. Instead he discussed it with Martin McGuinness, who was then 'instructed to proceed'. Later in the lengthy series of exchanges of written communications and clandestine meetings, McGuinness was joined by Gerry Kelly, who had been a close associate of Adams since at least October 1971 when he was noticed by the security forces as one of the IRA guard of honour at the funeral of Adams' close friends, Cumann na mBan members Maura Meehan and Dorothy Maguire. Subsequently Kelly was jailed for his part in bombing the Old Bailey court buildings in London, then was transferred back to the Maze jail near Lisburn. In 1983 Kelly was one of the leaders amongst thirty-eight IRA inmates who escaped from the Maze. When he was recaptured in Holland, Adams travelled over to observe the court case.

On the government's side the Mountain Climber, MI6 agent Michael Oatley, was initially involved – establishing a sense of continuity not only with the days of the hunger strikes but also with the mid-1970s when he had played a key role in laying the groundwork for the IRA ceasefire and when Adams had been regarded as a dangerous hardliner who should be taken off the streets. According to Martin McGuinness, Oatley made an approach informing the Provisionals that he was shortly to retire and wanted to re-establish contact and introduce another government representative who could take over his role when necessary in the future.

Within the government knowledge of the secret contacts was confined to an extremely small group of civil servants at Stormont, none of whom had been born locally, and an equally tight-knit group at Downing Street. In public the position remained that there could be no negotiation of any kind with the Provisionals unless the violence stopped, but while the government comforted themselves that the secret contacts did not amount to negotiation the principle was clearly less sacrosanct than appeared on the surface.

Little by way of substance passed through the secret channel in the first few months after its initiation. The government were mainly concerned with their long-drawn-out efforts to convene round-table talks which could be attended by both unionists and the Irish government. Gerry Adams, excluded from this process, spent his time shouting from the sidelines that people would eventually have to talk to him whatever they might think. But what appeared to be a static position was about to change again – this time with another new face, not at the Northern Ireland Office, but at Downing Street.

CHAPTER NINETEEN

Peace Comes Dropping Slow

Republicans never forgave Margaret Thatcher for what they saw as her obduracy during the hunger strikes and they were bitterly disappointed by their failure to kill her at the time of the bombing of the Grand Hotel in Brighton. Gerry Adams did take comfort, however, from the fact that the bombers got so close, commenting at one stage that Mrs Thatcher's belief that the hunger strike was the 'IRA's last card' 'exploded in a cloud of dust around her ears' in the Brighton bombing.

Predictably Adams shed no tears when a palace coup inside the Conservative Party led to Mrs Thatcher's removal from Number 10. Instead he viewed the end of her long reign as providing 'the opportunity to end her failed policies and begin the process of building real peace and justice in Ireland'. He expressed hope that Mrs Thatcher's successor John Major would be the man to set about this task.

Major took over at the end of November 1990 – a month later at Christmas the IRA called a three-day ceasefire. Such a break had been custom and practice but it was significant that for the first time in many years the IRA decided to announce it formally in advance. Not all the movement was on one side, as the Christmas parole arrangements agreed to by the government for paramilitary prisoners in 1990 were undoubtedly more generous than ever before.

The lull was brief. The IRA began 1991 with a series of fire-bombings on commercial premises estimated to have caused £25 million worth of damage. Still, even for observers who were of necessity unaware of the secret contacts between the government and republicans, it was evident that something appeared to be stirring in the undergrowth. Martin McGuinness indicated that the three-day ceasefire was a deliberate signal to John Major of what could be possible. 'There has been an awful lot of speculation about what that meant,' McGuinness commented,

> and all sorts of ludicrous and nonsensical suggestions that people within Sinn Fein, like myself and Gerry Adams, were preparing a six-month ceasefire programme that was going to be put to the IRA. I mean it's total and absolute nonsense . . .
>
> But in terms of the suspension of IRA operations at that three-day period at Christmas I think the British government could take it as a sign of republican goodwill in a situation where Margaret Thatcher has gone and a new administration has come into being in 10 Downing Street. I think that the British government could take that as a sign of goodwill, that republicans are serious about entering into meaningful discussions which will bring an honourable settlement to the problem. Mr Major, since he has taken over, has been very quiet and subdued on Irish affairs, has made very little comment about it, and I think we would be hopeful that his new administration will signal the possibility that there could be developments some time in the future which will resolve what has been an ongoing problem for all of us.

McGuinness went on to point out that there had been several instances in the past twenty years when republicans had successfully observed ceasefires. But at this stage such a possibility was still being couched as a distant prospect, conceivable only in the event of 'meaningful talks'.

One former IRA member prepared to talk about a ceasefire in more immediate terms was Mark Lenaghan, who was disgusted by the Enniskillen bombing and inspired by a reinvigorated religious faith. He looked around at the developments in Eastern Europe and decided the time had come for change in Ireland. 'If we want change, political change and social change, it can be done in another way, other than armed struggle,' he argued in an interview with one of the authors in early 1991. 'Recently I was in Czechoslovakia, and I also talked to members of Solidarity from Poland and to many young people who were involved in the whole movement for peace and they were very, very dynamic. They did many, many things, they started off simply: marches, petitions, dialogue. They challenged all these entrenched hardline positions. They constantly challenged. We can do that in the North and South of Ireland.' Lenaghan tried, with little success, to organize a mass youth petition to be presented to the IRA, calling for a ceasefire.

Lenaghan appeared very much a voice crying in the wilderness, but as a former IRA volunteer from Twinbrook, an estate not far from Gerry Adams' home patch on the outskirts of West Belfast, he was well placed to evaluate Adams' potential role in bringing about the kind of change he envisaged. Gerry Adams couldn't necessarily tell the IRA what to do, Lenaghan argued, but he undoubtedly had great influence upon it:

> I wouldn't imagine that Gerry Adams calls the shots or the leadership of Sinn Fein calls the shots. But they do have obviously a massive bearing and a massive influence on the policy, on the direction that is taken, the tactics that are taken at the very highest levels of the IRA. I would assume so. It's often Gerry Adams has to carry the can for the likes of the fire bombing and the car bombing and the loss of innocent life. I would say this, that Gerry Adams and people like him have an awful lot to say, have an awful lot to offer and they have a great influence on the IRA ... I believe Gerry Adams should use that influence and so should the councillors and other people around him ... They must begin to debate, to dialogue with IRA volunteers and the leadership of the movement, to talk peace. They must begin to look at that tactically as well as morally. They have to do that. I think the onus is on them, a responsibility from our people.

The most vociferous debate which Gerry Adams was engaged in at this time concerned the fire bombings – except it wasn't with the IRA but with the British minister responsible for the Northern Ireland economy, Richard Needham. Needham had been a colourful feature of life in Stormont Castle since 1985 when he was given charge of the health service and the environment. By early 1991 he had moved on to the economy and particularly concentrated on trying to create jobs in the deprived areas of North and West Belfast covered by his 'Making Belfast Work' scheme. Needham was noted for never being slow to talk to reporters, whether it be promoting his own efforts at economic regeneration or attacking the paramilitaries, whom he looked on as his natural enemies. This prompted the comment, which Needham credits to Adams, that every time the minister picked up a sweet paper along Belfast's main shopping street, Royal Avenue, he would hold a press conference to tell the world about it.

Needham looked on Adams as a racketeer, who held his people in thrall by fear. While in charge of social security in Northern Ireland the minister paid a visit to the office where Adams claimed his unemployment benefit. 'Everybody was very frightened of him. I remember going up to the West Belfast Supplementary Benefit Office and looking as they told me with hushed voices, "That's where Mr Adams comes and collects his money every week."' Needham believed that Gerry Adams cynically wanted to keep his people in poverty, because prosperity would have weaned them away from the IRA's control. By contrast Adams argued that unemployment in the area he represented as West Belfast MP was down to the economic policies of the Conservative government.

The fire bombings of the New Year of 1991 seemed to Needham to be proof of Gerry Adams' hypocrisy when it came to job creation, so the minister set about a high-profile campaign taking every opportunity to launch personal attacks on the Sinn Fein president in the pages of the local papers, describing him as 'an apologist for those who burn jobs'. Adams in turn accused Needham of indulging in 'theatrical hysterics'. Day by day the two men traded insults as the bombs and the fire bombs went on detonating around them. Needham saw what the IRA was doing as being deliberately opposed to his efforts both to create jobs in outlying areas of North and West Belfast and to attract young people from the hardline estates there into the melting pot offered by the city centre.

> We had a very sophisticated and coherent strategy. For example when we opened stores in Belfast or offices, we would take the young unemployed from West Belfast and get them trained for the specific jobs. Many of them would have been the children of paramilitaries and that was a way of trying to wean them off the mother's milk, if you like. Adams knew all that but what was so intolerable about Adams was that he knew perfectly well that the only way he was ever going to keep his people loyal to him was to keep them poor, keep them hungry and keep them intimi-

dated. That's why I've never had any time for the man, because it's always struck me that he's too intelligent a man to believe the complete utter rubbish that he used to speak.

Needham's schemes were, in large part, dependent on the co-operation of those who wielded influence within North and West Belfast but who were not republican supporters. In practice this meant that the role of the Catholic Church, and in particular the Bishop of Down and Conor, Cahal Daly, was crucial. As the abstentionist MP for West Belfast, Gerry Adams often found himself in conflict with Daly, who missed no opportunity to condemn IRA violence, and who lent his considerable support to the efforts of Needham and others to transform the ghetto areas. In a series of exchanges which ran from the mid-1980s through to the early 1990s, Adams acused Daly of taking a more extreme line than the rest of the Church hierarchy, and argued that the Bishop endorsed the RUC, 'an armed organization on the payroll of a foreign government', while condemning the IRA, 'a volunteer Irish citizen's organization'.

Daly, for his part, went on speaking out against the IRA, even though on occasions it provoked walk-outs from his churches and once, in front of one of the authors, led to a mourner at the funeral of a Catholic victim of loyalist violence spitting in the Bishop's face. Adams frequently asked Daly to meet him – Daly consistently refused, reasoning that Adams was seeking the meeting not as an individual member of his diocese but as president of an organization 'which openly and publicly supports a campaign of physical force . . . which it declares to be "morally correct". This is completely contrary to the moral teaching condemning this physical-force campaign as morally evil – teaching which I, in the name of the Catholic Church . . . have consistently given.'

While this battle for hearts and minds continued in the streets of West Belfast, Gerry Adams wrote a letter to John Major seeking a face-to-face meeting. In practice Adams knew there was no realistic chance of such an encounter while the government were pressing ahead with their plans for talks involving the other parties at Stormont and while the IRA's campaign ground on. A few days after Adams' letter arrived at Downing Street the IRA delivered a rather more blunt message. They abandoned a white Transit van in Whitehall and triggered the firing mechanism on three large mortar bombs. To the astonishment of passers-by, the mortars shot out of the roof of the vehicle and arced their way towards Downing Street, narrowly missing Number 10, where ministers were meeting for a cabinet session, and exploding a few yards away in its rear garden.

The Gulf War was being fought at the time of the mortar attack, and Adams had criticized the 'hypocrisy of those who, while condemning the armed struggle of the IRA, support the use of wholesale violence against the Iraqi people'. Perhaps he took satisfaction from the fact that the IRA mortars caused what the cabinet minutes noted as 'a brief interruption' to the government's war committee, which was discussing the progress of the struggle against Saddam Hussein. Adams declined either to condemn or condone the mortar attack, but said that it showed that the IRA could not be defeated and called once again for a United Ireland.

Sinn Fein's strategy was to try to put increasing distance between themselves and the IRA. Perhaps the arm's-length diplomacy conducted by Peter Brooke had given the Provisionals a vision of the future, and it appeared more advisable to build an image as a political party like any other prior to any future negotiations. Perhaps the embarrassment of apologizing for IRA mistakes had got too much. Clearly the plan from now on was to repeat *ad nauseam* the mantra that Sinn Fein were not the IRA and the IRA was not Sinn Fein. Even if that might provoke sceptical looks from Belfast's more experienced journalists, it had the cumulative effect of creating a fire break between the two organizations. In future Adams' and McGuinness' first line of defence when the IRA committed some particularly nasty atrocity would be to instruct reporters that they had 'better put that question to the IRA'.

In line with this policy, briefings about IRA matters such as how many British helicopters they believed they had hit by heavy machine-gun fire, which had previously been given in the Sinn Fein press centre on the Falls Road, now dried up, became more difficult to arrange and were most certainly not carried out on Sinn Fein property. The Sinn Fein press office stopped issuing faxes carrying the various IRA brigades' claims of responsibility for recent attacks. Martin McGuinness stressed that 'nowhere in the Sinn Fein constitution does it state that if you become a member or supporter of Sinn Fein do you have to support armed struggle. It doesn't say anywhere whatsoever that you have to support the IRA and I think personally from within the republican movement that that is a position which we should be moving towards in the future. That we have to say to people that you can support Sinn Fein and you can support the republican analysis of what's wrong in the six counties and you don't necessarily have to support every single IRA operation which takes place.'

Occasionally, however, the mask slipped. Less than a fortnight after the mortar attack on Downing Street the closeness of Gerry Adams' personal links with the IRA was again illustrated when his brother Sean appeared in court to receive a fourteen-year jail sentence for his part in a gun attack on the New Barnsley police station, the base just beside Adams' home estate of Ballymurphy. Together with Anthony Gillen from Divismore Park – the street where the Adams family had grown up – Sean Adams was convicted of attempting to wound a soldier and a police officer inside the base and carrying a rifle with intent to endanger life.

Three months later one of Gerry Adams' closest confidants, the former editor of *Republican News* and Sinn Fein spin doctor Danny Morrison, stood in the dock at Belfast's Crumlin Road court waiting to hear the judge pass sentence on him. Morrison had been caught in the house next door to one where the IRA had held captive a police informer, Alexander 'Sandy' Lynch. Morrison had escaped when the RUC launched a raid to rescue Lynch, but when he ran in at the back of the next-door house the neighbours told the police that contrary to his story they had never set eyes on him before. Morrison maintained he was arranging a news conference so Lynch could tell his story to the press – the police believed he had been called upon to sanction an IRA 'execution' of the informer. The judge found Morrison untrustworthy and sentenced him to eight years for falsely imprisoning Lynch.

In April 1991 the government used their secret channel of communications to inform Sinn Fein and the IRA that the loyalist paramilitaries, the UVF and the UFF, were about to call a ceasefire to facilitate progress in the talks which had now been succesfully arranged by Peter Brooke to convene at Stormont.

Adams saw the purpose of these talks, from which Sinn Fein were excluded, as being to halt the advances made by republicans since the early 1980s. He told a rally in West Belfast that 'every single political development and the present relationship between Britain and Ireland can be traced to the hunger strike ten years ago, including Peter

Brooke's talks process. Today the objective of the British government is the same as during the hunger strike – to undermine the republican movement. But we are still demanding our freedom.' He said the talks were 'wholly dependent upon the co-operation and the presence of the SDLP', but in fact held out less for nationalists than had been on offer to them in the 1970s. 'There must be a depressing sense of *déjà vu* for the SDLP leadership involved in discussions similar in content to Sunningdale eighteen years ago but holding out the promise of less influence and power at the end of this particular road than Sunningdale did.'

Adams expressed alarm that the Irish government might consider giving up Articles 2 and 3 of Eire's constitution, which contained its historical territorial claim to Northern Ireland, as part of any bargaining process they might enter into with unionists. He said the Articles had never been used by the IRA to justify its campaign – after all the IRA had never recognized the legitimacy of the twenty-six-county state – so their removal wouldn't have any impact on the IRA's armed struggle. But he nevertheless regarded the Articles as important as 'a statement of commitment to the national integrity of the Irish people'.

Given the length of time it had taken Peter Brooke to coax the various participants into the talks and the diametrically opposing nature of their aims, most observers didn't rate very highly the chances of any dramatic progress. Brooke himself has indicated that he was happy to have persuaded the unionists to come out of the cul-de-sac in which they had been since the signing of the Anglo-Irish Agreement, and that any progress beyond that was a bonus.

Curiously then, given the likelihood of failure, Adams allowed himself to ponder in one interview what the consequences of the Brooke talks succeeding would be for him, stuck on the outside. In a mirror-image world, where accommodation between others would be defeat for his philosophy, Adams mused that even if the Brooke talks reached their most optimistic conclusion, 'the most they'll do is put the lid on it'. An internal settlement within Northern Ireland, he argued, wouldn't solve anything in the long term, although it might defeat Sinn Fein and the IRA for a number of years. If such an agreement was reached, he concluded, 'the rest of us could just end up yawning, shrugging our shoulders and going home, but we're back to Churchill's dreary steeples'.

As the Brooke talks proceeded the IRA appeared to be doing its best to crank up its campaign – killing three Ulster Defence Regiment soldiers with a lorry bomb left outside their base at Glennane, bombing a series of Protestant estates and shooting Robert Orr, a Protestant who had been so long retired from the RUC that his targeting seemed to have more to do with the fact that he was a leading Orangeman than with any connection he had once had with the security forces. The Orr murder and the bombing of Protestant areas led to increasing criticism that the IRA campaign was becoming more blatantly sectarian. The loyalists, for their part, were hardly magnanimous with their ceasefire – using the period to venture across the Irish border into County Donegal and murder Sinn Fein councillor Eddie Fullerton. They claimed subsequently that their gesture had only ever applied within Northern Ireland itself.

In July the Brooke talks finally ground to a halt, with no sign of progress. The talks about talks which had been required to arrange them had taken far longer than the Stormont negotiations themselves. Gerry Adams appeared relieved at the failure, claiming that it should show unionists that they had to recognize that their future lay with the rest of the Irish people.

In a tactic to be employed by successive ministers in these circumstances, Brooke presented the end of the discussions not as a terminal breakdown but as a temporary suspension. Brooke's theory was that it was always possible in a long process to pick up the pieces and move on:

I used to liken it to a steeplechase course and I produced this phrase that we've always got to be able to camp on the course. If the race breaks down so we can't get over the next hurdle what we can't have is everybody dispersing to the four corners of the island.

We've actually got to camp on the course so that when we're ready to go we can do so, and that's exactly how I envisage it. I read a leading article which said the route to peace is a very long and devious one and nobody knows how many turns of the road it will take and who will do what to get them there. But unless you believe that, unless you believe that there is a way to peace then you might just as well pack up and go home. What you can't predict is actually how it's going to happen. But each time somebody's put to the test and gets through the test then it makes it more likely they'll get through the next one.

After the breakdown of the talks Adams intensified his calls for republicans to be involved in discussions. 'I want to see an end to all the violence. How do we go about doing that? That is the challenge. Are those who are so vocal in their denunciation of Sinn Fein prepared to move forward and try and find a way out of the impasse? Because we are.'

Adams' old sparring partner Richard Needham was unimpressed. 'The only message I have for Mr Adams is that he should call off his rottweilers and if he ever wants to be remembered for anything good in his life, he can help bring peace to this place by stopping the terrorist activity which his party supports.'

Although Adams was receiving assistance from Father Alex Reid and his fellow Redemptorist priests, the Catholic Church hierarchy continued to keep him at arm's length. After the death of Cardinal Tomas O Fiaich, Adams' *bête noire* Cahal Daly took over as head of the Church. At the end of 1991 Daly together with the leader of the Church of Ireland Archbishop Robin Eames, and the heads of the Presbyterian and Methodist Churches, rejected yet another request from Adams for a meeting.

The Church leaders welcomed Adams' words that Sinn Fein was committed to working towards 'bringing the conflict to an end' and was 'prepared to take political risks'. But the clergymen retorted, 'in our opinion, these are merely words – fine words certainly and welcome – but nevertheless, only words. Until Sinn Fein gives public, tangible and credible proof that it is actually taking the only "political risk" which is meaningful in our situation, namely calling for the cessation of violence, then your words will lack credibility. No party which supports violence can seriously claim to be "discharging its responsibilities in a positive and honourable way" in so far as the establishment of peace is concerned. Since no credible proof has been given, or is now being given, by Sinn Fein of its readiness to abjure all violence, we cannot meet with yourself or with other representatives of Sinn Fein.'

CHAPTER TWENTY

How the West Was Lost

At Christmas 1991 the IRA observed another three-day ceasefire and Gerry Adams followed through in the New Year with his ritualistic demand that the government enter into dialogue with Sinn Fein. They had done so in the past, he said, and would do so again.

Although they were in contact with the Provisionals in secret and the attempts to recommence talks with the other parties were not going well, the government were never going to be tempted into abandoning a cardinal principle of their policy, as Peter Brooke made clear when he said ministers could only become involved in talks in the event of a 'cessation of violence' not a 'temporary ceasefire'.

Just as Adams' letter to Downing Street a year before had been followed promptly by a volley of mortars, so these diplomatic exchanges were swiftly overwhelmed by the impact of violence on the ground. On 17 January the IRA detonated a landmine besides a van carrying eight Protestant construction workers returning home after a day employed on a contract at the Lisanelly army base in Omagh. Seven died instantly in the massive explosion at Teebane crossroads, an eighth worker, Oswald Gilchrist, succumbed to his injuries four days after the attack.

Teebane marked the start of another vicious ratchet of violence – a fortnight later three men were shot at the Sinn Fein office on the Falls Road from which Adams had made his victory speech after winning the West Belfast seat. The killer, an off-duty RUC officer, had been looking for Adams and later took his own life. Then the loyalist Ulster Freedom Fighters attacked a bookmakers' shop, Sean Graham's on Belfast's Lower Ormeau Road, coldly shooting down five Catholic punters. The youngest was just fifteen, the oldest sixty-six.

The targeting of Sinn Fein, Adams alleged, was a product of 'the climate of McCarthyism that has been created' around his party. In his comments on Teebane, Adams tried to walk a tightrope, on the one hand saying nothing which could be taken as criticism of the IRA, on the other trying to shed the image of the bombers' mouthpiece which had contributed to the 'McCarthyism' he claimed to resent. With the bombers in mind, Adams argued that the death of eight Protestants was 'a horrific reminder of the failure of British policy in Ireland' and republicans accepted that people had 'a legitimate right to use armed force'.

So far as the wider audience was concerned, Adams stopped well short of openly defending the bombing. 'I think it was a horrific incident and my heart does go out to the families of the people who were bereaved. I have experienced the same type of loss in my own family when incidents have occurred within the broad republican community. I regret very much the loss of life in this situation and it doesn't matter whether it's British soldiers or IRA volunteers or civilians or people in between them all. I think it diminishes all of us.' He stressed that there were 'no organic links' between Sinn Fein and the IRA, repeating the mantra, 'Sinn Fein is not the IRA, it is a political manifestation of republicanism.'

A few days after the UFF launched their attack on Sean Graham's, Sinn Fein published a policy document entitled *A Scenario for Peace*. Although it rejected the partition of Ireland and denied that the majority of people north of the border had the right to decide how they wished to be governed, the paper did place a greater emphasis on consulting Protestants than had been the case in previous Sinn Fein documents. Adams explained the shift in republican thinking in the following terms. 'There was a fairly popular republican notion maybe twenty years ago that the IRA would fight the British Army to a standstill; and the British Army would shake hands and say, "Well, we are sorry we are beat, we are going to leave next week, next year," and that unionists would become reconciled to this new scenario. That, put in a sort of very exaggerated way, may have been the republican notion. This new document at least shows that republicans have come away from that kind of thinking.' Adams told the *Irish Times* that whereas a few years ago he would have felt it necessary to declare himself publicly in favour of the IRA's campaign, 'I don't feel the need to do that now.' While Sinn Fein was in favour of a centralized all-Ireland government, Adams acknowledged that they might have to compromise. 'Republicans would have to argue for our view of the type of model, but we would also have to have an open mind about other confederal, federal, interim phased arrangements, all have to be taken into account.'

All this was pie in the sky. Northern Ireland was in the midst of a renewed IRA commercial bombing campaign and as a consequence of the Teebane massacre members of the Dublin city corporation banned Sinn Fein for the first time from using the Mansion House for their annual conference. The party was forced to decamp to an uninviting community centre in the working-class estate of Ballyfermot. It was a move which symbolized Adams' continuing rejection by the mainstream of Irish society.

Back north of the border Adams' opponents had begun to gear up for another general election campaign. Most commentators didn't rate the chances of his main rival Dr Joe Hendron, a general practitioner whose clinic lay in the shadows of the strongly republican Divis Flats and the towers of the Catholic cathedral of St Peter's. Hendron was regarded as a nice man and a good councillor, but without the cutting edge or street-fighting qualities necessary to take on Adams' well-oiled political machine.

However, for his 1992 campaign, Hendron employed a new campaign manager, Tom Kelly, a shrewd political operator who invested money in a survey of voters to try to identify those who hadn't bothered to vote previously and find out their concerns. The Church also weighed in on the side of constitutional nationalism, much to Adams' chagrin. Cahal Daly may have denied that he was telling people how to vote, but no ordinary Mass-goer could fail to understand what the Bishop was getting at when he said he hoped people would 'reflect very carefully not only on the vote that they are going to give but on the possible interpretations put upon their vote . . . and I hope that whatever people do, they will vote for a peaceful future'.

In the event, though, the election was probably decided by people who didn't give a fig what a Catholic Church leader said one way or the other. In January 1992 a loyalist from Londonderry, Ken Kerr, then a member of the UDA's political wing, suggested that Protestants on the Shankill Road, which fell within Adams' West Belfast constituency, might consider voting tactically to unseat their hate figure.

Sinn Fein employed the loyalist card as often as they could throughout the election campaign: Hendron would find himself making his way into his surgery past graffiti insulting him personally and accusing him of being in league with UFF murderers. The SDLP for their part retorted that Provisional supporters were busy printing off fake medical cards – essential equipment in Northern Ireland's long-standing tradition of personation, or vote-stealing – to increase their chances of winning what was lining up to be a tight race.

On polling day some 3,000 Protestants put their crosses against Hendron's name, a tactical vote which was far bigger than the support which any UDA candidate had ever managed to muster in past elections and which was sizeable enough to give Hendron a 589-vote majority.

Adams tried to pass the result off as 'a shallow victory' and the theft of the seat by the UDA. But in private he acknowledged it was a devastating blow to his strategy and personal esteem. 'It's a matter of personal disappointment to me,' he admitted, 'and remember it was with the assistance of the loyalist forces that the seat was actually stolen and with the assistance of a propaganda campaign of moral blackmail by leaders of the Churches, particularly the Catholic Church in this area.' He took heart from the fact that his own vote had remained almost exactly static – the shift, he argued, had occurred instead in unionist allegiances. 'The election was depicted by you beforehand and by others quite correctly as a battle for the hearts and minds of nationalist West Belfast,' he told one of the authors. 'The battle for the hearts and minds of West Belfast is not over, they may have won one round in relation to winning the seat, but they certainly haven't won the battle for the hearts and minds.'

One of the ugliest encounters between Adams and Hendron came after twenty-six-year-old Philomena Hanna was murdered at her chemist's shop on the Springfield Road by the Ulster Freedom Fighters, a fortnight after the election. Hendron, as the local MP, was confronted at the scene by a group of Sinn Fein-supporting women who crowded around him, claiming that it was his political allies who had carried out the murder. The RUC, concerned for Hendron's safety, offered to help, but Hendron's aide Alex Attwood declined, mindful of the negative impact it would have for a nationalist politician to be seen to be requiring the protection of the police against his own nationalist constituents.

Suddenly Adams appeared on the scene and began to usher the women away – a move which appeared eminently reasonable but had the added political benefit of making him appear statesmanlike and Hendron inadequate. Attwood swiftly assessed the situation and moved in alongside Adams, joining in as, apparently, an equal partner in the process of crowd control. Adams turned venomously on Attwood, telling him, 'Don't you ever do that to me again.' As Attwood recalled later, 'The mask slipped.'

The day after Adams' defeat in the Westminster election, the IRA exploded a massive bomb in the City of London wrecking the Baltic Exchange and causing £700 million worth of damage, more than the entire cost to the Exchequer of the last twenty-two years of violence from the Troubles. Three people died, including a fifteen-year-old girl. The scale of the damage and the ensuing publicity delighted the IRA, who realized that the British nation's financial heart was the government's Achilles heel.

The general election of April 1992 not only saw Adams removed from West Belfast, but also led to the replacement of Peter Brooke as Northern Ireland Secretary. Brooke had embarrassed himself on the evening after the Teebane massacre when he appeared on the Gay Byrne chat show, one of the most popular programmes broadcast by the Irish state television service RTE, and allowed himself to be persuaded to give a rendition of 'My Darling Clementine'. The Prime Minister refused Brooke's immediate offer to resign, but in a post-election reshuffle he appointed the Attorney General Sir Patrick Mayhew to take over at Stormont.

In May when the initial furore associated with the Baltic Exchange bombing had died down, Brooke confided in an interview with RTE that he would have liked to have met Adams. 'As a matter of history because he had quite a significant role in the development of events, yes, but that is only a human reaction. The basic position of the government was absolutely firm and unless certain things happened it was not going to be possible.'

Brooke later felt his comment had been somewhat misunderstood, telling the authors that what he meant was that he would have liked an IRA ceasefire to have been in place during his time in office rather than that he had any particularly earnest desire to see Adams. That said, Brooke as a close observer of the Provisionals had clearly developed a curiosity about the movement's central figure. Brooke always found the columns in *Republican News* which he believed Adams penned 'extremely well written and very well informed . . . I did always regard him as being very significant just simply because of the quality of his thinking and indeed of his knowledge.'

Others had been better placed than Brooke to act on their curiosity and find out what the man 'on the other side of the hill' was like. Adams had been engaging in a series of meetings with Protestants, including the Reverend Ken Newell, since late 1990. Initially Newell had found the encounters relatively unproductive – stalemated on the question of violence – but from the spring of 1992 on he detected a greater warmth on Adams' part and a greater commitment to build some kind of peace.

In the spring of 1992 two other Presbyterians, former moderators Jack Weir and Godfrey Brown, met Adams. Weir had been involved in the talks with the IRA at Feakle which had presaged the 1975 ceasefire. Motivated by the killings at Teebane and on the Ormeau Road, Weir and Brown decided it was time to tell both the UDA and Sinn Fein that enough was enough. In the tense atmosphere of the time some criticized the churchmen for having anything to do with those associated with violence, but Weir justified his decision by arguing that 'these people who do the most horrible things are flesh and blood like ourselves and that's part of the horror of it. They're not devils. They are people who have reason, who have conscience.'

Adams, for his part, welcomed what he termed the 'frank and useful' meetings with the churchmen. They were part of his party's wider strategy, 'which embraces talks with anyone who has a policy of trying to promote the need for the demilitarization of the situation'. Reacting to Dr Weir's view that republicans continued to live in 'never-never land', Adams countered that 'the British claim jurisdiction over a major part of our country. This is in fact a major part of the problem. That isn't never-never land. That's quite a valid, legitimate and I would say logical common-sense viewpoint of the situation.'

Even if there was no meeting of minds with some of those he held talks with, Adams' view was still very much that such dialogue had to be encouraged. The logic was that while the government might refuse to have anything to do with the Provisionals the process of informal discussions with other groups would slowly but surely break the ice surrounding Sinn Fein.

While the Mayhew talks – inherited from his predecessor – continued, Hume knew that the unionists would walk away from him if it became known that he was still talking with Adams. But he did stay in touch with Adams, assuring him that he had no intention of agreeing to a return to the old Stormont-style internal Northern Ireland government. More important, Hume passed Adams a series of documents which he had drawn up with assistance from some of the Irish government's most high-ranking civil servants. They represented the SDLP leader's development of his thinking about Irish self-determination which had dominated his discussions with Adams in 1988.

In 1989 Hume tried to circumvent the dichotomy between those who supported unification and those who said Northern Ireland must remain British by suggesting that an all-Ireland conference should be held and its recommendations should then be tested by referenda north and south of the Irish border. Adams was not impressed, but undeterred by his initial hostility, Hume continued to think laterally about national self-determination, and in his first written document, drawn up in late 1991 in the form of a draft declaration on behalf of the British and Irish governments, he suggested that Dublin should recognize that its exercise could not be achieved without the agreement of the people of Northern Ireland.

He also proposed the creation of an 'Irish convention'. These key ideas were batted to and fro over the succeeding months, with Adams consistently trying to harden up the 'green nationalist' tinge to the document. After several exchanges the drafts became the basis of what was to be the Downing Street Declaration signed by John Major and Albert Reynolds, who had taken over as Irish Prime Minister in February 1992. By that stage, however, both governments were, for diplomatic reasons, hotly denying that Adams had any hand in the drafting process.

So, as the Stormont talks convened by Sir Patrick Mayhew occupied the foreground of politics, there was a whole network of separate, secret and in the long term probably more significant processes going on in the background. Drafts were being exchanged between the Irish government, Hume and Adams. And, through Martin McGuinness, Adams was being regularly updated on the information provided by the secret back channel to the British government, which contained such nuggets as details of the supposedly confidential discussions under way at Stormont, revelations about how the government hoped to 'ghost-write' reports supposedly drawn up by the independent chairman Sir Ninian Stephen and advance copies of important speeches ministers were due to make.

When the Mayhew talks failed in November 1992, Adams was therefore not at all surprised. He had already been told via the secret contacts that the government believed the discussions were going to collapse, and he would have known that John Hume in particular had a great deal of his political attention focused on documents which were not part of the Stormont process. When Sir Patrick then stood up at Coleraine and made a speech widely interpreted as an overture to the Provisionals, saying troops could be withdrawn to barracks in the event of an end to the IRA campaign, Adams would have again been well briefed, having obtained a copy of the speech through the back channel.

Adams chose to play down those aspects of the address, which unionists claimed amounted to a 'surrender,' and instead concentrated on Mayhew's insistence that until republicans repudiated violence they would exclude themselves from discussions. 'Perhaps Mr Mayhew harbours the hope that republican resistance will be worn down,' Adams retorted, studiously avoiding any reference to the Northern Ireland Secretary's British knighthood. 'It will not. Peace will have to be negotiated and peace-making is about bringing hostile parties together to seek agreement through negotiation.'

At the close of the year Adams could congratulate himself that far from being the isolated figure portrayed by his opponents, excluded from ordinary political discourse because of his links with the IRA, he was in fact at the centre of an extensive web of contacts well beyond the boundaries of the republican movement, some of them overt, others covert. In many ways he knew more about the overall picture than almost any of the other major players. Unlike the British government, he knew all about the interchanges with Hume. Unlike the Irish government, he was kept abreast of the secret contacts with British secret agents, and unlike the unionists, he knew exactly how the government were hoping to manipulate the Stormont talks. These multiple contacts which kept Adams so well informed were maintained despite the continuation of IRA violence. A major bombing campaign had forced many of Northern Ireland's Protestant towns to shut their security gates for the first time since the 1970s.

But despite being at the centre of this impressive political web, Adams could not regard 1992 as a good year. He had lost his treasured Westminster seat and would have to work hard to regain the status that being an MP had provided. Setting politics to one side, he had also suffered a more personal loss. In September 1992 his mother Annie died after suffering a stroke. Gerry junior stood beside his father during the requiem mass. All the family walked in the cortège, led by a piper, as it made its way from the family home to the church. Among them was Gerry's brother Sean, who had been refused compassionate parole to visit his sick mother in hospital, but was given twenty-four hours out of prison to attend her funeral.

CHAPTER TWENTY-ONE

'The Conflict Is Over'

In October 1992 the Northern Ireland Security Minister Michael Mates received word from the security services that the IRA Army Council was considering extending its Christmas ceasefire from three days to ten to test the water so far as the government's likely response was concerned.

Mates told his family he wouldn't be coming home for Christmas and waited for what he expected to be a significant development. 'Then on 20 or 21 December,' he later recalled, 'the Army Council met and decided three to two against it. The two who were present and in favour were Adams and McGuinness . . . They had toyed with a long ceasefire and decided marginally against it. I think the inference is that if the other two members of the [seven-strong] Army Council had been present it would have been five to two against.'

Nevertheless, it was a sign that things were moving. In February 1993 the secret channel between the Provisionals and the British erupted into life. In the previous few months the channel had been used mainly for exchanges of information, rather than any proper negotiations, but over the next few weeks the messages passed to and fro had an altogether more urgent tone, and made a mockery of the government's later insistence that this wasn't a form of negotiation.

Quite what sparked this change of gear is open to debate, as the versions given by both sides differ markedly. The British government say that in February Martin McGuinness sent a message reading, 'The conflict is over but we need your advice on how to bring it to a close.' Sinn Fein insist that no such message was ever sent. In Gerry Adams' words, 'They say that republicans are ready to surrender. This is a lie. Our commitment to struggle is firm and undaunted.'

But Mates insists that the 'conflict is over' message was received and that it did not come as a total surprise because the intelligence information received the previous Christmas had given the government a fair idea of what was going on in Adams' and McGuinness' minds. 'That was the message, it came down several links, it wasn't signed by Martin McGuinness. It was brought ultimately by a churchman who was the last link in the chain,' he told the authors. Mates points to the nature of the British reply, which began, 'We understand and appreciate the seriousness of what has been said. We wish to take it seriously and at face value . . .' as evidence that the government's version was true. 'The first message was the one that set the whole chain in motion. If the first message was never sent why did they respond positively to the second one, the reply? I'm not telling you those were the exact words because they were sent down a line, but if the content and the purport of that message was not to the effect that we want to talk about ending the conflict why the hell did they send the second one, and the third and the fourth? That's a question they can't answer.'

In truth questions are left begging on all sides by what happened – the Provisional version of the contacts, published by Gerry Adams and Martin McGuinness, had more internal consistency than the British one, which had to be corrected after it was first given to the House of Commons. Sir Patrick Mayhew admitted there were twenty-two inaccuracies in the initial British account. The government's timetable for the communications, starting in February 1993, was also proven to be less accurate than the republican account, corroborated by Peter Brooke, which began in late 1990.

What is clear is that there were intensive exchanges between the two sides during the spring, with the possibility of a two-week IRA suspension of violence under discussion, suggestions for talks in Scandinavia, Scotland or the Isle of Man, and promises that evidence of an end to violent activity would lead to a reciprocal reduction in security force patrolling. Much of the content was couched in language referring to 'the Bank' or 'the national Chairman' as code to disguise these discussions of national importance as business communications.

Politically the contacts revealed the Provisionals pushing the British to 'persuade' the unionist community into an accommodation with the rest of the Irish people, while the government insisted that they could not adopt an approach which had as its objective 'the ending of partition'. By the time the exchanges broke down during June and July of 1993, however, what were referred to as 'economic events', 'events on the ground' and 'headline events' had clearly made a disastrous impact.

One of the most horrific 'headline events' occurred in the English town of Warrington on 20 March 1993. Two young boys, three-year-old Jonathan Ball and twelve-year-old Tim Parry were out shopping with their families when the IRA exploded two bombs. Jonathan Ball was killed instantly, Tim Parry died five days later from his injuries. Fifty-six people were also injured in the blast. The murder of young children caused a wave of revulsion both in Britain and in the Irish Republic, where tens of thousands of people attended peace rallies.

Adams described Warrington as unacceptable and said it should not be repeated. He would not call on the IRA to stop its campaign but pledged to work to get 'a political package' which he would take to the IRA if he was satisfied it could move the situation forward. Such a package, he argued, would involve an agreement by the British and Irish governments that their objective was to end partition. 'How long that takes, how it happens, what stages it takes, I think is all a matter for finding consensus and agreement. We would like to jump from the present situation into a democratic thirty-two-county social-ist republic, but that isn't going to happen. But when the British government says yes, we are going to do away with partition, then that does away with the reason for armed struggle.' Adams made these comments ten days after receiving the government's firm message that such a policy could not be adopted.

Some months after the Warrington bombing the parents of one of the victims, Tim Parry, visited Northern Ireland for a BBC *Panorama* documentary. Colin and Wendy Parry requested to meet Adams and for the encounter to be filmed, but he refused to meet them. His press aides argued that it would be voyeurism of the worst kind. Colin Parry was scornful of this response. 'I wanted to look at the man and hear his voice and ask him directly how he could be in league with an organization like the IRA. I feel that he would be extremely uncomfortable looking back at me, holding my gaze and trying to tell me that the loss of Tim was merely the unfortunate by-product of a war against Britain. The answer that we received was that to talk to us on film would be voyeurism at its worst. I think that that is an absolutely disgusting thing to say, to appear to make voyeurism a greater sin than the murder of my son.'

On 7 April 1993, the day that a memorial service was held in Warrington attended by the Prime Minister and the Irish President Mary Robinson, representatives of the IRA met Gordon Wilson, who had lost his daughter Marie in the IRA's Enniskillen bombing. Wilson, who had been made a senator in the Irish parliament, wanted to plead directly with the paramilitaries for an end to the killing and based his arguments not on politics but on raw human emotion. He came away disappointed. 'They seemed unmoved . . . their position is entrenched . . . nothing that I had said had in any way moved them from their stated position,' he admitted sorrowfully.

If there was no meeting of minds between Gordon Wilson and the IRA, then another encounter, this time involving Gerry Adams and a former senior Irish civil servant, appeared far more political in content and potentially more fruitful in its implications. Michael Lillis had been one of the prime architects of the Anglo-Irish Agreement in 1985 and as such he believed passionately that the accord provided a mechanism for the peaceful advance of Northern nationalist interests. This side of the Agreement, he believed, had been lost in its presentation as a means of marginalizing Sinn Fein and the IRA. Adams read a newspaper article by Lillis calling for a rejuvenation of the Agreement and found some of the ideas so interesting that he requested a meeting.

Lillis used the encounter to make clear to Adams 'in very strong terms that I disagreed with the use of violence by the Provisional IRA and was ashamed of it as an Irish person'. Adams listened to what Lillis had to say but didn't concur. 'I think it would be inaccurate certainly to suggest that he was in any way ashamed of the campaign of violence of the Provisional IRA. On the contrary, I would say that he believed that it had produced useful political effects and had produced whatever progress that they were prepared to see in the attitude of Britain . . . I do believe that he felt a good deal of grief and concern about the suffering that had been caused, but I think that his view was that this is a war situation, that these things happen, they are terribly regrettable, but given his view – which I absolutely reject – that it was a war, that these things are inevitable and unavoidable consequences of that kind of campaign.'

Lillis was impressed by Adams' personal qualities. 'I'm someone who has spent a great deal of my life talking to politicians and listening to politicians, but he impressed me as one of the most serious and intellectually gifted political people that I have met.' But more importantly, Lillis detected a shift in Adams' attitude away from the old simplistic 'Brits Out' notions. 'I think it's fair to say that he had moved intellectually quite a distance in his analysis of the problem. I think he had moved to a position much closer to the analysis which John Hume has been putting before all of us, for most of the past generation, which is that this is a divided community which requires a much more complex response than simply the imposition of one nationality over another.' Lillis drew the conclusion that what Adams said in public was often at variance with what he thought in private – certainly he believed the Sinn Fein president's real assessment of the Anglo-Irish Agreement was a good deal warmer than his public utterances indicated.

A few days after his encounter with Lillis, Adams was spotted leaving John Hume's home at West End Park on the edge of Derry's Bogside estate. The two men were trying to keep their continuing contacts under wraps but a local man, Tony Gillespie, tipped off the freelance journalist and socialist activist Eamonn McCann. McCann phoned the Dublin *Sunday Tribune* and broke the story – the first evidence of a meeting between the two nationalist leaders since their talks ended in disagreement in 1988. For Hume the timing of the revelation was particularly difficult given the widespread anger still felt over the Warrington murders.

A fortnight later, after a further meeting, the two men issued a joint statement on their discussions. The statement coincided with a rather more dramatic development – the explosion of an IRA bomb beside the National Westminister Tower in the centre of the City of London. The bomb, containing more than a ton of home made explosives, killed one person, injured more than thirty and caused an estimated £1 billion worth of damage.

Ten days after the bombing the Provisionals contacted the government through the secret channel to ask why there was a delay in the British responding to a recent message. 'Are there problems?' they inquired, shortly after having devastated the country's financial centre. The government replied, 'Events on the ground are crucial, as we have consistently made clear. We cannot conceivably disregard them.'

The discussions between Hume and Adams were prompting increasing talk from unionist politicians of the existence of a pan-nationalist front. Such comments had potentially deadly implications given that the loyalist paramilitary UDA had made it clear in January 1993 that they planned to target pan-nationalists, a group in which they included members of the SDLP, the Gaelic Athletic Association and the Irish government, as well as Sinn Fein and the IRA. As the year wore on the UDA, using its terrorist front name of the Ulster Freedom Fighters, made good its threat by killing or injuring a number of Sinn Fein members, party supporters and their relatives. The homes of SDLP councillors and the West Belfast MP Joe Hendron were also attacked. But the prestige target of greatest importance remained Gerry Adams himself.

Shortly after midnight on 9 June 1993 a red Vauxhall car pulled up at Norfolk Drive, the road where Gerry Adams maintains a home in West Belfast. A man got out of the vehicle and hurled a grenade at the Adams family home. The device bounced off a security screen and caused minor damage to the front porch. Adams wasn't at home but his wife Colette and his nineteen-year-old son Gearoid were. 'My son was studying at the time and my wife was in bed. They are shaken. The damage appears to be superficial. Everybody is thankful they are not injured,' he said.

Despite the increasingly wide network of discussions in which he was involved, Adams remained a pariah in the eyes of the public. So there was considerable astonishment when the Irish President Mary Robinson took up a long-standing invitation to visit West Belfast and shook the Sinn Fein president's hand in his capacity as 'founder member of the West Belfast festival'. The media was excluded from the meeting so as not to record the encounter.

After the IRA announced its 1994 ceasefire, President Robinson reflected on the dilemma she had faced about whether or not to meet Adams. 'It was a very difficult decision, one I thought deeply about. It was not easy to know whether you were doing the right thing. I underestimated what the media response would be afterwards. It was as though I had gone to Northern Ireland to shake Gerry Adams' hand. I tried to say that there was a story of local community vibrancy, of what was being done for young people, the drop-outs from school, the old people, but there was no interest in that. The only interest was on focusing on shaking hands with Gerry Adams. It was clear that it had been extremely important for those communities in West Belfast. In a small sense I think I helped them make the changes that they were making.'

Gerry Adams could reflect that the ice around him was beginning to break. Although President Robinson faced criticism not just from Britain but also from some sections of the Irish media, and, privately, from the Foreign Minister Dick Spring, she did appear to have the backing of the majority of the Irish people in holding out a hand of friendship to Adams. Polls showed more than 70 per cent support for her decision.

The support that was beginning to build around the notion of reaching out to Adams wasn't confined to Irish shores. In the United States republicans had always enjoyed a hardcore of support, but as Gerry Adams talked more and more of his 'peace strategy' a new brand of Irish Americans, who had previously dissociated themselves from anything to do with IRA violence, now became interested in investigating whether the new rhetoric might presage a decisive move towards peace.

In September 1993 a four-strong delegation of influential Irish Americans led by the former Congressman Bruce Morrison visited Ireland for six days. In Dublin they were given a lengthy briefing by Albert Reynolds. North of the border they met the Northern Ireland Secretary Sir Patrick Mayhew and representatives of all the main parties with the exception of the DUP, whose leader Ian Paisley referred to them as 'troublemakers'. The Irish Americans also met David Ervine and Gusty Spence, two former UVF men who were in the future to emerge into the public eye as the political representatives of the loyalist paramilitaries. The delegation finished their visit with a meeting with Gerry Adams, Martin McGuinness, Mairead Keane, the head of Sinn Fein's women's department, and executive member Lucilita Bhreatnach. The two sides had what Morrison termed 'a lengthy, very intense session' in which the Americans concentrated on telling the Provisionals how they could promote their political interests on the other side of the Atlantic in the event of a cessation of IRA violence. Afterwards Morrison said he wanted to see total demilitarization: 'That is a goal that I very much have and I want to see Gerry Adams and others lead the way in that direction if we can possibly achieve it.'

What was more significant than the content of the discussions was the fact that they took place in a peaceful atmosphere. Before leaving America, Morrison's delegation sought and received assurances that the IRA would not carry out any attacks during their visit. Dublin was also informed in advance. Between Friday 3 September, when an IRA bomb wrecked the courthouse in Armagh city, and 13 September, when another attack badly damaged the Stormont Hotel in East Belfast, there were no IRA attacks. Two gun attacks on RUC stations were blamed on the republican splinter group, the INLA. Adams later told journalist Conor O'Clery that IRA commanders had only given him a qualified commitment about the ceasefire, saying that they would not plan any new attacks, but nor would they stop anything which had already been arranged, if the opportunity arose to carry out an attack.

Six months after their continuing contacts had been exposed in the Dublin *Sunday Tribune*, Adams and Hume issued a brief statement to the press reporting that their discussions had made considerable progress and that they were forwarding a report to the Irish government. Pending a response from Dublin they were suspending further detailed discussions. The British government remained deeply suspicious. A few days later Sir Patrick Mayhew commented: 'On Saturday Mr Adams says, "We are convinced that a process can be devised which will provide a solid base for peace." On Monday the Provisional IRA – who had carefully laid off while American politicians were here – are back with another bomb. It is plain that their campaign of violence is what they see as the basis for future peace – on their terms.'

The Irish government was also less than pleased. Albert Reynolds was working closely with John Major in the hope of incorporating the drafts provided by Hume and Adams into a future joint declaration. But it was vital from the British government's point of view that the fingerprints of Adams should not be traceable on any text which they eventually agreed. Now, by publicizing their 'report to the Irish government' Hume and Adams had made this process far more difficult. There were two other reasons why Dublin was more than a little perplexed. First, they hadn't received any report from the two politicians. Second, John Hume departed immediately for America and was incommunicado. It left Irish ministers and civil servants wondering whether the pressure of events had simply got too much for the SDLP leader.

Hume's absence left Gerry Adams fronting up to the press, saying little about the contents of the report to the Irish government, which, unlike the reporters who were hounding him, he knew didn't exist. Asked if he thought he could bring all the republican movement with him he replied, 'I will not do anything that doesn't have that intention. I will not mislead anyone I am dealing with about that . . . There has been an evolution of republican policy for some time . . . Sinn Fein has not ceased to be a republican party. We want to see an Irish republic. We were never simply a "Brits Out" party at any time in our history, but we have adopted a different approach which is more in keeping with the reality of Ireland in 1993 than perhaps harking back to Ireland in 1918.'

A few days after the Hume/Adams joint statement, Kevin Myers, whose columns in the *Irish Times* were always biting in their invective towards the IRA, wrote prophetically in his 'Irishman's Diary': 'A prediction: thanks to those incredibly productive talks with John Hume (so vital that John Hume feels it more important to buzz off to the US than to tell anybody in Dublin what actually happened in them, although we may be sure that the Army Council of the IRA knows the lot) nice pipe-smoking, story-telling avuncular Gerry Adams will certainly be Westminster MP for West Belfast for all time after the next election. No wonder that whenever poor Joe Hendron appears on television, he looks as if he has spent the entire night trying to defuse a bomb taped to his eyelids.' On a more personal note, Myers continued, sardonically: 'And how splendidly the avuncular image suits Gerry! How much more would it suit him if he stopped dyeing his hair and his beard that inky and unconvincing black. Let it go, Gerry. Go on. Let the grey assert its natural self; you could, in addition to looking avuncular, be equally statesmanlike and be an ornament for West Belfast and a joy to behold.'

In between assessing the reaction to his talks with John Hume and liaising with IRA commanders, Gerry Adams took some time out to pen a rejoinder to this verbal assault on his appearance:

For years I have admired Kevin Myers. The clarity of his writing and quality of his wordmanship (wordpersonship?) has often been ample compensation for his frequent, unbalanced, disinforming and eccentric polemics in regard to the British connection and its effects in Ireland. But last Saturday's 'Irishman's

Diary' was a diary too far. Poor Myers has lost his marbles, I thought to myself upon reading it. He has gone over the top and it's my fault! I almost shaved. Such was my remorse. To think that my facial hair was responsible for reducing him to such wired up whingeing! And then I read his piece again. Reflectively. He gets paid for this. Probably quite a lot. You pay him. He presents it as journalism. Mad? Myers? Not by the hairs of my chinny, chin chin! Keep it up, Kevin. Fair play to you. It's easy money. Never say dye.

CHAPTER TWENTY-TWO

Carrying the Coffin

Gerry Adams had just finished attending a meeting in Belfast when a Sinn Fein aide told him there had been an explosion on the Shankill Road, the proudly loyalist enclave of West Belfast. A bomb had detonated in Frizzels fish shop, directly beneath the offices of the loyalist paramilitary UDA. The IRA said that the UDA members were their intended target, but the operation had been conceived with reckless abandonment of any thought for the likely consequences. The bomb killed nine people, including the shop owner and his daughter.

The explosion also killed Thomas Begley, a twenty-three-year-old member of the Belfast IRA's 3rd Battalion, based in the strongly republican North Belfast area of Ardoyne, who was held in low esteem by his peers in the neighbourhood. Commented one nationalist of some standing: 'I never thought I'd see the day when the IRA used people like him.'

Adams claimed: 'I was shattered when I heard the news. There was a sense of shock at what had happened. Republicans need to be very circumspect about being involved in any actions against the loyalists. They always need to be aware that such actions, no matter what their intentions, could have the awful human consequences that we have seen so clearly on the Shankill Road. It is of little comfort to anyone involved, but the fact that an IRA volunteer was killed is at least proof that it was a premature explosion.' Although he expressed shock at what had occurred he defended the IRA's plan. 'Their intention was to attack the leaders of the death squads who have been killing Catholics almost with impunity in this city. That was their intention. But of course, as we know, and as the families of those killed know, the tragedy was one where civilians were killed – and an added tragedy for the IRA itself where one of its own volunteers was killed in the course of the action.'

Challenged that simply saying the bombing was 'wrong' was insufficient, Adams hinted that his real views might be stronger. 'I live in the reality of this situation. I do not always publicly express myself to the exact extent of my private feelings.' These professions of sorrow held little credibility for the daughter of George and Gillian Williamson, a couple in their sixties who both died in the blast. Michelle Williamson said, 'I want to see Gerry Adams face to face. I want to tell him that the people who did this to my mammy and daddy are nothing but scum. I want to tell them they are evil bastards.'

Adams claimed comments implying he was directly responsible for the blast were 'despicable and irresponsible'. 'If you are asking me,' he told one journalist, 'can I as an individual stop the IRA the answer patently is "No". No one individual has the ability to stop the IRA.'

Martin McGartland, who worked as a police agent within the IRA in the late 1980s, says that eighteen months before the Shankill Road bombing the IRA in Belfast had been planning an attack on the UDA office using coffee-jar bombs, but the operation was aborted after he warned the RUC. But the office remained a priority target, not least because it was the base for Shankill loyalist Johnny Adair, whose involvement in planning UFF attacks had earned him an especially fearsome reputation. The IRA commander in Ardoyne, who had authority over Thomas Begley, was widely reputed to be intent on pursuing a personal vendetta against Adair, who was later jailed for directing terrorism.

Immediately after the explosion, press reports indicated that the IRA leadership were carrying out an inquiry into the attack, which had been sanctioned by the Belfast Brigade. But the man who led the Belfast Brigade stayed in his job and was later promoted within the IRA. Security sources say the IRA Army Council, who were allegedly so concerned about the impact of the bombing, included both Adams and Martin McGuinness. The diaries of the late Ian Phoenix, who was a detective superintendent in the RUC's Special Branch, record that the Shankill bombing, and the clear evidence of dual membership at the highest levels between Sinn Fein and the IRA made the police extremely sceptical at this time about Adams' much touted peace strategy.

After the deaths came the funerals, and for Adams that meant deciding whether to shoulder the coffin of Thomas Begley, the young man whose actions had caused the carnage which he had so publicly deplored. For those who had watched Adams over the years, regularly attending IRA funerals and taking his turn at 'lifting' the coffin in time-honoured Irish tradition, there was little doubt what course of action he would take. 'I am not going to abandon Thomas Begley, a lad in his early twenties, or hurt his family any more than they have been hurt,' he said. Acknowledging that the television pictures of him doing so may have inflamed the families of the innocent victims, Adams said he accepted their reaction but he hit out at 'the sort of hypocrisy from the Mayhews of this world or the Paisleys who tried to make political capital out of a grief-filled occasion for the Begley family. It seems to me very unChristian of these elected clergymen to be exploiting an unfortunately all too frequent occurrence, funerals of people who have died because of the violent situation in this country.' But a source close to Adams said: 'Although he was appalled, his thinking was he was not going to turn his back on a republican family. He may be a shit but he's our shit.'

The sight of the man who claimed to be involved in a peace process honouring someone widely regarded as a mass murderer was too much for British newspapers, which fell over themselves in trying to express their disgust. The *Daily Mirror*'s headline read 'Bloody Hypocrite'; the *Sun* editorialized: 'Gerry Adams: The two most disgusting words in the English language'. The *Daily Mail* commented that 'in the sanitised phrase, Sinn Fein is usually described as the "political wing" of the IRA. In grisly reality they are as close to each other as those two heads of bomber and bearer, divided only by the thickness of an undertaker's plank.' The sense of outrage was also felt in Dublin, where the *Irish Times* asked, 'Could there be an image more calculated to anger even the most moderate hearts than that of Sinn Fein President Gerry Adams carrying the coffin of the Shankill bomber Thomas Begley to Milltown cemetery?'

The media outcry was reflected in the corridors of power, where Albert Reynolds faced a tough job convincing John Major that Adams had had no other choice than to shoulder the coffin. 'Who knows,' Reynolds told Major, 'if he hadn't, maybe his body would be in the next coffin.' Reynolds struggled to keep the British on board with the ongoing work on a joint declaration. After a meeting in Brussels, Major and Reynolds produced a six-point statement which looked like the rejection of Hume's and Adams' efforts. The prime ministers praised what they termed John Hume's 'courageous and imaginative' work but made it clear that they could not adopt the Hume/Adams proposals. On the face of it the Shankill bomb had blown the two nationalist leaders' initiative out of the water.

John Hume's depression at the position taken by the two leaders darkened further the day after the summit, when UFF gunmen walked into the Rising Sun bar in the village of Greysteel outside Derry. The gunmen wore Halloween masks, and in a display of sick humour called out 'Trick or treat' before opening fire indiscriminately in the bar, murdering six Catholics and one Protestant. In a series of separate incidents in the week after the bomb attack on the Shankill Road, loyalist paramilitaries killed a total of thirteen people. When Hume attended the funerals at Greysteel, the daughter of one of the victims approached him and told him the family had prayed at the graveside for him, and what he was trying to do to achieve peace. Hume turned away in tears.

Immediately after the Shankill bombing, the British government reimposed an exclusion order on Adams. The intention was to head off a visit Adams was planning in response to an invitation from the left-wing Labour MP Tony Benn. Benn had consistently held the view that some political rapprochement between Adams and the government was inevitable. 'I think Gerry Adams will be outside Number 10 shaking hands with the Prime Minister on some peace accord before the end of the decade,' Benn reasoned. 'A few years ago Yasser Arafat was banned from going to New York to address the UN by the US government. Now we see him on the White House lawn signing a peace deal with Clinton and Rabin.'

A few days after the order was imposed Benn's fellow left-winger Dennis Skinner questioned John Major about the rights and wrongs of dealing with those associated with violence. 'People outside parliament understand only too well,' Skinner argued, 'that the government have dealt with terrorists over the decades.' Major was unequivocal in his reply. 'As ever, the honourable gentleman is very lucid and, as almost ever, he is entirely wrong. If the implication of his remarks is that we should sit down and talk with Mr Adams and the Provisional IRA, I can only say that that would turn my stomach and those of most honourable members; we will not do it. If and when there is a total ending of all violence, and if and when that ending of violence is established for a significant time, we shall talk to all the constitutional parties that have people elected in their names. I will not talk to people who murder indiscriminately.'

But in private Major had already given his authority for written communications which he knew were being sent to Adams' closest associates. In mid-November Gerry Adams began hinting that the government denials should be 'taken with a pinch of salt'. Soon he hardened this up, claiming there had been protracted contact and dialogue between the government and republicans which, he claimed, John Major had broken off at the behest of 'his unionist allies'. Downing Street denied that any negotiation had taken place and said the only written contact with Sinn Fein had been about local or constituency matters. Sinn Fein were not prepared at this stage to provide documentary evidence but hinted that more proof might be forthcoming. The government insisted that the reports were rubbish, describing them as 'unsubstantiated gossip and rumour' which belonged 'more properly in the fantasy of spy thrillers'.

Despite the denials the rumours continued to wash around Belfast. At a reception at Hillsborough Castle for Douglas Hurd, who was over giving a lecture to local Conservatives, Jonathan Cain, the special adviser to Sir Patrick Mayhew, was approached by David Fell, the head of the Northern Ireland Civil Service. 'Fell came up to me and said to me, "Jonathan, have you got any idea what's going on, because I haven't?" To which I had honestly to reply, "No, David, I don't."'

On Sunday 28 November the dam burst on the government, courtesy of an old-fashioned scoop by the *Observer* newspaper and Belfast's energetic Downtown Radio reporter Eamonn Mallie. He continued to pursue the story in the face of government denials on the basis of, first, a tip-off from the DUP MP William McCrea, then a document faxed to the MP by a senior source in the Northern Ireland Office. When they saw the document the *Observer* passed it to their political editor Tony Bevins, who then approached the Northern Ireland political affairs minister Michael Ancram in the lobby of the House of Commons.

Even though Ancram was in charge of handling the government's highly sensitive dealings with the Northern Ireland parties, evidence of a back channel to the IRA came as news to him. Jonathan Cain remembers that 'it was an extremely small loop, hardly anybody knew about it ... it was kept incredibly tight, so much so that other ministers didn't know this was going on. Michael Ancram didn't know it was going on until Tony Bevins of the *Observer* came up to him in the lobby the Thursday before the story was due to appear and challenged him about it. And then of course the following morning there was frenzied activity as other people were told.'

Confronted by the documentary evidence obtained by the *Observer*, those 'in the loop' frantically briefed those outside it and the government prepared to limit the damage.

For Sir Patrick Mayhew, who had swatted away the questions about secret contacts in an almost contemptuous manner, the process of coming clean must have been a sobering exercise. The government's line was that no negotiation had taken place – only contact in a written form explaining the publicly stated official position. Although it was acknowledged that some face-to-face meetings had occurred, these were said to have been unauthorized – 'a spook freelancing' in the words of one senior Northern Ireland Office source.

As a verbal war continued to rage, London and Dublin were coming close to finalizing their discussions on a joint declaration, intended to open up future political possibilities and challenge the paramilitaries to abandon violence. Although the Hume/Adams proposals had clearly influenced the text, both governments were at pains to ensure that the wording of any eventual document would take into account not only nationalist but also unionist concerns. Loyalist paramilitaries were sounded out for their views, via the Church of Ireland leader Archbishop Robin Eames. Mainstream unionists were kept on board by co-operation with the veteran Ulster Unionist leader, James Molyneaux.

Jonathan Cain believes that 'if the government had bought into what John Hume was initially putting on the table then it probably would have got an IRA ceasefire. It would also have in my view provoked the other side into even greater atrocities. There is no way that the unionists were going to buy into what was on the table in terms of Hume/Adams and the early drafts of the Downing Street Declaration. Which is why it was very important to get Jim Molyneaux's involvement during those crucial couple of months before the Declaration was signed, and Michael Ancram and Jim Molyneaux worked very closely in ensuring that unionist interests were safeguarded in the final text.'

Some of the nationalist content in the early drafts of what became the Downing Street Declaration upset Molyneaux so much that he went 'absolutely white'. Major pleaded with the Ulster Unionist leader, 'Don't you believe me when I tell you I'm a unionist?' To which Molyneaux's response was 'Well, I did until last night.' Major then promised Molyneaux, 'Well, okay, all bets are off.' From that stage Molyneaux was involved in the drafting and, Jonathan Cain recalls, 'Until the last minute if Jim didn't want a comma somewhere, that would have to be taken on board. Not that he wrote the document but his involvement was crucial to it and to unionists accepting it.'

When the Downing Street Declaration was announced, on 15 December 1993, it was bereft of the principal objectives which Adams had been looking for, namely that the British government should 'persuade' the unionists of the benefits of Irish unity and that it should be subject to the outcome of an all-Ireland convention of political parties. As consolation the Provisionals did get the recognition that a future agreement 'may, as of right, take the form of agreed structures for the island as a whole, including a united Ireland achieved by peaceful means'. Borrowing heavily on John Hume's lateral thinking ever since his 1988 talks with Gerry Adams, the Declaration went on, 'The British government agree that it is for the people of the island of Ireland alone, by agreement between the two parts respectively, to exercise their right of self-determination on the basis of consent, freely and concurrently given, North and South, to bring about a united Ireland if that is their wish.'

The government challenged Adams to respond swiftly to the Declaration, coupling this with an assurance that if the violence ended Sinn Fein could be in talks within three months. Subsequently Sinn Fein were to claim that this meant that round-table talks would begin within this time period, whereas the government pointed out they had only been referring to exploratory discussions, initially with civil servants. The world looked to Adams to say yes or no to the Declaration. He replied with a resounding 'wait and see'. Just a few days before the Declaration was announced by John Major and Albert Reynolds under the Downing Street Christmas tree, Adams had defined the package with which he could 'go to the IRA' in far more explicitly nationalist terms than the language contained in the Declaration. It would, he said, involve the British government accepting the

Irish people's right to national self-determination, making this a policy objective, and agreeing a process with Dublin aimed at implementing the measures necessary to bring about agreement among the people of Ireland. On the question of the unionists and Northern Ireland's British status, he insisted, 'the six counties cannot have a right to self-determination, that is a matter for the Irish people as a whole to be exercised without impediment [on the part of the British]. However, the shape of a future Ireland is a matter to be determined by all groups in Ireland, obviously including the unionists.'

As the clamour continued for a response to the government's challenge to the Provisionals to end the violence and enter talks, Adams hit on the idea of asking for 'clarification'. The Declaration was a complex document, he insisted, and its presentation by the British and Irish prime ministers had been different in tone. The British government saw this as a ruse, an attempt by Adams to draw ministers into negotiations, without delivering the IRA ceasefire which they required. John Major insisted he would not fall for the tactic: 'What is intended by Mr Adams in his present activities is to seek bit by bit to draw the government into negotiation upon the Joint Declaration. That is not on offer to Mr Adams now. It will not be on offer to Mr Adams in the future.' In fact clarification was probably a ruse aimed not so much at the government as at the IRA's own grassroots supporters. By this stage Gerry Adams would have been fairly confident in his own mind that the correct course of action was to continue with the process he had embarked on with John Hume and to move into talks. But it required time to win the approval of hardliners throughout Ireland and to prepare the movement psychologically for a new phase. The search for 'clarification' bought that time.

On the face of it the Declaration fell far short of traditional republican aims, and among Gerry Adams' supporters there was a great deal of scepticism about it. John McComb, who served a seventeen-year sentence for conspiracy to cause explosions in six British cities in the late 1970s, went to his local post office to get a copy of the Declaration. 'It was being passed down to me through a smokescreen. I couldn't even see the person, but I heard this voice saying, "You would be better off buying yourself a book and having a good read, because there is nothing in that for anybody."'

McComb considered the Downing Street Declaration 'a load of

nonsense' and 'gobbledygook' which could 'mean all things to all people'. Asked about a ceasefire, he responded, 'I don't think there is anything in that document that would persuade republicans, or the IRA for that matter, that anything substantially has changed in the last twenty-five years. That document doesn't provide any basis for change in my opinion'. Nevertheless, McComb remained firmly loyal to Adams to the extent that he supported his decision not to reject the Declaration immediately but instead to call for clarification. 'I think it is very important that no doors are closed. I think the avenue should be explored.'

McComb's scepticism was repeated around Northern Ireland – inside the locked doors of a hall in Derry where Sinn Fein executive members were given a rough ride by grassroots IRA supporters, and at Loughmacrory in County Tyrone where prisoners out on Christmas parole debated the way forward.

Some of those implacably opposed to the Declaration believed that they had majority republican opinion on their side and that Gerry Adams would therefore find it hard to proceed any further with his initiative. The former MP Bernadette McAliskey said, 'I read the document and to me it requires clarification in as much as one has to decide what part of "get lost" you don't understand. I mean the document is as simple as that to me from a republican point of view. This document basically says get lost.'

During an Irish-language debate on the Declaration in West Belfast she brandished a copy of the document and told the audience, 'It cannot be sold, that's the difficulty Gerry Adams is in . . . Gerry Adams cannot sell this thing, that's the beginning of the story and the end of the story in reality.'

A representative of the IRA leadership, interviewed by one of the authors during the clarification period, said: 'Just because Albert [Reynolds, the Irish Taoiseach] bottled it [the Downing Street Declaration] doesn't mean we're going to give up now. All we want to know is, are the British leaving? Because if they're not, we'll bring London down around their ears.'

Adams, however, outsmarted his opponents. He knew it wasn't necessary to sign up to every dot and comma of the Declaration; indeed it was quite possible for Sinn Fein and the IRA to reject what they saw as the document's continuing support for partition. But if a substantial ceasefire were to be declared, republicans would nevertheless be able to get involved in talks and start arguing about the political balance of the British and Irish governments' policies.

Adams defended himself against the purist republicans' criticisms. 'Our concern and me as a leader of Sinn Fein is to deal with the wider issues,' he argued, 'and whether it has been tactically handled correctly or not is a matter for history to tell . . . The Sinn Fein project is quite clear. It is to establish, to be part of establishing through a negotiated settlement, a lasting peace in our country. We've been through a very substantial and important and significant phase of that in the last number of years. The end of that phase could be marked with the first response from the two governments embodied in the Downing Street Declaration. We have to move on into the next phase.'

Alongside the philosophical discussion of the Downing Street Declaration, the Provisionals were conducting the more basic exercise of preparing the ground for the ceasefire to come. On the surface this was vehemently denied – but informed observers knew that this was what lay beneath the political rhetoric. In January 1994 the late, lamented Derry journalist Domhnall McDermott predicted on a BBC Northern Ireland *Spotlight* television programme, 'There is a very good chance of a ceasefire. I think we are still at the process where everybody's jockeying for position. They are refusing to react quickly. They also have to be seen as not surrendering and any sorts of noises from the British government which are suggesting that what's on the cards is an IRA surrender will actually draw them into a situation where they won't call a ceasefire. The republican movement believe they are capable of continuing this war, as they see it, and will do so if there's nothing on the table for them. But I think they would like something to be there at the table and I think at the end of the day we will see a ceasefire within a matter of months rather than weeks.' After the programme's transmission, Gerry Adams' press aides privately rubbished this prediction, asking, 'Who on earth has Domhnall McDermott been talking to?' But McDermott's prophecy was to prove highly accurate – though he would never know it, as he died of cancer before the IRA declared its ceasefire seven months later.

Calls for clarification continued alongside IRA violence. Another three-day Christmas ceasefire in December 1993 ended with a mortar attack on a police station in Fintona, County Tyrone. A few days later a soldier, Guardsman Daniel Blinkoe, was killed by an IRA sniper in Crossmaglen. Much to the embarrassment of some of the more literary-minded Provisionals, one IRA unit decided to plant an incendiary device in Belfast's historic Linenhall Library, damaging some of its irreplaceable stock.

In the past Gerry Adams' connections with this kind of violent activity had circumscribed his influence beyond Ireland, and most significantly had prevented the US authorities giving permission for him to visit America and fully tap the vast potential pool of support represented by forty million Americans claiming Irish descent. But shortly after the publication of the Downing Street Declaration and Gerry Adams' call for clarification, President Clinton signalled the possibility of a breakthrough. 'As you know Gerry Adams was refused a US visa earlier this year,' he told the *Irish Times*. 'That decision followed a careful review of his case and was consistent with our own immigration laws regarding terrorist activity.' But he then added a crucial rider: 'we will, of course, keep the issue under review as the developing situation warrants'.

TWENTY-THREE

The Clinton Factor

From the days of Michael Collins and Eamon De Valera, Irish republicanism has enjoyed a sizeable degree of sympathy and support on the other side of the Atlantic. Indeed during the Irish War of Independence De Valera travelled to the United States to rally support for the cause, staying for a time at New York's Waldorf Astoria Hotel. Many of the forty million Americans who claim Irish ancestry, brought up on their families' stories of having to leave the old country because of famine and discrimination, harboured no affection for the British. Some sang rebel songs, others gave money to collections for prisoner welfare, a few zealots bought guns and set about shipping them across the ocean. The onset of the troubles in 1969 stimulated these natural sympathies once again. But so far as official America was concerned, once the civil rights protests had given way to no-warning bombs, Irish republicans became stigmatized as terrorists with dangerous Marxist leanings.

During the 1970s Gerry Adams was too busy taking part in the conflict on his doorstep to consider how best to tap the potential Irish American pool of support. But after his election as West Belfast MP in 1983 he became the pre-eminent figurehead of the republican movement. As such his services as an ambassador for Sinn Fein and the IRA were far more in demand. In the summer of 1984 his first visa application was turned down; according to the US Consulate in Belfast, 'in the light of Provisional Sinn Fein's public support for the Provisional IRA terrorist campaign in Northern Ireland and Mr Adams's own advocacy of violence in Northern Ireland he was found ineligible for a visa'.

The pattern continued throughout the 1980s. Adams replied to successive visa denials by criticizing the US bombing of Tripoli, its support for the Contras in Nicaragua and its role in the Iran–Iraq war. When President Reagan used a St Patrick's Day address to attack the IRA, Adams replied, 'It is President Reagan whose administration finances international terrorism and destabilizes democratically elected governments.'

In January 1989 a US Defence Intelligence Agency document listed the IRA as one of the fifty-two most notorious terrorist groups in the world, naming Gerry Adams and Martin McGuinness as its leaders. A Pentagon official stated, 'As far as we're concerned there is no distinction between the Provisional IRA and Sinn Fein.'

Three months later six Irish American groups began legal action to force the US government to grant Adams a visa. The State Department said that Adams' visa application had been denied because of classified information it had received that he was a member of the IRA. Adams argued in his court papers that 'I am not and I never have been a member of the Irish Republican Army.' The action on behalf of Adams did not succeed.

In late 1989 Adams' cousin Sean and two fellow republicans, Siobhan O'Hanlon and Richard May, discovered that entering the US was a hazardous business. Fifteen FBI agents, some of them carrying guns, arrested Sean Adams while he was making his way to a republican support dinner in Chicago. They also arrested Richard May in New York and Siobhan O'Hanlon in Los Angeles. All three were deported after being charged with withholding information about prior criminal convictions on their visa waiver forms.

In 1991 Adams called on President George Bush to pressurize the British to withdraw from Ireland. But this was no more than rhetoric – Bush enjoyed almost as close a relationship with John Major as his predecessor Ronald Reagan had with Margaret Thatcher, and there was little prospect of any fundamental shift in American policy under his lead. Knowing that, Adams adopted a critical stance towards Bush's and Major's role in the Gulf War, criticizing the 'hypocrisy of those who, while condemning the armed struggle of the IRA, support the use of wholesale violence against the Iraqi people'.

The spring of 1992 was not – on the face of it – a particularly promising time for Adams' political career. On 10 April, he lost his West Belfast seat to Joe Hendron, a defeat which robbed him of his ability to present himself as a man with a substantial mandate on the world scene. But, just three days before his defeat, Adams was thrown a lifeline by a contender for the US Democratic Party's nomination for the American Presidency. The lifeline was, in time, to become almost as crucial to Adams as the status he had enjoyed as an MP.

Bill Clinton had taken a battering during his progress through the Democratic primaries – revelations about his alleged affair with a cabaret singer and accusations of draft dodging and marijuana smoking had eaten into the early promise shown by his campaign. Still, by the time the candidates reached the important New York primary Clinton remained in the race – a potentially powerful influence for any lobby group to have on their side. Certainly, the Irish Americans organizing a forum on Irish issues at the Sheraton Hotel in Manhattan thought so. They used all their wiles to ensure that Clinton would turn up.When he realized that his rival, former California Governor Jerry Brown, would be attending, Clinton felt he had no choice but to accept the invitation. To do otherwise would be to court bad publicity within the Irish American community, not a good idea on the eve of the New York primary.

Clinton answered a series of questions from a panel of Irish Americans, among them Adams' friend Martin Galvin, who for many years was publicity director for Noraid, the Irish Northern Aid committee, which was the IRA's main support group in the United States. Galvin asked Clinton if he would let the Sinn Fein president enter the country. Adams was still three days away from his election defeat and Clinton was aware of his elected status, even if slightly hazy about how precisely to describe it. The presidential contender replied, 'I would support a visa for Gerry Adams and for any other properly elected official that was part of a government recognized by the United States of America. I think it would be totally harmless to our national security interests and it might be enlightening to the political debate in this country about the issues involved.'

The answer provoked a round of applause from the strongly nationalist audience. Clinton's aides must have been relieved – their man had yet again successfully tackled the detailed concerns of one of New York City's many caucuses.

What made the statement more than just rhetoric was Clinton's victory over George Bush in November 1992. The US election appeared a very promising development from an Irish republican point of view – not only had Clinton made a commitment on the Adams visa and on a number of other issues which were part of Sinn Fein's agenda, such as extradition and the appointment of a US peace envoy. What provided additional pleasure was the fact that the British Prime Minister had, rather unwisely, appeared to take sides by letting some of his political advisers go to the USA to assist the strategists behind George Bush's campaign.

Adams was gleeful when, shortly after Clinton's victory, John Major visited the United States and Clinton pointedly declined to meet him. 'Can you imagine that happening with Thatcher in the Reagan and Bush administrations?' Adams asked, concluding that 'there is a potential for a different attitude'. Adams announced that in the light of Clinton's stated views, he would shortly be reapplying for a visa, and one of his allies in Congress, the New York representative Peter King, said he would be inviting the Sinn Fein leader over to witness Clinton's inauguration in front of thousands of people in Washington DC.

But the trip to the inauguration never happened. Adams was to find out, along with other special-interest groups, that what a presidential hopeful says on the campaign trail is not necessarily the same as what he says once elected to the White House. In May 1993 the US authorities again refused to give Adams a visa. The Clinton administration defended itself by pointing out that the candidate's offer of a visa had been made on the assumption that Adams was an elected MP, but three days after the Manhattan forum he had lost his seat. The visa application, the administration maintained, had been turned down on advice from its intelligence services.

If gaining entry to America seemed to Adams like beating his head against a brick wall, some chinks of light began to appear around the autumn of 1993. An Irish American delegation, led by former Congressman Bruce Morrison, was impressed by what it saw of Adams during a visit to Northern Ireland in September 1993. The Morrison delegation represented a whole different echelon of Irish America from the committed republicans such as Martin Galvin who had always given their support to Sinn Fein. Individuals like billionaire businesssman Charles 'Chuck' Feeney and Bill Flynn, executive in the New York insurance company Mutual of America, provided respectability and financial clout to the mission organized by Morrison and the publisher Niall O'Dowd.

Flynn was absolutely opposed to the use of violence, but in 1991 he had visited Northern Ireland and had also been favourably impressed by Adams. 'He pulled no punches,' Flynn told journalist Conor O'Clery. 'If he couldn't answer a question he said so. I liked that about a person rather than blarney.' Once again Father Alex Reid proved a useful emissary for Adams, when the Sinn Fein leader accompanied Flynn to Clonard Monastery. 'I'm a Catholic,' said the insurance executive. 'Adams is a Catholic, a communicant. I would see these priests and brothers, living there, trying to help people, under poor conditions. To see them, and their respect and friendliness for Adams, I knew he had to be a man of peace.'

The month after the Morrison mission returned from Northern Ireland, the Democratic Mayor of New York City, David Dinkins, who was fighting a battle for re-election, said he would officially invite Gerry Adams to the Big Apple. Dinkins had consistently backed pro-republican Irish American lobbyists, who were an influential group in New York. But Dinkins' decision to issue an invitation to the Sinn Fein president couldn't have been more badly timed. It coincided almost exactly with the IRA's bombing on the Shankill Road. Pictures of the atrocity were broadcast widely in the United States and its reverberations undoubtedly reached the White House. In November 1993 President Clinton wrote to Mayor Dinkins telling him his invitation was not a good idea:

I continue to believe that we should not grant Adams a waiver. Credible evidence exists that Adams remains involved at the highest level in devising PIRA strategy.

Moreover, despite his recent talks with Social Democratic and Labor Party leader John Hume, Adams still has not publicly renounced terrorism. Unfortunately recent events provide no grounds for reconsidering Adams' visa request. The PIRA's October 23 bombing in Belfast that killed ten people – including two children – has underscored the brutal and terrorist nature of the organisation and undermined efforts to resume the political dialogue among the parties. Neither the British nor the Irish government favor granting Adams a visa. My administration's policy continues to support the early resumption of political talks as the most promising way to seek peace and reconciliation in Northern Ireland.

Those Irish Americans who had been working to improve Adams' image in America were dismayed by the tone of Clinton's letter. Gerry Adams himself said the letter contained 'the usual lies concocted by the British. I have no involvement in terrorist activity. This type of unfounded allegation is used by the British government as a cover for its real intention which is to prevent any informed debate about its involvement in Irish affairs.'

Irish government sources denied that they had been consulted before the visa denial. In fact the Irish Prime Minister Albert Reynolds was becoming convinced that letting Adams into America for a brief visit could be a positive move, in order to give him a taste of what politics could deliver and strengthen the arguments within Sinn Fein and the IRA for an end to violence. Reynolds believed 'it was a question of convincing them by demonstrating that politics could achieve things that they couldn't achieve and they never would achieve through violence. Naturally John Major was not supportive of that – you could hardly expect him to be. But I told him up front before I ever did it what I was going to do, that I was changing the policy of the Irish government. He reluctantly said, "You probably have your own reasons, but I can tell you I'll be fighting this one in Washington with all I have," and I said, "Fine, let President Clinton decide the issue at the end of the day."'

Reynolds' change of policy over the visa question was crucial, but Adams' Irish American backers realized that they needed a more credible excuse to invite Adams to America than something like the Dinkins invitation, which could easily be construed as a political ploy during a hard-fought mayoral election race. The publisher Niall O'Dowd and the businessman Bill Flynn came up with the idea of staging a Northern Ireland Peace Conference to which all party leaders would be invited, including Adams. The conference could be organized under the umbrella of the National Committee on American Foreign Policy, a respected organization which Flynn chaired.

In early January 1994 the *Irish Voice* newspaper carried a report giving a date and a venue for Bill Flynn's Peace Conference. A one-day event, it was to be staged at New York's Waldorf Astoria Hotel on 1 February. On 14 January Gerry Adams travelled to the US embassy in Dublin, now the fiefdom of Jean Kennedy Smith, sister of the assassinated President John F. Kennedy and the Massachusetts Senator Ted Kennedy. He handed in an envelope containing his passport and visa application and left without attracting any media attention.

Kennedy Smith, not long in her post, had to make one of her first important decisions. Aware that the Irish Prime Minister Albert Reynolds and, more recently, the SDLP leader John Hume had both come out in favour of granting a visa, Kennedy Smith recommended to Washington that the long-standing US policy of exclusion should be changed. Allowing Adams to make a short visit, she argued, could play a positive role in promoting progress in Northern Ireland.

Kennedy Smith's decision prompted a rebellion in her embassy – two officials profoundly disagreed with their ambassador's recommendation and sent a cable to the State Department in Washington registering their dissent. The officials believed, like the British government and the US State Department, that there should be no visa for Gerry Adams until Irish republicans explicitly renounced the use of political violence.

A battle royal for the heart of the White House ensued, with both sides to the argument deploying their best allies in Washington to press their case. The British had their ambassador Sir Robin Renwick and his embassy's long-established influence. They were able to count on powerful backing from the Speaker of the House of Representatives, Tom Foley, who believed that letting Adams in would be playing politics with people's lives.

But those in favour of a visa could rely on the active support of senior Democratic senators like Edward Kennedy, Daniel Moynihan, John Kerry and Chris Dodd. In a letter to the President they argued that granting Adams a visa would strengthen the peace faction within Sinn Fein and the IRA. 'While no one can be certain that a visa for Mr Adams will result in the IRA's accepting the conditions established by Ireland and Great Britain,' the senators reasoned, 'the United States cannot afford to ignore this possibility and miss this rare opportunity for our country to contribute to peace in Northern Ireland.'

Adams was requested to attend an interview with a US official to answer a series of questions about his attitude to political violence and the Downing Street Declaration. His answers to the US consul in Belfast appeared to be an unremarkable reiteration of Sinn Fein policy. But those within the White House, like Nancy Soderberg, who were leaning towards granting a visa seized on a press release Adams issued after the interview in which he bent over backwards to use language which would appeal to the Clinton administration: 'My sole purpose in coming to the United States is to advance the cause of peace and move the process forward. I want to see an end to all violence and an end to this conflict. I don't advocate violence. It is my personal and political priority to see an end to the IRA and an end to all other organizations involved in armed actions. I am willing to seek to persuade the IRA to make definitive decisions on the conduct of its campaign.'

The White House had more or less made up its mind to give Adams what he wanted. But there was one rather bizarre hitch, when reports came in that a hitherto unknown group calling itself the 'South California IRA' had placed hoax bombs in British stores in the city of San Diego close to the Mexican border. Amid last-minute jitters the Americans insisted that Adams should publicly dissociate himself from the incident. Adams thought it was a joke that he should be required to comment on such an unlikely and far-off threat, but once the seriousness of the situation was impressed upon him by Niall O'Dowd he duly obliged with an overnight press release: 'I unreservedly condemn these incidents as I do all attacks on innocent civilians everywhere. It is absurd to even associate the incident with Irish republicans. It appears to be the work of elements who seek to sabotage efforts to rally support in the United States for the peace process in Ireland.' The politics of condemnation, it appeared, were easier to espouse when a US visa was at stake and the innocent civilians involved were Americans than when security-force members or Shankill Road shoppers were being murdered by the Provos.

The morning after the San Diego statement was issued Clinton gave the go-ahead for Adams to get a forty-eight-hour visa, enabling him to attend the New York Peace Conference. He was restricted to an area no more than twenty-five miles from the city. Adams had already set off to Dublin in order to be able to catch a plane if permission came through.

Albert Reynolds had played a crucial part, prepared to get on the phone himself to the White House to press the case for a visa. Throughout Reynolds believed that the Provisionals had never really been convinced that success was within their grasp. 'They didn't think that it was possible to get a visa for Adams and that was a big victory on the international stage. British diplomacy is very strong. To take them on internationally and win in Washington was a big issue.'

Once in New York, Adams was treated as an instant celebrity. The whiff of cordite only served to whet the appetite of Americans for their unusual visitor. British displeasure was clear and the international media knew that whatever happened they had a good story on their hands. Unionist leaders had declined their invitations to the Peace Conference, which they saw as little more than cover for the Adams' visit. The leader of the middle of the road Alliance party, John Alderdice and the SDLP's John Hume were there, but, notwithstanding Hume's impressive American connections, both politicians were entirely overshadowed by Adams, the new kid on the block.

Adams was escorted through a pack of waiting reporters and camera crews at John F. Kennedy airport by Bruce Morrison and the New York Republican Congressman Peter King. At a brief airport news conference King introduced Adams as 'a former political prisoner, a writer, a former member of the British parliament and Irish statesman, President of Sinn Fein, Gerry Adams'. From the airport, Adams went on to the Waldorf Astoria – the hotel which De Valera had stayed at seventy-five years beforehand. For security reasons he registered under a false name – Shlomo Brezhnev.

After freshening up in the hotel, Adams headed for the studios of CNN, to appear on the network's *Larry King Live* programme, a show available to some sixty million households in the United States alone. CNN introduced the broadcast as an interview with 'a man so controversial, his very voice is barred from English television. The political leader of the Irish Republican Army, Gerry Adams, on a precedent-breaking mission that all sides hope will bring peace in Northern Ireland.' In one phrase CNN had proven what critics of the British broadcasting ban had always maintained – that its negative impact in terms of Britain's international image would eventually far outweigh its usefulness as a tool against Sinn Fein. CNN took a decision not to broadcast the Adams interview live on its European service – instead it was aired later with an actor's voice to comply with the British restrictions.

King's style of interviewing was relaxed, giving Adams plenty of opportunity to present himself as a spokesman for an oppressed people. He spelled out a potted history of his life – jailed without trial, beaten in custody and the survivor of a murder bid. He repeated that he wanted 'to see an end to all violence' and that he would gladly shake hands with the UFF men who tried to kill him if it would bring peace closer. The one dissenting voice on the broadcast was that of John Alderdice, the Alliance leader, who unlike Adams was on the end of a telephone line rather than in the studio. Adams welcomed Alderdice casually with a 'Hello John, how are you doing?' Alderdice countered that 'We'd all be doing a little bit better if there was some peace in Northern Ireland.'

As Larry King warmed to Adams' words of peace he asked Alderdice, 'Can't we both agree to stop killing?' As the leader of a party with unimpeachable anti-violence credentials, Alderdice didn't know how to answer this point. Spluttering on the other end of the phone line, he came over as apparently more intransigent than Adams, the man of peace. Questioned about ending the killing he said, 'That's what I would like to hear.' King broke in, 'But you are hearing it, Gerry has said it.' Alderdice retorted, 'But saying it is not in any good whenever the bombing and the killing continues on.' Alderdice later commented that Adams had been given a 'very easy ride' because American broadcasters were 'not used to the kind of very clever, rather cunning use of language with which we are familiar in Northern Ireland'.

But Alderdice was an isolated voice among the Irish American well-wishers who phoned in from places such as Atlanta, Georgia, Columbus, Ohio and Silver Spring, Maryland. Many of them shared the view of the Maryland caller who said his 'people were kicked off a farm by British people about a hundred years ago' and who looked forward to 'peace in Ireland and a unified Northern Ireland'.

King concluded the broadcast by proposing what sounded like CNN-sponsored peace talks in Belfast. 'If we were to come over to Belfast would you sit down with all the parties?' he asked Adams, who replied, 'Of course I would.' 'You'd be very welcome,' Adams told the broadcaster. 'I'd also invite you for a pint of Guinness on the Falls Road.' 'I won't be shot though?' King asked. 'No, no, you'll have your pint of Guinness,' Adams assured him.

When Gerry Adams addressed the Peace Conference he said that he needed to know what would follow on from the Downing Street Declaration so 'I can sell the agreement to every Irish republican . . . What we have at the moment is a free-standing joint statement. Where does it lead to?' He ended his speech by promising that 'it is our intention to see the gun removed permanently from Irish politics'. The performance won him a standing ovation from at least half the audience.

Adams' reception in the American press was just as favourable. The *New York Daily News* put Adams on its front page under the banner headline 'My Aim Is Peace'. The *New York Times*, which had previously been regarded by Britain as generally sympathetic in its coverage of Northern Ireland, described the Sinn Fein leader as 'an articulate and enigmatic partisan leader in a centuries-old struggle'. In a colour piece the Irish author Edna O'Brien compared Adams to Michael Collins. 'Where Collins was outgoing and swashbuckling,' O'Brien wrote, 'Gerry Adams is thoughtful and reserved, a lithe handsome man with a native formality . . . Given a different incarnation in a different century, one could imagine him as one of those monks transcribing the gospels into Gaelic.' O'Brien, in her romantic vision, bracketed Adams with Nelson Mandela: 'no doubt on his journey from violence to the negotiating table he sees parallels'.

The American IRA historian J. Bowyer Bell summed up Adams' appeal: 'He's gotten first place in the news while he's been here. It's exotic that he's been so long denied and suddenly he appears, not a monster at all, but a gentleman with a beard and a tweed coat and articulate and reasoned explanations, seeking peace in a funny accent.'

For Adams, New York had been politically triumphant but personally exhausting. He had joked at the Peace Conference that if his monotonal delivery might send his audience off to sleep, then his jet lag threatened at any moment to have him dozing off. The schedule had whisked him from place to place with no time to see the sights. Asked what he would remember about New York he responded, 'Nice rooms and lifts.' In his own nice room, though, he had difficulty finding anything to eat while working on a speech with a companion in the small hours of the morning. He had not managed to get a meal on his first day in America, so he struggled with the minibar in his hotel room, hoping that something edible might be inside. 'It would have been easier,' Adams wrote later, 'to get holy water in an Orange lodge. Ian Paisley would have been proud of my intransigent larder. It gave "not an inch". Its door was like the Derry gate and not a Lundy in sight. So we settled for a jar of jelly beans between us, one for me, one for him.'

On his way to JFK airport Adams was accompanied by the president of the National Committee on American Foreign Policy, the organization which had invited him over, Professor George D. Schwab. Schwab claims that Adams said to him, 'George, I promise you we will never return to the old ways.'

The Americans who waved Adams off at the airport thought that was what they had achieved, a practical demonstration to Irish republicans of the benefits of 'going political', of such power that it would obviate the need for any more violence. Many on the other side of the Atlantic weren't so sure. When Adams emerged from the terminal at Dublin airport he was at once confronted by a large figure in a sheepskin coat, Maurice Healy, who claimed to have been beaten by the IRA. Healy shouted, 'Did you tell them about the torture chambers, Gerry?' and called the Sinn Fein leader a 'fascist, psychotic bastard' before being pushed away by one of Adams' bodyguards, Paul 'Chico' Hamilton.

Another protester, Alan McBride, whose wife Sharon had been killed in the Shankill bombing, stood silently, clutching a banner reading, 'My wife was murdered by the IRA.' Later McBride took what comfort he could from the protest: 'At least today I stood up and said to Adams, "How dare you! How dare you go to America and pretend to be the Prince of Peace when in fact you lead the movement that slaughtered her."'

The protesters weren't the only ones angered by Adams' brief sojourn in New York. Britain's press and politicians were livid about what they had seen. Downing Street had accused Adams of using his American trip to mount a 'smokescreen of evasions and falsehoods' while the IRA fired off mortar bombs in Northern Ireland. The UK's ambassador in the USA, Sir Robin Renwick, went on CNN to try to mitigate the effects of Adams' PR triumph, and evoked memories of the Nazis' chief propagandist. 'When I listen to Gerry Adams, I think, as we all do, it's reminiscent of Dr Goebbels. It's an extraordinary propaganda line. The line is "I want peace but only after we've won." And the line is also that "I'm not prepared to call on the IRA to end the shootings, the bombings, the killings of innocent people in Northern Ireland and Great Britain."'

In Northern Ireland the decision of the two main unionist parties to boycott the New York conference, leaving the field open to Adams, became a talking point. Even some who despised Sinn Fein thought unionists should have responded more positively. Gerry Adams found himself in the unusual position of being asked to advise unionists on whether they should have flown out. 'I'm obviously not an advocate of the unionist case,' he pointed out, 'but how is the unionist case to be advanced by what is to be seen as an act of political cowardice, a failure to put their piece of the equation up for scrutiny? What are they afraid of?'

The unionists professed to be less than impressed. The DUP's deputy leader Peter Robinson said it would have been counter-productive for unionists to act as 'extras on the Gerry Adams freak show', but that they would try to develop their own profile in America. The Ulster Unionist security spokesman Ken Maginnis also claimed that it would have been wrong for him to 'hang on the coat-tails of the elephant man of Northern Ireland politics'. But beneath this bluster, unionists realized they were being outmanoeuvred on a bigger stage, and Ken Maginnis was soon keeping an eye on the travel plans of 'the elephant man' in order to make sure that he wasn't too late to catch a ride on his coat-tails.

CHAPTER TWENTY-FOUR

Spectacular Reminders

The month after Gerry Adams returned home from New York City, the IRA launched a mortar attack on Heathrow airport. Four mortars were fired from a van left in the car park of the Excelsior Hotel. Two mortar bombs hit a runway, two others fell short. None exploded. The failure of the mortars to detonate led security specialists to wonder quite what the attack had been intended to achieve. The simultaneous failure of four fuses seemed unlikely – perhaps the IRA was just demonstrating what it was capable of, rather than seriously trying to cause damage or injure passengers?

But Heathrow is the world's busiest international airport which deals with travellers from all four corners of the globe, and the broadbrush picture provided by newspaper headlines was an alarming one. The impression, especially in the United States, was that the Provisionals were prepared to cause carnage to civilian passengers, irrespective of their nationality. Two days later the IRA launched another mortar attack, from a series of tubes buried in the ground around the perimeter of the airport. The mortars were triggered by a timing device. The outcry over why this second launcher had not been discovered in the security searches which followed the first attack had barely died down when yet another mortar attack followed. This time a bomb hit the roof of Terminal 4. The mortars again all failed to explode.

The IRA had successfully demonstrated its capability and exposed the difficulties of defending a sprawling complex like Heathrow airport against terrorist attack. But it had done nothing for Adams' carefully cultivated image as a peace-maker. The *Sun* newspaper, in its reaction, showed that it hadn't forgotten Adams' trip to New York the previous month. 'The Americans let Gerry Adams take them for suckers,' the newspaper claimed. 'He told them the IRA only attack military targets. And they believed him. How do they feel in the US after the rocket blitz on Heathrow?' Adams compounded his difficulties by commenting in one interview that 'the conflict is ongoing. Every so often there will be something spectacular to remind the outside world.' The Heathrow attack would focus international attention on Ireland and 'should have a major accelerating effect on the British government'.

Comments like that enraged some of those who had been coming around to the view that Adams was moving towards a peaceful path. William Rutherford, the doctor who had treated Adams after he was shot, was depressed that Adams seemed 'very pleased that the armed struggle had put this on in order to up the political pressure'. The Irish Foreign Minister Dick Spring described Adams' comments as 'outrageous'. In the United States, Senator Daniel Patrick Moynihan passed a note to Senator Ted Kennedy asking, 'Have we been had?'

Adams launched a damage-limitation exercise, claiming he was 'taken completely out of context and misreported and misinterpreted'. With his peace-maker hat firmly back on, he contended that 'The peace process is not finished. I have always said there were no quick fixes, that building a developing peace process is going to be difficult and problematic. At times perhaps there are going to be aspects of it that look confusing, but all in all the peace process is not finished. It's going to be difficult but I think it can be done. We need cool management and calm heads. The process will go through various phases and it will have ups and it will have downs and it will have difficulties.'

In a St Patrick's Day message Adams reiterated his conciliatory tone: 'I remain convinced that the IRA is willing to deal positively with any new eventuality. It is crystal clear that the IRA are interested in developing the search for peace.'

Heathrow may have been a peculiarity on the international stage, but in Northern Ireland the IRA campaign rolled on, not subject to 'confusing ups and downs' but a well-oiled killing machine efficiently continuing the task for which it had been designed. RUC Constable Johnston Beacom, a married man with three children, was killed by an improvised grenade while out on patrol in the Markets area of Belfast. RUC Constable Jackie Haggan was shot dead watching greyhounds at a racing track in the north of the city. His wife, who was pregnant with their third child, was next to him when the gunman shot him at close range. As Adams sat next to John Hume in New York, Provisionals in South Armagh were dragging out John Fee, personal assistant to Hume's deputy, Seamus Mallon, and subjecting him to a vicious beating.

At Easter, after coming under considerable pressure to prove that its commitment to peace was more than just words, the IRA announced a three-day ceasefire. Gerry Adams saw this as no mean achievement, telling reporters that 'The IRA have moved to break the stalemate . . . the significance of this initiative is in its potential to open up an entirely new situation and move us on from it.' Adams wrote to the White House assuring the Clinton administration that the brief cessation should be seen as a genuine sign of intent. He told other Irish Americans that the seventy-two-hour ceasefire had not come easily. In his traditional Easter speech, Adams used the word 'peace' thirty-nine times. The IRA was observing its first non-Christmas ceasefire since the 1970s.

But if Provisionals considered it mould-breaking, their opponents regarded it as an insult – a commitment only to postpone murdering anyone for three days. John Major branded the ceasefire a 'cynical exercise'. The RUC Chief Constable Sir Hugh Annesley also regarded the gesture as derisory, but suggested that at one point the IRA might have been contemplating a more significant one. 'I don't think it was deliberately intended at that stage just to be a three-day ceasefire by the leadership of PIRA. I suspect at that time it was all they felt they could get, but I think the condemnation both inside and outside Northern Ireland from all shades of opinion was quite staggering.'

After the Easter gesture, the IRA returned to business, targeting drugs dealers in Belfast and attacking serving and former members of the security forces. Fred Anthony's crime was to work as a cleaner in Lurgan police station. The IRA attached a booby-trap bomb to his car, killing him and critically injuring his three-year-old daughter Emma. At first the doctors didn't believe Emma would survive, but after several weeks battling for her life the little girl recovered.

Albert Reynolds decided to break the impasse over Adams' demand for clarification of the Downing Street Declaration by offering himself as intermediary: 'I adjudicated on what I believed were fair questions to ask John Major and what I believed were not fair questions and eventually we got agreement on that and so we moved on from there.' The British, who had insisted that they wouldn't be drawn into negotiation with Gerry Adams, insisted that the responses which they published to a series of written questions from Sinn Fein were not answers, but merely a 'commentary' on the questions. But Sinn Fein were jubilant when Downing Street replied that the 1922 Government of Ireland Act – which they regarded as the cornerstone of partition – would be 'on the negotiating table'.

On a trip to the Basque country in Spain in May 1994, Adams expressed his view that the Northern Ireland conflict had reached its endgame. 'I remain convinced,' he said, 'that we are in the final phase of the Anglo-Irish conflict. This is a new area of struggle for us. I do not know how long this phase will last, but I do know it will be difficult and dangerous.'

What was undoubtedly proving difficult was the slow process of convincing IRA units around Ireland that a more lengthy ceasefire had to be declared. On the surface, the process of assessing the Downing Street Declaration was being carried out by Sinn Fein's Peace Commission, which held a series of public meetings around Ireland. Just over a third of the 228 submissions made to the commission argued either for an end to the IRA's campaign or for a substantial three-month ceasefire. But the more important consultations were taking place far away from prying eyes.

Adams' envoy during much of the process of contact with IRA units was the Sinn Fein vice president Pat Doherty who was brought up in Glasgow but had lived for many years in his family's native Donegal. Doherty's brother Hugh was serving eleven life sentences in jail in England for IRA bombings carried out by the 'Balcombe Street Gang'. Doherty toured the country pushing the Adams line, arguing for a ceasefire in places where he felt he was getting a sympathetic hearing, but being more circumspect in areas where the Adams analysis was meeting significant resistance.

If the hardliners continued to remain sceptical, Adams was bolstered by support elsewhere. His lawyer, Paddy McGrory, was a respected figure in nationalist circles, with a long track record of defending both IRA and some loyalist paramilitaries. McGrory's most high profile case had been representing the families of the three IRA members killed in Gibraltar at the inquest held in the colony. McGrory now took part in a series of discussions with Adams and his close assistant Aidan McAteer. They talked about constitutional matters such as the wording of the Government of Ireland Act, which underpinned Britain's rule in Ireland.

To McGrory, Adams' interest in such topics was a clear indication that he saw himself heading towards a talks table. Paddy McGrory set his own views down on paper. By this stage he was convinced that Adams wanted to end the IRA's campaign, but he was aware that Adams needed every argument he could lay his hands on to back his case. McGrory was at pains to separate the two strands which had become entwined in the public eye: a decision by the Provisionals to accept or reject the Downing Street Declaration, and a decision by the IRA to give up violence.

'The most important decision is not acceptance or rejection of the Declaration,' McGrory argued,

> but a decision as to whether more is likely to be gained for the republican cause by armed struggle than might be won through political means. Only madmen make war for fun, and the republican struggle has been waged for a specific political purpose, and only because of the total failure of conventional politics to advance the Irish cause. I hold the view that armed action is unlikely to secure any significant political advance, and certainly nothing to compare in importance with the political achievements to date.
>
> And the grave danger is that it could undo spectacular recent gains. Will political activity achieve more? I think it probably will, given the climate that has been created, and the status and credibility which the republican movement now enjoys. I believe that peace now will garner a rich harvest of support for the republican movement, such as it has not known for decades. Conversely, I think failure of the movement to seize this hour will in all probability mean a virtual collapse of Sinn Fein electoral support, and a rejection of the republican position all over Ireland and in America. I believe the tide is at the flood, and is beginning to ebb. This is the hour.

But before the IRA was ready to take that advice, more deaths were to follow. In mid-June 1994 Northern Ireland experienced another convulsion of violence, reminiscent in its horror of the previous October which had seen the Shankill bombing and the

Greysteel shootings. This time the IRA weren't directly involved. Instead the spiral was sparked by the republican splinter group, the INLA, which launched an attack on the Shankill Road, killing three Protestants, two of them members of the loyalist UVF. Every nationalist knew that the the UVF would seek revenge, and the risk appeared particularly high two nights later when Republic of Ireland football supporters gathered around their TV sets in homes and pubs all over Northern Ireland to watch their team take on Italy in the World Cup.

The game was in its second half when a group of UVF gunmen burst into O'Toole's bar in the little village of Loughinisland twenty miles south of Belfast. The locals were turned with their backs to the door, intent on the game, when the gunmen opened fire. Six Catholics were killed, including Barney Green, who at eighty-seven years of age was the oldest victim of the Troubles.

Gerry Adams was in Dublin when he heard the news. No soccer fan, he was nevertheless following the fortunes of the Ireland team in its crucial game. As the final whistle blew and people erupted into wild celebrations of Ireland's success, Adams received a phone call letting him know about Loughinisland. 'Most nationalists were waiting for such an attack,' Adams later wrote. 'It did not come out of the blue . . . nationalists knew that the prospect of large groups watching the World Cup in pubs and clubs throughout nationalist areas was too good an opportunity for loyalists to ignore. The people of Loughinisland could hardly have guessed that they would be chosen. The brutality of the attack was also premeditated. The intent was to terrorize.'

Adams called for 'calm and restraint' in the face of what he described as a 'premeditated attack aimed at deflecting those engaged in the peace process'. He said there would be no response from the IRA as 'retaliation has never played a part in IRA strategy . . . I set my head and my face against any action similar to this premeditated sectarian assault on people on the basis that they were just Catholics.' While acknowledging that the blame for Loughinisland lay with the UVF members who had carried it out, the nationalist *Irish News* also described Adams' reaction as 'deeply unsatisfactory'.

'Instead of calling for calm and restraint,' the newspaper's editorial argued, 'he should have been pleading for an end to the IRA's campaign of violence . . . The only lasting memorial to those who died in Loughinisland on Saturday night, and in the rest of Northern Ireland over this past quarter of a century, would be peace. Mr Adams spoke yesterday of "the challenge facing us". Let us hope that he and his party can live up to that challenge.' The *Irish News*' logic was rejected by Adams, who said that loyalist attacks like Loughinisland had 'never been reactive . . . Loyalism has always had its own agenda and has always been capable of the most horrible, premeditated atrocities.'

Adams' strategy had its own undeniable political logic. The 'pull factors', winning influence in America, uniting the nationalist family and drawing support from the Irish government, were undoubtedly the most significant arguments Adams could deploy in convincing the IRA that the time for some more significant cessation had come. But the 'push factor', intensifying loyalist violence, undoubtedly provided part of the context in which the debate within the republican movement was taking place. In the years before 1994 loyalists were murdering far more people than republicans were. The arguments posed in the *Irish News* editorial were also being put within Catholic communities throughout Northern Ireland. Despite Gerry Adams' claim that loyalist violence was 'not reactive', ordinary Catholics knew all too well that the IRA were not the defenders they liked to imagine themselves; they could only hit back in revenge. The majority looked on an IRA ceasefire as the best chance of relieving the pressure.

The influence of loyalist violence was reflected in the divisions within republicanism as the debate over a future ceasefire gathered pace. There were two divides, one between the leadership, who had almost all been converted to the Adams strategy, and the grassroots IRA members, who remained far more sceptical. The other divide was geographical and clearly reflected the UVF's and the UFF's main areas of threat. Put simply it was easier to be a purist, demanding no compromise of republican principles, when you lived in a relatively safe village in strongly nationalist territory near or beyond the Irish border, than if your home was in North Belfast, the killing zone for loyalist gunmen. No wonder that the 'hardliners' were to be found in rural areas like, Fermanagh and Tyrone, Kerry and Limerick.

The IRA remained intent on carrying out its own carefully planned murders. One victim, loyalist Ray Smallwoods, had been involved in the attempted UFF murder of the former MP Bernadette McAliskey, but had recently developed a profile as an articulate spokesman for the UDA's political wing, the Ulster Democratic Party. During a series of discussions he won the trust of Clonard Monastery priests close to Gerry Adams like Father Alec Reid and Father Gerry Reynolds. The murder of Ray Smallwoods robbed loyalism of what would undoubtedly have been one of their most impressive spokesmen during the peace process and was probably the overriding motive in his killing.

Caroline Mooreland, a thirty-four-year-old mother of three, was also murdered, an IRA 'court' finding her guilty of informing. Mooreland, who raised money for the West Belfast Muscular Dystrophy Association for several years, was kidnapped, held and 'questioned' by the IRA for three days before she was shot dead and dumped near the border at Roslea in County Fermanagh. The priest called to give her the last rites said her face was 'mutilated beyond recognition and her head completely disfigured'. Gerry Adams regretted, but would not condemn, the young mother's murder. 'A death diminishes us all,' Adams acknowledged. 'A death which has as its victim a mother and a woman diminishes us even more. And when we put it into the context of the use of informers – of the whole murky, cajoling, persuading, tricking, buying people to inform on their neighbours, on their comrades, and the whole web of deceit which must have marked that woman's life for the last number of years – all I can say is that we have to bring about a situation as speedily as possible where that never happens again.' Adams appealed for informers to come forward and give themselves up to the IRA's tender mercies.

In July there was an air of expectancy that a ceasefire was on the way as Sinn Fein delegates gathered in Letterkenny to give their definitive response to the Downing Street Declaration. Most of the meeting was held in private, but when the media were allowed in they were to be treated to resolutions and speeches which did not appear to represent any significant shift in the Sinn Fein position. The Downing Street Declaration had been compared unfavourably by the delegates with the more nationalist Hume/Adams initiative already endorsed by the IRA. The conference was still looking for Britain to make concessions by 'bridging the gap' between the two positions. It looked like a qualified rejection of the Declaration, and that was the message which the press sent out.

The Irish Premier Albert Reynolds had been briefed not to expect anything momentous, but to keep the faith. Under pressure, Reynolds reverted to his instincts as a businessman and told Sinn Fein and the IRA to close the deal or walk away from it:

> I had no more to give, I had no more to put on the table. Okay, I accepted that they had watered down, for want of a better word, some of their hardline positions. But they still didn't feel they had enough and so I said, 'Well that's it, decision time, either you go with what's on the table now, I've no more to give, or we just pull down the shutters and everybody goes their own way.'
>
> I wrote to them before I went away on holiday. I said when I come back from holiday in the first week of September either you make up your mind to go with it or not to go with it. But beyond that I am not prepared to wait. The initiative is over because there's no point in continuing. I felt that they had a fairly good platform for building a peace process at that stage.

At the start of August Adams revealed that he and Martin McGuinness had provided the IRA leadership with a considered and detailed briefing around the time of the Letterkenny conference outlining what they thought the political possibilities were. Security sources might have been more than a little sceptical about the choreography of such a 'briefing', since they were certain that both Adams and McGuinness were key players themselves in that leadership.

Nevertheless the decision to reveal that such a briefing had taken place was clearly designed as a signal that change was afoot. Questioned about whether a ceasefire had been discussed, Adams replied, 'Well, obviously a ceasefire was discussed, but it would not be, I think, sound or even right at this time to get into detail.'

The key to understanding Letterkenny was in the lawyer Paddy McGrory's statement that acceptance or rejection of the Downing Street Declaration was not as important as deciding on a ceasefire. Although it was hoped by mainstream nationalist politicians that in time Sinn Fein could be won over to the principle of consent central to the Declaration, at this stage it was perfectly possible for the party to remain true to its republican principles and reject large sections of the document, while at the same time the IRA called a halt in order to open up the political possibilities.

In the middle of August, Gerry Adams told Paddy McGrory, 'Some frightening decisions are going to have to be made in the next two weeks.' Around the same time Adams' one-time close confidant Danny Morrison, out on parole from the Maze, gave a news conference to promote his novel *On the Back of the Swallow*. Morrison found the journalists less interested in the plot of his novel than in the state of the peace process. In jail, Morrison had had no day-to-day experience of the protective PR operation which his successor as Sinn Fein press officer, Richard McAuley, had thrown around all questioning about the ceasefire.

His answers were consequently more straightforward than those of other senior republicans. 'The republican movement vowed years ago there would never be another ceasefire until the British government gave a clearcut decison to withdraw,' he told one of the authors. 'We have moderated that position and we have shown an attempt to unblock the logjam . . . Republicans are now attempting to explore whether or not the possibility exists of an unarmed strategy which can bring us a just settlement, however defined.'

In further remarks which added weight to theories and rumours circulating in Belfast a year later that the British had given the Provisionals 'a ten-year notice', Morrison said that the government 'has to state clearly whether it wants to stay or whether it wants to go'. What if Downing Street said 'stay'? 'Then it's an occupying force in our country.' But if John Major was to say, 'I cannot see us being in Ireland for ever,' 'that would have a dramatic effect on the situation'.

August 1994 marked the twenty-fifth anniversary of the arrival of soldiers on the streets in Northern Ireland. The anniversary attracted considerable attention, and TV screens were full of black and white images from the archives depicting the brief honeymoon period enjoyed by the troops or charting some of the worst moments of the conflict that followed. Sinn Fein had their own particular spin on the commemorations, holding a rally outside Belfast City Hall attended by a crowd of several thousand people. There were chants of 'IRA, IRA' as people gathered for the rally, and when Gerry Adams came to the platform to speak he claimed a victory of sorts over the soldiers.

'Twenty-five years after they came, we can say that we have defeated the British Army. All of us have defeated the largest, best-equipped and best Army in Europe and the state police, the RUC.' But there were also strong hints that things might not always be this way. 'I am especially confident that after twenty-five years of unparalleled courage and self-sacrifice the nationalist people of this part of Ireland are prepared to show the way to a new future while at the same time reaching out the hand of friendship to the unionists.'

The anniversary of the arrival of the troops dominated press coverage around this time. But Gerry Adams, while looking to the future, may have had a more personal anniversary on his mind. Twenty-one years earlier his brother-in-law, IRA man Paddy Mulvenna, had been killed in a gun battle with soldiers in the Adams family's heartland, Ballymurphy. Adams wasn't telling the outside world, but he had chosen the exact anniversary of Mulvenna's death as the day on which Sinn Fein's rhetoric of peace would at long last be matched by an impressive initiative from the IRA.

CHAPTER TWENTY-FIVE

A Taste of Peace

It was a victory rally of sorts, but many of the thousands gathered outside Sinn Fein's Connolly House headquarters to hear Gerry Adams speak might have been wondering what they were supposed to be celebrating. A few hours earlier the IRA had released a statement to the media announcing a 'complete cessation of military operations' from midnight onwards. In fact the press had slightly jumped the gun; the message to Reynolds' office from the Provisionals was to 'Listen for the Angelus bell, o'er the Liffey swell, ring out on the foggy dew' – in other words they meant the announcement to be first broadcast on the 12.01 headlines on RTE immediately after the daily noontime call to prayer.

Adams faced the crowds with a bouquet of flowers in one hand and a bottle of champagne in the other. A well-organized Sinn Fein cavalcade had already toured the Falls, horns blazing, flags waving. Peace, certainly, was good news by anyone's standards. But had Adams and his colleagues achieved some kind of secret deal with the British government which would see the IRA's goals achieved? Or had the graffiti artists on the Protestant Shankill Road got it right when they promptly wrote on the walls: 'We the Loyalist People Accept the Unconditional Surrender of the IRA'?

In his speech, Adams was at pains to stress that the ceasefire was not a surrender. He told the crowd that he wanted to say a word about 'the volunteers of the IRA'. 'This is a generation of men and women,' Adams proclaimed, 'who have fought the British for the last twenty-five years and who are undefeated by the British. I want to salute the courage of the IRA leadership and the historic and bold and decisive initiative that they have taken and which they announced this morning. They have created, if you like, a crucial moment, a decisive moment in the history of this island and of Anglo-Irish relations and I applaud and commend the leadership of the army.'

Adams began his speech on this momentous day by mentioning the dead and those present who had 'family who have died on this day'. It was a day of mixed emotions, he said, 'when we remember all of our friends, our neighbours and our comrades who have died throughout this last twenty-five years'. He then paid special tribute to his own brother-in-law 'Volunteer Patrick Mulvenna' and to his friend 'Volunteer Jim Bryson'. Adams had known many IRA men who, to use a phrase he once put in a death notice for his comrade Tommy 'Toddler' Tolan, had gone 'away to join the big battalion in the sky'. Bryson and Mulvenna, who had been married to Adams' sister Frances, had been carrying guns in the centre of the Ballymurphy estate exactly twenty-one years before this momentous occasion when they came under fire from soldiers belonging to the Royal Green Jackets. Mulvenna died instantly, Bryson died from his injuries three weeks later.

Twenty-one years later Adams had his own highly pragmatic reasons for moving the IRA away from gun battles and towards another strategy. For most of the 1970s he was a hawk, a hardliner who viewed ceasefires as a sign of weakness. But in the long, crushing years of violence since then his thinking had changed radically, politically and personally. In 1975 when the leadership of Ruairi O Bradaigh and Dave O'Connell opted for a ceasefire, the modern Troubles were only six years old and Adams, the young militant, was only in his twenties. By 1994 Adams was in his late forties, his beard sometimes jet black, sometimes flecked with grey. He was at the helm of the republican movement and the twenty-fifth anniversary of the Troubles had come and gone. Aside from Adams' belief that his 'peace strategy' represented the most feasible political way forward, the loss of so many lives, including those of close friends and relatives, had taken its toll. By pursuing a ceasefire, he hoped both to win political advantage and, in simple human terms, to break the relentless round of death, revenge and further death.

The ceasefire had been in preparation long before the 31 August announcement. But some very specific pieces in the jigsaw fell into place only in the final days running up to the ceasefire. One was another public expression of Irish American support. Bruce Morrison, Niall O'Dowd and their colleagues were asked to fly over again on a repeat of their September 1993 mission. But this time they were assured that a significant gesture from the IRA was much more imminent. The Irish Americans arrived in Dublin on 25 August 1994 and went first to meet the Irish Prime Minister Albert Reynolds. Morrison and O'Dowd were unsure what the IRA had in mind and were pondering whether it might be a time-limited ceasefire of, say, three or six months' duration or one with a significant qualification, such as a statement that the IRA reserved the right to take 'defensive' action against loyalists.

When they met Reynolds, who was also aware of the rumours about temporary ceasefires, the Irish Americans found him in combative mood. Knowing that they would be seeing Gerry Adams the next day, Reynolds told Morrison's delegation to pass on the message that Dublin wasn't interested in anything less than a permanent ceasefire, with no ifs and no buts. Reynolds made it clear that it was 'either all or nothing'. If the IRA announced a temporary cessation or they reserved the right to defend nationalist areas, the deal was off. 'I've told them if they don't do this right they can shag off,' he told his press officer Sean Duignan. 'I don't want to hear anything about a six-month or six-year ceasefire, no temporary, indefinite or conditional stuff, no defending or retaliating against anyone, just that it's over period, full stop. Otherwise I'll walk away. I'll go off down that three-strand talks/framework document road with John Major and they can detour away for another twenty-five years of killing and being killed – for what? Because, at the end of that twenty-five years, they'll be back where they are right now, with damn all to show for it, except thousands more dead and all for nothing. So they do it now, in the name of God, and be done with it, or goodbye.'

Reynolds added that John Major did not believe the IRA had any intention of ending the violence permanently. 'But he's going to get peace and he deserves it, because he did more than any other British Prime Minister to bring it about.' If the IRA announced a temporary cessation Reynolds would not make good his promises to meet Adams within a week, invite Sinn Fein to a peace forum in Dublin or lobby for their entry to all-party inclusive talks on Northern Ireland's future.

The Irish Americans headed to Belfast with some misgivings, believing this would be a tough message to deliver face to face with Gerry Adams. When they made their way through a scrum of reporters outside Connolly House and found themselves sitting opposite Adams they were therefore relieved to be told, 'We're talking about a complete cessation.' The Americans were sworn to secrecy until the official announcement was made, but Adams also told them that there remained a hitch, which had to be sorted out. 'If not,' confided Adams, 'the army feel there is no way they can go forward.'

The hitch involved another man from Gerry Adams' past, Joe Cahill. Adams had escorted Cahill through the streets of West Belfast in the days when Cahill was the IRA's commander in the city. Cahill had been sitting in a condemned man's cell in Belfast prison when Gerry Adams' father had fired his shots at the RUC back in the 1940s. Cahill's youth had saved him from the hangman's noose then, and now he was an elder statesman of the IRA, bald-pated and hard of hearing, but respected for his years of commitment, his gun-running exploits from America and his grasp on the finances which earned him the reputation of being the IRA's 'Mr Money'.

Cahill's stature was confirmed by the fact that the IRA leadership insisted that he had to travel to the United States to brief units there before the ceasefire could be given the go-ahead. This was if anything more difficult to achieve than getting Gerry Adams a visa, because Cahill, unlike Adams, was a convicted murderer and gun-runner. Reynolds realized that the IRA was attaching such importance to it because they wanted to avoid a split among their hardline American supporters. Adams was well aware that when he advocated taking seats in the Dublin parliament in the mid-1980s and parted company with the former IRA chief of staff Ruairi O Bradaigh, he had lost some valuable American backers, veterans like Michael Flannery and George Harrison, who until Colonel Gadaffi came on the scene had for many years been the IRA's main source of arms.

Reynolds believed that the fear of a further haemorrhaging of support was playing on Adams' mind as he tried to get the choreography of the August 1994 ceasefire right. 'Everything was done to avoid a split . . . that was the reason for trying to get Joe Cahill into the States, because [of] the American situation at the time of the previous split, when Ruairi O Bradaigh split from the present leadership. The American units of support over there were supportive of Ruairi O Bradaigh and the leadership were afraid that if this thing came out on television or over the radio that it could have engineered another split, if Cahill didn't get over, who would be a respected individual and an authoritative source, to say look we're changing policy, we're changing direction. If he wasn't there in advance to keep it together, we might not have got a ceasefire.'

President Clinton, who still felt as if his fingers had been burned over the last visa for Adams, leafed through Cahill's CV and did not like what he saw. Reynolds spent much of the night on the telephone, relaying information between 'the priest' Father Alex Reid and Nancy Soderberg, who as staff director of the US National Security Council had exerted a powerful influence on the decision to grant Adams his American visa. Reid began to annoy the Taoiseach with his persistent message that the IRA Army Council was preparing to meet in emergency session and that nothing would happen unless Cahill made it across the Atlantic. Soderberg confirmed to him that the British embassy in Washington was strongly opposing the visa and trying to have it delayed at least until after an IRA announcement. Soderberg began to outline to Reynolds the distinction between Adams and Cahill the convicted murderer in terms of their criminality rating, at which point the Taoiseach snapped: 'Dammit, Nancy, I never claimed we were dealing with saints.'

In the end Albert Reynolds employed his trademark direct approach and got put through on the phone to the President. According to Reynolds, Clinton said, 'But I didn't get a result, I never got a return on the first visa for Adams.' Reynolds replied, 'Surely to God, you didn't expect to get a return that quickly, you had to bring him over and restrict his movement, give him a taste of politics and send him back so he'd spread the message.' The President asked, 'How can I be sure I'll get a return this time?' Reynolds assured him, 'This time you will get a result, you will get the ceasefire.' Clinton remained sceptical asking, 'How can I be sure? Give me something to prove it, give me one line of the IRA statement, so I can check it.' Reynolds obliged, reading out a line from the ceasefire statement and telling the President, 'If they don't make that statement within twenty-four hours, send Cahill home.'

Cahill flew out, dodging past reporters at John F. Kennedy airport, telling them only that he was on a private visit. According to one report of a meeting he held in Philadelphia his message was not that there was any wholesale change of policy but that this was a variation on the same old theme. 'It's the same today as it has been all along,' Cahill told his American audience. 'We want to see the Brits out of Ireland. We want to see a United Ireland and we want our people to rule our country any way we want.' That message, no doubt similar to the one which had been repeated to IRA units around Ireland, was designed to quell doubts and repel any suspicion that what was happening was a dignified surrender. But it also contained in it the seeds of danger for the new ceasefire. Adams had sold the cessation as the best way of moving things on. But now there was an expectation of swift and radical movement.

Gerry Adams used his ceasefire-day speech to press for such immediate change. 'The onus is on the British government, the onus is on Mr Major,' he declared, 'to seize this moment. I also want to appeal to unionists to join with all the people of this island in shaping out a new future for all the people of this island, for all of the Irish people. We have waited for too long for our freedom. We are demanding of Mr Major's government that he takes decisive steps now to move the situation forward in a fundamental way, and that means fundamental political and constitutional change, it means the demilitarization of the situation, it means our prisoners home from England and home with their families from prisons in Ireland . . . This struggle is not over, this struggle is into a new phase, all of us have a role to play in moving the situation forward.'

They were resounding words, but the unionists remained to be dealt with, representatives of the majority of people in Northern Ireland and opposed to the fundamental changes of which Adams spoke. On the day of the ceasefire they had swiftly embarked on an analysis of the IRA's language and found an essential ambiguity in that the cessation had been described as 'complete' but not 'permanent'. Were the two the same? asked the unionists. Speculation was raised further when *An Phoblacht*, the weekly paper of the republican movement and traditionally more aligned with the military than the political wing, called the ceasefire a 'suspension'. Some unionists subscribed to the theory, later shown to be groundless, that the IRA would not have called such a ceasefire unless some kind of dirty deal had been done with the British and betrayal lay around the corner. Others started talking about the need for a disposal of weapons and a process of verification of handing over arms, an issue which was to grow as a stumbling block in the months to come.

If the unionists remained an uncomfortable reality which Gerry Adams found hard to deal with, so British ministers remained in power in Downing Street and at Stormont Castle, wary of doing anything radical which might upset the delicate balance in Northern Ireland. The government had obviously been aware of the speculation about the ceasefire in the preceding weeks, but they were taken aback by the open-ended nature of the IRA's gesture. Security sources detected some last-minute wrangling about the precise terms of the ceasefire. The RUC Chief Constable Sir Hugh Annesley made no secret of the fact that the wording of the IRA's statement was more than he had thought possible or likely. One of the government's most senior security advisers told the authors: 'I was expecting a ceasefire perhaps of three months' duration. But an open-ended unconditional cessation – the government was initially all over the place and didn't know how to react.'

'We were being cautious,' the political affairs minister Michael Ancram admitted to the authors, 'saying we want to look at this, because if it's tactical then it's damaging. We want to see whether we think we can have confidence in it. We had set out already a pattern of what we would do, wait for a three-month period, then go into exploratory dialogue with republicans. So those keys were there but we had to have some confidence in the ceasefire before we could get that clock running. We were looking for a permanent renunciation. So we were looking at all of that in terms of their language and we came out with a welcoming but fairly cautious reaction to it on that basis.'

Caution remained the watchword north of the border as the security forces waited to see if the ceasefire would hold. Albert Reynolds said the loyalist paramilitaries had given him a simple assurance that if he got the IRA to stop they would stop. But for now the loyalists remained to be convinced. They debated whether the constitutional position of Northern Ireland was safe or whether, as politicians like Ian Paisley claimed, a secret deal had been hatched. While they made up their mind they carried on killing, testing the IRA's resolve. In a matter of days they killed a young Catholic man, John O'Hanlon. Then they detonated a no-warning bomb outside Sinn Fein's press office on the Falls Road. The IRA – which had gone out of its way to ensure that the loyalists would not call a reciprocal ceasefire in the last days of their campaign by murdering two prominent loyalists on Belfast's Ormeau Road and then bombing a loyalist pub in the north of the city – did not respond.

If John Major and his ministers were determined to take things slowly, Albert Reynolds believed that speed was of the essence. He had made a number of pledges to the Provisionals, one of which was that he would meet Gerry Adams in public within a week of any ceasefire announcement. Reynolds was determined to keep it even though he had some difficulty scheduling the meeting at a time when the SDLP leader John Hume could also attend, which some Dublin officials put down to rivalry and jealousy between the two men as they jostled for their place in the history books.

In the event John Hume made it to the meeting, but Dick Spring deliberately absented himself from the country, unhappy at the haste with which the encounter had been arranged. Arriving at Government Buildings in Dublin, Adams strode in on foot, carrying a bulging Filofax, accompanied by his minders as well as Jim Gibney and Sinn Fein's head of publicity Rita O'Hare, the Garda Special Branch glaring at them. Reporters mobbed Adams, asking him whether he now felt like Michael Collins, the IRA leader who had signed the deal with the British and brought about an end to the War of Independence. 'Regrettably, Michael Collins didn't bring an end to partition,' Adams replied. The Collins question reflected the sense that by walking through the gates of Government Buildings he was stepping into a whole new era. But such comparisons were at this stage unwelcome, as Gerry Adams would have been well aware that the members of his own movement had been brought up to think of Collins as a traitor to the true republican cause.

As Reynolds remembers it the meeting had a peculiar human dynamic. Adams had relied on Reynolds for high-profile support and encouragement for many months. But because of the IRA's campaign the two men hadn't been able to meet face to face until now. Reynolds found Adams 'a bit silent . . . I could well understand his frame of mind coming in to Government Buildings, what do you expect, what's this all about? This was new territory to him, risky territory as far as I was concerned, there was a lot of people who wouldn't agree with me meeting Gerry Adams within five days of a ceasefire. But I believed it was all necessary to cement the ceasefire.' After getting beyond the silence Reynolds decided Adams was 'extremely nervous. It was a historic moment and I think the atmosphere of that got to everybody. I can understand that it was a big move to walk through those gates into Government Buildings because here they were joining a political process. But I believed we had taken a major step along the way. In the full glare of everybody they were coming into the political process.'

Once inside the Irish Prime Minister's offices Adams and his companions abandoned politics for a moment to get some mementoes:

> I do remember them having their own little cameras and they wanted photographs with me before I went out on to the plinth. I think it was Rita O'Hare taking a photograph of me and Gerry Adams and I said, 'Rita, join the photograph yourself.' One of my security guys was there and I said, 'Will you take a photograph?' and he took the photograph. It was actually one of the guys who on many occasions over the years tracked Gerry Adams down here and searched him and questioned him. I didn't realize it at the time, but he took the photograph and he handed back the camera to Gerry, and Gerry said, 'That's the first time I ever got anything back from you guys!' There were light moments, and it helped to take away the tension and the nervousness. Gerry Adams came into the office upstairs and we spoke in Irish, which settled him down a bit. We had a cup of tea and John Hume joined us and we drew up the statement between us and we had it ready – a historic statement for a historic day, no question about it.

While Adams drank tea inside, his bodyguards sat around in the courtyard of Government Buildings outside. 'Well,' a reporter asked Terence 'Cleeky' Clarke, 'Albert Reynolds today, John Major tomorrow?' 'No reason why not,' the bodyguard replied, 'haven't we been there before at Cheyne Walk?' This was a reference to the 1972 meeting when the young Gerry Adams had represented the IRA in talks with the British, and when the distinction between the 'army' and the 'party' was not so religiously followed.

In their statement after their brief meeting the three nationalist leaders declared, 'We are at the beginning of a new era in which we are all totally and absolutely committed to democratic and peaceful methods of resolving our political problems. We reiterate that our objective is an equitable and lasting agreement that can command the allegiance of all. We see the Forum as a major instrument in that process. We reiterate that we cannot resolve this problem without the participation and agreement of the unionist people. We call on everyone to use all their influence to bring this agreement about.'

Reynolds felt that Adams had shown courage in signing up to this communiqué because its references to the role of unionists indirectly 'embodied the principle of consent without specifically spelling it out'. Unionists would almost certainly quibble with that assessment, and the principle of consent was to become a major bone of contention in the proceedings of the Dublin Forum. But as he stood on the steps of Government Buildings, clasping Adams' hand, Reynolds believed the three leaders had shown that 'there was a new beginning here for everybody and it's constitutional republicanism from hereon in. Nobody, no Irish leader, had achieved that from the 1920s. Nobody had brought everybody under the one umbrella. It was a momentous occasion.'

While Reynolds rushed forward to cement the ceasefire, John Major and his Northern Ireland Secretary Sir Patrick Mayhew remained sceptical, keen to keep the unionists on side and to do nothing which would fuel their suspicions of secret deals. In an ironic reversal of the situation which followed the Downing Street Declaration it was now John Major who demanded clarification from Gerry Adams – the British wanted to know if the IRA's term 'complete cessation' could be translated into 'permanent ceasefire'.

For many years Adams had been used to reporters repeatedly hitting him with one question: 'Will you condemn the latest IRA atrocity?' Over the last few months that inquiry had been replaced by a continual 'When is the IRA going to call a ceasefire?' Now Adams became used to another refrain: 'Is it permanent?' He became expert at dodging the question, professing to be bewildered by the importance the government was attaching to the word 'permanent'. 'London was talking to us until recently when the IRA campaign was going full blast in Britain and the occupied part of Ireland,' he said in a reference to the series of secret contacts. 'There weren't any preconditions. There weren't any of these nigglings. Now when the IRA's stopped they're refusing to talk. It just doesn't make sense to me.'

The stand-off about the word 'permanent' continued through September, prompting Adams to accuse Major of 'trawling about for excuses not to engage in discussions'. The Prime Minister, visiting Saudi Arabia, expressed the view that Sinn Fein were 'very close' to providing the government with the assurances which were required, but still the logjam over permanency continued. The government announced some moves which Adams welcomed. Almost immediately after the declaration of the ceasefire, they had confirmed the transfer of Adams' close friend, the Brighton bomber Patrick Magee, back to a jail in Northern Ireland. This was widely interpreted as a payback for the ceasefire, but Downing Street let it be known that the timing was coincidental and unfortunate. Other moves followed, such as the dropping of the British broadcasting ban and the reopening of cross-border roads which had been closed off for many years for security reasons.

But other pronouncements by both London and Dublin followed which were less to Adams' taste. He found Major's pledge that any future settlement in Northern Ireland would be put to a referendum, thus giving unionists a fail-safe option, to be 'premature and presumptuous'. Nor was he any happier with Reynolds' assertion that it would take a generation or more before a United Ireland could be achieved. The *realpolitik* underlying such statements was that both prime ministers felt they had the IRA's ceasefire in the bag and were looking to copper-fasten the prospects for peace by reassuring unionists in a bid to encourage the loyalist paramilitaries to follow suit.

At the end of September, Adams flew out from Dublin airport for a coast-to-coast trip around the USA. This time the unionists, aware of the march which they had allowed Adams to steal on them during his New York trip, made sure that they got out to Washington ahead of him for talks with the US Vice President Al Gore. Before flying out Adams again accused Major of 'tactical manoeuvring' over the wording of the IRA ceasefire. 'I think what we have here is a little subterfuge by Mr Major.'

He proved, however, that he himself was not beyond a little terminological sleight of hand by using the word 'permanent' but not quite in the context which the British had been looking for. 'We want a permanent peace' was a carefully worded phrase guaranteed to make headlines but which didn't clarify anything about the IRA's long-term intentions. Adams used the many interview opportunities he was afforded in America to keep stressing what commentators began to refer to as the 'p' word, but again never quite giving the answer which he knew John Major wanted to hear.

In contrast to his first visit, Adams wasn't any longer an unknown quantity as he travelled around the States. But the fact that he now had no restrictions on his movements meant he could meet first hand far more of his American supporters than had proved possible in his previous forty-eight-hour visit. When he arrived in Boston, Senator Ted Kennedy described Adams as a 'great peace-maker'. In Springfield, Massachusetts, Adams joked with his Irish audience that some members of the Tory government in Britain 'think they still rule America'. Boiling down his peace strategy for beginners he said, 'It's a serious proposition we're putting up to the Brits. Can they leave our country in a way which leaves behind a stable and peaceful country? I'm convinced Protestants and Catholics, unionists and nationalists, can live in peace.'

Most of Adams' comments during an exhausting tour of the USA were deliberately upbeat, encouraging his American audiences to be 'guarantors of the peace process'. As he said in Springfield, 'I'm not coming here to make war or look for guns.' But with the IRA ceasefire less than a month old he did, in one interview with the *Boston Herald*, strike a warning note. While he said there was 'not even a whisper' of the ceasefire being broken by republicans, and that he wanted 'to see the gun taken permanently out of Irish politics', Adams cautioned that 'none of us can say two or three years up the road that if the causes of conflict aren't resolved, that another IRA leadership won't come along. Because this has always happened . . . the history of Ireland is filled with phases of armed struggle and then of quiet and then of reprised phases of armed struggle.'

Like the unionists, the British government had learned lessons from Adams' first trip to America and so made strenuous efforts to counter his message. The Foreign Secretary Douglas Hurd, visiting the United Nations, ridiculed Adams as a man with a very limited mandate. 'There's a tendency in some places here to put him on some kind of level with someone like Nelson Mandela,' Hurd acknowledged. 'We know – because it's measured in free elections – exactly what support Gerry Adams and Sinn Fein have in Northern Ireland. It's 10 per cent. He's Mr Ten Per Cent. He's a minority within the minority in Northern Ireland.' Hurd's counter-attack made the news back in Britain, and to that extent probably pleased Downing Street. Whether it did much good in America was another matter. Hurd came over to Americans as rather patrician and his policy differences over Bosnia with the Clinton administration had not made him very popular with the White House. Adams responded adroitly by defying 'any British politician to get 1 per cent in any election in Northern Ireland at any time'.

Douglas Hurd, though, hadn't been charged with carrying the main thrust of the British counter-attack in the United States. That task had fallen to the former Northern Ireland security minister Michael Mates. Mates had lost his ministerial job after admitting accepting a gift from a businessman wanted on corruption charges. But he still retained the government's confidence to speak with a degree of authority about Northern Ireland and to handle himself competently under the glare of any US network cameras which might be pointed in his direction. As Mates remembers it, the mission to counter Adams was decided upon only at the last minute. 'The whole American thing opened up, there was a great wave of sentiment and the government thought that someone ought to go and, you know, answer. Paddy Mayhew rang me and asked me to go and I went twelve hours later. That's why I went on Concorde, it was the only way to get me there on time. Paddy just said he wanted me to get on the media and do some stuff in New York and Washington.'

By his own assessment Mates' mission to explain didn't get off to much of a start. 'I had sat in Washington for two or three days while Adams had been up to Hartford, Connecticut for a hero's welcome and I was due to go home. I thought this has achieved absolutely bugger all.' Then Mates discovered that Peter Snow from the BBC's *Newsnight* programme was in town. He rang Snow and told him that he was prepared to go live on the programme in a head-to-head with Adams. At this stage no senior Conservative or former minister had ever come so close in a public debate to the republican figurehead. Snow understandably jumped at the chance of staging such an encounter.

'It was quite dramatic,' Mates recalls.

I took stringent precautions not to be seen, as it were, socializing with him. My arse could have been in a bit of a sling here. Peter said, 'Well, you've got to shake the man by the hand, will you do that?' I said, 'Yes,' because if I hadn't the whole of that story would have been Mates refuses to shake Adams' hand. As it happens then they filmed the handshake live, and Adams said, 'There, that wasn't too bad, was it?' Then I spotted his minders, one of whom was Terence 'Cleeky' Clarke [who had been convicted for his part in the attack on the two corporals in Andersonstown in 1988]. I thought, Jesus wept, I could be in the deepest possible shit here. I had mentally taken six valiums – don't get cross, don't get angry. I had never been so nervous before.

The encounter was described in the papers the next day as a bad-tempered exchange. On several occasions the two men cut in over each other, rendering both contributors unintelligible. Adams asked Mates why they could not have a similar discussion back in Belfast. Mates replied that such an encounter would happen 'in due course . . . We have now had just over twenty-five days of peace, after twenty-five years when you have supported violence to achieve your ends. You must not be surprised if the British public are still a bit sceptical.' Adams retorted that as someone who had served in the British Army, Mates was 'a person who defended the killing of Irish citizens'. As the debate went on the two men clashed over bigger questions such as the principle of consent or, as Gerry Adams put it, the unionist veto. Adams accused Mates of being in the USA 'on a junket'. The tone of the discussion prompted Peter Snow to remind both men 'not to exchange insults'. Adams accused Snow of bias, claiming at one point, 'There are two Englishman here arguing with one Irishman. It's very unfair.' Snow replied, 'No. I'm asking you to be fair to Mr Mates.'

Afterwards the former Northern Ireland minister feigned insouciance, claiming that Adams had 'ranted' and that the *Newsnight* debate had therefore been 'a waste of time'. In truth he was glad to have come to such close quarters with his quarry and believed 'the interview went rather well. Afterwards I got up and I walked out, and I saw Clarke again. He then said, "Well, aren't you going to shake hands?" I walked straight on and out. The BBC monkeys were looking for anything off-camera.' Mates believed that he had 'softened Adams up' so that the Ulster Unionist MP Ken Maginnis could 'knock him over' a few days later. Like the encounter with Mates, the decision by Ken Maginnis to go into head-to-head combat with Adams was a first. It marked a dramatic departure from the unionists' policy back in Northern Ireland, which had been to avoid any platform or discussion which might bring them into close proximity with republicans.

The debate was staged on CNN's *Larry King Live*, the same programme which had provided Adams with his most high-profile interview opportunity during his previous visit to America. Maginnis enjoyed some natural advantages over Mates – first and foremost, his rich Ulster accent. There was no question of Americans easily accepting that such a man was simply an agent of British imperialism. Symbolically the encounter represented the division between Irishman and Irishman, not the conflict between the Irish and the British. Unlike Mates, Maginnis decided not to shake hands with Adams. When the Sinn Fein president held out his hand, stating that it was time 'to put out the hand of friendship', Maginnis contemptuously rejected it as a 'gimmick'. Maginnis claimed that Adams wasn't just a Sinn Fein leader but also held a senior position in the IRA. He gave a litany of what he claimed was Adams' curriculum vitae: 'Commander of Ballymurphy in 1971, commander of Belfast Brigade 1972, taken as an IRA leader to the talks with William Whitelaw, along with Martin McGuinness, IRA leaders went to those . . .' Adams retorted that 'part of the difficulty is that Mr Maginnis seems to be very well misinformed about this situation. He has problems, I think, about joined-up thinking.'

Having survived nine attempts by the IRA to kill him Maginnis was emphatic that he didn't trust republicans' recent talk of peace. 'I most certainly don't trust Gerry. I don't know who Gerry is. I don't think he knows who he is. We know him as the leader of the IRA, Sinn Fein spokesman for the IRA. But sometimes he tells us that he is not that person. So I wonder who he is. He is someone who fronts a vicious organization, which has killed almost two thousand during the last twenty-odd years. If someone is sitting on over a hundred tons of arms, how on earth do you trust them?' Adams replied that trust had to be built. 'I have acknowledged in Ireland the suffering inflicted by republicans.' He pointed out that he had been shot and injured by loyalists and accused Maginnis of 'looking for excuses not to look for peace'.

Throughout Adams looked straight at Maginnis and edged closer towards him. Maginnis avoided eye contact and kept his distance, a strategy which some commentators thought might have been misguided in terms of how Americans would judge the encounter. Maginnis, however, began to look at Adams more as the broadcast went on. At one point a Northern Ireland woman caller from San Franciso questioned Adams about IRA punishment beatings and Maginnis held up a large photograph of one of the victims lying in a hospital bed. Adams claimed the call was a set-up and the picture 'cheap propaganda,' but he went on to distance himself from punishment attacks. 'If the IRA are involved in punishment beatings it's wrong, but the community also has a right to defend itself.'

Maginnis concluded by trying to rubbish the impression Adams had cultivated in America of being some kind of Irish Nelson Mandela or Yasser Arafat. 'Arafat represented a nation of Palestinian people, so did Mandela in South Africa, he represented a majority. Gerry Adams represents 10 per cent of the people in Northern Ireland . . . He is exercising a veto and has done so for twenty-five years following Mao Tse-tung's philosophy of power coming down the barrel of a gun.' Afterwards Maginnis professed to be very pleased by the encounter. He declared it a worthwhile exercise which had shown Americans 'the other side of the story'. Mates and Maginnis had indeed adjusted the focus of British and Irish TV coverage, but Adams himself could be satisfied that in the end they had been forced to come out and debate him. However one scored the actual encounters, the fact that they had taken place had breached long-standing British and unionist policy.

Moreover in America the Adams bandwagon rolled on – in New York he was presented with peace awards and a crystal apple, receiving a formal welcome at the City Hall which only two other Irish political figures, Charles Stewart Parnell and Eamon De Valera, had received before. In Hollywood Adams attended a party hosted by the Irish actress Fionnuala Flanagan. The boy from Ballymurphy rubbed shoulders with film stars and directors like Barbara Hershey, Anjelica Huston, Oliver Stone, Martin Sheen, Gabriel Byrne and Sean Penn. The partygoers finished their evening by singing 'The Foggy Dew' and other Irish ballads. More important than all this showbiz razzamatazz, Adams won yet another battle over British diplomacy when the White House announced that its officials would meet him and no less a person than the Vice President Al Gore honoured him with a phone call.

Adams was in Canada by 13 October, when the loyalist paramilitaries declared they would 'universally cease all operational hostilities'. The loyalists had decided that there had been no secret deal with the IRA and that 'the union is safe'. They hedged their ceasefire with the condition that its permanence 'will be completely dependent upon the continued cessation of all nationalist/republican violence. The sole responsibility for a return to war lies with them.' The loyalists also took the surprising step of expressing their 'abject and true remorse' to the relatives of all their innocent victims. Adams welcomed the loyalist ceasefire, but pointed out that it was 'a direct result of the IRA's very courageous initiative on 31 August, and now we have the irony that the only force that will remain in military operations after midnight will be the Army of the British government'.

The declaration of the loyalist ceasefire opened up the options for the government, who were now no longer so fearful that an overture towards Sinn Fein would spark off loyalist violence. Just over a week after the loyalist ceasefire began, the government announced that they would make a 'working assumption' that the IRA's cessation was permanent, thus enabling the 'clock to start ticking' towards exploratory meetings between Sinn Fein and senior civil servants.

Just like the stand-off over clarification, the dispute over permanency turned out to be a situation in which the British blinked first. The Northern Ireland political affairs minister Michael Ancram says the government decided to give ground because they realized that the IRA, going by its own rule book, understood the word 'permanent' to imply something rather different from what British ministers were looking for. 'I'm told you can actually get permanence, but in order to get it you have to have a General Army Convention, even then you can't bind the next generation, but you can say it for yourselves. That is really why we moved away from permanence, because we realized what we meant by permanence was the confidence that it was for good, whereas what they understood by permanence was requiring them to do this thing which then requires all sorts of constitutional and doctrinal adjustments to be made. That's when we came off it and said we would look for a working assumption that, in our view, it was permanent.'

The proverbial clock, which had supposedly been standing still thoughout the preceding weeks, had in fact been ticking all the time. Exploratory meetings got under way at the start of December, roughly three months after the IRA ceasefire and therefore broadly in line with the pledge John Major made at the time of the publication of the Downing Street Declaration.

In the run-up to those exploratory talks Gerry Adams busied himself in Dublin, where Albert Reynolds had hastened to set up his Forum for Peace and Reconciliation. The Forum had been specifically referred to in the Joint Declaration, where it held a much less prominent position than in an earlier draft of the Hume/Adams document. The Forum had started life as an idea for the all-party, all-Ireland negotiations which would be binding and free of British government input. Now it was downgraded to a place where politicians from north and south of the border could come together and talk about the problems of Ireland on political, economic, social and cultural levels.

Before the Forum's first meeting Gerry Adams said the body should be used to convince unionists that they had nothing to fear and that peace need not be unattainable or impracticable, and war need not be inevitable. But unionists, warned by Jim Molyneaux of its dubious origins, were notable by their absence at the Forum. For them, the very existence of the body was repugnant as it institutionalized the view that Ireland was a single entity and that Northern Ireland's difficulties could only be solved on a North–South basis. Thus the SDLP and the Alliance Party were the only Northern Ireland-based parties which sat around the Forum table. The main Southern Irish parties were all represented alongside three groups which organized to a greater or lesser degree on an all-Ireland basis: Sinn Fein and two parties which had their historical roots in the old Official IRA, the Democratic Left and the Workers Party.

At a formal dinner in Dublin Castle to mark the inauguration of the Forum, a very senior Irish diplomat was amused by Adams' pretensions. 'Here he was sitting in the old seat of British rule, with oil paintings of former viceroys gazing down at him, and when the wine waiter approached, Adams gave him a nod that he should pour him a drop to sample. He held it up to the light, swirled and tasted. Then with another curt nod, indicated to the waiter that it met his approval and he could fill the glass. It was a picture to behold, and I thought at that moment that once Adams had a taste for this style of living he would never want to give it up.'

Reynolds believed the Forum performed a useful function because it brought Sinn Fein into the world of conventional politics. He regarded it as 'a very good exercise in reconciliation. There was such a diverse attendance at that Forum. It just proved the point that over a period of time the barriers slowly but surely were taken away and that a very good understanding began to develop.'

That understanding, though, hit its first serious obstacle the month after the Dublin Forum began its proceedings. Armed robbers tricked their way into the main postal sorting office in Newry and shot dead a worker there, Frank Kerr. The RUC arrested two men in the countryside of South Armagh a short time after the raid and soon the word was leaking out that the IRA was involved. The Irish government was on the brink of authorizing the early release of nine IRA prisoners. The Justice Minister Maire Geoghan Quinn moved swiftly to halt the releases.

Initially the IRA denied involvement, issuing a statement saying that its position on the ceasefire had not changed. Gerry Adams expressed his shock and regret and tried to turn the blame on to the police, claiming, 'Many people will be concerned at the way in which the RUC has sought to blame republicans for the killing. The RUC is engaged in a transparent attempt to damage the peace process.' But within days the IRA changed its story, saying that, 'We have established that Frank Kerr was shot in the midst of an intense scuffle with one of our volunteers and we take this opportunity to offer sincere apologies to his family and friends.' The IRA said none of its members had been authorized to use firearms and the Newry raid had been the result of 'an identified problem in the IRA chain of command'.

Albert Reynolds got a fuller explanation from the Sinn Fein leadership:

People were saying to me, ah, you've been fooled, this thing isn't for real, and I asked for a total explanation immediately. It was up to me to accept it or otherwise. I got one, either from Adams or McGuinness or both. I said I had a serious question mark and I had to be convinced. I never accepted, I never believed, that the whole ceasefire was going to be without problems along the way, there were always going to be problems. But, to me, there was a man shot in that incident, that was a very serious one as far as I was concerned. I was told that the discipline that followed the ceasefire had fallen into place perfectly in Northern Ireland, but there were gaps in the chain of command south of the border that allowed this thing to happen. After a while I accepted it. But I said I would not accept a second incident like that. A repeat of that would just send me away as far as I was concerned.

Shortly after the Newry raid, Adams made his first visit to Westminster since the IRA ceasefire and the lifting of the exclusion order which had been in force against him. His reception in England was always likely to be less frenzied than in America, but media interest was nevertheless high, with sixteen camera crews wanting to join him on his flight across the Irish Sea. Adams swept into parliament at speed, prompting one of the policemen on the gate to joke, 'He came by so fast, we didn't even have time to plant anything on him.' Inside, Adams took tea with his host, Labour left-winger Tony Benn. Some MPs on the right of the Conservative Party still found the mere sight of Gerry Adams hard to bear. David Evans described the visit as 'outrageous'. Alan Duncan approached him and asked for an apology for the murders of Airey Neave, Ian Gow and other MPs, to which Adams replied, 'I regret any killings, be it of British MPs by the IRA or republicans by the British.' Duncan decided then to make a positive gesture. 'I said to him, "Right, I shall shake you by the hand and I hope this handshake is worth something." I then shook his hand.'

The scrum of photographers and reporters at Adams' news conference in parliament grew so disorderly at one stage that he jokingly appealed for calm: 'I have come to bring peace to the press corps.' But despite this attention Adams had in fact been upstaged in the headlines by the man who had brought him into the political mainstream. Albert Reynolds was experiencing a little local difficulty and disagreements in his coalition government with Labour's Dick Spring were spiralling out of control. Adams had balanced his ceasefire strategy on the existence of a political three-legged stool. In November 1994, less than three months after the IRA called a halt to its campaign, one of the legs dropped off.

CHAPTER TWENTY-SIX

'King of America'

The demise of Albert Reynolds seemed to happen in agonizingly slow motion. The origins of his downfall were obscure but they boiled down to a fatal breach of trust between the Taoiseach and his Tanaiste, the Labour leader Dick Spring. All through the months that peace was being built in Northern Ireland, war was looming in the cabinet room. Ironically the seeds of his undoing were sown on what should have been Ireland's happiest day in generations – 1 September, the day the IRA ceasefire was called.

It was no surprise – and some believed no coincidence – that the Provisionals' announcement had overshadowed a Dail debate on the Beef Tribunal report, the republic's longest ever and most expensive investigation into allegations of irregularities in the Irish meat industry. Spring warned: 'The government would fail if delicate and sensitive situations were to be played for party or personal advantage.' The news at the end of October that an RUC extradition warrant for a priest wanted in Northern Ireland for molesting children over a twenty-four-year period had lain ignored for seven months proved to be the last straw. Spring demanded that Reynolds' choice for the vacant post of president of the High Court, the Attorney General Harry Whelehan, should publicly explain the delay before the appointment went ahead. When Reynolds refused, Spring led his Labour colleagues out of cabinet. Reynolds appointed Whelehan in their absence and all hell broke loose.

Over the next few days Reynolds made a doomed attempt to survive, abasing himself before Spring in the Dail, apologizing profusely and desperately seeking answers to the 'paedophile priest' affair, all to no avail. He admitted that he could offer no satisfactory explanation, but said it would be a great pity if a government which had achieved the biggest breakthrough in Northern Ireland in the last twenty-five years should be jeopardized by misunderstandings. 'It is my profound conviction that we have to give the fragile peace process the best possible chance of permanent consolidation,' he said.

That view was shared by British ministers across the Irish Sea, one of whom told the *Guardian* that Reynolds was the Irish politician best placed to deliver Sinn Fein, since they trusted him. The Foreign Secretary Douglas Hurd insisted publicly that the peace path was irreversible. At the start of the week Adams ventured the opinion: 'There could be a crisis, it's dangerous and risky . . . this government has done more about moving the whole issue of peace forward than any other Dublin government ever. We can't afford to abandon it.'

Spring professed another view: 'The peace process is not now as fragile as some commentators would have us believe . . . there is no leader in this house who would not be willing to carry on the work started by the Taoiseach in the spirit in which he started that work if the necessity arose.' In the future that task would fall to Spring himself, as he buried his doubts about Sinn Fein along with his previous views that terrorist weapons had to be handed in before political talks.

With the die clearly cast Adams put a brave face on the change in government, saying that the peace process was 'bigger than Mr Reynolds' and declaring that Sinn Fein's commitment to the process remained 'absolute, no matter who is in power in Dublin'. He promised that Sinn Fein could do business even with the party which historically accepted partition, Fine Gael – which Spring in due course invited to form a new government with him and Democratic Left, descended from the Official IRA from which the Provisionals split in 1969.

But republicans were well aware that things weren't going to be the same for them under the leadership of the Fine Gael leader John Bruton, who had been known jocularly as 'John Unionist' by some nationalists because of his consistently anti-IRA line. As the political transition worked itself out over the course of several days in Dublin, a senior Sinn Fein press aide confided to reporters, 'The on-the-record line is we will work with whoever is in power. The off-the-record line is "oh shit."' The very last words spoken in the Dail by Reynolds – the cement in the alliance forged between militant republicanism and constitutional nationalism – as he stepped down as Taoiseach and

Fianna Fail leader stood as his own epitaph and expressed some of the genuine bafflement he felt at what had happened: 'It's amazing, you cross the big hurdles and when you get to the small ones you get tripped.'

The Dublin crisis put back work on the Anglo-Irish Framework Document on Northern Ireland's future, but all did not seem to be doom and gloom. Major made a 'working assumption' that the IRA ceasefire was intended to be permanent and opened the door to 'exploratory talks'. For the plain people of Ireland, North and South, the politics was secondary to the sheer novelty and joy of peace. Gay Byrne, RTE's top broadcaster, ran a competition to take Southerners who had never dared venture north in their lives across the border, revealing a host of heartwarming stories in the process. A staggering 75 per cent of the Republic's 3.5 million citizens had never spent a night in the North. 'I simply cannot believe that I'm here,' said Anne Reddin, an Ulsterwoman who lived just a short journey from the border. 'I've been near the border so many times and would have heard of a shoot-out or a bomb going off and it just put the fear of God in me. Even crossing yesterday the fear came over me. Then I looked up and saw that there was nothing there and it was wonderful, sheer relief. Now I've broken the spell I'll be coming up to do the shopping. I always thought the place was a wasteland but I would never have thought I was in the Falls Road yesterday, you could have been in the middle of Dublin.' The increased traffic, heavily made up of cars bearing Southern registration plates, told their own story of change. On the Republic's first autumn bank holiday after the IRA and loyalist ceasefire declarations every hotel room in Northern Ireland seemed to be booked by Southerners breaking a lifetime's taboo.

When the first talks between Sinn Fein and British government officials finally took place in December, a little over three months after the IRA ceasefire was called, a last-minute hiccup led to their postponement for forty-eight hours. It was to be the first of many signs that all was not well. A raid on a petrol station in West Belfast, in which a number of known republicans were said to have taken part, prompted John Major to issue a stern warning that there was no guarantee the Northern Ireland peace process would end in success. 'We offer a fair place in Northern Ireland's political life to those who commit themselves exclusively to peaceful methods. I do mean exclusively. No more punishment beatings, no more robberies, no more racketeering, no more blackmail.' Speaking at the same London conference Sir Patrick Mayhew said that a commitment to give up IRA weapons must be made during preliminary dialogue if Sinn Fein was to be admitted to the body politic.

Sinn Fein announced a hardline talks team for the Stormont meeting: Siobhan O'Hanlon, who was jailed for seven years in 1983 after her arrest in a Belfast bomb factory and who later was allegedly the fourth and only surviving member of the IRA's Gibraltar team, shot dead as they prepared to bomb a regimental band on the Rock; Gerry Kelly and Martin McGuinness, both of whom had IRA prison convictions and who led the secret talks with British government officials during the early 1990s; Sean McManus, a Sligo Sinn Fein councillor whose son Joseph was shot dead as he attempted to murder a part-time Ulster Defence Regiment member and full-time county council dog handler; and Lucilita Bhreatnach.

The absence of Adams led to lively and mostly uninformed speculation. One version had it that as the party's president he was being held in reserve for later on when Sinn Fein would sit down with government officials, another that McGuinness was the man best able to inspire loyalty and confidence among the IRA volunteers. But for some observers it also conjured up comparisons with the Anglo-Irish Treaty negotiations of 1921, when De Valera sent a reluctant Michael Collins to negotiate with the British and, when he failed to return with the republic, washed his hands of his former colleague and refused to accept the terms for a partitioned Ireland.

At an eve-of-talks rally in torrential rain outside Sinn Fein's Falls Road office, McGuinness assured his supporters that he was well able to handle the Oxford- and Eton-educated British negotiators because, first and foremost, 'I am Martin McGuinness, from Derry, from the Bogside.' There seemed to the many journalists who outnumbered the public something decidedly flat about the 'historic moment'.

When the Provisionals arrived at Stormont, the imposing symbol of unionist control of Northern Ireland for fifty years, it was not in tanks as Adams must have fondly dreamed in his militant twenties, but in an old black London cab and an armour-plated Ford Granada. Some Sinn Feiners had carried out a reconnaissance trip the day before, so frightened were they of driving through staunchly Protestant East Belfast. After three hours of talks McGuinness led his team down the imposing steps at the front of the old parliament building to say: 'Well, the meeting has just broken up. This is an historic opportunity which needs to be built upon and we've arranged another meeting for December 19. We've told the representatives of the British government that it is now time to liberate the oppressed and the oppressor. Thank you.'

It was the first official contact between Sinn Fein and the British government in more than seventy years. The British civil servants involved in the exploratory discussions were under orders to inquire about the 'practical consequences of the ending of violence' – diplomatic language for the thorny question of paramilitary disarmament. In a letter to Major, Adams said his party wanted to address three broad issues, 'political and constitutional change, demilitarization and associated issues, and democratic rights for all Irish people, nationalist and unionist'. The civil servants were never likely to get far down the road of the bigger political issues and Adams himself pointed out that 'bilaterals are important, but it is in multilaterals that real progress will be made'.

But elsewhere, in a number of debates and interviews, Adams was giving what appeared to be a fairly fundamentalist version of his movement's aims. He would compromise, he told an audience in West Belfast, on 'how long the British will be here and how we can get them to leave' but not on the principle that they must go. He told the *Irish Times* that 'an internal settlement is not a solution . . . We would have a preference, obviously, of ending the British jurisdiction and bringing about an agreed, new, Irish jurisdiction. And within that context all these matters take on a new significance.' He was, however, rather more respectful towards Hume's suggested fudge of Irish national self-determination, namely the holding of referenda north and south of the border at the same time, with the same questions. Previously he had dismissed the idea as 'rather silly'; now he said, 'It would not constitute self-determination by the Irish people. But it could constitute a very worthwhile way of measuring agreement on whatever had been agreed [by the political parties].'

Just before Martin McGuinness' first trip to Stormont, Adams returned from America, where he had made more inroads with the Clinton administration, making his first visit to the White House for a meeting with President Clinton's National Security Adviser, Tony Lake. He also talked to the US Commerce Secretary, Ron Brown.

Soon after, Brown travelled across the Atlantic to Belfast to attend a special economic conference on Northern Ireland convened by John Major. The British again signalled their refusal to put Sinn Fein on a par with other parties by keeping republicans off the invitation list to the conference. Eventually the government shifted their ground, inviting six Sinn Fein members in their capacity as councillors from Belfast and Londonderry.

Sceptics believed the conference had been arranged hastily in order to ensure that the US administration did not steal a march on the British government by pressing ahead with its own plans for an economic conference. Certainly the British handling of the Belfast event was amateurish, given the preference of their invited American guests to include all sides. In the event the government provided an opportunity for Sinn Fein to demonstrate outside the Europa Hotel where the conference was being held, and for their belatedly invited councillors then to stage a largely unnoticed walk-out. Adams wrote to delegates claiming that the conference could have played a positive role in building on the peace process but 'instead it has become an instrument of discrimination against Sinn Fein and those who vote for our party'. In this instance, as in others, there was more than a sense that British caution was dictated not by concern for upsetting the delicate balance in Northern Ireland, but more by the difficulty of seeing republicans as anything other than the implacable enemies they had been for twenty-five years.

On the day of the conference Major chose his visit to Northern Ireland to make the removal of terrorist weapons his top priority in the peace process. 'I am not pedantic about whether these weapons are surrendered or decommissioned or destroyed with some form of verification. That is the significant point, that they are no longer available for use and a political party would not go back to a nice, neat stockpile of weapons if something goes wrong.'

Just before Christmas 1994 Adams had his first preliminary meeting with the new Irish Prime Minister at Dublin airport. Bruton was just on his way back from a meeting with John Major, while Adams was heading towards Paris to launch a French translation of his prison memoirs, *Cage 11*. Irish government sources described the two men as having established a 'solid working relationship'. But by now the issue which, above all others, was to pose problems for the peace process was growing too large to ignore. Bruton and Adams discussed the decommissioning of paramilitary weapons, but both stressed that it had been just one item on their agenda. Adams acknowledged that 'Everybody, I think, sees the sense of needing to get all of the weapons out of the Irish politics as part of an overall settlement.'

In the New Year he changed tack, accusing the British government of using the issue to try to split the republican movement. 'One has always to be mindful that the British government in dealing with this peace process never came to it willingly,' the Sinn Fein president argued. 'There is always a temptation, I presume, for a government to be involved in tactical manoeuvring. Perhaps they want, and I would not dismiss this, to cause a split in the republican ranks. But I can tell you with certainty there will be no split.' Adams characterized the question of disarmament as an 'artificial issue' and began to suggest that it was a new precondition. 'We must be quite clear how the government work these issues. This was not an issue in the exchange of papers or going back over the years of dialogue or public exchanges between ourselves and the British.'

John Bruton was soon doing his best to overcome his instincts when in opposition and to reflect Adams' concern about arms, saying it should not be a 'blocking item'. The concern sprang from the course of the exploratory dialogue, where British officials were making it clear to Martin McGuinness' negotiating team that, when they talked about decommissioning, the government were looking for weapons not words. Bruton's predecessor Albert Reynolds believed that being too insistent about disarmament would pose problems with both the IRA and the loyalists:

Both sides were equally adamant and equally intransigent about getting rid of guns at a very early stage or indeed in advance of the talks process. That was never ever a runner in my view. The biggest single mistake that was made was to allow decommissioning to be put on the table as a precondition, because it started to sour the whole relationships that had been built up ... I absolutely abhor violence, but listening to both sides I could see how their minds were working ... From the republican movement side on decommissioning they would be seeing that as surrender, while at the same time the British Army and they themselves, the IRA, they had accepted that neither of them was going to win this war, it was deadlocked . . . Yet handing up guns in advance of talks and the way you did it was going to be seen as surrender. There's a certain pride in that organization, nationalist pride. And on the other side there was genuine fear on the loyalist side – we're going to leave ourselves defenceless against this lot.

Reynolds was convinced that the paramilitaries weren't opposed to disarming themselves in principle, it was more a matter of timing. 'You couldn't have a genuine peace, at the end of the day, if there were still guns around. There would have to be a formula found. But I got an acceptance from both sides that, come a certain stage of development, the guns issue would not be a major problem. Because there was a recognition on both sides that they would have to be got rid of. It was a question of when and how, it wasn't a question of if. The if didn't come into it . . . That's why I think that issue was very badly handled, because there wasn't an understanding of the problems associated with it. I think that's where people made a mistake.'

By mid-January 1995 Adams was accusing the Northern Ireland Secretary Sir Patrick Mayhew of setting unacceptable preconditions and allowing the arms issue to cause a crisis in the process. After three exploratory meetings between his party and British officials he wrote, 'I believe the British government is engaged in a strategy which involves, at best, stalling the process through the deliberate erection of barriers to progress on a bogus pretext, at worst, attempting to create and sustain a crisis in the peace process around the issue of IRA arms.' Adams contended that 'Sinn Fein's position on the weapons issue is transparent. The entire logic of a peace process is that through peace talks we arrive at a peace settlement which removes the causes of the conflict and removes the guns for ever from the political equation in Ireland.' The government, however, found it impossible to take the IRA's long-term good intentions on trust in the way Adams wanted. 'Decommissioning is one issue which illustrates the great gulf between Tory or any British ministers and Irish republicans – it's almost an unbridgeable chasm in culture, background and temperament,' reflects Jonathan Cain, special adviser to the Northern Ireland Secretary, Sir Patrick Mayhew. 'The British government didn't understand that republicans felt that there was no way they could decommission. The British thought they might get some sort of gesture.'

In public, Mayhew tended to reply to Adams' criticisms in robust terms. But in a private question-and-answer session with sixth formers from University College School in London, Sir Patrick revealed what Jonathan Cain calls the 'schizophrenic relationship' which had developed between the government and the Sinn Fein president. Sir Patrick told the sixth formers that the government didn't trust Adams but realized it would be 'a disadvantage to everybody' if he was replaced. The government needed him to control the 'hard men' of the IRA and Adams needed support, otherwise he might be forced to take 'a long walk on a short plank, and be replaced by someone much harder'. The Northern Ireland Secretary concluded that 'to some extent, we have got to help Mr Adams carry with him the people who are reluctant to see a ceasefire, who believe they might be betrayed by the British government'.

The Secretary of State's unusual transparency was due to the fact that he didn't realize that a reporter from the London *Hampstead and Highgate Express* newspaper was present. The publication of the remarks caused some embarrassment as unionists expressed their alarm that, in Ian Paisley's words, Sir Patrick was 'prepared to sustain a terrorist leader and give in to some of his demands in order to hold together something which he calls a peace process when in fact it is a surrender process'.

According to Jonathan Cain, the off-the-cuff remarks, which the Northern Ireland Office refused to confirm or deny, reflected the reality of the British view of Adams' importance:

It is a schizophrenic relationship. On the one hand you've got this man who's viewed as an apologist for the most unspeakable horrors, such as the Shankill bombing, all the things that have happened in the past twenty-five years, and who's been implicated himself in some of them. A man who, it wouldn't be unfair to say, is hated because of that, what he's done, not so much what he stands for, Irish republicanism, but what he apologizes for and what he seeks to justify.

Yet at the same time he's viewed as the man who is the best hope that the British government has of delivering a peaceful solution. The British government believed, certainly by mid-'95, that he was genuine about wanting a peaceful way out and that's reflected really in Paddy Mayhew's comments in the school in Hampstead, when he was speaking to a sixth form without the knowledge that a journalist was there, when he said that we've got to help this man. Much as the government found it distasteful, he's our best chance, and if he goes, then the chances are that he will go because hardliners ousted him, and we're not going to be able to do a deal with the hardliners. So it's a very schizophrenic relationship. He's not trusted, he's hated for what he is and what he justifies, yet at the same time he's the only one that they can really deal with, he holds the key.

As Mayhew's private thoughts on Gerry Adams were being made public his predecessor Peter Brooke hit the headlines with some comments made on camera to the BBC's *Panorama* reporter John Ware for his documentary: *Gerry Adams – The Man We Hate to Love*. Ware, who had clinically demolished Adams' political façade in his 1983 profile *The Honourable Member for West Belfast*, decided that the events since the 1994 ceasefire merited a re-examination. In the new documentary he traced Adams' increasing interest in conventional politics to the mid-1980s and the introduction of the Anglo-Irish Agreement. Peter Brooke told Ware that he admired Adams' courage in delivering the 1994 ceasefire. 'In my view he was a brave man – and I hope he will be justified. That step was a crucial step. I describe it myself as a rubicon. He led them across that rubicon. It was like many acts of leadership. In my view that was a courageous step. He had a leadership role. He performed it. And I think the whole of Ireland and the whole of these islands and I think arguably the whole of the world is grateful to him for having done it. Irish history is littered with occasions when people have, in fact, been attacked from behind. Therefore, understandably, anybody who does take so forward a step is, in my view, taking a courageous one.'

Brooke's generosity wasn't appreciated in all quarters. The DUP deputy leader Peter Robinson rejoined: 'As for the world having much for which they might thank Mr Adams, I believe the world might have greater cause to curse the day he was ever born.' Colin Parry, whose son Tim died in the IRA bombing in Warrington, counselled caution: 'I do give credit to Gerry Adams for the role he played in persuading hardline elements in the IRA to abandon violence and back the peace process instead . . . But just now exaggerated and as yet unwarranted praise is being heaped upon Gerry Adams. And it concerns me that so much of this praise is emanating from unexpected quarters, people who should understand better than they apparently do that their remarks can cause considerable pain and offence to those who have suffered at the hands of the IRA . . . For all that those of us on the outside of the IRA know, the "courageous step" with which Gerry Adams is credited by Peter Brooke may have been no more than a change of tactics.'

The nationalist *Irish News* came to Mr Brooke's defence, describing his remarks as 'timely given the niggardly behaviour of the British government since the ceasefire'. But the unionist *Newsletter* went on the attack. Under a heading 'Babblin' Brooke shores up Adams' a *Newsletter* editorial expressed concern that 'Peter Brooke may be perceived as a bumbling old fool, but one suspects that the comments he made about Gerry Adams were said deliberately to pave the way for the Government to engage in talks with the Provo leaders.'

In an interview with the authors, Peter Brooke said his comments were 'slightly hyped' but defended his remarks within their historical context. 'I was saying on the basis of the experience of Michael Collins in signing the Treaty in 1921 that the consequence is that the people who in fact take those sort of steps are being personally brave, personally courageous. I wasn't making any other observation about him, but it was genuine, I did think he was. I think in a history like Ireland's people who take those sort of steps are being brave and part of the problem in Irish history is that the fear of betrayal is so strong that it inhibits very positive actions.' Asked whether the end of the IRA ceasefire showed Gerry Adams wasn't genuine or merely illustrated the limits to his influence, Brooke responded, 'I think it shows the limits to his influence, and understandably. For somebody who is a member of my own political party which has been having a fairly major debate about Europe over the last five years [1992–7] it would be perfectly ridiculous for me to imply that in other political organizations you don't have a similar kind of debate.'

If, as *Panorama* argued, Gerry Adams had seen some potential in the Anglo-Irish Agreement of 1985 for advancing the nationalist agenda, this was as nothing compared to the warm reaction which he gave another agreement reached between London and Dublin in

February 1995. The Framework Document was intended to provide a vision of the way forward for the North and South of Ireland – the vision was subscribed to by both John Major and John Bruton. But when both prime ministers presented it to the outside world at a launch inside the Balmoral Conference centre in South Belfast, they stressed that the document was merely a basis for discussion, which unionists and nationalists could accept, reject or amend as they saw fit.

The Framework Document amounted to an attempt by the governments to exercise the judgement of Solomon on the division between those who favoured permanent partition and those who desired an all-Ireland solution. It proposed that Northern Ireland should have its own elected assembly with devolved powers, but an important role was also envisaged for a variety of cross-border bodies which would seek to harmonize tourism, education, economic development and a variety of other areas across the island as a whole. The cross-border bodies would have an 'open dynamic role', meaning that if agreement was obtained their remit could be widened as the years passed. This mixture of Northern Ireland and cross-border elements led one political wag to dub the Framework Document 'Sunningdale for slow learners' as it mirrored many of the elements which had made up the suggested solution under discussion at the Sunningdale conference in 1974. A short-lived agreement produced a powersharing executive and a proposal for a Council of Ireland – the initiative foundered after the loyalist Ulster Worker's Council strike.

An old-style Gerry Adams might have been expected to dismiss such a vision as an unacceptable fudge which did not amount to the United Ireland he believed should exist as of right. But the extent to which Adams had journeyed away from his old absolutism was illustrated by the warmth of his welcome for the Framework Document. He hailed the document's publication as proof 'that partition has failed, that British rule in Ireland has failed and that there is no going back to the failed policies and structures of the past'. He believed that the document recognized the need for fundamental political change: 'It is undeniable that the document embraces an all-Ireland character and that it deals with the general notion of one-island social, economic and political structures.' The Sinn Fein president believed the Framework Document opened up a 'new phase in the peace process' and expressed confidence that there would be swift movement towards all-party talks.

The Northern Ireland political affairs minister Michael Ancram was surprised that Gerry Adams' reaction to the Framework Document was so favourable. 'It still surprises me because the Framework Document is predicated on the continuation of the union and any movement away from that, within the Framework Document, can only be achieved with the agreement of an assembly in Northern Ireland, which by the nature of politics in Northern Ireland is likely to have a unionist majority.' This guarantee to the majority, Ancram says, held despite the fact that the cross-border bodies had been given a dynamic role:

> The only way that dynamism could be operated, after the original structure had been put in place, the only way they could be dynamically improved from an Irish point of view was with the consent of the Northern Ireland Assembly, which by its nature is going to have a unionist majority, and therefore is always going to be in a position to say no, we won't do that. Well, that is very firmly written into the Framework Document. So if you read it what we were trying to create was not a slippery slope but a level plain which you could only move forward from if there was a general consensus including unionist consensus in Northern Ireland to move forward from it. And in our view that's called democracy.

According to this view, Adams was engaged in putting a brave face on something which didn't match up to traditional republican demands. He said his party would have liked to see the all-Ireland aspect 'more deeply rooted, prescriptive and thoroughgoing' but added that Sinn Fein was making its judgements 'pragmatically in the context of our objectives, policy and strategy'. He was able to draw on the elements favourable to his agenda, while British officials like Sir Patrick Mayhew's special adviser Jonathan Cain were highlighting different aspects of the Document to others:

> To the unionists we kept saying of course none of these North–South bodies can do anything without reference back to the Assembly, everything is accountable. They can't take any powers without agreement and consent and therefore there's no slippery slope and that was the line that was used *ad nauseam*.

No slippery slope, no threat of a United Ireland and of course the union remains intact, so there's nothing to worry about. But you talk to republicans and you can say well, here you are, you've got all these great North–South bodies. We don't put any limits on how far they can grow, what they can do, that's all for you to decide. North–South bodies do have this dynamic, they're not just talking shops, but they'll have real and significant powers, executive harmonizing and all of that. And that played very well with republicans.

You can look at the Framework Document as unionists did and say actually this is a staging post on the way to a United Ireland, and I think it's fairly clear that republicans accept that they're not going to get the United Ireland tomorrow and so in the first instance they have to prepare for something less than that. What was important about the Framework Document is that it's an interim settlement, but you can sell it to republicans by saying that there is within the arrangement a dynamic which could lead to greater things in their terms, i.e. it's a dynamic which these institutions have and they can take on more powers and eventually be the instruments of a transition of sovereignty.

Soon after the Framework Document's publication Gerry Adams stood up in front of the 1995 Sinn Fein *ard fheis* inside the Mansion House in Dublin. It was the first time since he had taken over as Sinn Fein president that Adams had addressed his party's annual conference without the backdrop of IRA and loyalist violence. Adams acknowledged that the ceasefire had, for many republicans, been an 'unsettling, difficult and traumatic' time. 'For over two decades,' Adams continued, 'IRA volunteers had conducted an unprecedented and unbroken period of armed resistance. For many republicans this was one of the certainties of our time and our struggle. The 31 August statement changed all that.'

A couple of delegates from south of the border called for a return to the armed struggle. But Adams brushed these isolated comments aside as healthy internal debate and presented his strategy as the one with which 'great new possibilities have opened up'. The president was keen to channel his party activists into tackling more achievable tasks than the immediate ending of partition. The government should be pushed, he argued, to remove 'all anti-nationalist symbols and appearances' from the Northern Ireland state. A platform of 'parity of esteem' should be pursued which would cover equality in employment, education and economic development.

It left Adams dangerously open to the assertion that he was settling for reforms of a partitionist state rather than seeking its overthrow. But he avoided the charge by arguing that 'the achievement of equality of treatment for nationalists in the North will erode the very reason for that statelet. The unionist leaders know this. That is why they so dogmatically turn their faces against change.' By this logic, Adams could direct his supporters towards more short- to medium-term goals, while still maintaining that 'an end to partition' remained his movement's primary objective.

The month after the *ard fheis* both the British and Sinn Fein turned their attention back across the Atlantic. Britain had long since lost its battle to stop Gerry Adams getting a visa, but it was pushing hard to ensure that he wasn't allowed to raise funds while he was in the USA. The British argued that the concession should be held up until republicans indicated that they were prepared to move on the question of decommissioning weapons. In early March, the Northern Ireland Secretary Sir Patrick Mayhew travelled to Washington to lobby against any changes on the Adams visa. Sir Patrick thought he had done well, reporting that the US Secretary of State Warren Christopher was 'aligning himself squarely with how we see the matter'.

Sir Patrick also used his visit to America to make a keynote speech on the disarmament issue, which government sources indicated as a 'softening' or sign of flexibility. Prior to this, unionists and Conservative backbenchers had assumed that the government would insist on the actual decommissioning of large quantities of IRA arms before Sinn Fein would be admitted into what were termed 'substantive' talks, and probably before the discussions with the party could be upgraded from civil-servant level to include government ministers. Sir Patrick spelled out three objectives: the government were looking for 'a willingness to disarm progressively', a practical understanding of the 'modalities' of decommissioning and, what became known as the Washington Three condition, 'in order to test the practical arrangements and to demonstrate good faith, the actual decommissioning of some arms as a tangible confidence-building measure and to signal the start of a process'.

Unionists accused the Northern Ireland Secretary of backing down on previous demands and 'betraying the union'. They called for his resignation. But equally Gerry Adams didn't accept that the speech represented a 'softening' of the British line, claiming that it was 'totally unacceptable' for the government to link the weapons issue with Sinn Fein's involvement in talks. In time Washington Three was to be portrayed by republicans as a barrier to progress, erected as a deliberate attempt to keep them out of talks. But what the government had really been trying to do was to introduce a formula which would allow them to move matters on, and upgrade the talks with Sinn Fein by introducing a government minister, Michael Ancram.

As Jonathan Cain recalls:

> There had to be a distinction between Michael Ancram joining the exploratory talks and ministers engaging in inclusive negotiations with Sinn Fein. So we came up with what became Washington One, Two and Three. It's to help draw a distinction between ministers engaged in exploratory dialogue and ministers engaged in negotiation. What we said was that they couldn't be involved in inclusive negotiations until three things had happened and they were a willingness to disarm, commitment to peaceful methods and some actual decommissioning, as a sign of good faith.
>
> Well that itself was taken by most Conservative backbenchers at the time as something of a climbdown by the government. The backbenchers had previously assumed that great lorry-loads of weapons would have to be handed in before a minister would sit in the same room as Adams, McGuinness et al. I had Andrew Hunter [Chairman of the Conservative Backbench Northern Ireland committee] on the phone after Paddy's speech in Washington saying, 'What the hell's changed? Why's the government engaging in this climbdown?' Far from imposing a great new hurdle or obstacle into the equation the British government and certainly most Conservative backbenchers saw Washington One, Two and Three as actually a retreat from, not a strengthening of, the existing position.

The speech may have eased the Northern Ireland Secretary over the planned change in policy regarding the talks with Sinn Fein. But

Sir Patrick's trip to America served little purpose as a diplomatic mission. US administration figures found Sir Patrick too haughty – his accent and bearing put them off. The British view was that restrictions on Gerry Adams should be kept in place as a stick to beat republicans into decommissioning. The Americans were, as they had been before the ceasefire, more inclined to dangle fund-raising as a carrot in return for something which might be considered progress.

Adams' American supporters were fortified in their demand that he should be allowed to raise funds by the fact that there was no ban on the Sinn Fein president soliciting money within the United Kingdom. What Adams could do at home, senators like Ted Kennedy and Chris Dodd argued, he should also be allowed to do in America. When it came down to it Adams was assisted by the fact that Senator Dodd was a golf-playing buddy of the President. During a round at Arlington, Virginia, Dodd said to Clinton, 'I'm sorry to bring up business, but I think you should give Adams fund-raising.' Clinton gave him cause for hope, replying, 'All the advice I'm getting is not, but I think I might.'

In what appeared an almost exact rerun of the visa episode prior to the ceasefire, the White House contacted Adams and looked for a statement of commitment to decommissioning arms as a *quid pro quo* for a move on fund-raising. The request was conveyed in a phone call from Nancy Soderberg to the publisher Niall O'Dowd – the White House, Soderberg explained, wanted Adams to undertake to 'seriously discuss' disarmament. Adams responded by issuing a statement which acknowledged that in his party's talks with the government 'no issue including decommissioning of arms can be excluded. We look forward to discussing all issues with a view to their resolution.' 'Demilitarization,' he argued, 'requires movement on a range of issues including repressive legislation, prisoners and the decommissioning of weapons.'

In return for this undertaking to discuss decommissioning, as opposed to actually engaging in disarmament, the White House lifted the ban on fund-raising. In addition Adams would be invited to the White House to attend the President's St Patrick's Day party. Predictably Adams was extremely pleased; he said President Clinton had made the right decision about his first visa. 'I believe he has engaged positively and his decision will enhance the peace process.' British officials did little to disguise their 'anger and fury' at yet another diplomatic rebuff from their most powerful ally. They believed that

major concessions were being ceded for what was regarded as a
'vaguely worded' statement on the arms question. Tory backbencher
Lady Olga Maitland summed it up as 'a slap in the face for John
Major. It is outrageous to do something as insensitive as this at such a
crucial time.' Major refused to take Clinton's phone calls for five
days.

When Adams flew out to New York, Major was boarding a plane
to Israel. The Prime Minister used his visit to the Middle East to
launch a 'compare and contrast' style attack on the Sinn Fein
president. He was asked by reporters why he objected to President
Clinton meeting Adams when he himself was about to meet the PLO
chairman Yasser Arafat. 'Terrorism has now been renounced by
Chairman Arafat. I have not seen it comprehensively denounced by
Mr Adams. Chairman Arafat has signed a declaration of principles.
Sinn Fein have not yet committed themselves to the Downing Street
Declaration and they are not party to any agreement in Northern
Ireland. The Israeli government entered diplomatic contacts with
Chairman Arafat after he had explicitly renounced terrorism and had
committed himself unambiguously to peace. It was only after Chair-
man Arafat had signed a declaration of principles that I met him last
year in Downing Street.'

But Adams, on a roll, was able to shrug this off as so much sour
grapes. 'What I have is what Arafat never had, an electoral mandate,
which John Major doesn't have in my country, and I think it's a bit
insensitive of Mr Major to make those comparisons. It's right for him
to talk to Yasser Arafat and it's right for him to talk to Sinn Fein. If
John Major says we'll talk tomorrow, I will catch the first plane back.'
Adams was cheered at a fund raiser in the Tower View ballroom in
the Bronx area of New York. A short time after, he officially launched
the Washington Office of the Friends of Sinn Fein, a new fund-raising
group which had far more influential backing than the old Noraid.
Four hundred supporters of the group turned out for a $200 per head
dinner at the Essex House Hotel in Manhattan. The great and the
good of New York society turned out to rub shoulders with Gerry
Adams and put money in his coffers. They included the millionaire
Donald Trump, the former model Bianca Jagger, the screenwriter
Michael Moore and the former mayor of the city, David Dinkins. Not
all the rough edges had been rubbed off though – when one guest
on his way in saw a small but vocal picket from the group Families

Against Intimidation and Terror, he aimed a punch at a Belfast man whose son had committed suicide after being subjected to an IRA beating.

As Gerry Adams was socializing with New York's high society in Manhattan, in the Bronx eighty-year-old George Harrison, wearing trousers, braces and a string vest, was making a cup of black tea and cutting a heel of bread. Harrison remembered the barbarity of the Black and Tans, the irregular soldiers used by the British during Ireland's struggle for independence. His view of the problem had crystallized then and hadn't changed, and after emigrating to America he had down the decades set about supplying his fellow Irishmen with the only thing he believed the British understood – guns and ammunition. One conservative estimate is that he shipped 2,500 weapons from America to Ireland. The single biggest source of IRA weaponry until Colonel Gadaffi came on the scene, Harrison had parted political company with Adams from the time he changed the policy on abstaining from the Irish parliament. Adams' high-profile visit to America left Harrison equally cold – it wasn't true Irish republicanism, he argued, and the struggle was not going to be won in America. 'That it has focused a lot of attention is correct. The fact is that the Brits are still there, and the bottom line for all of us who have followed the republican tradition of resistance has to be "Brits Out" and a plebiscite of the whole people of Ireland followed by a constituent assembly which will restore our last republic.'

Having split away from Gerry Adams' Sinn Fein, Harrison had put himself beyond the fold – but his understanding of and undeniable commitment to the republican creed put him in a good position to gauge the tensions within Adams' camp:

I have an idea that there is a lot of hidden disappointment ... I have no intentions of criticizing those who seek a different road, but we'll continue on the old road to the Republic ... I see a lot of dissatisfied people planning for the future and for another round of armed struggle. You can ask me, well, what weapons or whatever? Well, I quote James Connolly on that and he said, 'You use the weapons closest to hand.' The job isn't finished, the job that the heroes of 1920, and who fought the betrayal of 1922, the job that those men faced the British hangman for, faced the firing squad for, it's not finished, the job that Pearse and his comrades died for is not finished, and the thing to do is there's unfinished work to be done.

Within the ranks of the IRA, there were many who felt, like Harrison, that the only language the Brits understood was violence and that the unfinished work had to be completed. It was these hardliners whom Adams had in mind when a few days after his New York fund raiser he had breakfast with one of the authors in a Washington hotel and asked the rhetorical question, 'What if a section of the IRA told me to fuck off? Then where would I be, how could I deliver? If I danced to the British tune and a section of the IRA detached, then I could not deliver . . . It is important the likes of me and Martin McGuinness are not undermined in the process.' Adams was pondering on the difficulties posed by the government's continuing insistence on paramilitary disarmament, and he used an analogy which he was to develop and use several times over. 'If the dog's asleep,' he asked, 'why wake it up? What is the point of kicking the dog to see if it will bark?' The dog in this context was the IRA – the ceasefire had put it to sleep but the demand for weapons might wake it up and provoke it to attack.

These expressions of concern, significantly, came at what was arguably the highest point of Adams' political offensive. Days earlier he had been at the Capitol building, home of the US Congress, for a luncheon organized by the Speaker, Newt Gingrich. Sensitive to British pressure, Gingrich initially decided not to invite Adams to his luncheon. But then he heard the news that the President was inviting the Sinn Fein leader into the White House itself for his St Patrick's Day reception. Aware that it would have been unwise to have been out of line, so far as the powerful Irish American lobby was concerned, Gingrich swiftly despatched an invitation in Adams' direction. Adams, in the company of his old friend New York Republican Congressman Peter King arrived on Capitol Hill as the President was greeting visiting dignitaries. An American cameraman yelled, 'Who's the guy with the bald patch?' as the Irish Prime Minister John Bruton arrived. 'And where's the IRA guy?'

Inside the Congress building Adams and Clinton sat down to lunch, in the same room for the first time. After a few minor diplomatic hitches, John Hume escorted Adams over to the President. Clinton put his arm around the SDLP leader's shoulder and then stretched out his hand in Adams' direction.

During their brief conversation the President mentioned the pressure he'd been coming under from Britain. Adams told him, 'Now you know, Mr President. You've found out in the last two weeks what I've had to live with for forty-seven years.' Clinton responded by telling Hume and Adams, 'We're going to make this thing work!' and punching his fist in the air.

When the other diners noticed what was happening, they broke off from their boiled corned beef and cabbage and broke into spontaneous applause. Outside, when he met the press together with Peter King, Adams was in jubilant mood. The cameras may have been excluded but he had shaken the hand of the most powerful man in the world. No presidential pressure had been placed on him regarding the decommissioning of IRA arms, he maintained. He had enjoyed 'a very nice lunch'. He did acknowledge, though, in the face of one pointed question from a British reporter, that there was 'no such thing as a free lunch'.

The President's own reception came the next evening. A certain frisson was added to the atmosphere by the presence of three loyalists, Joe English, Billy Blair and Gary McMichael, who had been added to the guest list at the last minute to provide balance. McMichael was the pre-eminent spokesman for the small Ulster Democratic Party, the political wing of the loyalist paramilitary UDA and UFF. His father John, as UFF commander, is believed to have sanctioned the loyalists' attempt to kill Adams, before he in turn was murdered by the IRA. McMichael and Adams avoided one another, but getting them into the same room together was no mean achievement.

At breakfast the next morning with one of the authors, Adams was clearly on a high, recounting stories of how the filmstar Paul Newman had asked for his autograph, how he had persuaded a waiter to find a small bottle of Guinness hidden deep within the vaults of the White House. He also talked about the sing-song which had taken place in the White House's East Room after the President and First Lady had made their excuses. Adams had joined John Hume on stage, clutching microphones, for an impromptu rendition of the ode to Derry, 'The Town I Loved So Well'. Everyone had had a wonderful time. Or perhaps not quite everyone. Asked about the sing-song a day or two later the loyalist Joe English grimaced. 'I have never heard such terrible caterwauling in my whole life.'

CHAPTER TWENTY-SEVEN

They Haven't Gone Away, You Know

A week after Adams left Washington, an Ulster businessman visiting the US capital got talking with his taxi driver, who asked the visitor where he came from. 'Northern Ireland,' came the reply. 'Oh, Northern Ireland,' said the cabbie. 'We had your President over here last week.' No wonder Adams was keen to return, and return he did, spending almost as much time, it appeared, in America as in Northern Ireland itself.

Adams was a welcome guest in Washington, but by contrast Major had difficulty visiting a city where he was meant to be Prime Minister. When Major arrived in Londonderry in May 1995 he found his planned visit to a museum in the centre of the city disrupted by republican demonstrators. Although the injuries were relatively light, the pictures of mayhem in Derry's Guildhall Square and a gas canister being hurled through the rear window of a police car produced striking television images. The Prime Minister eventually made it into the centre of the city but only after a delay and a considerable security operation. Adams, continuing his new career as an international statesman, was in Switzerland picking up a peace prize at a gala reception in a medieval castle. He blamed the trouble on the RUC, who, he claimed, had 'harassed and hassled' the demonstrators. Perhaps Swiss TV had not carried the pictures, which clearly showed a senior member of his party kicking a lone policeman from behind before turning and running. 'British ministers coming to my country,' Adams warned, 'need to be mindful that they are in Ireland and that they are in a new situation.'

Adams had set great store by upgrading the talks between Sinn Fein and the government to ministerial status. Predictably when the landmark moment came and Michael Ancram, survivor of the IRA

Brighton bombing, stepped into the same room inside Stormont's Parliament Buildings to talk to Martin McGuinness' negotiating team, Gerry Adams was away – once again in America. The fund-raising trip was designed to culminate in Washington in late May, where the President was organizing a conference to promote Investment in Northern Ireland and the Irish Border Counties. The event was ostensibly economic – but in content it was inevitably highly political. The Americans had invited all Northern Ireland's political parties, the British and Irish governments and dozens of business and community leaders to the gathering, scheduled to take place in the Sheraton Washington Hotel.

Somewhat ironically, delegates checking in at the hotel found themselves rubbing shoulders with guests at another conference, devoted to the latest in small arms and weaponry. As muscle-bound men from the US Army walked past carrying briefcases labelled 'Beretta' and 'Colt', the Ulster Unionist negotiator Reg Empey could be clearly seen in the foyer shaking hands with Richard McAuley – it appeared that he didn't know quite who Gerry Adams' personal press officer was.

In the run-up to the conference, Sir Patrick Mayhew announced that he would hold a meeting in Washington with the Sinn Fein president. The move prompted one Conservative backbencher David Wilshire to accuse Mayhew of 'bending the knee to terrorism' and 'abject surrender'. Unionists were also furious at hearing the news. The Ulster Unionist leader Jim Molyneaux said Mayhew's decision to meet Adams was 'Washington driven'. Pressure had been put on Mayhew to agree to the meeting and 'he had very little option – that is not to say I agree with the decision'. Molyneaux and Ian Paisley stayed away. But, with the exception of their party leaders, the unionist delegations still got on the plane.

The junior Northern Ireland minister Malcolm Moss was at a reception early on in the event explaining to journalists how he himself wouldn't have too many difficulties shaking Adams' hand when the Sinn Fein leader's entourage entered the room. A senior civil servant whispered in Moss' ear, 'Here comes trouble,' and without further ado the minister reversed swiftly out of the room, narrowly avoiding a public encounter with Adams. Mayhew's chief press officer Andy Wood and Adams' aide Richard McAuley put their heads together to arrange the choreography of the Mayhew/Adams meeting. No details were given about where it would take place. The understanding was that nothing would be captured on camera. Mayhew would already be inside a hotel suite and Adams would join him for a brief meeting.

Reporters and camera crews were reduced to dogging the steps of the two protagonists in the hour running up to the encounter. As Adams made his way through the hotel he was followed by a crocodile of reporters and television cameras – the future Ulster Unionist MP Jeffery Donaldson looked on apparently aghast at the media circus in front of his eyes. Richard McAuley jumped into a lift. A reporter jumped in with him. 'Where are you going?' asked McAuley. 'Same floor as you,' came the reply. In the event the destination became clear – Suite 6066. Sir Patrick arrived first, to be followed a minute later by Gerry Adams. For thirty-two minutes the door of the suite stayed closed, then the two men came out in turn to give impromptu news conferences to about seventy reporters and photographers crowded into the corridor outside.

The Northern Ireland Secretary was accompanied by his parliamentary private secretary James Cran and his principal private secretary Martin Howard. Adams had Richard McAuley and the head of Sinn Fein's Washington Office Mairead Keane. Andy Wood, who was also there, said the meeting was 'civil'. Mayhew presented Adams with a two-page document calling for Sinn Fein to use 'its influence with the IRA to get substantial progress on the decommissioning of their stock of arms and explosives'. When asked how he had felt shaking hands with Adams, he replied that he 'didn't care for that experience very much'. Gerry Adams also gave the government a lengthy submission which said that Sinn Fein was 'wholly committed to the permanent removal of all guns from Irish politics'. Adams described it as 'a useful meeting, a frank and friendly and positive exchange of views'. He claimed not to mind that the historic handshake between the two had taken place off camera. 'We are concerned more with making peace than taking pictures.'

Mayhew's special adviser Jonathan Cain told the authors that the Northern Ireland Secretary was in fact quite impressed with Adams. 'There is this view among most people that Mayhew hates Adams so much that the mere mention of his name is enough to provoke him to anger. Yet actually he found Adams had quite a good personality and was rather an engaging and interesting character and not at all as cold and calculating as you would have expected. Of course, he met him again on a couple of occasions and I think was probably convinced by Adams that he was for real in the sense that he wanted a peaceful way out of this, that violence was going nowhere, getting them nowhere, and he wanted a political way forward.'

At the end of the week in Washington the delegates set off in buses to the White House for a reception hosted by the President himself. Ironically a bomb scare in the US capital held the buses up, leaving Gerry Adams and his fellow delegates stranded in traffic for ninety minutes. The mixed collection of Protestants and Catholics decided to make their own entertainment and burst into song on the bus. Gerry Adams joined in, singing the Orange anthem 'The Sash My Father Wore' as loud as the rest. When the bomb scare turned out to be a hoax Adams and the others made it to the reception, held in a big marquee in the White House grounds. But torrential rain and loud thunder hampered the gathering, and the public address system broke down, meaning that most guests couldn't make out the President's joke that 'We arranged the Irish weather here tonight, to remind you that we are here under a very large tent in more ways than one.'

The rain notwithstanding, Adams enjoyed his second visit to the White House. But he claimed a few days later in an interview with a Catholic magazine not to have forgotten those whose sacrifices had made the trip possible. 'I think quite often of Bobby Sands, not just in the quiet times but as I go about my business. When I went to the White House, I thought of Bobby Sands.' In the same interview, he named Nelson Mandela as one of the men he most admired. The month after President Clinton's Investment Conference, Adams went to South Africa to meet his hero. At the start of an eight-day tour, Adams said, 'We have come to learn and listen and take lessons from the struggle in South Africa, which has been inspirational all over the world. There are many similarities . . . those of conquest and discrimination. How South Africa emerged from all of these, we have come here to find out.'

Adams visited Soweto and the grave of the former head of the ANC's military wing, the communist leader Joe Slovo. Adams was greeted at Avalon cemetery by a band of about twenty ANC supporters who chanted happily 'Viva the ANC, viva! Viva Sinn Fein, viva! Long live IRA, long live! Viva Joe Slovo, viva!' At a nearby squatter camp Adams was followed for more than a mile by a chanting band of warriors bearing their traditional African weapons. He managed to join them in a few steps of the ANC's *toyi-toyi* freedom dance. The ANC supporters were polite and curious, but one confessed to the *Irish Times* that they didn't know a great deal about their visitor: 'The leadership told us that there is a person who is coming here, but we don't know that much about him or where he comes from.'

The next day Adams held a half-hour meeting with Nelson Mandela at the ANC's Shell House headquarters in Johannesburg. A statement described the talks as 'friendly, constructive and extremely relaxed'. Afterwards the ANC leader came close to backing Gerry Adams' view of the arms issue when he talked about his organization's own experience. 'When we made a statement suspending armed struggle,' Mandela said, 'we totally rejected the demand from the then South African government that we should hand in our arms, and we said that is a decision that we ourselves will take at an appropriate time.'

On his return from South Africa, Adams addressed a rally in the Short Strand, a Catholic enclave in Protestant East Belfast. The rally commemorated the twenty-fifth anniversary of the defence of St Matthew's Catholic Church when it came under attack from loyalists in 1970. The incident was one of the episodes from the early Troubles where republicans could with conviction claim that guns had been used for the defence of nationalist areas rather than in offensive action against soldiers, police or loyalists. A statement from IRA prisoners from the Short Strand area was read out to the rally. It said, 'Today those guns are silent, but they are still very well oiled.'

The arms stalemate prompted Adams to use his 1995 Easter speech, delivered at Glasnevin cemetery in Dublin, to warn of a wave of protests in support of 'parity of esteem' for his party. He told those gathered in the cemetery that 'if the British refuse to listen to reasoned and reasonable argument, then let them listen to the sound of marching feet and angry voices'. In time the strategy of 'marching feet and angry voices' was to become especially associated with the issue of Orange parades. But in mid-1995 the event which brought the marching feet on to the streets was the case of a soldier released early from jail. In July Sir Patrick Mayhew approved the release of Private Lee Clegg, a Paratrooper jailed for the murder of a young girl, Karen Reilly, a passenger in a car stolen by joyriders.

Sinn Fein viewed the decision to free Clegg as especially objectionable given the government's lack of response to their demands for an amnesty for IRA prisoners. Graffiti appeared on the walls demanding,

'Clegg out, all out,' and a wave of rioting broke out in nationalist areas across Northern Ireland. John Major claimed that the riots were orchestrated by Sinn Fein. Adams countered that his party had been involved in purely peaceful protest. That said, cars and lorries were hijacked and burned quite openly just yards from Sinn Fein offices with senior party members doing nothing to restrain the young people involved. Most of the disturbances had a high level of organization, but as in all disorderly situations not everything went entirely according to the IRA's plans. In Derry an IRA prisoner out on a short period of leave from jail found his car taken from him by over-zealous teenagers. And on the Falls Road in West Belfast, youths told a motorist that they were taking his car for burning, only to find out that the vehicle owner was none other than Sean Reilly, the stepfather of the girl killed by Private Clegg.

The Clegg riots, through their timing, merged with disturbances associated with Orange marches that same month. Adams expressed concern about what he termed the 'curfew' imposed on Catholics in the Lower Ormeau area of South Belfast and said that unionist politicians David Trimble and Ian Paisley had been 'triumphalistically dancing around like Orange Lils' after the Drumcree Orange parade made its way down Portadown's mainly Catholic Garvaghy Road following mediation with the residents.

Sinn Fein continued their organization of street demonstrations – a tactic which brought some protest from the Irish government. Adams defended the protests as a way to 'manage' its constituency. While this surface activity continued, Sinn Fein's pressure on the British to maintain and upgrade discussions was beginning to pay some dividends. On 6 July Martin McGuinness held a private meeting with political affairs minister Michael Ancram in a house in Londonderry, to explore ways around the logjam over paramilitary arms. Then on the 18th another meeting took place in a different house in Derry where Ancram and McGuinness were joined by Gerry Adams and Sir Patrick Mayhew for an hour to an hour and a half of discussions.

This was Ancram's first encounter with Adams, barring a brief handshake under the gaze of the television cameras at a conference in Belfast's Europa Hotel:

> The colour to that meeting was that Martin McGuinness appeared to be much harder than he'd appeared in the private

meeting with me. But Adams was appearing as much the more flexible in terms of the conversation, although it was also clear that he was very much in charge of the conversation ... At that meeting, I think the first fly was floated which eventually led to the twin track approach and the setting up of the Mitchell Commission. But it was, at that time, a very gentle exploratory suggestion, between us, as we talked about the ways in which we could find some key to this. The line they were taking was that they could not be put in a position where they appeared to be surrendering.

And we were making it clear to them that we were not looking for that but we had a genuine problem here that unless something moved on this we didn't see how we would get into a talks process of the sort we wanted and they wanted. All the way through they had said to us, 'Decommissioning is no problem because when we reach an agreement it will happen. And we don't need to discuss the modalities because it will happen like that when the time comes for it to happen.' What we were arguing with them was not the question of actual weapons, but the question of how you created the confidence to bring others around the table, which is the key to all this.

At the end of the discussion Adams indicated there was a need to 'brainstorm' more on the problem and on 27 July the four men held another meeting in the Stormont office of the then security minister Sir John Wheeler. Wheeler, who took a more hawkish line than his ministerial colleagues, had vowed never to meet Adams until he drove a 'pantechnicon of Semtex up to the steps of Stormont Castle'. He didn't take kindly to the idea that the two Provisionals had been in his room. During the discussion, Ancram recalls some progress being made with the tentative suggestion that disarmament could occur alongside political discussions: 'We began to float rather more strongly the idea of the twin track again, not completely formalized at that stage, but the idea that you could somehow run the two things in parallel ... I think in fairness to them they didn't sign up to it but they gave us sufficent indications of interest for us to think it was worth pursuing.'

Adams described the meeting at Stormont Castle as 'constructive' and having had 'a good focus'. But he remained firm on the arms issue, which he said was one on which Sinn Fein had 'no room for manoeuvre'. He accused the government of inventing the hurdle after the 31 August ceasefire, and implied that the cessation would not have taken place if the problem had been raised beforehand. He drew support in this from the former Irish Prime Minister Albert Reynolds, who said decommissioning should not be a precondition and had not been raised as an issue prior to the Downing Street Declaration. British sources suggested that both Reynolds and Adams were suffering from 'memory loss' and pointed to a message sent via the secret contacts in late 1993 which had said there would have to be discussion of the 'practical consequences of ending violence' as proof that the issue was not a new invention. They could also point out that, when demanding clarification of the Downing Street Declaration in early 1994, Adams had specifically said he wanted to clarify whether the talks would turn into a 'decommissioning conference'.

Michael Ancram recalls of his meetings with McGuinness and Adams that 'All the way along there was always a general sentiment that the ceasefire is here, but unless we make progress we're not certain how long it will hold. There was always that sort of aura behind our conversations. There was never a direct threat but that was always in the background.' Ancram says he was talking to Gerry Adams in the belief that he spoke for the whole of the movement, not just a peace wing within it:

> If you're saying to me is there a peace wing of republicanism which is different from the rest, the answer is we thought we were talking to people who influenced the whole, that this was a leadership of the republican movement, and it was on that basis that we talked to them. It was on that basis that I met them originally. We weren't talking to them on the basis that they were a party with 12 per cent of the vote and no connection with anything else. And had we been doing so we would not have been talking to them about the decommissioning of arms for a start. The whole thing was that we took the view we were talking to the republican leadership.

A fortnight after Gerry Adams sat on Sir John Wheeler's sofa, he was addressing a rally held outside Belfast City Hall to commemorate the anniversary of internment. In response to a heckler who shouted,

'Bring back the IRA!' Adams replied, 'They haven't gone away, you know!' Later he made the intentions of the republican movement clear: 'Let no one tell you that we won't have Irish unity. We will. Let no one tell you that all our political prisoners will not be released. They will. Let no one tell you that we will not break the British connection. We will.'

But if the IRA hadn't gone away, what was its battle plan? A clue seemed to be provided by the leaking in 1995 of an internal IRA discussion document circulated among IRA members the previous year, preparing them for the declaration of the 31 August ceasefire. The document explained that 'Our goals have not changed. A united 32 county democratic socialist Republic.' But it went on to admit that 'republicans at this time and on their own do not have the strength to achieve the end goal'. Because of the problems faced by the IRA in winning its military campaign and Sinn Fein in expanding its political base, the leadership had concluded that it was time to strengthen the struggle by drawing support from three different quarters – the Dublin government, the main nationalist party in Northern Ireland, the SDLP, and the Irish American lobby, which was enjoying increasing influence under President Clinton.

The document defined the three legs of the stool as follows:

Hume is the only SDLP person on the horizon strong enough to face the challenge.

Dublin's coalition is the strongest government in 25 years or more. Reynolds has no historical baggage to hinder him and knows how popular such a consensus would be among grassroots.

There is potentially a very powerful Irish American lobby not in hock to any particular party in Ireland or Britain. Clinton is perhaps the first US President in decades to be substantially influenced by such a lobby.

The document concluded that there was 'enough agreement to proceed with the TUAS option ... TUAS has been part of every struggle in the world this century. It is vital that activists realise the struggle is not over. Another front has opened up and we should have the confidence and put in the effort to succeed on that front. We have the ability to carry on indefinitely. We should be trying to double the pressure on the British.'

Because of the frequent use of the acronym this briefing paper became known as the TUAS document. But what did TUAS stand for? For several months the assumption, fed by republican sources, was that it meant 'Totally Unarmed Strategy'. The translation of the acronym appeared to make a good deal of sense – had not Danny Morrison referred to 'an unarmed strategy' during his brief period out of jail in the run-up to the ceasefire? If this was true, the obstacle over arms was in essence a question of pride – men with a tradition of fighting not wishing to be seen to bow the knee to their enemies. But if the acronym meant something else, then the refusal to hand over a single bullet could be interpreted as rather more sinister. In the summer and autumn of 1995 nobody outside the ranks of the IRA could know for sure what the bottom line was. TUAS appeared to embrace the high politics of meetings with ministers and the agitation of the 'marching feet and angry voices'. But could it also include a return to violence? Within a few months a rather less benign explanation for the TUAS acronym emerged in public.

The conversations between Adams and the British ministers circled around the notion of engaging in disarmament in parallel with talks, but failed to bridge the gap between the two sides. A meeting at the start of September 1995 between Adams and Mayhew went badly. Further trips to the United States by both Ancram and Adams produced little movement. In late September the former Northern Ireland security minister Michael Mates was quoted as arguing that the British should 'call the IRA's bluff' and move on without Sinn Fein if no guns were forthcoming. Adams responded by saying that this phase in the peace process was 'doomed to collapse . . . the more people's heads go down, the more those of us who have created this opportunity are marginalized'. Adams appeared to be running out of adjectives to hint at how bad things were behind the scenes. He said he was 'sick of saying the peace process is in crisis'.

His strategy was endorsed by a special Sinn Fein delegate conference held in Dublin at the end of September. But the mood was becoming ever more dark. One former long-term prisoner from Adams' home patch of Ballymurphy used a boxing analogy when he told the conference that after the ceasefire the republican movement had shown 'good ring craft but no punching power'. A Belfast delegate told the *Irish Times* that he hadn't bothered addressing the conference because 'there are people who do the talking and people who do the fighting'. The republican said that if the stalemate over arms continued, the IRA should restart its campaign after a visit to Northern Ireland by President Clinton, which had been set for the end of November. 'If they don't, then the INLA or somebody else will.'

Adams said the only possibility for breaking the impasse was the dynamic inherent in Clinton's arrival in Ireland. Before the day came, Adams made another trip to the USA, where he gave a bleak assessment of the future. 'I think if the British don't move speedily to set up all-party talks as soon as possible then we're all in deep, deep trouble . . . What should be an organic process for change has been reduced to a high-wire act and the high wire is stretched like elastic . . . If I am of any service to this process or even to the republican cause, and the more pressing and wider cause of peace, it is in my ability to bring republicans to the negotiating table. It is in my ability to deliver and I cannot deliver on the terms that the British government is putting.'

On the eve of the Clinton visit the British and Irish governments, keen to deliver their distinguished visitor a breakthrough, called a late-night summit at Downing Street and announced their joint intention of pressing ahead with what they termed 'the twin-track approach,' which consisted of attempting to move matters forward on one political track, while appointing an international body, chaired by the former US Senator George Mitchell, to examine the question of disarmament on the other. But, crucially, the British refused to abandon their Washington Three condition of a token gesture on IRA disarmament before Sinn Fein could enter talks, or cede the right to the international body to decide whether the condition should be dropped. John Bruton disagreed with John Major about this but the difference was thinly papered over in the language of their joint communiqué. Adams lampooned it as illogical: 'Flann O'Brien could not have scripted it better, because the most important point of agreement between the two principals was that they agreed about that which they disagreed about – which was a rather English way of looking at matters.' Clearly, Adams added, 'What we got last night was a fudge. We want to interpret it positively and make it work. John Major may not. He may be buying time. We don't know.'

Despite Gerry Adams' caveats that President Clinton was visiting 'a police state which is governed by emergency legislation which has

been there permanently', the presidential visit was generally acknowledged as a resounding success. Adams played a significant role with
his well-choreographed handshake with the President on the Falls
Road, followed by his attendance later that evening at a reception
held in Belfast's Queen's University. Ian Paisley went to the same
event but stayed in a side room so as not to have even the possibility
of contact with Adams.

But the politicians were bit-part players, the real stars were the
people of Northern Ireland, who turned out in droves, enthusiastically
endorsing their newfound peace. On the day even the most hardened
and cynical observer of the flawed Northern Ireland peace process
found themselves believing that the emotions of the day could create
a momentum for lasting peace which it would be difficult to stop.
Outside Belfast City Hall, where Gerry Adams told his supporters that
the IRA 'hadn't gone away', the Northern Ireland rock musician Van
Morrison played to a far larger and much more varied crowd. His
band broke into a version of Morrison's song 'Days Like This'. The
tune had been appropriated by the Northern Ireland Office for
television adverts which attempted to underscore the peace process.
As Van Morrison sang that 'My mama always told me there'd be days
like this' the message seemed loud and clear, embodied in the line
from another Van Morrison song 'Coney Island' – 'wouldn't it be
great if it was like this all the time?'

Not everybody shared in the feel-good factor. Within days of the
presidential visit, slogans appeared on a wall on the Andersonstown
Road: 'Adams – Remember Collins'. It was a clear warning to the
Sinn Fein president that if he capitulated to British demands he would
go the same way as the earlier IRA leader, shot dead by his own
erstwhile comrades. The *Belfast Telegraph* reported that the slogan
was the work of a republican activist in his twenties from Andersonstown who was dissatisfied with the peace process. He had been helped
by six or seven friends in what was a spur-of-the-moment action rather
than part of an organized campaign. Sinn Fein workers spent hours in
the mid-winter cold scrubbing the offending slogan off the wall. Two
of the culprits were summoned to the party's Connolly House
headquarters in Andersonstown to explain themselves.

Despite Gerry Adams' doubts over the 'twin-track' process on
arms and politics, he and his party colleagues went along to meet the
three-man International Body when it started taking submissions in

December 1995. The IRA, by contrast, put out a statement saying that it would have no contact with the body and reaffirming its hard line on any weapons handover. Adams pronounced himself impressed with the way in which Senator George Mitchell and his two colleagues, Canadian General John de Chastelain and former Finnish Prime Minister Harri Holkeri, were going about their business. In a submission Sinn Fein revealed that they had supported the notion of 'DIY decommissioning', in other words that paramilitary organizations should dispose of their own arms.

On 24 January 1996 the International Body presented its report. Besides formulating six principles on democracy and non-violence, the three-man team decreed that a sensible compromise would be starting disarmament not before talks, as the government and unionists wanted, nor after a settlement, as the IRA preferred, but during the process of negotiations. The Mitchell report suggested that the process of disarmament could be used to build trust and confidence. The initial response from nationalists and republicans appeared positive. The International Body hadn't got the power to overturn the government's policy, but in pointing to an obvious way of breaking the deadlock over arms it would clearly exert a powerful influence. Gerry Adams claimed that the international team had accepted that the demand for disarmament before talks was impractical and that their report provided a basis for moving forward.

But when John Major stood up in the afternoon in the House of Commons and gave his response to the Mitchell report, the tenor of the day changed radically. Major would have found it hard to make a speech simply backing down on his government's prior insistence on the actual handover of some guns. He also knew that if he simply accepted the Mitchell report as it stood it was going to prove very difficult to persuade unionists to move towards inclusive talks. The Ulster Unionists, now led by Jim Molyneaux's younger successor David Trimble, had themselves suggested that there might be alternative ways of building confidence, namely by calling elections as a precursor to talks. Sinn Fein didn't like the idea, not because it had any doubts about its ability to get its vote out, but because the election would be held in Northern Ireland alone and smacked of an internal settlement, a precursor perhaps to some new form of Northern Ireland assembly which would once more enshrine the unionist majority.

In the Commons, Major welcomed the Mitchell report, but moved swiftly on to announce a plan for elections leading to talks. John Hume, well aware of Gerry Adams' severe misgivings, accused Major of 'playing politics with people's lives'. Sinn Fein issued a statement quoting Gerry Adams as accusing John Major of having 'dumped the twin-track process'. Adams claimed Major was 'quite clearly acting in bad faith by swapping one precondition for another.' And, in a reference to the Conservatives' dwindling Commons majority Adams added that, 'Mr Major has now adopted an entirely unionist agenda in an attempt to buy unionist votes in Westminster.' What was more ominous than the wording of this statement was the fact that for the best part of the day Sinn Fein spokespersons, normally readily accessible to put their point across on a big political day, were unavailable for comment.

In what had become a regular feature of the peace process Gerry Adams set off once again to Washington to enlist American support in fighting his corner. He was treated with kid gloves by the White House, being granted a ten-minute meeting with Bill Clinton. But in America, which cherishes its democratic traditions, selling the notion that an election was inherently a bad thing was always going to be difficult. One White House source later said that Adams had been told that he 'ought not to rule out' elections as a way of moving on.

While Adams was in America attending more $100 a plate fund-raising lunches, Sinn Fein refused to endorse a report by the Dublin Forum on Peace and Reconciliation which recognized the principle of consent – that the majority of people in Northern Ireland should have the right to determine their own future. Sinn Fein had hitherto tiptoed around the consent issue, arguing that they wished to give the unionists the 'maximum consent possible' while refusing to give them a 'veto'. Adams argued that it was wrong to ask his party to 'abandon core positions before negotiations even begin'. The founder of the Forum Albert Reynolds agreed. 'The one mistake at the Forum, if I may say so, was that they pushed for the principle of consent to be accepted in the report – because the circumstances weren't right at the time for it to happen, and the Forum was never meant to take decisions like that. It wasn't set up to take decisions like that, it was set up to break down the barriers and help people to reconcile each other's points of views.'

To accept the principle of consent would have indeed been a

crossing of the political rubicon for Gerry Adams, who as a republican continued to regard the only valid unit for self-determination as the entire thirty-two counties of Ireland. Albert Reynolds believed it was an ace card which they would play eventually. 'They could only play that card at the real negotiations and I had every confidence that they would have played it in real negotiations. I still believe they'll play it in real negotiations.'

In truth, though, the timing of the Forum report could not have been worse. Far from being ready to make concessions Sinn Fein and the IRA were in hostile and alienated mood. The Clinton visit and the appointment of George Mitchell's International Body on Disarmament had won a bit of breathing space. But President Clinton had proven of no use in turning around the British determination to press ahead with their 'partitionist' election, the government still had their demand for a gesture on arms on the table and no firm date had been set for Sinn Fein's inclusion in round-table talks. Rather than make an historic concession, the IRA was about to act on the basis of a decision it had taken in the autumn of 1995.

CHAPTER TWENTY-EIGHT

The Genie Is Out of the Bottle

On Friday 9 February 1996, as the cities of Dublin, London and Belfast were beginning to wind down for the weekend and weary office workers made their way home, two members of the Provisional IRA parked a lorry bomb under a bridge at South Quay railway station in the heart of the British capital's prestigious docklands Canary Wharf development, home to the majority of the national press. The massive bomb was timed to explode at seven o'clock. By then, its departing custodians believed, the world would know that the ceasefire was over.

But across the Irish Sea a journalist in the Dublin newsroom of RTE, the state broadcaster, didn't want to believe what the man claiming to represent the IRA and using a recognized codeword had to say. He scribbled down the statement that the seventeen-month ceasefire was at an end, but still refused to believe what he was hearing. Frantic efforts were made to contact Charlie Bird, the station's chief reporter, who was breaking the habit of a lifetime by choosing to go home early and join the commuting bustle homewards because of a sore throat.

After several attempts Bird was finally contacted on his mobile telephone by the IRA man. 'Charlie, you know who this is,' the voice said. There had been no announcement by RTE, why not? 'It's the real thing, go with the statement,' he was instructed. By now the rumours were sweeping newsrooms across both islands and the police in London were investigating a call to Belfast's Irish News that a bomb had been left in Docklands. As RTE finally decided, on Bird's word, to run a newsflash the bomb exploded. Two newsagents, John Jefferies and Inan Ul-Haq Bashir, were killed outright and a wide area was devastated. So too were the politicians on both sides of the sea who had invested so much work in the peace process.

Gerry Adams was in Belfast when he first heard news of the announcement. A senior British security source told the authors there was 'irrefutable evidence' that he did not know what was about to happen, although he was aware that the decision to end the ceasefire had already been made some months before President Clinton's visit. The Irish view dissents from that opinion. In government circles there was a conviction that Adams not only knew in advance but was party to the decision. The question of his foreknowledge was intensely explored in Washington. Shortly before the explosion Adams rang the White House to say that he was hearing some disturbing news. The Americans were keen to find out if he had been stringing President Clinton along during their meeting the weekend prior to the Canary Wharf bomb.

For his part, and given that he had met Clinton in Washington only the week before the Canary Wharf bomb, Adams was desperate to convince the President that he knew nothing of the ceasefire ending. A senior Belfast Sinn Fein figure was the origin of United States newspaper reports that the IRA Army Council decision to end the ceasefire was made while Adams was out of the country on his Washington trip, therefore leaving his hands clean and allowing him to be presented as the last hope of salvaging the peace. The same papers quoted Irish government sources as saying that both Adams and Martin McGuinness had quit the Army Council several months earlier. On the evening of the bombing Adams called Tony Lake, head of the National Security Council, to assure them of his non-involvement, as well as Senator Ted Kennedy, another key Sinn Fein ally. 'I think I do believe he wasn't in the loop. If he's not telling the truth he's the best damned actor I've ever heard,' said one White House aide.

In spite of the damage-limitation exercise, Adams was personally damaged in the eyes of his nervous allies outside the republican movement. Either he knew and was therefore lying, or he didn't and therefore his ability to keep the IRA on-side was in question. Sinn Fein sources argued that the decision to end the ceasefire had been taken as early as June the previous year and that it was Adams who had managed continually to postpone the return to violence, urging IRA leaders to explore every avenue before abandoning the peace process. But if Canary Wharf plunged politicians back into despair, within the IRA the decision had the effect of consolidating support for Adams at a time when the cries of 'sell-out' were clamorous. Attendance at protest meetings and sales of the movement's newspaper had been in decline, both seen as indicators of growing disenchantment. The *Belfast Telegraph* summed up the mood of the province. 'Along with the massive destruction caused by the bomb the IRA has destroyed at a stroke whatever trust in the republican movement has been built up over the past eighteen months. If Sinn Fein knew nothing about the bomb plan, as it says, what are its relations with the IRA? Why should the views of its leaders be taken seriously, if they have no influence over the bombers?'

In its statement the IRA blamed John Major for the ceasefire breakdown and a few days later Adams endorsed that view. He told the *Irish Times*: 'It was the absence of negotiations and the consequent failure to address and resolve the causes of conflict which made the re-occurrence of conflict inevitable.' But the Irish Taoiseach John Bruton was not impressed, ruling out a meeting with Sinn Fein and demanding a renewed IRA ceasefire which this time would have to be be clearly signposted as permanent.

John Major defended his role in the peace process and accused Sinn Fein and the IRA of not being serious about abandoning violence from the very beginning. 'All the time that Sinn Fein were calling for all-party talks we knew that the IRA continued to train and plan for terrorist attacks . . . It remained ready to resume full-scale terrorism at any time. We could never be confident that its behaviour was that of an organization which had decided to renounce violence for ever. The IRA peace was not true peace. I regret to say that the events of last Friday showed that our caution about the IRA was only too justified.'

But the most damning indictment of the IRA came from Fianna Fail, the political party most closely related in historical terms. Those who carried out the bombing, said Bertie Ahern, the new party leader, 'raise the doubt as to whether any reliance can be placed in future on Sinn Fein's influence with the IRA or on Sinn Fein assurances with regard to the IRA's future intentions. The bomb has damaged the credibility of all of us who urged people to put their trust in the commitment to peace of the movement which combines Sinn Fein and the IRA.'

The speech, written by Fianna Fail's chief conduit to the

Provisional movement, Martin Mansergh, was the most detailed critique of modern republicanism yet delivered and set out once and for all the Irish Republic's largest party's unambiguous position on Northern Ireland. In words which gave no comfort to Adams, Ahern told the Dail: 'While we consider that partition was a grave injustice and contrary to the principle of national self-determination, if it had been correctly observed at the time, we cannot ignore the lapse of time and treat Northern Ireland seventy-five years on as if it had never existed. Most of the Irish people, while they would like to see a United Ireland brought about in due course by peaceful means and agreement, have no wish to coerce an unwilling unionist majority into a United Ireland against their will . . .' Ahern then warned: 'The IRA, if it continues down its present path, will infallibly destroy the current peace process . . . If that violence goes on I predict they will ultimately destroy themselves and their movement, because without support among the Irish people they will not survive in the longer term.'

In the midst of the apportioning of blame the Irish politician who could claim the lion's share of the credit for securing the 1994 ceasefire made a relatively overlooked intervention. Albert Reynolds forsook his previous principled stand of refusing direct contact with the IRA's political wing while their violence continued to hold a meeting with Adams. At the end of it he declared his belief that if a definitive date was set for all-party talks then the IRA would immediately call another ceasefire.

It was such 'expert analysis' which no doubt persuaded Major to press on with efforts to convene peace negotiations, including Sinn Fein, even though by doing so he left himself open to jibes that when the IRA was on ceasefire he did nothing and when it returned to violence he acted. In spite of public outrage over the bombing he authorized further contacts between Martin McGuinness and Stormont officials, before which an IRA volunteer, Eddie O'Brien, blew himself up and seriously injured passengers on a London bus. A tribute in *An Phoblacht* said 'his daring and courage in assisting his comrades in carrying out a variety of attacks in the heartland of Britain's war machine did not go unnoticed'.

The meeting was a failure – the government wanted Sinn Fein to accept elections to all-party talks in return for a place at the table once the IRA restored its ceasefire. 'I'm afraid it appears that the British government is still not prepared to take risks for peace. I think the situation is very grave indeed,' McGuinness told reporters afterwards. In spite of his opposition the British and Irish governments agreed a formula which Dublin was still confident could bring Adams back in from the cold. Just twenty days after the IRA bombed Canary Wharf the two prime ministers unveiled their proposals, at the head of which was an immutable date of 10 June for the start of all-party talks. Major, in the face of unionist opposition, had given important ground to Adams, just as his former Irish counterpart Reynolds had urged. In return a complex voting system would lead to a new Northern Ireland Forum, lacking all real powers, to placate unionists. It would not be long before Adams' aides would be whispering in journalists' ears that Major had messed up yet again, giving the IRA hardliners the proof that violence was the only language the British understood.

As the signatures were drying on the Major/Bruton initiative, the SDLP leader John Hume was sitting down with Gerry Adams to meet representatives of the IRA leadership. Unionists were furious with Hume for bolstering Adams' image as being entirely separate from the IRA, even while security intelligence on both sides of the Irish border placed him still on its Army Council. To a Northern Ireland public, and more particularly the nationalist/Catholic population, desperate for peace, the fact that Hume, a life-long pacifist, was willing to lend his reputation to Adams did not go unnoticed. An IRA statement – which Major called 'a sick joke' – said the meeting was arranged at Hume and Adams' request. Later Adams said that he did not know if or when the IRA would restore its ceasefire but he was in favour of that course of action. He added that he had told the IRA of his 'sadness and regret' at the breakdown of the ceasefire. He claimed that he was told that the Army Council's credibility was on the line and that 'We sued for peace, the British wanted war. If that's what they want we will give them another twenty-five years of war.'

Hume confirmed that Adams had 'recommended' to the IRA that it restore its ceasefire. The IRA had observed a total silence during its seventeen-month ceasefire. Now hardly a day passed without a statement. On the day that McGuinness said he was prepared to go back to the IRA and ask for a new ceasefire if all preconditions to talks were abandoned, the IRA said it did not want 'military engagement' with loyalists, by now speaking openly of returning to their offensive. Within less than twenty-four hours another statement said there was a need for armed struggle 'given the current political conditions'. It continued: 'There will be no surrender of IRA weapons under any circumstances and to anyone. We will accept no preconditions whatsoever . . . We pursue armed struggle because of conditions in the six counties and the British claim to sovereignty in Ireland. We know the conflict has to be ended but this requires a real peace settlement. In that context we can live with the pursuance of republican objectives through unarmed political or social struggle.'

As Adams arrived in the United States for another support-seeking tour, the IRA confirmed that it had placed a bomb in a litter bin in the Earls Court district of West London, which caused some damage but no injuries. Adams found the five star treatment previously accorded to him by Americans no longer available, his fund-raising rights withdrawn and no invitation to the prestigious annual St Patrick's Day party at the White House. Even his former ally Senator Ted Kennedy, who kissed and embraced Adams upon his first arrival in Boston two years before, declined to meet him. Adams made do with the New York St Patrick's parade, and tried not to get drawn into the row over the organizer's refusal to let gays take part. Back in Ireland signs of an internal debate were allowed to be glimpsed when the republican paper *An Phoblacht* published a letter from a veteran IRA prisoner, Joe O'Connell. Writing from his cell in Full Sutton prison, England, O'Connell said the bombing of Canary Wharf was the 'most stupid, blinkered and ill-conceived decision ever made by a revolutionary body anywhere'.

With the prospect of the Forum/all-party-talks election only weeks away, it fell to Martin McGuinness to confirm Sinn Fein's participation, not wanting to leave the field clear for the SDLP. As he did so he made an admission that seriously embarrassed moderate nationalist leaders. Repudiating his comment that the 1994 IRA ceasefire would 'hold in all circumstances', McGuinness told BBC Radio Ulster that the cessation had never been permanent and anybody connected with the peace process had never been under any illusions about that. A few days later a bomb placed under London's Hammersmith Bridge, containing 30lb of Semtex, failed to detonate properly.

On 30 May Northern Ireland went to the polls, propelling Sinn Fein's vote to a record 15.5 per cent and bringing them, with seventeen seats, within snapping distance of the SDLP's twenty-one seats. In West Belfast Gerry Adams gobbled up more than half of all the votes cast and twice those of his SDLP rival Dr Joe Hendron, who only a week earlier had branded Sinn Fein a 'sectarian, fascist organization'. The SDLP accused Sinn Fein of massive vote-stealing organized with military precision, but the reality was that the peace process had brought Adams within touching distance of his ambition first stated in the early 1980s to supplant the moderate SDLP as the leading voice of Northern Ireland's Catholic nationalists. Sinn Fein beat the SDLP into second place in the sectarian cockpit of Mid-Ulster, pipped them in Fermanagh and South Tyrone, left them level-pegging in Newry and Armagh and in John Hume's Foyle fiefdom got Martin McGuinness and Mitchel McLaughlin elected. As one young female voter in Strabane said: 'I voted Sinn Fein but only because they need the encouragement of people like me to go for it. Come the general election I will be voting SDLP as usual.' That may have comforted many of the more sceptical SDLP stalwarts, now increasingly questioning Hume's strategy, but Adams knew that what had once been achieved could be repeated and even improved upon, so long as careful management of the peace process continued.

As 10 June drew nearer, ever more frantic efforts were being made by the two governments to reach a formula whereby the IRA would call a new ceasefire and permit Sinn Fein to enter the talks. Weekly meetings took place between Sinn Fein leaders and three of Dublin's most senior civil servants – Paddy Teahon, secretary of the Taoiseach's office, Tim Dalton, secretary of the Department of Justice, and Sean O hUiginn, head of the Department of Foreign Affairs Anglo-Irish Division. John Major published an article in Irish newspapers spelling out that he wanted Sinn Fein involved in the talks and that the agenda would be 'open', with nothing ruled in or out. President Clinton's special Irish envoy, the former US Senator George Mitchell, was given the role of talks chairman, as well as chairing the crucial subcommittee responsible for overseeing the best means of handling terrorist weaponry. The British government shifted on arms, now signing up to the idea that they should be discussed separately and in parallel with the political negotiations. While unionists vented their fury, one nationalist politician smugly observed: 'The conflict has been internationalized, there can be no going back now.'

The Anglo-Irish moves stoked up hopes that the IRA might call a new ceasefire to enable Sinn Fein to enter the all-party talks. But almost on the eve of the talks an IRA statement dashed those hopes.

In a call to the BBC's newsroom in Belfast an IRA spokesman said that a ceasefire was 'remote in the extreme . . . Let us nail completely the position on decommissioning. The IRA will not be decommissioning its weapons through either the front or the back doors. We will never leave nationalist areas defenceless this side of a final settlement.' The statement was delivered as British and Irish ministers were completing a marathon final session on how the talks would proceed, at which a hard-won agreement showed just how far both governments – and the SDLP – had moved since the days in 1993 when all sides were agreed that weapons would have to be given up before terrorist representatives could be involved in political peace negotiations.

But the governmental diplomacy appeared almost irrelevant when a Provisional IRA unit shot and murdered a Garda officer, Jerry McCabe, and seriously wounded another in a bungled cash raid in the picturesque village of Adare, County Limerick. In spite of the identity of at least one of the killers being known to the Irish police, the Provisionals denied involvement. While Dublin dithered in its response, senior Garda officers were making little secret of their anger. As news of the murder – the first time a police officer had been killed in the Republic in more than ten years – filtered out, Gerry Adams was attending what some journalists were moved to describe as a Nuremberg-style rally of Sinn Fein supporters at Belfast's Ulster Hall to celebrate their Forum election success. Young children dressed in black performed a Riverdance-type dance before Adams, to an appreciative roar, entered the hall in presidential style. Adams' speech gave few clues to the intentions of the IRA, concentrating instead on Sinn Fein's inexorable electoral rise. There would be no peace settlement if republicans were locked outside the talks. 'Unless Sinn Fein is in there, there can't be a peace settlement. For a long time our history has been frozen in a deep freezer of British policy. We know that the ice has yet to break, but the thaw has begun. Whatever ups and downs there are in this process, it is my conviction that we are going to have a peace settlement.'

He made no comment on the murder of Garda McCabe, but in a statement later he criticized 'a continuing political effort to link this killing with Sinn Fein's efforts to restore the peace process . . . It is clear that the killing at Adare can form no part in the republican struggle. On the contrary, actions such as those would be a disservice to that struggle. Those who are trying to use this killing to undermine Sinn Fein know this. In fact it is their political agenda. The IRA last Friday said that none of its volunteers or units were involved in the Adare incident. I accept that position.'

With the shadow of an IRA murder in Ireland hanging over it, the Stormont talks finally opened amid pomp and farce. The two governments were so nervous of unionist protests that at the last moment they decided not to provide a live television feed of the opening statements by Major and Bruton. Outside, Adams timed his arrival to make it on to the lunchtime television news bulletins. Almost swamped by a tide of international reporters the Sinn Fein president, accompanied by Martin McGuinness, Gerry Kelly and other key Sinn Fein personnel, walked slowly up to the gates of the talks venue to wrangle with an unlucky civil servant. 'We come as peace-builders,' he declared to the cameras, 'not to protest but to participate. We feel cheated that we have been denied the right to be part of a collective process to build peace.'

Four days later the Provisionals delivered what could only be regarded as their verdict on the talks in the loudest possible terms. A bomb, made of up to a ton and a half of fertilizer-based explosive, exploded in the heart of Manchester during the busy shopping period of Saturday morning. More than 200 people were injured, miraculously none was killed, and a square mile of the city centre devastated. The Irish Foreign Minister Dick Spring for the first time since August 1994 publicly questioned the merit of further relations with Sinn Fein. 'We always felt we were dealing with people who were trying to bring the IRA into democratic politics, but now . . . we don't know who we're dealing with,' he said.

The signals in Belfast were confusing. In a four-paragraph statement Adams did not even refer to the bombing and made a call for 'inclusive dialogue'. A number of media outlets received calls from apparent IRA dissidents claiming that the Army Council no longer had the confidence of key areas and units. 'We have called on them to stand down, we're not happy with them, they've short-changed us. The Manchester attack wasn't sanctioned by them,' an anonymous caller told the Press Association. While the bombing at first sight seemed to have been organized without the usual methodical delivery expected of the IRA, security sources in Belfast, London and Dublin all discounted theories that a split was emerging. Indeed, the prevailing view was that more violence should be expected, since the IRA was determined to avoid a split.

Many also noted that the huge bomb attack took place after Sinn Fein's electoral campaign was safely concluded. If the republican movement was genuinely split, some argued, then surely the dissidents would show their hand at a time most calculated to damage the 'politicians'? If a further illustration of the Provisionals' twin-track strategy was needed, one only had to cast one's mind back a month to the Sunday on which Martin McGuinness sent doveish signals via the Jonathan Dimbleby programme, when he said he believed the IRA was 'open to persuasion' if the decommissioning obstacle could be surmounted. Within the same hour, however, another leading Provisional, the Belfast bomber Brian Keenan, was delivering an altogther different message to supporters gathered at the Belfast graveside of IRA volunteers. Keenan told them not to be confused by the politics of the situation 'The only decommissioning republicans will accept is of the British state in Ireland . . . we will have our victory.'

A further piece of evidence to suggest the duplicity of republicans was the emergence of the true title of an internal briefing document which had been deliberately leaked a year earlier. The typed document was entitled 'TUAS', under which an unknown hand had written 'totally unarmed strategy'. By the early stages of 1996 at least one senior Provisional in Dublin was telling reporters this was false and urging them to discover the true meaning. Eventually Ed Moloney of the Dublin *Sunday Tribune*, who had originally unveiled the TUAS document, revealed its true title: 'Tactical Use of Armed Struggle'. Rather than meaning that the Provisional movement had abandoned violence as a political weapon for all time, the document's real title suggested that bombs and murders were still part of the republican strategy, to be used in a more focused way, so that if the political route towards British withdrawal appeared to be flagging then a judiciously targeted attack might force the UK government to 'face up to its responsibilities'.

This was the grimmest of scenarios, for in these circumstances all confidence in peace negotiations involving Sinn Fein would be fatally undermined. Yet the evidence provided by Manchester suggested it was so. Those who were not prepared to give up entirely on the peace process and enjoyed the occasional confidence of senior republicans were encouraged to believe that, like the two-headed Janus figure of Greek mythology, the leadership had no choice but to sell the strategy to two different constituencies. Thus the hardline grassroots would be reassured that there was no sell-out of traditional republican principles but at the same time Sinn Fein's powerful new allies would not be frightened off. According to this version, once the talks began to gather pace and an irreversible momentum towards a political settlement was in train, both meanings of the document would be rendered obsolete.

This was certainly the view taken of the meaning of TUAS by Albert Reynolds, who maintained his contacts with the republicans after his fall from power. 'Which is right? Did you ever get it confirmed either way? You will find sources that will tell you one and sources that will tell you the other. Is this part of the internal debate? I think it means both ... I may be wrong. This is one of the crunch issues when they come to it where everything will be done to avoid a split, to avoid a split they create this fudge ... a very clever way of doing it. I'm not satisfied that it was ever intended to be one or the other.'

Whatever the machinations of the republican movement, Adams was exposed to media and political scrutiny as never before in the days after Manchester. What everyone wanted to know – what they had wanted to know for decades – was 'What is the precise relationship between the IRA and Sinn Fein?' 'I have told you, we are not the IRA and the IRA is not Sinn Fein,' he told reporters gathered at a training centre in West Belfast. Is there any relationship? 'I have told you, we are not the IRA and the IRA is not Sinn Fein.' If he refused to condemn the Manchester bombing, did that mean that, to use his own phrase, he supported 'armed actions'? 'Sinn Fein's manifesto is very clear, we have a peace strategy. That's the basis on which we received a negotiating mandate when we stood in the elections,' he said, now visibly sweating as he strained to keep his language neutral and to the narrow path upon which neither IRA supporters nor democrats could be offended.

But then he was asked the big question: did the IRA respect the mandate that he was forever claiming on behalf of Sinn Fein? 'That's a question I'm not going to get into,' he stumbled. 'The reality is that the people who voted for us voted for an inclusive process of dialogue and for a negotiated settlement ...' The answers were insufficient to satisfy anybody, least of all those in Dublin who had invested so much in the peace process. The Irish cabinet decided to pose two specific questions: had he yet gone to the IRA to ask for another ceasefire and, if not, why not? And did his party support the armed struggle of the IRA? The answers must be 'simple, genuine and convincing, not tactical nor semantic', a spokesman said.

The following day an interview with Irish radio hinted at the depths of the struggle of ideas taking place within the republican movement. Adams said Sinn Fein wanted 'to see an end to the armed struggle . . . we're not involved in it and we do not advocate it', but he understood how in certain conditions armed actions were seen as legitimate: 'That has been the international experience . . . The reality of the situation is that there was no armed struggle for a year and a half. The reality of the situation is that those of us who were trying to move the process forward were slapped in the face by the British government.' Admitting that he now accepted that the IRA had murdered Garda Jerry McCabe and then lied about it, he said: 'I believe that it should not have happened and the news that individual IRA volunteers were involved makes it even worse from my perspective. I wish that the bomb had not happened in Manchester. I wish that there weren't British soldiers on the streets of the six counties. I wish there wasn't discrimination. I wish there hadn't been unionist domination. I wish that our island wasn't partitioned. But the reality is that we deal with the objective situation and the conditions which exist in making peace. And making peace is very difficult.'

He accepted that it was his responsibility, along with others, to try to end the violence. 'The question, I think, in terms of what the IRA can or should do is one which obviously I am working at and will continue to work at.' Asked if he had indeed 'gone to the IRA for a ceasefire', he replied: 'I don't think it's helpful for me to speculate about exactly where that is at this time.' The interview was followed a day later by an IRA statement issued in Dublin which 'sincerely regretted' the injuries caused in Manchester and hinted at the possibility of a renewed ceasefire. An IRA bomb factory was discovered in County Laois, west of Dublin, and three men charged.

On the same day the RUC Chief Constable Sir Hugh Annesley, delivering his final annual report before retiring in the autumn, predicted more IRA bombs in the short term but sounded confident that the Troubles were into the endgame. A very serious debate was being conducted in republican ranks over whether the future was to be war or politics. 'It's extremely difficult to read, I simply do not know what they will do tomorrow. They might call a ceasefire tomorrow, in a week, a month or two years. Part of that is because they are unsure themselves.' Sir Hugh said that the IRA and Sinn Fein were unquestionably linked and that the two major figures were Gerry Adams and Martin McGuinness:

> I do not see this artificial distinction that's being drawn. I believe Messrs Adams and McGuinness are very, very influential people and I think they have a major say in the conduct overall of the republican thrust. There are of course other members on the Army Council and it seems that those not arguing for a resumption [of the ceasefire] may from day to day just be marginally in the majority.
>
> The difficulty is it seems to move from day to day. There are people in Sinn Fein who devote themselves solely to politics but the control of the movement at the top is clearly linked. There are members of Provisional Sinn Fein on the Army Council and there are members of the Army Council on the political talks level of Sinn Fein.

Sir Hugh was demonstrating that he was just as nimble with the English language as Gerry Adams, always stopping just short of placing the Sinn Fein president in a commanding role within the IRA, even though privately the police view on both sides of the border was that Adams had been an Army Council member since the late 1970s.

But he added that he did not believe Adams and McGuinness could themselves deliver an IRA ceasefire. 'You would need another two or three to come along with them. That can change, because people talk about the seven-member Army Council, but other people can be co-opted, so it is isn't often a straight vote. I think they play the situation as it's going and they're not sure which way to go.' As for a split, 'I don't think the IRA's going to split and I think they would go to enormous lengths to ensure that it did not split. I have no doubt significant sections of the Army Council want peace. I think the difficulty is that some have been associated with violence for so long they don't trust the British, they don't trust the unionists and now they're at loggerheads with the Americans. I do not see a split in those terms [Adams and McGuinness leaving the IRA behind] and you could potentially see more violence rather than have a split.'

Sir Hugh Annesley had accurately predicted the return of violence to Northern Ireland, but the quarter from which it came in the summer of 1996 may have been surprising. The Siege of Drumcree from the previous July, for which commemorative medals had been struck by the victorious Orangemen, returned to haunt Ulster. But if the RUC professed to have been taken unawares by the ferocity of loyalist resistance to the police refusal to allow them to march down the mainly Catholic Garvaghy Road, few civilian or paramilitary Protestants were in any doubt that Drumcree '96 was to be a turning point, a line in the sand.

The extent of the resistance was swiftly felt as the RUC buckled under the pressure of nightly riots in Belfast, roadblocks across the province, the blockading of Northern Ireland's international airport and the steadily growing numbers lining the barbed wire outside Drumcree church itself. Dissident loyalist terrorists from Mid-Ulster murdered Michael McGoldrick, a Catholic taxi driver with no republican connections, in Lurgan, just a few miles from Portadown. The murder led to the expulsion of Ulster Volunteer Force members by the Belfast leadership. On the fifth day of the siege and after talks led by church leaders failed to reach a compromise, the RUC performed a U-turn and facilitated the Orange march down the Garvaghy Road. As one senior police officer critical of Sir Hugh commented: 'He made the wrong decision and then he made the wrong decision.' The force's morale and reputation was in tatters, to the delight of Sinn Fein members, who gloated at the immediate reversal in their fortunes. In the world's eyes Northern Ireland was once again an Orange state where the Catholics had their civil rights trampled into the ground.

The U-turn prompted a nationalist backlash, with widespread and ferocious rioting. In Derry a man was killed in clashes with the Army. In Belfast Adams made an appeal for nationalists to respond in a restrained and disciplined manner. Three hours later a group of militants who said they were disgusted by his comments hijacked an Ulster Television van on the Falls Road and set it alight. 'That's the only way to move the republican struggle forward,' said one of them.

The Belfast IRA ordered pubs and off-licences to close in West Belfast in an attempt to prevent after-hours rioting and senior members stood by at flashpoint areas to break up trouble. The *Irish Times* reported that 'the situation was particularly volatile in Andersonstown where IRA "lieutenants" were involved in a serious confrontation with their own lower echelons who wanted to riot. It nearly ended in a fight. A compromise allowed the grassroots activists to burn a few vehicles.' Sinn Fein also contacted the RUC through intermediaries and the force agreed to keep a low profile in the area. Earlier in the week one of Adams' closest allies, Tom Hartley, was forced to abandon a speech he was trying to make in the Lower Falls when he was nearly attacked. It fell to Gerry Kelly to restore order, which he managed with some difficulty.

As the Irish Taoiseach John Bruton and the Catholic Primate of Ireland Cahal Daly joined in accusing the British authorities of failing to handle the policing of Orange parades with impartiality, Adams gave his verdict. 'I want to say clearly that the peace process lies in absolute ruins. The responsibility for that and the responsibility for restoring it also lies with John Major,' he said.

British government officials and unionist politicians strongly suspected that far from trying to avert the Drumcree crisis Sinn Fein had been actively working to ensure that Northern Ireland would go up in flames and in so doing take the pressure off the republican movement to restore its ceasefire. Drumcree, in this view, could be seen as an extension of the 'marching feet and angry voices' stategy which Adams had first enunciated during the ceasefire. Evidence to support that view finally came many months later from, of all places, the flagship current affairs programme of the Irish Republic's Radio Telefis Eireann, *Prime Time*, which had obtained a speech given later in the year by Adams at an internal Sinn Fein conference. Adams said: 'Ask any activist in the North, did Drumcree happen by accident and they will tell you "no". Three years of work on the Lower Ormeau Road, Portadown and parts of Fermanagh and Newry, Armagh and in Bellaghy and up in Derry. Three years of work went into creating that situation and fair play to those people who put the work in. They are the type of scene changes that we have to focus on and develop and exploit.' The programme said it was 'clear evidence that Sinn Fein is behind the protest'. Adams reacted angrily but did not dispute the version of his comments. The Orange Order noted that in the key places where a residents group had sprung up to oppose its parades, the leading spokesman was a convicted IRA figure. Just as hardline loyalists treated the civil rights movement of the late 1960s as a cover for the IRA, their attitude to the residents groups had not moved on after almost thirty years.

In a sense they were right, but not in a way that they wished to understand. It was true that some former IRA activists were now channelling their energies into community-based activities without forsaking the republican principles which they once held as active service volunteers. But Adams was trying to demonstrate that there was another, more successful way than the failed policy of armed struggle, hence his increasing references to the old civil rights movement. His problem – and it wasn't a new one – was that in order to convince the hardliners he had to produce tangible results. This was to be civil rights with a harder edge and to many observers of the peace process it simply did not add up.

On the one hand Adams was reaching out in his many speeches and statements to his 'Protestant brothers and sisters,' while on the other he was encouraging confrontation with them. Many moderate Protestants were confused; surely if republicans were serious about peace they would use the ceasefire to encourage the building up of trust between the two communities with acts of generosity rather than fostering further polarization? Imagine the transformation of the political atmosphere if Sinn Fein had been publicly and privately working to get the Garvaghy Road residents to welcome the Porta-down Orangemen, on the understanding that an act of generosity deserved another in return.

If Adams was serious about this new direction then it was a welcome development but hardly evidence of new thinking. It was uncannily reminiscent of the path which the 1960s IRA chief of staff Cathal Goulding had attempted to take, an endeavour which had failed because of the opposition of hardliners like Adams himself. The best that could be said of the present Sinn Fein president Gerry Adams in these circumstances was that he had finally seen the error of his ways, in which case, what had the last twenty-six years been about? Had more than 3,000 people been killed in a conflict based on a pursuit of a United Ireland which Adams now understood was unat-tainable? And if he did believe that, as his opponents – once comrades – in the hardline Republican Sinn Fein, his nervous allies in the Dublin government, Washington and the SDLP all thought, at what point in time had Gerry Adams made that leap of the imagination?

After the events of Drumcree, the peace process looked as if it was beyond repair. A bomb destroyed the Killyhevlin Hotel in Enniskillen, County Fermanagh. Attributed to the Continuity Army Council of the IRA, widely believed to be the military wing of Republican Sinn Fein, it demonstrated that if the Provisionals were having doubts about the merits of the armed struggle there were others eager and willing to fill the vacuum. A boycott of Protestant businesses in country areas by Catholics led to further bitterness and the closure of several long-established shops. Robert Rainey, a thirty-three-year-old father of two young daughters, finally shut up his butcher's business in the Tyrone village of Pomeroy after months of waiting in an empty shop for his regular customers to return. 'It's been very well organized by Sinn Fein/IRA. I've customers who've told me they have been threatened with getting their cars burned or beaten up if they go into my shop,' he said.

As the atmosphere worsened in Northern Ireland John Major was seen as no longer operating the impartiality which once brought him a rousing reception in the staunchly nationalist border town of Newry. He met and shook hands with John White, a member of the Ulster Democratic Party, which is linked to the illegal Ulster Defence Association. White is a convicted double murderer who stabbed to death a popular SDLP Stormont senator, Paddy Wilson, and his girlfriend in what was described in court as a frenzied attack. The meeting closely followed the murder of Catholic taxi driver Michael McGoldrick and a hoax bomb alert in Dublin. At a time when the loyalist ceasefire looked close to breaking down, Gerry Adams could only observe with bitterness that Major's constant refusal to meet him had contributed to the IRA's return to war.

By mid-September security sources on both sides of the Irish border were briefing that a General Army Convention, the supreme body of the IRA, was expected in the near future. The last such gathering took place in 1986 when Adams was campaigning to get abstention from the Dail lifted and which precipitated a split in the movement. Garda and RUC sources speculated that the convention would elect a new IRA executive, the body which in turn selects a new Army Council and chief of staff, but more importantly it would debate the issue of a new ceasefire. The discontent within the grassroots over the way in which the 1994 ceasefire had been imposed was going to be avoided in the event of another cessation. 'Those in favour of a new cessation are in the ascendant but the hardliners who favour continuation of an armed campaign could equally swing a convention,' said a Garda source. Adams dismissed the reports. Echoing a phrase he had used a week before the IRA declared its 1994 ceasefire he told reporters, 'It's the first I've heard of it,' and added 'You have to ask why British military intelligence are putting out these speculative reports. It's to cause confusion in republican ranks and it's not helpful.'

While the speculation mounted the IRA suffered a severe blow to its England bombing campaign when five terrorist suspects were arrested and an IRA man was shot dead in London. The police raids also netted ten tons of home-made fertilizer-based explosive, prepared car bombs, timers, Semtex and vehicles. It was proof that the IRA was intent on launching another major offensive in England and a major setback to those who still believed that the only language the British government understood was the sound of large bombs exploding in the City of London.

Perhaps it was the stunning blow to their prospects of mounting an offensive in England which finally prompted the Provisionals to end their ceasefire at home. On 8 October a bomb exploded without warning inside the grounds of the British Army's headquarters in Northern Ireland at Thiepval Barracks, Lisburn. Fifteen minutes later, as the injured were being ferried to a medical centre and civilians working at the base tried to find safety a second device exploded. The clear intention was to kill as many as possible. Miraculously only one soldier died. Warrant Officer James Bradwell, a career soldier with three children aged fourteen, sixteen and twenty-three, was only two months into his first ever tour of duty in Ulster. He died exactly as the bombers wanted: caught in the first blast, he was fatally injured in the second explosion. The IRA had restored its morale with an audacious attack at the very heart of the British 'military machine' in Ireland and one which exposed serious security deficiencies at Thiepval. But a terrible and potentially final blow had been paid to Gerry Adams' peace process.

The Irish Taoiseach John Bruton compared the Provisionals to the Nazis. 'The Irish state cannot be hostage to tactical manoeuvres by a violent movement that is only willing to give up the option of violence if it gets the terms that it has dictated to everyone else. Those are the classic tactics of the National Socialists and fascists during the

1920s and 1930s.' John Major used the attack to maximum effect at his party's annual conference in Bournemouth, addressing Adams directly. 'For many months Sinn Fein leaders have mouthed the word peace. Warrant Officer James Bradwell was forty-three with a wife and with children, Mr Adams. He joined the Army prepared to lose his life defending the British nation. Soldiers do. But he was murdered in cold blood in the United Kingdom. I sent him there, Mr Adams, so spare me any crocodile tears. Don't tell me this has nothing to do with you. I don't believe you, Mr Adams, I don't believe you.'

When the IRA met it was not for a full army convention but for a caucus meeting of command groups, a battalion-level gathering according to security sources in the Republic, where the leadership structure was overhauled in order to impose a stronger political direction. The intended effect was to undermine attempts by hard-liners to move the organization back on to a military footing and to put strategy firmly in the hands of senior Sinn Fein figures acting in their capacity as IRA leaders. On each side of the border the security view was that Adams remained a key figure across both wings of the movement. A new chief of staff was appointed, a veteran South Armagh IRA militant.

The new RUC Chief Constable, Ronnie Flanagan, concurred with the Taoiseach John Bruton that over the first weekend in November the IRA had been going through a serious rethink of strategy. 'I think there may have been a meeting of some sort. There is an internal debate going on into the exact nature and structure of the republican movement's future,' he said. 'There are those in the republicans who realize that even though they can carry on perpetrating attacks for another twenty-five years, it probably does not progress them towards achievement of their objectives. It doesn't mean they are morally reformed. It doesn't mean they believe violence is morally wrong.'

While the name remained unspoken it seemed clear that the Chief Constable was talking about Adams, a man who now found himself in similar circumstances to those experienced by his first chief of staff Cathal Goulding. A lot of hopes were riding on Adams. Two weeks later at Sinn Fein's internal conference in Athboy, County Meath, Adams spelt out the political realities and strategy to senior and middle-ranking Provisionals. 'We all understand why we have to deal with Fianna Fail,' he said. 'We all understand why we have to deal with the SDLP. It would be far better if we were bigger than them, we could ignore them. It would be far better that we were in a better situation than both of them on this island.'

He went back to John Hume and the two men began work once more on the conditions for a renewal of the IRA ceasefire. Hume's contribution was once again to act as intermediary, shuffling backwards and forwards down the channels of communication to British and Irish officials. When word leaked out about the meetings, neither man was willing to say much. 'The least said sometimes on these matters the better,' commented Adams on a report that the government were about to publish a statement outlining their conditions for admitting Sinn Fein to all-party talks in the event of a new ceasefire.

It was Adams who had renewed the contact, with the approval of the IRA's Army Council, in order to spell out their terms. These became known as the 'Hume/Adams Mark II paper', with its four key demands for immediate entry into talks, the dropping of prior decommissioning, a talks time-frame and confidence-building measures such as the release of prisoners. There was little sign from Major, now nearing the end of his government term, that the proposals held any attraction for him. Nevertheless he was prepared to make one final offer to Adams for the restoration of the peace process. The new Hume/Adams had crossed his desk. In a few days' time he would deliver his verdict.

Adams claimed to know the answer in advance. In a briefing to selected journalists at the Felons Club, the drinking and social club established by his father, he gave a depressing résumé of the situation. He said that he had verified on more than one occasion that what the British required was 'an unequivocal restoration of the IRA ceasefire, *sin e*'. All that was being asked was for the IRA to restore its August 1994 cessation. Adams said that it would be impossible to persuade the IRA unless the British dropped their demand for a weapons surrender. 'An IRA leadership would be laughed out of office if there was a restoration and then two months later the Brits said, "Now . . . [it's time to deliver some guns]",' he said. The leadership would leave itself open to criticism that it should have boxed the issue off beforehand. As for the broader picture: 'My personal view is that, for whatever reason, the unionists don't want change and John Major isn't prepared to preside over that change.' The British had received the new Hume/Adams proposals six weeks earlier and Adams wondered if they were waiting for the next IRA operation. 'Is this a hand being played very slowly, playing it down to the wire?'

'This government hasn't yet brought its mind round to the idea of a negotiated settlement, because that means that nobody can win,' he said, before ruling out his party's entry into the talks process as envisaged by Major. The Prime Minister wanted an immediate IRA ceasefire so that Sinn Fein could use the period of the Christmas break to complete their 'purdah' – a matter of weeks in which to demonstrate to a sceptical world that the cessation was 'genuinely unequivocal' – and join the other parties up at Stormont when they resumed in the New Year. Adams said he thought one week was reasonable, 'but if everyone is off for Christmas eating turkey and Sinn Fein is up there eating humble pie, that's not acceptable'.

In spite of the impasse he was keen to stress to the journalists that there would be no change in direction. 'They can only postpone, they can't cancel. The Sinn Fein strategy, in my view, is at this point the single biggest focus of the party and will continue to be so. There are new concepts in that for republicans, of course.' A lot of anger too, he reflected. 'The summer hasn't been good.' But he cast his mind back to the funerals of IRA volunteers a decade earlier, when sometimes only a sparse attendance could be mustered and the RUC was giving them a hard time. 'If it doesn't work this time we have to go back and be resilient and pick up the pieces and go at it again.' Adams thought it was remarkable that he had brought the process back once more to its present stage after the Manchester bombing. 'We brought the IRA to a position in August 1994 that they probably didn't envisage in July 1994.' Turning to the loyalist ceasefire, he did not hide his contempt. 'The loyalists are at best the dodgy wing of the establishment. They want their prisoners out, that's it. The status quo as it is. You also have to watch who's the Brit agent in there, so I'm not surprised it has held.' As for the Continuity Army Council, 'they are obviously having a go at the Brits and obviously don't have the wherewithal to go at it. Killyhevlin [the Enniskillen hotel which was blown up] I believe was dirty tricks.'

Returning to his party Adams said he was of the view 'that our biggest aid to ending British rule is our increasing political strength. The job of getting a political settlement will necessarily be tortuous, tedious and up and down.' He saw the election of David Trimble as the Ulster Unionist leader as a lurch to the right. 'We have been talking to more unionists in the last eighteen months than we have done in the previous eighteen years. There has to be more fight-back from liberal unionists. The only incentive for them is that it's for real.' He was not concerned about a unionist walkout if Sinn Fein were allowed in to the talks. 'It will take time, unionists will go in and out as they see fit.' Although he was pushing for a time-frame of between six and twelve months he admitted that he did not envisage the process being wrapped up in that time.

Growing expansive, he made the seemingly outlandish claim that he had spoken with Sir Patrick Mayhew 'on many occasions and you might think it difficult to imagine us as intimate but we did spell out how you build confidence without giving up your own position . . . I have never believed that this is an intractable conflict. Some people have said it was the wrong time, the wrong British government. Perhaps it could have been done five years, ten years earlier. Twenty years ago I wouldn't have even thought of it.' He smiled briefly. Pushed on whether the IRA would call another ceasefire he responded: 'There's no point in trying to persuade an IRA that was not defeated in 1994 and is clearly not now to call another cessation in these circumstances. Everything can be finessed up to a point but we're not even sitting down with British officials.' But he ducked direct questions about why the IRA was stockpiling weapons in London in the spring of 1995 when the ceasefire was still in its infancy. 'To the best of my knowledge the IRA wasn't doing any of those things, intelligence gathering, targeting. I went and checked it two or three times because I thought it was stupid.'

One journalist put it to him that the strategy of the bomb and the bullet would never bring about a United Ireland. Adams replied: 'I would never admit to anybody in a republican family what you have just said.' Summing up, he said: 'I don't foresee any unilateral IRA cessation – the dynamic and the mood isn't there for it.' His final words made him sound as if he too was in a strange way a prisoner of the IRA, its past, present and future, a movement which would only release its grip once its historical objective had been achieved and which did not really take into account the individual, whether they were volunteers, opponents or even passive bystanders. The cause was self-justifying enough to sustain any amount of pain indefinitely. 'In the fullness of time, God knows how many years' time, if an IRA leadership, and God knows it might become more hardline, decides to dump arms . . . well, I think that the situation is that the IRA is undefeatable . . . it is just impossible in this situation.' The only outcome, he seemed to be saying, which would end the pain on all sides was a British withdrawal. 'This summer just gone has probably created the dynamic for the IRA to fight on for the next two generations.'

A few days later John Major launched his final, pre-doomed attempt to restore the peace process. The devil was in the detail and much of the language was deliberately borrowed from Sinn Fein's style book. There was no longer a demand for a 'permanent' ceasefire, as Albert Reynolds had once demanded and believed he had secured. Instead it was to be 'genuinely unequivocal, i.e. lasting and not simply a tactical device'. Adams also got his 'indicative time-frame', but where the package fell apart was where it stated that 'sufficient time' would have to elapse before Sinn Fein was welcomed inside Castle Buildings. That open-ended phrase raised the fearful prospect of another indefinite period of decontamination.

Adams accused Major of sabotaging his and John Hume's efforts to achieve a settlement. Hume announced angrily: 'If he had a clear majority we would have had peace in Ireland quite some time ago.' The truth was that Major had indeed moved in Sinn Fein's direction, but only so far as his dependency on the Ulster Unionists and his own personal instincts allowed him. He shared the view of his Irish counterpart John Bruton that the Provisionals were not serious about accepting democratic norms and were prepared to run with politics only while it paid to do so. The moment at which Adams ran up against the brick wall of consent, the IRA would be letting bombs off again in the British capital.

As Major was delivering his final offer the IRA was manoeuvring one of the largest bombs ever seen in Northern Ireland towards an Army base close to Armagh city: 2,500lb of home-made explosive had been set on top of a trailer, which had to be abandoned because its sheer weight had buried the wheels in the soft ground. That weekend the old faithful were gathering around Adams' former comrade Ruairi O Bradaigh in Dublin at the annual conference of Republican Sinn Fein. O Bradaigh's criticisms of Adams had become increasingly forthright; the peace process, it seemed, had left him unrestrained. 'The Provisionals are in no-man's land. We said in 1986 that he was going to try and ride two horses that would be leading in different directions. To have an underground military revolutionary organization and above ground a constitutional political party which has totally different priorities means all the pigeons are coming home to roost now. It has worked itself out to its inevitable conclusion.'

Adams could content himself with the knowledge that O Bradaigh was still only able to attract a small, generally older fringe, even if he could not shrug off the public attacks so lightly. In fact O Bradaigh was only saying what every other party in Ireland felt: Adams could not go on leading a 'slightly constitutional party', demanding real negotiations one day and refusing to condemn the latest IRA atrocity the next. The time was fast approaching, if it had not already passed, when he would have to choose.

A few days before Christmas the Provos launched one of the most sickening attacks in years when they tried to murder Nigel Dodds, a leading light in Paisley's Democratic Unionist Party, as he and his wife visited their child who was seriously ill in the intensive-care unit of the Royal Children's Hospital on the Falls Road. Two IRA men wearing wigs were spotted by plainclothes police officers guarding Dodds and his family. Shots were fired, one of which left a bullet hole in an incubator and another of which injured one of the RUC men. Even though it represented a new low in terrorism Adams refused to condemn the attack.

On New Year's Eve 400 guests at a wedding reception had to be cleared from Belfast Castle in the north of the city when the IRA abandoned a 1,000lb bomb in its grounds. The RUC accused the Provisionals of attempted mass murder and claimed that their plan was to lure security force members into its killing range before detonating the device. Six days later the IRA fired a PRIG – propelled rocket improvised grenade – at the High Court building in Belfast city centre, the first such attack in years. An RUC officer was treated for his injuries. Adams gave his response a few hours later: 'The genie in many ways is back out of the bottle. I want to see that rectified. I think we will still be able, when all of the main players focus their attention, to bring about a negotiated settlement. In the meantime we are living once again in dangerous times.'

CHAPTER TWENTY-NINE

An Honourable Member Again

If there was a sense that time was running out for Adams as 1997 dawned it was greatly sharpened when the SDLP leader John Hume finally broke his policy of offering tacit support to the Sinn Fein leader in the pages of the Irish *Sunday Independent*, a paper which had in the past been critical of their nationalist double act. The spur for the article was the impending Westminster and local government elections, for which Sinn Fein had been urging an electoral pact with the SDLP. If the nationalists joined forces they could sweep all the unionist representatives west of the River Bann clear off the board, the clearest evidence yet that, with the demographic shifts taking place in Northern Ireland, the polarization of the two communities and the 'white flight' scenario which saw Protestants moving in ever increasing numbers to the east of the province, real change was coming.

Hume had been under pressure from the more sceptical wing of his party ever since the IRA ended its ceasefire at Canary Wharf to rethink his association with militant nationalism. In Belfast the party was in a state of near panic as the hardening of community divisions after Drumcree threatened their traditionally dominant moderate constituency. Many ordinary SDLP-voting Catholics had 'lent' their vote to Sinn Fein at the Forum election in May 1996 to encourage them towards the political path. Now it appeared that some were doubtful about returning to their traditional representatives, particularly since Sinn Fein was so much more youthful and dynamic than the staid, well-meaning, middle class types who ran the SDLP. One of the reasons for this discrepancy in energy levels was that most Sinn Fein activists were effectively working full-time for the movement, living on the weekly state handouts of the government they wished to see removed from Ireland.

So it was that Hume revealed his price for entering an electoral pact with Sinn Fein: Adams must dump the central republican tenet of not taking their seats in the Westminster parliament. 'What exactly is the motivation of those who insist on fighting for seats in a parliament they do not recognise – seats which they refuse to take if they won them?' said the article bearing Hume's name but which in reality had been written by committee. 'Is their concern really to maximise nationalist representation or is it rather to win partisan advantage within the nationalist community by exploiting nationalist frustration? Is their real target unionism or is it the SDLP – and if it is the latter how does that fit into their expressed desire for a consensus among Irish nationalists?'

Adams responded angrily, his first comments containing the implict threat that Hume's article 'marks the beginning of the British general election campaign between our two parties'. He claimed that the refusal to swear an oath of allegiance to the English Queen had not prevented Sinn Fein from representing its electorate. While the rest of his party entered the fray with gusto – a Belfast SDLP councillor successfully challenging the electoral register in West Belfast where in one instance thirteen adults were registered to vote at one address – Hume returned to his quiet diplomacy.

On the first anniversary of the Canary Wharf bomb the IRA briefed RTE and BBC journalists in Dublin. Stressing its continued support for the Adams/McGuinness leadership, the spokesperson dismissed press speculation that a 'phoney war' was being waged, in spite of the long list of failed, aborted or botched attacks. Because there was no evidence of a change of heart by the British a ceasefire before the Westminster election was 'most unlikely'. The focus was now on the elections and the SDLP continued its somewhat belated attempt to regain lost ground. A BBC Northern Ireland documentary revealed details of widespread electoral malpractice. Among the charges was that Adams' chief bodyguard Terence 'Cleeky' Clarke was registered to vote in several addresses across the city.

The Provisionals' border sniping campaign returned when Lance Bombardier Stephen Restorick, a twenty-three-year-old single man from Peterborough, was shot dead by a single high-velocity round while checking a woman's driving licence at a checkpoint in the South Armagh village of Bessbrook. Lorraine McIlroy was grazed by the same bullet which killed the soldier:

The soldier took the licence off me and was smiling and handed it back to me. When it happened I don't even think he had the licence out of his hand. There was what I would describe as a flash and a crack and there was blood pouring from my head.

I hear the soldier groaning. He was on the ground but there was nothing I could do. The hospital is only down the road but the journey was probably the most horrific thing I've ever endured because I was watching a young man dying. I just wanted to hold him because he was so alone and he was dying. So often you hear on the news that a soldier was shot, but he was a man, a young man, a person. He was smiling at me when it happened. He was just there and so nice and somebody killed him. Last night all I could think of was his face smiling at me. My heart just breaks for his family.

Sinn Fein refused to condemn the killing, calling it a tragedy which could have been avoided.

If the horror following the killing had not been so great more might have been made of the bitter irony that whereas Mrs McIlroy, a native of South Armagh, had only words of contempt for the IRA and Sinn Fein, the parents of the soldier issued what sounded almost like a Sinn Fein statement. The best monument to their son would be that all the political parties finally sat down together and agreed a common future. 'All parties have got to talk, there's no point excluding anybody,' said John Restorick. In Northern Ireland a common view was that Mrs McIlroy, a distant cousin of the convicted IRA bomber Donna Maguire, understood the Provisionals better than the English grief-consumed parents of a murdered soldier. But in any case Mrs McIlroy suddenly no longer had an opinion to offer and did not even attend a commemoration in the village to which the dead man's parents came. The word in the neighbourhood was that she had been told by republicans to keep her opinions to herself.

While John Hume continued his policy of not attacking Adams personally he returned to the fray in print. In the Belfast nationalist daily the *Irish News* an article in his name confirmed the reason why there could be no electoral pact between the SDLP and Sinn Fein: 'It would be the equivalent of asking our voters to support the killing of innocent human beings by the IRA.' Hume asked *Irish News* readers, traditionally supporters of the SDLP, to consider the impact on Irish citizens south of the border 'if northern nationalists were seen to throw in their lot with the movement that murdered [Garda detective] Jerry McCabe and so many other innocent people.' And he suggested, perhaps mischievously, the need for a time-frame for his talks with Gerry Adams about a ceasefire. 'It would be unreasonable to expect me and my party to go on, month in month out, going over the same arguments endlessly.'

Some voters, Hume said, thought that at the Forum election they could have the luxury of voting for Sinn Fein to encourage the IRA to make peace and tell John Major they wanted inclusive talks. 'The result was that the republican movement claimed an increased mandate for their strategy and within weeks they had broken their *de facto* ceasefire in the North, threatening to plunge us back into a full-scale resumption of violence.' As the election campaign got under way the opposition Labour Party's spokesperson on Northern Ireland Mo Mowlam offered Sinn Fein a place in talks within three months if the IRA immediately restored its ceasefire. Although the suggestion was in substance no different to what John Major had put forward before Christmas, Adams told a republican rally it was 'very encouraging'.

At an Easter rally in Ardoyne, the hardline republican enclave in North Belfast, two balaclava-wearing IRA members suddenly appeared among supporters waving semi-automatic rifles aloft. Sinn Fein councillor Francie Molloy said it was 'fitting that we had the presence of the IRA on our streets, the defenders of our people over the last twenty-five to thirty years'. Molloy continued: 'The road ahead is two-pronged. We go down the road to negotiations and settlement or the British government could take it down the road to conflict.'

When the IRA forced the cancellation of the Grand National at Aintree, one of the world's best-loved horse races, it was a classic example of the power of a terrorist codeword. All it needed was for a volunteer to ring a news station with a recognized codeword to cause havoc. Over the next few weeks the IRA proceeded to do just that in England, issuing threats first thing in the morning to ensnare commuters and dominate the political parties' main press conferences. The beauty of it was that most of the time the Provisionals did not have to do anything to endanger their volunteers, and it was taken as yet another sign that while the republican movement was threatening to resume its violence on a grand scale they were still holding out the prospect of a ceasefire restoration.

In fact ceasefire speculation built to fever pitch, with press reports that the IRA was about to call a ceasefire in Northern Ireland at 4.00 p.m. on Thursday 10 April, although it was not certain if it would be announced. At ten minutes to four that day a forty-six-year-old mother of four children, reserve RUC constable Alice Collins, was shot in the back as she guarded the courthouse in Londonderry. Inside, the court was hearing public order charges against Sinn Fein members involved in demonstrations against John Major's visit to the city the preceding year.

It was the last act of violence perpetrated by the IRA before the general election. The same day the RUC, with Army support, arrested several men in South Armagh along with an American-made Barrett high-velocity rifle, a type which might have played a part in the deaths of so many security-force members along the border. A few weeks later a man was charged with the murder of Stephen Restorick, the 'smiling soldier'.

As polling day in the Westminster election drew nearer, the Irish Taoiseach John Bruton endorsed John Hume's view of Sinn Fein when he warned voters not to give their support to the Provisionals: 'A vote for Sinn Fein is a vote of support for the IRA and the IRA's campaign of killing and murder.' He admitted that his patience with Adams had run out, accusing him of squandering the opportunity to enter political negotiations in favour of staging a 'meaningless demonstration' at the gates of Stormont. 'The only reason they weren't there was because they hadn't the courage to call a ceasefire.' Hume also weighed in: 'Everybody knows that Sinn Fein and the IRA belong to the one movement and as long as they are committed to what they call armed struggle a vote for them is a vote for that strategy.'

Adams accused Bruton of 'blatant electioneering' and added: 'I am not a member of the IRA.' Asked if he ever had been, he replied: 'No.' But if the leaders of constitutional Irish nationalism had hoped, at this late hour, to swing ordinary Catholics away from Sinn Fein they were to be bitterly disappointed. As the days passed Adams sounded at his most doveish. His Easter speech at Milltown cemetery was near-textbook 'Stickie'-speak with its invocation of Wolfe Tone and the United Irishmen, a litany of republican struggle and nary a mention of the Provisional IRA.

Addressing directly the Protestants with whom he and other republicans had been talking in recent years, he said: 'Some unionists believe that we do not comprehend or appreciate the effects of the last twenty-five years upon them. We do. Or at least some of us do and we are trying to reach out because we who have suffered grievously do understand your sense of hurt also. This conflict has hurt all of us . . . we want to make peace with unionists; to work with you; to accommodate and celebrate our diversity as equals.'

It was clear to the SDLP even before polling day on 1 May that Sinn Fein was about to score a historic victory. The only question remaining was just how great it would be. The results were stunning. Adams retook his old West Belfast seat from Dr Joe Hendron with a majority of 8,000. His close ally Martin McGuinness captured Mid-Ulster from the DUP hardliner Willie McCrea, in the process causing a collapse in the SDLP vote. In the new seat of West Tyrone the SDLP stayed ahead of Sinn Fein by just 562 votes, the split Catholic vote putting an Ulster Unionist into a naturally nationalist seat. Overall Sinn Fein gained 16.1 per cent share of the vote, making it the third largest political party in Northern Ireland behind the Ulster Unionists and the SDLP. There were scenes of wild jubilation bordering on triumphalism as Belfast's City Hall was invaded by hordes of Adams supporters who jeered and jostled a frightened-looking Joe Hendron before hoisting their hero on to their shoulders and bearing him off down Royal Avenue in a sea of Irish tricolours.

John Hume was forced by television interviewers to repeat his contention that the Sinn Fein vote was a vote for violence, but he betrayed his true feelings when he went on to say, 'My clear hope is that on 3 June all parties – all parties – will be at the table in a totally peaceful atmosphere.' His deputy Seamus Mallon, on the other hand, could barely disguise his anger. 'It was a vote that gives a blank cheque to the IRA,' he said. Adams' party's campaign had been 'cynical and manipulative' and every one of their voters should remember that every time somebody was killed, injured or beaten by punishment squads they had contributed to those actions.

McGuinness said the most urgent task facing the new British Prime Minister Tony Blair was the rebuilding of the peace process. 'We in Sinn Fein will do all in our power to assist the reconstruction of a new peace process.' When John Bruton met the new British leader in Downing Street a week later he raised the hope that Sinn

Fein could be in the Stormont talks on 3 June if the IRA called an immediate ceasefire and 'threw away the crutch' of violence for good. Blair was cautious, saying he thought it unlikely that there was enough time.

With more elections looming on both sides of the border, violence resumed in Northern Ireland. A young police officer, Darren Bradshaw, was shot dead in a Belfast gay bar. The murder was claimed by the INLA. A Portadown Catholic, Robert Hamill, died after thirteen days in a coma from injuries sustained when he was beaten up by loyalists. And Sean Brown, a popular figure in GAA circles, was abducted by loyalist paramilitaries in Bellaghy, shot in the head and left for dead.

As hundreds walked behind Brown's coffin, Tony Blair was underlining that Northern Ireland was a priority for him by making the province his first destination as Prime Minister outside of London. In a keynote speech at the Royal Ulster Agricultural Show at the Balmoral showground, he made the offer that Sinn Fein had wanted – a renewal of direct contacts between them and British officials. But there was a sting in the tail. Blair sounded, if anything, more unionist than his predecessor John Major, to whom he paid fulsome credit for bringing the peace process so far down the road. Burying old Labour's policy of a United Ireland by consent, he declared: 'I believe in the United Kingdom, I value the union. My agenda is not a United Ireland – and I wonder just how many see it as a realistic possibility in the foreseeable future ... none of us in this hall today, even the youngest, is likely to see Northern Ireland as anything but a part of the United Kingdom. That is the reality, because the consent principle is now almost universally accepted.' The SDLP leader John Hume was rapturous in his praise, calling the speech the most comprehensive statement on Northern Ireland by a British prime minister in twenty-five years.

Adams could barely conceal his disappointment, but the offer of talks was accepted with alacrity. A few days before the local elections he and McGuinness travelled over to London for a spot of lunch in the Commons. Both were entitled to be there, in spite of their refusal to swear an oath of allegiance to the Queen, but only for another thirty-six hours. The Speaker of the House, Betty Boothroyd, had decided to ban them from the Palace of Westminster 'in the interests of the House', changing Commons rules which previously permitted the use of MPs' facilities if not the salary. Leading politicians such as the former deputy Labour leader Roy Hattersley – no friend in the past of Adams and the Provisionals – were outraged by this attack on democracy. Adams and McGuinness were more concerned with garnering as much publicity for the party before the next round of elections. Standing on the Commons terrace, with its unrivalled views of the River Thames, Adams commented: 'This is the most restful period we have had in twenty-five years.'

Back in Northern Ireland, unionists were angered by the extra publicity the new Labour government were dishing out when the Northern Ireland Secretary met representatives of nationalist residents groups opposed to Orange parades and her officials met a Sinn Fein delegation up at Stormont as the province voted in the local elections. The Ulster Unionist Ken Maginnis claimed those actions were worth 25,000 Sinn Fein votes, but when the results began coming through on a Friday lunchtime it was clear that the party had just completed a resounding hat-trick of rising votes, finishing with an unprecedented 16.9 per cent share. Unionists could only look on in despair as they lost control of Belfast for the first time ever as well as councils in Fermanagh, Strabane and Cookstown. In Londonderry Sinn Fein captured three more seats to end the domination of the SDLP. Where Adams' party scored particularly well was in convincing thousands of nationalists to vote for the first time in their lives. But the Chief Electoral Officer Pat Bradley also confirmed there had been a 'planned campaign of malpractice' with massive abuse of proxy and postal votes.

For Gerry Adams the lesson was obvious: 'This election sends a very clear message that our strategy is being endorsed. The British government should recognize that and treat Sinn Fein on the same basis as every other party.' In Washington Mo Mowlam was making positive noises about a new US visa for Adams if the IRA renewed its ceasefire. In spite of the new British government and the electoral successes a ceasefire seemed as far off as ever. Adams and colleagues turned up at Stormont when the talks resumed for the ritual of being locked out, posing photogenically behind the padlocked gates. On 6 June there was one last hurrah for Sinn Fein when Caoimhghin O Caolain was elected to the Irish parliament, the Dail. Martin Ferris, the prominent Provisional and convicted gun-runner, also polled strongly in the traditionally republican area of North Kerry. And there was more good news: John Bruton's 'rainbow coalition' failed to get re-elected, leaving the more republican-friendly Fianna Fail to form the next government.

Most political observers of the Irish scene, particularly those with some sympathy for Adams and who took his peace mission at face value, now assumed that a new IRA ceasefire was inevitable and just around the corner. While there were still hurdles for him to leap over, the run of election successes and the changes of government in both London and Dublin had left the opportunity for real political progress looking never rosier. British government officials were conducting what were in effect ceasefire negotiations with Martin McGuinness and Gerry Kelly under the guise of 'clarification' talks. Three out of the Provisionals' four preconditions were met or on the verge of being met. Mo Mowlam had set May 1998 as the talks time-frame, there was movement on prisoners and other confidence-building measures in the pipeline.

But in the midst of all the optimism the Provisionals struck again. Two RUC officers, David Johnston and John Graham, were on their local beat just a few yards from the police station in Lurgan, County Armagh, when they were both shot in the back of the head at close quarters, dying immediately. Children were playing in the street when the murders happened. A getaway car was quickly found in the town's strongly nationalist Kilwilkie estate, set on fire to destroy any forensic evidence.

There was shock and astonishment in Dublin and London, where both prime ministers concluded that the proximity of the murder scene to Drumcree, where the contentious Orange parade was due to take place in a fortnight's time, was deliberately and cynically designed to stoke up tension. Blair immediately cancelled all further meetings with Sinn Fein. 'Their cynicism and hypocrisy are sickening,' he said. 'It is not just a murder that has been absolutely callous, brutal and without any justification, it is also something that has been done to frustrate a process that is bringing hope.' Only three days earlier he had sent an *aide-mémoire* to the Provisionals, explaining that in the event of an IRA ceasefire Sinn Fein could join all-party talks just six weeks later. He and John Bruton had also been working flat out on a joint paper that would finally remove the stumbling-block demand for a handover of terrorist weaponry before talks got under way.

Adams was signing copies of the paperback edition of his auto-biography in a Belfast bookshop when he was told by *Times* reporter Nicholas Watt of the Lurgan murders. According to Watt, the Sinn Fein president looked straight ahead without a flicker of emotion, nodded and said: 'At a personal and at a human level I am shocked. I think that any death in this situation diminishes all of us. These deaths must act as a huge incentive on those of us in political leadership to redouble our efforts to get the peace process restored.' It was back to the same, tired old script, and the outgoing Irish Taoiseach John Bruton summed up the mood of the island when he denounced Adams' 'weasel words' and said: 'I am appalled by the way in which Mr Adams ransacked the dictionary to find new words to avoid condemning this brutal murder.'

Criticism from that quarter could hardly have surprised Adams, but even the normally sympathetic *Andersonstown News*, often seen as a barometer of public opinion in his own republican heartland of West Belfast, could not contain its outrage on this occasion. 'The IRA', wrote the paper, 'is fast becoming not a symptom of the problem, as they have liked to portray themselves, over the past 28 years, but part of the problem itself. What happened in Lurgan was wrong, brutal and counter-productive and demands to be condemned outright. It is no longer good enough for the leaders of Sinn Fein to stick to the tired old mantra of refusing to indulge in the politics of condemnation. If the thing is wrong, it is wrong, and demands to be branded as such.' The consensus among senior officials in Washington, Dublin and London was that Adams had a very limited time-span in which to deliver on his promises, which could probably best be measured in weeks rather than months. 'This is a defining moment,' said one well-placed diplomat. 'If this is not put right in weeks then Adams' access to the White House is dead.' For others it raised the old unanswered question of just exactly where Adams stood in the IRA and Sinn Fein. Either he had approved the Lurgan murders, in which case he was an untouchable again, or else he was not in control and therefore what use was he to the three governments?

Blair's gut instinct told him to cast Adams out into the wilderness by immediately revealing the contents of the negotiations between his officials and Sinn Fein. Poised to make a statement in the Commons, he was talked round by Hume, who suggested that the game was not yet over even though there was only a final roll of the dice to make.

That came when, in almost his final act as Taoiseach, Bruton announced that he and Blair had reached agreement on a formula for overcoming the decommissioning obstacle. The announcement was made by Blair in the Commons that he had finally laid to rest the demand for a handover of weapons in advance of talks. The proposals were a near-carbon copy of what the Mitchell report had suggested. Since one side wanted weapons before talks and the other only after talks, the only reasonable compromise was weapons during talks. An independent commission would be established to deal with the issue while the substantive political negotiations ran on in parallel. The hardline Democratic Unionists denounced the plan as another British sell-out, but the Ulster Unionist leader David Trimble was more measured. So long as decommissioning actually did take place during the talks, rather than merely endless discussions relating to it, he could work with the plan. The ball was left firmly planted in Adams' court.

Adams put out a holding statement, saying that the proposals would be given his 'fullest attention and consideration', but appealing for further meetings with British officials for the sake of 'clarity'. These were turned down. The mood in Downing Street was that enough time had been wasted and that the moment of truth had now dawned. Adams had three and a half out of four of his wishes granted. No more could be done on decommissioning, in spite of the IRA's insistence that it would never hand over its arms until a political settlement was signed. The time had come for the republican movement to decide.

CHAPTER THIRTY

Another Chance . . . and a New Beginning

Shortly after Tony Blair announced his proposals on the Northern Ireland talks in the House of Commons at the end of June 1997, his Northern Ireland Secretary Mo Mowlam confessed that, within government, there was still great uncertainty about the IRA's intentions. 'My advisers,' she told one of the authors, 'are just as confused as the rest of you. Sinn Fein say something positive one day and they say, "Oh that's looking good." Then something dreadful happens and the advisers say, "Oh dear, maybe they aren't serious."' Mowlam confessed that the Prime Minister was close to pulling the plug on the government's courtship of the republican movement. 'He really takes these things personally,' she said, referring to the IRA murder of the two RUC officers in Lurgan. 'I'm concerned that if nothing happens soon he's just going to say that they can bugger off for good.'

The proposals announced by Blair may have put the ball in Gerry Adams' court but nobody believed that the IRA was likely to declare a new ceasefire before the middle of July. Not with another Drumcree looming – the by now annual crisis surrounding an Orange Order church parade in Portadown. Adams described the march as the litmus test for Tony Blair. 'The response and approach of the British government to this critical issue will be monitored very closely, both here in Ireland and internationally. Mr Blair's government must not behave as the Major government did. To do so would send a strong signal that one British government is much like another. It would say to nationalists that unionists rule, whether it is on the streets or at the negotiating table.'

It was precisely for the reason that Sinn Fein was perfectly happy to see the government face such a litmus test that Mowlam's frantic efforts to broker a compromise were inevitably doomed to failure.

Both communities wanted to see the colour of Labour's money – would their massive parliamentary majority give them the sinew to face down the Orangemen and the unionists, as had been tried unsuccessfully in 1996? Or would the ability of Northern Ireland's majority community to render the province ungovernable mean that once again the march would be forced down?

In the middle of the night before the Drumcree parade was due to set off, the RUC and the Army moved in to clear Catholic protesters off the Garvaghy Road. For nearly an hour there was a fierce running battle in the dark before the protesters were beaten back into their estate. The Garvaghy Road was left strewn with bricks and bottles, but clear for the Orange marchers to complete their parade. The RUC Chief Constable, Ronnie Flanagan, defended the action as the only way to protect Catholic lives in the face of a likely loyalist paramilitary backlash if the march was stopped.

Emotions in the Garvaghy estate were running high. Soldiers formed a cordon to allow some local people to go to church, but the people decided that the route, via a dirt track, was demeaning. The negotiations broke down and nobody was allowed to attend Mass inside the church – instead the local priests organized an outdoor Mass, turning a table into a makeshift altar. As a soldier stood in the way of some would-be churchgoers, one man threatened him. 'The only Mass you are going to is in a box,' he shouted. As the Orangemen walked impassively down the road, protesters broke into a chant of 'No ceasefire! No ceasefire!' The IRA responded, launching sniper attacks on the police and Army in Belfast and elsewhere. The splinter group, the INLA, also fired shots at Protestants across the Peace Line, hitting a fourteen-year-old boy. On the other side of the wall another fourteen-year-old boy was hit and seriously injured by a plastic bullet. Adams called for 'peaceful but militant' protest and attacked a government which stood 'indicted before the bar of public opinion internationally'. He called for an end to the hijacking and burning of vehicles in nationalist areas, intervening to retrieve a lorry from a group of teenagers, quipping, 'Don't you think I've got better things to be doing than spending my time getting cars off kids?'

Although he said the prospects for a ceasefire had been made 'much more difficult' by Drumcree, he was careful to avoid blaming the Northern Ireland Secretary. 'It was not Mo Mowlam who was in charge, it was the police and the military and that is a very dangerous situation,' he said. Three days later, even after the revelation of a secret government contingency plan to force a controlled parade through the Garvaghy Road, Adams still seemed less inclined to blame ministers than their advisers. 'Last weekend's decision and the way it was implemented shows once again that it is the security/military and intelligence people who are in charge,' he said.

What seems to have conditioned this restrained reaction to Drumcree in 1997 was the expectation that he was on the point of winning all the preconditions for his party's entry into talks. Blair's proposals gave the Provisionals a time-scale both for their inclusion in negotiations and for the duration of the discussions themselves. A letter written by the Northern Ireland Office to Martin McGuinness at the height of the Drumcree disturbances made it clear that regular reviews of progress on paramilitary disarmament would not act as a means of ejecting Sinn Fein from talks if the IRA did not hand over weapons. The letter also promised more rapid movement on the question of IRA prisoners seeking transfers to jails in the Irish Republic. The consensus among outside observers began to form that Sinn Fein would wait for the tempers raised by the Drumcree march to cool. The IRA might launch a revenge strike, but it would deliver a new ceasefire. Only the timing seemed to be in doubt.

Wednesday 23 July was a critical date because the political parties at Stormont were due to vote on the British and Irish decommissioning proposals, which Blair hoped would finally release the logjam. To garner unionist support the British government would have to harden the arms proposals – but such a move would risk alienating republicans and make a renewed ceasefire less likely. Several events conspired to knock the pundits' timetable to one side. First, on the night of 10 July the Orange Order announced a series of unexpected concessions regarding contentious parades which were due to take place on the 12th, the biggest day in the Orange calendar when the order celebrates the anniversary of the Battle of the Boyne. The Orangemen pulled back from confrontation with nationalists in South Belfast, Armagh city, Derry and Newry. The decisions defused the potential for further serious violence in the wake of the Drumcree parade and won the Orangemen a belated piece of the moral high ground. Gerry Adams, cheated of what would certainly have been a leading role in a likely stand-off in South Belfast, acknowledged the significance of the decision.

In the lighter atmosphere Mowlam met the new Irish Foreign Minister Ray Burke in London to review matters ahead of the big decommissioning vote. Although she had been coming under pressure to toughen her stance on weapons she steadfastly refused to budge. Standing on the steps of the new Northern Ireland Office Building, an edifice which the department had inherited from MI5, she stood by a document which would see Sinn Fein enter talks without significant pressure for an early handover of IRA arms.

In the moments before Mowlam and Burke defended their approach to the disarmament issue, a wave of rumours began to sweep Belfast, Dublin and London that something big was in the offing. A joint statement appeared under the names of Gerry Adams and John Hume expressing optimism about the prospects for peace. The statement was reminiscent of similar joint announcements by the two nationalist leaders in the run-up to the 1994 ceasefire. The word was that the IRA might have something to say later in the day – but surely they would wait until after the vital decommissioning vote the following Wednesday before making any significant announcement?

In fact, events moved rather more quickly. At 5.00 p.m. Sinn Fein issued a faxed statement announcing that Gerry Adams and Martin McGuinness had urged the IRA leadership to call a new ceasefire and that they were hopeful of a speedy response. Given the conviction of senior security officers that both Adams and McGuinness continued to sit on the IRA's Army Council there appeared to be little doubt about what that response would be. Adams pointed out in his statement that throughout the course of the most recent IRA campaign he had consistently said that he would never urge such a step without a firm belief that the IRA's response would be positive. The choreography of the request and the response, then, was all part of the elaborate game of maintaining distance between the party and its armed wing.

In contrast to the painstaking run-up to the 1994 ceasefire, the speed of the events was breathtaking. On Friday Adams issued his statement. On Saturday the IRA followed through with its own communiqué, announcing an 'unequivocal restoration of the ceasefire of August 1994'. At noon on Sunday 20 July the new ceasefire came into effect. As parishioners filed out of Clonard Monastery in West Belfast, the base for Father Alec Reid and the religious centre for the peace process, one woman confided, 'I think it's wonderful, that no other mother will have to go through the pain of losing her son. I lost my son through the Troubles and I felt the pain for every mother and I just thank God that all pain and bitterness will vanish from the hearts of Irish men and women.' Another Mass-goer chimed in: 'We've got another chance and I think it will be good. I don't think it will be broken. Good on Gerry, he's worked hard for this.'

Second time around things felt different, something which Adams himself acknowledged when he stood on a table outside Connolly House facing a crowd much smaller than the one which had turned out after the announcement of the 1994 ceasefire. He put it down to the holiday period. When in a repeat of his 1994 speech he paid tribute to the 'leadership and volunteers of the Irish Republican Army', Adams got a predictable cheer. But among the many happy that peace was being given another chance, there were some hardliners who warned that the second ceasefire in three years was doomed to go the same way as the first. 'We should have blown London apart and tested the Blair government,' a man from Twinbrook told the *Irish News*. 'Blair is just another unionist.'

The very speed of the ceasefire raised questions about how broadly based support for the initiative was. Martin McGuinness and Gerry Kelly went in to visit IRA prisoners in the Maze to reassure them about Sinn Fein's intentions after the announcement. In 1994 the prisoners had been extensively canvassed beforehand. The day the ceasefire came into effect, the Dublin *Sunday Tribune* carried a report indicating that the restoration had been approved not by the seven-strong IRA Army Council but by the slightly bigger twelve-member Army Executive, which it said was more hardline than the Council itself.

The cutting edge to the report, though, was the claim that the ceasefire had only been approved for four months at which time the Provisionals would review political progress and then perhaps return to violence if they didn't believe politics was getting them what they wanted. Adams reacted with apoplexy, pronouncing himself 'disgusted' and accusing the well informed author Ed Moloney of being a 'jumped up journalist', guilty of 'irresponsible reporting'. The vehemence of the denial prompted a widespread belief that Moloney had touched a sore spot – the substance of the report was repeated in a series of other newspapers in the next few days. Certainly there were persistent rumours that senior IRA members, including the former

Belfast Brigade commander, were distinctly unhappy about the new direction. Predictably, the INLA and the hardline republican Sinn Fein loyal to Ruairi O Bradaigh denounced the ceasefire as a false peace and part of a programme of pacification of nationalist resistance.

Some security sources expressed doubts about whether a fixed four-month timetable had been set – the process of keeping the cessation under review, they suggested, was more open ended. But the point was, as both Martin McGuinness and Adams' press aide Richard McAuley had readily admitted during the preceding months, that there is no such thing as a permanent IRA ceasefire. Any suspension of violence is conditional on political change. If the status quo in Northern Ireland remains frozen the IRA will put its guns to use. The question remained unchanged since 1994: what was Adams' bottom line? Only during talks involving unionists could Adams' true attitude to the principle of majority consent within Northern Ireland be tested. Only during such negotiations could the IRA's resolve be assessed.

Mo Mowlam lost no time. True to her word, she invited Adams to Stormont in early August, a first since a Sinn Fein delegation and a British minister met in early 1996 when the IRA ended its seventeen-month ceasefire. 'We want an Ireland free and independent,' he told her, welcoming her as the first woman to take the poisoned chalice of Northern Ireland Secretary. 'We also want her to be the last British Secretary of State,' he said he told her. 'As far as we are concerned the main item on the agenda was about ending the Union.' After the meeting Mowlam told Adams that she welcomed the two-week-old ceasefire. 'The advice is that it is holding very well,' she told reporters. She gave no guarantee that Sinn Fein would be at the Castle Buildings talks when they resumed on September 15, but the mood music was right. This time there would be no delays.

On the other side of the Atlantic there was just as much haste. Adams was granted a new visa, with no restrictions this time on his fund-raising activities: no meeting with President Clinton, but a tumultuous reception from 600 American supporters who paid $500 each to crowd into the Starlight Room of the Waldorf Astoria to eat Aberdeen Angus beef and hear Adams speak. What they heard was a more measured assessment of what Irish republicans could realistically secure from the talks process, the first signal that the Sinn Fein leader was beginning the delicate task of lowering his supporters' expectations.

'Compromise, compromise, compromise. It is in a spirit of generosity, accommodation and preparedness to come to a compromise that we go into these talks,' he told a Washington press conference. Asked about Prime Minister Tony Blair's view that a united Ireland was a long way off, he retorted, 'We just say the opposite. There will be and there should be and there can be a united Ireland in our lifetime. Our commitment to a negotiated settlement is for ever. It isn't a whim, it isn't temporary: it is for ever.'

The death of Diana, Princess of Wales, in a car accident in Paris, overshadowed Adams' trip to America. He was inevitably asked his opinion and offered his sympathy to her family, praising her for her humane work and compassion towards Aids victims. Having seen her sons, Princes William and Harry, on the television, 'no one could but be moved at observing the plight of those two young fellows'. Scoffing at a question over whether the IRA had ever targeted the British Royal Family, he admonished a reporter for 'repeating nonsense stories that sometimes have their birth and inception in *Alice in Wonderland*.' A senior Sinn Fein official said, 'She wouldn't have been at the top of our list.'

It was back to Belfast for the by now inevitable invitation to join the Stormont talks. Adams went armed with some good news from Washington. Janet Reno, the United States Attorney General, had blocked the extradition of six former IRA men, wanted in Northern Ireland to face serious charges. Reno was responding to a request from the United States Secretary of State Madeleine Albright, who said the suspension of the extradition warrants 'could advance the peace process'. Fighting his way through the press and some two hundred loyalist protesters outside Castle Buildings, Adams formally committed himself and Sinn Fein to the Mitchell principles of democracy and non-violence. None of the main unionist parties were present at the ceremony, but Pearl Sagar, a Protestant from East Belfast and Women's Coalition delegate, was there. 'Sitting down with Gerry Adams was the hardest thing I have ever done in my life,' she said later. 'If we want peace in Northern Ireland we don't have the luxury of who we speak to.' Adams had given a 'sensitive' speech, she added.

If he had created a favourable impression in some quarters it was immediately spoiled by an interview with the Provisional IRA in the newspaper *An Phoblacht*, which said they would 'have problems with sections of the Mitchell principles' but that what Sinn Fein did was 'a matter for them'. For his part, Adams said the timing was 'unfortunate . . . the political storm created by the IRA interview is quite astonishing and offensive when one considers the lack of comment on the loyalist, unionist and British breaches of the Mitchell principles. It appears that for some, IRA words are more offensive that the very real violence of the loyalist death squads and the British forces.'

Ulster Unionist leader David Trimble, reassured over the summer by private meetings with Tony Blair at Chequers, stayed in the talks even while expressing his regret that Sinn Fein had been allowed to reach the table without a single bullet surrendered by the IRA. 'We are not there to negotiate with them but to confront them, to expose their fascist character,' he said. Nevertheless, it had not been easy to convince his own hardliners. In a deft move, Trimble turned the devastation of the mainly Protestant County Armagh town of Markethill by a 400lb bomb, planted by the splinter Continuity IRA, into a reason for entering Castle Buildings. 'Sinn Fein's presence in the talks must be challenged,' he argued. That was fine by Adams, who described the Ulster Unionist leader's threats to have Sinn Fein thrown out as 'some synchronized posturings'.

At their first face-to-face encounter at the talks table the Ulster Unionists launched an 'indictment' to have Sinn Fein thrown out. The attempt failed but in his reply Adams welcomed the unionists and loyalists:

> I acknowledge that it is likely that republicans don't fully understand or comprehend the suffering which unionists and loyalists have endured, or the suffering of the families of the British soldiers. It is also likely that unionists and loyalists don't understand what republicans and nationalists have suffered and endured. But the difference between us and the Ulster Unionists is that Sinn Fein is prepared to listen to them and to engage with them and to try to reach out to them. Nineteen members of Sinn Fein have been killed, family members have been killed, and scores have been injured in attacks. That's an awful lot of pain, an awful lot of funerals. People who stood for our party or who worked during elections knew that when they signed up for us they could be signing a death warrant and they did so to uphold democratic principles and the democratic rights of our electorate

... I could indict the British government, I could indict the loyalists. I don't want to do that. I want to get on to the business of making all of this a thing of the past ... Sinn Fein signed up to the Mitchell principles. We didn't do so lightly. We will honour our commitments.

But it was that commitment which finally was to begin what Adams had insisted right through the early years of the peace process would never happen again – a split within the Provisional movement. Not even a claim by Martin McGuinness on the eve of the commencement of the 'substantive negotiations' that Sinn Fein was going to the negotiating table to 'smash the Union' could forestall the parting of the ways.

On 10 October around a hundred IRA delegates converged on a roomy barn in remotest Gweedore, in the Gaelic-speaking west of Donegal. To further reduce the chances of being spotted many of the IRA men were piled into the backs of lorries, which drove straight into the huge barn. Among the visitors were Gerry Adams and Martin McGuinness, who were about to put down an attempted coup. Its mastermind was the Provisionals' quartermaster general, a hugely powerful man who controlled the IRA's extensive network of arms dumps in the South. The quartermaster, who lived in north County Louth, just south of the Northern Irish border, had been disenchanted with the peace process ever since the first ceasefire had been tried and failed. He was a key figure in the return to violence in February 1997.

Believing that he had canvassed sufficient support among similarly disaffected hardliners in Belfast and South Armagh, the quartermaster and his allies on the IRA's twelve-member Army Executive, demanded that a convention be held at which the adoption by Sinn Fein of the Mitchell principles be tested with a vote. Expecting to win, the quartermaster would then demand a return to war and the removal of key pro-peace process figures. He had not reckoned with Adams' vice-like grip on the Provisionals, the product of two decades in leadership during which he had promoted all his most loyal allies to the detriment of anyone who might pose a threat. While serious discontent was growing within the ranks, Adams' cultivation of the command structure left him as the unrivalled leader whom most chose to follow blindly.

The quartermaster general argued that the Mitchell principles were a bridge too far for militant republicanism, because they removed the right of the IRA, in the name of the Irish people, to wage armed struggle against the British occupier. He demanded an end to the ceasefire. Adams and Martin McGuinness argued through a long night with the gathering. By the early hours they had won over most of the delegates. The motions put forward by the quartermaster general were heavily defeated, with a vote against of 80 per cent. Shortly afterwards the quartermaster general and his allies in the attempted coup quit.

'I think the meeting was very carefully arranged so that the leadership at the meeting had very strong support,' RUC Chief Constable Ronnie Flanagan told BBC's *Panorama*. 'I think the opposition wasn't properly martialled and was rather easily routed at that meeting.' Asked what he had told the IRA convention in Gweedore by reporter Peter Taylor, Adams said he was playing one of his journalistic tricks before adding, 'I have never ever gone into with any journalist or with anyone else, the mechanisms of how we deal with the IRA.'

Although it would not be long before some Sinn Fein and IRA activists in the more hardline areas of Ulster followed the quartermaster general, the spotlight remained focussed on the novelty of seeing, for the first time, political opinions of all shades battling it out under one roof up at Stormont.

Three days after looking the rebel quartermaster general in the eye, Gerry Adams was back at Castle Buildings, face to face with the British Prime Minister Tony Blair. The two men talked for nearly half an hour during their discreet ice-breaking meeting. The photographers were denied sight of the handshake, but afterwards Blair told reporters, 'I treated Gerry Adams and the members of Sinn Fein the same way as I would treat any human being. If we don't seize this opportunity now we may not see it again in our lifetime.' Adams recalled that the last time a Sinn Fein leader had met a British prime minister was in 1921. 'I hope we make a better job of it than we did the last time,' he told Blair and went on to suggest that if he had been born in West Belfast he too might have joined the IRA.

Later in the day Blair made an ill-advised visit to a shopping centre in the heart of staunchly loyalist Democratic Unionist territory in East Belfast. He was pursued by elderly women wearing surgical gloves who screamed at him that, having clasped Adams' hand, his own hand was now covered with the blood of the IRA's victims. Blair faced his tormentors and made his way back through the boos and chanting to his car. A valuable lesson for the prime minister in the realities of Northern Ireland's politics, but a day too on which the period of symbolic events seemed finally to be drawing to a close. The new Irish Foreign Affairs Minister David Andrews said that a united Ireland was 'not achievable in my lifetime' and the US State Department dropped the Provisional IRA from its list of terrorist organizations. A comment made by former Defence Minister Alan Clark at a fringe meeting of the Conservative Party conference that 'the only solution for dealing with the IRA is to kill six hundred people in one night' sounded even more anachronistic in the light of the historic steps being taken.

The talks seemed to settle back into their old ways. Christmas was fast approaching and delegates could not even agree on what they disagreed. About a dozen Sinn Fein members in the Irish Republic's border town of Dundalk, traditionally seen by Northerners as a bolt-hole for Provisional activists, resigned from the party in protest at the acceptance of the Mitchell principles. The dissidents formed a pressure group which they called the Thirty-two County Sovereignty Committee, making up for their small numbers by proudly proclaiming that their main spokesperson was Bernadette Sands, the sister of the IRA hunger striker Bobby Sands. Adams called the resignations 'a spat' but admitted that 'one or two' more Sinn Fein members might leave the party. It was the first official comment on the growing evidence that a split was occurring since reports began circulating about the IRA meeting in Gweedore. Speaking after a Provisional statement which revealed that a small number of its members had left the organization but assured supporters that it remained united, Adams said the ceasefire was 'by any measure a good and genuine cessation'.

> I think the IRA as an organization is cohesive. It is bigger than any individual or number of individuals ... Coming at a time when there has been no real movement – beyond most of the parties actually getting into the same room – of course all of this is risky, it is dangerous. But it is always going to be testing, the search for peace. That is what we have to see our way through. I see this as part of the process that we are all going through: it's all part of this phase of the struggle. There has been a huge

whirlwind of change within republican politics for the last ten, eleven or twelve years. We are not a monolith.

In South Armagh, however, Sinn Fein councillor Francie Molloy, unaware that members of the press were present, told a republican meeting that if the multi-party talks at Stormont failed then they could always return 'to what they know best'. When the story emerged Molloy claimed he had been misquoted and denied he was threatening a return to violence. Conor Murphy, a leading republican activist in South Armagh told a Sinn Fein meeting at Belfast's Europa Hotel – a favourite target for IRA bombs, that press reports of thirty-five defections from the IRA in the area were wrong, 'on behalf of the entire republican movement in South Armagh – and I speak with a little bit of authority – we are a hundred per cent, a hundred and ten per cent behind the leadership of Sinn Fein. If there was, which there wasn't, thirty-five people left in the republican movement in South Armagh, there would be three hundred and fifty people to take their place tomorrow.'

Adams left for Paris to enjoy some Gallic hospitality. After addressing the French parliament's foreign affairs committee, the former Culture Minister Jack Lang thanked him 'for the struggle you have led for your country and for your humanism'. Adams told his audience that Sinn Fein's goal of a united Ireland would endure but 'we have to be prepared to compromise. The effort to bring about Irish unity will continue until it becomes a reality.'

A further piece of symbolism was left to be performed before the year was out. The Sinn Fein leader had already met the British prime minister in Belfast, but wanted and needed the historic images of a grand entry into the heart of the enemy establishment, a feat not repeated since Michael Collins negotiated the Anglo-Irish Treaty of 1921. Adams' visit to Number Ten Downing Street was scheduled for 11 December. The Sinn Fein leader, addressing the annual Kilmichael commemoration, where the IRA's West Cork flying column under Tom Barry ambushed and killed seventeen auxiliaries in 1920, explained the purpose of his journey. 'For the first time since 1921 a British prime minister is going to hear Irish republicans politely but firmly tell him that it's time to go.'

Politeness – hardly a traditional word in the Irish republican lexicon when it comes to dealing with the British – seemed to be the hallmark of the Number Ten meeting. After an hour of talks a happy-looking Adams emerged to declare 'a good moment in history'. Contrary to the media image, Adams said he found a prime minister

> who engaged and listened'. [He had] a real sense of exploring each other's analysis ... I think for the first time in my life a British prime minister was able to hear from an Irish republican that the relationship between our two islands, which has meant so much suffering and death and pain and agony, can be put to one side, can become part of our history, and that Mr Blair is significantly placed to be the British prime minister who brings about a new history, a new relationship between the people of these islands.

Facing Adams directly across the table Blair told the Sinn Fein leader he was committed to the principles of consent, and that he was 'not a persuader for Irish unity'. The two men sat together in the Cabinet Room, just yards from the spot where an IRA mortar exploded in 1991. Blair told Adams, 'This is a choice of history – violence and despair or peace and progress'. Alastair Campbell, the Downing Street Press Secretary, briefed journalists that it had been important for Gerry Adams to look him in the eye and say he was committed to peace. 'That's what Alastair was saying, was it? Yes, Alastair's very good at his job. I don't think any of the drama of that romantic-type notion occurred,' Adams later told BBC *Newsnight*. On his way into Downing Street Adams was greeted by Rita Restorick, mother of Stephen, the British soldier murdered by an IRA sniper in Bessbrook, South Armagh earlier the same year. She handed him a Christmas card with a note attached asking all political parties in Northern Ireland to 'do all in their power' to ensure the talks were successful. Adams said he knew 'many, many, many Mrs Restoricks', and praised her for her courage.

Even the escape from the Maze prison outside Belfast of Liam Averill, who was serving two life sentences for murder, couldn't dampen the mood of optimism in London. Adams wished the escapee luck. 'There will be prisoners who try to escape. I tried it myself. Liam Averill succeeded where I didn't. Good luck to him.'

But more than good luck would be required to keep the talks on the road in the early months of the New Year. The murder of a loyalist leader, Billy Wright, by republicans inside the Maze prison unleashed a new wave of sectarian killings. Wright, a well-known hate figure for republicans, who had terrorized the Catholic community in Mid-Ulster, had once attempted an impromptu assassination of Adams. Spotting the Sinn Fein leader at a local function in West Belfast as he cruised the streets, Wright raced off to the Shankill Road to pick up a kalashnikov from a weapons dump, but on his return found that Adams had already left.

As the death toll mounted, and a 500lb bomb was defused in the County Down town of Banbridge, Adams said that the IRA was 'the only group in ceasefire mode'. 'We certainly expected a more robust action from the Provisional IRA which in real terms never came,' said David Ervine, leader of the Progressive Unionist Party. 'It proved to us that that strategy was strong, that people were in control and that indeed moving towards a democratic path was more important than hitting back out of an emotional sense. I think Sinn Fein have done that. The Unionist populace perhaps can't see the wood for the trees.'

One of the Catholic victims, twenty-eight-year-old Terry Enright, was married to a niece of Adams. 'This young man was a valued member of this community. He was married to a niece of mine, but that should not be used as an excuse for killing him. He was heavily involved in community affairs and with young people. He was a good, or as he probably thought, a brilliant Gaelic footballer,' said Adams. Terry Enright's wife Dierdre was the daughter of Adams' sister Margaret, whose husband Mickey McCorry had sided with the Officials during the republican parting of the way back in 1969. He was killed while working as a doorman at a club owned by the sister-in-law of one of Adams' fellow negotiators at the talks, the loyalist David Ervine. As an athlete and an outdoor pursuits instructor the murder victim was a hero to many young people in West Belfast, and his community work took him to both Catholic and Protestant parts of the city. At his funeral, attended by thousands, Adams gave his niece a comforting hug as Bishop Patrick Walsh told the mourners 'Terry was born in 1969, a fateful year. Will 1998 be a fateful year in a different sense, a year that will see the agony over and the darkness of bitterness, suspicion, hatred and terror scattered in the light of tolerance, respect, love and peace?' Davey Adams, a loyalist member of the Ulster Democratic Party's talks team, said it was obvious that the murder of Terry Enright affected Adams. He just looked to me to be someone who was sick, sore and tired of all that had been going on and was genuinely concerned about trying to move the situation to a peaceful plane.'

The talks limped on, hitting a new obstacle when Sinn Fein rejected the British and Irish governments' *Heads of Agreement* document, their best guess of a possible settlement which proposed the establishment of a Northern Ireland assembly, a North-South ministerial council, and incorporated an equality agenda for Catholics and Protestants. The document was welcomed by the unionist parties in the talks and the SDLP leader John Hume, who accused Sinn Fein of failing to address realities. As often seemed the case during the peace process at moments identified by Adams as ones of crisis, the Provisional IRA leadership issued a statement condemning the 'pro-unionist document'. Adams flew to London for his third meeting with Blair in six weeks. 'An internal settlement is not a solution,' he said afterwards. 'There must be at the very least an all-Ireland dimension to this, and we, of course, as nationalists and republicans want to see Irish unity. We accept that others have a different view. That's a matter for negotiation. But at the very least those negotiations have to be conducted on a comprehensive agenda.'

The killing continued, with irrefutable evidence from the RUC that the Ulster Freedom Fighters, represented in the talks by the Ulster Democratic Party, was involved in the murders. The UDP was ejected from Castle Buildings. The loyalist ceasefire, now unofficially broken, teetered, and threatened to fall – until Mo Mowlam took the risky but successful step of going to the Maze prison to speak directly with loyalist inmates and persuade them to swing behind the talks process once more.

In an attempt to inject a greater sense of urgency the talks were moved to Lancaster House in London. Ever since his first meeting with Blair at Downing Street before Christmas, Adams had sought a meeting with the Ulster Unionist leader David Trimble, but to no avail. The depth of the enmity was illustrated by an off-stage encounter between him and Trimble's colleague Ken Maginnis, MP for Fermanagh and South Tyrone. The clash occurred in the tea-room when Adams tried to engage Maginnis in conversation. 'In the plenary session Ken went on a long rant, a long and personal invective against Martin McGuinness and myself. He was not acknowledging at all the very real anger there is in the community about the recent murders, or reflecting on it at all,' Adams told *An Phoblacht*.

'Afterwards, when I went over I just very quietly said that his remarks were a disgrace and at a time when people are being killed we need to start talking and inject some sense of urgency into the negotiations in the interests of peace. He called me a fucking murderer and walked off.'

The prospect of the expulsion of Sinn Fein from the talks now loomed as suspicion that the Provisionals were behind the murders of loyalist Robert Dougan and an alleged drugs dealer Brendan Campbell climbed. As RUC Chief Constable Ronnie Flanagan resisted calls to go public with his assessment of the killings, Adams said the talks would collapse if his party was removed. The pressure on the Sinn Fein leader was clearly seen when he accused ITN reporter Johnnie Irvine of being 'smart-arsed' for asking questions about Sinn Fein's links with the IRA. 'I am absolutely pissed off with trying to make this thing work and those who have no interest in making it work seize upon two men being killed to exploit it and to bring this process down,' he exclaimed. Dr Philip McGarry, a member of the Alliance party's talks team and a psychiatrist, said it was evidence of the conflict between what the IRA wanted and what Adams knew he could deliver. 'Although Adams' image is very collected and smooth, when you scrape away the veneer of peace, love and platitudes what you get is the sectarianism. He's very good on soundbites but when he's put on the spot he's just bluff and bluster like Paisley.'

Given the circumstances it seemed a little bizarre that Adams was addressing a £19.50-a-head lunch for two hundred business leaders in Belfast on his party's economic strategy. Sinn Fein was about to be expelled from the talks and the peace process was going to 'crumble into dust', yet here he was, proposing harmonization of tax rates throughout the island to a well-fed Chamber of Commerce gathering. The chamber's President Colin Anderson said he was pleased with how the event had gone. 'Although I thought Mr Adams' economic analysis was a little naïve in some respects, he gave us plenty of food for thought. I would say further dialogue with Sinn Fein is more rather than less likely, and feel that at least the door is now open.'

When Adams climbed Vinegar Hill in County Wexford, where the rebellion against the British by the United Irishmen was decisively beaten two hundred years earlier, the five thousand people present on that bright February day may have been full of foreboding and gloom. A few days earlier Sinn Fein had finally been 'sin-binned' – ejected from the talks for a token period of two weeks. Noting that remarks had been passed about the use of photographs of two young IRA volunteers who had both been killed in London during the lapse in its ceasefire the previous year, Adams said that no apology was necessary. 'It is a sign of the failure of those in power, of those who pay lip service to the ideal of national freedom that young men like that . . . should die in the way they died and should feel moved to take up armed action. And the responsibility on responsible politicians – and may I say on responsible republicans – is to make sure that no more of our young men and women die in the service of the freedom of our country.'

The appeal to republicans in that important sentence exposed the seismic shift in Adams' thinking, a transformation which had taken him from the former apologist for Provisional violence to the man who was now trying to bring its failed campaign of violence to a gentle close. Only a few weeks earlier Adams had given an audience in London containing hostile elements a similar lesson. 'I could give you some *Tiocfaidh ar La* speech, but we are in the business of making the revolution. That's what we care about and no one should be sitting back waiting for one of us to fall off our high wire.'

When he finished speaking at Vinegar Hill Adams was presented with a replica Wexford pike, which provoked some jollity. One man asked what the RUC's reaction would be when the Sinn Fein leader tried to bring the centuries-old weapon across the border. Nobody asked him if he was about to stick the pike in the thatch, an old Irish phrase meaning to give up the fight.

Two bombs which devastated the centres of the mainly Protestant towns of Moira and Portadown in mid-Ulster prompted another statement from the Provisional IRA, after speculation that it was helping dissident republican groups to continue the campaign of violence while keeping its own hands clean. The statement denied the claims, rejected stories about splits and emphasized that its ceasefire remained intact. But it was the appalling murder of two friends, a Catholic and a Protestant, in a bar in Poyntzpass, County Armagh, by loyalist mavericks which deeply shocked the Northern Ireland public and gave talks chairman George Mitchell an opportunity to set a firm deadline for completion of a settlement agreement by the Thursday before Easter.

Into the final lap, the British and Irish governments signed a document saying they believed the IRA ceasefire was genuine and officially invited Sinn Fein back inside Castle Buildings. Adams chose not to go back immediately, but flew to London for yet another meeting with Blair, who said that an agreement was 'agonizingly close', and then on to the White House for President Clinton's annual St Patrick's Day dinner. Dignity restored, he led the Sinn Fein team back into Stormont on his return. As the parties raced towards the finishing tape, Adams went public in the newspapers acknowledging that there would be no united Ireland emerging from any agreement but setting out his wish-list of minimum demands, including strong cross-border bodies, the repeal of emergency powers and disbandment of the RUC.

As the deadline of midnight 9 April drew near, Sinn Fein hunkered down inside their Castle Buildings offices. Adams made the point to Blair that he had never done business with a British government during office hours. 'We were well prepared for the Easter week negotiations. We got a bed into the office: we knew it was going to go down into the small hours of the morning.' Stalwarts like Aidan McAteer and Ted Howell, the unseen backbone of Adams' talks operation, were joined by those who represented Irish republicanism down the decades from every corner of the island: veteran Belfast commander Joe Cahill; from Kerry the convicted arms runner Martin Ferris; the Old Bailey bomber, Maze escapee and former Adjutant General Gerry Kelly. Lord Alderdice, leader of the cross-community Alliance Party later recalled, 'The republicans and loyalists in the last few days brought a lot of their colleagues in and it really became a very different kind of place in terms of the sort of people that were there. Indeed, I joked to one of my colleagues that if they had wanted to introduce internment all they needed to do was close the doors . . . they would have had most of the significant figures in Northern Ireland, I suspect.'

The first stab at an agreement – a document put out under the name of the talks chairman George Mitchell – had republicans smiling. It contained a long list of cross-border bodies with wide-ranging responsibilities. But unionists who wanted the roles of such bodies to be defined by a Northern Ireland assembly threw up their hands in horror. With days to go the talks hit a crisis. Prime Minister Blair flew in on a rescue mission throwing in a memorable phrase which he almost sounded embarassed to release, 'A day like today – I mean it's not a day for sort of soundbites really, you can leave those at home, but – I feel the hand of history upon our shoulder, I really do.'

Blair was joined by his Irish counterpart Bertie Ahern, braving personal tragedy as he persisted with the negotiations despite the death of his mother. Adams, aware that his party's objections to a new Stormont assembly had long since been brushed aside by the other negotiators, concentrated his party's firepower on the cross border bodies, the repeal of the legislation underpinning Northern Ireland's position in the UK, and, most crucially for the IRA, the early release of IRA prisoners.

Gerry Kelly took a leading role in the prisoner negotiations, levering the British government back from a position which would have seen some inmates remaining in jail until 2005. Kelly hoped the government could be forced to accept a one-year time limit, but worrying reports reached the Sinn Fein offices that the loyalists two floors down had agreed an early release scheme over a two-year period. Kelly marched down to the offices of the Progressive Union-ists, the political wing of the UVF, and demanded to see the party leader David Ervine, much to the bemusement of more than fifty loyalists crammed into the PUP offices, including some leading UVF paramilitaries. Kelly said he wanted to get Ervine's prisoners out but the loyalist failed to bite. He believed a twelve-month release scheme wouldn't have been sellable to the wider Northern Ireland com-munity. He told Sinn Fein they were being selfish and the prisoner proposals on offer were 'as good as it gets'.

It was left to Gerry Adams and Martin McGuinness to sort out the crucial prisoner release in a meeting with Tony Blair and Bertie Ahern. Adams emerged with the pledge contained in the agreement that an accelerated programme for the release of prisoners would be set in train and 'the intention would be that, should the circumstances allow it, any qualifying prisoners who remained in custody two years after the commencement of the scheme would be released at that point.' Adams and McGuinness decided to clear their heads, so sauntered outside Castle Buildings, discussing the details of the deal as they wandered around the car park wrapped up against the freezing cold. Aware that the constitutional section of the agreement fell far short of republican principles, they knew that the elements which dealt with prisoners, policing, justice and equality issues would be vital to them in selling it to their grassroots. During the night, as they had seen the unionists claw back significant ground on the cross-border bodies, Sinn Fein had appeared to wobble. But by breakfast time Adams had made up his mind, dictating a press statement which made it clear that he would go with the deal, on the understanding that he still had to seek the formal approval of his party's annual conference.

Punch drunk with fatigue, the parties assembled at 5 p.m. for a final plenary session to ratify the agreement. The delay had been caused not by rumblings in republican ranks but by division among the Ulster Unionists. Adams told his fellow negotiators. 'For now it is time to draw a breath; it is time to reflect. Republicans and nationalists will come to this document with scepticism but also with hope. They will ask, does it offer a chance of a way forward. Is it a new beginning?'

The words might have stopped short of a formal endorsement, but those closely involved in the negotiations knew that the Sinn Fein leadership meant business. 'When the broad shape of the agreement became obvious, then I wondered as everyone did, whether they would find some excuse to leave the process or whether they would stick at it, and they did stick at it,' said the UDP's Davey Adams.

'Even in the remarks that each leader made at the final plenary session it was pretty obvious that even though they weren't in a position to accept it there and then, and they had to go through the process of the party, the leadership were determined to do as much as they could to sell it to their movement. When one looks at the agreement and the nature of it, it's nothing short of miraculous that mainstream republicanism as we have known it found themselves able to buy into it.'

From the opposite end of the political spectrum Martin Mansergh, the Irish government's chief architect of the peace process, shared Davey Adams' sense of wonder. 'Undoubtedly complete lack of sleep does dampen euphoria; a little bit of incredulity which took at least two or three days over Easter to properly sink in; but I think an immense sense of achievement, almost a miracle that we had actually got an agreement that in principle the spectrum from Sinn Fein to the unionists and loyalists could subscribe to.'

The Good Friday Agreement dominated Easter Sunday's proceedings, the holiest day in the Republican calendar, when the blood sacrifice of the volunteers of the Rising of 1916 is annually recollected. Adams travelled to Carrickmore, in the heart of hardline East Tyrone, where the IRA had traditionally fought 'a good war' but had also suffered punishing losses at the hands of the loyalist UVF and the security forces. Speaking before 4,000 people Adams commended the 'courage, tenacity and commitment' of the IRA and said he was not being provocative or paying homage to the hard men. 'When I pay tribute to IRA soldiers, I pay tribute not just to their role when they make war, but also to their role when they provide the opportunity for peace.' The conclusion of the previous two days had brought 'another phase of our struggle to an end'. The impetus generated 'through thirty years of struggle will see us through to make further significant advances towards our goal of a free and independent Ireland'.

Adams' audience seemed confused if grudgingly supportive. 'This deal is the best we can get for the moment and we move on from here,' said one man. 'Hopefully there will be a diminishing role for an armed campaign but nobody is saying we gave up the armed struggle because we were tired of it,' said another. 'Every inch is an inch. No one is saying it's over. There's a long road ahead.'

In Belfast's Milltown cemetery the wilder fringes of republicanism were wearing their Easter lilies and berating Adams for selling out their cause. Gerry Byrnes of the Irish Republican Socialist Party, the political wing of the Irish National Liberation Army which had recently been murdering loyalists, said, 'This agreement is nothing more than capitulation to reactionary unionism . . . we call upon those republicans remaining within the Provisional movement to send a clear message to the Adams leadership that while the occupation continues we reserve the right to engage the British forces and those who target the nationalist working class.'

Declan Donnelly, a man barely out of his twenties, told a scattering of republican Sinn Fein supporters that the Irish freedom struggle faced its greatest challenge ever. 'Just as the Treaty of Surrender was met by Republicans with scorn and derision in 1921, so too the second Treaty of Surrender, which has just been launched at Stormont, should be treated as a sell-out and a betrayal.' He ended by quoting the same words which had so inspired Adams' father as a boy, written by Belfast IRA volunteer Tom Williams shortly before he was hanged for killing a policeman: 'To carry on no matter what odds are against you, to carry on no matter what torments are inflicted on you. The road to freedom is paved with suffering, hardships and torture; carry on my gallant and brave comrades until that certain day.'

The next four weeks would see Adams deploying his by now tried and tested tactic of winning approval for a new policy by avoiding committing himself publicly but sending out his most loyal allies to test the water. It had paid off handsomely in the mid-1980s, minimizing the first serious split that the Provisionals had faced since their own birth out of the 1970 break with the Officials. The difference a decade later was that the time-scale in which he must perform what many thought would be a miracle was to be judged in weeks rather than years. When Sinn Fein delegates gathered in Dublin the weekend after Easter it was obvious that no conclusive decision would emerge so soon. Two Sinn Fein members, now sporting dual membership of the breakaway Thirty-two County Sovereignty Committee, which had links with the Provisionals' recently retired quartermaster general, were barred from entering the conference.

True to form, the Provisionals' middle managers gave the Good Friday Agreement qualified support while dissent was voiced by a few grassroots members. Joe Reilly from the Sinn Fein executive said, 'My view is that we should give the document a qualified welcome. I also hold a personal view that we should change our constitution and enter a new assembly.' But Christine Beattie from North Belfast said, 'I cannot advocate a yes vote for an agreement which legitimizes the Six-County statelet and enforces a unionist veto over our people. I believe for Irish republicans to enter such a body could become political suicide.'

The most impassioned speech was made by Tom McNulty from Tyrone, who invoked the memory of an old comrade Paddy Carty who was killed at the age of twenty-six, together with two other IRA men, when the bomb they were transporting exploded prematurely near Omagh in 1973. McNulty's speech was all the more affecting for its emotional, unpolished delivery, and it went to the heart of the old dilemma for republicans of being ruled from the grave.

If I had to go to the grave of Paddy Carty in Dungannon and stand at the end of his grave and say 'Paddy, can this agreement complete the ideals that you died for. Did you open the door for us so that we can walk through and achieve our goals without any more young men and women going down to an early grave or spending the best part of their lives in jail?

'And can I take on this peace process, Paddy, without walking away from your grave and feeling that I let you down because you didn't die in peace? Paddy, you died in the middle of the battle.' But at the same time I know that if Paddy could speak back to me he would be willing to say to me, 'If there's a way that you can do it without any more deaths and without any more destruction, without any more tears and without any more suffering', I would say that Paddy Carty would say to me, 'Tom, you take that way because I gave my life for the freedom of this country'. And I don't know whether this agreement is enough to do that but all I can say is that if we stick together in whatever decisions we do make in the years to come the end result of whether it's good enough or whether it's not will be when I can stand at the end of Paddy Carty's grave and say that 'Paddy, the doors that you opened with your supreme sacrifice, we have the free democratic Ireland that you died for'.

As the day wore on and the debate raged, Adams interjected with a piece of news from the enemy camp. Back in Belfast the Ulster Unionists were voting on whether or not to endorse their leader's support for the agreement. 'We've just heard the word that David Trimble won the vote at the Ulster Unionist Party meeting today and we welcome that. Well done, David. Republicans are never sure whether to clap or not to clap but that's alright. I think the whole sense of the political landscape here is changing and we republicans are in the forefront of that change.' More of an exercise in flushing out the dissenters and gauging just how strong the opposition was going to be, the meeting broke up with a promise to reconvene in three weeks. Before everyone went home to ponder the republican dilemma Adams ventured, 'While the agreement is not a settlement, it is a basis for advancement, it does herald a change in the status quo, and it could become a transitional stage towards reunification.'

Just a few days before the Sinn Fein conference resumed its work, word began to leak out that the Provisional IRA had held yet another Army Convention. The main business involved granting IRA members with a dual role within Sinn Fein a dispensation enabling them to take seats in a future Northern Ireland assembly. According to Paragraph Two of the so-called Green Book rules of the IRA's constitution, 'Participation in Stormont or Westminster and in any other subservient parliament, if any, is strictly forbidden.' The result was a foregone conclusion but, according to a security source, Adams still faced doubt and concerns over the long-standing demand for the decommissioning of IRA weapons as part of the final settlement. Asked by a delegate what would become of its arsenal, Adams batted the question back. 'Are you going to give your guns up?' he asked, leaving it hanging in the air. 'It was a classic Adams move, answering a question with another question, so that he could look as if he was on the man's side without ever having committed himself to a position at all,' the source told the authors.

Just as in 1986, when the IRA convention's decision to back Adams in recognizing the legitimacy of the Irish parliament was made public a few days before the crucial Sinn Fein conference at which the traditionalists, led by Ruairi O Bradaigh, were routed, the same sequence of events emerged. As Sinn Fein delegates gathered once more in Dublin they were informed that the IRA had decided to, in effect, back the taking of seats in a new Northern Ireland assembly. The Sinn Fein leadership tabled two resolutions, endorsing the Good Friday Agreement and, albeit with reservations, assenting to significant changes in Articles Two and Three, the parts of the Irish constitution which contained Dublin's territorial claim to Northern Ireland.

The conference itself was a choreographer's masterwork. Speaker after speaker came out in favour of the leadership, with only a few delegates such as Geraldine Cusack from the Liberties in Dublin spelling out in clear terms what the significance of the day's main vote really meant for Irish republicanism.

> Sovereignty within a thirty-two county republic has always been a core principle for Sinn Fein. Resolution One recognizes that fact but then it goes on to talk around it by suggesting that what we are being asked to do today is to accept a transition period in which the principle of sovereignty is virtually abandoned.
>
> We can use all the sophisticated talk we like to cloud the

issue. But the fact remains that when we vote yes to changes in Articles Two and Three we accept the fact that the six northern counties of our country will become a legitimate part of Great Britain. That is a fact: there is no space on the ballot paper for a reluctant yes. To suggest that there is something intrinsically wrong with the Articles on the basis that the twenty-six-county-state failed to pursue them or to suggest that their defence is based on emotional ties is wrong. They are a legitimate and clear constitutional definition of our country. It is nowhere else.

The republican struggle has always been based on our legal and moral right to work towards the reunification of our country in whatever way the situation demanded at the time. The struggle was part of a just war against the occupation of the North of our country. If Sinn Fein subscribes to the changes in Articles Two and Three we will be choosing to give up that right, we will be accepting the reality that any attempt to undermine the northern state will be an act of treason for those who live in the North and an act of terrorism for those who live in the South. There will be no political status. It is important that republicans recognize the cul-de-sac that we are walking into.'

The line of argument was clear and stark, but nobody was listening. At the back of the hall there was a hubbub of activity as Adams' minder Cleeky Clarke and his aide Richard McAuley led in four of the Provisional IRA's longest-serving prisoners: Hugh Doherty, Eddie Butler, Joe O'Connell and Harry Duggan. Although the Balcombe Street Gang admitted the Guildford and Woolwich no-warning pub bombings of 1974, killing seven people, they were never convicted of those crimes, the sentences passed on Irish innocents instead. But the gang members were each charged with twenty-five separate offences linked to a wave of bomb and gun attacks and their more than twenty years inside English prisons stood as a warning to future generations of Irish bombers.

Now they were home, or at least close to home having been transferred to Irish prisons a short time before as part of the peace process, and once more in the bosom of the Provisional movement. Asking for the temporary release of the Balcombe Street Gang and other prisoners, Adams had given the Irish Prime Minister Bertie

Ahern an assurance that there would be no triumphalism. But the crowd inside the conference hall had other ideas, and the four bombers were given a heroes' welcome by tearful women and men punching their fists in the air. The chair of the proceedings provided a running commentary 'This is a wonderful day to welcome all our comrades home. These are the comrades, these are the people, all of them, the stuff that this struggle is made of, and we're delighted to have them here.'

Adams embraced Hugh Doherty, the brother of Sinn Fein's Vice President Pat Doherty. He said Hugh stood unbowed and unbroken, although, he quipped, he had less hair than Pat. 'We said there could be no political settlement and no peace settlement until all of the prisoners are free, and we mean and we meant that.'

The approval of the prisoners had been vital throughout the peace process, and Adams had worked hard to keep them on side during the final vital days. He had asked the British and Irish governments to grant a handful of important prisoners weekend parole so they could attend the conference and bolster the yes camp. So desperate were Dublin and London for Adams to succeed that they released twenty-seven inmates, among them the Provisional IRA's officer, commanding at the Maze prison, Padraic Wilson, who told the conference, 'Today we as Irish republicans must take decisions and decide upon a course of action which can only be considered if it has the potential to move the struggle forward. We are confident in ourselves; we have created the dynamic for change: this must be developed. Our struggle is not over. There is a lengthy road ahead yet.'

When the card vote was called the doubters were all but forgotten amid the euphoria. Ninety-six per cent voted in favour of ending the republican boycott of a Stormont assembly and for the party to take its seats alongside unionists. 'It's huge. It's a watershed. It is historical,' Adams told one of the authors immediately after the vote. 'But the real history will be made when we get freedom, and we haven't got that yet, and that's where our focus has to be. But today was big business done here by a big party which is going to get bigger in the time ahead.'

Asked if most republicans thought that thirty years of an armed campaign was a fair exchange for a new Northern Ireland assembly and cross-border bodies he said:

Well, the struggle isn't over . . . There were thousands of people here today who have given thirty years of their lives to struggle, who have come from prisons, who have come many times from graveyards to be involved in republican activism and we keep moving forward. The struggle will not be ended until British rule in our country is ended and as I made it very clear the Good Friday paper marked an end of a phase of negotiations. We collectively and democratically worked out today how we're going to approach the next phase so let's get into that and let's keep moving forward.

The historic Sinn Fein decision wiped away the news of a belligerent statement from 'the real IRA', the group associated with the former Provisional quartermaster general which security sources estimated had about 150 members and access to some of the Provisionals' arms dumps. The statement, threatening war on the British cabinet, had been accompanied by a mortar attack on an RUC station in Belleek, County Fermanagh. The group called on all IRA members to switch allegiance from 'the old leadership', which they claimed had betrayed republicanism, to their own caretaker army executive. Few Provisionals seemed to take the invitation seriously.

Having taken the leap of faith Sinn Fein kept a remarkably low profile in the days running up to the joint referenda in the North and South of Ireland on the Agreement. Given a straight choice between a yes and a no, Adams knew there was little point in drawing too much attention to the fact that he and the Ulster Unionist leader David Trimble were now running on the same ticket, particularly since Trimble claimed a strong yes vote would strengthen the Union while Adams argued precisely the opposite.

When the unionist camp wobbled over the appearance of the Balcombe Street Gang at the Sinn Fein conference, Adams even made a semi-apology, explaining that the reception given the prisoners was not meant to have been triumphalist. 'I misjudged the raw emotion of delight which gripped the Sinn Fein *ard fheis* when these four men came in . . . it was I who asked for them to be there. I'm glad they were there. I can understand why some elements of our society were outraged by that.'

Unionist no campaigners tried to frighten voters by dangling the thought of Sinn Fein leaders holding key posts in a future Northern

Ireland cabinet. Willie Ross, a hardline traditionalist MP for the Londonderry East seat, reduced one rally to a chilled silence by telling them 'Just think of it: Gerry Adams as Minister for Education. Gerry Adams in charge of your child's school.'

At a quarter past three on the afternoon of Saturday 23 May Gerry Adams sat on a BBC referendum special television set inside Belfast's King's Hall alongside the lynchpins of the Good Friday agreement, John Hume and David Trimble, waiting to hear the result of the vote. The turnout was massive – the people of Northern Ireland had recognized that they were being asked to give their verdict on something which would shape their destiny for decades ahead. The returning officer Pat Bradley stepped up to make his announcement under a large statue of the British monarch. The votes had been sorted into red, white, and blue trays – red for invalid, white for no, and blue for yes. But none of this royalist imagery unsettled Adams, who knew that, unlike the far more nervous David Trimble, his position remained assured.

When Bradley announced the result, 71.12 per cent in favour, the crowd inside the hall erupted. There were rowdy exchanges between the deal's supporters and its opponents, but they were confined mainly to unionists and loyalists. As the UDP leader Ian Paisley was taunted as a loser, the republicans present were able to look loftily on. Adams reacted to the vote by aiming a dart at Trimble, who, despite the dawning of a new era, was still refusing to talk to him. Talking, Adams argued, was what the decisive vote was all about. 'The people voted for dialogue, and voted for equality, and voted for inclusiveness, and all of this was a partnership, with people from all sorts of different positions, voting yes because they took a leap of faith into the future.'

After taking a back seat during the referendum campaign, Adams notched up a gear, recognizing the Northern Ireland assembly elections as a chance to close the gap on the SDLP. He challenged his partner in the peace process, John Hume, to agree a formal voting pact, an offer he knew was bound to be rejected by the SDLP leader who was readying himself to act as deputy minister in a future government to Trimble.

Within days of the referendum Adams boarded another plane to the United States, brushing off unionist demands that IRA decommissioning must start immediately. Once again his itinerary included a host of plush fund-raising events, including a $250-a-head cocktail reception at the Plaza Hotel in Manhattan, and a $1,000-a-head event on the top of the World Trade Centre. But in contrast to his previous visits he now faced some opposition from diehard Irish Americans. A group calling itself the Irish Republican Movement in America handed out leaflets, featuring a one-cent coin, demanding that not one cent should go to funding 'British rule, British partition, British dominion or any participants' in the future Stormont assembly. John McDonagh, whose New York Irish community radio programme advocated a hardline republican position, argued that 'Gerry Adams is now on the British payroll and we should not be supporting anyone who helps to prop up the British state. We used to picket Charles Haughey and Garret Fitzgerald, and Adams is no different.'

While in America news leaked out that Adams had been invited to the Northern Ireland Secretary's annual garden party at Hillsborough castle, where he might have the opportunity to rub shoulders with the guest of honour, the Prince of Wales. Mo Mowlam thought changing times necessitated an invitation to Sinn Fein's two MPs, if not to Northern Ireland's seven lord lieutenants, the Queen's official representatives in the province, nor to Belfast's most senior law officers. The furore that ensued, however, was shortlived as both Adams and McGuinness declined to attend because of Prince Charles' role as Commander in Chief of the Parachute Regiment, the unit involved in the Bloody Sunday killings.

In comparison to the referendum on the Good Friday agreement which had featured visits by Tony Blair, John Major and even celebrities like the enterpreneur Richard Branson and the pop group U2, the election to the 108 strong Northern Ireland assembly appeared a lacklustre affair. Sinn Fein tried to inject some interest by cheekily standing Adams' mentor from the early days of the troubles, the veteran Belfast IRA leader Joe Cahill, against Ian Paisley in North Antrim. The ploy had little effect on the general sense of election fatigue, but when polling day came the voters knew the new assembly could soon wield power over their hospitals and schools, so they still turned out in healthy numbers, if not quite with the same vigour shown during the referendum.

Gerry Adams was one of the first handful of politicians to know for certain that he would have a place in the assembly. Emerging from the counting room inside Belfast City Hall he pushed his way through a scrum of media people to break the news – he had topped the poll in West Belfast with 9,078 votes, more than 3,000 votes ahead of the SDLP's Joe Hendron. Adams quipped that he had in fact received too many votes – under the proportional representation system Sinn Fein were endeavouring to spread their support amongst less well known candidates to try to get as many as possible elected.

In the end Adams had plenty of reason to be cheerful – his party's share of the vote at 17.6 per cent was its best ever. It gave Sinn Fein eighteen seats in the new assembly and entitled the Republicans to two seats at the cabinet table in a devolved Northern Ireland government, sharing power with the unionists. All of this had been achieved without fatally harming the SDLP which still emerged as the most popular party in Northern Ireland – Adams put it down to his party attracting dormant voters out, those nationalists whose confidence was growing with the advance of the peace process.

Ian Paisley, whose Democratic Unionists had a similar share of the vote to Sinn Fein, vowed never to sit down in a government with IRA terrorists. But Adams brushed this off – his party would take what it was entitled to. He denied suggestions that by becoming a Northern Ireland minister he would be selling out to the establishment, telling the BBC, 'I'll always be a subversive. I think that's the only respectable position for any Irish person to be in while we have so much inequality and injustice, and this assembly doesn't stand alone. The assembly is inextricably linked to the cross-border bodies, to the council of ministers and through the cabinet is the only route to that all-Ireland dimension. So I am modest enough to believe that we can do a good job because of the strength of our struggle and I've always had a conviction, and I've said over the years, that we'd be talking to the British, we'd be talking to the unionists and we'd have a peace settlement. Now we haven't got a peace settlement yet, but I think we're moving in that direction and it's my conviction that we'll get there.'

CHAPTER THIRTY-ONE

The Adams Family

Sinn Fein supporters at the party's *ard fheis* in Dublin's Mansion House in February 1995 chortled over a copy of a Valentine message which appeared in the *Belfast Telegraph* a fortnight before. The message was a little delphic, as Valentines always are, but for observers of the peace process who'd been subjected to countless images of Gerry Adams and the brunette Sinn Fein executive member Lucilita Bhreatnach heading together into political talks, the joke was obvious. '–E–RY –D–MS Forget Colette. Love Only Me Sexy. Your tickly beard drives me wild at night. Luc-L-Ta. hot breath. xoxox'. The Valentine, clearly a spoof, was removed from later editions of the *Telegraph*, but not before dozens were photocopied and circulated among republicans and journalists.

The message was part of a 'nudge-nudge' process of rumour-mongering which gathered pace following the ceasefire as Adams' fame outside Ireland grew and the media became interested in more than his attitude to decommissioning arms. There was no more to the rumour than idle chatter – in various interviews Lucilita Bhreatnach was at pains to point out that she was happily married. Shortly before the Valentine appeared, the *Sunday Express* sent one of its reporters, Maria Trkulja, to carry out the impossible job of knocking on Colette Adams' door in Norfolk Gardens in West Belfast, seeking an exclusive interview. As Mrs Adams almost never exchanged a word with the media, such a task was bound to end in failure. Ms Trkulja found the Adams family home easy to spot because of the precautions which had been taken since the UFF's grenade attack upon it in June 1993:

Mrs Adams now lives behind green bullet-proof glass. The venetian blinds on every window are shut. There is a padlock on the front double gate and a security camera mounted on the front of the house. There are three locks on the front door. There is no doorbell or knocker, only an intercom. I pressed the intercom once, but there was no reply. A black and white spaniel started yapping at the gate to the path at the side of the house. A very English-style family pet seemed a strange choice for the Republicans' leading light. I waited and pressed the intercom again: still no sign of life. There was a wooden plaque on the wall engraved with 'Tir na nog' (which means the land of eternal youth, a piece of Irish folklore). It was the only personal touch. I tried the intercom a third time and was about to give up when a female voice answered. Was this Mrs Adams? 'Linda, is that you Linda?' she asked hesitantly. I asked again if she was Mrs Adams. 'Yes, who is it?' I told her I was a journalist and asked if she would speak to me. 'No, no, no' she shouted in a frightened voice.

Colette hadn't always been quite so invisible to the media. In the early days of the troubles she was actively involved in street politics, every bit as committed to the women's side of republicanism as her close friends Maura Meehan and Dorothy Maguire, who were killed by soldiers in 1971. Reports of Colette's distress when her husband was arrested in July 1973 figured strongly in the Belfast papers. Ten years later she was by his side with their ten-year-old son Gearoid when, shortly after winning the West Belfast seat, he put in an appearance at a rally in Kilmichael in County Cork.

But when in 1987 *The Times* approached her to take part in a series of articles on wives of party political leaders, she declined. Through a Sinn Fein spokesman Colette said she felt she would be seen as 'an appendage of her husband and this was not the case, as she was a political activist in her own right'. The year before, however, she had described her husband as 'very romantic and understanding. He never forgets an anniversary or a birthday.' Mrs Adams confided to Belfast journalist Eamon Mallie that when she first met Adams back in the heady days of the early Troubles in Ballymurphy, he presented her with a rose plucked from a front garden. When the *Sunday Express* tried for their 'exclusive' Richard McAuley, Adams' press officer, told them, only exaggerating slightly, that Colette 'had never given an interview. She doesn't like the media. She wants her privacy and republicans respect that.'

It is undeniable that, down the years, Adams and his wife have led separate lives. From the early days of the Troubles he had to move from house to house to stay one step ahead of both the security forces and potential loyalist assassins. Then there were the long years in jail when he was kept apart from both his young son and the long-suffering 'St Brownie's wife', as Adams' fellow prisoners dubbed Colette. The peace process brought a different kind of separation as Adams jetted off to the United States or South Africa to pursue his handshake diplomacy with the likes of Bill Clinton and Nelson Mandela. After the IRA ceasefire, public sightings of the two together continued to be extremely rare. One occasion when they went out as a couple was during the West Belfast Festival in August 1995 when Colette and Gerry arrived for the première of Dubbeljoint Theatre Company's *Women on the Verge of HRT*. Watching the comedy about middle-aged women whose romantic longings had been reawoken by a trip to Donegal, the two seemed a slightly odd couple – Colette appearing very much the conventional West Belfast housewife, whereas Gerry looked more like a mature student or a trendy lecturer, wearing jeans and a tee shirt.

If Colette has remained silent about her personal life the same cannot be said of her husband. In a television interview with the noted Dublin psychiatrist Anthony Clare, Adams revealed that his first sexual fumblings as a teenager had been with Protestant girls. 'Our first explorations were in the Moyard area, which was loyalist, and our first encounters with young women were with Protestant young women, simply because they were just across the road.' According to neighbours, the young Adams wasn't noted particularly as a 'woman chaser'; indeed in his duffle coat and spectacles his early image around Ballymurphy didn't attract too much notice from the girls. But those aware of his position within the IRA knew that he was no 'nerd', and, as the Troubles began, that contributed to his personal status. The women he associated with, like Colette, he met during his protest activity – ironically, organizing pickets to stop other women meeting young men by going to the Army's discos.

In more recent years, as the *Vanity Fair* writer Maureen Orth pointed out in a lengthy profile, women found the smartly turned out, internationally renowned Adams attractive. But while Adams told Orth that he enjoyed 'the company of women' he made it clear that he wasn't going to be seduced by any 'groupies' who might have been attracted by his movement's shift from Tiocfaidh Ar La – the IRA slogan meaning 'Our Day Will Come' – to what columnists dubbed 'Tiocfaidh Armani'. 'The sex act, if you're very lucky, lasts fifteen minutes. Why even jeopardize a relationship which is based on loyalty and love and working through? So it's just not an issue. Colette is a very strong woman and she has her own identity. I often make the joke that in front of every great woman a man has foisted himself . . . I genuinely couldn't do what I do if my domestic situation crumbled.'

The priest who married the couple, Father Des Wilson, remains a close friend. He says Adams and his counterparts aren't given enough credit for maintaining a degree of normality in their personal circumstances despite living in what has been anything but a normal situation. 'The whole political situation of the last twenty-five years especially has been devastating on people and on their marriages. Imagine what it's like for someone going into prison for ten, twelve, twenty years and then coming out, finding that a family has grown up without them and finding that they hardly know their wives and husbands any more. People who've managed to keep their families and marriages intact deserve a great deal of credit. What kind of person can engage in very intensive political activity and yet keep his or her family together and be faithful to each other and all that, what kind of people are they?'

Despite the jet-setting, Father Wilson says Adams has always kept hold of his Ballymurphy roots:

We have just watched him develop as a political person with a great amount of admiration. There are some people, and I would be among them, who would view with reservation some of the alliances that you have to make, whether it's in the USA or elsewhere. I mean, I'm not sure that the interests of the people of Ballymurphy are going to be served by any kind of alliance with some of the rich multi-millionaires in America. But that's another day's work, you have to make your alliances where you can, and I think Gerry has shown a great amount of skill, first of all in making those alliances and secondly making sure those alliances did not separate him from the people that he came from. I think one of the reasons for that may well be that he comes from a family which has very deep local roots and very deep political republican roots and it would be very difficult for anyone like Gerry to become totally separated from the people that he grew up with. I don't think that his family and his relatives and friends would take a very good view of that. So he's got a good safeguard there.

Gerry Adams continues to rely on his family and friends. When he won back his West Belfast seat in 1997 one of his close companions taking part in the celebrations on the steps of Belfast City Hall was his younger brother Paddy, now no longer the child who played with Gerry during their youth. Paddy is a smaller man than Gerry, but strong looking. His hair is greyer than his elder brother's.

Also outside the City Hall were Gerry Adams' other family – the close band of minders who travel with him wherever he goes. Terence 'Cleeky' Clarke has been beside Adams' shoulder since the days when they were both locked up together in Long Kesh. Clarke was jailed for his part in the mob attack on two British Army corporals at an IRA funeral in West Belfast in 1988. Released early from jail because he was suffering from cancer, Clarke, who prefers to be known by his Irish name Turlough, took up duties as Adams' principal bodyguard. He is not to be trifled with if the going gets tough, but has a wry sense of humour with which he deflects the banter of the Belfast press corps. Clarke was once sitting in the Royal Victoria Hospital waiting for a check-up on his condition when he was unceremoniously frogmarched out by RUC officers. The Northern Ireland health minister was due to visit the hospital and the zealous police decided Clarke was a security risk. The aggrieved bodyguard complained to reporters, 'I was just having a smoke waiting for my cancer check-up when they bundled me out.' 'Cleeky' Clarke stayed with Adams throughout the ups and downs of the peace process, and in the build-up to his boss's re-election in West Belfast BBC Northern Ireland's *Spotlight* programme reported that Clarke and two other bodyguards were registered on the draft Northern Ireland electoral roll at multiple addresses.

Two other bodyguards with chequered careers were Paul 'Chico' Hamilton and Jim McCarthy. In 1979 Hamilton was jailed for twelve years for his part in the attempted murder of a British Army major. Two years previously McCarthy was convicted of possession of weapons and ammunition. The RUC Special Branch agent Martin McGartland identified both men as active members of IRA punishment-beating squads – a practice which Adams says he disagrees with. McGartland says Hamilton and McCarthy abducted him from Sinn Fein's Andersonstown base, Connolly House, and took him off for interrogation. McGartland escaped certain death by leaping out of the window of the flat in which he was being interrogated and surviving a fall of forty feet. Neither Hamilton nor McCarthy has ever been charged with the abduction, but after McGartland had got considerable mileage out of the story on radio and television 'Chico' would jokingly ask reporters, 'How's my old friend Marty?' McGartland – who went into hiding in England – later received a funeral Mass card from 'Your friends in Connelly House [sic] Crumlin Road and Long Kesh'.

Before Gerry Adams' bodyguards caught up with him, McGartland had spent much of his career inside the IRA working in the same unit as Gerry's cousin, Davy. McGarland describes Davy Adams as an indefatigable planner of IRA attacks – in 1995 Davy Adams was sentenced to twenty-five years jail for his part in an attempt to murder a senior RUC officer in East Belfast, described by the judge as 'a sophisticated, carefully planned and serious murder plan'. Five years previously another cousin, Dominic Adams, was jailed for ten years in the Irish Republic for his part in an IRA armed bank robbery. His namesake, Gerry's brother Dominic, served fourteen years after being found guilty of having a revolver and an anti-personnel bomb in 1986.

Adams is rarely to be seen in public without his personal press officer Richard McAuley by his side. McAuley is without doubt the most skilled spin doctor in Northern Ireland – the master of selling a movement which indulges in frequent bouts of indefensible violence as if it is the most reasonable group of people on the scene. McAuley was jailed for ten years after being stopped riding a motorbike with another youth in Andersonstown. An Army patrol discovered McAuley had a .45 Colt revolver and seven rounds of ammunition on him; his pillion passenger had an M1 carbine rifle and two magazines. Another gun was found at McAuley's home. During his time in jail he wrote frequently for *Republican News*, once paying tribute to the extreme left-wing German Baader–Meinhof gang, who had kidnapped and killed businessmen in their country, as 'folk heroes'. After emerging from jail, McAuley supplanted Danny Morrison as the chief purveyor of the Provisional message, and, as Adams shifted position, so McAuley abandoned his left-wing rhetoric and militant approach to appear far more moderate.

McAuley travels everywhere with Adams – and at President Clinton's Investment Conference held in Washington in May 1995 he found himself in the unusual position of having to liaise with his British government counterparts. The Northern Ireland Office press officer Andy Wood offered to buy McAuley a drink while they discussed arrangements, only to be told that the whole Sinn Fein party had made a group decision not to drink while they were abroad. McAuley is rivalled in his influence on the movement's external image only by Sinn Fein's chief press officer, Dublin-based Rita O'Hare. At the internal conference which the party held in Athboy in November 1996, McAuley was asked why all the senior IRA men and Sinn Fein leaders present were drinking milk. 'It's white, the colour of peace,' he joked. 'No, it's to give us good healthy Provos,' Rita O'Hare quipped.

McAuley, like Sinn Fein figures Tom Hartley and Jim Gibney, is an essential part of Gerry Adams' kitchen cabinet – the young Belfast-based 'think tank' of the late 1970s matured and developing in their political thought. One other member who doesn't get quite so much attention is Aidan McAteer, one of Adams' main policy advisers. McAteer sat in on most of the internal discussions Adams held before delivering the 1994 IRA ceasefire. McAteer was jailed for twelve years in June 1975 for his part in a bomb and gun attack on the Army. He is kept out of public view, according to one security source, because his appearance doesn't fit the new smart Sinn Fein look. The alliance between McAteer and Adams has historic resonance – McAteer's grandfather Hugh was the IRA chief of staff who appeared before the same court during the Second World War as Adams' father, Gerry senior.

If the image of the majority of those with whom Adams surrounds himself is one of unbroken republican tradition, one crucial exception to the rule is his relationship with his son Gearoid. Although Gerry Adams senior encouraged his sons to join the IRA, Gerry junior did exactly the opposite with his own child. The authors are assured by those close to Adams that his son is *not* a member of either Sinn Fein or the IRA. Gearoid, a strong and talented Gaelic football player, turns out on a regular basis for the Antrim side. Although his father is no doubt proud of this sporting achievement he is fiercely protective, and with good reason, of his son's privacy. When a BBC current affairs programme used some footage of Gearoid during a Gaelic match to illustrate the political match which Adams had to win in West Belfast, Adams rang the reporter personally to complain. Gearoid could play in full view of several thousand people at Casement Park in West Belfast, but to associate him with his father's politics is to overstep the mark in Adams' view.

The fact that Adams has chosen to steer his only child away from active republicanism has to be significant in understanding his long-term aims. Adams may be no Mahatma Gandhi, and is clearly prepared to contemplate tactical manoeuvres involving people's lives which would leave most conventional politicians gasping. But the stark contrast between Gerry senior and Gerry junior in this respect appears to indicate that, if he can get terms acceptable to him, Adams would much prefer to be living in a more stable society, bequeathing to his child a more peaceful future.

In the summer of 1997 Gearoid qualified as a primary school teacher specializing in physical education. In West Belfast, he will not have been brought up to expect anything of an inheritance from his father beyond a famous name. But the family's financial fortunes have been changed by Gerry Adams' renown. For many years, when not on the run or in jail, Gerry Adams was, to use West Belfast slang, 'on the brew'. Periodically the decision of Britain's 'Public Enemy Number One' to draw public money promoted controversy in the press.

In November 1989 it was reported that the unemployed barman would be called to an interview at a job centre to be offered work or retraining. If he refused both, a decision would be made as to whether his benefits should be stopped. Adams responded by claiming that the information on him had been leaked by a senior Northern Ireland Office source. 'If the British are going to attempt to cut off statutory benefits to political dissidents this represents an extension of their policy of political vetting. It is important that the trade unions involved make clear that they will not be used to politically vet recipients.' Danny Morrison pointed out that since 1983 Adams hadn't taken his pay cheque as a Westminster MP, then £24,000 a year. Therefore, he was costing the taxpayer less than if he was drawing his salary.

Adams continued to draw benefit, and in March 1995 there was a further spate of stories about how he could be claiming money while at the same time earning considerable sums from his books. March 1995 was the last month in which Gerry Adams drew the dole. By that stage it was becoming a bit incongruous, perhaps, alongside his lunch engagements with President Clinton and Donald Trump. On his American trips Adams was drawing $17,000 or more for a lecture – funds which were going not to him personally, but to the Friends of Sinn Fein support group. Adams, however, kept his earnings from his writing – in 1995 these were estimated at £50,000 over the previous thirteen years. This was before the publication of his autobiography, *Before The Dawn*, in 1996. The advance Adams was paid by his publishers, Brandon, has been estimated at £100,000. The book went on to top the Irish bestseller lists for several weeks. The Irish market, however, was tiny by comparison with its potential sales in the United States, Australia and Europe, where it was released in translation.

So even though Gerry Adams abandoned his trade as a barman, and never went on to qualify as the teacher he had once wanted to become, his son Gearoid is set to embark on a teaching career, not get sucked into the IRA, and even, maybe, inherit a sizeable sum which his father has earned by the pen, not by the sword. If he could inherit a long life lived in peaceful times, not only Gerry Adams, but also the majority of the population in Ireland would be happy about the turnaround in the family's fortunes.

CHAPTER THIRTY-TWO

Man of War, Man of Peace

A statesman, a traitor, a terrorist, a peace-maker. Few public figures can prompt so many contrasting assessments as Gerry Adams – a respected community leader in his home patch of Ballymurphy, a hate figure for many loyalists, who would happily see him dead.

Judging Gerry Adams is not an easy task because of both his lack of candour about his past and the uncertainty about what the future may hold for him. In Adams' world, where the direct meaning of words has long since become twisted, actions are more important. If he succeeds in what appears to be his personal objective of delivering a lasting settlement, then history is likely to prove forgiving about his previous involvement in and apology for violence. If violence persists there may be those who will argue that Adams did his best.

When the authors broached this project with Adams' spin doctor, Richard McAuley, he breathed in deeply. 'You could land yourself in the shit,' he warned, 'because you will have to address the whole question of Gerry's secret life, or' – he quickly qualified his statement – 'whether or not he has a secret life. And whatever you say about that, you're liable to annoy somebody. And that's the name of the game.' Adams himself gave no assistance to us in compiling this book – rather he took the view that it was an impertinence. He would prefer people to stick to his own autobiography. Unfortunately while he is the best-placed person to provide information about his own life, he is probably the least qualified to assess it.

We hope to have lifted some corners of the blanket which covers Gerry Adams' secret life, but this process is far easier in regard to his earlier years than it is when you begin to approach the present day. The evidence that Adams joined the IRA in the early 1960s seems clear, that he was involved in carrying out and planning violence in the early to mid-1970s appears to us unquestionable. But what of Adams the politician, Adams the peace-broker? Did he leave the IRA? We think not. And what does that say about his role during the 'peace process' of the 1990s? Truly he is, to borrow Winston Churchill's famous phrase, 'a riddle wrapped in a mystery inside an enigma'.

There are, for want of a better phrase, valid reasons why Adams cannot tell the whole truth. As he pointed out to psychiatrist Dr Anthony Clare, 'It's an illegal thing to join the IRA . . . The history of these times will have to be told some time when it is not illegal.' But on top of this 'white lie' has been built a web of deceit which has become an integral part of Adams' strategy. Sinn Fein is not the IRA and the IRA is not Sinn Fein, therefore I did not kill anyone, therefore I have no weapons, therefore everybody else is being unreasonable when they have difficulty in talking to me. The separation strategy fostered during the 1980s and come to fruition during the 1990s has brought benefits, enabling Adams and his party to slip through a variety of political loopholes and broaden their circle of friends and sphere of influence around the world. But no wonder that his opponents refuse to believe him even when he is telling them that two and two makes four. He lacks not only Nelson Mandela's democratic majority, but also Mandela's honesty and relative transparency.

To say that Adams continues to be an IRA leader, though, is not necessarily to put a balaclava on his head and a gun in his hand, eager to carry out any act of violence irrespective of its consequences. As one senior policeman remarked to the authors: 'I would be more concerned if he wasn't on the IRA's Army Council.' Within the IRA there is a sense of discipline which stifles external signs of debate, but nevertheless there is clearly a range of views. Adams' analysis and tactics are undoubtedly different in kind to, for instance, Brian Keenan, the hardline Marxist who has been credited with masterminding many of the IRA's bombing campaigns in England. Were it not for Adams' status within the IRA, he would not have been able to neutralize Keenan at a time when his fellow Army Council comrade was deeply unhappy about the course the Provisionals' peace strategy was taking. Nor would he have been able to face down the challenge, when it came, from the quartermaster general at the decisive IRA convention of October 1997.

Before the 1994 ceasefire Adams maintained that he 'went to the

IRA' to give them political briefings. After the return to violence he even took John Hume along to one of these affairs, where the two men put their respective analyses to the IRA leaders. Adams claimed he needed political information and promises to 'go to the IRA' and ask them for a new ceasefire. But, to see the IRA, does he have to do any more than look into his bathroom mirror? Both security personnel and former IRA members who have talked to the authors refer to Adams as 'the chairman of the board'. The best British guess available places him at the time of writing on the IRA's seven-strong Army Council. He is not the IRA's chief of staff, but in the past that has not mattered as the chief of staff has done his bidding.

The IRA informer Sean O'Callaghan maintains that from October 1982 onwards 'Adams stopped playing an operational IRA role and never actually resumed a day-to-day IRA involvement, while he remained probably the most senior person at the leadership of the IRA. But he certainly distanced himself from day-to-day IRA activity. He was only really attending Army Council meetings. Prior to that he was adjutant general of the IRA, he was never chief of staff.' O'Callaghan says that in the mid-1980s Adams and Ivor Bell came up with the idea of a 'Revolutionary Council. It was a think tank, basically, which incorporated some senior IRA people and some senior Sinn Fein people. I was at a couple of its meetings and the idea was that this would eventually be the ruling body of the republican movement. I'm pretty certain that, although it's not called the Revolutionary Council now, what we're looking at is a committee composed of senior IRA people, Army Council people and people perhaps like Adams who can say they're not on the Army Council and people are not really aware of another ruling body but that there is a committee composed of senior Sinn Fein people and they are in fact the people who are running the republican movement now. I have no doubt that Adams and McGuinness are firmly in charge.'

Whether such a committee still formally exists is very doubtful, but it is the same small group of people who make key decisions on behalf of Sinn Fein and the IRA. Adams derives his authority in the main from his membership of this clique. He has moulded it and formed its objectives down through the decades. Superficially he appears to govern by a form of consensus, not pushing his own views but letting others voice them, answering questions with questions. But more often than not he knows the direction he is heading in well in advance. If you share his analysis, your career path within the organization is likely to be steep. If not, you will soon find yourself marginalized and isolated. According to one former IRA comrade, 'His stock in trade is manipulation. He took over Belfast before he took over nationally and he did it the exact same way by targeting individuals to get rid of them and pushing people into their positions.'

These days, though, Adams has a wider power base and a wider prospectus than his IRA clique. As an MP with a healthy majority and the man whose strategy helped bring Sinn Fein a second seat in the British parliament and the first seat it could actually occupy in the Irish parliament, Adams is in some senses bigger than the movement from which he emerged. This, politically, is an incredible achievement for the former Ballymurphy military commander – to be seen by ordinary nationalists not as a man responsible for contributing to the conflict but as an honest broker with a difficult job. A cynic may see the rise of Adams as the victory of personality over principle, but a believer is entitled to hail the transformation of a figure willing to break the bonds of his upbringing and tradition.

Adams is also the man who met the President, against the odds. Niall O'Dowd, the US-based Irish publisher, who did as much as anyone to make that possible, says that when Clinton chatted with Adams the two men were able to draw on common interests:

> I think President Clinton was impressed with Adams. I think that from the start Adams made clear that he was trying very hard to deliver a long-term IRA cessation. I think President Clinton took him at face value . . . They are men of similar age in many ways influenced by the same things. The generation thing was important. As far as I know they discussed many of the same influences, Martin Luther King and the history of the civil rights movement in the United States. I believe they got on quite well. But Adams is an impressive figure and I think whatever his opponents think of him in terms of Northern Ireland politics he stands out as a bright, intelligent, articulate figure irrespective of his politics.

What Adams has going for him, be it with President Clinton or with other figures outside Northern Ireland, is a sense that he lives in the modern world, in contrast to the often fusty figures which unionism tends to throw up. He is able to talk about literature, the cinema, the arts, issues beyond the confines of the immediate conflict. Even some who would be Adams' implacable opponents recognize a personal charm and ability to relate with different kinds of people. One senior RUC detective who had to interrogate him confessed to having 'actually enjoyed the interview'. 'If I was going out for an evening and I had a choice of him or Ian Paisley I know who I would pick.'

He is attractive to young people too. When he arrived at the Centrepoint building in Belfast where a schools political forum was being staged in 1997 he was mobbed by children anxiously seeking his autograph, according him the status of pop star. By the time he left, though, his presence seemed to have had a divisive influence on the hitherto amiable nature of the pupils' debate. They were almost at one another's throats, the tension boiling between Catholic and Protestant teenagers.

But this is at a superficial level. Beneath the affable exterior there clearly lies a very cold and shrewd tactician, one who could contemplate the mayhem, tragedy and disruption which Drumcree 1996 brought into ordinary people's lives as an opportunity to be 'developed and exploited'. One can grant Adams a modicum of humanitarian motivation in devising and developing his 'peace strategy'. But he has at times remained willing and able to stir the pot in Northern Ireland until it boils – occasionally throwing in an ingredient which might appear to be helpful, but which he knows is likely to have far from positive repercussions. Despite these caveats, though, Adams remains in the view of many the only person on the horizon who can possibly deliver an end to IRA violence – so censure of his tactics, censure of his refusal to condemn violence, must be qualified by the crossing of fingers that one day, somehow, peace can be found and Gerry Adams will have made a significant contribution to it.

After the Docklands bombing Adams told Albert Reynolds, 'We lost the debate, it's as simple as that.' Despite the end of the ceasefire, first in England, then back in Northern Ireland, the former Irish Prime Minister remained convinced that Adams wanted to bring about a permanent end to political violence. 'That's his objective in life. I think that's what he wants to do.'

Reynolds took heart fom the restoration of the ceasefire in 1997 and Sinn Fein's subsequent historic endorsement of the Good Friday Agreement, not only because of what they represented in themselves, but also because he felt no other republican leader could have delivered in Adams' stead.

> Because if he can't do it I think you're another generation away from somebody who'll command the respect from both sides within the republican movement, from both the military hardline men and the others. I don't know of anybody else.
>
> If the thing doesn't work out, if you lose Adams and McGuinness, which you could well do, I don't see anybody else on the horizon for this generation. I would hate to think that the hardline men would take over and we'd face another twenty-five years. Because I think it would be worse than the last twenty-five years.

For an entirely contrasting assessment you can turn to Sir John Wheeler, the man who was the British government's security minister in Northern Ireland at the time of the IRA ceasefire. Wheeler says the ceasefire was bogus and he would never have met Adams unless he had been driving a 'pantechnicon of Semtex' up to the steps of Stormont Castle to hand it over. How then did the Conservative government's hawk think history would judge Adams? 'It depends whether history is judging him on fact or on myth. Given the propensity of all things in the island of Ireland to be cloaked in a myth of romantic idealism, probably as a sort of hero. But in a world where there is a more critical analysis of his character and involvement he would be seen for what he is, a racketeering criminal thug.'

Another sceptic, although coming from a very different quarter, is the Dungannon priest Denis Faul, who crossed swords with Adams during the hunger strikes and who has ever since been a persistently outspoken critic of the IRA. During the 1994 ceasefire, Faul met Adams at a funeral and the Sinn Fein president urged the priest, 'Don't be so hard on us . . .' Faul responded that as long as IRA violence continued, be it punishment beatings or bombings and murders, so would his criticism. Father Faul believes Adams is a good politician who clearly achieved something by building his political party. He also believes Adams has moved away, in his heart of hearts, from purist republican aims. But he is not convinced that he can take the IRA all the way with him:

The trouble with Sinn Fein and the Provos is that they only talk to Sinn Fein and the Provos, they're not in the real world. There has to be some kind of compromise and an appreciation of a person's point of view. They're not into that. The thing about the Provos, you see, is that they're ruled from the grave. 1916, Milltown cemetery. Each Sinn Fein association is run by the youngest volunteer in the IRA. If somebody gets up in a Sinn Fein meeting and says, 'I think we should talk to the Brits and work for a United Ireland by political means alone and take our seats in Westminster,' some young fella is going to get up and say, 'My brother was shot by the SAS, he wasn't shot for you to go and take a seat at Westminster.'

Interviewed again after the Good Friday Agreement, Faul was heartened by what had occurred, although still unwilling to back away from his previous caveat that he didn't believe Adams would be the man who delivered lasting peace.

I hope he's on that road. I was pleased to see he did denounce the Continuity IRA people and those who sided with Bernadette Sands. Sinn Fein had the guts at least to expel them. They were good signs. I think Gerry actually would like to be a full-time politician. He's good at it; he's clever; he's patient; he would love to go to Westminster. His ambition is probably to out poll the SDLP. But there must be that moral part, that's what worries me. There must be that morality that you respect human life, put it in no danger, and get away from any element of violent force, and that you reach out above all to your Protestant neighbour and, of course, the Protestant leaders should be doing the same.

I've always seen Gerry Adams as a very patient politician – patience is a virtue he has more than any other politician in Ireland – and I would say that when Sinn Fein voted yes it was what they could see two, three, four, five years down the road and that would worry me. Throughout the last six months Gerry Adams and his followers simply went on to say they were looking for a united Ireland. The farthest they would go is that this was a phase, another phase on the road to a United Ireland ... I've seen nothing said by Gerry Adams and his followers which would reach out in trust to the Protestant people. And that is the biggest need we have in Northern Ireland, we need to build trust. We need to stand in the shoes of our neighbour and realize what has kept the Protestants in fear since 1921: a lot of it is the IRA ... Gerry is in a powerful position now to create an element of trust on the other side.'

From the Protestant side of the community the Reverend Jack Weir holds a unique position in understanding the Provisionals. In 1975 he met the IRA leaders Dave O'Connell and Ruairi O Bradaigh at Feakle, County Clare, to discuss a ceasefire. Weir says that he heard later that Adams was strongly opposed to the meeting and the talks taking place.

Weir renewed his Provisional contacts after the IRA massacre of Protestant construction workers at Teebane, County Tyrone, and the consequent UFF murders of Catholics at the Sean Graham bookmakers in Belfast's Ormeau Road, out of the same sense that Christians had a duty to try and stop the cycle of killing. He began a series of meetings with Adams and Tom Hartley, driving to private houses in West Belfast under terms of strict security and secrecy. 'He was very civil, you could argue with him. He had his standpoint and the logic flowed from there.' But for all Adams' studied image as a man of letters and an intellectual, Weir considered the man whom Adams helped topple, Dave O'Connell, as having a better brain:

His main concern was that he wanted to get into discussions with the political authorities and thought that perhaps through us he might. My impression was that his objective was to be accepted as an equal partner in political circles, that he claimed his mandate and so forth, regardless of the IRA violence.

I told him that was not the basis for democratic discussion, that democracy meant abjuring the use of force.

Over tea and buns they chatted for many hours and from these contacts Weir formed the impression that the Provisionals had not really moved on that much from his meetings in 1975, which he said annoyed Adams.

They still had the same idea that if the Brits went the Irish would march arm in arm to the dawn of a new day. He was angry because he felt there had been a great many changes. He was going on about the Brits, the problem was the British government and everything was other people's problems. We tried to say forget about the British government, think more about the people here who don't like being treated like puppets, as if they didn't have their own point of view, it wasn't as if the British government was pulling their strings.

He said that unionists might believe themselves to be British but they were mistaken. 'If their eyes would only open they would know that they really belonged to us.' In a sense he had to say that because that was part of his analysis and if he moved from that his logic fell down – the logic of the IRA campaign, the republican campaign was on a shaky basis. We knew that was incorrect and that was what we were trying to impress upon him. In a sense he was prepared to adjust it somewhat but not basically. I hoped that while he was not admitting this, he was absorbing it.

Asked if Adams recognized that he had to come to some agreement with unionists, Weir says: 'Certainly it moved on to that and yet I felt it hadn't really stuck with him. With part of his head he accepted that, but in his heart he was reacting in the old way. I don't think that the republicans have changed their basic analysis. But human beings are illogical creatures and can live with logical incompatibles, that's the best that can be hoped for here. There are going to be a lot of loose ends.'

Weir recalls meeting Adams shortly after the 1993 Shankill bomb, where the minister did not hide his anger with the Provisionals. 'He said he was very sorry, but in a war these things happen. "I regret it like any soldier would regret any incident in wartime." Just as he regretted the casualties on his side. There was no acknowledgement that the whole thing was wrong: regret, yes, but part of the price of a campaign.'

Weir felt that Adams would not share the 'abject and true remorse' expressed by the loyalist leader Gusty Spence for all the victims of the Troubles when he announced the Combined Loyalist Military Command's ceasefire.

Regret and grief, grief most for his own casualties which he came back to, the way that they had been shot up by the forces. He felt that they had been suffering. He was full of their own sufferings, just as all parties here are much more conscious of the way they've suffered than the way others are suffering. He said he was being demonized, not being treated as a rational human being. And he's not a demon, he's just another human sinner in a sinful world. I said to him, 'Just as you demonize the Brits and the Orangemen and they are just as human as you are.' Whether he accepted that or not, he didn't admit it.

I took it that according to his lights he was a Christian. I remember seeing him take communion at the enthronement of Cahal Daly [the Catholic Primate of Ireland]. It might be compared with the Christianity of generals in a war. I don't want to question his sincerity any more than I would question the sincerity of a general. I see him seeing himself in those terms. I don't accept that as my estimate of it, but that's the way he sees it. Or if not a general, a politician who sends the generals out – a Churchill.

One observer who has no illusions about Gerry Adams' past is General Sir James Glover, the former head of Army intelligence. He believes that, whatever one thinks of him, Adams is a man with whom the British government are likely to have to do business. 'My own judgement now, would be that Adams is probably the one person who can actually deliver the IRA. In that respect I think he actually does stand above McGuinness . . . because of his terrorist background he is accepted by the terrorists as a man who knows really what he is talking about and not someone who's just been imposed on them. So he has the operational background. He is obviously highly articulate; he's intelligent; he's got considerable political flair, and despite some of the more unattractive things which he's obviously done over the years, because of his dominant position, I personally don't think that the government has got any alternative but to negotiate with him, like they've done with his counterparts elsewhere in the world over the last twenty or thirty years.'

General Glover admires Adams' skill in dealing with his own backwoodsmen. 'I think that's a measure of the astuteness of the man that he's been able to keep the IRA together and that the extreme elements, whatever label they may now like to put upon them, have by and large responded to his authority. But as soon as he starts in any way to be seen to be discredited, that authority will disappear and things will become very difficult.' Glover believes the key alliance Adams has depended on throughout has been with Sinn Fein's chief negotiator Martin McGuinness. 'I used to wonder if there was a power struggle between the two of them and again I sense that that is not so, that they complement each other. I don't think there can be much personal jealousy separating them. They do share a common cause, a common aim. They make quite a good pair because they can each play the same or a different tune whenever circumstances demand. Standing on the touchline today, I can't see their position actually being threatened by any other individuals at the moment.'

Having survived the IRA bombing of the Grand Hotel in Brighton, an attack which claimed the lives of two of his close friends, Michael Ancram often found himself asked what it was like to sit opposite Gerry Adams in the discussions with Sinn Fein during the ceasefire. The Northern Ireland political affairs minister saw Adams as a product of long years of Irish history. 'I think he comes from the tradition of Irish republicanism that sees no contradiction in being a man of war and then seamlessly moving into the democratic process. If you look back through Irish history, there's a number of examples of that. It's part of the tradition, De Valera being a very good example of it, and I think he may see himself in that context of, you know, moving seamlessly without betraying any principles on the way from what he would describe as the armed struggle into the commanding heights of democracy.'

On a personal level Ancram found Adams and his colleagues impressive, but blinkered. 'All of them are well read, all of them know their side of Irish history. I think one of the weaknesses that exists right throughout Ireland is that they haven't bothered to study the history of the other side particularly fully. They are all fundamentalists and that came through to me very strongly. The point of fundamentalism is that you have such a commitment to your own beliefs that you can justify all sorts of other things, and that came through from Adams, just as strongly as it did from Martin McGuinness and from Gerry Kelly. But if you said to me, "What is he like as a person who you can sit down with and have a meal with?" . . . I don't know because I never met him on that basis.'

Someone who has known Adams for many years on just such a personal basis is the radical Ballymurphy priest Father Des Wilson. Wilson reflects the sense of pride felt in Ballymurphy for a local boy made good:

> Most people would look upon him first of all as a neighbour, and his family as neighbours. In other words you introduce an element of normality into what is a very emotional kind of reaction to him. They would also look upon him as a man that they could trust. All through the years he has taken a very active part, of course, in republican politics. But he would be looked upon here, and I would share this view, as one of the very few people who could actually bring a military campaign into a political campaign.
>
> He could do that successfully and I think people would want him to do that. I have tremendous respect for him. I would certainly interpret what he has done in a very benign way because I have seen him so closely. I would hope that the future would be one in which he could take his place, which I think he deserves, and one in which I think he could contribute a great deal in a political settlement. I can't see how it's coming and I can't see the mechanics of it. All I know is that if we have to do without people of the quality of Gerry Adams then it will be a very much diminished democracy in my view. I think we need him and we need people like him, and his presence there has helped other people to emerge who would have exactly the same kind of quality.

Gerry Adams chose to try to transform the fortunes of the Provisionals and pursue his ambiguous TUAS strategy at a time when he and his allies were in complete control. His desire to be at the helm therefore has to be taken into account in assessing him, because it is easy to forget that he was one of the hardliners who opposed the 1975 ceasefire of Dave O'Connell and Ruairi O Bradaigh, as well as the determined youth who told William Whitelaw in 1972 that 'all bets are off'. Maturity and contemplation of his son's future may have had a part to play. But being the man in charge, rather than a bit player in somebody's else's process, is also an obvious element.

The young Adams always had an interest in politics, but his family ties and the force of violent circumstances meant that he wasn't going to follow Cathal Goulding and his Official IRA down the road to peaceful politics. Then as the bloodshed worsened he applied his considerable tactical skills to taking on the enemy and outmanoeuvring those on his own side who he believed could pose a threat. The hunger-strike period gave him the momentum to build a powerful political front and dabble his toes in the water of electoral campaigning. The dual strategy enabled that political base to be expanded without any threat of a split with the militarists. Adams was prepared to contemplate and ride out a split in the mid-1980s, over the issue of abstentionism. But he did this only after being absolutely sure of his ground with the IRA. It was also a useful step in his campaign to consolidate the control he and his allies exerted over the movement.

The dual strategy, however, inevitably limited Adams' political potential, hence the 'peace process' of the 1990s. A benign observer would say that the middle-aged leader was at last able to return to the conventional politics and agitation which he had dabbled with in his youth. A sceptic would point out that the endless toll of deaths had actually blunted the political force of IRA violence and that it was a master stroke to increase the power of the bomb and the bullet by holding out the possibility that the weapons could be silenced for ever. Whatever the case, Adams pursued the process more suredly to its conclusions than many would have believed.

Which will take precedence in time, Adams' early violent career or his later search for alternatives? Adams once paid a backhanded tribute to the Northern Ireland Secretary Peter Brooke, who he said was more thoughtful than 'some of the dimwits they have sent'. Brooke says of Adams: 'I think like all human beings he'll go down on the totality . . . If his contribution has been genuine and single-minded to bring these matters to a conclusion, it is the fact that he had the earlier role which will have given him, if you like, the centrality to be able to seek to achieve what he's been seeking to achieve and therefore is very important to the second part. He wouldn't have achieved the second part if he hadn't had the first.' Well aware of the lessons of Michael Collins, it was Brooke who paid tribute to Adams' courage as he made his choices during the peace process.

Another variety of tribute, however backhanded or indirect, came from the Irish film director Neil Jordan in his epic movie on the life of Michael Collins. The great IRA leader's fortunes as an icon had risen and fallen, but mainly fallen, down the years since his assassination at the hands of former comrades who swore he had sold out on the republican ideal of an independent United Ireland. The republican socialist and former MP Bernadette McAliskey shrewdly noted in 1995 that the revival of interest in all things Collins was like a barometer. Suddenly it was all right to be a compromiser. And a Belfast IRA man told the authors: 'Collins was all right really. He spoke the Brits' language, he was good at whacking [killing] them.'

When Jordan came under a barrage of hostile attention from the British press, he denied their claims that his film was a thinly veiled paean to Adams and the peace process. With cinema managers in Belfast holding private screenings to assess if it might stir up violent passions and the film becoming the most successful box-office hit ever in Ireland, it was undeniable that to the vast majority of Irish people it certainly spoke to them of this moment in their history. In the Irish newspapers Jordan had already admitted that the events of 1994 and 1995 had a bearing on his film. And in interviews with Spanish newspapers, he went further, telling *El Pais* in September 1996: 'Gerry Adams would be the Michael Collins of today, a heroic and positive figure who tries to stop the armed movement and transforms it into political strategies.' Curiously, in the same newspaper a month later he had slightly revised that opinion, saying that comparisons with Adams were irrelevant. 'But if one insists on making comparisons I would say that when the ceasefire was broken the response of Collins would have been to split the republican movement. Adams decided to press on with the political process.'

So how would the screenwriters of the future immortalize the most important Irish republican since Michael Collins? Adams would maintain that he remains true to his ideals. It is clear that he has seen the limitations of the simple 'trenchcoat and revolver' approach typified by his father. More can be gained, he believes, by pursuing the political path and joining the other 'men in suits'. But he has not left his youth behind. Indeed in a sense he is specifically drawing on that brief period of 'political' activity within the old IRA before the 1969 split, when he urges that he should not be left alone in the negotiating room, but should be backed up by a militant campaign of street protests. After the 1997 ceasefire he said that 'side by side with the demand for talks, nationalists should mobilize and agitate and talk tactics and strategy'.

This agitational approach is a way of keeping the IRA volunteers busy. It has also contributed to a political climate which has seen the electoral growth of Sinn Fein at the expense of the SDLP. Moreover, it has proved important in consolidating Adams and his supporters at the helm of the republican movement – in contrast to previous generations of leadership Adams has called a lengthy ceasefire, which arguably failed, and survived that failure strong enough to try the same tactic all over again and succeed.

Adams has won admirers in unlikely places. Davey Adams, his loyalist namesake, was disconcerted to find that, inside Castle Buildings as the talks progressed, he was forced to reassess the Sinn Fein president. 'I think, although not many unionists and loyalists would admit it, all of us could not help but be impressed by Sinn Fein in general and Adams in particular – their ability and the detail of their discussions and papers and how much they actually put into the whole thing. I think it became pretty obvious that they were very concerned about trying to move the situation forward to bring about some sort of a resolution.'

Davey Adams doesn't believe that the Sinn Fein president has experienced a Road-to-Damascus-type conversion but he does foresee a considerable future for him. 'I have never been of the view that it was entirely to do with the question of morality or conscience that the Sinn Fein leadership have moved to where they are; it's to do with the acceptance of reality. The fact that once you enter into politics in its broader sense, and particularly the democratic end of politics, there are rules that impose themselves on you. I think what Sinn Fein are going through is a natural process of transition. Militant republicans are always afraid that as soon as their members start involving themselves in politics they will end up at some stage as 'constitutional', but that's what's happening. Adams has talent, there's no doubt about that. He has major talent, and so has McGuinness to a lesser extent, and I think if we move to a situation where we can resolve the conflict and we have structures that are working and that most people can owe their allegiance to, I think those two people will have major roles to play in our society here. I don't think there's any doubt about it.'

Davey Adams' party, the Ulster Democrats, is the political wing of the Ulster Freedom Fighters, who came close to killing Gerry Adams in 1984 and then again at Milltown cemetery in 1988. A more grudging but perhaps more remarkable reassessment of the Sinn Fein president is provided by Michael Stone the man who, inside the cemetery, had his finger on the trigger. Asked to reflect on Gerry Adams and Martin McGuinness' role in the Good Friday Agreement and whether with hindsight, he was glad they survived his murder bid, Stone thought long and hard:

> With hindsight ... hindsight's a wonderful thing, but, yes, I suppose so. That's a begrudged 'I suppose so' because ten years ago I was willing to sacrifice my life for what I believed in. The Enniskillen tragedy wasn't justification for what I did but the Milltown thing was just something I believed I had to do. As you've said, Adams and McGuinness have brought the republican death squads on and they are seemingly making the transition into a democracy. If they believe in that democracy, then the majority rules and they have a political mandate, I accept that. They should have their place at the talks. It would really be a no comment on whether or not I regretted trying to take Adams and McGuinness out.

Some former IRA prisoners cannot see the transformation of Adams in a positive light. Anthony McIntyre, who served seventeen years for murdering a loyalist paramilitary, has put his IRA past to good use in writing a Ph.D. thesis on Northern Ireland politics. He was forced to reflect on the Provisionals' Long War, in which he participated and believed, on seeing the Maze prisoners' Officer Commanding Padraic Wilson endorse Adams at the extraordinary Sinn Fein *ard fheis* which voted to recognize a Stormont-style assembly.

Having served part of his sentence at the Maze under the leadership of hunger striker Bobby Sands, McIntyre feels that the historic vote was 'an indication of just how defeated the orginal Provisional republican project is'. Responding in the *Guardian* to his old comrade Danny Morrison's argument that the IRA had not been defeated by accepting the Good Friday Agreement, McIntyre said he too hoped that the war was over. 'But it would have been over twenty-plus years ago, and in less ignominious fashion, had the post-truce leadership [of Adams and McGuinness in the late 1970s] not insisted on fighting to an inglorious conclusion. And then we would have been spared the twin sorrows of one jail Officer Commanding

[Sands] dying to resist British state strategy and a second [Wilson], through no fault of his own, appearing to legitimize it.'

Bobby Sands' sister, Bernadette, believes the struggle must go on, and that by taking the road of the peace process Gerry Adams has left Irish republicanism behind.

> I am very saddened that we have witnessed a day come when once again we have seen those who have decided to leave a republican position and shift into a constitutional position, whereby they're recognizing the legitimacy of British rule in our country and partition . . . I was very cautious in relation to the first ceasefire because I couldn't understand why all the jubilation was taking place. It was apparent that there was nothing really there. People had hoped there was something there, perhaps some sort of hidden development, but that has not been the case at all . . . When, prior to the negotiations, Gerry Adams stated that no leader would have the authority to negotiate for anything other than the dismantling of partition and the withdrawal of Britain from our country, I would have agreed with him. But it soon became apparent that that was not what was on offer. This left me very worried and confused as to why republicans were involved in that process when it was obvious it was not going to deliver and could not possibly deliver what was necessary to solve this problem.

Questioned about whether Gerry Adams has betrayed the cause which her brother died for, Bernadette Sands avoids personalizing the issue.

> People do not go out to give their lives in order to create a political base or to increase a voting strength. People, and it's not unique to our country, go out and do these things with great courage because the courage of their conviction is that it's for the independence of their country and their freedom, and yes, that is where they feel it's worth dying for. Nothing else less than that would be acceptable . . . The IRA was a reaction to the British occupation of our country. IRA men and women went out to fight to uphold the republic and to oppose British rule in our country. If at the end of this agreement we still have that

situation then we will still have an IRA, and unfortunately we will still see it manifest itself once again . . . I would just wonder and question by what authority not only Gerry Adams, but John Hume and Bertie Ahern, who are supposedly representative of the Irish people in general, by what authority did they take part in negotiations that brought about a situation which was usurping the sovereign position of our country?'

The fact that, across Ireland, 85 per cent of people backed the Good Friday Agreement shows that Bernadette Sands represents a tiny minority, albeit a minority which may prove capable of disrupting the peace for which so many others yearn. But the juxtaposition of her views and Anthony McIntyre's alongside those of Michael Stone and Davey Adams illustrates just how much Northern Ireland has been turned upside down in the years of the peace process. Praised by loyalists and damned by some former comrades, Adams will clearly have to go on working at convincing the sceptics for many years to come. To those who say he should have taken his present course twenty or more years ago he could argue that the settlement which emerged in the 1990s could never have been achieved in the 1970s because unionists and loyalists then were adamantly and violently opposed to it. It is not only republicans who can be treated to the taunt that the Good Friday Agreement was 'Sunningdale (the 1974 solution) for Slow Learners'. To those who argue that he should not continue on his chosen path he can point to the referenda North and South in May 1998 as the ultimate proof of where the hearts of the people of Ireland really lie.

Researching this book has led us to believe that Adams was unready to settle all those years ago, when Sunningdale was on offer, for the compromise which he has now bought into. But his learning curve has followed the same trajectory as tens of thousands of other Irish and Ulstermen and -women. It was the SDLP leader John Hume who first urged his fellow citizens to draw a line under their troubled history and make a fresh beginning and perhaps that is the best verdict of all on the astonishing career of Gerry Adams. Blame can be apportioned to the few and the many for the thousands of deaths which have occurred in Northern Ireland since 1969. It is a far more difficult task to praise those who have indeed taken risks to make peace.

Belatedly, perhaps, Gerry Adams took on the challenge of persuading his IRA comrades to be ruled, not by the graves of their dead comrades, but by their hopes for their children. It has been a high-wire act, requiring all his resources of patience, cunning and sheer leadership. Historians will pick their parallels, be they Michael Collins, Eamon De Valera, Sean MacBride or Cathal Goulding, all IRA leaders who in time took a different road. Throughout his long years at the helm of the Provisionals, Gerry Adams has been undoubtedly a man of war. In the light of the peace process of the 1990s and the extraordinary evolution of Sinn Fein and the IRA it appears to the authors that he must also be recognized as a man of peace.

Select Bibliography

Adams, G., *Falls Memories*, Dingle, Brandon Book Publishers Ltd, 1982.

Adams, G., *Free Ireland: Towards a Lasting Peace*, Dingle, Brandon Book Publishers Ltd, 1986.

Adams, G., *The Politics of Irish Freedom*, Dingle, Brandon Book Publishers Ltd, 1986.

Adams, G., *Cage Eleven*, Dingle, Brandon Book Publishers Ltd, 1990.

Adams, G., *The Street and Other Stories*, Dingle, Brandon Book Publishers Ltd, 1992.

Adams, G., *Before the Dawn*, London, Heinemann in association with Brandon Brook Publishers Ltd, 1996

Baroid, C. de, *Ballymurphy and the Irish War*, London, Pluto Press, 1990.

Beresford, D., *Ten Dead Men, the Story of the 1981 Irish Hunger Strike*, London, Grafton, 1987.

Bishop, P., and Mallie, E., *The Provisional IRA*, London, Heinemann, 1987.

Clarke, L., *Broadening the Battlefield, the H-Blocks and the Rise of Sinn Fein*, Dublin, Gill and Macmillan, 1987.

Collins, E., with McGovern, M., *Killing Rage*, London, Granta, 1997.

Devlin, B., *The Price of My Soul*, London, André Deutsch in association with Pan Books, 1969.

Dillon, M., *Stone Cold, the True Story of Michael Stone and the Milltown Massacre*, London, Hutchinson, 1992.

Duigan, S., *One Spin on the Merry-Go-Round*, Dublin, Blackwater Press, 1996.

Holland, J., and Phoenix, S., *Phoenix, Policing the Shadows*, London, Hodder & Stoughton, 1996.

Keena, C., *Gerry Adams – A Biography*, Cork, Mercier Press, 1990.

MacStiofan, S., *Memoirs of a Revolutionary*, London, Gordon Cremonesi, 1975.

Mallie, E., and McKittrick, D., *The Fight for Peace, the Secret Story Behind the Irish Peace Process*, London, Heinemann, 1996.

McGartland, M., *Fifty Dead Men Walking*, London, Blake Publishing, 1997.

McGuire, M., *To Take Arms, A Year in the Provisional IRA*, London, Macmillan, 1973.

O'Clery, C., *The Greening of the White House, the Inside Story of How America Tried to Bring Peace to Ireland*, Dublin, Gill and Macmillan, 1996.

Report of the Scarman Tribunal, *Violence and Civil Disturbances in Northern Ireland in 1969, Report of Tribunal Inquiry*, Belfast, HMSO, 1972.

Rowan, B., *Behind the Lines, The Story of the IRA and Loyalist Ceasefires*, Belfast, Blackstaff Press, 1995.

Sunday Times Insight Team, *Ulster*, Harmondsworth, Penguin, 1970.

Index